True Gospel Revealed anew by Jesus

Volume III

Second Edition

Received by: James E. Padgett

Original Editor: Dr. John Paul Gibson

Current Editor: Geoff Cutler

Published July 2014.

True Gospel Revealed anew by Jesus

Volume III

No Copyright is claimed in this work.

This is the Second Edition: 2014

This volume was initially published in 1969 as "True Gospel Revealed anew by Jesus" by the F. C. N. B., Inc.

It is believed that Victor Summers, acting as president, put all these messages into the public domain on December 25th 1984.

July 2014, Bayview, NSW, Australia.

Editor: Geoffrey John Cutler.

ISBN: 978-1-291-95744-0

Other Divine Love related publications
By Geoff Cutler.

A Gospel of Truth and Light to Mankind. Published November 2011. This is the full set of Padgett Messages arranged in date order. It contains the contents of the four volumes known as the *"True Gospel revealed anew by Jesus"*, Volumes I to IV. This is the most up to date of various similar publications, in that the most recent date research is as per this book. Available at Lulu only. A very large hard cover book (11 inch by 9 inch) of over 700 pages.

Judas of Kerioth. Conversations with Judas Iscariot. Published December 2012. This is a 600 page book (9 inch by 6 inch) of communications from Judas. It contains many previously unknown details about the life of Jesus of Nazareth. Available at Lulu and Amazon.

Is Reincarnation an Illusion? Published March 2011. 191 pages. This is an original work based on ten years research into the subject, and drawing on many sources in order to evaluate all the issues that lead people to believe that reincarnation is true. Available at Lulu and Amazon.

Getting the Hell out of here. What happens after you die? Published March 2011. This is a small book of 45 pages summarizing the fascinating details of life after death. It draws on many sources, but particularly the Padgett Messages and the Judas Messages. Available at Lulu.

Many of these have pdf or Kindle eBook versions available either free, or at a nominal cost. Check the new-birth.net web site for details.

Introduction to Volume III Second Edition

By Geoff Cutler

This was the third volume of Padgett messages produced, in this case completed by Rev. John Paul Gibson in 1969, forty six years after the death of James Padgett. In publishing these messages initially the date of the message was ignored, but as the years rolled on and further Volumes and editions were produced, dates started to be attached to some messages. James Padgett maintained a diary that indicated who communicated and a short summary of their message. When this diary surfaced around the year 2000, efforts began to date each published message and those published on web sites could now be dated and indeed be indexed and read in date order.

In recent years a significant number of new publications have appeared, by various editors, many of them using the now freely available dates of the messages. As one of the people deeply involved in matching the often terse summary in the daily dairy, with these published messages, I am familiar with the benefit offered by reading the messages in the very sequence in which they were received. However I have also recently become aware of the difficulty in correctly absorbing this material, when one is required to read some 1250 communications, to cover all the subjects fully.

The benefit of these original publications lay in the fact that messages were collated together on a topic particularly in Volumes I and II, and it is far easier for a reader to absorb these new spiritual concepts, particularly as one is able to read in sequence messages that may have been received years apart. In this edition dates have been added where known.

There are 69 messages in Volume III which are repeated in either the earlier or later volumes. Every instance of a duplicate is slightly different, indicating it was re-transcribed from the original, and not simply copied. The number of duplicates may appear higher to the reader as every instance is flagged, and hence each duplicate is flagged twice at some stage. In this Volume seven messages were repeated, and in order to reduce the size of the volume, the second instance has been removed. I do feel that it is important to publish the most accurate of these repeated messages, on a word by word basis. This of course means that the resultant message that has been used is not exactly the same as any of the originals from which it was derived. In each case, a footnote to

i

that effect has been included here. Footnotes from earlier editions are also included. As Reverend Dr. John Paul Gibson himself used footnotes, each footnote is marked (J.P.G.) or (G.J.C.) to indicate which editor is responsible. The details of these duplicates are set out in some detail on my web site – www.new-birth.net.

While I respect the desire by this last publisher (of the First Edition) to never change a single comma in their publication, publishing standards have moved on considerably since that time. One simply no longer uses capitalization for emphasis, as an example. It is in the interests of readability that I have adopted modern standards of typography. Where a word has fallen into disuse, I have added its current equivalent in () brackets, rather than changing the word. I certainly have punctuated extensively, creating smaller sentences where in some cases the sentences were almost unreadable.

In the process of discovering the dates of the messages, it became apparent that Dr. Stone particularly, and to a lesser extent Rev. John Paul Gibson had concealed the names of many of James Padgett's legal acquaintances who came through as spirits in darkness. This was a very sensible approach at that time, but now that it is 100 years later it is more useful to see the spiritual progression of these individuals over time. Accordingly in every case where I have been able to discover the real name of the spirit, that has now been used. Similarly where additional detail regarding "preachers" was in the diary, this too has been added as background.

This content was first published in Kindle eBook format in January 2014.

Geoff Cutler. Bayview, NSW, Australia.
July 2014.

Foreword

By Rev. John Paul Gibson

After a sudden passing of Mr. Padgett's wife Helen in 1914 and with the help of a friend started to investigate spiritual communications and at one of the church meetings Mr. Padgett was told that his wife was present and wanted him to know that she was very much alive and wanted to communicate with him. The medium described her perfectly and told Mr. Padgett that he had the gift of automatic writing and his wife wanted him to pick up a pencil and pad at home that she would try and control him to write. After several attempts the name of Helen appeared that was discovered by his friend among a lot of scribbling that took place on the pad. And a little later on, a paragraph was written with a message, and more followed on Christmas Day.

"Let your thoughts turn to God and His love and you will be the happiest man on earth, for you have His love to a great degree, and you also have Jesus to love and care for you in a way that we all wonder at."

"Later Mr. Padgett's grandmother wrote advising him to try and do as well as learn exactly what the Master wishes for him to do, and then do it with all his might."

Do (sic) to a message received from the Master giving him instruction on how to receive the Divine Love of the Father.

What you will discover in reading this True Gospel Revealed Anew by Jesus Vol. III that there were still many important messages from Jesus and other Celestial writers that could not be printed in either volume I or II and that there is great value not only what the Celestial writers have said, but many others as well that are in the Natural Love Spheres.

Mr. Padgett also permitted the dark spirits to write and set aside certain evenings when they could come in and be permitted to write regarding their problems in the Spirit World. The help that they received was so great, that when Mr. Padgett entered the spirit world, he was greeted by thousands of dark spirits that he helped to progress into the light.

Mr. Padgett received spiritual communication over a period of approximately 10 years from 1914 to 1924 which began with his wife and then the parents of both as well as grandparents and of course the Master as has already been mentioned. And by earnest sincere prayer Mr. Padgett commenced to receive the Divine Love of the Father which permitted Jesus to write more and come more often.

Jesus in an early message wrote as follows:

"That the Spirit writings are governed by law in regards to the kind of messages that they may communicate through Mr. Padgett which is governed in accordance with his development. And he must be in good condition to permit these laws to be complied with. And that the spirit writers are powerless to use his brain for the purpose of delivering their messages, when he is not in good condition."

And Jesus further says,

"That you of course know now the remedy and that defects may exist at any particular time and we have urged you to seek this remedy and thereby get in the proper and necessary condition that will enable us to make the rapport with you. So continue to pray to the Father to receive His Divine Love in great abundance."

And as Mr. Padgett received the Divine Love of the Father in greater abundance, more important messages were received which are now printed in both Volume I & II of the True Gospel Revealed anew by Jesus.

However, there will be a fourth volume honoring Dr. Leslie R. Stone and his work in behalf of the Kingdom, where greater space will be given to soulmate love. And permitting more dark spirits to tell their story of distress in darkness and read of their progress into the light. And many of them have progressed out of darkness into the Celestial Heavens. With the help of Mr. Padgett and many Celestial Spirits that were always on hand to help those in trouble in whatever level they were in.

Mr. Padgett began his writing by asking questions of all spirits that wrote through him during the appointed writing periods, so that closer ties existed between him and the spirit writer to permit them to better express themselves and to explain to them the higher spiritual life that he was already familiar with as a result of receiving communication from Jesus and other Celestial writers.

And as you will note from time to time in reading these messages that I have added the words Questions and Answers. Of course we do not know what the questions were, but the answers are clear enough for anyone to understand. But in my close association with Dr. Stone, I was informed that such was the case during Mr. Padgett's writing periods and he was present a great deal of the time when these writings were being received and heard the various conversations between Mr. Padgett and the spirits writers. And you will also note that there is a constant conversation between Mr. Padgett and his wife Helen in permitting the various spirits to write and then confirm the authenticity of the various spirits who wrote and often gives her opinion regarding their various stages of spirit understanding and development that permits them to write on any given subject that is first approved by Mr. Padgett's band of workers.

Rev. John Paul Gibson.
Editor of the First Edition.

James E. Padgett

Background

JAMES E. PADGETT

Mr. James E. Padgett was born August 25th, 1852, in Washington, D.C. and attended the Polytechnic Academy Institute at Newmarket, Virginia. In 1880 he was admitted to the bar in Washington, D.C. and thereafter he practiced law for 43 years until his death on March 17th, 1923. During his student years, he became friendly with Professor Joseph Salyards, an instructor at the Academy who, after his death in 1885, wrote him many interesting messages. His wife, Helen, died on the 14th February 1914, and was the first to write him from the spirit world. Padgett never practiced the gift of mediumship as a means of earning money. He was dedicated wholly to the reception of the great messages signed by Jesus and his many disciples.

Mr. Padgett passed into the spirit world on March 17th, 1923; this first message was received through Eugene Morgan four days later. And the second message followed about a month later

March 21st, 1923.
Received by: Eugene Morgan.[1]
Washington D.C.

I am here, James E. Padgett.

We are all here and at last I am where I so often desired to be. And when I arrived I was met by Jesus and other high spirits who were formally with me so often and also by a great crowd of spirits who were unknown to me, but said that I had enabled them to get out of darkness and become Divine Angels.

Was ever such beauty and happiness conceived of as is now mine. My soul mate is with me and says that a joyous mansion awaits me and that in a little time we will occupy it. I am in a beautiful place, but have not as yet asked its location. As many are seeking control, I must now stop.

James E. Padgett

I am here, James E. Padgett.

Well Morgan, here I am again, I must say that nothing I ever conceived of compares to the marvelous beauty of my home as you are aware. We are making as it were a mighty effort to progress. I mean those in the same plane as myself. When I entered this life, I was met by many thousands of spirits who said that I had helped them and you cannot conceive of the happiness the knowledge brought me. We must continue in this work, as my coming here will only change my location. I

---

[1] Mr. Eugene Morgan was also a lawyer and was selected by Jesus shortly after Mr. Padgett and Dr. Stone were selected as his disciples on earth in the same manner that Jesus selected the original 12 disciples. (J.P.G.)

am trying for more of the Divine Love with all the powers on my being. I of course desire this for myself, but I also desire it that I may be better fitted to become a member of your band and participate in the work more fully than it is now possible for us to do.

Tell the doctor that I was with him the other morning, and that he actually had the experience of leaving his body and looking upon his old friend. You are many times more developed in your amazing and wonderful powers of making clear and simple and obscure truths, than I ever thought you were. I also want to say that you are the mightiest force upon the earth and that you are known and spoken of, as I am told, all through the spirit world from the highest heavens to the lowest hells. Oh, my friend, if I had only put my energy and determination in the work as you have, how different I would now feel, but some comfort is left me, and that is, for a long time I did, and this has enabled the work to be begun. I am most anxious to see it started, and I am most anxious to make up for my delinquency by my efforts in this life.

Jesus often comes to me and comforts me with his love like others of the Celestial Heavens do. Well, I must stop, as it seems that millions are seeking to get control to write.

Your brother in Christ,
James E. Padgett.

The next important message that was received by Eugene Morgan from Mr. Padgett was about two years later on July 1st, 1925

July 1st, 1925.
Received by: Eugene Morgan.
Washington D.C.

I am here, James E. Padgett.

Among those present tonight is your old and much astonished friend Padgett. Yes, astonished for I never had the slightest conception when we so intimately associated as to your marvelous intellectual possession. Morgan[2] you are able to grasp what you are actually accomplishing.

Wumas, a marvelous spirit, is your great admirer, and says: That, as a mundane man you have no equal in respect to the use of the reasoning faculties and powers to disclose their processes. I am engaged in the work and find untold happiness in the thought that I contributed what I did to its success and at the same time a sadness will creep into my very soul when I recall that I did not do this to the extent I might.

---

[2] Mr. Morgan worked with dark spirits mostly and helped them to see the light. And he mentioned that Wumas was over enthusiastic in his estimate of him. (J.P.G.)

Well that cannot be remedied and I can now only try to make up for my delinquency.

My home is in the Celestial Heavens[3] and Helen and I are together and supremely happy. She also participates in the work and in fact does, as you say, every spirit of the Celestial Heavens does in some way. For as a fact, you have awakened the desire of such countless numbers of spirits outside of our world that it requires the service of all of us to look after them.

I have wanted to write for a long time, but conditions have not been such that I deemed that I was justified in gratifying my desires, but tonight it is possible and I have availed myself of the opportunity.

When the Dr. is with you, read this message to him and say that I am with him a great deal as well as are spirits of the Celestial, whose love is always about him.

Washington[4] is a marvelous spirit and is second to Samuel in his capacity as an organizer.

Let me say as a spirit of the Celestial Heavens that all men outside of these heavens, you are as the mouthpiece of the Master, the most transcendent in respect to position, as no king, ruler of nations or people are your equal.

Wumas must write, as he says, soon as I finish, so I will give him the control.

James E. Padgett.

Wumas, a dark spirit, was helped by Eugene Morgan to see the light

July 1st, 1925.
Received by: Eugene Morgan.
Washington D.C.

I am here, Wumas.

Since entering this world many experiences have been mine. When you made your statement as to our laws and that which provided the means of escaping from our environments, with all my intellectual development, I did not for sometime grasp their significance, yet I am possessed of marvelous intellectual development, and should have immediately grasped what I failed in doing, which demonstrates that you in obtaining what I did not as the result of my intellectual effort independently made, demonstrated the possession of intellectual

---

[3] The term "Celestial" is used throughout the Padgett Messages to indicate that the spirit has moved beyond the highest Spirit Sphere, which is the seventh, and entered the eternal realms. (G.J.C.)

[4] Washington was part of Eugene Morgan's band. (J.P.G.)

faculties that enabled you to perceive the marvelous relevancy and marvelous significance of the laws as to which there was no analogy on the earth to enable you to grasp them as a natural result of ordinary mental functioning of the mind. Emasas a marvelous spirit as myself also concurs in the conclusion I have obtained to, and that is, as to unusual intellectual powers, you are without a superior on this earth.
    Wumas.

Introduction

By Dr. Leslie R. Stone

I met Mr. Padgett, to the best of my recollection, sometime in September of 1914 as a result of our mutual interest in Spiritualism, which became a bond of friendship, mutual respect and brotherly love that grew in time and was never broken in his life until his death on March 17th, 1923.

At Mr. Padgett's home, I met his two close friends, Eugene Morgan and Dr. Goerger. The first time there, I was informed of his gift of automatic writing and of the fact that he was receiving from his wife, Helen, who had passed into the spirit world the early part of 1914, and who has written to him many things about the spirit life, that she was living as normally as he was on earth, describing her experiences at the time of her death, the sphere of her abode, her great love for her husband in the flesh and disclosing the fact that he was her true soulmate.

Mr. Padgett had no knowledge of spiritual communication before being advised at a séance in Washington that he possessed the psychic power to obtain automatic writings from spirits who urged him to try. When he decided to do so he found that his pencil started to move and produced circles and scribbling so that sometimes the writings looked like "fish hooks," but after several tries he deciphered a message signed by his wife Helen. It was a short personal note that he understood could have only been written by his wife, although feeling skeptical that it was in any way possible for his wife to write through him. When he asked for proof, she was delighted to comply and write about conditions with which he would be impressed. But in spite of all the evidence submitted by his wife, Mr. Padgett still thought that the material was coming from his own mind, with one exception: that the messages came in too fast for his mind to formulate such thoughts about the spirit world that he knew nothing about. In order to obtain more confidence about this revealed gift of his, he began to read books on the subject of Spiritualism and attended several séances where I also was present, and I can substantiate that Mr. Padgett heard his wife speak to him in which she reassured him that it was really she who was actually writing through him, and this was corroborated by his mother and grandmother, Ann Rollins, as is made clear in messages contained in this book.

With this assurance Mr. Padgett continued to take messages from his wife and many friends in the spirit world which included his former partner in the practice of law. While he was exploring the contents of various books on spiritualism, one book in particular that I recall he read was J. M. Peeble's "Immortality". This book interested him very much and gave him more confidence and spiritual belief that his wife could write through him. He became intensely desirous for her spiritual progression, and her many writings in this book show her spiritual progress from the lower sphere to the Celestial Heavens. During these writing periods Helen became a channel through which the first religious note was injected. As the writing progressed, additional writers began to replace the personal material that Helen was inserting to convince Mr. Padgett of her spiritual development. As a matter of fact, he took the advice of the higher spirits to the effect that progress could only be obtained by earnest prayer to the Heavenly Father for His Love. This knowledge of Divine Love and possession of it, constitutes the reason for the organization of our Church of the New Birth.

    It was not too long before Helen found out that her prayers to the Father for His Love were answered, inasmuch as she has written that she had done what Mr. Padgett had wanted for her to do. Not too long after, she progressed to the Third Sphere and urged that Mr. Padgett, too, should seek the Father's Love to better his condition on earth as well. With Helen's help, as well as other writers' encouragement, above all of Jesus himself, who began to write about this time, Mr. Padgett did receive the Father's Love and that condition of soul to permit him to obtain the many wonderful messages that are now printed in the two volumes of the True Gospel Revealed Anew.

    There is one very important message by Helen "on the several kinds of love" that I have selected especially for this introduction to Volume III.

November 26th, 1918.

    I am here, your own true and loving Helen.

    After I passed over, I saw that I must seek a way to communicate with you in my spirit existence, and you may not know, but it is a fact that I was with you when you visited the mediums who informed you that you were a medium, being possessed of the gift of automatic writing; and I, having learned this fact from some of your spirit relatives, and principally your father, impressed these mediums to tell you of the fact of your mediumship. And when, at last, you made the experiment, I was present with you and exerted all my powers, and had the help of other spirits, in making your experiment a success. And when you commenced to receive the messages I cannot tell you how happy I was and thankful that the way was opened up that enabled me to tell you what, above everything else, I was so anxious to tell you. And if you will think for a moment of the nature of my communications, you will remember that the burden of all my messages was my love for you, and no matter how important other portions of the messages might be, yet in them was the continuous assurance that I loved you with all my heart and soul.

There are various kinds of love existing between humans and also between spirits and humans, each having its source in different conditions of fact and in varying causes; and of all these loves, only one is or can be the true and eternal one. The love of husband and wife is a beautiful thing, and may exist during the life on earth and bring much happiness to its possessors even though that love is temporary, and, in the workings of the law of attraction in the spirit life, may entirely cease its existence and become forgotten. And so, I may state, will be the destiny of the paternal and maternal, and brotherly and sisterly love. All these are based upon causes or conditions that are merely temporary—that is, may last during time and for a more or less longer period in eternity, but finally must end.

These loves, as I understand, are provisions of God which are necessary to enable mankind to work out their progress through the human life in the way that will produce the greatest harmony and happiness among mortals as they contend with the difficulties, cares and disappointments of the earth life. In the spirit world there is no need for these loves, for a greater bond of affection is provided, and is created or brought into operation by the great law of attraction, which causes the merely personal relationship that may have existed between spirits when inhabiting the earthly forms, to cease to be forgotten. This law of attraction is based upon the condition of the soul, whether that soul possesses the development created by the Divine Love or only that created by the purification of the natural love.

In the early stages in the spirit life the conditions of the earth life may remain for a time, because the spirit's state of soul and desires and affections may continue to be as they were when on earth; but as stagnation is not a quality of the soul in spirit life, these things which may have bound the humans together in the relationship mentioned do not long continue as they were, as there is no way of avoiding the workings of this law and its results. In order for this state to continue any great length of time, it would be necessary that all the spirits bound by these affections or conditions should remain without change in their souls, and that rarely happens, for in our world the individual becomes the individual in fact, and the real is apparent and spirits see one another face to face, and pretense or effort to hide the true condition of love or affection, or want of the same, becomes futile; so that, as is the real state of the spirit, so is his relationship to other spirits.

Again, this law of attraction operates in other directions than that of determining the mere affections, for men's mental conditions and aspirations are determining factors in establishing relationships among themselves. When men become spirits they are at the time of transition, and for a longer or shorter period afterwards, the possessors of the same knowledge and aspirations as they were immediately preceding their passage, with this difference: that to a more or less extent this knowledge and these aspirations, when in spirit life, are made apparent to others, not necessarily in words and professions, but by the power of seeing, which all but the very depraved spirits possess, so that, pretense and dissembling being absent or of no avail, these spirits, under the law, attract those affections arising from their human relationships cease to bind these several spirits, and they obey the law. The temporary love has fulfilled its mission and object, and to continue to exist under the circumstances mentioned would work injury and retardation to the progress of these spirits, no matter what may be the nature or cause of that progress.

Now, while what I have said is all true, yet there is another provision of the Father's law, designed for the happiness of men while mortals, that causes the love arising from the human relationship to continue with the spirit so long as the object of that love continues in the flesh, and no matter what the progress of that spirit may be or what its attractions are, yet it continues to love the mortal during his earthly career, and to watch over and help him, and all this even though this love which once existed for other mortals in the same relationship, and who have passed to spirit life, may have ended and been forgotten. This human love is subject to change and death, and those of earth life who console themselves with the thought that when they pass to spirit life they will meet their loved ones who have gone before, never to part again, will be disappointed, but not long distressed, for they will soon thereafter learn and experience the workings of the great law of attraction, and in that experience will be happy.

But there is another and differing love, not of the temporal, but of the everlasting, in its nature, and all humans have it, though probably unaware of the fact, but which at some period—and this may be for some time—in eternity they will become conscious of, and then never deprived of, for it is the perfect fulfillment of this law of attraction. I mean the soulmate love, of which I have written you so often. It was born before any man appeared in the flesh, and was a part of his very soul's creation, and of which he could never be deprived, though so often does it lie dormant in the souls and consciousness of man. I and others have written you as to how when the souls of men were created by the Father these souls were made male and female, though constituting only the one soul—two in one, the perfect one. And with their creation was bestowed upon them a love—not two loves, but only one—which was possessed equally by each part of the complete soul, and which will always remain one in its complete workings, although these two parts of the soul have to be, and are, separated in their incarnation in the human body, which incarnation is for the purpose of giving the male and the female parts of the one soul a separate individuality, without severing or disuniting this love, which through all eternity binds together these two parts as one.

The love of which I have first spoken is the love for time only; the soulmate love is the love for all eternity, and this great love which requires that at some stage in eternity these two parts of the one soul shall become one again, should be one of the most convincing proofs that all men, sooner or later, will come into harmony with the will of the Father and with the laws creating such souls. The fundamental law of the universe is that all things shall come into harmony with the will of the Father, and as the hells and all that they comprehend are out of such harmony, men may believe that in the ultimate working out of this law no soul will remain in the hells or in the condition or state of existence that primarily makes the hells, but that all souls in their perfected union will become inhabitants of either the spiritual or the Celestial heavens.

And further, I must say, as you have been told before, that this soulmate love is the only love that can have a separate and individual existence in the Celestial heavens, where the Divine Love exists to the exclusion of every other love save the soulmate love; and the more the spirits—the united two in one—possess the Divine Love, the greater will be their possession of this soulmate love.

As you know, I am your soulmate and come to you so often in my love and you realize the fact and respond, and at times are very happy. You have experienced on several occasions the depth and yearnings of my love to such an extent that your soul has come to me in my spirit world and enjoyed moments of unspeakable bliss; and as you may not know, left me with protestations against its return to your mortal body, and, if my love had not been wise as well as intense and wonderfully absorbing, your protests would have been heeded and you would have remained with me to enjoy the happiness which can be yours only when you come to the spirit world to find your home everlasting.

It has been said that the man in love is a fool, and that may be true in regard to the merely human love, but as to this soulmate love the more of it we possess the wiser we become and correspondingly happy.

I cannot tell you the depth and height and wonders of my love, and only say that it fulfils to the uttermost the great law of attraction, and there is nothing, save the Divine Love, in all the universe of being that can excel it or take its place, or make two souls so united that even death cannot sever it.

I will be with you as long as you continue to live on earth, in all the fullness of my love, and when the time of your passing comes, I will be present; and so much love will be around you that you will forget the dying and the awakening, and know only that your soulmate is with you telling you of love and happiness and the beauties of the life that will be yours, and showing you to a large degree how splendid and heavenly this love can make a spirit that possesses the Divine Love also.

Well dear, baby is here and says she has read what I have written and is so glad that you have me for your soulmate. She is very happy and is growing all the time in beauty and in the possession of the Father's Love, and so wants you to seek more and more for this love, and says, "How rich Daddy is to have the soulmate love of my beautiful mother and the certainty of the great love of the Father, if he will only seek for it; and in addition, which may not count for much, he has the love of his own Baby, who is now so happy."

And Mary says that I must not neglect to say that she is here also, and has read my message with great pleasure, and wants me to tell the Dr. that if he will only substitute himself in your place and her in my place and read the letter he will know something of her love for him; that he is her soulmate and can never be another's and she is with him so very often trying to impress him with her presence and love.

Well dear, you have written a great deal and I will stop. I am so glad that I could write.

Good night, my dear Ned.
Your own true and loving,
Helen.

I selected this message for it is beautiful in its love contents, also because in it there is reference to my Mary and to her love for me. Believe me when I say I am grateful to Mrs. Helen Padgett for the many wonderful messages that she has written to me and especially for the fact that she located my soulmate for me, Mary Kennedy, who once lived near my home in England. Although we never met on earth, I have been blessed with so much of her great love from the spirit world throughout many decades of my 90 years on this material plane. I possess her constant companionship on this material plane, as I feel her presence whenever I have need of spiritual strength and love, and her love for me is expressed continually throughout all her writings, some of which are printed in this volume.

In closing I also want to express my love and gratitude to the two magnanimous ladies, who wish to remain anonymous, for their financial support to permit our work to progress in behalf of the Kingdom, a task that the Church of the New Birth is organized to perform. Without their assistance, the reprinting of the last Volume II of the True Gospel Revealed anew by Jesus, and this Volume III, would have been very greatly delayed.

Dr. Leslie R. Stone.

Contents

Introduction to Volume III Second Edition i

Foreword iii

James E. Padgett vii
    Background vii
    Wumas, a dark spirit, was helped by Eugene Morgan to see the light ... x

Introduction xiii

Volume III Messages 1

Ann R. Padgett
    Says that his father has found his soulmate and tells of his spiritual progression 1

White Eagle
    Discusses the health of Mr. Padgett that he is constantly watching .. 2

Jesus
    First effort to deliver a formal message, but Mr. Padgett was not in condition to receive it completely 2

Ann Rollins
    Confirms that it was Jesus who just wrote and reassures him of the great love that Jesus had for him 4

Helen Padgett
    Advises Mr. Padgett to give all his thoughts to God and to His Love and he will soon realize that only His Love is necessary to become a very spiritual man 5

A. G. Riddle
    Mr. Padgett advised his old friend and law partner on how to obtain the Love of the Father in a previous communication, which he is trying to do and advises him of the fact 7

Table of Contents

Helen Padgett
Christmas night, Helen writes for Mr. Padgett to be true to God and to himself and that he need not care what the future may bring 11

An early personal message to love her more with all his heart as she loves him, and advises him to be careful as to where he attends séances 12

John H. Padgett
Tells of soulmate records and the work that his son does in helping the dark spirits to progress out of darkness and in leading them into the light with the help of Celestial spirits 16

Helen Padgett
Confirms the effort made by Mr. Padgett to bring his two friends now in the spirit world to the Light of the Father 21

Bright Star
Mr. Padgett met Bright Star at a séance and is now helping her to progress spiritually and she says that automatic writing is superior to independent voice séances 21

Helen Padgett
Wrote that she is studying spiritual laws and learned that a spirit can only communicate with mortals when they are in rapport, and that the same law applies to mortals and that her home is in the Third Sphere 23

Jesus
Promises to come and reveal the truth and untruth of the Bible to Mr. Padgett 27

Writes that he is truly the man who was crucified on Calvary that comes to him and writes. And that Mr. Padgett is doing the greatest work that God has given to any of his creatures to do 28

Helen Padgett
Is happy that the Master explained the lost soul meaning to Mr. Padgett and that he should be happy to have Jesus as a friend 29

Writes about her progress from the Third Spirit Sphere to the Fifth Spirit Sphere where she is now living with Mr. Padgett's mother and describes the beauty of her new home and that she is now continuing with earth hobbies, such as painting and voice study 30

    Writes about the sudden passing of a friend and how she tried to convince her that she could not re-enter her body, which was similar to her own experience 34

Vespasian
    Roman Emperor gives his experience. Why he learned English 36

Hannah Somerville
    A spirit who believed in the eternal punishment of those who denied the vicarious atonement of Jesus 37

Semiramis
    Once a Pagan and now a Christian 38

Sebastobel
    An ancient spirit decides to search for the Divine Love, which he learns is the cause of the beauty and brightness of Helen Padgett, a Celestial Spirit 39

Helen Padgett
    Now a Celestial spirit, relates her early spiritual development in the Third Sphere with the help of Mr. Padgett 41

John H. Padgett
    Agrees with the suggestion made to form a band to protect his son in his spiritual investigation through automatic writings 42

Helen Padgett
    First preserved message from Mr. Padgett's wife Helen: Who says that she looks on Jesus as a man of God, but not as God Himself. Also informs him regarding his parents and grandparents 44

    Reassures Mr. Padgett that it was truly Jesus who wrote Saturday night. And for Mr. Colburn to also believe 45

John H. Padgett
    Reassures him that it was Jesus who wrote on Saturday 47

Ann Rollins
    A Celestial Spirit also reassures him that it was truly Jesus of the Scriptures that spoke and wrote to him on Saturday 48

Jesus
    An early message from Jesus to enable Mr. Padgett to get into a spiritual condition before the important Truths were written 49

> *Jesus is the Way, the Truth and the Life for all mankind to believe in* 50
>
> *In his first formal message informs Mr. Padgett to go to the Father for His help*.. 52

Ann Rollins
> *Writes that the New Birth is the inflowing of the Spirit of God into your soul and that the disappearing of all that tends to turn your heart from the truth and love of God* 53

Ann R. Padgett
> *Talks about her soulmate and the love that she has for her son*...... 54

Ann Rollins
> *In an early message describes her home in the 7th. Sphere—all the blessings the Father promised—friends—her work, and they are not singing all the time* 55

Bright Star
> *Mr. Padgett asked questions of the spirit writers and in this early one the question asked is written in his conversation with Bright Star*... 55

Helen Padgett
> *In the beginning of his work in behalf of the Kingdom, Mr. Padgett received this message from his grandmother through his wife Helen to encourage him to pray to the Father more sincerely and not Jesus as he once believed*.. 57
>
> *In an early message Helen wrote that Mr. Padgett was too much taken up with his business matters and does not devote enough time to prayer to the Father to receive the gift of the spirit*..................... 58

Ann Rollins
> *Answers many questions for him on the Holy Spirit and the Heavenly Father, as well as better explains Jesus' power on earth and in the spirit world*.. 60

Thomas Padgett
> *Wants to assure Mr. Padgett that important spirits actually write* . 63

Ann R. Padgett
> *Says that Mrs. Mary Baker Eddy sees the error in her teachings and is living in the same sphere with her*.. 64

Ann Rollins
Says that the Father's Love for Mr. Padgett will help him in his material problems 64

Helen Padgett
Locates Mr. Padgett's father's soulmate that is very lovely and a Celestial Spirit 65

Mr. Padgett spent the day with his friends, Judge Syrick and Col. Woods, and Helen writes that they both believe in spiritualism 67

Jesus
That it is that degree of belief that enables you to know a Truth. And that faith is the only thing to make you realize that I am who and what I declare myself to be 71

Admits that his power is limited in some things and does not always know the answer without going to the Father, the Source of all knowledge 72

Ann Rollins
Writes that the Master is so close to Mr. Padgett to make him feel like a true brother 74

Helen Padgett
Writes that she is happy that the Master wrote and he was so loving and brotherly 75

Jesus
Comments on a book that Mr. Padgett was reading about fallen angels, which some churches believe in 77

Assures Mr. Padgett that when the messages that he is now receiving will be printed that they will be accepted 79

When Mr. Padgett's soul condition was sufficient to permit Jesus to write, the following informative message was received 81

Second formal message "His Father's Nature as my God and your God" 83

Ann Rollins
Gave additional explanation on the same day 85

Jesus
Explanation on the love of man 86

Table of Contents

> *Explains that coming to Mr. Padgett as he does is not contrary to any law of the spirit world*.. 89
>
> *Is amazed at the power that Mr. Padgett has with the dark spirits and approves of his work in this respect* 90
>
> *Is pleased with Mr. Padgett's declaration and will help him to become At-One with the Father* 91
>
> *Advises Mr. Padgett to give more time to prayer and that the Father's Love is coming into his soul* 92

Professor Joseph Salyards
> *Writes about the great work that Mr. Padgett is doing and will help him also* 93

Helen Padgett
> *Says that as her love increases for the Father so also her love increases for him as well*... 93

Jesus
> *Will cause Mr. Padgett to feel the Great Love of the Father for him* 95
>
> *Relates the importance of getting the New Birth in order to become Immortal*.. 96
>
> *Tells Mr. Padgett that he will reveal the Truths of the Father which is now timely to do so, and was not as a result of any previous instruments or writers* 97

Gomeses
> *Greek who lived in the time of Christ, is now a Celestial Spirit*......... 98

Jesus
> *Writes about a visit by Mr. Padgett to spiritualist medium and advises him to help her to discover the Divine Love of the Father that is now justly due her since she has been seeking the greater Love since early childhood* 99

St. Sebastian
> *Interested in the work of the Master through Mr. Padgett*............ 102

Jesus
> *Affirms that Mr. Padgett is now receiving the Divine Love of the Father in more abundance* 102

> *Was very much interested in the way that Mr. Padgett helped to prevent two suicides by instructing them on the consequences of such an act* 103

Jayemas
> *Atlantis teacher of arts and sciences, writes about his lost continent and the high intellect that it possessed* 104

Jesus
> *The preacher was limited in describing one of the Attributes of God, and that is the Loving Care that He has for His children* 105

> *Wanted Mr. Padgett and Dr. Stone to know that he was present during their discussion of spiritual things* 106

White Eagle
> *Under Jesus' direction helped to correct Mr. Padgett's digestive organs, as a result of his prayer to the Father for help* 107

St. Stephen
> *Writes about Jesus as Head of the Church in the Celestial Heavens. And confirms that Paul wrote on the resurrection* 109

Helen
> *Has written that Jesus is not very happy during the holidays and removes himself from the earth plane into the highest Celestial Heavens until the holidays end. Because he does not want to hear the worship of him as God* 110

Bright Star
> *Became a friend as a result of a séance that Mr. Padgett attended* 110

Helen Padgett
> *Telling about one love (soulmate love) that is in store for them as they both seek the Divine Love of the Father* 111

John H. Padgett
> *Has been selected by the Higher Powers to be the guardian angel of his son as long as he may live on earth as a mortal* 113

Helen Padgett
> *Writes that the Master is with Mr. Padgett a great deal and even prays with him at night* 114

Table of Contents

Ann Rollins
Tells about the errors in the book that he was reading about the hells 115

Herod
Writes on the hells. Corroborates Swedenborg's message on the hells 117

Helen Padgett
Confirms that Herod wrote on the hells 118

John
Confirms that Swedenborg and Herod gave true descriptions of the Hells 119

Jesus
Man was given the possibility of becoming in his nature Divine like the Father. But this gift was never possessed by him, until my coming to earth, and making known such possibility 120

Cornelius
Tells of the great spiritual audiences that attend the writings received by Mr. Padgett and listen to what is said 121

The centurion of the Bible and the first gentile Christian. Now in the Celestial Heavens 122

Jesus
Explains the phrase: He that liveth and believeth on me shall never die 123

Urges Mr. Padgett to believe in him and trust the Father that he will not be forsaken or left alone 124

Ann Rollins
Says that the Master had a great love for him 125

Helen Padgett
Writes that she has progressed into the Celestial Heavens within one year after leaving the material plane 126

Ann Rollins
Tells of her spiritual progression from first Celestial sphere to the second Celestial sphere 127

Gives reasons why so many of the higher spirits wrote on Divine Love 129

Helen Padgett
Tells of her love for Mr. Padgett 130

Ann Rollins
Answers Mr. Padgett's question on baptism 130

Writes about the unpardonable sin that is of the greatest importance 131

Again writes on the Kingdom of Jesus being closed to all those that do not receive the Divine Love of the Father 132

Writes on the importance of knowing the Way to the Celestial Heavens 134

John H. Padgett
Informs Mr. Padgett that his soul is developing very rapidly 136

Writes about the infidel's first realization when they come into the spirit world that there must be a God 136

Is one of his guardian angels that is protecting him from undesirable spirits and is now a Celestial Spirit, living with his soulmate 137

Helen Padgett
Describes the various writers that wrote on this night and the help that each is given and her work in locating soulmates 139

Father of Dr. Arbelee
Writes to his sick son Dr. Arbelee, regarding his life in the spirit world 139

Helen Padgett
Confirms that the father of Dr. Arbelee wrote to him, giving advice 142

Has progressed into the Third Celestial sphere and says that there are no words to describe its beauty 143

Tells about her new beautiful garment as a result of her spiritual advancement 144

Judge Syrick
Confirms Helen's beauty 145

Table of Contents

Helen Padgett
Writes that she was impressed with what Mr. Padgett said to Dr. Stone about the Love of God flowing into the heart; also locates Judge Syrick's Soulmate 145

St. Chrysostom
Gives his testimony on the errors of the church in not knowing about Divine Love 148

Wishes to be included in book since he is also helping Mr. Padgett in his work 150

Descartes
A French philosopher who rejects the idea of Divine Love and places his faith in reason and intellectual development 150

August Comte
A French philosopher that is not interested in the Divine Love of the Father, but is willing to put his faith in reason and investigations . 152

Helen Padgett
Comments on spirit who wrote and went with Prof. Salyards 155

Hortense
Stepdaughter of Napoleon, now knows the Way to the Celestial Heavens 155

Gregory
A former Pope of the early days of Catholicism has now reached the Celestial Spheres; stresses the importance of soul religion 157

Gen. Ulysses S. Grant
Has had his spiritual eyes opened and is seeking the Father's Divine Love 158

Gen. Wm. T. Sherman
Is the same as he was on earth; but seeing his former friends so changed by the Divine Love causes him to go with Mr. Riddle to learn the reason 159

Helen Padgett
Is grateful that through Mr. Padgett the two Generals were able to find out about the Divine Love 161

Table of Contents

Gladstone
Was Premier of Great Britain. Has deep feelings of horror at the war that is raging. Wonders why he is not in a higher sphere; still believes in the sacrifice of Jesus 161

St. George
Confirms the Master communicating through Mr. Padgett 162

Jas. A. Garfield
Has been seeking truth with his mind. Mr. Padgett tells him about seeking truth with his soul 163

A. G. Riddle
Comments on Mr. Garfield's writing, and his own progress 165

Helen Padgett
Confirms that Garfield wrote 166

Galileo
Writes of his studies of the material universe 166

Sam Ford
How the spirits progress in knowledge of the Truths 167

Helen Padgett
Wants Mr. Padgett to write on Sunday 168

John C. Calhoun
Still working for his country 169

Julius Caesar
Gives his experiences after receiving help from a Divine Spirit 170

Helen Padgett
Confirms that Julius Caesar wrote 173

Julius Caesar
Is seeking for the Divine Love. Light is breaking into his soul 173

Writes that earthly position does not determine one's spiritual abode 175

Helen Padgett
Confirms that Julius Caesar wrote 176

Grover Cleveland
Expresses gratitude to Mr. Padgett 177

Table of Contents

    Comes to Mr. Padgett for help 179

Cousin Alice
    Writes of her happiness in the Third Sphere 181

Francis Bacon
    The limitations which mortal man places upon his perception of the laws governing the universe 182

    Comments on an article written by James Hyslop on Christianity and Spiritualism regarding laws which operated in certain miracles of Jesus 184

Anaxylabis
    The designer of the Great Pyramid of Gizeh in Egypt 186

Leander Albright
    A spirit who has received the Divine Love writes of his efforts to awaken other spirits to the true religion 187

Jay Hudson
    The Truths that an author has learned since passing into the spirit life 188

Ann R. Padgett
    A Celestial Spirit wants to assure Mr. Padgett that they are really the spirits they represent themselves to be and do not doubt them 189

Helen Padgett
    Is sorry that she cannot permit an old friend of Mr. Padgett to write but is happy with Jesus' letter to him and that of his mother 190

Jesus
    Had all his disciples and apostles and those called saints attend his writings to convince Mr. Padgett that he really selected him to do his work on earth 191

    Advises Mr. Padgett to take his daughter to a séance to prove to her that there is truth in spiritualism 191

Helen Padgett
    Writes that as his soulmate, her love for him is greater than for her children, who will not need her in the great future of eternity 193

    Explains the Sabbath and for Mr. Padgett not to take the pamphlet he was reading seriously, that is an Adventist belief 195

> Comments on the book that Mr. Padgett was reading (The Great Controversy) says the author regrets its contents 196
>
> Explains that the book that he was reading (Pastor Russell On Spiritualism) did not have a good influence on him 197

Pastor Russell
> Writes about his passing into the spirit world 198

Helen Padgett
> Enlightens Mr. Padgett on the closeness of spirit and mortals during the earth holiday festivities, which Jesus does not participate in ... 198

Mrs. Mitchell
> Is very happy that her son is preaching the Truth of God's Love 200

Helen Padgett
> Confirms that the preacher's mother was very happy because her son will put away his dogmatic beliefs 200

Francis Bacon
> Explains the difference between the spiritual and material elements 201

Helen Padgett
> Confirms that Francis Bacon wrote on the subject of the spiritual and material elements which are purely scientific 202
>
> Explains the sudden passing of their daughter, Nita, as a result of a serious operation, and the great progress she is making in the spirit world 203

Jesus
> Comforts Mr. Padgett regarding his daughter's sudden passing into the spirit world and the love that now exists between them, and the greater love of his soulmate wife 205

Helen Padgett
> Wants Mr. Padgett to know that "Baby", their daughter that just passed into the spirit world is with her and sends her love to him. 207

Nita Padgett
> First communication from Mr. Padgett's daughter, Nita, that is also known by Baby, tells of her progress to the Third Sphere 208

Table of Contents

Helen Padgett
Explains that the power of communication can be shut off by the instrument as Mr. Padgett did for a while to even prevent his closest love tie to write. Explains the progress that is being made by their daughter, Nita, now in the spirit world 209

Nita Padgett
The second writing could not be the long letter that she wanted to write to tell of her experience in passing into the spirit world, but happy to wait for a better time 210

Helen Padgett
Confirms their daughter Nita's progress and the Truth of Jesus' second coming on earth. 211

Wishes for Mr. Padgett to be ready to receive the Master's message and that she will write on soulmates 212

Nita Padgett
Describes her experiences in passing into the spirit world 212

Helen Padgett
Is very happy that her daughter Nita was able to write the way she did to disclose her happiness and spiritual progress 215

Jesus
Writes on faith and glory of the Father 215

Paul
Writes about the resurrection of the body 216

Luke
Discloses the names of the guides for Mr. Padgett, Mr. Morgan and Dr. Stone and that above each of them is Jesus 217

Helen Padgett
Confirms that it was Luke who wrote 218

Luke
Never said that Jesus came to earth as the only begotten of the Father, which is not true 218

Helen Padgett
Arranges for Mr. Padgett to see her in a vision with all her beauty and love that she has for her soulmate 219

Jesus
  Jesus listened to a conversation that Mr. Padgett had regarding his blood saving from sin, which was based on ignorance.................. 220

John H. Padgett
  Mr. Padgett's father writes about his friend's present spiritual condition and the suffering that he must undergo before he can begin to see the light 221

John P. Newman
  Methodist minister would like to tell his people on earth what he has learned to be the Truth about the soul............................ 223

Last of the Mohicans
  Mr. Padgett helped spirits from all walks of life and the early Indian who asked for help was not denied to write...................... 224

John
  Reassures Mr. Padgett that all his material requirements and plans will be realized 224

Helen Padgett
  Writes that Mr. Padgett will receive great love and power to do the great work of the Master as well as other high spirits 226

John
  Explains the soulmate separations in the event that both do not obtain the Divine Love of the Father................................. 227

Helen Padgett
  Responds to Mr. Padgett's call to write............................ 228

John
  Explains what takes place on death of the body and what does the spirit of man do when it leaves the body.......................... 228

Helen Padgett
  Shared the happiness of Mr. Padgett today when his soul was so filled with the Love of the Father..................... 231

John the Baptist
  Strongly urges him to get in condition to receive the Celestial messages that are more important than the personal ones that he is receiving 232

Table of Contents

John
Explains that Jesus has already come the second time, which subject he will discuss at a later date 233

Helen Padgett
Does not approve of Mr. Padgett's idea to send messages to a man that would not appreciate it 234

Jesus
Does not think that that message could do harm and may do some good 234

Is with Mr. Padgett often and prays with him to help his soul development to permit him to receive his writings 235

Ann Rollins
Confirms what the Master said and encourages him in his work ... 236

Jesus
Jesus' help spiritually is without limit but the material depends on the individual himself 236

Attended a church service with Mr. Padgett and tells of what the preacher should have said regarding the blood sacrifice 237

Helen Padgett
Writes that although the Master was anxious to write tonight, He was not displeased with him 238

Frank Davis
Mr. Padgett's boyhood chum expresses his gratitude for the help given to him 239

Samuel
Expresses his love for Mr. Padgett and the work that he is doing in behalf of the Kingdom 239

Jesus
That the only part of man that is immortal is the soul, the spirit is merely the active energies that manifest life and these energies for their existence depend upon the soul from which they emanate ... 240

There are very often spirits present who listen to those on earth when they read spiritual truths 240

>
> Due to Mr. Padgett's heavy schedule with the dark spirits that even Jesus had to make definite appointments to fit into his schedule .. 241

Helen Padgett
> Tells Mr. Padgett that he has the power to prevent the dark spirits from writing as Jesus has just written 242

Jesus
> That the world is becoming more spiritual and requires spiritual food, and that war causes people to think more of the hereafter 243

> Explains the difference in the work of Mr. Morgan and Dr. Stone and the importance of each, but his revelations can only be made through Mr. Padgett 244

Seligman
> A Muslim never knew or heard of Divine Love with all his many years in the spirit world until Mr. Padgett informed him and helped him to seek and obtain It. Says his prophet never taught us about Divine Love 245

Frederick, the Father
> Agrees with what Bismarck has said about freedom of the German people from one man rule and that the end is very soon 247

Helen Padgett
> Comments on St. John not being able to finish his message and the two German writers' predictions on ending the war 248

Stainton Moses
> The medium whose book Mr. Padgett was reading, explains why his book "Spirit Teachings" did not contain the Truth of the "New Birth" as taught by Jesus 249

John
> Approves of Mr. Padgett reading the book by Stainton Moses as there are many things in it that are true 250

> The guardian angel of Mr. Padgett has said that Jesus, our leader, is making a great effort to establish a Kingdom of God in the Celestial Heavens 251

> Writes that Mr. Padgett is very near the Father in His Love and not to doubt that the Master is not with him 252

Table of Contents

    Explains that even Jesus can lose power of communications when it is exhausted according to Law of Communication.............. 253

Luke
    Also mentions that even Jesus in his writing can exhaust his power according to spiritual laws.............. 254

St. Sebastian
    Wants Mr. Padgett to know that he is in condition to write 254

Helen Padgett
    Confirms that those who wrote were actually who they said that they were, because she knew them.............. 255

St. Celestia
    Tells of how she was killed in Rome and her work now trying to help Mr. Padgett to do the work of the Master to better understand Jesus' mission.............. 255

Aaron
    Was a very powerful man when on earth.............. 257

Soloman of Old
    Also became a follower of Jesus and knows that Jesus is the only way to the Father.............. 257

Anabalixis
    Promised to come again and write on the lost continent.............. 258

Helen Padgett
    Confirms that the ancient writers were just who they represented themselves to be.............. 258

Soloman of Old
    Encourages Mr. Padgett and stresses the importance to receive these important Truths without delay as mankind is turning more to spiritual things.............. 259

Matthew
    Will be a part of Mr. Padgett's band.............. 260

Mark
    Assures Mr. Padgett that the Master is now doing the great work for the redemption of mankind.............. 260

Helen Padgett
Writes about the importance to receive the Master's Truths......... 261

John
Confirms the thought that he is the St. John of the Bible 261

Samuel
Writes that there is no reason why Mr. Padgett cannot get the Divine Love of the Father.. 262

Lot
Is also trying to help Mr. Padgett 262

Helen Padgett
Describes the discussion in the park between Dr. Stone and Mr. Padgett.. 262

Samuel
Says that the only Way to redemption is through the Divine Love of the Father 263

Elohiam
Says that Jesus was crucified because the Jews failed to recognise Jesus as the looked for Messiah... 264

Caligula
A Roman Emperor and murderer of Christians, suffered all the horrors of hell and has paid his penalties and is now a follower of Jesus, who helped him out of darkness... 267

Overheard a conversation between Mr. Padgett and Dr. Stone on operations of the soul development upon the physical mind after death... 269

Gottfried Liebnitz
A German philosopher, now in the Second Sphere, wrote on immortality and the uncertainty of obtaining it even in the spirit world... 270

James G. Blaine
A friend of Mr. Padgett's praises him for his work and tells about his spiritual pursuits 272

Helen Padgett
Wonders about the many beautiful spirits that are around him at times 273

xxxvii

Table of Contents

James G. Blaine
Visits the councils of all nations to learn the objects of their efforts and desires and surprising as it may seem the German's feel that God is on their side 273

Bismarck
A former statesman places the blame on England for the economic conditions in Germany that forced them to go to war 276

Helen Padgett
Confirms that Blaine and Bismarck wrote about the war and were most serious about what they said 279

Elias
Writes that he is the prophet of the Transfiguration that actually occurred 280

Talks about the importance in getting into proper condition to permit the spirits to write 280

Salaaida
A Muslim, helped to defend Jerusalem from the Christians, is a very happy spirit and a lover of God 281

Los Trenos
Was murdered in the Inquisition of Spain because he believed in God and was a Bible student, tells of his progress into the Celestial Heavens 282

A. G. Riddle
Confirms that the Spanish martyr is whom he represents himself to be 283

Loyola
Is a follower of the Master and an inhabitant of the Father's Kingdom 283

St. Salatia
Is now in the Celestial heavens and a follower of Jesus, but began in the spirit world in darkness and suffering because of a false life as a teacher 284

St. Camelia
A Catholic nun, is no longer a nun or a Catholic, but a Christian redeemed by the Father 285

Amoulomol
A resident of the North Pole when it was green and warm 286

St. Clement
Errors of the Church in which he was a member must be destroyed 286

Martin Luther
Writes that Mr. Padgett will not be in error as he was because his writing came only from spirits and angels who know God's Truth. 287

Andrew Johnson
An ex-president is still in darkness due to some earth desires 288

Longiticus
Tells of his spiritual progression, but knows nothing of Divine Love 288

Helen Padgett
Mentions the fact that Mr. Padgett was not satisfied with what the wise men were writing about 290

Mother in Spirit
Spirit mother of a material preacher writes about her spiritual finding and new beliefs and would like her son to know and believe as she does 291

Helen Padgett
Progresses to a higher Celestial Sphere and tells of her work in revealing who their soulmates are and in bringing them together, but since Mr. Padgett is her soulmate, her work is mainly with him so long as he is on earth 293

Answers a dream call from Mr. Padgett 295

Jesus
Is not willing to write on the subject of soul because Mr. Padgett's condition is not what it should be although Mr. Padgett is anxious to receive it 297

John
Explains the writing received by Mr. Morgan and the relative importance of each, and that their work will become more important after Mr. Padgett finishes his work in behalf of the Kingdom 298

Jesus
Explains the great importance of his being in condition to receive the many truths that are still to be written while Mr. Padgett is still here 299

Helen Padgett
Is so anxious to reveal the Truth that he knows for the good of humanity 301

Jesus
Postpones writing to correct Mr. Padgett's thinking before he can write again 302

Helen Padgett
Is happy for the improvements in Mr. Padgett's spiritual progression 302

Layfayette
The lover of liberty, and a friend of Washington and our country, expresses his thoughts regarding France as well as Germany and the outcome of the war 303

Bismarck
Disagrees with what Lafayette has just written about the German emperor, but claims that the war was forced on him and of course made the wrong prediction as to its outcome 305

George Washington
Is a follower of the Master and has progressed to the First Celestial Heaven, and is still interested in the individual souls of men as well as their spiritual welfare 306

John Brown
Gave his life for the freedom of the slaves and the purification of the nation; and is still fighting for truth and liberty in the spirit world 308

Helen Padgett
Explains the effect on babies who come into the spirit world as a result of abortion 309

Laura Burroughs
Mr. Padgett's cousin seeks his help, which she has learned about in the spirit world from the dark spirits that received his help 310

Ann Rollins
    Reassures Mr. Padgett to have faith in the Master, the true Jesus of the Bible, and others truly are who they represented themselves to be 311

    Describes her home in the Second Celestial Sphere 312

Jesus
    Confirms Luke's message and that he is the representative of the Father to help His work on earth 313

Ann Rollins
    Writes on the great love of Jesus for him and his work of greatest importance 314

Helen Padgett
    Writes of the great love of Jesus for him and the interest he has in both material and spiritual work 315

Jesus
    Writes about the increase in the love for the Father will help Mr. Padgett both materially and spiritually 315

    Was praying and helping Mr. Padgett to receive the Divine Love of the Father to permit the writing to be received by him 316

John
    Let not your faith be shaken by what anyone says 318

Helen Padgett
    A message from Helen 318

Jesus
    Often went with Mr. Padgett to the church services that he attended in Washington and then wrote about the preachers belief and spiritual development 318

John
    States that Mr. Padgett is very near the Kingdom and that Jesus is with him in all his love and blessings 321

    Writes that the Truths that are now being received by Padgett will fill the void in man's search for the Truth that is not being taught by the Churches 322

Table of Contents

> *Writes that only the Father can give you His Divine Love through earnest prayer to Him* 324
>
> *Advises Mr. Padgett to give up reading unrelated material and apply himself to the writings given him by Jesus and other Celestials* 325
>
> *Attended a spiritual meeting with Mr. Padgett and then wrote about the speakers that they did not know what oneness with the Father means* 327
>
> *Often attends Church services with Mr. Padgett as well as many other Celestials; says: The inexperience of the preacher to fully describe the subject of spiritualism was due to insufficient knowledge of the continuity of life* 328

James
> *Writes about his visit to Church with Mr. Padgett* 329

Helen Padgett
> *Writes of the ignorance of preachers to explain the Truth of the Gospel* 329

Saul of Old
> *A member of Mr. Padgett's band is happy that he was selected to do the Master's work on earth* 330

Elias
> *Introduces himself to Mr. Padgett and makes arrangement to write and be included in the Book of Truths* 331
>
> *Describes the feelings of the congregation of an orthodox minister, whose sermon was spiritual enlightenment and believed to be a true spiritualist* 331

Helen Padgett
> *Was also present and heard the sermon of the orthodox minister* 333

Elias
> *Talks about the Law of Compensation and that God will not alter same* 334
>
> *Comments on the lack of knowledge by the preacher of the truths of spiritualism* 335
>
> *Encourages Mr. Padgett to get into condition of soul to enable the Master to write his important messages* 337

John
    Expected to complete an important message, but the soul condition of Mr. Padgett did not permit it 339

Helen Padgett
    Confirms that both Elias and John were anxious to deliver important messages tonight but could not due to improper soul conditions.. 339

Samuel R. Smith
    Mr. Padgett once called an old friend "a man with a ponderous mind"; came back to tell him of the wonderful help that he received from his band of spirit helpers 340

Judge Syrick
    Tries impersonation to test Mr. Padgett's soul perception 341

Helen Padgett
    Confirms the test that was made by Judge Syrick 342

Judge Syrick
    Confirms many things that Mr. Padgett told him about life in the spirit world... 342

Helen Padgett
    Explains Judge Syrick's spiritual condition as well as their cousin Laura who was not known to either on earth................................ 343

Elizabeth Barret Browning
    Although a bright spirit and happy, she has never seen spirits as bright as those that surround Mr. Padgett when he is receiving these communications 346

John
    Discloses that allowing the lower spirits to take control of him has depressed him to the extent that he lost faith in the Celestial Spirits 347

Ann Rollins
    Explains disappointments in both spiritual and material world 349

Helen Padgett
    Also reassures Mr. Padgett that the sun will shine on his material as well as spiritual affairs.. 350

Table of Contents

John
    Says the preacher has very little knowledge of the "Truth" as has been revealed in the writings received and does not advise attending these services 351

Helen Padgett
    Agrees with John that Mr. Padgett was not benefitted by attending meeting, but pleased with his improved condition of soul 352

John
    Came in to encourage both Mr. Padgett and Dr. Stone to have faith in the outcome of a plan that the spirit forces have outlined to them 353

Helen Padgett
    Comments on Billy Sunday's sermon to the effect that his teachings are directed towards the progress of the soul and the perfect man 354

Jesus
    Comments on a sermon delivered by Rev. William Sunday entitled: "There is appointed once a time for man to die and after than the Judgment." 356

Helen Padgett
    Was also present at Rev. William Sunday's services with many others including his special guardian, John, and is happy that Jesus was able to make a good rapport with her husband 358

    Writes that a large majority of men will exist in eternity as perfect men and enjoy the happiness which it brings, hence it is important that men should know the moral Truths of Divine Love 359

John
    That the most effective way of re-establishing the rapport is by praying more sincerely and frequently to the Father for the inflowing of His Love 360

Helen Padgett
    Urges Mr. Padgett to bend every effort to get in condition as John Helen Padgetthas written 361

Informs Mr. Padgett that his reading about the old prophets had little effect on his soul, because our Father never had the feeling of wrath against His children as the Bible quotes................................ 362

Job
Comments on the book that Mr. Padgett was reading, which only incorporates the natural love and not the Divine Love................... 364

Helen Padgett
Is pleased with the improvement that Mr. Padgett is making in his recovery, but he is not strong enough for the Celestial Spirits to write 365

John
Mr. Padgett's guardian angel is with him a great deal and advises him on the talks given by various lecturers 366

Advises Mr. Padgett about a Plan of Independence that will be disclosed in detail at a later date... 367

John D. Mastry
Selected to help Mr. Padgett with his personal problems 367

Helen Padgett
Confirms both John and stranger by the name of Mastry wrote.... 368

A. G. Riddle
A former law partner of Mr. Padgett, has progressed sufficiently in receiving the Divine Love of the Father to be able to help other spirits in the lower spheres... 368

Helen Padgett
Writes about her experience with some spirits that Mr. Padgett sent to her that did not believe in prayer, although one said that he did pray as a child... 370

John
Gives reasons why corrections have to be made in the New Testament and that James is the real brother of Jesus 372

Martin Luther
Has met the two popes responsible for his trials and they have now progressed in the Spirit World 373

Helen Padgett
Is happy with Mr. Padgett's improved condition........................... 373

Table of Contents

Lazarus
Confirms the writers as being who they represented themselves to be and that both Mary and Martha, his daughters, are living together in the Celestial Heavens 374

Helen Padgett
Confirms the writing from Lazarus 375

Goliath
The famous giant Goliath of the Philistines affirms that there is no reincarnation after death of the mortal body 376

Helen Padgett
Helen confirms the statement, that there is no reincarnation 378

Judas
As a brother and friend, urges Mr. Padgett not to permit his material mind control his spiritual consciousness, which darkens the soul faculties and prevents rapport with higher spirits 378

John
Comments on the mediums' ability to prophecy and says, that no spirit has the gift of prophecy, as mortals term it, arising from a supernatural or omniscient power; as well as encouragement for Mr. Padgett 380

Samuel
Agrees with what John has written concerning Mr. Padgett's material and spiritual progression 381

Helen Padgett
Confirms the opinion of John regarding the ability of the medium to prophecy 382

John
Writes that there is no one in all the world at this time who is fitted to do the work which you are now doing and which you must continue to do while on earth 382

States that very soon a great effort will be made by the Christian spiritualist to spread the Truth 384

John the Baptist
Writes that there is no doubt among the Celestial Spirits that Jesus has selected Mr. Padgett to do the work of communication between earth and the spirit world 385

Mark
Reassures Mr. Padgett that the writers truly are who they represent themselves to be 385

St. Stephen
Is working to strengthen Mr. Padgett's faith 385

William A. Meloy
A brother lawyer explains his spiritual progress and is happy that Jesus is able to write through his old friend 386

Helen Padgett
Confirms the various writers this night and they all were who they represented themselves to be 387

John
Informs Mr. Padgett that he is surrounded by a band of Celestial spirits sending their love and best wishes for his spiritual progression 387

John the Baptist
Also speaks encouraging words to Mr. Padgett to help increase his faith 388

James
Also encourages Mr. Padgett to have faith in what Jesus said today 389

Luke
Assures Mr. Padgett of the great love and power of the master and the Celestial power that surrounds him 390

John Critcher
A brother lawyer, dropped in to pay a visit and explain his disappointment on entering the spirit world 390

A. G. Riddle
A former law partner of Mr. Padgett's, is now a part of his band of workers as well as protectors from the spirit side of life 391

Table of Contents

Helen Padgett
Attended a Church Service with Mr. Padgett and tells of the various relatives that tried to contact him that he never knew 391

William R. Woodward
A friend of Mr. Padgett's writes that when on earth he believed in the New Birth but found It quite different upon entering the spirit world 392

George C. Calvert
A school acquaintance is seeking help from Mr. Padgett 393

Samuel R. Phillips
A brother lawyer, in darkness, learned that Mr. Padgett was helping spirits in darkness and thought that he would not refuse to help him 394

Sarah J. Wilson
An abortionist realizes only too late the great wrong she performed on earth and is seeking help 395

Bill Tucker
Claims to have been bad when on earth, is trying to get out of darkness 397

Soloman P. Brown
A wandering spirit is looking for help as he is more or less lost 397

Samuel Williams
Is seeking help because on earth he made many animals to suffer 398

Julius Soloman
Is in darkness and is seeking help 398

Louisa R. Connell
Had a theatrical career and is in darkness with others of the same profession 400

White Eagle
A message from White Eagle 401

Helen Padgett
A message from Helen 401

Joseph G. Godfrey
    A grateful spirit writes to thank Mr. Padgett for the help, he had received from him 402

John G. Carlisle
    Writes about his suffering and darkness that he is in and is asking for help 403

Helen Padgett
    Tells Mr. Padgett why she called him to write 404

John G. Carlisle
    A friend of Mr. Padgett's, is seeking his help to get out of darkness 405

Frank Davis
    An old friend and chum of Mr. Padgett's, describes his condition on entering the spirit world and tells about the help that he received there to obtain the light 406

Helen Padgett
    Writes that she sees both Carlisle and Davis and is trying to help them both to come into the light 408

John G. Carlisle
    Has progressed into the light within the past year with the help of Mr. Padgett and his Celestial Spirits 408

George Butler
    Writes about his progress from darkness into the light with the help of Mr. Padgett 410

Stephen B. Elkins
    Is in a condition of darkness and suffering, is asking Mr. Padgett for help 413

Helen Padgett
    By this message, admits that she is not always present when Mr. Padgett receives communications 413

Stephen B. Elkins
    Was helped by Mr. Padgett and has progressed out of darkness. When on earth, he did not believe in things of the soul, or Jesus, or even in a God 413

Table of Contents

Helen Padgett
Explains that White Eagle is in charge of the dark spirits and only permits them to write at the proper time, and reports on the progress made by spirits that he helped.. 415

Ralph Waldo Emerson
Does not believe in the Divine Love; his home is in the Sixth Sphere 417

Thomas Paine
While on earth, did not believe in Jesus as the Son of God............. 417

Clara Barton
Founded the Red Cross Society, and is still in the earth plane and not too interested in spiritual progression.. 419

Helen Padgett
Says that Miss Barton is now with Mr. Padgett's mother, who is explaining to her the Great Love of the Father................................ 420

John Bunyan
The writer of Pilgrims Progress, now a Celestial Spirit, and a follower of Jesus 420

Ann Rollins
When on earth was both blind and deaf, but was not unhappy, and the secret was, that in her soul she had the Love of the Father..... 421

John Bunyan
Heard the message of Ann Rollins that was filled with deep Truth and love of the Father. If I had this love I would have saved many hours of worriment 423

Helen Padgett
Reassures Mr. Padgett that Bunyan really wrote. And she wants him to read his grandmother's message 425

Laura Burroughs
Tells of meeting her soulmate 425

George E. Luckett
Is surprised to hear about soulmates, as written by his cousin, so moved to write 426

John D. Parker
   A Seventh Sphere inhabitant wants to assure Mr. Padgett that the writers are truthfully who they represent themselves to be 427

Josephus
   Assures Mr. Padgett that he is receiving communications from spirits living in the Celestial Spheres 428

Helen Padgett
   Says that spirits that wanted to write were stopped by his Indian guide because Mr. Padgett was too tired 428

Franklin H. Mackey
   Is grateful and never will forget Mr. Padgett's kindness in helping him to see the light 428

George W. Harvey
   Wants to know why Mackey and Taggart have changed so: Was it because they have received the Love of God? 429

Hugh Taggart
   Is grateful for what Mr. Padgett has done for him and the wonderful results that followed from the advice given to him 429

James A. Garfield
   Writes that Mr. Padgett's grandmother has had a beneficial effect on him and has helped him to get into the light 431

   Would like to be able to impress our President that he is overlooking matters of greater importance close to his peace stand 432

Professor Joseph Salyards
   Describes his entry into the spirit world and his spiritual progression 434

Helen Padgett
   Assures Mr. Padgett that Prof. Salyards loves him and that it was really he who wrote 438

Professor Joseph Salyards
   Has progressed to the Third Sphere and has located his soulmate with the help of Mrs. Padgett and knows that she is his forever 441

   Is prevailed upon to write his prose or poem as he mentioned in an earlier writing 443

Table of Contents

> *Has progressed into the Seventh Sphere and never ceases to thank God for His Love and Mercy* 444
>
> *Writes on the effect of the Divine Love on the soul of spirits and its great power to purify* 445

James
> *Is helping Dr. Leslie R. Stone with his spiritual progression and is with him a great deal* 446

Professor Joseph Salyards
> *Writes that the Law is the unchangeable factor in determining the status of men on earth and spirits* 446

Helen Padgett
> *Informs Mr. Padgett on the conditions surrounding a medium that he visited to learn about the kind of work they did in behalf of the Kingdom, on advice of a friend* 448

Professor Joseph Salyards
> *Mr. Padgett was once a pupil of Prof. Salyards and now the tables are reversed* 449

Helen Padgett
> *Learns that Mr. Morgan will have an Indian guide called Red Fox.* 450

Barnabas
> *Says he goes to the Father in time of trouble* 451

John Wesley
> *Also encourages Mr. Padgett* 451

R. Ross Perry
> *An old friend of Mr. Padgett's wrote about his suicide and his condition in darkness and explains the reasons for taking his own life, but is astonished to learn that Jesus is working today, as always, in helping the fallen and dark spirits* 452

Hugh Taggart
> *Helps a friend of Mr. Padgett, a suicide spirit that lost all hope of ever being forgiven to realize that there is hope for him in the spirit world* 455

R. Ross Perry
> *Is feeling better and is grateful for all the help given to him by Mr. Padgett and other loving spirits* 456

Perry's Mother
  Expresses her gratitude to Mr. Padgett for his efforts in permitting her son to see the light 456

Helen Padgett
  Perry is praying for Divine Love and is commencing to realize the great love that his mother has for him 457

Edwin Forrest
  A brother lawyer and once an associate of Mr. Padgett, seeks help, since he heard that others received help 458

  Writes that he is out of darkness and in the light of Love, that he has been praying, and the bright spirits in his behalf and especially Helen, Mr. Padgett's wife 458

  Is commencing to realize that there must be a God of Mercy and Love with the help of Mr. Padgett's wife and grandmother 460

Helen Padgett
  Writes that Forrest is praying earnestly for the Divine Love and is progressing, and was so anxious to write 461

Perry's Mother
  Writes about her son's soul, that is now opening to the Truth and that he is relieved from the awful belief that held him in darkness, and is praying to the Father 463

Helen Padgett
  Confirms that Perry has been helped by Mr. Padgett in the direction of Divine Love 463

R. Ross Perry
  Has progressed sufficiently out of darkness that he is now helping other dark spirits that are going through the same conditions that are similar to his 463

  Is very happy to tell Mr. Padgett that he is praying to the Father with all the longing of his soul for an increase of His Love, and that he will soon be in the Third Sphere 465

Helen Padgett
  Glad Perry wrote 466

Table of Contents

Luke
> *Was the first to compile material now contained in his Gospel, which is not the same as he compiled it* *467*

Jesus
> *The Prayer for Divine Love* *467*

Volume III Messages

Says that his father has found his soulmate and tells of his spiritual progression

December 20th, 1914.

I am here, your mother.

I am your mother and I want to write you a few lines for you have not let me write lately, so do not think that you are not very dear to me, for you are still my own darling boy.

I am very happy as your father is now in a sphere where he is more spiritual and happy, as he has told you. His soulmate is with him very often and she loves him very much, but he does not yet seem to realize that she is the only one for him to love. He still has some of the old love for me which he had on earth, but that is not the true soulmate love, and he will soon realize it. So do not think that he is not very happy because I am not for him. He is a very bright spirit and needs only more of God's Love to make him perfectly contented with his lot. Oh my darling boy, I am so glad that your soulmate is Helen. She is so beautiful and lovely now that she has found God's Love that I can hardly tell you how beautiful she is.

I am very happy also, but my soulmate is still in the earth plane[5] and does not seem to progress as rapidly as he should. I wish that you could talk to him as you did to your father, for I believe that it would do him good. You seem to have a wonderful influence with the spirits of men who are in a condition of sin and darkness. God is certainly good to you and has favored you beyond my greatest expectations. You seem to have the faith that calls for an answering ear and for a love that reaches to the very throne of God, and I believe that you will in some way do a great deal of good in the spirit world as well as in the earth.

Jesus is also interested in you and loves you with more than ordinary love. He seems to think that you will be of great help to him, and he is trying to show you the way to the Father's Love and favor. So do not doubt what I say.

I know that, but you will meet him or I will bring him to you before long, and have him write to you, and then you can tell him of what you know about God's Love, and the necessity of his believing that he must give his whole heart to God.

---

[5] The reference to "earth plane" is probably the astral plane, which is not described in any detail in the Padgett Messages. (G.J.C.)

Yes, I can, and will later, when I bring him to you. I have a very good influence over him but not sufficient to cause him to believe in the Father's Love being a necessity to his advancement. He is not a very spiritual man, and never was, but he is goodhearted and will listen to you. I know as you seem to have the power to make spirits listen to you. I do not understand why but it is so. So be very careful of this great power which God has given you, for if you should not do what I believe God has in store for you to do He might not continue the power, or might withdraw himself from you in the way that I mention.

I will still believe that you are his special object of love and favor, only do not neglect to do His will.

I must stop now for you are tired.

Your mother.

Discusses the health of Mr. Padgett that he is constantly watching

August 28th, 1915.

I am here, your Indian Guide.

I am not going to give you a treatment tonight as you are not in condition. Take the pills and you will feel better tomorrow night when I will treat you.

Do not let me keep you writing longer for you must stop writing now. Yes, I do. I have everything necessary. And I will succeed as I know in about three months if you sit regularly about twice a week.

I think that you are in the right way to God's Love and will soon be in condition to do what the Master wants you to do.

So good night.

White Eagle.

First effort to deliver a formal message, but Mr. Padgett was not in condition to receive it completely

December 17th, 1914.

I am here, Jesus.

I have come to write to you my first [formal] message and you are too weak to take it, but I will come again when you are stronger. You are not in a condition for me to tell you of what I have to write because you are too much worried by what you think of your earthly affairs. So I want you to let these things pass from you entirely as I cannot give you the thoughts that I desire you to write, until you are wholly free from your earth cares. Be more faithful and you will be more in condition to do as I desire. I will not come again until you are free from these worries, for you are not in a condition to receive what I wish to write while these worries exist.

Question asked by Mr. Padgett, unknown

Yes I know, but you have not succeeded as I can see the condition of your mind and know that you are too much worried by the things that you have been thinking about during the day. You must trust more in the Father.

Other questions and answers.

Yes, I do. So let that question rest.

Yes, I am that Jesus, and the men you have been reading about were my disciples and they are now enjoying the reward which their work and faith entitled them to. They are not in the heavens singing psalms or riding on clouds, as some of the alleged Christians of the present and past times believe and teach, but are still working for the salvation of human and spirit souls. They are with me still and are doing the same kind of work as when they were on earth.

They did not actually mean that, but spoke only in allegory, and meant that I was in the heavens where they all supposed God to be; but as to my sitting on the right hand of His Throne, that is not true. I am in a sphere that is of the highest and closest to the fountainhead of God's Love, But I am also working to save mankind from their sins, and bring them in unison with God's Love, which is all around men and angels, but not necessarily in or forms a part of them. Only when a soul is filled with this Love, can it be said to be in the Kingdom of God. So do not think that because God's Love is all through and around the world that every man is a partaker of it. I tell you that only the man who has received this Love into his soul and lets it fill that soul so that there is no room for anything that tends to defile it, can be said to have received salvation or to be at-one with the Father.

You are trying to learn the truth in this regard and are progressing to a degree that you will realize what the New Birth means, and without this New Birth no man can come into the full enjoyment of the Father's Love or be supremely happy. Men may when they come into the spirit world think that they are happy by reason of a great moral excellence or because of wonderful mental acquirements, but their happiness is not the kind that the Love of God, filling a man's soul, will bring.

So let your faith in the one necessary attainment increase, and when you have realized it to the full, you will be very happy and in God's

Kingdom. I must stop writing now, for you are not in condition to write more.

Question and Answer

No, I will soon come again, for you will be in condition to receive me. Yes, I will love you with all my heart and let you feel that I am in closer rapport with you and lead you to a greater happiness from now until you can find the more extensive and greater Love of the Holy Spirit. It is with you to a large extent now, but not so full as you need.

You are very dear to me and I will never forsake you, so rest in that assurance and I know that you will be happier, for no man has ever yet been in condition of unhappiness who has my love as you now have it. Be only my own true follower and I will be with you to the end.

Your own dear teacher and friend,
Jesus of Nazareth
who was crucified but rose again from the dead, as you will rise and live again in the Favor and Love of the Father.

Confirms that it was Jesus who just wrote and reassures him of the great love that Jesus had for him

December 17th, 1914.

I am here, your grandmother.

You are certainly blessed and favored. It was Jesus and he was so loving and gracious that I hardly know what to say. But of this you can rest assured; you will never be without his love and help. He certainly loves you to a degree that is beyond my comprehension. You seem to be so close to him that I wonder at your great fortune. Only believe in his love and he will never forsake you. When he told you that your worries would soon leave you, he knew and you can rest assured that you will soon be rid of them. He is so wonderfully grand and lovely, that I wonder that you could have attracted him to you in the way that you have. Be a true follower and you will soon realize that what he told you will come to pass. He is not only lovely, but he is powerful [enough] to do what he said; and you seem to have his love to a degree that we do not possess. I don't know why, but it is so. And you must believe it to be true. You are my own dear boy and we all love you so very much, that when you are given so much love of the Master, we all rejoice and thank God.

Question and answer.

Yes, he was the real Jesus and you must not doubt it, for to doubt is to show that you are not loving him as you said you wanted to. He will show you by his treatment of you and your happiness in his love that he is the one that was crucified as he said.

Be my own true son and believe and everything will be yours for the asking. He can help you beyond all conception, if you will only believe and call upon him for his assistance.

I am not going to write more as you are tired.

Question and answer.

Yes wonderful. He (Mr. A. G. Riddle[6]) is now seeing that prayer is the only thing that can help him and he is praying and listening to the advice of your mother and father. He is much changed since you wrote him[7], and I believe that he will soon be able to understand what it is to have the Love of God in his soul.

So let your prayer go to God for him as we all are doing.
Your grandmother
Ann Rollins.

Advises Mr. Padgett to give all his thoughts to God and to His Love and he will soon realize that only His Love is necessary to become a very spiritual man

December 27th, 1914.

I am here, Helen.
I am very happy, and so are you.

Let me tell you that you are very near the kingdom as your grandmother says, for you have a faith that will soon bring you so close to God that you will not let worries or the things of earth trouble you very much. Give all your thoughts to God and to His Love and you will soon realize that only His Love is necessary for you to become a very spiritual man and one whom the Master will soon use to carry out his work of teaching the people what truth and love are. So do not hesitate to give yourself to God unreservedly and without doubt, and also to believe that the Master is writing to you, and that he loves you in the way that he told you for he does, and you are favored above all others that I know of. He says that you are very close to him and need only more love towards God and more belief in him to become his own dear brother and disciple.

---

[6] Law partner of Mr. Padgett. (J.P.G.)
[7] Read Mr. Riddles' discussion of his spiritual condition and what he's doing to "make a better man of myself." This is in Vol IV (2nd Ed.) page 329.(G.J.C.)

I wonder how that can be when I know that you have been a sinful man, subject to all the temptations of the flesh, and having indulged in these things to a great extent. But it is so, and his selection of you is a surprise to us all, and we can only thank God for his goodness and Love in so blessing you. Be only faithful and you will not have to worry about the material things of life for you will be taken care of at all times and in every way that is best.

I know because the Master has told me and he will not tell an untruth or can he be mistaken as he has told you. You will be before very long. He will help you to get what is necessary that you may give him your time and work. So do not be too anxious to commence this great work, for in his own time it will be provided for you so that you can give up your professional work, as we have all told you.

Yes, he is with you quite often and is helping you to increase your faith and to love him more, and to believe that he is helping you. He is not one who will forsake you or leave you to go back to your life of sin and doubt. Only be true to him and he will be with you to the end of time; and then when you come over he will receive you and take you to the home that he has prepared for you, which will be a grand one far up in the heavens near the Father's place of Love and truth. This I know because he has told us all that you are to be with him in the spirit world and live in his home of happiness and bliss supreme. I will try, and if you will pray for me, as I know you will, there is no doubt that I will be with you.

Yes, it does, but he knows best, and we must only rejoice that it is so. Your grandmother says that she does not understand why he should have selected you, but he has done so, and you are the most highly favored one on earth, as he says that you shall be so close to him in your love and faith that men will wonder how you could possibly become so filled with God's Love and know the mysteries of his kingdom and the way to life eternal in a heaven of perfect happiness and peace.

So be my own dear Ned, and love me with all your heart and soul—only, I mean, next to the love you have for God and the Master—their love is greater than mine and so must your love for them be greater and more divine.

Yes, I was with you and I saw that you were so very much influenced by the Love of God and of the Master that I was greatly helped myself, and felt that if you continued to receive their love in such abundance you would soon be in a state of love that would carry you way beyond me in your progression, and that I would be left behind, and so when this great Love came to you I prayed that I might have it with you and receive a portion, so that I might progress also, and I did receive it and now I am on my way to the higher sphere that I told you I wanted so much to go to. Your mother says that soon I will be with her, and that your prayers and faith will help me so much—so pray for me with all your heart and faith and I will soon realize my fondest hopes.

Oh my darling, to think that after all our earthly troubles, we should now be so much one in love and happiness. It is beyond my comprehension but I can only thank God and praise Him for His mercy and great Love.

They all know, even Mr. Riddle, sees that something wonderful is taking place in your spiritual nature and in mine, and he asks us what it all means. We tell him that it is the Love of God filling your soul and the love of Jesus taking possession of your heart, which is causing your spiritual nature to undergo such a change, and he says that he does not understand, but that he must try to learn the meaning of it all, and he is now asking us to show him the way, and to pray for him and help him to obtain this wonderful Love.

He is here now and wants to write to you a long letter and tell you of his present condition and how much he loves you as his friend and helper. He is not yet firmly convinced that he needs the Love of God to make him a redeemed spirit and one with his Father; but he is thinking very deeply and will, I believe, soon realize the truth, and then he will be free indeed, and will love God with an earnest and confiding love, for he is a spirit of great conviction of principle when he has once become convinced of the truth. So try to tell him what he must believe, and you will have much influence with him for he has the greatest confidence in you and your faith and the influence of your prayers.

So if you are feeling well enough let him write to you now, and I will stop, but will write to you again tonight when you come to your room. Yes, go to the church that you have in mind—it will do you good, as the subject matter will be interesting, and the preacher knows something of the conditions of the spirit world.

So goodbye for the present,
With all my love, I am your own loving
Helen.

Mr. Padgett advised his old friend and law partner on how to obtain the Love of the Father in a previous communication, which he is trying to do and advises him of the fact

December 27th, 1914.

I am here, your old partner and friend.

You are very kind to have me write to you again[8] and I want to

---

[8] Read Mr. Riddles' previous message about his spiritual growth. This is in Vol IV (2nd Ed.)

tell you of my present spiritual condition, which is somewhat changed from what it was when I last wrote you, as I have thought very much of what you then told me, and have seen some things that have made me think that there is something more in the teachings of Jesus and in prayer than I then believed.

You told me that while I was a man of considerable intellectual attainment that fact would never take me to the sphere where Love and happiness existed in their greatest degree and that the only way to obtain that Love and happiness was through prayer to God, and faith in his power to give them to me.

I have thought of what you said very much and have tried to pray with all my heart, and have felt the result of that prayer and of your prayers which you made for me every night as you promised. I am not yet in a condition of faith that enables me to fully understand what this process of obtaining God's Love is, or how that the mere fact of praying can cause me to get it, but as I see so many evidences of the result of prayer as shown in the wonderful change in the appearance and happiness of your wife and Prof. Salyards and your father, I cannot but believe that even though I do not understand the process by which these great changes are made, yet there must be some great power in operation which answers prayer, and why not God, as you all tell me.

I want you to pray for me with all your heart and faith when you pray, that I may have the faith that you tell me about. I must obtain this change in my condition as I feel that it is absolutely necessary to my future happiness, and if I can only get the faith, I feel that I may possibly receive this Love that has apparently so transformed your wife and the others that I have mentioned.

I am comparatively happy and realize that I am a spirit wholly of the spirit world, and no longer a part of earth; but the realization does not satisfy my longings for something higher, as I look around and see that others enjoy what I have not, and they seem to be so very much happier than I.

You seem to be changed also since I first wrote to you[9], (only 11 days ago) and your mother tells me that it is because you have more of God's Love in your heart and are trying to love Him more, so everywhere I look at those whom I knew on earth, except those who don't believe in the power of prayer, I see changes and progression, which cannot be accounted for in any other way than by the one you and the others tell me is the only way to this great happiness and transformation.

You are very dear to me as I have told you, and I have the

---

page 329. (G.J.C.)
[9] Read Mr. Riddles' previous message about his spiritual growth. This is in Vol IV (2nd Ed.) page 329. (G.J.C.)

greatest confidence in what you tell me, and believe that what you tell me is the truth, but I cannot understand it all, and hence my faith is not very strong. I understand what you say and I see that you are right, and I will try to do as you say. My mind is such that I have required proof of everything before I could believe; but now I see that there are some things which cannot or need not be proved in order for me to believe, and I must accept them as true by the mere exercise of faith; so I will now try, and pray God to give me this Love and increase my faith. You must also pray for me. Yes, I know what you mean. He has told me that you are to do his work and you certainly are a favored man, for I cannot conceive of any mortal being given that great office, and having the Love of God and of Jesus to such an extent as to make him worthy or qualified to do it.

But rest assured if you need any help in any way, and I obtain that great possession for which I will strive, I will be with you and help you in every way possible. You are very close to Jesus as I am informed, and he certainly is a wonderful spirit—the brightest and most lovely that I have ever seen in the spirit world. He tells me of the way to the Father as he calls God and I listen to him and try to believe what he tells me, but somehow I have my doubts and he turns away as if in great pity and love. He will not let me alone very long, but keeps telling me of the wonderful Love of God, and how willing God is to give me His Love and blessings. But I do not understand as I have told you.

You seem to help me more, for you are somehow closer to me and more in accord with my condition of mind and thought. You are too much given to what I call right thinking about these spiritual matters to ever try to tell me what is not true.

Yes, that is what they all say, but until I do have this faith and Love I cannot realize that he is a very great teacher. I mean that I cannot believe what he tells me so easily as what you tell me.

I am praying all the time, and now I will pray with more understanding, or rather belief that it is not necessary for me to understand the process of obtaining this Love, but that it is mine if only I believe that it is.

Yes, I hope so, and if I am so blessed you will know just as soon as you give me the opportunity to write; and you will know in no uncertain terms, for when I am filled with this happiness that I see the others of the band have, you will hear me shout it out[10] as you used to hear me shout in my speeches in court — only this will be entirely from the soul and not merely a matter of mind.

I see them (Wm. R. & Bert) quite frequently and they are still in a

---

[10] Read about Mr. Riddles' changed perceptions of God and Jesus and the changes that followed in Vol II (4th Ed.) page 12. (G.J.C.)

condition of spiritual darkness as I before told you—but I try to tell them what little I have learned from you and the others mentioned, and they do not seem to want to learn of spiritual things so I do not know what to do.

Your wife and mother talk to them also and tell them of the wonderful things that they may obtain if they will only give their thoughts to God and His Love, but they do not seem to comprehend just what is meant, and think that they are still to some extent connected with earthly matters. They are not so very unhappy, but their happiness is not of the kind that I see your wife have, and I want them to obtain it, for they are very dear to me as you may know. Mrs. Riddle is not my soulmate but I love her very much and want her to become happy as she possibly can.

No, not set, but I am hoping to soon. I do not know why, but it is so. I will ask her when I next see her for she is a very beautiful and loving spirit. She certainly does love you and I wonder that she does to the extent that I see, for you are not so much interested in her as I think, for you are not a man that loves anyone very much, so you see you are a very blessed man in having the love of such a spirit.

Yes, I know you do and I was only jesting a little. You do love her as I know and you will be very happy when you come over and live with her.

Yes, I hear of her home as one of such beauty and it must be so for she is so beautiful that I couldn't imagine that her home is anything other than beautiful. Or, if I could only get into the sphere where she is I know that I would be very happy and I certainly would visit her and listen to her music and her beautiful thoughts, for she has beautiful thoughts which you cannot imagine she possesses. You will be the most surprised man in the world when you come over and meet her.

Yes, infinitely more beautiful. I did think her one of the most beautiful young women on earth when I lived, but her beauty then is as a mere faded shadow to what it is now.

Yes. I see the Professor quite often and he is progressing very wonderfully in his spiritual growth, for he is really a beautiful spirit and you know he was not so beautiful on earth. But now he is a spirit that shows that he possesses what he says is the Love of God to a wonderful degree. He is still studying and writing, and says that he will soon write you some of his thoughts, if you will let him and I advise you to do so for they are wonderful even for this spiritual world. He is here now and says that he wants to thank you for your inquiry, and also wants you to know that he is thinking a great deal of you and will soon write you if you will only permit him to do so.

You are tired and I must stop.

I am as ever your own true friend and partner,

A. G. Riddle.

Christmas night, Helen writes for Mr. Padgett to be true to God and to himself and that he need not care what the future may bring

December 25th, 1914.[11]

I am here, Helen.

You are much better tonight and I am so glad for you needed to give up all your worries and learn to trust God for all your wants. He will take care of you in every way, and you will not lack for anything that is right for you to have. So, do not worry anymore and you will not only be happy but will be successful in all your efforts of a material kind. Yes, do that and you will feel like a man out of prison, for cares and worries are the things that make a man captive. His Love will set you free indeed as Jesus says and he knows. Be true to God and to yourself and you need not care what the future may bring, for it will bring everything which the Father knows to be for the best.

You are now my own true Ned, and I love you so much that I cannot tell you of its intensity. Let your thoughts turn to God and His Love and you will be the happiest man on earth for you have His Love to a great degree, and you have Jesus to love and care for you in a way that we all wonder at. He seems to think that you are his special care, and will not let you need for anything that he sees you should have for your material good. He is here and will write to you tonight[12] and tell you what you must do in order to be able to carry out his mission, which he has designed for you. So listen to him very attentively and try to follow his instructions and you will be a very happy and fortunate man.

We are all so grateful that he has selected you for the work, and when you engage in it we will all be with you to assist you in doing everything that is possible for you to do.

Your grandmother is here and says that you must try to learn exactly what the Master wishes you to do, and do it with all your might.

She is full of love for you and so happy that you have been chosen by Jesus to do this work that she is praising God all the time and giving thanks for his Love and favor.

Do not think that you cannot do what he may tell you to do for you can if you will only try. But you must have faith in his teachings and not let the other spirits or any of your friends on earth lead you to

---

[11] This message was received Christmas night. (G.J.C.)
[12] Read Jesus' message to Mr. Padgett about what he "must do in order to be able to carry out his mission", in Vol I (5th Ed.) page 331. (G.J.C.)

believe that Jesus is not writing to you and asking you to be his true disciple. He is with you in every hour of need and loves you with a love that knows no limit. He is so very holy and pure that what he says must impress you that it is he that writes to you; so do not doubt in any particular. He says that you are his chosen one, and you will be a great man in teaching mankind what the truth is and what God's Love means to all humanity. So let him teach you and you believe.

We are now all here and are trying our best to make you feel our presence, and know that love is all around you waiting for you to feel its influence and cause you to give more of your love in return.

I am very happy tonight for you seem nearer to me than ever since the night that you prayed so very earnestly for my progression to my present home. It was a glorious night when your prayers were answered and I felt the Love of God flowing into my heart in such abundance and in such perfect peace. Oh, my darling, if you could only see how happy I am. I know that you would praise God for His goodness and thank him for being so kind to your little wife.

You must now let Jesus write, and I will write you afterwards if you are not too tired for me to do so.

So goodbye for the present,
Helen.

An early personal message to love her more with all his heart as she loves him, and advises him to be careful as to where he attends séances

December 5th, 1914.

I am here, Helen.

You are not doing the right thing by not loving me as you did. Try to think of me more in the way that you did when you were in your last meeting at the Colburns. The way for you to love me is to let your heart believe that I am with you and [that I] love you with all my heart.

You should try to throw off the feeling that you speak of. Do not be so despondent as everything will come right as I told you. Be more hopeful and you will feel better.

I will help you if you will only trust me as I have told you for I know that you will be able to do what you want to in reference to Nita. You will sell the apartment in time or I would not say so. Yes. I am and if you do, you must promise to never doubt again. So you see that I am willing to risk a great deal on my prophecy. Be true to me and you will succeed.

Yes, it was and I know what you have in mind. I thought of you then and of the influences that were surrounding you. The woman was influencing you in the way that you think. But you must not grieve about it but try to turn your thoughts to me and my love.

The conditions were not good because the young medium was not surrounded by the spirits that could help in producing the results that you are seeking. She has too many spirits that are merely of the earth plane and whose thoughts were of the kind that will not help you very much. Do not sit again with her or with the other woman for they only retard the success of your efforts.

She saw some things, but not all that she spoke of—the baby was all right and so were the hearts in the woman, but the comment on Mr. Colburn's front or the newspapers on your lap were not there. She only imagined them. Yes, she saw the pirate for he was there and the room was full of Indians, but they were not of the kind that I admire. Mr. Colburn's Indians were not there in any number. Some were, Swanee and Wolf and Rolling Cloud and another whom I don't know. Bright Star was not there nor was the guide of Miss Colburn. Your guide, White Eagle, was and he was not in good humor because of the great number of spirits. He wanted to talk but he did not try, neither did any of us.

Yes, that was the result of an effort on the part of some spirits trying to make themselves felt by you. They were not any that we desire to have present.

Yes, your father was, but not your mother or grandmother. They would not attend, as they said that the conditions were not such as they desired to have when they attended. No they were not either.

I was not at Mrs. Ripple's, but I believe that your father went there. He said that he was going as you were there and he desired to send you a message, so that you might know that he desired to speak to you. He is not here now and I don't know what he said.

Yes, I can. He is here now, and says that he wanted to send you word that your Uncle William wished to be remembered to you. He is here also and says that he wants you to pray for him and think kindly of him when you try to write as he needs your help so much. Yes, he says, but he wants you to think more of him and he will progress much faster. He says that Fred is with him in the spirit world and that his mind is improving very much, that he was not of such a mind on earth that he was able to commit any very great sin, and consequently that his progress here is much faster because of that fact, and that he is as a child and needs only enlightenment to learn the way to God's Love. He is a bright spirit, but is not so well informed as he will be soon.

You have me, only believe I am yours now and always will be, my own darling Ned.

You will be more satisfied with Takoma Park after you get rid of your troubles and get the money that you need. I don't think that you would like California after you should get there for it is not so desirable a place as you may imagine for the purposes that you have in mind and for which you have been selected. It is not a good country for the development of spiritual things. You had best be contented with the place we have selected for you.

No, I don't. It (Baltimore) is too much given to the old way of thinking about the religions that have been taught so long. The people are conservative and would not easily be brought to see the real and new truths that you are to teach to the world, so let your mind be fixed on the Park. Besides it will be best for Nita and her ambition. She will have much better opportunities in Washington than elsewhere. Because you are not satisfied with your present condition, let the matter rest until you are in position to choose, and then you will not be so unsettled as you will see that the plans we mention are the best. Yes, I know, but they will be more likely to be with you in the Park than in California or elsewhere.

Let your mind rest on that point. We are not witches but your own dear departed loves. We do not think that that church will be the one for you to join, but if you must associate with some church, join the Universalist, as that is the one that is more in accord with the truths as you will be taught. No, it does not. It merely believes that he is the son of God as I am informed.

The Unitarian Church is not very spiritual because the people do not give much of their thoughts to the things of the spirit. They depend too much on their ideas of morality and the teaching that God is a being that will not let anyone be punished for sins that he did not think were contrary to his ideas of right or wrong. They have no knowledge of the Holy Spirits mission or that God is a God of Love and ready to flow into men's souls whenever men call upon Him. Yes they do but they do not really understand the full meaning of His Love as you do: but I think that you could associate with them to advantage your spiritual being. I mean that their ideas that God is Love and is the only one that can help mankind to become spiritual and at one with Him. They are not right though, in all their teachings, for they would deprive mankind of one of the greatest consolations that they can have while on earth. That is the communication with their departed friends. They are very good in other particulars, but they would not suit you on the question of spiritualism.

Yes, I know and I am glad of it. It will help her (Nita) to learn of God's Love and she will be much benefitted by it and when the time comes she can easily believe that her mother comes to her.

You will not be benefitted very much by attending the séances of the mediums who hold séances for pay, as they have all kind of spirits come to them: but I think that your sitting with the Colburns will help you as they are good people and have spirits of a more exalted condition come to them: and the help that you may get from these spirits will soon enable you to get the voices.

Yes, sometimes but not often. Mr. Colburn's grandmother is a spirit of spiritual excellence and so is his mother to some extent, but they have not the full realization of God's Love, but they are helpful.

Yes, they are very bright spirits, but they don't come to him anymore. They are in the higher spheres and do not come to the earth plane very often, as I am told their loved ones are not on earth and they are not attracted to the earth plane very much. They know what God's Love is too, but they are not so far advanced as your grandmother or mother. I have heard them talk and know what they say.

Yes, we do, only once more, for I want you to see me as I promised you should.

Yes, I do, and I will write you very often and so will the rest of us. You need not go to the séances if you will only believe that we write you and are with you as we say.

I will try and so will the others, but I cannot tell whether we will be successful or not. But we will try very hard. Yes, she (B.S.) will and she says that she will try to speak as she promised you. Yes, and says that your friend was at the séance last night and that your father spoke to him and sent a message to you. She says that you are too mean not to visit her as she wishes to talk to you. She says that you were not in condition to talk because you were only trying to see if she would tell you that she understood what you wanted her to say so that you might know that she had written to you. She says that when you believe that she comes to you and writes sometimes she will not speak to you at Mr. Ripple's. She says that you are her brother and that she loves you, but that you must not think that she will do what you may desire, if it is not for the best.

She says that she was not impatient but that the French woman tried to monopolize too much of the time with her inquiries about her business affairs. She does not deserve another husband. She says that the spirits spoke French and that Mr. Ripple did not speak at all. She is an honest medium and does not try to deceive the people. She says that she is not in love with Mr. Ripple but that she is the one that she must help, and that in doing her duty she tries to like Mr. R. as much as possible. She does not feel attracted to her in a spiritual way.

Yes, to you and to Mr. Colburn and to Mrs. Colburn, but to scarcely any others.

She says that he (Colburn) is a very good man but is not yet spiritually enlightened and sees only the moral things. She is not in rapport with him as with you and the Colburns.

She says that she is willing that you do that, as she feels that you will he much better satisfied, and that the conditions will be much better if you do so. She will try very hard to let you hear her very soon. She says that she will be glad to tell you of those things, and to do so whenever you feel that you desire to have her write. She says that she will pray for you and try to help you in every way in her power. She says good night.

He (W.E.) says that he has not get learned to write but will try to learn. That he made the pictures for you so that you might know that he was present. He was an artist when on earth. He says that you may depend on him.

Yes, I am so I will stop. Good night and may God bless you and love you as I do, my own darling husband.

Helen

Tells of soulmate records and the work that his son does in helping the dark spirits to progress out of darkness and in leading them into the light with the help of Celestial spirits

December 31st, 1914.

I am here, your father.
I am very happy and am glad that you seem to be also.

Question and answer:

Yes, because of your experience the other night in loving Helen and her loving you. You certainly were filled with love and you must be perfectly happy, to have had such a demonstration of love and the realization of the actual sensitive presence of your wife. for I tell you that she was with you and was so filled with her love for you, that we all wondered at her love. She is a spirit that seems to have no limit to her love for you, not many spirits seem to have such abundance of love as she has for you. So you must consider yourself a very blessed man to have such a wife and a soulmate.

Yes, as I told you many years ago, there is of record in the heavens—a book of lives, as I might call it, which contains the names of those who are decreed by God to be one through all eternity: and when I want to know who is the soulmate of one who desires to know his or her soulmate, I consult that book, and there I find who the soulmate is. I am not permitted to give the name of the soulmate if he or she is on the earth life, for it might create discord or unhappiness to the living, but if the soulmate is not married then there is no restriction upon me, but if the soulmate is married then I must not tell the name, such is the law of God in this particular. The reason is that I have that duty assigned to me, and as Helen has told you I have taught her to perform this duty and she is now engaged in it, and is most successful in the performance of her mission. She seems to have a wonderful ability, or you might call it, intuition for locating the soulmates in the spirit world as she never fails when she undertakes to find one. She also finds great happiness in doing this work and in seeing the happiness that comes to them who ask her to perform this task. I do not engage in it with so much enthusiasm as she does, but I do the best that I can, and I am rewarded also by seeing the happiness of those soulmates when they are brought together.

No, not if they are not assigned to do this work. It is one of the provisions of the spiritual world that each person has some work of a certain kind, or several kinds to do, and in that way are helped by the higher powers, or, as we believe, the Love of God to perform. A spirit who is assigned to do a particular work, such as helping the spirit when it first enters the spirit world, will not attempt to engage in other work of a wholly different kind.

Yes, as to attempting to awaken a spirit to a conception of the Love of God that is waiting for it, all spirits may do this, and when a spirit succeeds in causing a darkened or blinded spirit to feel or realize that God's Love is waiting for it, then the spirit who has caused that awakening is most happy.

Of course, it is only the spirit who has had that awakening himself, who can cause or lead another spirit to that desire for spiritual enlightenment that will finally cause it to get this Love to his full and complete happiness. I am not yet in a condition to be fully able to do this with much success, but your grandmother and mother are very powerful in this particular, and they are the cause of many spirits becoming reconciled to God and His salvation. So you see, the one great thing to obtain, either while on earth, or after you come here, is this great awakening and Love of God in your own heart. It is of all things necessary, the greatest. I know to a considerable degree what it means and the happiness that comes from it; but I am not satisfied and am striving to obtain more of this Love, and to rise higher in the Kingdom of God. So you must try also, for you need not wait until you come over.

She has it to a degree that almost enables her to go with your mother, and I think that in a very short time she will leave us and rise to the higher sphere, and we will miss her very much.

Yes, he (Mr. A. G. Riddle[13]) is becoming more in condition to receive this Love and believe in what your mother tells him. She is the one that is trying to show him the way, more than anyone else. He seems to have great confidence in her and in her love.

He is also progressing very fast, and I expect that he will soon be with me in this sphere. So you see we all are doing well in the way of progressing and your prayers help us very much.

I have seen him (Taggart) very recently and he is in the same

---

[13] The law partner of James Padgett. (G.J.C.)

condition as when I wrote you first about him. He does not seem to realize that he needs any assistance to help him to become happier or to progress to a better condition and it is difficult to convince him. I tried several times, but he said that I was mistaken in what I told him, and that he knew that he was just where it was intended that he should be, so I have not tried lately.

No, I do not, but I can find him (Mackey) if you desire that I shall. He might want to say something to you, but only through me, as you must not get into rapport with these strangers to our band, for it will do harm, and we must not run the risk.

We are here. Mr. Mackey and Mr. Taggart. They say that they are very glad that you have given them the opportunity to say a word.

He (Mackey) says that he is much happier than when he first came over, as he has commenced to see the things that are necessary to make him happier. He says that he wants you to tell him of your experience with some of the other spirits, with whom you have come in contact; as he says, he has recently learned from earth sources that you have had considerable experience with spirits who have been in a condition of unrest and spiritual blindness, and have helped them some.

He says that he is in the earth plane, and that when he came over it was a very dark and dreadful road that he travelled, that he was all blind and left alone after he first entered the spirit world, and that only recently has he commenced to see a ray of light, that his condition now is not one in which he receives much happiness, and he is not very hopeful of ever becoming very happy, as he sees nothing around him but darkness and depravity, and evil spirits who delight in trying to make everyone around them feel that there is no hope for any spirit; but that their lives must be spent in a condition of suffering and unhappiness, in other words, that they are in hell and have no hope of getting away from it.

He says that he has gotten some little light from a spirit who has been telling him, that there is hope and a better place if he will only believe it to be so, and let his soul open up to the better influences; but that he cannot believe that there is any God or any Savior or any better place for him. He says that if there is a better place or any reason to believe that there is a God or Savior he wants to know it, and if you can help him any, to please do so.

He says that he has not seen Mr. Riddle and did not know that he is in the Spirit World. He says that he will try to find him, and may be he can get some help.

He says that I am much more beautiful than Mr. Taggart, and more happy looking. He further says that I am not so very different, as he sees it, to cause him to ask that question, but as you request it, he will do so. He has asked me and I told him that my appearance and happiness was caused by my having gotten the Love of God in my soul, and the realization that God is my Father, and loves me so very much that he wants me to be his child and become one in thought with Him.

He says that that may be true, but he does not understand it, and that if it is the cause, he would like to know the Way, for he certainly wants to be rid of the awful darkness and despair that is with him almost continuously. Because, as he says, that you are his friend and that he will try to do as you suggested; but he says that he cannot yet believe that there is a God who can help him to get out of his awful condition. He says that he will try to pray and try to believe and that if there is anything in what you say, and you really believe what you say that you must pray for him also.

He says that for the sake of what you say, that if any of these spirits that you speak of, should come to him, he will listen to them, even though he may not believe—that he cannot promise to believe.

He says that he will come to you tonight and try to pray as you say, but he doubts that it will do any good, but he does not think that it can do any harm. He is willing to pray and will try to believe, you must not feel bad, if when he does so, he tells you that he doesn't believe in prayer or God

He says that he is not willing to run the risk of having his conscience lash him or of his suffering any more than he is now. He does not believe that he can do so and live.

He says, that what you say sounds as if there might be some truth in it, and he will think about it, that is, if his happiness or future state depends upon his will, he will very soon determine that question, for if what you say is true, then he will be a big fool to remain where he is, when by the mere exercise of his will he can get into places of happiness and light. So he says, he will think of what you say.

He says that what you say may be all true, but the difficulty is that he can't understand, and, therefore, can't believe.

He says that he can say what you have just said and mean it, and he is ready to do so now. "If there be a God, and if that God has a Love for me, and is ready to fill my soul with that Love and make me happy and full of light, and whether I receive that Love or not depends upon my will, then if this is all true, I will that God give me this Love with all my strength and desire."

He says that he is feeling some strong sensation now and that he will repeat this and pray to God and ask for faith; and will continue to repeat it, as you have taught him, and he hopes that he may receive this Love and light. He says that you have shown him that there may be some such thing as this Love of God, and that he is willing to pray, and if his receiving it depends upon his will, he is willing it with all his heart. He says that as you seem to have such faith in this Love and in prayer that you do not forget to pray for him.

Yes, Mr. Taggart has heard it all and he says, that you certainly did put it up to Mackey to try the experiment, but that he is very doubtful if you will see any good results flow from it. He says that he will wait and see what effect it has on Mackey, and then he may be willing to consider the matter. He does not believe that prayer is anything more than a mere wish that emanates in and goes no higher than mind; and that, consequently, there is no God to answer, for if there was the prayers of all the people of the warring nations, would bring about such conflicting answers that confusion would be worse confused.

He says that he never thought of it in that way, but, if as you say the prayer should be that this Love which you say would make men love not only God but one another, and make every man strive to make happy every other man, then if that prayer should be answered, the war would soon stop, and the nations as nations and as individuals would undoubtedly be happy and peace would reign over all the land. And if this is the Love that you are trying to tell us about, then I am not so certain that it is worth striving for.

You are a very ingenious reasoner, and I commence to see that there may be some logic in what you say, but how am I to attempt to do that in which I have no faith? I know that I ordinarily, when on earth required everything to be proved, and unless things were proved I was not willing to accept conclusions, and I have not changed in that particular since I have come to the spirit world and I find it hard to change; but, as you say, I should be reasonable enough to let my mind be open to a conviction, if such conviction can possibly be brought about by any means, whether they arise from the knowledge that I gained when on earth, or whether they arise from things connected with this spiritual world of which I have very little knowledge. So after all I guess Mackey is not such a big fool to try the experiment; and having confidence in you as a friend that has at heart my welfare, I will do the same as Mackey has promised to do. So you can pray for me too, and I will pray also—but of course I will not be able to have any belief that my prayers will be answered. So you see I am not only hard headed, but hard hearted also.

Yes I am, if it depends on my will I am more than willing, not only that, but if there be a God and the Love that you speak of, I will forever thank that God for taking me away from this condition of blindness and unhappiness.

Yes, I am willing to pray to God to help me to believe, and if that will bring relief, then there will be no difficulty, for I will make such a prayer with all my heart.

You are the most persistent man that I have ever met in these spiritual matters and if what you say happens, I will certainly thank you with all my heart and soul, for I can conceive of nothing more desirable than to have the great blessings and possessions that you tell me about. So I will keep faith with you as I said when next you give me the opportunity to write, I will frankly tell you what the result of my experiment is.

Yes, and I appreciate what you have done and I say to you that this violation of your law, which the band you speak of has prescribed, has caused me to think more deeply of your interest in me and what you said, than I can express.

So goodbye for the present, the next time I come I will try to observe your law, and write through your father, if he will permit me to.

Yes, you certainly did give the gentleman a struggle to get away from what you said to them, and I believe that you have impressed them to such a degree that they will be lead to learn the truth. You are tired and must stop.

Your father, John H. Padgett.

Confirms the effort made by Mr. Padgett to bring his two friends now in the spirit world to the Light of the Father

December 31st, 1915.

I am here, Helen.

Yes, and you know that I do love you. You certainly did try hard to lead the two friends[14] to the light, and my darling I am so happy that you are so filled with the Love of God that you can do this work as you are tonight. They are most certainly impressed with what you say, and I believe that they will soon see the necessity for a spiritual awakening, and turn their thoughts to God and His Love. What a blessed work for the Master. Be only true yourself and you will be able to do much good.

You are tired so, my darling, with all my love and many kisses I am your own true sweetheart and wife,

Helen.

Mr. Padgett met Bright Star at a séance and is now helping her to progress spiritually and she says that automatic writing is superior to independent voice séances

December 24th, 1914.

I am here, Bright Star.

Yes, I know, I saw and felt that your love for your wife was so great and so pure, that I felt better too. You certainly do love her and she

---

[14] See the previous message regarding Mr. Taggart and Mr. Mackey. (G.J.C.)

loves you even more for her love is something that I have never seen surpassed. She is such a beautiful and sweet spirit that we all love her. So you must feel that you are more blessed than most men.

I am very happy but I would like to talk to you more often than I do, as you help me so much when I come to you, for you love me as a true brother and realize that I am not a mere Indian squaw, but a spirit of light and truth having been redeemed by the Love of God. Oh my dear brother, if you only knew how I love to hear of spiritual things of my Father, and not of those things which I have to listen to so much, you would think of me more often and give me many thoughts that would help me in my work. I am not one to complain, but I am also one who loves the beautiful thoughts that tell of God's love and the love of the Master and of the spirits of the higher planes. So you see you are the only one in all the earth who knows what I am in my spiritual nature. So think of me sometimes and especially in your prayers. Yes, I know you do pray for me sometimes, and I am so grateful for they help me.

Yes I do, and if you will only sit in the dark for a little while, I believe that we will be able to talk as you suggest. I certainly will try my best, and I know that your wife and father will, and so will White Eagle, who is such a powerful spirit that we should not have any great difficulty in establishing the rapport necessary. So try tonight after you stop writing, and maybe some result will follow.

Yes, I know, and it is a wonderful thing to us all. We do not understand it, but see that it is so. You are certainly blessed and you must do your work with all your strength and ability. I will try all that I know how to help you. You are not so very far behind some of our spirits who are very near the kingdom in your love for God; and I believe that if you continue to receive that Love you will have a most wonderful influence with God and also with men. The Master certainly loves you and you are his favorite one to do his work, so believe implicitly.

Be my true brother and love me as such for your love is true as I can see.

Yes, you can pray for me as I said, and give me your best thoughts. I want to get closer to God and his heaven of love, even though I have to spend so much time in the earth plane. But thank God my duties will soon be over in that respect and then I can live more in my home higher up, where your mother lives. She is a lovely and pure spirit and is filled with God's love, so try to be like her and you will be very happy.

Tell Mr. Colburn that I was at his house last night about six o'clock and tried to impress him with my presence but I could not. He is one who is very dear to me and I want him to seek for the love too, so tell him. And when you go to his home again try to get the voices, for I believe that they will soon come to you all.

Yes, I do, your father was there and called his name, and Mr. Colburn answered and your father told him that your Uncle William wanted to give you a message. Your father was actually there also.

They do not have to come there to talk to you. What can compare with the way they do talk to you. You are one of the most favored persons that I know in the way of receiving communications. The independent voices do not convey such messages as you get and cannot, for even if the spirits speaking could talk in the way that those who communicate with you write, yet there would not be power sufficient to support such extended communications. I would rather have the power of automatic writing, as it is called, than any I know of. Yes, we can say some comforting things but cannot have long communications.

Yes, she is an honest medium or I would not sit with her. So you may rest assured of that. You do love me as such and your prayer has filled my soul with happiness. So I must go, but I will come again soon and so good night

Your loving sister,
Bright Star.

Wrote that she is studying spiritual laws and learned that a spirit can only communicate with mortals when they are in rapport, and that the same law applies to mortals and that her home is in the Third Sphere

December 29th, 1914.

I am here, Helen.

I am in my home in the Third [Spirit] Sphere still, but soon I hope that I will be with your mother who is waiting for me to come to her; she is trying all she can to help me, and she says that if you continue to pray as you did last night for me that I will soon be with her.

Your father is also very anxious to progress to the same sphere so that he can be with his soulmate, who is very anxiously waiting for him. He is now a very beautiful spirit and he loves her with a very great love, but not so much as I do you.

No, I am not. I know for I can see the love in the souls of spirits and I know that his love is not the equal of mine even if he does love her so much. You will know also when you come over and you will say that I am not mistaken. So do not think that I am biased in the matter, for I am not.

Most of my time when I am not with you is given to helping the spirits who do not know the way to God's love, and the necessity for obtaining it in order to obtain perfect happiness. I am also engaged in studying the laws pertaining to spirit intercourse with mortals, as I have told you. I find that a spirit can only communicate when it is in a condition of rapport with the mortal, and only then when certain conditions exist.

Even if a spirit is in rapport it cannot exercise any influence over the mortal unless the mortal is in a certain condition to receive that influence, so it is absolutely necessary for the mortal as well as the spirit to have these conditions around him in order to get the communications. You and I have no difficulty because we are in the condition that enables us to communicate at all times, although sometimes the conditions are not as good as at other times.

No, you are in complete condition with all your band, and also with some others who occasionally write to you. Bright Star is one who finds no difficulty in writing to you, and she is very anxious to have you permit her to write as soon as possible. I will tell her and I have no doubt that she will take advantage of the opportunity. But you must not let these outside spirits write too often, for, as we have told you, it will injure our rapport and condition. No, of course not. He is privileged at all times and has the first right. No, White Eagle is a part of us and his writing will not interfere.

Yes, I have, and she has met him (Mr. R.), and they have become acquainted and have exchanged greetings. She is in the fifth [spirit] heaven and is a very spiritual woman. No, not on earth. It seems that she lived in the State of Illinois and he in Ohio; so they never met, but he says that she is a beautiful spirit, and he is so thankful that he has found her, and keeps telling me that I am his guardian angel, and that he will help me to watch over you and keep you from all harm and trouble. He is a very powerful spirit although he has not yet gotten the great love which we are all trying to help him get, but he will have it very soon now, and then he will realize what true happiness is.

I feel that you are not so close to me tonight as usual for some reason, and it doesn't make me very happy to feel so. Tell me what the trouble is that keeps you away from me, and I will try to remove it, if possible. I see and I am sorry for I have tried my best to help you, and if I am not successful it is not because I did not try. I understand and I do not know what to say for I don't see how I can give any more convincing evidence. I see what you mean, and I am sure that you will not have to feel that I am not your Helen on that account, though I am not infallible, and something might intervene to prevent the happening of what I have told you, but I do not see anything now, and, consequently, I am quite sure that you will be relieved in the way that I say.

No, she can do what you want her to do in a very short time as she has the securities, and Harry can help her get the money as I see it, but I am sorry that you do not believe sufficiently to set aside this contingency.

Yes, I know, but you might get a little more this week from local matters, and will have enough for your own purposes.

He meant just what he said, and you must believe him. He will surely see that you will want for nothing as he told you, so you have so many assurances that I don't see why you should worry.

Yes, I have met quite a number and have spoken to them; though many of them did not know me, for I had changed so much that they did not recognize me in the spirit that I am now. They are nearly all in the earth plane, and I have tried to help them, but somehow the spirits do not seem to have so much power in that regard as do the mortals by their prayers. I do not understand this, but it seems to be so. Many of the spirits, whom I knew on earth, have not had the spiritual awakening yet, so they do not see the necessity for seeking for a higher sphere. They are pretty well contented with their condition and are comparatively happy.

Yes, she is in the Third [Spirit] Sphere as she was a spiritual woman, and had a great deal of God's love in her heart.

He is not with her—he is in the earth plane. He was a very good church member, but not very spiritual. He seems to be quite happy though, and is not worrying much about progressing to the higher spheres. He is not her soulmate. She has one who is still on earth but very old, and will soon come over.

Well, I am specially endowed with the power to find the soulmates of the spirits. I don't know why it is, but I am. So is your father. He first instructed me and I am now working with him in that regard. You would be surprised to know the number of spirits here, who have no conception of what a soulmate means. They seem to think that they have to remain all alone, until some day they may meet a spirit to whom they may become attached and live with. So you see I am doing some good in that particular; for when they find their soulmates they become ever so much happier, and seem to think that I am their best friend, and special angel to guide them.

Yes, they could meet and not realize that they are soulmates. I don't understand how this is, but I know from observation that it is so. Some spirits are so in want of the power of observation that when their soulmates come to them they do not recognize them until some length of time has elapsed. I remember one case where a bright spirit from the third plane came to her soulmate in the earth plane, and tried to make him understand that she was his soulmate, but was unable to succeed until after a long time, when he awoke to the fact that he should have a soulmate allotted to him, and even then she had to tell him that she was his soulmate. He did not seem to have any longing for a mate. He was so much engrossed with things of earth that he did not think of soulmates or anything else of that kind. So you see the spirits who understand that they have soulmates are so much better off in the way of obtaining happiness than those who have no knowledge of that fact.

Question: Who will find my soulmate for me?

When that time comes, you won't need anyone to find your soulmate, because she will be right at the portals of the spirit world with her arms open and her heart so full of love for you, that you will know yourself who your soulmate is, without having to have someone find her for you.

Yes, I know how happy you are and you make me happy too, my own darling Ned. Oh, how you must love me to feel that way for me; and I love you with all my heart and soul too. Dry your tears and know that for every teardrop that falls from your eyes I have one to correspond in love and joy. Oh how I wish that you could see me now!, and then you would know that I am your own Helen and that every drop of my love is for you and no one else. So do not cry more my own dear boy. You make me so happy that I can scarcely write.

You love me now as you never loved me before and I cannot tell you how happy I am, my own sweetheart. So do not cry more but continue to always love me in this way, and you will find more happiness than you have ever known before.

I do thank God for his goodness in giving you to me, and keeping you for me in all these years that we lived together and apart. But my dear we will never live apart again through all eternity. Be all mine in thought and desire as you are now and we will know no sorrow in the time to come, my dear boy. Only to think that you will be mine in all the years that are before us, and that no matter what may happen in the few short years intervening, the time will soon be with us that we will have each other without any veil of flesh to separate us. We are one now, my Ned, and you need never fear again that your Helen does not write to you. Now you know and you will never doubt again.

Bless you, my darling, for this evidence of your love for me, for now, never again will I have a thought that you are not mine.

Yes, I will, and he will be so happy when I tell him for he loves you very much. Tell me again what you quoted: "Steeped in the luxury of tears". Oh, isn't that beautiful!, and how I enjoy those tears, but do not shed more now, for I know that they are all for me, and that your love is all mine.

No, not now. More close than ever before. No more distance. No more feelings of separation, only one close eternal one. My dear, how can I tell you my feelings this night?

Oh, night! I will never forget the happiness that you give me! Nor the love that comes to me from my own true soulmate! He is mine and I am his, but we cannot ever know the extent of our bliss!

Please, my darling, dry your tears, and let me stop a while—you need not stop writing for the night—only stop awhile that I may rest.

I am rested now.

Yes, that is the way that I feel too. Isn't it glorious that such love has come to us. The Father is good to us, and how we ought to love him and thank him for His goodness. So when we pray together tonight we will let our whole hearts go out to Him in thanksgiving and gratitude that He has given us so much of His love, and so much love for each other, for our love must come from Him, without Him we would not have the love we do for each other.

You are my lover as well as my husband and no woman could ever have been loved more than you loved me tonight. So do not let us further write as I am tired.

I will be with you in your prayers, and watch over your slumbers tonight and try to make you have pleasant dreams.

So good night my own darling Ned.

Your own

Helen.

Promises to come and reveal the truth and untruth of the Bible to Mr. Padgett

I am here, Jesus.

Let me write just a line, since I have been with you as you read and saw that you thought that many of the sayings attributed to me could not have been said by me in view of what I have revealed to you of the truths of God. In this you are correct, and many of these things I never said and for men to think that I did is foolishness and untruth. I will come and reveal to you the truth and the untruth and until I do, you must believe only those things that I have written you.

I waited that tonight I might tell you of these things and many more but it is too late and you are not in condition to receive my writings, but I will come and the world shall know the truth.

Good night, my dear brother. Do not despair for I have said it,

Your brother and friend,

Jesus.[15]

---

[15] This message is a composite of two, being published in this Volume III twice. These repeated messages have different titles, so they cannot be discerned by simply reading the table of contents. The second instance has been removed in this edition. (G.J.C.)

Writes that he is truly the man who was crucified on Calvary that comes to him and writes. And that Mr. Padgett is doing the greatest work that God has given to any of his creatures to do

April 3rd, 1914.

I am here, Jesus. I know that what you say is true, but it is I, Jesus, the man who was crucified on Calvary, that comes to you and writes. These persons, who will not believe this fact will someday become convinced, especially your friend.

I am with you, as I have told you, because I have work for you to do, and also because I love you very dearly. So you must not doubt me in any way; and if you do not, you will soon see from my messages, and also from your own spiritual development, that I am the Jesus that I represent myself to be. So believe in me and you will be happier and prosper in every way. I want soon to commence my messages again. Yes, you will soon be in condition, and then we will continue our work.

Well, he was so overshadowed by the results of his confining all his thoughts[16], when on earth, to his mental development, that his soul was permitted and compelled to starve, and as he now believes, to leave him. Of course, he has his soul, and only needs an awakening of his spiritual perceptions to realize the fact; but as long as he remains in the mental condition that he is now in he will never find his soul, as he says. The only thing that will get him out of that condition of mind is an opening of his spiritual nature, and then a belief in the Love of the Father. Your grandmother is now endeavoring to bring about his awakening, and she will succeed, for she is a very wise as well as highly developed spirit in her soul qualities.

The spirit is not what you might call a wicked one, he only committed the great error of believing that the mind was everything in existence, and as he said, the soul and all spiritual faculties were myths. Many a spirit is in this condition of mind over-shadowing the soul to such a degree as to cause the soul, so far as the knowledge or belief of the spirit is concerned, to be lost[17]. He is not one that will find much difficulty in recovering his soul, as soon as the soul faculties are awakened. The unfortunate spirit is one who knows that he has a soul, and knows that that soul is filled with sin and error, and has no apparent way of becoming cleansed. I know of no spirit more to be pitied, or who needs more of the influence and help of both spirits and mortals.

---

[16] See message titled "A spirit who is suffering intensely comes to Mr. Padgett and begs him to help him to find his lost soul" in Vol IV (2nd Ed.) page 323. (G.J.C.)

[17] Jesus answers "what is a lost soul?" in Vol I (5th Ed.) page 314. (G.J.C.)

Let me tell you right here that when you help a spirit to find the way to salvation and God's Love, you are doing the greatest work that God has given any of his creatures to do—and when that spirit, through your help, finds that way and realizes the truth and receives this Love, he is forever your most thankful friend and worker in forwarding the interests of your own spiritual being. So when the Bible says, for every soul saved there is a new star added[18] to the crown of one who is the instrument in saving such a soul, it only declares a truth which exists and which never changes. So in your work of helping these poor sinful and darkened spirits you are laying up spiritual jewels, which, when you come over into the spirit world, will form a part of your soul's existence.

Of course, there are no jewels, as such; but they represent great qualities of happiness and Love, which the Father will give you. Men do not realize of what momentous importance the saving of a soul is, and what results come to him as such a savior.

I am not going to write more on this subject now, as in my other messages I will deal with it. So, I will now say good night, and may the Love of the Father be with you and in you this night. I will give you all my love, and help you to obtain your desires, spiritual and material.

Your true brother,
Jesus[19]

Is happy that the Master explained the lost soul meaning to Mr. Padgett and that he should be happy to have Jesus as a friend

April 3rd, 1914.

I am here, Helen.

Well, did not the Master explain what the lost soul[20] means in a way that makes it very plain? I am so glad that you asked him and received the answer that you did.

He is the only Jesus of the Bible and you are right when you say you believe that he is. Let not what men say cause you to doubt this fact, for it is a fact. He is the greatest son of his Father, and when you have him for a friend, you are rich indeed. So my dear Ned continue to believe in him, and listen to his teachings, and follow them.

Well, I love you, as you know, with all my heart and soul, and with a love that increases as the Father's Love fills my heart more

---

[18] See Daniel 12:2-3, the best match I could find. (G.J.C.)
[19] This message is a composite of two, being published in Volume II and Volume III. (G.J.C.)
[20] Jesus explains what is needed to recover "a lost soul." In Vol II (4th Ed.) page 47. (G.J.C.)

abundantly; and when I am so filled with more of this Love, I will tell you, and you will know that my love for you has increased correspondingly.

So my darling Ned, I must say, good night,
Your Helen.[21]

Writes about her progress from the Third Spirit Sphere to the Fifth Spirit Sphere where she is now living with Mr. Padgett's mother and describes the beauty of her new home and that she is now continuing with earth hobbies, such as painting and voice study

January 7th, 1915.

I am here, Helen.

I am very happy and you are a little better, and there is no need to worry about Nita as she is now very happy in her school. I will try tonight to tell you of what I am now doing in my new home and in the earth sphere where I am most of the time, helping spirits.

Well in my home I am so very much engaged in studying the laws of communicating with you that I have hardly time for anything else. I am now quite certain that I understand how to talk to you in an independent voice and also to materialize. So you must not be astonished anytime to hear my voice or see me in the form of a materialized spirit. I am also trying to help the spirits who are in a condition of blindness and doubt.

I am living with your mother in her home, but I am not as spiritual as she. We are both very happy though, and have everything that heart could wish for. The music is so beautiful that I cannot describe it to you, and even the love which helps to make the music is of such an intensity that you could not possibly understand if I should attempt to tell it to you. My home here is much more beautiful than that which I had in the third (spirit) sphere, and everything is beyond what I conceived when I lived there. The house and trees and flowers and fruits are very much more beautiful and delightful. No one could be anything but happy in such a home. We have nothing to interfere with our happiness and every one is a delightful companion and full of love and beauty. I have met many spirits that I did not know either on earth or in the spirit world before I came to this place, both men and women.

Yes, we have rivers and lakes and fields and mountains and all the beautiful landscapes that you can imagine, I not only enjoy these things, but they are more real than those of earth. I am sometimes engaged in painting these flowers and landscapes, and have many

---

[21] This message is a composite of two, being published in Volume II and Volume III. (G.J.C.)

pictures which others painted. I find that I can paint with a more artistic touch than when on earth. I have no trouble in drawing as you know I had some in my earth pictures. I am also studying music, and especially my vocal lessons. You will be much surprised when you hear me sing as you cannot conceive what a different voice I have. Sometimes I try to sing some of the songs that I used to sing to you, but they are not pretty in comparison to the songs we have here, either in the music or the sentiments.

Well as you are not so much interested in my description, I will not attempt further portrayal of the things here. Yes, I can see it in your brain—you are thinking about other things, so you see, I know. Yes, but you must think of what I write for that is necessary in order for you to write. While I can guide your hand, yet I have also to use your brain to express my thoughts. You could, if you will try—that is one of the things that I want you to do, for then you can hear what I say at anytime, and it will not be necessary for you to write.

Yes, it is better to presume what I write, for sometimes it does you good to read over what I have said and feel over again the emotions which you felt at the time of your receiving my messages.

I love you all the time, and you know it, but sometimes it is beneficial to reread my expressions of love, even though you doubt that they are mine. Let me tell you that you are not to remain in this state of doubt much longer, for I will so indubitably show my presence to you that you will never again doubt that I am with you. Then when you write you will feel that I am indeed writing as convincingly as if I sat beside you and you could see me. It may happen any night as you sit and write or when you are lying in bed thinking of me and wondering if I am really with you. So you must be prepared to have anything happen which will show you that I am with you. Yes, I believe that I will be able to do that when you are all alone, and so you will hear my voice when you are alone.

No, this is the most satisfactory means of communicating that I know of. You can exchange your thoughts for mine, and can write so much more than I could possibly speak. Yes, I will be able to speak for a little while, at a time, but not as I write. No spirit can gather such power as would be required to continue to talk for any length of time. Even Bright Star, who is an adept, could not carry on an extended conversation, as she says.

The power that I now have enables me to manifest myself in several ways—such as the independent voice, materialization and writing—I do not know about the slate writing, but I believe that I can do that too—at any rate I will try to accomplish it sometime. I don't think that I will be able to manifest on the same night in an independent voice and also materialize, for each manifestation requires great power. Yes, I can knock on the table, but that does not give any special satisfaction—all earth bound spirits can do that—it is the lowest order of manifestation. We of the higher spheres do not care to do that if we can manifest in any other way, and I would rather not try it.

I mean that I am stronger physically, spiritually and mentally than White Eagle. I do not know the exact extent of my power, but the spirits with a better knowledge of these things, say that my power is so very unusual that I can do most anything that I may try. Of course, they mean within reasonable limitations. I could not take a mountain and move it, or even a very heavy substance, but I could lift you and will sometime just to show you how strong I am.

Spiritually, I am now in a sphere that enables me to know what the Love of God really is and that in his Love I have almost complete happiness. I have gotten rid of those things, I now love everybody, and am trying my best to help every soul that I possibly can; feelings of dislike or envy or hatred has no place in my heart, for which I thank God.

The conditions of all spirits are determined by their goodness and love. No distinction on account of what a spirit might have been on earth is known here. The poorest working man is as of as great importance as the most famous man according to his earthly standing. In fact more of the poor and humble of earth are in the higher spheres than are those who were wealthy and held high positions. This is so, not because there were more of the poor, but because their spiritual conditions were better, and they are more susceptible to the influences of the good spirits, who are doing the Father's work. So you see high standing on earth is not a thing which determines the condition of the spirit here.

I know a number of spirits who, when on earth, were prominent in society, and wealthy, but who are now in the lowest sphere, simply because they did not know anything of God's Love, and wholly failed to observe his laws and truths while on earth. You will be surprised at the number of friends of yours who were prominent on earth, and who are not as happy as they were while on earth. Their desires are very much the same as on earth, and yet they have no means of gratifying them, and, consequently, they are very unhappy.

I think that the sin of suicide is the worst, and then the murderer, the drunkard and the prostitute. The last is a person who seems very difficult to (discover) things spiritual because he or she does not realize the enormity of his sin so much as the suicide or murderer. A prostitute has ruined many, and when she at last realizes that fact her sufferings are very, great. They are in very low planes—lower than the earth planes, and they are generally trying to pursue the occupation that they had on earth, and imagine that they do. I say imagine, because I have no better word to express it. But they really believe that there is some kind of happiness that comes to them from the belief that they have, that they can still engage in such things. You would be surprised to see the great number of men and women who occupy this plane—some of them who on earth were not considered such. But prostitution is not a thing of act altogether, but of desire or lust. A man may look on a women and lust after her, and, as Jesus said, he already commits adultery in heart; and so, many mortals committed adultery in that way and the sin arising there from follows them here, and can only be gotten rid of by prayer, and the consequent forgiveness and Love of God in their hearts. A man or women may get rid of this sin while on earth, if he repents and prays God to let His Love come into his soul. When this Love takes possession of a man's soul all sin is cast out and is no more remembered against him—this is what is meant by washing away sin.

Neither the blood of Jesus nor his vicarious atonement, as it is called, ever washes away sin—the only effective thing is the Love of God in the heart. So you see men may believe all that they possibly can that the blood and sufferings of Jesus, and his death on the cross, saves them from sin and its consequence, and yet, if they are not possessed of this Love, these sins will remain and they are not saved.

I have written more than I intended on this subject, but as you are so much interested I thought it best to tell you what I have learned from the Master himself.

I mean by having more powerful mentality that I have progressed so very much in knowledge and in my will power. I am not yet a wise woman, but in a certain line I have acquired a great deal of knowledge as regards, for instance, the way in which spirits and mortals (function) while in the flesh. I am not any more versed in the science of what controls the heavenly bodies, or why one star differs from another in glory, or what are God's mysteries as you may consider them—these matters are being investigated by other and older spirits. But as regards love, both of God and spirits and mortals, I have learned a great deal. Let me tell you that of all subjects that should interest men, love is the greatest, for love is the fulfilling of all law; and the man who knows what love is, I mean the real, genuine love both for God and his fellow mortals and spirits has that which is not equaled by knowledge of anything else in all the Universe.

Jesus has this knowledge to a greater extent than any other spirit, and, consequently, is the greatest power in all the heavens or earth, and those who listen to his teachings and follow them will be when they come over, and even while on earth, the strongest and happiest of all beings. So do not neglect to learn this great knowledge. You are very far in the possession of it, and when you shall have had his teachings and followed them you will be a powerful and happy spirit when you come over.

I am told by him (Jesus) that he is forming his own kingdom in the spirit world of those who listen to and follow his teaching, and get this great Love in their hearts; and their home or sphere will be entirely separate from the other spirits, and will be in the highest heavens, where happiness the most supreme will be.

So I am trying to become one of his followers and a subject of his kingdom. He will not let sin of any kind of inharmony find a resting peace in that kingdom, and hence no man or spirit who has not been fully purified can possibly enter into it. He is now forming that kingdom and when his work is done, and he leaves the earth plane and mankind to themselves, he will go into that kingdom and remain there, and rule for all eternity. So strive to become worth of becoming a subject of that kingdom.

You must stop writing now as you are tired. Well as you are my soulmate and the only one that I will ever have or want, I must tell you that I love you with a love that can never grow old or less, and that when you come over you will realize that your Helen is a spirit who knows how to love. But she loves you now with all her heart and soul and you must believe it.

So good night my own darling Ned.

Your loving, Helen.

Writes about the sudden passing of a friend and how she tried to convince her that she could not re-enter her body, which was similar to her own experience

January 27th, 1915.

I am here, Helen.

Yes, we will try—you are in a better condition than you were tonight, at the office, and I will be able to write in a more connected manner. Well, I was present when Jen passed over, and took her in my arms and carried her to a place in the earth plane where she will live until she progresses to a higher sphere—she was very glad to see me for she recognized me and said: "Oh, Helen; where am I? It seems so strange that I should be with you."

I told her, she had passed from the mortal to the spirit life, and that now she must not think of her body or that she can ever enter it again. She did not quite understand me, but said that she did not see why she should not re-enter her body, as it was only asleep, and would want her as soon as it should awaken. I told her that never again would she enter her body, that she had ceased to be a mortal, and that just as soon as her body should be buried she would realize that she is a spirit, and that no more would she live on earth as a mortal, but that she would visit her dear ones on earth many times, but not in a physical form.

She is still in darkness as to this matter, but I am trying my best to help her realize that she is a spirit. She is somewhat confused, because she tries to talk to George (her husband) and he won't listen to her. She says: "My dear is very deaf and that is why he doesn't hear me"; But I tell her that he cannot hear her, as her voice is only a spirit voice, and his ears are not attuned to hear spirit voices.

She will soon realize to some extent, that she can no longer talk to George or any of her friends, and then will come the full understanding that she is really a spirit.

She is with her body now, and sees the presence of her husband, and relatives, but as I said, does not comprehend why they do not notice her presence, or tell her why they do not notice her presence, or tell her what the trouble is. She sees them sorrowing, and yet she does not understand why they should do so, as she says, she knows that when she awakens she will become a part of her body again; and so I can do nothing more now, but to let her know that I and her other spirit friends are with her and will not leave her until after she realizes that no more is her body to become her home.

Her mother is with her, and so is her father, and they are trying to help her, also. Her mother is a very bright spirit, and is filled with God's love, and has her home in the fifth (spirit) sphere, where she is very happy.

Her father is in the earth plane, yet. He is not very spiritual, but thinks more of earthly matters; and does not turn his thoughts to higher things—but some day he will, and then will see that real happiness, can only be found in the things which are of God, and his love.

Jen's soulmate is here and is in the third (spirit) sphere. He has never met her on earth, but he knows that she is his soulmate, and that as soon as she awakens to her condition, he will meet her and tell her that she is his for all eternity, and that his happiness is her happiness; and that they must both try to progress to the higher spheres where true happiness may be found. He is a very beautiful spirit and is in possession of much of God's Love.

George's soulmate is still on earth, but she does not live in Washington, and he will probably never meet her. She is a woman of about thirty-six years of age, and is not very spiritual, but is a great church member. So he will never again meet Jen as his wife, for she is another's.

Jen's body will be buried in the earth as was mine, but, sweetheart, she won't be there any more than I am there; and when her body is finally laid away, she will never go to the place where it is buried, unless her folks go there and weep over her grave, and in that way attract her to them. But she doesn't want them to do that as I know from my own experience.

More questions and answers unrecorded, but will print what is written.

Well, we will see. Maybe she will not want to. But if she does, I will certainly communicate it. She thought that she did, but really did not, and now, when she learns the truth, she will not feel any attraction towards him—but maybe she will, as we cannot so soon forget our mortal loves, even though we find the real Love after we come over—and when I think of that, it may be that she will want to send him a message of comfort.

Yes, that was singular coincidence. But you see, we never know when the summons will come for us to pass over. We both expected to return home soon, as we were feeling much better, and were happy in the thought; but in a moment, the summons came, and quickly we passed to this home of delight and freedom from care and suffering.

Your own true and loving,
Helen.

Roman Emperor gives his experience. Why he learned English

July 22nd, 1915.

I was a spirit who, when on earth, was known as the man who conquered and destroyed Jerusalem. I am Vespasian, the Roman Emperor.

I became a Christian even before my death, but I never was more than a Christian in name. I knew nothing of the true doctrines of Christianity, or of the Love which the early Christians professed to possess, as such Love was taught by Jesus. My espousing Christianity was a matter of political expediency, and was not the result of any fixed faith in the truths of that religion. But since I became a spirit I have become a true Christian, and am now a follower of and believe in the truths of the Master. I live in the Celestial Spheres and am a redeemed spirit and have the happiness which such condition ensures. You must not think that because I was once Emperor of the great Roman nation that therefore I am a person of more importance than are those who were of less importance on earth. That fact does not enter into the determination of what place I shall occupy in the Celestial Spheres. Only the soul's development determines that question.

But I am a high spirit, nevertheless, and I want to tell you that I am interested in your work among men and the unfortunate spirits. So believe me when I tell you that I am in sympathy with your work and will aid you to the best of my ability. I know that you have your doubts as to my writing to you, and I can hardly blame you, for it is not natural to suppose that the spirit of one who passed over such a long time ago would have the interest in you or in humanity to cause him to come to the earth sphere again, and attempt to write to you or to help mortals. But it is a fact, nevertheless, and you must believe me.

Well, we do not stand still in our spirit life, and we have learned many languages since we became spirits; and knowing sometime ago that mortals would be called upon to do the work of assisting in the redemption of men, we have prepared ourselves so that we can understand and write most of the languages of earth. But in the case of the English language, we saw that the greatest number of mediums come from the race speaking that language, and hence we paid particular attention to the learning of the English tongue.

We can learn so much more readily the various languages since we became spirits and men must not think that spirits do not progress in their knowledge of nearly every kind of learning. I am not now the one-sided person that I was on earth—the whole universe is open to me to learn whatever it contains, and I have studied with great interest and assiduity ever since I became a spirit.

Well, I must stop, but will come again and tell you of many things that my studies have brought to my knowledge. So, with the best and kindest of feelings, I am,

Your brother in Christ,
Vespasian, the Roman Emperor.

A spirit who believed in the eternal punishment of those who denied the vicarious atonement of Jesus

January 16th, 1916.

I am here, Hannah Somerville.

I am the spirit of one who lived on earth the life of a leader of a sect that believed in the resurrection of the body and the eternal punishment of those who refused to believe in the vicarious atonement of Jesus and his sacrificial death.

I have been in the spirit world a great many years, and have long ago learned the great errors of my beliefs and teachings, and now know that the earthly body does not rise again and Jesus did not make a vicarious atonement, nor did His death on the cross satisfy the justice and demands of an angry God.

I know that other spirits have written you this same denial of a false belief, but I wanted to do so also, for I realize to such a great extent how harmful such beliefs are. I was in the spirit world a long time before I was relieved of these beliefs, and I stood still in my progress for many years waiting to be called to heaven and meet my Lord face to face, and receive from Him the great commendation of, "Well done, good and faithful servant." But I received no such call, and I never got any nearer to God, apparently, than when I first entered the spirit world. And all this time I was in such a condition that I was not susceptible to the teachings of other spirits who know the truth and attempted to show me the errors of my belief.

This may seem strange to you, but I want to tell you that the conviction of a strong belief is one that is not easily removed or shaken, and I did not find any greater and convincing force in the assertions and arguments of spirits, than I would have found in the arguments of mortals, had I remained on earth.

I saw many spirits and talked with them, and they told me that Jesus was not God, but merely a spirit like myself, only the perfect on; but I would not believe, for my earth belief could not be shaken.

I even saw a spirit who said he was Jesus and that I must not believe in him as God, or in any vicarious atonement; but yet I would not be convinced of my errors.

This earth belief is a wonderful thing when it once possesses a man as it did me, and so many spirits have suffered from it, as I suffered.

At last the light came to me, and my soul was set free to progress to the higher spheres. But how much time I lost, and how much unhappiness I needlessly endured I cannot tell you. Now I am in a Celestial Sphere, where I know that Jesus made no vicarious atonement and is not God, but my loving elder brother.

I have never written before and I wanted very much to write, and your band was kind enough to let me do so. My name was Hannah Somerville, and I lived in England, and died in 1682.

I have forgotten the name, but it was a sect of dissenters. Yes, and I have given you my correct name. Yes, I can. I believe and know that Jesus was and is the son of God, and the most beloved son, too.

I will say good night.
Hannah Somerville.

Once a Pagan and now a Christian

November 2nd, 1915.

I am here, Semiramis.

I was a Greek maiden, and I only wish to say that I desire to tell you that I am a Christian, and live in the Celestial Heavens where the Master is forming his New Jerusalem.

I was on earth a pagan, as I was called, and believed in the philosophy of the Greeks and also of the Egyptians, who had written many works dealing with the soul and its destiny. I then believed in the immortality of the soul and the Elysian Fields for those spirits who should obey the gods, and do those things which caused the soul to seek the higher planes of truth and happiness. But after I became a spirit and met some of the beautiful Christian spirits, I had an awakening and I became convinced of the truths of Christianity, and the wonderful plans of God for the salvation of mankind.

So I merely wanted to say this and to write, and your band permitted me to do so. I will not detain you longer, but must stop, and will say that I am

Your sister in Christ,
Semiramis.

An ancient spirit decides to search for the Divine Love, which he learns is the cause of the beauty and brightness of Helen Padgett, a Celestial Spirit

September 24th, 1915.

I am here, Sebastobel.

I am a spirit who has never written before, and I desire to say a few things which I consider of importance to mortals as well as to spirits.

I live in the highest sphere where intellect rules supreme,[22] and where spirits are happy in the knowledge that their spirit existence is free from all the cares and limitations which a life in the body imposes.

I am a student of the laws governing the relationship of the various planets to one another, and to the earth, and of the influences which the sun and moon and stars exert upon mortals of the earth. I am an ancient spirit and have been in spirit life many thousands of years—long before the great flood which submerged a great continent which men know as Atlantis.

When that continent existed and was peopled by living, active, intelligent beings, I had been a spirit many years and was in communication with the prophets, as they were called—or rather seers—of that happy land. The development of these people far surpassed that of the present inhabitants of earth in not only the purely intellectual qualities in the abstract, but also in their knowledge of what you call the arts and sciences. Then the inhabitants of that fair land not only did not have the necessity for using horses or automobiles or steam cars or boats, or airships, for moving from place to place and travelling,

---

[22] The Sixth Sphere. (J.P.G.)

but they knew of the existence of and the way to utilize certain forces of nature which enabled each individual or group of individuals to transport themselves from place to place by mere operation of their will power, using these forces. These forces still exist in nature, and are just as ready to be utilized now as they were at the time these people of whom I speak brought them under their control.

Some day it will be given to man to understand and control these great forces and utilize them to their fullest extent. Just when this time will be I don't know; but considering the rapid strides that mortals have made in discovering and utilizing some of the heretofore hidden forces in nature during the last half century, I do not think it will be long before these great forces will be discovered, or rather revealed, to man. It will not be so revealed until the higher powers consider the time ripe for man to have the knowledge of these forces revealed to him and to control them.

I know what these forces are, but I am not permitted to make them known to you or anyone else at this time. I should otherwise gladly do so.

Well, while they had this great knowledge and power of transporting themselves, and could have done so had they been given time, the submerging of the continent was so sudden that no man knew the moment when the catastrophe took place. It was in the twinkling of an eye, as it were, and men were drowned before they had time to think or attempt to save themselves.

No, it was not like the Bible description of the flood, which never occurred; that was merely allegory and existed in other books, in a little different form, long before the Bible was written.

These Atlantians are now inhabitants of the spirit world, living in different spheres, and more or less developed in their intellects.

Well, I merely want to say further that I am somewhat surprised that you can receive my thoughts in the way of written communication, for I never before in all my spirit experience have written my thoughts this way. It is a wonderful gift and one which I consider superior to any other method that I know of for communing with mortals. You may ask me any question and I will answer it if I can.

Yes, I see other spirits here—some dark and ugly and some bright and beautiful. I have spoken to one who says she is your wife, and she is a most beautiful and bright spirit—the brightest that I have come in contact with.

Well, I must confess that I have never seen in my sphere any spirit so beautiful or bright or pure looking or lovely as she, and I wonder why it is. I am at a loss to know, and I would like to know, I assure you.

No, my intellect does not tell me, and I see that there is here presented a phenomenon which is worthy of all investigation and study.

Well, she has told me, and I am astonished at her explanation. I never before knew or heard of the existence of such a thing as this New Birth or Divine Love, and even now I cannot comprehend what she means, but I see a result or effect for which I can find no cause, and it seems reasonable that I should accept the cause which she gives me. But I am astonished, as I thought that there is nothing in all the spirit world equal to the mind, and nothing which brings such happiness. But she tells me of a happiness of which I had no conception. Well, as you say, I see an effect and there must be a cause; and as I am an investigator of the truth, I feel it my duty to search for that cause, and I will.

She has invited me to go with her and meet her band, and also one who, she tells me, is the most magnificent and beautiful in all the spirit universe. I will go with her and investigate this matter; and will come to you again. So I will say good night.

My name when on earth was Sebastobel. I lived in the Upper Nile when the human race was very early developed into thinking beings.

Sebastobel.

Now a Celestial spirit, relates her early spiritual development in the Third Sphere with the help of Mr. Padgett

November 16th, 1914.

I am here, Helen.
I am very happy.

Yes, I am and I feel that God is filling my soul with His Love. I believe that He is my Father and that I am His child. He is very near me and the Holy Spirit is coming into my soul more and more. I have commenced to have more faith in His Love and Grace, and I believe that He is waiting to fill my soul with His Love as you have told me. I am so happy that I can realize that He is my own true Father of Love. He is with me so very much now, that I know that I have been born again, as your grandmother has told me I would be if I would only believe and let His Holy Spirit enter into my soul. I will soon be in the Third Sphere that I told you about, and will then be so very happy. I will come to you just as soon as I realize the change in my condition and tell you of the glories that your mother tells me will be mine. So do not worry more about me as you have done and pray for my salvation. I am soon to be in my new home and then you will know that I am a spirit redeemed.

Yes, it will and you will be so very happy also. Let us both thank God for His Goodness and Love. Let us try to progress more and more until we join each other in this world of light and happiness.

Yes, it has more love for you than ever before and when you

commence to really learn what the true meaning of God's Love is you will see that all our past happiness and love are merely shadows of what the real Love and happiness is that we may enjoy when the Holy Spirit takes full possession of our souls and makes us feel that the Father's Love and Care are only the one thing necessary for our true happiness and love.

Yes, I will just as soon as I reach that home.

Yes, they all rejoice that I have at last found God and have His Love to that extent that makes my soul free from sin and error.

Yes, and so could I but I must not write much tonight as you are tired and sleepy.

Good night, my own true love,
Helen.

Agrees with the suggestion made to form a band to protect his son in his spiritual investigation through automatic writings

May 31st, 1914. (Date doubtful).

I am here, your father. (John H. Padgett)

Yes, I am. And I will try to tell you what you must do to form a band of spirit workers. Let me select them, and then you will not be troubled by bad spirits. You must not try to talk to every one who may come to you, for that will work injury to you and you will not be able to get the best results.

Let me tell you who you should have form the band: your grandmother, your mother, Helen, Professor Salyards, Mr. Riddle, and myself—these are enough to help you in the investigation of spiritualism.

Will they join?

Yes, I will have them come, and you can ask them.

Grandmother, Ann Rollins.

Yes, I will, and you will be a successful medium, and will not need to go to the séances where you went on Friday night, as they are not helpful to you in the way of progressing in your investigations.

Mother.

Yes, I am. I certainly will, and you will not be troubled by bad spirits, for your father and grandmother will keep them away from you.

Prof. Salyards.

Yes, I am, and I will be one of the band to help you. You will be my mouthpiece in my writing to the world the thoughts that I desire to make known on subjects that are of interest to mankind. Keep well and I will soon let you write my ideas of this life and of what I find to be the real truth of the Love of God and the love of mankind.

Asks him to write a verse.

Yes. I am not in condition tonight, as you are too weak to write much more. Yes, I will show my face in the photograph, and then you will know that I am one of your band.

Mr. Riddle.

Yes, I am, and I will be one of the band. You will not be annoyed by any others than the ones your father has named. I will write you what my beliefs and thoughts are of the life here so that you may know that I am just a spirit in search of the truth. You will see that I am not one who knows everything, but will try to learn whatever is possible and will tell you what I learn. Yes, and will let you see that I have my moustache and goatee just as in my earthly life.

Father.

Yes. You can go to the photographer as soon as you find it convenient and we will be there, and you will see us all. I will be in my naval uniform and then you will be convinced that I am living.

At the séance on Friday last, J. Shellington spoke to me and asked that he be permitted to join my band of spirits. I had not then thought of or had suggested to me a band of spirits. I suggested his name to my father, who wrote.

Father.

He is not of the spiritual kind that will be helpful to you, and I do not think it wise for him to join. He is too much of the earthy yet, but will soon progress, and then we may have him join.

Go to bed and rest.
Your father,
John H. Padgett.

First preserved message from Mr. Padgett's wife Helen: Who says that she looks on Jesus as a man of God, but not as God Himself. Also informs him regarding his parents and grandparents

May 31st, 1914.

I am here, Helen.

Yes, I love you and you know it. Come to bed and I will let you feel my arms around your neck and will hug you and put you to sleep so that you will feel better in the morning.

Were you at the Bahai meeting?

Yes, I was. I did not think much of the address of the woman from India, because it did not tell of what the Love of God is to the lost souls of man. You were not benefitted much by it, as you were very lonely and needed the Love of God to be preached. The other address was better, but it does not tell the way to truth and light that the Bible does. Be a Christian and love the God of the Bible and ...

Yes I am, and you know that I am in the spirit world. I can see that the things taught are the truth, for I am not in the flesh and am not bound by the limitations of the flesh as I was when alive.

Yes, and I am trying to help you all that I can. Yes, you do and I will continue to help If you will let me.

Yes, I look upon him (Jesus) as a man of God, not as God Himself. He is the one that should be your guide and friend. He is a very bright spirit and is far up in the Heavens and is close to God. He does come to us sometimes, and keeps us in holy rapport with the Father. He is the loveliest of all the spirits in the Heavens. He is not angry with you, for he loves you with his whole heart, and will do everything to help you.

Yes, I am, but I am not in the Heavens yet, but I will soon be and then you will learn much more from me.

He (her father) is getting better; he is beginning to see that this life is not for the Christians who have not the Love of God in their hearts, but for those who love God with all their hearts and souls. He did not love God truly; he put too much faith in the literal words of the Bible, but did not have the spiritual love that he should have had.

She (her mother) is progressing, too.

Your father is in the Heavens, and is a bright and shining spirit and is your Guardian Angel. He is with you very much and he will help you to progress and to become a more spiritual man.

Your mother is far up in the Heavens, and she is with you often and is trying to help you also. She is an exceeding bright spirit and is very strong and is filled with the Holy Spirit to a very high degree. She is one of the brightest spirits that I know. She comes to me often and helps me progress.

Yes, she (Mr. Padgett's grandmother, Ann Rollins) is too pure and holy to come to me very often, but she is much interested in you and will come to you when you write sometimes. She says she will tell you of the life in the higher spheres, and also will come to you when you sit for a photograph, in her illumined form, so that you may see that she is living and is part of the Kingdom of God. She is the brightest spirit that I know. She is a very strong and powerful spirit, and will not let you be bothered by the evil spirits, or those who try to impersonate those spirits who are here and try to talk to you. She is here now and wants me to say that she is the loving grandmother that she always was, and will love you with her whole heart and …

He is not with her in the high Heavens (Mr. Padgett's grandfather), but he is a very bright spirit, and he loves you, too.

Yes, they are in the Heavens (Grandmother and Grandfather Padgett). Their love was so pure and holy that they went to the Heavens of holy love. They are not …

Yes I am, and must stop. Good night.
Helen.

Reassures Mr. Padgett that it was truly Jesus who wrote Saturday night. And for Mr. Colburn to also believe

September 14th, 1914.

I am here, Helen.

I do, with all my heart. I was and I was so happy. You must not be unhappy because I am with you all the time, and you will not be lonely if you love me as you did this morning. You are my only darling one and this is my one dear privilege of having you for myself. Be true to me and you will be happy.

Yes the Master was with you on Saturday night and he is the only one who can help you to feel the Love of God as you did

The following question referring to Mr. Colburn, who said it might be a false impersonation.

Yes and I heard what was said—he is not correct in saying that I do not know Jesus when he comes among us. He is so luminous with the Love of God and the spirit of righteousness in his whole being that we all know that he is the true Christ. Do not let any doubt exist in your mind that the one who wrote to you was not Jesus; he was the true Jesus of the Bible.

Yes, and I have seen the spirit of Rector, he is not the spirit that he represents himself to be, he is a wicked spirit who goes about to deceive the mortals on earth, he is a wicked spirit who has no love for God or man, and he is trying to lead mankind to believe that he is the Christ, he will be severely punished at the time of reckoning. Yes and I know what I am talking about as I have been warned against him. Your grandmother who is in one of the highest planes of the spirit world has told me of him.

He (Jesus) is a very bright and handsome spirit. He is not the same as the picture on earth represents him to be. He is very lovely and kind and filled with love, and has a face that seems to glow with the spirit of the Love of his Father. He is a most holy looking spirit and does not know that he is a lovely one, but seems so humble and ready to serve all who need his help and love.

Yes he will and you must believe in him and follow his advice. He wants you to become a good and pure man. He saw that you were longing to know the truth and he was anxious to help you. He saw that you were distressed and that you needed the assistance of his great love and teaching.

Tell Mr. Colburn that he must believe that Jesus is ready to come to him and show him the Truth and Love of God and that he must not think that the Christ is not teaching mankind the way of truth and love. He is only hearing the cry of the penitent and the lost soul.

He will come when you earnestly call for him and will teach you the true and secret meanings of his sayings as recorded in the Bible, only have faith and love the Father. He has told me that he is only waiting for you and your friend (Mr. Colburn) to call on him in faith and earnestness and he will come to you both.

Yes, and I am progressing very rapidly and will soon be in the third sphere. You must not wish for that now, be contented a little while and you will soon be with me.

No, I will wait for you and we will go together to the higher planes of love and light. We will always be together as husband and wife.

Padgett asked the question, did she love her children very much?

Yes, I love them and am with them very often, but they are the love mates of others. They will find their happiness in the society of these others, they will not need me after a little while, except that I shall help them to feel that their mother is watching over them and loves them as a mother. Do not let their lives be too much a part of yours as you are not the one that God decreed should be with them as their true loves forever. Let your love for them only help them to learn that they must live right and love their God.

Yes, she (Nita) is in the school and is very happy and only wants to have her school commence its exercises. She loves you very much and is a true daughter, and is learning the truths of Christ's teachings.

You are my dearest and only love and you will be my soul-mate when you come to me in the future. Let me feel that you love me as I do you and I shall be very happy.

Yes, and I saw the book that you were reading, the last one is not helpful, let it alone, as it is but the philosophy of a man that has a hobby and he will not convince you of any helpful truth.

Be a true follower of Christ and you will need no other knowledge or help. Yes, and I do not agree with him as to Spiritualism or Christian Science. He is not well enough informed on either to form a correct judgment. He is too bigoted and has not a true conception of the Bible. Let him alone.

Good night, with all my love and many kisses.
Helen.[23]

Reassures him that it was Jesus who wrote on Saturday

September 14th, 1914.

I am here, your father. (John H. Padgett)

I am happy and so is your mother, and you are very much better spiritually than when you were a very young boy. You are commencing to see the true teachings of the Bible. Let your teachings be in Christ as he is the truth and the way and the light.

It was Jesus of the Bible that came to you on Saturday night[24]. I know because I was with him and know it was he. He is not an impostor, as your friend thinks might come representing himself to be the true Christ, but he was Jesus of Nazareth and he was the only one in all the spirit world who has the wonderful countenance of love and truth. He is the one true son of God that can save you and your friend from your sins, believe in him and do not let the teachings or false statements of the other spirits cause you to have doubts as to his being the true Christ—keep his love fresh in your hearts. He will come to you again and also to Mr. Colburn if he will only believe and earnestly pray to him. He is not the spirit that Mr. Colburn thinks may impersonate him. He is the true Jesus that was hanged on the cross and arose again from the dead—be not deceived by the spirits who say that he cannot come to you or your friend. He is your friend and Savior and he loves you both as his younger brothers. Give your love to God and he will show you the way to

---

[23] In a message from Judas, which was received January 9th, 2002, he comments on the likelihood that this communication is not exactly what Helen would have said. (G.J.C.)
[24] Read Jesus' message in Vol II (4th Ed.) page 1. (G.J.C.)

salvation.

Jesus is the personality that took the form of man and lived on the earth, teaching the truths of God. Christ is the truths that Jesus taught, and these truths are the everlasting things that will save the human race from their sins. He is a spirit just as we are, but he is so very far above us in the spirit life and knowledge of God that we all, who believe in God look up to him as our teacher and savior from our sins.

Believe that he is your savior and you will not be deceived. Let his love for you keep you in the true way to eternal life and happiness.

Good bye and may God bless you.

Your father.

A Celestial Spirit also reassures him that it was truly Jesus of the Scriptures that spoke and wrote to him on Saturday

September 14th, 1914.

I am here, your grandmother.

I am exceedingly happy and am glad that you are seeing the truth as it is in Christ. He is the truest son of God as I have found in my life here. He is not a savior of the merely churchman, but of them who have received the New Birth of the Spirit—do not let the thought that you must be a member of any church keep you from seeking his help and love for he is the savior of the individual and not of the aggregate of people who happen to belong to a church.

He was with you on Saturday night and he talked to you[25]. I am well acquainted with him and often see and converse with him, so I know that he was the true Christ of the Scriptures. He was only trying to let you feel that he is interested in your spiritual welfare, and you must believe that he was with you.

I know the spirit that Mr. Colburn referred to and he is not a good spirit. He is a spirit that has an inordinate amount of vanity and often impersonates Jesus and other spirits of high station. He is not to be believed when he makes the assertion that he is the Christ. Let him alone and he will not trouble you or your friend in the way of impersonating the true Christ.

Give my love to your friend and tell him that I am very much interested in his spiritual welfare and will try to help him and lead him to the realization of the truth as I know it in the spirit world. He is only a little way from the Kingdom and he will soon see the truth in all its beauty and purity. Tell him to have faith in his God and pray to Him for light and he will get it more abundantly. He is a very good and loving man

---

[25] Read Jesus' message to Mr. Padgett in Vol II (4th Ed.) page 1. (G.J.C.)

in his spiritual life and he will soon feel that God is his true and loving savior.

Good night and may the Love of God rest with you and keep you from all sin and unhappiness forever.

Your grandmother,
Ann Rollins.

An early message from Jesus to enable Mr. Padgett to get into a spiritual condition before the important Truths were written

October 5th, 1914.

I am here, Jesus.

You must not be too anxious for me to explain all the mysteries of God's creation. I must not teach you all of them now, but will later, when you have become purified and are at-one with Him.

You are the messenger that I shall use to carry my gospel to mankind and I will teach you those truths which you cannot now understand. I will explain all the qualities of the soul and spirit so that mankind need no longer remain in darkness as to what my teachings mean and as to how very necessary it is that it shall understand and follow my teachings.

Do not be over anxious at this time to know the mysteries of pre-existent of the difference between the soul and the spirit. You shall know in the future and you will then be able to receive the truths of God in their respects to your fellow man.

Go to the Lord in prayer and he will remove from your soul all that tends to defile it and make it an alien from Him.

He is the one that will clean it from all sin and error. Do not believe all that you read tonight in the books that you are reading at the library. Some statements were true and some were not. Only the teachings that I shall give you will tell the wishes of my Father.

Let not your heart be troubled or cast down for I am with you always and I will help you in every time of need. Only believe that I am the Jesus of the Scriptures and you will not be long out of the Kingdom.

You are my chosen one on earth to proclaim my glad tidings of life and love. Be true to yourself and to your God and He will bless you abundantly.

Keep His commandments and you will be very happy and will soon receive the contentment that He gives His true children. Go to Him in all your troubles and you will find rest and peace.

Unknown questions

Yes, in a very short time you will be free to devote your whole attention to my objects and to your work. You will soon be in a condition to let the things of this world alone as I need you for my service. Let me tell you that you will get your home as you desire and have your surroundings all harmonious for receiving my messages. And you will be with your daughter to keep you happy and free from care.

Let me bless you and leave you now for you are too nervous to write more at this time.

With all my love and my blessings and those of the Holy Spirit.

Jesus.

Jesus is the Way, the Truth and the Life for all mankind to believe in

January 13th, 1915.

I am here, Jesus. Yes, I am that Jesus. You should not doubt as I have told you before that I am.

They are in a condition which prevents them from seeing that I am the true Jesus, and they will all be lost unless in some way they get an awakening to the fact that only through me can they obtain the Love of the Father which will enable them to enter His kingdom. I am the Way, the Truth and the Life, as I long ago said. They will be forever shut out of His kingdom and will live in the spirit land without this love to comfort and make them happy. I do not mean to say that they will all suffer eternal punishment, for they will not. The Father loves them all, but their state will be one of only comparative happiness and they will not have within them that Love of the Father which is necessary to make them supremely happy.

You will know in proper time all these things which make for the happiness of my followers. You must wait until I am ready to explain these matters to you.

Yes, I know you are helping the darkened spirits and some mortals; but you must not let every spirit who seeks your help cause you to give your strength to them in the way of writing, for as your wife has told you, the laws of communication must be obeyed, or you will suffer in your power to receive these messages.

Yes, very much. You have great faith and I am somewhat surprised at it myself, but you have it, and God hears and answers your prayers. You must continue to pray and believe.

You must not doubt that I am with you and wrote to you; neither must you doubt that I can help you in every time and need.

Yes, you will receive that inflowing of the Holy Spirit as they did, even while you are on earth, and will be able to know that God is your Father to the extent that they knew. Only you must pray more and believe more. You will not only receive that but you will also receive power to convince men of my teachings and lead them to my Father's Love, and also to show that you possess this Love by being able to heal the sick by merely praying for them.

This I tell you now, because you will soon commence to take my messages and you must have these powers and faith.

Yes, I hear your prayers to the Father and I try to let you feel my love, and you do sometimes. But you must not let your prayers come to me as God; I am only your friend and brother. Yes, I know, but these sayings I did not say at all. I merely claimed to be my Father's son and messenger. I did not claim to be God.

Yes, I said that my Father sent me and that is true. I did live before I came to earth with my Father in the heavens and so did you.

I meant that in the Kingdom of God there are homes and that I would go and prepare a place where my followers should have a home with me, separate from the homes of the spirits who are not believers in or followers of me; that my kingdom was to be a separate kingdom from the other parts of the spirit lands, and that those who wanted to live with me would have to get this Love of God in their hearts to do so. My kingdom is one where Love is supreme and where it is manifested in the purest and highest degree. I have not seen God in the sense that I have seen you, but that in the sense that my love is so very abundant and so truly His Love that He appears to my soul's eyes just as plainly as you appear to my natural eyes.

Many of my sayings were merely symbolical and not intended to be taken literally. My Father cannot be seen by anyone of His children, and no man has ever seen Him, for He is not of form or substance that can be seen. You are now very near where you will see Him with your soul's eyes, as I did, and when you do, then you will be able to know that His Love is in your heart to its fullest. Why you are so greatly blessed with this Love and Faith I really do not know, even though I do know so much of His truth and Love. But I see that you have great possibilities of faith and love which will make you a most wonderful man doing His work of saving souls for His kingdom.

Well, I can readily see how you may doubt; but as I know, you must believe me for I am telling you the truth. It will leave you as the Love flows in, and you will then be able to realize that you are free indeed. They will not after the time appointed shall end. No more will the opportunity come, and no more will God give His Love and Grace to men or spirits. They will love only with the natural love that belongs to them as mortals. They will never receive this great Love which comes by the operation of the Holy Spirit. They will continue to live forever, but their happiness will not be of the kind that my followers will have and they will not be contented in that happiness. They will forever long for something that they can never get.

I will not let you write more tonight as you are now in a condition of more happiness. Well, I love you with a love that will never end and that will keep you in all your troubles and worries free from everything that tends to make you doubt God's Love or my teachings.

So with this Love I now bless you, and pray that God's Love may come into your heart more abundantly.

Jesus.

In his first formal message informs Mr. Padgett to go to the Father for His help

September 28th, 1914.[26]

I am here, Jesus.

You are my true brother and will soon have the Love of our Father in your heart. Do not be discouraged or cast down for the Holy Spirit will soon fill your heart with the Love of the Father, and then you will be most happy and full of light and power to help yourself and fellowmen.

Go to your Father for His help. Go in prayer, firmly believing and you soon will feel His Love in your heart. My teachings, I know, you will receive in the course of time, and you will then see that your understanding will be greatly enlarged so that you will know that I am the Father's son as I explained it to you a few nights ago[27]. You can and will receive the Father's Love so that you will not need to go through the expiation in the spirit world.

I was not conceived by the Holy Spirit, as it is taught by the preachers and teachers who are now leading mankind in the doctrines of the churches. I was born as you were born, and my earthly father was Joseph. I was conceived by God's Spirit in the sense that I was born free from sin and error, while all other human beings were born in sin and error. I never was a human being so far as my spiritual existence is concerned, as I was always free from sin and error, but I had all the feelings and longings of a human being which were not of sin. My love was human as well as spiritual, and I was subject to all the feelings of sympathy and love that any other human being was. Do not understand that I was with desires and longings for the pleasures of the world which

---

[26] This is the third message from Jesus received by James E. Padgett. The term "formal" was used to differentiate the meaty communications from the more social. (G.J.C.)

[27] Jesus explains that he is not God, and what he meant by "I am the Way, the Truth and the Life" in Vol II (4th Ed.) page 3. (G.J.C.)

the human passions created. I was not, only I was capable of deep feeling, and could feel and know the suffering and distress of humanity.

Yes, I will, and you will learn that many errors were written by the writers of the Bible. I will show you that the many alleged sayings of mine were not said by me or did not express my teachings of the truth. Her teachings of Christian Science do not express the true meaning of truth and love as I taught them. She is in error as to the ideas that God is spirit only, a spirit of mind. He is a spirit of everything that belongs to His Being. He is not only Mind, but Heart, Soul and Love.

You are too weak to write more. You have my blessing and also that of the Holy Spirit.

Jesus the Christ.[28]

Writes that the New Birth is the inflowing of the Spirit of God into your soul and that the disappearing of all that tends to turn your heart from the truth and love of God

September 15th, 1914.

Yes, I am your grandmother.

Yes, and I am in close touch with the Lord. God is a spirit. He is the one mind and spirit that teaches all other spirits that the truth is the only thing that can save from sin and error. Do not let the teachings of the Savior become mere idle sounds in your ears—believe in them and you will be soon in the possession of the precious and glorious jewels of the truth—let him lead you to God. Love him and he will be with you and teach you the truths of his Father.

The New Birth is the flowing of the Spirit of God into your soul and the disappearing of all that tends to turn your heart from the truth and Love of God. It comes by the workings of the Holy Spirit that conveys the Grace of God. It is not a working of your own will or power—it is the Love of God that causes the change. You cannot of yourself change the evil workings of your heart but you can pray and the Holy Spirit will come into your soul and then you will realize the change.

The Spirit is the power of God which he uses to influence men to seek His Favor and Love. It is not God Himself, but only one of His instrumentalities with which he works for the salvation of mankind. Let your love for him be the holiest and best kind that you can give to Him. And pray for the Divine Love with earnest sincere prayer.

Yes, Jesus is the teacher, and the Holy Spirit is God's messenger or instrument that carries into the soul the Divine Love that is bestowed on the truly penitent man. Jesus is the savior of men by his teachings and

---

[28] This message is a composite of two, being published in Volume I and Volume III. (G.J.C.)

his example and the Holy Spirit is the Comforter that carries into the soul the Divine Love. Jesus is still teaching and influencing men to turn to God. He will continue to teach until the Celestial Kingdom is closed. He will come as a still small voice that will reach men's souls and lead them to the Father. He will not come as the Adventist preach.

Jesus will come quietly into each man's heart and in that way establish the millennium. He is not going to have a kingdom all his own. He is the son of his Father and will remain in the spirit world to teach men to progress to the heavenly planes that reach up to the presence of God. He is the most glorious spirit in all the heavens and he is the greatest spirit under the dominion of his Father.

There is only one God. Jesus and the Holy Spirit are merely the forces which God uses to carry out his great plans for the redemption of man.

Let me stop now as I am tired.

Your grandmother, (Ann Rollins)

Talks about her soulmate and the love that she has for her son

September 15th, 1914.

I am here, your mother.

You are the best son in the world. Yes, and you must love me more than you do. Give me more of your heart and you will feel that I am with you more. Yes, and I am very often with you. No, he is in the lower sphere, but he will soon be with me. He is progressing very fast and is a lovely spirit.

Yes, I do not believe in hell and eternal punishment—they are the false teachings of the orthodox churches.

The yes & no are answers to questions asked by Mr. Padgett.

Jesus is the same as I believed him to be on earth. Yes, he is my savior still, but I do not worship him as God. He is not God, but a spirit of the greatest perfection and goodness. He is with me quite often. He talked to you on Saturday night and he will come to you again very soon and explain the true teaching of the Bible. Let him be your friend and adviser.

I have a home and live with a spirit that is the same in progression as myself. We are very happy together and she is the soulmate of your father. No, I am not, but he is waiting to come here and be with the one who is. Yes, but he is not in the same sphere with me. He is in the one with your father and he is progressing too. No, I did not and only met him when he came to the spirit world. He was living in the City of Chicago, and was a very wealthy man, but a very great sinner. He is now in a state of progression and will be with me soon. Yes, but I am not his and he is not mine.

Yes, they are, but he is not with her yet, he is too earthly, but is progressing. Yes I do—she is Helen. She does and you must love her too.

You must go to bed. good night my son.

Your mother.

Ann R. Padgett.

In an early message describes her home in the 7th. Sphere—all the blessings the Father promised—friends—her work, and they are not singing all the time

September 15th, 1914.

I am here; your grandmother.

You are too much troubled in spirit to enjoy my visit as you otherwise would, but I will try to help you to be more happy. I am in a state of contentment and have my home in the seventh heaven and have all the blessings that my Father promised me when I was on earth, but I had no conception of them then. My home is a wonderful mansion, built of the most beautiful material that you can imagine. There are flowers and beautiful pictures and lovely rooms filled with all kinds of furniture that you could possibly wish for. I am not the only one that lives in my home, there is also a beautiful spirit that was on earth, a great follower of Christ and lover of her fellow man. Our home is full of the finest kind of everything that makes a home lovely. We have many friends who visit us and whom we visit. We do the work of the Lord in helping the spirits in the lower spheres to see the truths of the Love of their Father. We are not singing all the time, but we have a great deal of beautiful music and laughter and love.

Good night.

Your grandmother,

Ann Rollins.

Mr. Padgett asked questions of the spirit writers and in this early one the question asked is written in his conversation with Bright Star

June 8th, 1915.

I am here, Bright Star.

Yes, I did. Let me tell you that I am with you tonight for the purpose of helping you get out of your despondency. You must not be so downhearted. You are too lonely to be left alone. Go to the Lord for help. I am not the only one here. Your wife and father and mother and grandmother and Christ and Prof. Salyards are here. I know him very well, he is your friend and my friend. He is not the only one that you will hear from tonight.

Come to the Savior's Love and you will be helped.

Question: Are you Bright Star?

Yes, I am, and you must believe that I am. Yes, very often I come to help you and try to let you know that you are not to be left to your own ways of thinking.

Shall I go to Mrs. R. B.?

Yes, you must come soon and I will talk to you and you will know that I am the Indian Squaw that you spoke to when you were present on the two occasions that you visited the medium.

Question by Mr. Padgett: Who wrote Saturday night?

You were written to by your father and mother and grandmother and your wife, also Jesus. Yes, he will if you will call for him, he will teach you the truths of the Bible and of his own knowledge. He is the greatest of all teachers. He is a lovely spirit and loves you and all mankind. Be a true follower of his teachings and you will become a very spiritual man. He is the only one for you to follow. Yes I do, and he teaches me and all of us who have the Love of God in our hearts.

Question: Are you Indians in the earth plane?

I am in the fourth sphere. We are only in the earth plane to help you mortals. Our home is not here, but higher up.

Question: Are visits to Mrs. R. especially beneficial?

No! it is not, but you may be helped some by learning that your friends are not dead, but living.

Question: Did the spirits actually speak to me at the séance?

Yes, they all spoke to you and you cannot help but believe that they did.

Question: What was the meaning of the light?

It was merely the power of the spirit manifested. No, it did not mean anything in particular; it was merely an evidence of the presence of spiritual power. Yes; your wife is the one provided for you.

Question: Do you know Mr. Colburn?

Yes, I do. He is a very good man and is gifted with the power of clairvoyance and having taps come to him. He is not a very strong medium, but is going to become such in the near future. You will be able to help him develop as a medium in the way of writing with the planchette. You are too spiritual to be long without the power of seeing the truth of the Lord's ways. Yes, but not in as great a degree as you will soon have. You are very near the kingdom. Keep trying for the light and you will soon get it, and then you will be able to help mankind in a spiritual and a physical way. Be only true to yourself and God.

Question: Did not the people at the séance think of her only in a material way?

Yes, that is the way that they thought of me, but I am more than that. I have a spiritual side to my being as well as the side that they know of. You however can see the spiritual side for you are spiritually minded and not satisfied with mere phenomena and with you I like to talk of spiritual things.

Let me go now.
Good night,
Bright Star.

In the beginning of his work in behalf of the Kingdom, Mr. Padgett received this message from his grandmother through his wife Helen to encourage him to pray to the Father more sincerely and not Jesus as he once believed

November 8th, 1914.

I am here, Helen.
Yes I was, and you were benefitted by the services although you did not enjoy the full blessings of the fact that Jesus writes through you. You should not let that thought enter into your worship as it is only one

of the blessings that you can enjoy if you will try.

You did not pray to God as you should have done. He was the one that you should have thought of more.

Question and Answer.

Yes, I know, but they were only trying to feel the presence of God and the Holy Spirit. You did not get the full benefit of the service. Yes, that is so, but you must not let that idea prevent you from worshipping God, as He does not want anyone to worship Him in any other way than in Spirit and in Truth.

I am your grandmother who is dictating this message to Helen. Because she does not understand yet, the fullness of God's Love and I am trying to let you know that you must worship God only, and let your heart go out to Him in thankfulness and love.

Jesus of course is the one for you to keep in holy rapport with, so do not let the thought that he is not a God prevent you from loving and serving him. You must not think of him as your savior from sin and error, but merely as one who is interested in you and wants to write through you, and this will help you to progress.

His blood does not save you, nor does his death, but his love and teachings do save you from sin and death. He is not going to let you feel that he is not your friend, unless you turn away from him to get the love of earth, by things and pleasures.

Question and Answer.

Yes, but you were not praying to the Father as you should have done. Do not let the thought that you are going to write for him, keep you from praying to the Father or you will not advance in your spiritual life. You are not in condition to write more tonight or I would write fully on just what you should know and will do so later. You will soon know just what I mean. Go to bed and rest.

Good night, your grandmother

Helen, good night, with all my love.

In an early message Helen wrote that Mr. Padgett was too much taken up with his business matters and does not devote enough time to prayer to the Father to receive the gift of the spirit

November 3rd, 1914.

I am here, Helen.

You are too nervous to write. You must go to bed early and rest. You are my darling Ned, and I love you with all my heart, so do not think that you are not loved by me, and your father and mother and grandmother. We all love you.

Question and answer.

Yes I have. And he (Jesus) says, that he is waiting for you to get in condition to write. He will write to you as he said and you must soon get in condition. You will get it by prayer as I am told by your grandmother, who is here. She says that you must believe more thoroughly in the promises of the Master and you will receive the gift of the Spirit. She says that you are too much taken up with your business matters to let the Spirit enter into your soul in all its truth and love. She says that you must not let the thoughts of what you shall do in the future keep you from praying to God and loving him as you will be taken care of.

She says that Jesus is the one for you to believe in and love as he will be your friend and will help you to progress in your spiritual life, as well as in your temporal life. He is the one who can help you more than anyone else.

She says that the Christian Scientists Church is the one that will help you most as the people who attend there are more in accord with the teachings of Christ than are the Spiritualists of the church of Mrs. Kates. And she further says, that the Spiritualists are not teaching the true religion of the Master, and that is the only one that will lead to God; they are merely showing the possibility of communicating between the dead and the living, which is desirable so far as it goes, but which does not save men from their sins or bring them at-one with God. So I would not attend there very often, but rather go to some church that teaches that Jesus is the savior of men from their sins. Go to the Methodist, or Congregational or Universalist church. Each of them will help you to progress in your spiritual development.

Yes, he (preacher) is all wrong and you will not be benefited by him. He is not in the true way of light. He is too imaginative and visionary. He does not see the things that he preaches and he is not doing any good to himself or to others. Go to the Lord and He will lead you aright. I mean the Father whom Jesus taught about, and that he will help you to see the Truth and the things that are necessary for your salvation. Yes you should, as they are the mediums by which God lets His Love and Favor come to man. They are the only true instrumentalities of the Father which He uses to show the way to salvation, and to confer His Love and Grace on man.

Yes, you do, only believe more and you will soon receive the gift of the spirit in all its fullness. Yes, you will and so will those that you come in contact with. Give the Lord your whole heart and soul and you will soon realize the difference in your life. Yes, she does, and is with you often and prays to God to bless you.

She says, that she is willing for once to attend such a séance, but that it is not beneficial as a general thing, as it does not help the spiritual development of the person, but only convinces the man that the spirit is a living being and can come back to earth and show himself in a form that may be realized.

The writing phase is the most satisfactory as you can preserve what is said, and can commune in a more extended and enlightening manner.

She (Mrs. Kates) is talking through her own mind. No spirit talks through her. She sees the forms and scenes which she describes and she hears the voices of spirits talking to her and she merely repeats what she hears. (Irish control) She merely repeats the language that she hears.

You will be a strong medium of communicating by the pencil. You will not be a clairvoyant as that is a phase that is not intended for you to possess. Yes, and you will not only be able to write for us, but for Jesus, as he desires. You will become a true follower of him, and then you will be able to write with much facility and success. He will tell you when he writes. I do not know what he will write, for he has only told me that he will write on the Truths that the Bible does not contain or rather that he will correct certain passages contained in the Bible.

Yes, you must love me as I love you and then you will be happy. Yes, and you must believe that I am. Yes I am, and will soon be in the third (spirit) heaven, and I will then be so much happier. Yes it is, and that is what I want you to do.

Good night my own love.
Helen.

Answers many questions for him on the Holy Spirit and the Heavenly Father, as well as better explains Jesus' power on earth and in the spirit world

November 11th, 1914.

I am here, your grandmother.

Yes, I am here and I wish to tell you that you must not let what I said to you last night discourage you for I was only trying to let you know that you must not forget to pray to God for His Blessing. You were not in a condition to fully understand what I wrote. You were only in a condition of doubt as to what it was that you should do in order to feel the influence of my meaning.

Question and Answer.

Yes it is and you must not so worship him. They were not only wrong in that particular, but they did not understand that Jesus does not want to be worshipped in that way. They may follow him in his teachings and example, but must worship only God. You can help them to see the Truth and you should try to do so.

Yes, I know, but nevertheless you should make the effort for they must learn that Jesus is only a son of God and is not the God or any part of Him. He is the one for them to seek and ask his aid in order to learn the truth. Yes, I know, but they will have to learn sooner or later that the Holy Spirit is of God and not a medium of Jesus to bring about their New Birth and entrance into God's Kingdom. He (God) is the one that confers the blessings of the Spirit and they will realize it when they receive the Spirits inflow of Love and Grace. Yes, many have and their influence is good and helpful, their spirit friends are with them at their meetings and help them to realize that God is Love and Truth.

Yes, sometimes, but they do not enjoy being there and consequently do not remain very long or take any part in the services. He is not present at the various meetings that are held in the several churches over the whole country, but his truths are there in the character of spirits who are ordained to do the work of teaching the truths which he taught and which are the truths of God.

The Holy Spirit is the one that can cause the inflowing of God's Love and it is present in all meetings as it is without form or personality. It is the messenger of God and it can be in all places at the same time so that the penitents no matter how far apart can receive it's influence and feel its saving Grace and Love. It is not necessary for it to use other spirits to carry its Love and influence. It of itself is able and all comprehending enough to influence the persons who seek for its inflowing. So do not think that you have to have Jesus present in order to obtain the blessings of the Holy Spirit. He meant that when they are gathered together for the purpose of seeking the Love of God he would be able to help them feel the influence of the Holy Spirit, he would not have to be present himself for that purpose, but he would be represented by the Holy Spirit. No, he cannot, for he is a person and has all the limitations that belong to the individual. Jesus is not a spirit in the sense that God is a spirit. He is only an individualized spirit as you are. He is only a spirit of such wonderful development that he can control all the spirits of his own manner of thinking and who have been Born Again into God's Kingdom so that he can have them do his work just as he teaches them to do. Yes, he can direct the Holy Spirit in the sense that when the penitent prays for help the Holy Spirit will respond and fulfill the work that the Father has provided it to do.

Jesus is the truest exponent of his Father's Truths and he alone (only) through his teachings can cause the Holy Spirit to enter the hearts and souls of mankind. No, it is not, for the Father has given him the power to control all the spirits that are of the Father's Kingdom of Truth and Love. Christ is not only a spirit of the Father, but is the one that God gave to Jesus when he anointed him on his earthly mission. He is the one spirit that cannot be made to do anything that is contrary to God's Love and Law. No, not in addition to the spirit that Jesus had, but the spirit that God gave to Jesus at the time of the anointing.

The spirit that Jesus had before that time became one and the same with the Christ Spirit—they are now one—Jesus is not a man as is taught by some writers, but is the Christ of God—a spirit that is full of God's truths. He is the great dispenser of truths and he cannot lie nor do anything but what the Father has given him to do.

Yes, Jesus the Spirit is only a spirit as you have a spirit, but Jesus the Christ is a Spirit that is without form or limitations, so that he can be everywhere at the same time. Yes, he meant that he as the Christ would be with all peoples wherever they might be gathered together seeking his help and teachings, but as Jesus the mere spirit, he did not mean that he would be with them.

So you may believe that he is with you always in the sense that he is your Christ. It is Jesus the teacher of truth and not the Christ, the latter is with you and everyone else at all times. Only the penitent must ask that he let them feel his influence and teach them the Truth of God, and the fact that the Holy Spirit is waiting to enter into their hearts and fill them with the Divine Love.

Go to the church where you were last night, as you will be much more benefited than you will be by attending the other churches. You will be under the influence of more spirits who have received the New Birth.

No, not in the sense that the Holy Spirit is in their hearts, they are only letting their minds become confused with the idea that Jesus' blood or crucifixion saves them when the fact is the blood of Jesus or the crucifixion is not necessary, as a matter of belief to their salvation. The only thing that saves them from their sins and reconciles them to God is that they must become conscious of God's Truths and receive the Holy Spirit into their souls. No vicarious suffering on the part of Jesus is necessary to save them. He never taught that erroneous doctrine and it is not doing any good by being taught by the preachers who claim to represent his cause.

No, only in the sense that these things (his blood and crucifixion) call the attention of mankind to Jesus and his mission on earth. As between God and man, no blood of Jesus or vicarious suffering can appease God or save man. God is a God of Love and does not have any wrath to be appeased. He is only too glad to have his children come to Him and be at-one with Him. He is not waiting to punish them or have them suffer because of any wrath that He may be supposed to have towards them. They suffer only because they have violated his laws and they must do that which will remove the causes of their violation of these laws.

Mankind are not the object of God's anger, but are the dear children of His Love. He is not pleased when they do wrong or when they do not obey his precepts. Let not the idea that God delights in the punishment of the wicked make you think that God wants any one of His children to suffer. He is only too ready to save and have the sinner come to His Love and Care. He is the one Perfect Love that exists.

You must stop writing now as you won't go to your dinner.

Your loving grandmother.[29]

Wants to assure Mr. Padgett that important spirits actually write

November 14th, 1914.

I am here, Thomas Padgett.

I am Thomas Padgett. I am your father's uncle. I lived in St. Mary's County, Maryland, and passed over in 1831 at the county seat, Leonardtown. I was not a very good man when I passed over, but I am now in the fourth sphere and am progressing very rapidly.

I was his (my grandfather's) brother. He is here and is very happy. He is in a condition of love with his wife that makes them perfectly happy and contented.

Yes, I have and often talk to him about you and your gift of writing. You must believe that the spirits write to you, for I assure you that they do. You must not let any seeming inconsistencies cause you to lose faith in the power of communicating, or you will lose the greatest consolation that you can ever obtain. Be a true medium and you will not only become much happier yourself, but will help to make others happy.

Let me come to you occasionally and write and I will help you in your investigation.

Your grand uncle,
Thomas Padgett.

---

[29] This message is a composite of two, being published in Volume III and Volume IV. It would benefit greatly from being recreated from the original. It is clear that Ann Rollins is having difficulty expressing her meaning. However it's also likely that Padgett simply did not have the soul condition at this time to receive as accurately as he later did. (G.J.C.)

Says that Mrs. Mary Baker Eddy sees the error in her teachings and is living in the same sphere with her

December 5th, 1914.

I am here, your mother.

My boy I am so glad to write you again. It seems so long since I wrote to you. I love you so much and feel that I must tell you.

Go to the Universalist Church as Helen told you. It is the best one now in existence because it believes more in God's Love without having to worship Jesus. As you say, the Christian Scientists are good people but their position on spiritualism is all wrong and Mrs. Eddy now sees her error and wishes that she could undo it. She is in the same sphere with me but she does not enjoy so much of God's Love as I do; and I talk to her sometimes and she tells me that she is very sorry that she made the mistake of teaching that spirits could not communicate with mortals. She is a very bright spirit but does not know all that she thought she knew when on earth.

She may, I do not know, but I will ask her. Yes, I will pray for you my dear boy with all my heart. So good night,

Your mother.

Says that the Father's Love for Mr. Padgett will help him in his material problems

December 5th, 1914.

I am here, your grandmother.

You must not be so despondent. Pray to God and he will bless you. Try not to let the things of the material kind keep you from loving God. You are not doing right by thinking so much of the troubles of earth life. Trust in God. He will take care of you and you will not be left alone to worry over those things which will soon pass by. Give more of your thoughts to God and believe more in His love and care, and he will help you more than you can comprehend.

Yes, even as to them. He is not so weak that His Love cannot help you in those things. Be true to Him and yourself and you will not want for anything that is for your good. I know, for my experience in life has proved to me that I am speaking the truth.

Yes, I am with her (Nita) very often. She is a good girl and has much of God's Love in her heart. She is trying to learn the true way to His Love, and she will become a very spiritual woman as she grows older. Yes, I will and she will love you too, for you seem to her now as both father and mother. Yes, you will for I will try to help you to the fullest of my power, only believe and she will stay at school, and come home to you in the summer and feel that you have been her true and loving father, as you are.

You must believe that we communicate with you and when you do so without doubt, and then I do not think that you should go to the séances. They are generally of such a mixed condition that you are not helped by what you come in contact with.

Yes, I would advise you to go there, while they are not what I consider spiritual people, yet the spirits who attend their meetings are of a very good kind and will benefit you in the matter of your belief. Yes, I do, and your wife and guide, White Eagle, and your father will be able to talk to you soon. Bright Star will be a great help. She is a very spiritual person and loves God, as I know. But she is not yet entirely in the blessings of His full Love, but she is trying to obtain it very hard. Yes, she is, though many Indians are very spiritual. White Eagle is a very spiritual man and lives in the fourth plane [spirit sphere]. He is a strong spirit and seems to think a great deal of you. He will protect you in all emergencies and you can rely on him. He has never been the guide of anyone before and has not tried to learn English as he says, but he will soon learn as he is now making the effort. Only you must not let him write to you too often for he is not of the writing band.

Yes, it would. He is a powerful guide in certain ways, but he is not one who can help so much in spiritual matters. While he is good himself yet he cannot instruct you in those things that you need to learn at this time.

They (Mr. R. & Prof. S.) are not so spiritual but their knowledge of certain other things in the spiritual world will be beneficial to you. You must not confine your investigations to purely spiritual things, for while they are the things absolutely necessary, yet there are other things that you should learn, and we formed our band of such persons as we thought would serve the purpose that we had in view.

I doubt that he can cause the truth to grow but you can try him. I don't know just what power he has with reference to physical things. I believe that he can help your eyesight and liver. So let him try to do what he says. He is honest in his belief and he may succeed.

Good night my own dear boy,
Your loving, grandmother.

Locates Mr. Padgett's father's soulmate that is very lovely and a Celestial Spirit

I am here, Helen.

I will tell you of your father's soulmate as I promised. She is a very beautiful and spiritual woman and loves him very much. She is not so spiritual as your mother or so beautiful, but she is in a condition of spiritual love that makes her seem more beautiful than she really is. Her eyes are not so large as are mine but very bright with her soul's love, and features are not so regular as mine but are very mobile and seem to give her an appearance of extreme gladness and happiness which I know she enjoys. She is in a condition of love that makes her feel that your father is the only one in all the spirit world that is worth loving as she loves him, and I know that he is well worthy of her love. But you don't know that my love for you is even greater than hers for him. Yes, but I do, for my love is so very great that I am almost consumed with it, as your grandmother says, for you are the only one that I know as regards soulmate—that is you are my soulmate, and I know it, and love you with a love that only one of my intense disposition can possibly love with. Yes I know, but I do not believe it. She is very glad that he does and comes to see him more often than when he was on the earth plane because it is easier for her to do so. The spirits who live in the higher spheres feel some difficulty in coming to the lower plane, just as you would if you should go into an atmosphere that was all dark and murky with dampness and unpleasant smells. So you see what I endure when I come to you, but if the atmosphere were fifty times as bad I would come to you.

Let us talk of our little girl in Chicago. She is now trying her best to accomplish her lessons and is so full of enthusiasm about doing it successfully that she does not think of getting tired or of letting other things interfere with her efforts. She certainly is trying hard to make a success and she will for she does everything that comes to her to do. She is also giving her thoughts to higher things and is very much interested in Christian Science.

She will come home to you next summer a very different girl from when you saw her last and will make you feel so thankful that you sent her to school as you did. Do not let the thoughts that you will not be able to keep here there bother you for you will, and will also be able to give her a nice home when she returns to you. So let me help you to feel that everything will be for the best.

No, I have not been with her for some hours, but will go very soon and tell you what she is doing. Yes I will and will return by the time you come back. Yes I will.

I am back. She is in her own room and is studying her lessons, but not the ones for tomorrow's recitation. She is with several girls who are also studying but they are not so deeply interested as she is.

Yes, but I am not in condition. I don't feel strong enough to write more now.

Your own true and loving,

Helen.[30]

Mr. Padgett spent the day with his friends, Judge Syrick and Col. Woods, and Helen writes that they both believe in spiritualism

December 20th, 1914.

I am here, Helen.

I am happy, and I am so glad that you feel so much better. You are now in a good condition of mind and I feel that you are commencing to believe in what we have told you. You will soon be free from your worries and then you will be in such a spiritual condition that you will be able to take the Master's messages, for he is waiting for you to do so.

You must not let your mind get into the condition again that it was in during the past two weeks for it interferes very much with our communications, and also with your ability to work at your profession. You will be able to do what you want to for Nita, and then you will see that we can do much to assist you in material things; as well as in spiritual ones. Be only faithful and believe in what we tell you and you will be all right. So do not let me see you again in a despondent condition or I will not love you so much.

You have had a very pleasant day in your association with those people who believe in spiritualism and I am glad that you spent the day with Judge Syrick and Col. Woods. He is a very great believer in spiritualism, but he does not know anything about the spiritual side of it. He thinks that the fact that his spirit friends communicate with him is all that there is to learn or be contented with. His friends were with you today and they are not of the higher spheres, but they are very good spirits and seem to be quite happy in their condition. He was telling you the truth when he said that Jesus came to him and talked at Mrs. Miller's séances, for your grandmother told me that she knows for Jesus told her he would attempt to do so. I, of course, don't know anything about it, but your grandmother says it is so; and you must believe her. She says that Jesus did not show himself or attempt to materialize at these séances, for he has never yet attempted to do this, as he is not inclined to come into the earth influences. He is not one who will do this, for he is too holy to take on the form of flesh again, as I have told you before. He is now doing his work solely by influencing men in the way of teaching them the truths of God, by means of his suggestions and messages

---

[30] This message has had a date attributed elsewhere of 24th March 1915, but I can find no evidence for that. It must be before June 20th 1918, as that is the date Nita passed over. (G.J.C.)

through other spirits who are helping him so to do.

No, I don't. He did not materialize sufficiently for that purpose, the photograph that he has was that of a spirit who impersonated the Master, for he will not permit himself to be photographed by anyone on earth, or even here.[31] He is too pure in his spiritual nature to become an object of photography or even of clairvoyance, for he is a spirit that will not appear to man, except in the way that I have told you. So do not believe that he has ever appeared to any man either by way of the photograph or by clairvoyance. He will come to you in the way that he has told you and write his messages, but not in any other manner. I only know what your grandmother says about it and I am writing at her dictation. She says that Jesus has told her that he will not appear to mankind again only as a teacher through his writings or through that of his spirits. So do not believe any spirit who says that he has seen Jesus materializing for he has not.

That was his appearance in a dream only. He was there but not as a materialized spirit. You merely saw him in your dream, and he was not even in the spirit form with you; it was the result of your own conscience working on your mind. You felt that you had not done what you knew he approved, and your own conscience took you to task for it and made you dream as you did.

I do not attempt to reconcile these statements for they need no reconciliation. When we told you that he would not leave you again, we only meant that your conscience would not again accuse you of doing what is contrary to his teachings. You were not really seeing him, but only dreaming that you were. He was not present with you but was in your dreams only as your own mind pictured him to be. So do not let the fact that it was only a dream make you think that it had no significance, for it had, and it showed you that unless you commenced to give your thoughts to higher things and live a better life, you would not have his care and love for your welfare any longer. It was only a warning that you should change your course of thinking and living.

Yes, he told you but I have explained what was meant. We know, because we saw it in your thoughts and then we knew that you had dreamed it. So you see, we do not have to know of things actually happening in order to be able to speak about them. All we have to is to learn what your mind is thinking and we are then able to tell you just what you know and believe. Every man is the mirror of his own thoughts and we do not have to know of our own knowledge just what has taken place in that man's life in order to tell him of all his actions and doings

---

[31] It would seem that Jesus may have changed his mind, as the story told by Linda Green in "Love Without End" is compelling, and her painting matches the description we have of Jesus. (G.J.C.)

while on earth. We are able by our power of reading the brain of a man to know what he has done in his past life. His brain is a storehouse of all that he has done, even though he is not able to recall these things. But they are there in memory's halls and we can see and learn what is recorded.

So you see the past is as apparent to us as the present. We do not always resort to this method of telling a man what is in store for him in the future, but when we need to know his past all we have to do is to look into his memory's storehouse and we know. But dreams are not stored in memory always; some are mere fleeting shadows that leave no trace of their ever having passed through his brain, while others leave their records on his memory. So when you dream, if your dream has any significance or is worthy of being preserved, it is in memory's home; but in order to know whether it is there or not we have to search the hidden recesses of his memory as well as the more open places. So you see every act that a man is guilty of and every dream that has a significance or is worthy of preservation is kept on record for future reference. Then how careful ought a man try to do what is right in God's sight, and not do those things which will rise up before him when his spirit comes here and arises before him in judgment.

I am not going to tell you of what I saw at the meeting at Mr. Colburn's tonight. I saw a large number of spirits that wanted to communicate with Miss Colburn, but who were not able to, and who were very much disappointed. Her mother was one of the most anxious, as she has some information that she very much desires that her husband should know; and you must tell Miss Colburn that she must sit for her mother to write. She is a very beautiful spirit and knows that Mr. Colburn will not live much longer and that he should do something in reference to his affairs before passing over. So tell her to let her mother write as soon as she can.

Other spirits there were only attracted by their desires to make known their presence and tell some of their experiences in spirit life.

Yes, his (Judge Syrick)'s mother was there and also his soulmate. They wanted to tell him of their love and how much they are interested in his giving more of his thought to them and to things spiritual; for he is not going to live very long, as he has a bad case of Bright's disease (acute or chronic nephritis) and needs to be very careful with himself.

I don't know anything about what some spirit may have told him, but I am informed by his mother that she knows that he is not going to live very long, even if his spirit friend did tell him that he was going to live until he was seventy years old. He must not believe that or he will suddenly find that his life is not for him to live as a man of seventy. He must not think that he is going to live to be that age, for he will suddenly find that his life is not one that is to be extended to that age. I mean that he will suddenly die and realize that his information was not correct. (Judge Syrick did die suddenly soon after this message was given.[32])

No do not, for it would do him harm.

He is not a very bad man, but he needs the soul development in order to become a good man as his mother and soulmate wants him to be.

She is here now and wants to send him a message. So tell him that his soulmate does not think that he loves her as much as he should, and that he is only trying to let himself believe that he is not really her soulmate, and wants to marry the young girl at the University home. She is not for him, and he must not think of doing so, for he would be very unhappy if he should do so. If he must get married tell him to marry an older woman and he will find more happiness; or better still, not marry at all as he will only need his soulmate to love him and make him happy if he will only let her do so, he is not going to live very long and he will soon be with her to love and make him happy. So tell him to give most of his thoughts to her and he will be a very much happier man. She says that you must teach him the way to God's Love for you know how and he will listen to you, if you will only try and if you do he will bless you just as soon as he comes over, for he will have the benefit of that teaching and will not have to suffer the expiation of going through the earth plane. So she says please try to tell him of the only way that will lead him to happiness and to his soulmate who is so anxiously waiting for him. Be his friend in this particular and you will never regret it.

She is in the third sphere with me and is a very lovely spirit and is trying her best to influence him to become a more spiritual man, so that he may be able to come and live with her when he comes over. She loves him very dearly and will not let his love for her keep him away from the true place of joy and happiness.

I mean that she will not let his want of love for her keep him away from true joy and happiness. She sees that he is not thinking as much of her as he should, but when he comes over he will not fail to recognize that she is the only one in all the spirit world that is his own true soulmate. She says that he is now very dear to her and when she gets him with her she will be so happy that he will see that his happiness can only be found with her. So tell him to think more of her at his leisure moments.

The young girl that he is thinking of does not care for him as a sweetheart and if she should marry him it would only be because he would be able to take care of her, and relieve her of the condition which she is now in on account of her father's unsuccessful adventure in trying

---

[32] See the message in this volume from Judge Syrick on page 342 for confirmation of much of what Mr. Padgett told him about life in the spirit world. (G.J.C.)

to run a school and form a new church, which he will never do, for his ideas of religion are all wrong. I mean the peculiar tenets that he is trying to introduce. Some of his ideas are all right, but most of them are not. He is a very well educated man, but is very visionary in his ideas as to what he thinks he sees in the spirit life. He never talks to Jesus as he preaches, nor does he ascend into the heavens, for no man does that now until he has given up his earth life. So he will not succeed for his foundation principles are not true.

I am not in condition to write much more tonight. You are my very own darling Ned, and I love you with all my heart and soul. You loved me when the music was playing my song that I used to sing to you so often. Oh, my darling, love me with all your heart as I do you.

So good night,

Your own true wife, Helen.

That it is that degree of belief that enables you to know a Truth. And that faith is the only thing to make you realize that I am who and what I declare myself to be

March 25th, 1914.

I am here, Jesus.

(Faith:) It is that degree of belief that enables you to know, as a reality, that what presents itself to your consciousness as a truth is in fact a truth, and an existing condition. It is not a mere intellectual belief, but a belief of the soul which makes the belief a reality.

I know that this faith is the only one that can make you realize that I am who and what I declare myself to be. Let this faith take possession of your soul, and you will be a very happy and progressive man. I am not here tonight to discuss spiritual subjects, but merely to help you in your troubles over material things. When you get in proper condition to write my messages, then I will finish my last subject[33] which we left unfinished.

So my dear brother, and friend and worker, try to let these things leave your mind, and believe what I tell you, for I say again that they will come true.

Well, the devil is with you all the time. He is not a person as many think, but merely the evil suggestions that result from the operations of the thoughts of the unregenerate man. Every man has his devils, who cling close to him, and can only be gotten rid of by the operations of the Holy Spirit. So do not think that the devil is something

---

[33] Jesus explains what he meant when he said: "In my Father's house are many mansions" in Vol II (4th Ed.) page 38. (G.J.C.)

that has form or independent personality, for he is not. You are the creator and nourisher of your own devil, and until you get into a state which leaves no room for his presence he will abide with you.

Well, the influences and suggestions that come from evil spirits would not have any effect, if man were not in that condition of sympathy with such spirits as enables them to become, as it were, a part of him. I know that many men are possessed or obsessed by these evil spirits but if they, the men, would only seek the higher spiritual conditions these spirits would not harm them.

Well, that is one of the subjects of my messages, and I will delay to answer until I write that message. Yes the time will soon come when you will know these things.

I must stop now as you are not in condition to write much more, and your wife wants to say a word.

So with my true and brotherly love, I am
Jesus.

Admits that his power is limited in some things and does not always know the answer without going to the Father, the Source of all knowledge

March 24th, 1915.

I am here, Jesus.

Of course you must remember that I don't know everything that has happened or that is going to happen. I have my limitations as have other spirits but of course my knowledge and powers are more extended than are those of other spirits. This is true because I am nearer my Father, fountainhead of wisdom and power, and consequently can draw there from more than can other spirits. Yet I am limited as I said and should you ask me some questions and I not be able to answer them with knowledge, I will tell you and you must not be surprised or disappointed at my inability to do so.

I was not present and don't know and cannot guess. Well that is a difficult question to answer for it involves so much of my very existence that I feel that my ability is to tell you is limited.

I love you so very much that I have come from my celestial home many times just to be with you and help and influence you in right thinking and living; and no spirit who has never seen the grandeur and happiness of these Celestial Spheres can conceive what it means to leave these precincts and mingle in the forbidding earth atmosphere.

I love you so much that I am writing to exert my powers to help you in your material affairs and to keep you from worry and unhappiness as far as possible.

And I love you so much that I am trying to have you become so spiritual and good that you may be fitted for a home in my sphere when the time comes for you to come over; and this latter beneficence has never yet been given to any mortal. But if you will follow me and live with me in love and unison you will be able to experience this great transformation and become an inhabitant of my home as I said.

Well you are a sinner, as you say, but when I tell you of how you may become so spiritual and good you must believe me for I know whereof I speak and speak in all earnestness and truth.

Yes, I did, for you called me to you by your earnest aspirations and prayers to the Father. and what you then saw in your imaginings may very easily come true, except that I will never materialize again on earth. The other portions of your day dreams may become realities, and the happiness that you felt will be increased manyfold. The thought that you have as to fitting up a room in the way you pictured, is one that should be carried into execution; for such a room would be very attractive to the higher spirits, and would cause many of them to assemble and give you many truths of the higher spheres. I, of course, would do my writing there, and it would be much easier for us both, for conditions would not be mixed as they necessarily are now. So when you get your home carry out your ideas as to that room.

Yes, I have, and it was one of the first times that I ever communicated with mortals. The conditions were good both for the spirits and for Dr. Peebles and his companion. But of course I did not talk in any extended manner. The spirit who transmitted the communications was not in that degree of spiritual development that enabled us to teach the higher truths in all their fullness and beauty. Dr. Peebles is a good man and very highly developed spiritually, but he does not yet know the way, the truth and the life as I taught them. He does not know the mystery of the New Birth as I have taught it to you; and he is resting in the belief that if he loves God and his fellow man in the natural way that is all that is necessary for his highest development and greatest happiness. Some day he will realize that only the Divine Love can give him of a Divine Nature, and that no self development or cultivation of the Natural Love to the greatest and most sublime extent are sufficient to make him at one with the Father in the divine sense that I wrote of, and which makes the spirit a partaker of this Divine Essence of the Father. So should you ever meet him explain to him the difference between the two loves and what the New Birth means.

Well, as I have written you a long message and as you want to hear from some of your band I will close.

Yes he (Mr. Crowell[34]) has realized the New Birth and is teaching it to spirits. He seems very anxious to write more through you, and he will as soon as I tell your band that he is in a condition to not interfere with their rapport. So when he comes listen to him, and you will learn many truths which he has learned since he came over.

With my truest love and best wishes and blessings, I am your own spirit brother and friend,
Jesus.

Writes that the Master is so close to Mr. Padgett to make him feel like a true brother

March 24th, 1915.

I am here, your grandmother.

Well, my son, what a beautiful and comforting letter[35] you got from the Master. He was so loving and so interested in your happiness that he seemed almost like a new relative. I mean that in the human sense. Of course, he is nearer to you in love than any of us, because his capacity for loving is so much greater. But he seemed so very human in the sense of coming so close to you and making you feel that you and he are true brothers. I doubt if he has ever come so close to any mortal before, His love for you seems to be a thing of no limitation or bound. He loves you so much that he even lets his love do things which he does not engage in among mortals. I mean in interfering in the material things of their lives. As he said, spirits of lesser greatness and development help mortals in their earthly affairs, and we all wonder that Jesus should make himself so humble, as we say, to do what he has done for you.

But he knows what is best and you should feel yourself among the most blessed of men. I know that you cannot understand this and neither can we, but he is the wisest of us all, and the most powerful, and when he tells you a thing you may believe it.

Of course, his great mission is to teach the wonderful truths of his Father, and he sees the best way to disseminate them among mankind. You have been selected by him for this work and you will do it with all your heart and soul, I know. I know how you feel and you will be able to carry out your desires, for he has decreed it and it will be done. So my dear son, consider yourself as one set aside for this great work, and let all your ambitions and aspirations urge you to its performance.

Well, he knows, and when he said it he knew what your future would be. It is certainly marvelous, and we all thank the Father that you

---

[34] See Mr. Crowells' message in Volume IV. (G.J.C.)
[35] Read Jesus' comforting words in the preceding message. (G.J.C.)

have such wonderful promises. Only pray and have faith, and you will realize these promises.

Yes, I know that you are a very great sinner, but you know this great Love of the Father was created or rather has always been, for the redemption of the vilest sinner who seeks and believes.

Yes, and I was astonished at his answers. They involve so much that you will not readily comprehend their full significance until you have progressed more in your spiritual development.

But know this, that such love as he expressed is sufficient to help you in every time of trouble and to make you a wonderfully bright and happy man and spirit.

His love is past finding out.

Neither do I now, but some day you will and there will come such an avalanche of happiness as will almost transport you to the Celestial Spheres. Oh my dear boy, you have before you a wonderful future of love and happiness if you will only follow the Master's teachings and do his will, and reciprocate his love.

Well dear, I must stop now as others are here and want to write.

I have met Garfield[36] and have had a talk with him. He is a spirit of wonderful intellect, but of not much spiritual development. I told him of this great love and how it operates and what results it brought to the believing spirits. I think that he was somewhat impressed and is now thinking about the matter and frequently talking to Mr. Riddle on the subject. You will be surprised to learn how Mr. Riddle has progressed in faith and love, and is praying all the time for more light and greater abundance of love. He will soon be in the fifth (spirit) sphere where your father and Prof. Salyards are, and they will find congenial companionship. He will soon write you a long letter telling of his progress. He seems to love you with a very wonderful love and is with you very often trying to help you and comfort you.

Well I must say good night your loving grandmother.

Writes that she is happy that the Master wrote and he was so loving and brotherly

March 24th, 1915.

I am here, your own dear and loving Helen.

Well, see how obedient I am, but it was a very great pleasure to obey you in that way, as you know.

Well sweetheart, you have had some wonderful messages

---

[36] See Mr. Garfield's message later in this volume on page 163. (G.J.C.)

tonight[37] and I feel that they will help you very much in your moments of trouble and worry. I was so glad that the Master wrote you as he did. He was so very loving and brotherly and seemed to be so much interested in your welfare.

He is so beautiful that we all stand and gaze at him, as you say on earth, and so loving, that we feel that he is our great big, loving brother. I tell you that without him this spirit world would not be the place of happiness that it is to us who believe in him and love him and follow his teachings. So many spirits do not know him as their loving brother and way shower, and they are left to their own thoughts to find happiness. So you see the great privilege and opportunity we, who know him as the son of the Father, have over those who know him not. Having eyes, they see not, and ears they hear not. It seems so strange to me, but I tell you that it is true. The Master, with his great love and wisdom and power, passes them by and they see him not. I try so hard to teach many spirits what a knowledge of him means; but they seem so dull of comprehension and so darkened in their souls development, that my work is often in vain. Yet I have hope and continue my work, knowing that at some unexpected moment a ray of light may break in and they commence to think that God lives to give them his great Love, and take them to his care and protection in the way that we have told you of.

My heart yearns so for these blind spirits and willful rejecters of the truth of the New Birth. Many of these spirits are very excellent moral people and live lives of uprightness and love for their fellow spirits, and work very hard to help the less enlightened to progress to conditions of comparative happiness; and yet they, themselves, will not listen to our teachings of the greater truths, which if understood and obeyed would carry them to conditions of inexpressible happiness.

Well, such is the work of spirits on earth as well as here; and we are all trying to do the work of the Father in helping to redeem souls.

You are much better than when you came to your room tonight, and I am so glad of it. Only trust in the Master's promises and you will not be disappointed.

I heard what he said about your progressing to a condition, even while on earth, that would enable you to enter the celestial spheres when you come over, and I believe it to be true. Now you must try to get this very great development because when you come to me I want you to come to my home to live. Won't that be joyful! Yes, my dear Ned, I know that you will try, and I will help you so hard to accomplish it and so will all. But your great helper will be the Master, for you will be with him so much that his love will overshadow you so that your soul will have to develop. So you see how you are blessed in all this. Try to do his work

---

[37]Helen is referring to the preceding message from Jesus. (G.J.C.)

with all your heart and soul, and you will succeed.

Yes I heard, and when the time comes I will be with you to suggest and advise, and you will have a beautiful room for your purpose. And I know that we will have many joyous evenings together. We will bring heaven with us, and you will live in it for minutes at a time. You will then hear our voices in talk and song, feel our presence so palpably that you will know that we are with you. I am so anxious for that time to come, as are all of us.

Yes, we will all try to help you get the home and then you will be fixed for life.

Well, wait until the time comes, and you may change your mind. Of course, I would prefer that you should not, and if your comfort and happiness could be provided for otherwise, I would rather have it as you suggest. But you will have to wait.

Well, sweetheart, you have written much and must stop.

She is well and a little troubled, but it will soon disappear as you will do what the Master said.

So with all my love, and with many hugs and kisses, I am

Your own true and loving,

Helen.

Comments on a book that Mr. Padgett was reading about fallen angels, which some churches believe in

January 2nd, 1916.

I am here, Jesus.

I come to tell you that you have not been in a very good condition of spirituality since last night when you read that book.[38]

Well, in the first place I want to say that there are no such things as the fallen angels or any spirits except the spirits of those who once lived as mortals and who are living now as spirits. Of course many of them are what may be called evil spirits but they are not devils in the sense that the author describes them.

There never were any rebellions in heaven of any of the angels of God and whenever such a thing is mentioned in the Bible it has no foundation in fact for there never was a Seraphim or any other angel that fell and became the devil or Satan as he is called and you must not let your thoughts disturb your belief in our writing to you for we who profess to write to you actually do write. I know that it is very largely believed in the churches that there are such beings as devils of whom

---

[38]Helen explains the bad influence that Pastor Russell's book on Spiritualism had on Mr. Padgett and which is published further on in this volume on page 197. (G.J.C.)

Satan is the chief, but such belief is wholly erroneous and has worked a great injury to the cause of truth and to my teachings.

The men who teach this false doctrine will have a great sin to atone for when they come to the spirit world and especially will the author of the book you were reading[39] and not only for this false doctrine but for others which he teaches. He will find as soon as his breath leaves the body that there is a spirit world and that he is a living spirit and one who will find come to him the recollections of all his false teachings. I know that it may be said that he actually believes what he preaches but that fact will not alter the fact that his teachings are untrue and that he must pay the penalties of these false teachings until at last they shall no longer exist on earth.

This may seem unjust when it is considered that he may be honest in his beliefs, but as I said on earth, the man who believes these false doctrines and teaches other men to believe them will have to pay the penalties of results of these teachings—not because they injured him and not even if taught insincerely—but because they injured others and as a consequence placed those whom he taught in a condition which is not in unison with the truth or with the laws of God. And that condition can only be reversed[40] by the truth (or knowledge of the truth) being possessed by these misguided beings. They can only come into the possession of the truth by being untaught as it were these falsehoods and being taught the truths. This will be the work of the author mentioned and all those who assist him in teaching these doctrines until all who have ever been deceived by such teachings have been shown the error of the same and brought to a knowledge of the truth.

This will arise not because of any special punishment inflicted upon him by God, but because of his realization of the great harm he has done to those who believed in and followed him in these teachings. He will need no other punishment than that of his own recollection and his conscience.

So I say, give no further heed to what you may have read and believe that I Jesus am actually writing to you and that all the others who claim to write are the spirits that they actually represent themselves to be.

I was with you tonight at church and heard the lecture and while it was undoubtedly interesting to many in the audience, yet it has no basis of fact upon which to rest. The medium did not know the things that she predicted and no spirit controlled her to make the prophecies and if such had she would not have been able to make such predictions.

---

[39] Read of Pastor Russell's tragic awakening and penalties of teaching a faith that was wholly untrue in Volume IV (2nd Ed.) page 238. (G.J.C.)

[40] In the previous edition this read "reinclosed." (G.J.C.)

The only reason that the medium had for making the prophecies were the facts that she knows now exists, that will probably bring about the future as she stated it. But no reliance can be placed upon what she attempts to foretell, and if some of the things happen that she predicted, it will not be because she predicted them or because any spirit inspired her to make such predictions, but because they will be the natural effects of course that now exist or which will probably arise in the future.

Well, as to the discourse of which she spoke, she doesn't know any more nor have any greater reason to declare that such a disease will prevail in your country than you have, and she has no reasons upon which to found any such prophecy. I do not see any condition which will bring about such disease in the way that she describes it. Of course there are men dying all the time of some disease or other and men will continue to so die and some may die of the trouble that she speaks of or of those akin to the same. But such disease will not prevail in the way that she described. So, on the whole you need not give any credence to what she said in the particulars mentioned.

I have been with you a great deal today and I was glad when you went to the church of your birth this morning, while you do not believe in the wine and the bread as representing my blood and body, yet many of the people who partook of these have the Divine Love of the Father in their souls and are very close to the Kingdom, and the influence that attended this service was very spiritual.

Many of the spirits of mortals who had attended this church were present exercising a very spiritual influence on the worshipers and you could feel the presence of the same.

I must not write more tonight, but will say that you must trust in my love and believe that I am with you very often trying to help you and make your soul feel the great love of the Father flowing into it.

And with my love and blessings and that of the Father, I will say good night.

Your friend and brother,
Jesus.

Assures Mr. Padgett that when the messages that he is now receiving will be printed that they will be accepted

December 28th, 1915.

I am here, Jesus.

I came tonight to tell you that you did the right thing by sending the message to the person who wrote the article upon the subject of Christianizing the Bible, for I now believe that he will appreciate it to a very great extent.

He is not an orthodox Christian as I have learned, but is the preacher of a Unitarian Church in the little town in which he lives and is a very broad minded man. I have learned this by visiting him and saw the condition of his mind and beliefs upon subjects related to what you have written him.

He may have some doubts as to the source of the message and may not feel inclined to accept your statements as to how you received it as true, but yet his doubts will not be altogether of such a nature that he may not have some hesitation on saying that such a thing as your receiving my message could not be true.

At any rate he will become interested in the subject matter of the message and will find some thoughts that he never before had.

And I fully realize that when you shall publish my messages the great difficulty in their being accepted will be the doubts of the people as to their source, but you will have to compile the book in such a way that the testimony of the numerous writers will be so strong that the doubts will not be able to withstand the evidence of my being the writer of the messages. And when men read the same they will realize that the truths which they contain could only come from a higher source than mortal mind and that the hand of the Father is in them.

I merely write this tonight to show you that we will have a great difficulty to have people believe that I wrote the messages and that we will have to do everything possible to convince them of the truth of the source of the writings. But if this difficulty should appear almost insurmountable in the beginning, yet after a while when men come to appreciate the inherent truth and importance of the messages they will easily believe that I wrote them, and especially will this be the case with those men who are not orthodox in this belief.

So I will continue to write and you to receive the messages and when the time comes to publish them, I do not fear that they will not be gladly received.

Very soon I will write you another, which will be very important to mankind.

I will only say further that I am with you trying to influence you to do the right thing in your life and to believe with all your heart in the Divine Love of the Father and in my mission and your work.

I will not write more but will say with all my love that I am,
Your brother and friend.
Jesus.

When Mr. Padgett's soul condition was sufficient to permit Jesus to write, the following informative message was received

January 24th, 1915.

I am here, Jesus.

You are now in condition, and I will give you a short message. When I was on earth I was not worshiped as God, but was considered merely as the son of God in the sense that in me were imposed the Truths of my Father and many of His wonderful and mysterious powers. I did not proclaim myself to be God, neither did I permit any of my disciples to believe that I was God, but only that I was His beloved son sent to proclaim to mankind His truths, and show them the way to the Love of the Father. I was not different from other men, except that I possessed to a degree this Love of God, which made me free from sin, and prevented the evils that formed a part of the nature of men from becoming a part of my nature.

No man who believes that I am God has a knowledge of the truth, or is obeying the commandments of God by worshiping me. Such worshipers are blaspheming and are doing the cause of God and my teachings great injury. Many a man would have become a true believer in and worshiper of the Father and follower of my teachings, had not this blasphemous dogma been interpolated into the Bible. It was not with my authority, or in consequence of my teachings that such a very injurious doctrine was promulgated or believed in.

I am only a son of my Father as you are, and while I was always free from sin and error, as regards the true conception of my Father's true relationship to mankind, yet you are His son also; and if you will seek earnestly and pray to the Father with faith, you may become as free from sin and error as I was then, and am now.

The Father is Himself, alone. There is no other God besides Him, and no other God to be worshiped. I am His teacher of truth, and am the Way, the Truth and the Life, because in me are those attributes of goodness and knowledge which fit me to show the way and lead men to eternal life in the Father, and to teach them that God has prepared a Kingdom in which they may live forever, if they so desire. But not withstanding my teachings, men and those who have assumed high places in what is called the Christian Church, impose doctrines so at variance with the truth, that, in these latter days, many men in the exercise of an enlightened freedom and of reason, have become infidels and turned away from God and His Love, and have thought and taught that man, himself, is sufficient for his own salvation.

The time has come when these men must be taught to know that while the teachings of these professed authorities on the truths of God are all wrong, they, these same men, are in error when they refuse to believe in God and my teachings. What my teachings are, I know it is difficult to understand from the writings of the New Testament, for many things therein contained I never said, and many things that I did say are not written therein. I am now going to give to the world the truths as I taught them when on earth and many that I never disclosed to my disciples or inspired others to write.

No man can come to the Father's Love, except he be born again. This is the great and fundamental Truth which men must learn and believe, for without this New Birth men cannot partake of the Divine Essence of God's Love, which, when possessed by a man, makes him at one with the Father. This Love comes to man by the workings of the Holy Ghost, causing this Love to flow into the heart and soul, and filling it, so that all sin and error, which tends to make them unhappy, must be eradicated.

I am not going to tell tonight just how this working of the spirit operates, but, I say, if a man will pray to the Father and believe, and earnestly ask that this Love be given him, he will receive it; and when it comes into his soul he will realize it.

Let not men think that by any effort of their own they can come into this union with the Father, because they cannot. No river can rise higher than its source; and no man who has only the natural love and filled with error can of his own powers cause that natural love to partake of the Divine, or his nature to be relieved of such sin and error.

Man is a mere creature and cannot create anything higher than himself; so man cannot rise to the nature of the Divine, unless the Divine first comes into that man and makes him a part of Its Own Divinity.

All men who do not get a part of this Divine Essence will be left in their natural state, and while they may progress to higher degrees of goodness and freedom from sin and from everything that tends to make them unhappy, yet, they will be only natural men, still.

I came into the world to show men the way to this Divine Love of the Father and teach them his spiritual truths, and my mission was that in all its perfection, and incidentally, to teach them the way to greater happiness on earth as well as in the spirit world by teaching them the way to the purification of the natural love; even though they neglected to seek for and obtain this Divine Love and become one with the Father.

Let men ponder this momentous question, and they will learn that the happiness of the natural man, and the happiness of the man who has obtained the attributes of Divinity, are very different, and in all eternity must be separate and distinct. My teachings are not very hard to understand and follow, and if men will only listen to them and believe them and follow them, they will learn the way and obtain the one perfect state of happiness which the father has prepared for his children. No man can obtain this state of Celestial bliss, unless he first gets this Divine Love of the Father, and so becomes at one with the Father.

I know it is thought and taught that morality and correct living and great natural love will assure a man's future happiness, and to a degree this is true, but this happiness is not that greater happiness which God desires His children to have; and to show the way to which I came to earth to teach. But in some hearts and minds my truths found a lodgment, and were preserved to save mankind from total spiritual darkness and a relapse to worship of form and ceremony only.

I have written you this to show that you must not let the teachings of the Bible, and what men wrote or professed to have written therein, keep you from receiving and understanding what I write.

I shall write no more tonight, but I will continue to tell you the Truths which will be "my New Gospel to all men," and when they have heard my messages they will believe that there is only one God, and only one to be worshiped.

With my love and blessings I close for this time.

Jesus.[41]

Second formal message "His Father's Nature as my God and your God"

January 31st, 1915.

I am here, Jesus.

As I told you I will write my second message tonight. I am not going to tell you of my Father's Kingdom at this time, but of His Nature as my God and your God.

He is the only one who is supreme and all powerful and loving, and wise. He is not a being of form or individuality as men understand, but is a substance of being and soul. His soul is that part of Him which embraces all the affections and love, and which is bestowed on man in order that he may become like his Father.

I am not yet so possessed of that soul essence, as to make me just like the Father in all His attributes, but I expect that some time in the future, when I have received that divine essence in all its fullness, I will be likened unto the Father; and so may every one of His creatures, if he will only seek for it with true faith and earnestness.

The Father is not capable of being seen with the physical or

---

41 This message is a composite of two, being published in Volume I and Volume III. The correction suggested by Judas on December 27th, 2001 has been applied. This was to alter "all sin tends to make them unhappy." which now reads "all sin, which tends to make them unhappy, must be eradicated."(G.J.C.)

spiritual sight, but can only be seen with the soul's eyes of perfect love. He is not in any particular place, or seated on a throne in His Heavens, but His attributes are everywhere, and fills the whole universe. The earth is a very small portion of the universe, and men must not believe that God is only in the heavens, where the sons of earth go when they cease to live as mortals.

God is a God of Love, above everything else; and the sooner mankind learns and believes that fact, the sooner will happiness exist on the earth, as well as in the heavens. He is not a God of hatred, nor does He chastise His children in wrath or anger. His love is with all mankind, be they saints or sinners, and no man suffers punishment because the Father wants him to suffer. He is also a God of Mercy and Forgiveness; and will forgive the sins of men, and shed His Mercy over them, if they will truly and in sincerity ask His Forgiveness and seek His Mercy.

He is also a God of Wisdom; and His plans for the redemption and salvation of mankind are the only plans that can be adopted for men to try to follow, in order that they may receive this salvation. He is also a God of Power and in the days to come, when He sees fit to carry out and perfect His plans in their full fruition, He will through the working of His Spirit, which is perfect in its working, destroy all sin and error in His Universe, and perfect harmony will reign and man will be at peace and happiness.

So God is everything in nature and attributes which will not only redeem men from their sins, but will make them lovers of one another and brothers in the true sense of the word. The world will not be destroyed as it is taught by some, in the interpreting of the Bible, but when the great day of judgment comes, all sin will be eradicated from the world, and mankind will continue to live upon the earth, free from sin and unhappiness, just as it is supposed Adam and Eve lived in the Garden of Eden.

Never has man seen God, and the stories in the Old Testament about some of the prophets and leaders of the Jews in their early captivity and wanderings, are not true, for God cannot be seen as therein described. His angels and messengers who were at one time mortals of earth, were seen, and spoke to the prophets and represented themselves as being angels of God, but no angel or spirit ever represented himself to be God; not even the angels who delivered to Moses the tablets of stone, as it is written. God works always through His Angels, and never directly, as some of the Bible writers teach. I was His chosen son to do the work of redeeming the earth from sin, and I came as my Father's representative, I never was God, nor did I ever claim to be, either to my disciples or to the Jews or the Sanhedrin.

It is written in the Bible that the voice of God spoke to my disciples on the Mount of Transfiguration, and to John and those present at my baptism, but it was not the voice of God, but the voice of one of God's Highest Angels.

No man has ever heard the voice of God, for He has no voice. He works in a silent mysterious way, through the operation of His soul upon the soul of men, just as the coming of the Holy Ghost at Pentecost. While the Bible says that there was a noise as of a mighty wind, yet that was not perceptible to the physical ears of the disciples, but in their souls they felt the presence of such a manifestation, and in order to have mankind understand that there was this wonderful manifestation, they used the imagery of the voice of a mighty wind. So man must understand that God speaks to man through His angels, or through the communication of His Soul and theirs.

I speak thus because I want it made plain that God is not the person, loving or otherwise, which the Bible may teach man that He is. He is only the personification of love, power, and wisdom, and is without form or personal appearance. This is my knowledge of what God is.

I will not write further tonight. With my blessing and love.
Jesus.

Gave additional explanation on the same day

January 31st, 1915.

I am here, your grandmother.

You must not think that because the Master said that God is a personification of love, power, and wisdom, that there is no real God, but merely an abstract being representing these attributes. He is a real being, and these attributes are His, and not the combination of the attributes. He exists, and without Him, there would be no love, wisdom, or power. He is the creator of these principles, and not their creature.

As Jesus said He is without form or substance, such as mortals and spirits have; yet He has a spiritual substance, and that is real, and not shadowy or nonexistent. Pantheism is different from what God is.

While His attributes are everywhere, yet He is of an identical substance of spirit. So do not let the idea possess you that he is not a being, for he is, and even though we cannot see Him, or feel Him as a spirit, yet He exists as His one true self. So believe in a personal God in that sense.

I know that it is hard to comprehend the true conception of His being, but the higher we get in the scale of love, the more apparent becomes His real existence as a being. Do not let your inability to grasp the true meaning of this description of God and His nature, lead you to think that He is a mere essence. He is real, and to us who have received a large amount of His love and essence, He becomes as real as if we could see and feel Him with our spiritual eyes and hands.

I know the difficulties in the way of your finite mind to grasp the true conception of His being, but as love draws you closer to Him, the mind gives way to the perceptions of the soul, and God appears as a real existing being, the Creator of all.

I want to tell you further, that God, (the God of the Master), while He works through His angels, yet He, Himself, comes into our souls by His direct communication. The Holy Spirit is His messenger that causes the souls of men to hear and receive this soul communication; yet God's Love comes direct from Himself, and when man was created in the likeness of God, he was given a soul that was capable of receiving the soul essence of the Father. Neither in his physical nor spiritual form was man created in the image of his Father, because the Father has no such forms. But in the soul essence, the image was made alike.

Yet man is of such a great degree in God's creation that he can refuse to receive this soul essence, if he so wills. His soul is capable of receiving it, but is not compelled to do so, and while man has the image, yet if he neglects to receive the substance, he will never become at-one with the Father. That image will never be more than an image only.

God is so good, that He implanted in man's soul what may be called the natural love; and that love is sufficient to make him comparatively happy, and in the great day when sin and error shall be destroyed, man's natural love will be able to cause this happiness.

But man will not be at-one with the Father in the larger sense, and will not take on the divine nature of His God. So you see the necessity of seeking this wonderful union with the Father.

I must now stop.

Your grandmother (Ann Rollins).

Explanation on the love of man

March 4th, 1915.

I am here, Jesus. I want to write tonight on the love of man. This love is one that is not understood by humanity in its most important particular. I mean that this love is not one that is sufficient to give man the highest degree of happiness which he may obtain in either the mortal life or in the life to come.

This love is of a nature that changes with the change in the ideas and desires of man, and has no stability that will serve to keep him constant in his affections. No man who has only this love can ever be in condition to say that he will continue to have this love for a longer time than the present; and when he thinks that his love can never change, or leave him, he is only giving wish to the thought.

But this love is one that may last for a long time, and sometimes it seems that it can never die or grow less; yet, in it's very nature, it has not that constancy which ensures its lasting longer than a moment of time.

I do not mean to say anything disparaging of this natural love, for it is undoubtedly the greatest gift that the Father has bestowed upon mankind, and without it, men would be in a very unhappy condition. Yet, it is not the Great Love of the Father which all men may receive, if they will only seek and strive to obtain it by prayer and faith.

This natural love is that which unites men and women in unity while on earth, and enables them to approach nearer to a life of happiness than does any other human quality; but still it has the danger always accompanying it, that some time, in some way, it may cease to exist.

The mother's love is the strongest of all loves given to mortals, and apparently it can never end or grow old, yet a time may come when even that love will die or cease to retain all its vitality or beauty. I know it is said that love never dies; but that is not true as regards this natural love; and no man can say that his love of today will remain his love of a few years hence.

Yet, there is a love that may be called the natural love that will last forever, providing these souls seek and obtain the Divine Love, and that is the love that God has implanted in two souls that he has designed to become one in spirit life. This love is in reality not the love of two souls, but one and the same love manifested in the two opposite sexes, and which is only a complete one when these two apparently independent souls come together in perfect unity. This is what is commonly called the love of soulmates, and which is that essence of spiritual love which makes the happiness of the two spirits or mortals seemingly complete. Yet this love is not of a Divine nature, but merely the highest type of the natural love. (But still not God's Divine Essence.) So, when men speak of the love of one mortal for his fellow man, it means merely the love which his human nature is capable of having and giving to another mortal.

I do not wish to be understood as in any way implying that this love is not a great boon and blessing to mankind, for it is, and without it, there would not be the harmony that exists on earth even to its present extent; when hatred and anger seems to have taken its place in the hearts of many men who are now striving to kill and destroy. (World War I) But this is only for a season; the war will cease and then men will realize, more than for a long time that only their love for one another can make the earth a happy and desirable place to live on.

Love, I know it is said, is the fulfilling of the law,[42] but no man can thoroughly understand this until he knows what love is. I do not mean that in order to fulfill every law man must have the Divine Love of the Father, because there are laws that govern the Divine existence, and laws that govern the human and merely spiritual existence; and the Love of the Divine is the fulfillment of the former laws, and the natural love is the fulfillment of the latter laws. So you must see that only as men have the Love of the Divine can they fulfill the laws of the Divine existence; and so, as they have the natural love only, can they fulfill the natural laws.

But this natural love will not suffice to make them at-one with the Father, as I have before written; and the utmost of its powers and functions is to give them that happiness which they will receive in living the life of a spirit or man unredeemed.

I will not say that man should not cultivate this love for his fellow man to the greatest possible degree, for he should; and if that should be the only kind of love that he may have, either on earth or in the spirit world, the more of it that he possesses the happier will he be, and the greater will be the happiness of his fellow man and fellow spirit.

So when I said, while on earth, that men should love their God and love their fellow men as themselves, I meant that they should do so with all the possibilities of whatever love they might possess. Yet, if men would only learn, as they can, that there is no necessity for them to have only the natural love, but that they can all seek the Greater Love, and obtain the correspondingly greater happiness, and immortality. Men do not realize this, though, and seem to be satisfied with this natural love and the pleasures that ensue from its possession.

I would not have them do anything that would lessen this love or shut their hearts to its influence, when it is pure and good; but yet, I cannot help trying to impress upon them the great desirability of having this higher Love in their souls. I am a lover of all men, and I want them to feel the happiness of the inflowing of the Divine Love, and thereby learn what the Love of God means, and what they may have if they will only seek.

This love of the purely natural will not suffice for the temptations that beset men on earth; and, also, will not insure against temptations when they become spirits. I know this, and hence I say it with the positiveness of one who knows — you may say, with authority.

As you are tired I must stop. With all my blessings and love, I am,
Your brother in spirit, Jesus.[43]

---

[42]Read Romans 13:10. (G.J.C.)
[43]This message is a composite of two, being published in Volume II and Volume III. (G.J.C.)

Explains that coming to Mr. Padgett as he does is not contrary to any law of the spirit world

April 9th, 1915.

I am here, Jesus.

Yes, I am, and you will be enabled to fully understand what the Holy Ghost is, and what meaning should be given to it as you find it referred to in various parts of the Bible. I will say this though, that it is not God nor any part of Him. It is merely one of his instrumentalities, used by Him in doing His work for the redemption of mankind. I will not write any message tonight, but will commence next week, if you are in better condition.

Well, as you believe what I say as to my being a son of God, and not a God, you can easily believe that my coming to you as I do, is not at all contrary to any law of the spirit world. The fact that I have my home in the highest Celestial Heaven does not prevent me from coming to earth to do my work, which has not been carried on by those of earth who should have performed it. I am a spirit of love and sympathy, as well as of great spiritual development, and I desire that all men shall know what the great plan of the Father is for their redemption and happiness.

So, because I am such an exalted spirit, as you say, it is no reason that I should not come to you, and communicate with you freely and, in a way, confidentially. I love you, as I have told you, and I have selected you to do my work and hence, I am trying to make you wholly at-one with me. You must not doubt me just because I come to you so often and speak so familiarly with you, because I hope and expect that in the great future you will be very close to me and with me. I am trying to prepare you for so great a progression in your spiritual condition, that when you come over, you will realize the oneness that I speak of, and be fitted to live near my sphere.

Well, your grandmother is a wonderful spirit in her development, and by the time you come over she will be near me, in my home, and, as I believe, will your mother and wife. They are all filled with the Father's Love and are receiving it more abundantly all the time. They are now in the first (celestial) sphere of my Kingdom, and will find that their progress will be much more rapid.

So try to believe what I say, and do my will, and all will be well with you. Well, soon you will be free, as I told you, and then you can do the work without being interfered with by material things. I know that it is hard for you to lay aside these cares, and I am not disappointed or impatient that you do not, but only believe that the time will soon come when they will trouble you no more.

So as we have written somewhat long to night, I will stop now. I will pray for you as I always do. With all my love and the blessings of the Father.

I am your loving brother,
Jesus.[44]

Is amazed at the power that Mr. Padgett has with the dark spirits and approves of his work in this respect

April 7th, 1915.

I am here, Jesus.

Well, you have my love and help, and you must realize that I am with you very much, as I am.

I wish to tell you that you are not in such a good condition tonight for much writing as your nervous forces are not exactly suitable for the strain which writing imposes upon you. I know that you do not understand just what this means, but I know, and tell you, so that you may not write very much.

I do not think that in permitting the unfortunate to write as you have determined that they may write, will injure your rapport with your band or with me. You are doing them much good, and the influence that you seem to have with these unfortunate spirits is surprising, and to many other spirits seems a very remarkable thing. I know just what your kindness and desire to help means, and that you not only benefit them who come to you and are happy, but also benefit many who are not able to write, for these latter see that you have helped the former, and they naturally make inquiries as to what you said to them, and what course you advised them to pursue; and as a consequence of what they hear they seek the help of other spirits.

There are great hosts of these unhappy spirits who come to you or gather around when you are writing. Of course, they cannot all write; and yet, they who do not write are just as anxious to get relief from the condition of darkness in which they are, as are the others, and naturally try to learn the way out. Many of these spirits, after learning and seeing what benefit the few whom you advise have derived, of their own volition turn to the brighter spirits and ask advice. They seem to think that these brighter spirits may be somewhat interested in them, and, consequently, they seek their help. You are doing a good work and must not stop, for if you do, you will cause many spirits to remain in darkness for a much longer time than they otherwise would.

I want to tell you that I am anxious to continue my messages, and so have been very free from them, and your band should save you

---

[44] This message is a composite of two, being published in Volume II and Volume III. (G.J.C.)

from being bothered by them.

Your Indian guide is strong enough to keep them away, and he will do so, I have no doubt. Your band also is strong enough to keep away the strongest of these evil spirits and they will do so.

Yes, so far you have, and I have been very much pleased that you have. You certainly have a way that overcomes these evil spirits and turns them to higher things, and causes them to listen to the bright spirits. You must not doubt or become disheartened.

I will stop now as your wife wants to write a little.

With all my love, I am

Jesus.

Is pleased with Mr. Padgett's declaration and will help him to become At-One with the Father

April 6th, 1915.

I am here, Jesus.

Well, I am here to tell you of my great gratification in hearing you declare your belief in me again as you did today. This may seem to be a small matter to you, but I tell you it is one of greatest moment, not only to my cause but to you personally, because it puts you in close rapport with me, and helps you get into a condition which enables you to respond with a greater facility to my efforts to convey to you my messages. And also it has a reflex influence on your spiritual condition, and tends to increase your faith in what I tell you of the Father's Love and His great mercy and plan for man's redemption.

I am pleased with your declaration and will help you to become more at-one with me in my work. So let not doubt come into your mind as to my being who and what I represent myself to be, for if there is a truth in all the universe, that assertion of mine is a truth. Let your faith increase, and your life will be happier, and you will become better fitted to inhabit the sphere which I have determined you shall have for your home.

Oh, my dear brother, it is a great consolation to know that you will do my work as I desire it to be done on earth, and to feel that I can rely upon you to receive my "Gospel of Truth and Light to mankind."[45]

Yes, you were correct and I will soon write on this subject at length, and you will see that, before me, no man or spirit ever declared

---

[45] Although a number of different titles were used by Dr. Stone, including "Messages from Jesus and Celestials", "Book of Truths", and "True Gospel revealed anew by Jesus", and even "True Gospel revealed again from Jesus", this is not a title that was ever used until I published a volume of messages in date order. (G.J.C.)

the truth of immortality[46]. You have a right conception of what I meant, and you will sometime realize that that immortality is for you. You and all who believe as you do and seek for the Divine Essence, which alone can bring immortality to man.

Very soon now I will continue my last message and then we will progress faster in our work.

Well, I will not detain you longer tonight, as there are several present who desire to write.

Well, that is now a part of your work[47], and your band knows that you must do that work. It will not injure your rapport with your band, or cause your power of writing to diminish.

So with all my love and the blessings of the Father, I am your own true brother.

Jesus.[48]

Advises Mr. Padgett to give more time to prayer and that the Father's Love is coming into his soul

April 12th, 1915.

I am here, Jesus.

I want to tell you that you are now getting in a better spiritual condition than you have been for a long time. You have more of God's Love in your heart, and I think that very soon you will be in that condition of mind and soul development that will enable you to take my messages and as I desire that they be received.

I am with you very much and try to help you in your efforts to obtain this soul development, and also in your material matters. So do not doubt me, as what I tell you is true.

If you will only give more time to prayer you will find that your condition of happiness will be much improved and that you will realize that the Father's love is coming into your soul more abundantly.

So, let me feel that you are endeavoring to get this Great Love more and more every day, and I will try to help you with all my powers and love.

I will not write more tonight as there are some others here who desire to write.

So good night. With all my love and the blessings of the Father.

---

[46] Jesus discusses the truth of immortality in a lengthy and comprehensive message in Volume I (5th Ed.) on page 45. (G.J.C.)

[47] The work referred to is helping spirits who write through Mr. Padgett, and enable them to visualise the bright spirits who help them in their progress. (J.P.G.)

[48] This message is a composite of two, being published in Volume II and Volume III. (G.J.C.)

I am your own true brother,
Jesus.

Writes about the great work that Mr. Padgett is doing and will help him also

April 12th, 1915.

I am here, your old Prof.

I am very happy and am glad to say that I can see that you are, too. I want to say that I am prepared now to write you as I promised, and anytime that suits you I will be glad to do so. Well, that will suit me very well, and I will be here, and ready to give you the result of my best thoughts, and hope that you will find my writings interesting and profitable.

Yes, she is happy and is here. She says that you are very dear to her, and wants you to know that you are doing a great good to the poor unfortunate spirits who come to you for help. She is willing to help too, if you desire her to.

Yes, says Mrs. Salyards, that will be perfectly proper, and she will not hesitate to respond and do what she can. So she says, with all her love, she wishes you much happiness and success.

Well, I tried to help them, and some of them listened to me and tried to take my advice, and are now striving to obtain the Father's Forgiveness and Love. Some were not so easily impressed, but I believe that they will ultimately try to do as I advised them. Oh, it is a great and good work that you are doing, and we are helping you to do.

Yes, I heard the conversation between him and Mr. Riddle, and I enjoyed it very much. It was quite a revelation to me, as I could hardly conceive that a spirit, with all the surroundings that exist here, could be so self-opinionated, or believe that he had such an all comprehensive mind. It was certainly interesting as I heard him discourse on the wonderful knowledge which he possessed, or thought he possessed. Such minds, I doubt not, are very difficult to convince that there may be some little knowledge that they do not possess.

I will not write more now, but will say good night.
With all my love and best wishes for your happiness, I am
Your old Prof,
Joseph H. Salyards.

Says that as her love increases for the Father so also her love increases for him as well

April 12th, 1915.

I am here, Helen.

It was the Master. I want to tell you of my love for you, as I promised. Well, because I have not lately said very much about my love, and have let others write a great deal, you must not think that I do not love you as much as formerly, for I love you a great deal more as I told you a few nights ago.

As my love for the Father increases and I receive more of his Love in my heart, the more and deeper love I have for you, and I can only try to tell it to you. I am not able to find words sufficient to do so, for words cannot convey to you my feelings of love and happiness.

Oh, Ned, I never thought when on earth that there could exist such love as I have for you now, and I never thought that I could love you as I do now. But I do love you with all the capacity of my developed soul and feel that I am yours for all eternity. No one can understand what this love means, who has not received it in his heart, and no one can know the happiness that it brings when once such love becomes a part of him, until he has actually experienced it. I am waiting patiently, I hope, for the time to come when you will be with me and share my home and joys. I am now in such a state of happiness that nothing that can possibly happen can in any way take from one that happiness or diminish my love for you. I sympathize with you in all your troubles, but I know that they are only for a season, and that in a very short time, comparatively speaking, they will pass away and you will be free to turn all your thoughts to me, and love me as your own, and only true soulmate. I will not attempt to tell you what it will all mean to you and to me, but I assure you that in your moments when my love overshadows and fills your soul, as it does at times, you catch only a faint glimpse of what is here waiting for you. So, do not let yourself worry or doubt that I love you with a love greater than you can possibly imagine can exist.

Well, sweetheart, I must stop now as another wishes to write some.

I asked if Mr. M. has a guardian angel and soulmate.

Yes he has both. His guardian angel is his mother, who is a very happy and beautiful spirit, filled with the Love of God, and who watches over him with such tenderness and love. She is now trying to influence him to give his thoughts to higher things and to let doubts of the future and the possibilities awaiting him flee from him. She certainly does love her boy, and if he only knew what hours and days she spends with him overshadowing him with her love and beautiful thoughts, he would thank God for such a mother.

I do not believe that she will ever cease praying until he fully realizes the great truth that a man never dies; and that when he passes from the earth life to the spirit life, she will be waiting for him, ready to take him into her arms and loving care as she did when he was a very small boy.

She says that he never knew very much of her mother's love and protection, and that for that very reason she has for so long a time been so anxious for the time to come, when he will know and realize that he has a mother with so much love for him, that he will wonder how she can love him so much.

She is with him and tries to make him feel her presence and sometimes she succeeds, and he feels very happy, but does not know the cause. She is trying to help him see that there is something more of life than this mere earthly existence, and that when the time comes for him to leave his mortal body, there is another body which will show itself to him, and which will live forever in a world where, if he will only make the effort to find, he will find happiness and love beyond his conception.

Tell him that his mother is closer to him now than she possibly could have been had she remained a mortal, because she knows all his troubles and times of loneliness and aspiration for better and higher things. She will come sometime and write him a letter and tell him of her great love for him.

She says: "Bless my boy and keep him in ways of happiness and truth, of Father of Love!"

Well, as to his soulmate, I have not thought of finding her, but I will do so and let you know.

I am your own true and loving,
Helen.

Will cause Mr. Padgett to feel the Great Love of the Father for him

November 25th, 1915.

I am here, Jesus.

I am with you tonight in your spiritual exaltation and will show you the love that you crave for, and will cause you to feel that the Father is very near you in his Love and blessings. So you must let your thoughts go out to the Father and he will come to you with an abundance of Love that will make you realize that he is your loving Father. I was with you at the Colburn's and saw that your love was very great and that you needed a response and I tried to make you realize that I was with you and loved you very much.

The music was very beautiful and caused a rapport which drew us very close together, and you were very happy in the thoughts of love and peace that came to you. I am so glad that you are free from your cares tonight, as I want you to feel that the Love of the Father is with you and is filling your soul so that you can realize that His Love is a thing of reality and substance.

I will let you see how much you can become at one with Him, and what a joy and peace the Love of the Father brings to you. So, as I say, let your thoughts turn to him and let your prayers ascend to Him and you will soon know that His kingdom is within and of you.

I am now going to tell you what a loving Father he is, and what great desire He has that you believe in Him and in His Love for you. He is not a God of wrath and anger and His only desire is that you shall love Him with all your heart, and so become so close to Him that you will know that He is the Father that I have told you of. He does not want you to let anything on earth keep you from becoming his own dear son and a follower of His truths. I know that you are now very near the place where your soul will be filled with His Love, and your faith will have such strength that never again will it be shaken by troubles or doubts.

In the near future you will be able to receive from me my messages in that condition of soul knowledge that will enable you to get them just as I desire to give them to you and so to the world. Be more faithful in your aspirations for this Love and more in condition to believe what I may write. I am your own true friend and brother and have an interest in you that will enable you to overcome all temptations and all the worries of your earth life. My love will strengthen you in your faith and in your realization that I am your friend and brother, and that I am able to fulfill my promises that I have made to you. Let me again impress upon you the necessity of prayer and faith and the necessity to seek continually, the help of the Father.

I must not write more tonight but will soon give you another message.

I will do so, as I think it will be more satisfactory to write it anew. You were not in good condition when I wrote, and some things were not as clear as I desire. You will be stronger when I write again and the message will be more satisfactory. So try to obtain more faith and you will find that our writings will be more successful.

So, with all my love,
I am your friend and brother,
Jesus.

Relates the importance of getting the New Birth in order to become Immortal

August 23rd, 1915.

I am here, Jesus.

I am glad that you are feeling better tonight and I see that you will soon be in condition to take my messages again, and then I will be ready to write you more of my truths.

The messages that you have been getting from the spirits of those who have lived in the spirit world for a long time all go to confirm the truth of my writing to you and of the reality of the New Birth, and the necessity of men getting this new birth in order to become immortal.

So I think that these messages will work a great confirmation of what I write, and for that purpose you have been permitted to receive them and they to write to you. I thought, that considering the fact that men will be so loath to believe what I write through you, that it is wise that all these spirits should write.

I will not write more tonight, but will have you prepare to soon take another of my messages. I will rewrite the message that I last wrote you as it is not entirely satisfactory.

Well, that is a subject upon which I will write you fully later, and I can only give you a satisfactory explanation of that question in a message that will require me to write longer than I can tonight. So, wait until then.

I will stop now and say that you will soon be in the condition that we both desire you to be in. I give you my blessings and love.

Your friend and brother,
Jesus.

Tells Mr. Padgett that he will reveal the Truths of the Father which is now timely to do so, and was not as a result of any previous instruments or writers

August 24th, 1915.

I am here, Jesus.

I merely want to say that the book you have been reading is one that shows that spiritualism is an established thing in this world of mortals. It is beyond doubt that spirits and mortals communicate, and that spirits know just what mortals are doing on earth and how to influence them in their loves and actions.

Well, that is the very reason why I am communicating to you these truths, for as you say, they were never before communicated to any mortal. Well, because no medium was fitted to receive them and the world was not in condition to believe as it is now. All this was a part of God's plan to bring about a salvation of mankind.

If these truths had been communicated at the time of the occurrence that you read of in that book, they would have been received with incredulity, even by the spiritualists themselves; and so the date for the communication of these truths was postponed until we saw that mortals were ready to receive these truths, which is now.

Question asked by Mr. Padgett of Jesus, which was often the case during Jesus writings when he was giving advice to Mr. Padgett.[49]

I have read some of it, and it is more the imagination of spirits who attempted to impress the believers in Spiritualism with the idea that it was true and contained a true account of the creation of the world since, but it is not true, and has never been received as true by the people, and will not be so received, but will soon be forgotten.

My writings will contain only the truth and those truths must be received and accepted by men for in them is the eternal happiness or otherwise, for mankind. So you need not fear that they will not be received.

The power that is behind the present moment to spiritualize the world will not fail, and it will be accomplished through my messages which are being delivered through you.

You[50] will not pass over until my messages shall be fully declared to the world, and neither will your mental faculties be impaired, but rather increased and with all this will be given you power to do many wonderful things which will cause to think and believe in what you may give to the world as truth coming from me.

I cannot write more your friend and brother,
Jesus.

Greek who lived in the time of Christ, is now a Celestial Spirit

October 10th, 1915.

I am Gomeses.

I am a Greek, and lived in the time of Christ, although I never met him on earth, as I died shortly after he did. I was not a Christian, but a follower of Pythagoras and a believer in the immortality of the soul, but not in the sense that I have since been taught by Jesus.

I am a Christian now and believe in the truths as taught by the Master, and am trying to understand them more thoroughly and live by them. I am in the Celestial Spheres and am very happy.

I will not write more tonight.

---

[49] This is an insertion by Rev. John Paul Gibson to reflect the fact that questions were often asked. (G.J.C.)

[50] Mr. James E. Padgett received communications from Jesus from 1914 to 1923. (J.P.G.) Careful reading of the messages in date order indicates however that this is only partially true, as it appears that Jesus stopped communicating in 1920. (G.J.C.)

He is the greatest spirit in all God's universe and the one altogether lovely. He is your friend and savior as well as mine, and you must listen to him when he comes to you in the kindness of his love and the power of his humility, and tells you of the great mission which he has given you to perform. You are now in the way and you must pray more and seek more of the Divine Love.

Your friend in Christ,
Gomeses.

Writes about a visit by Mr. Padgett to spiritualist medium and advises him to help her to discover the Divine Love of the Father that is now justly due her since she has been seeking the greater Love since early childhood

March 30th, 1919.

I am here, Jesus.

Let me write a few lines, for I am anxious to tell you that you have not been in good company today, as the meeting[51] was filled with spirits who are of the earth plane, and know not the truths that will lead to a knowledge of the things that are necessary in order to secure a home in the Celestial Heavens. Many spirits were those of men who, when on earth, lived immoral and licentious lives, and who are in the same condition as they were when on earth. They have not yet answered to the Law of Compensation[52] and, of course, you will see that their influence is not of the kind that tends to develop those soul qualities that lead to the Heaven of the followers of me, in the true sense.

The medium with whom you conversed, and who delivered the messages of some of the spirits who were so anxious to reach their friends of earth, was influenced by spirits who are in a condition of more or less darkness and alienation from God, and consequently suffers from her association and the influence to which she was subjected. She has long been in this work of demonstrating to mankind the fact of communication between the spirits in the flesh and those who have passed the mysterious border line; and her work has been strenuous and served to demonstrate the fact for which it was intended, and she is satisfied with the reality of the fact of the continuity of life after so called death.

This has been a phase of mediumship that was necessary to be performed, and she has done her work faithfully and well, and is now

---

[51] Mrs Kates' séance was held in Washington, D.C. (J.P.G.)
[52] Read about the impartial Law of Compensation, in a message by John Bunyan published in Volume I (5th Ed.) page 312. (G.J.C.)

entitled to be relieved of this work that pertains to the lower order of spiritualism, and should be freed of this great burden and be permitted to come into a knowledge of the higher things of spirit life. I am glad that you will soon have the opportunity to tell her things that await her as a reward for all the sacrifices that she has been compelled to make.

Now, do not misunderstand me. Her work was necessary as a preliminary to the conversion of men to a belief in the truth of spirit communication and the fact that there is no death, and to the consolation that comes to men from the knowledge that their loved ones are with them, seeking to help and be helped in their conditions that the great law of cause and effect imposes upon them. Many a sad heart has been comforted by her ministrations and many a spirit has been helped by having opened up to them the way to make known their presence to mortals.

But she has from the very nature of her occupation been more or less injured in her spiritual progress, and the time has come when she shall have the opportunity to attend to and obtain her own soul's progress. She is naturally a good woman, and when she told you that she had a longing for something for which she did not understand, she was uttering a great truth of her soul, and one that has been present with her since she was a little child, for her soul has been calling to the great soul of the Father for His Love and the happiness that comes with the knowledge that the Father's Love is ever ready and anxious to respond to her longings. Her knowledge of spiritualism does not teach her what this Love is, even though her soul feels its presence, and in her under-developed longings realizes that there must exist that which will draw her closer to the great Love of the Father.

So I say, tell her the truths that have been revealed to you, and of your experience in seeking for and obtaining this transforming Love, and she will listen and seek and obtain, and with such obtaining will come a happiness she has never before experienced. And when she has believed in this Love and obtained it to a degree, she will become a powerful instrument in converting men to a belief in the only way to the Celestial Heaven and to immortality. Then will she have back of her the influence of the hosts of Celestial angels to inspire her and qualify her to preach the true Kingdom of God; and her faculties of clairvoyance will be opened up to see the things of the Celestial Heavens and the wonderfully bright and glorious spirits, who will come to her with their messages of truth and knowledge of the glories that belong to those who know that the Divine Love of God is the only thing that can transform the human soul into an angel of light, and the immortality that I came to earth to teach, and which I did teach, but which, alas, was so soon lost to the knowledge of men.

I am particularly interested in her, not so much because of her own soul, as because she has in her those qualities that can be used by us in making known to the world the truths which we of the Celestial spheres know will set them free from the false and damning teachings of the orthodox churches, and making my coming to earth and living—not dying—the way to the Truth and the Life. She may think that her knowledge—I mean intellectual—is all that needs to be known, but when she lets her soul's longings go to the Father and receives the response, which she will certainly receive, she will then know that spiritualism, as she conceives it to be, is the mere forerunner of that which will make all men at one with the Father, when embraced by man and lived.

The meetings, such as was held today, while as I have said was filled with spirits who are in darkness and suffering, yet also attracted many spirits who are bright and progressing in their natural love, and who tried to help those to whom they came and communicated, and to that extent did good, and also served to convince the unbelievers of the truth of the mere passing from the body of flesh into the spirit body; a continued existence, without changing of condition of happiness or misery. The great Law of Compensation—as you sow so shall you reap[53]—is taught at the meetings, and there is no truer or greater law in all the universe of God, and man must realize that it works without exception and to the last farthing[54], and that there can never be forgiveness until forgetfulness[55] takes place.

Well, my dear brother, I must stop as the power is weakening, but before closing let me entrust you to tell the medium that I, Jesus of the Bible, as I called my disciples when on earth, now call her to do the work which is so important to mankind, and that she must prepare herself by seeking for this Love. It is utterly impossible for a soul out of unison with the souls of the spirits who come to it to receive their communications and transmit the same to mankind. Her soul must respond to the souls of the spirits, and it will be so easy for her to get into the condition that will make this possible. Like attracts like, and this law applies to rapport and to other things of the spirit world, and of the earth as well.

I see that you are in better condition tonight, and I am pleased, for I will soon come and write another message with reference to the higher truths. With my love and blessings, I will say good night.

Your brother and friend,
Jesus[56]

---

[53] Galatians 6:7. (G.J.C.)
[54] Matthew 5:26. (G.J.C.)
[55] Read about the inner workings of "forgiveness until forgetfulness" in a contemporary message held on the new-birth.net web site published on November 6th, 2001 from Judas of Kerioth. (G.J.C.)
[56] This message is a composite of two, being published in Volume III and Volume IV.

Interested in the work of the Master through Mr. Padgett

July 22nd, 1915.

I am here, St. Sebastian.

I am the spirit of a man who lived on the earth a few hundred years after the death of Jesus and was a bishop of the church of Christ, and was crucified because of my faith and teaching of the truth of Jesus.

I was not a very great Christian in the sense of having a large degree of soul development, but I had the intellectual faith which caused me to pursue with energy and zeal the callings to which I had given my life.

I was not known to the world as a great disciple of the Master, but in the limited territory in which I lived and worked I was known as a zealous follower of the Master and a propagandist of his truths.

I am now in the Celestial Spheres and am possessed of the Divine Love of the Father and am happy beyond description. I am interested in the work which you are now performing and want to assure you of my cooperation in making known to the world the great truths which Jesus came to earth to teach and make known to humanity.

So, I will be of those who will sustain and help you to transmit these truths to mankind, and I will occasionally write you, as opportunity presents itself.

I lived in Italy and died there a martyr to my faith. So you see, I was like the disciples in this particular.

I will not write more tonight but will say that I am
your brother in Christ,
St. Sebastian.

Affirms that Mr. Padgett is now receiving the Divine Love of the Father in more abundance

January 5th, 1916.

I am here, Jesus.

I merely want to say, that I am glad to see that you are in condition of soul which makes you more at one with the Father, and which must convince you that the Love of the Father is flowing into your soul in more abundant streams of power and quantity.

I know that you have not been in the best condition of mind as regards your beliefs and doubts, during the past few days, but you must not let such experience discourage you, for such conditions will arise as

(G.J.C.)

long as you are in the flesh; and you must not think that, because of the doubts, you are not receiving this love in your soul, for you are, and after a while it will become so very abundant that the doubts will rarely appear to disconcert you.

I will not write much tonight, as I think you are in need of meditation over what has been written you lately, before more truths shall be presented to you. So think of what has been written you and you will find yourself much benefitted.

With all my love, I am your brother and friend,
Jesus.

Was very much interested in the way that Mr. Padgett helped to prevent two suicides by instructing them on the consequences of such an act

November 8th, 1915.

I am here, Jesus:

I want to tell you tonight that I am very much interested in the way in which you are doing your work among your acquaintances in the matter of bringing them to a realization of the truths of spiritualism, and the importance of believing in the truths which are communicated to you. I refer more particularly to the two instances in which persons who had determined to commit suicide have abandoned that idea and now realize that it would be a most grievous sin to take their lives. I heard what was said today by Mr. Morgan in reference to the young lady who had contemplated such an act.

But, for your encouragement I must tell you that the good that you are doing the darkened spirits in the method that you have adopted is beyond any conception that you may have, and beyond the powers of your spirit friends to inform you.

If all this is an indication of what good my messages will do when you shall have received and disseminated them to the world, then I know that success will attend your efforts, and the truths of my Father will quickly spread and be believed.

So you see the necessity for doing this work with all possible speed. I will write a message very soon.

I am with you a great deal and am trying to help you in every way.

So with my love and blessings I will say good night.
Your friend and brother
Jesus.

Atlantis teacher of arts and sciences, writes about his lost continent and the high intellect that it possessed

October 7th, 1915.

I am here, Jayemas.

I am the spirit of a man who when on earth was an inhabitant of the great continent of Atlantis which was submerged in a cataclysm and by which great calamity all the inhabitants of that country were drowned.

I am now in the sixth sphere where are many others of my countrymen, and wherein are enjoying much happiness and great intellectual pursuits that bring to us knowledge of the wonderful laws of the universe.

I was, when on earth, a teacher of the arts and sciences, and of the philosophy of life as well. I made many inventions which enabled my people to progress in the development of the use of forces which existed in the unseen world, and which are now still in existence and operating.

If mortals would only understand and had means for utilizing these forces; they would enjoy wonderful facilities for travelling and propelling the different engines of trade and manufacture that they are engaged in, and also for making easy much of the labor which is now done by hand or by imperfect machinery.

You must not think that the forces of nature have all been discovered by your great scientists and inventors for that is not true; and in the near future you will have revealed to your investigators some wonderful forces that will revolutionize many of the means of conducting the communications between nations, and of leading men to a knowledge of what the possibilities are.

Well, I am not permitted to disclose any of these secrets at this time, but in the near future they will be made known, and you will live to see some of these forces applied to the actual working out of what you suppose to be the ideas of your inventors.

I merely wanted to introduce myself at this time as I hope to come to you later and tell you about my life on the submerged continent. So I will not write more.

Your friend,
Jayemas
The Atlantian.

The preacher was limited in describing one of the Attributes of God, and that is the Loving Care that He has for His children

September 19th, 1920.

I am here, Jesus. Let me say a few words tonight as I see that you were disappointed in the sermon that the preacher delivered tonight.

Well, you must not be so disappointed because he knows only that which he could deduce from the teachings of the Bible and while what he said was true, yet it is not all of the truth for he discussed only one of the attributes of God and that is the loving care that he has for and exercises over the children of earth. To most men this view of God is satisfactory and give them much comfort and assurance in the security that arises from the knowledge that there is such a loving and caring Father; and to these men this assurance is of wonderful blessedness and comfort, and it is well that men can have this conception of God—a Father who is always solicitous for their happiness and welfare and to whom they can pray in the faith that he will hear and answer their prayers.

But as we have written you before, the things that men generally pray for and expect to receive in response thereto, are not the things that God in his own personality bestows upon men in answer to such prayers. His great gift is His Divine Love, and these things of the material—or earthly in themselves—he leaves to his ministering spirits to bestow, or, in other words, He delegates His angels to so come into contact with and influence the souls of men that they may feel that their prayers have been answered, as they have.

The preacher's conception of God does not extend beyond these attributes that in themselves are sufficient to answer men's wants and make them better and happier. I will come soon and write you of God's attributes, and hope that you will get in condition that I may make the necessary rapport.

It has been some time since I have written you of these higher truths that are so important to men, and regret that such is the fact, but now that you have had your vacation, and feel that you are willing and anxious that our communications be resumed, I will try to assist you in getting in that condition of soul that will enable the messages to be written you. But as you know, much depends upon yourself and you must try with all the energies of your soul to obtain a greater inflowing of the Father's Love, for only from it can come the condition that is necessary. Pray more and think deeply of the spiritual truths that have already been written you, and we will come together in closer communion and be able to give and you receive the messages.

I am glad that you have thought more of these things during the past few days, and hope that your thoughts will continue and that your longings will flow more to the Father. You cannot now appreciate the necessity for this condition, and if you could, I know you would give all your thoughts and longings and energy to the accomplishment of the work.

Well, I will not write more tonight, but will be with you and pray with you and try to influence you in the efforts to perform the mission that has been given you. Have more faith and believe that you will succeed and you will not be disappointed.

Your brother and friend,
Jesus.[57]

Wanted Mr. Padgett and Dr. Stone to know that he was present during their discussion of spiritual things

July 19th, 1920.

I am here, Jesus.

Let me write a few lines and see that you are in a better condition tonight and feel that you would like to hear from me. Well, my dear brother, you must know that always we are anxious and ready to write, and it is only because your condition is such that we cannot form the rapport that enables us to come to you and give expression to our thoughts.

I have been with you this evening as you and your friend (Dr Leslie R. Stone) discussed spiritual things of the future, and saw that a new awakening had taken place in your soul and I felt very glad that such was the fact. It is useless for us to attempt to communicate when you are not in condition, for you would not understand just what we desire to convey, even if we could transmit our thoughts. But in the mere physical act of writing you must have a soul development or opening up to the truths that are ours, and which become yours when you are attuned to receive them.

I will tell you of one fact that may be helpful to you both and that is, that many of your spirit friends are surrounding you, always ready to help you and inform you of their love. This is not said in the way of merely assuring you that you are very seldom alone, but of impressing on you the fact that only upon yourself depends the love-words of these

---

[57] This is the very last message received by James Padgett from Jesus, according to the daily dairy. However it also appears there are also some later messages that were not recorded in the daily diary, but were not from Jesus. It is clear from this message that Jesus had hoped to deliver more material, but this did not eventuate.
This message is a composite of two, being published in Volume III and Volume IV. (G.J.C.)

spirits in making known to you, consciously, that they are present and have thoughts to convey that are worthwhile. Nothing frivolous or immaterial to your soul's growth, but always that which will cause you to know that they are true, thinking, loving friends.

Very soon now, I will come and write again about the great vital truths of the Father that are necessary for man to grasp and understand. Keep up your faith and pray to the Father, and ask for a bestowal of this love in increased abundance, and you will be like the man who while all adrift at sea, yet realizes that around him are those things that will save him and bring him safely to shore. I will not write more now. Good night, and God bless you both.

Your friend and brother,
Jesus.

Under Jesus' direction helped to correct Mr. Padgett's digestive organs, as a result of his prayer to the Father for help

February 15th, 1915.

I am here, White Eagle.

You are much better. The Master helped you very much last night. I manipulated you as he directed, and your digestive organs are now doing their work. Your prayer to the Father was answered. He heard you as Jesus told you He would if you would pray in faith. You had the faith and the cure came. So it is with everything in life, only pray and believe and you will receive the answer. You are certainly blessed, and I wonder as do all of us, at your faith; but thank God you are the one that the Master has selected, and you will be in condition soon to do his work as he desires.

Yes, you are right. He is the only one that can help you in time of trouble. Only continue in your faith and you will realize that he is your Father and your helper. Jesus says that your faith is wonderful, and that you will be able to do many things that will help mankind. Only be true to him and you will never be forsaken.

No, you need not use any more medicine now, the work is done, and medicine is no longer necessary. Well, he (Dr Stone) may help you some in starting your various muscles and nerves to get into activity, but even his treatment is not necessary now. When God heals He heals effectively, and no other help is needed.

You are commencing to get that Great Love in your soul now, and soon you will be filled, and then your happiness will be complete, that is it will be of such a character that the worries of life will not make you unhappy.

Yes, he (Jesus) was present and he directed my movements. He is the all-powerful one. His knowledge is without limit, and he is so full of love, that when he tries to impress you, you cannot resist the influence of that love. So be more prayerful and you will become possessed of that Love to a degree that will make you love all mankind as well as God. Well, I am telling you what the Master tells us, and he knows. You had better not eat promiscuously yet, give the digestive organs a chance to get back their full strength.

So good night.
White Eagle.[58]

This photograph of White Eagle was published in Volume III without any comment as to how it was obtained.

White Eagle

Further comment accompanying this photograph reads as follows:

White Eagle is a powerful Indian and has often used his great healing powers to restore Mr. James E. Padgett to good health. He wrote often as he had considerable Divine Love in his soul that made him a bright and beautiful spirit.

---

[58] This message is a composite of two, being published in Volume III and Volume IV. (G.J.C.)

Writes about Jesus as Head of the Church in the Celestial Heavens. And confirms that Paul wrote on the resurrection.

January 17th, 1916.

I am here, Saint Stephen.

I merely want to say a word on the importance of the subject which Paul has written on the Resurrection.

This is one of the most vital truths in all the plan of God for the redemption of mankind, and for the preservation and existence of the church; and when I say church, I do not mean any church which claims to be the only Church of Christ, but that invisible church which is composed of the soul worship of men and women, who have received the Divine Love in their souls. It is not necessary that there be any formation of congregations and ceremonies of church worship as men understand it, but the true, sincere worship of men founded on a knowledge of the Divine Love and its possession in their souls.

While men on earth may never form large congregations and erect magnificent churches in which to worship the Father with the true soul worship and aspirations, yet when they come into the spirit world they will find that the Master has established his church in the eternal heavens, where none but the truly Christian can enter and partake of its glories and happiness.

Jesus is the head of that church[59] here in our Celestial Heavens, as he should be of the church on earth. And as he must be when that church has for its members only those who have had the resurrection from sin and error and death of the soul into the knowledge of the Divine Love and the life everlasting. Jesus referred to this Resurrection when he said: "I am the resurrection and the life," and not the resurrection of the body either physical or spiritual.

I see that you are anxious to have these truths come and I am also anxious, and a co-worker.

I will now say good night and in doing so say with all my love, God Bless you and keep you in his care now and always.

Your brother in Christ,
St. Stephen.

---

[59] This is an early message and I suspect that the term "church" would not normally be applied by the Master to the body of spirits in the Celestial Heavens. However Stephen has tried to redefine that word here. Certainly they are united in their beliefs, but the term church has far too many earthy connotations to be appropriate in my opinion. (G.J.C.)

Has written that Jesus is not very happy during the holidays and removes himself from the earth plane into the highest Celestial Heavens until the holidays end. Because he does not want to hear the worship of him as God

December 25th, 1914.

I am here, your own true and loving Helen.

On this Christmas Eve,[60] we rejoice that the people all believe that Jesus has risen from the dead. He is now in the higher home waiting for the worship of the people of him to end, as he does not enjoy the worship. He wants the people to worship God and God alone. He is not very happy when they worship him, for he says that he is only a son of his Father and that they should not worship him as God. He does not believe that he is worthy of such adoration and he is not pleased at it. So you must love him and not worship him, for he will not love you so much as he does now if you do.

What I tell you is true, for he has said it himself; and you must believe it to be true.

Let me tell you that you are very close to him, and he wants you to do just as he says, for he intends to give the world the true doctrines of God's Love and being and his own relationship to the Father through you as his messenger. So do not let the thought that you are wrong in believing what he tells you.

Now we must stop for you are not in such a good condition to write more at this time.

Your own true and loving wife,
Helen.

Became a friend as a result of a séance that Mr. Padgett attended

March 30th, 1916.

I am here, Bright Star.[61]

You are surprised to see me, but I have this opportunity and I desire to say just a word.

I am interested in you and your friend (Eugene Morgan) and I want to do whatever I can to help you in every way. Of course, when you hear my voice you feel confident that I am talking; now you must feel

---

[60] Although this message actually says "Christmas Eve", it is recorded in the Tablet as being on the 25th. (G.J.C.)

[61] Bright Star was a guide at Mrs. Ripple's séances. (J.P.G.)

just as confident that I can write for I am just as certainly here writing as I was at the séance talking. I say this because I heard your friend say that some spirit may impersonate your spirit friends who profess to write.

I saw the preceding two spirits write and I know that they are both Morgans but a little different in their appearance and conditions. But they are whom they profess to be and I know this for I have seen them many times before with you writing and one of them has been to my séance and talked a little. I of course don't know anything about the subject of the big noise[62] (Pierpont Morgan) man's communication but I see that he is in earnest and wants to tell you what he thinks is the truth.

Besides this your wife and the rest of your band are here and they say that the spirits who write are known to them and that they are the spirits of whom they represent themselves to be.

I will come soon and write you as I promised. Come and see me soon and bring the young chief for I like him.

So goodbye,
Your friend,
Bright Star.

Telling about one love (soulmate love) that is in store for them as they both seek the Divine Love of the Father

February 22nd, 1915.

I am here, Helen.

Yes, I am when you need me and feel that I am your own true wife. I am not yet ready to let you see that you are so necessary to my happiness, that I must be with you all the time, for if I do you will become so careless of my love and will think that all you have to do is say, "Come Helen," and I will be there. Thanks are not in order as you are too very much of a flirt to make me believe that you really mean "thank you". But you are my darling Ned, and I love you and you know it, and I am glad that you do.

You are too much in love with me to ever want another. I know and I thank God that He gave us to each other, for if I had not your love, I would not be so happy. Oh my darling, I so long to have you with me all the time, so that I could tell you of my great love for you, and that you are the only one that I love or have ever loved in all my life. Be so true to me that no doubt will arise in your mind that I am the one that God selected for you. Let us continue to love God and then we will love each other with a love that knows no ending or falling away. My love for you is

---

[62] This message is probably dated around March to May, 1916, as that was when Pierpont Morgan gave James Padgett financial advice. (G.J.C.)

not only for a time, but for all eternity, and we will never be separated after you come over to me.

Question and Answer.

Yes, it is possible, for I know that our love will become so real, that the mere fact of your being in the physical body will not prevent us from realizing that we are together in all the reality of our true being and love. You will not have to wait very long before you will hear my voice and feel my presence in a way that will convince you that I am with you in all my strength and real existence. Let us believe that we are one in spirit and love, and our realization of that fact will be strong that we will be certain that the union is true. Give me all your thoughts for a while and you will learn that I am not only yours in spirit and love but in real personal contact and actual presence.

So do not doubt that I am with you now, writing this love letter as I promised you this afternoon, for I am actually writing it and you have nothing to do with it but merely hold the pencil. You do not deserve the blessings which God has given you, but He is so loving and merciful, that He sees that you need His love and my love to make you happy, and in the end become a spiritual man and a true follower of Jesus who is also your true friend and teacher. He will tell you all things that the Father has in store for you and will not let you go astray again as you did when we were living together on earth. So do not let the thought that you are too worldly or too great a sinner keep you from seeking the love of the Father or believing that Jesus is interested in your welfare both on earth and in this world. Only believe what He may tell you and you will not be left to go wrong.

Try to let your thoughts turn more to God's love and to mine.

Yes they (parents and relatives) all love you very much, but not as I do, because their love is that of a parent, while mine is that of one whom God has decreed shall be the necessary part of a love that is one and a perfect whole. Our loves are not two but one, and if either part is not in true accord the perfect one is not in existence. So you see we must be sure that our loves are just in that accord that is necessary to make the perfect one. Let us not write anymore tonight as I am tired and so are you. Yes you did right—under the conditions—we could not do what you desired.

With all my love and best wishes for your happiness. I am your own true wife and sweetheart.

Helen.

Has been selected by the Higher Powers to be the guardian angel of his son as long as he may live on earth as a mortal

March 17th, 1915.

I am here, your father.

Well my son, I have not written you for sometime as you have not given me the opportunity, but it was best as you have received much valuable information from the others that have written you. Well, I am still your guardian angel and will be as long as you live on earth. I know that Helen is with you very much of the time, and of course is much more interested in you than any of us and tries so hard to make you happy, nevertheless, she is not your guardian angel. White Eagle is your guide in a great many things and is faithful one too, but he is not the one designated by the higher powers to perform the duties of a guardian angel. So do not think that I am not with you trying to help and sustain you in your troubles and cares, for I am.

We are all so much interested in you, that you are never alone even while you sleep. Even Mr. Riddle and Prof. Salyards are with you a great deal trying to influence you in your earthly affairs.

The last writer[63] was the spirit of the man who wrote the book that you are reading. I did not know him until he came to write and introduced himself as the author of the book and said that Jesus recommended him. Of course we consented for him to write.

He is a spirit of the fifth sphere where I live and I shall see more of him now, and it may be that he will join our band, for he is wonderfully intellectual man and well versed in spiritual truths. Yes, he is not filled with this great Love as are your grandmother and mother and Helen. But he will make a desirable addition, and I believe that all the band will consent, especially as Jesus has recommended him.

Yes, I am glad to say that Alice is now in the third sphere, and she is praying with all her soul for more love,—she is a beautiful spirit.

Yes she does, and she loves you very much, for your kind thoughts, and is with me very often, when I am with you. Call her Laura or Sola. Yes, look at your writings and you will see.

Yes, they are still praying and I see them quite often. Mackey is progressing more rapidly than any of them. Taggart is progressing, but he is so hard to convince, but sooner or later he will be convinced and then he will advance rapidly. Harvey is held back by his disappointment in not receiving what the priests had told him on earth. And McNally is still in darkness—his awful habit of drink has resulted in keeping him in this

---

[63] This is Mr. Eugene Crowell author of "The identity of primitive Christianity and modern spiritualism." His message is published in Volume IV. (G.J.C.)

darkness, but he is praying also. And we all hope that they will see the light.

Yes, especially Taggart, who says that he would like to have another talk with you before long, and he wants to ask you some questions and maybe you can answer them so that some of his doubts may be removed.

Yes she (Mrs. Emmons.) is not very happy and has not yet fully realized that she is in the spirit world exclusively. But Helen is with her very much and is trying to assist her to see the light and turn her thoughts to things spiritual.

Well I must stop, so good night, my dear son.

Your loving Father.

Writes that the Master is with Mr. Padgett a great deal and even prays with him at night

April 15th, 1917

I am here, your own true and loving Helen.

Well sweetheart, we did not get the opportunity to write our love message and I am a little disappointed but we will try tomorrow night to do so. The spirits who wrote were so anxious to do so and especially Mary, and I thought it advisable to let them write.

I see that you are feeling better and I am glad. Worries do not help and while they are difficult to throw off, yet if you can do so it will be best to let them go. I love you with all my heart and soul; and so want you to be happy and will do everything possible to make you so. Only love me and believe in me and you will find that your love will help you.

Well my dear, I am so glad to hear you say that, for there is nothing more desirable or more important to your present as well as your future and we all want you to get into a condition of greater nearness to the Father and to us all. Pray more to the Father and let your thoughts be of things of the higher kind and believe that we are with you in our love and especially that the Master is with you very often and brings to you his love and influence. You must believe this for it is true. He is with you very much and he loves you more than you can conceive of and is trying to help you in every way.

And this I must tell you, that he prays for you as you pray at night and I know that his prayers will be answered. His is a wonderful love and a wonderful faith. He knows no doubting and when he asks the Father for anything he knows that he will receive it. So you see you have so much to make you believe that this great Love that you long for will come to you and the happiness that always comes with it. You can get this Love in a wonderful degree if you will only earnestly seek and believe that your prayers will be answered and you will progress even though you have the worries and distractions of your earth life to contend with.

We all pray for you and will continue to do so and I believe that our prayers will have some effect in helping your progress in the spiritual way. I am with you very often, loving you and trying to help you.

Yes, I know and have a little patience and it will come. You are my own dear Ned and the husband of my eternity.

So sweetheart let us stop now. I love you and love you and want your love in return. Give me my kiss.

Good night and may the Father bless you with His Love and care.
Your own true and loving,
Helen.

Tells about the errors in the book that he was reading about the hells

January 8th, 1915.

I am here, your grandmother.

Yes, I see that you are desirous of some spiritual food and I have come to tell you of some truths of the spirit life. You have been reading a book which is not true for there are no hells as described in it, where mortals after passing into the spirit life have to undergo such sufferings and torments. There are no such places as described in the first part of the book.[64] You need not believe that there are any such places of punishment for the evil spirits. God loves all His children too much to have them pass through such experiences as are in that book described. I know what I am telling you for I have descended into the lowest spheres and have never yet seen or heard of such hells or any spirits who are in the condition described.

Evil spirits have to suffer for their sins and atone for every evil thought, but not by any such suffering as the writer of that book depicts. I am conscious of the fact that the churches teach of hells somewhat similar to the ones we have referred to, but neither the hells of the churches nor the hells of that book exist. So don't let the thoughts which the reading of that book may engender make you think that there is such a vengeful and cruel God, for I know that there is not.

My observations of the condition of the wicked shows me that they must all suffer before they can be relieved from the burden of their sins, and have a place where happiness, even to a smallest degree, is obtained; but when they have become truly penitent and seek the saving

---

[64] This is probably a reference to Dr. Peeble's book "Immortality". (G.J.C.)

Power and Love of God, they will always find it.

You are not much, impressed, I can see, by the statements in the book, and I am glad of it, for it might tend to make you have an idea of what God is, that is wholly erroneous. My own belief is that He is God of love to even the vilest sinner, and when such a sinner turns to Him and prays for forgiveness and love he gets them both. Let me tell you further that the Love of God, when it enters into the soul of a man is sufficient to wash away all sins, and make that soul happy and joyful. Not even the most evil man who is guilty of the greatest sin need think that he cannot be pardoned, and made happy and brought into harmony with God.

I am now going to tell you of what a love the Master has for all mankind. He is now working for their redemption by showing them the way to the love of God, and the light that they need is not one of belief in any ordinance of the church or creed or doctrine, but simply that a belief in God's Love and the exercise of the will of a man accompanied with a desire to obtain that Love, with an earnest prayer to the Father, are all that is necessary to bring true happiness and salvation. He (Jesus) is here now, and says that he is almost ready to write to you. That you must try with all your heart to get more of God's Love and become one with him, and then he will be able to write and you will understand just what he intends. So you see that you have a duty to perform with regards to your own self as well as to what the Master requires you to do.

Yes, the Master is now working to lead all souls to God and His Love, and some will follow him, but the vast majority will not, and they will be left to themselves when he stops his work. When that time comes, he will ascend into the Heaven where his home is, and all his followers will go with him and live there for all eternity.

He will not come again to the earth plane or even to the higher planes where the moral and intellectual spirits live, but they will be left to enjoy the happiness which their conditions may give them. His Kingdom will be one of supreme happiness and very near the center of God's Love, and will be one that will be entirely to itself. No spirit who is not of his kingdom can possibly enter therein. I don't know just when the time will come for him to leave the earth sphere and enter into this kingdom, but when he does, the gates thereto will be closed forever upon all spirits who are not followers of him, and never again will they be opened. He has told me this and I must believe him and so must you. He is now trying to teach mankind the great truth, that in order to become partakers of this great privilege they must permit the Love of God to come into their souls, as without it, no one can enter the Kingdom. Soon the privileges will be taken away and then will be the separation of the sheep from the goats, as mentioned in the Bible.

No other of the great teachers is teaching the truth of the New

Birth, except Jesus. All are teaching morality and, in a way, a love for God, but none teach the absolute entering into the soul of man this Love by means of the Holy Ghost. Many of the ancient prophets and teachers of God's Love will be partakers of this Kingdom, as I am told, and so will all who receive this love, whether born and living before the time of Jesus, or subsequently. The Kingdom will be created not merely by Jesus teachings, but by this Love of God; and all who have it will become inhabitants of the Kingdom. Jesus will be the ruler of it but not in the sense that you understand a ruler on earth to be: but he will be the greatest possessor of this love, and, consequently, the most powerful as well as the most loving spirit in the whole Kingdom. But his rule will be one of peace and love and ministration. You must try to become a member of this kingdom or you will not be happy as you might be by doing so.

Well as you are tired I must stop. Yes, there are many spheres beyond me and I am striving now to progress to a higher one. So you see there is no limit to what may be obtained.

As I understand that spheres of his kingdom will be the one close to the Father's home, and there will be none beyond. I of course don't know, but this is what I believe.

Yes, sometime I will tell you more in detail of the conditions and laws of the sphere where I am.

Good night, your grandmother
Ann Rollins.

Writes on the hells. Corroborates Swedenborg's message on the hells

December 18th, 1915.

I am here, Herod.

Let me write just a line before you close, as I am anxious to tell you of a matter that may be of importance to you in reference to the descriptions of the hells [65] which you received last night from Swedenborg.

He says that the hells are places as well as conditions, and that they have as a part of them certain appearances and surroundings that make the sufferings of the evil spirits increase. Well, this is true, and in addition I wish to say that not only are these appearances and surroundings real, and existing to the consciousness of the spirit, but are real as a fact, independent of the consciousness. If there were no spirits in these hells, these appearances and surroundings would exist just the

---

[65] This is published in volume II (4th Ed.) page 308. (J.P.G.)

same.

So you see, a great many mortals whom I have heard express their opinions to the effect that hell is a mere condition of the recollections of the spirit, and nothing more, are altogether wrong in such opinions, and they will find that the consolation, if any there be, from such opinions will not be found whenever they may become inhabitants of these hells. I have passed through all of them, and know whereof I write; for there is no teacher so efficient and convincing as the teacher called experience.

I know that if I had only my recollections and remorse as the cause of my sufferings they would have been much lighter and not so excruciating as they were. No, mortals will not find any consolation in such a hope, for there is no foundation for such hope, and the poor, deceived mortal who bases his ideas of hell on such a hope will be sadly disappointed. When you consider a moment, you will see that there is nothing unreasonable in the facts that I have stated.

You and all others who believe in the happiness of the higher spiritual spheres, not to mention the Celestial Spheres, believe that the happiness of the spirits who inhabit these spheres is increased and made more real by the beautiful surroundings and the fruits and living water that so many spirits have described as being a part of that higher existence. Then why is it not as reasonable to suppose that in the hells there are surroundings and appearances that will make the conditions of spirits whose evil lives have caused them to become inhabitants of these hells of even more unhappiness, and create more suffering and misery. This supposition is one that no reasonable argument can prove to be incorrect.

I merely wanted to add what I have said to what Swedenborg wrote, for I know that conviction must come where statements are based upon actual experiences and where knowledge is derived from sufferings which came from the actual existence of things that are sometimes alleged not to exist.

I will not write more now, but in closing will say that I have long since left these hells, and am now an inhabitant of higher spheres and a follower of the blessed Master.

When on earth I was known as Herod the King of Judea, and the poor, miserable, mistaken man who thought that by slaying the babes of Bethlehem he would maintain his power as ruler.

So good night and God bless you.
Herod.

Confirms that Herod wrote on the hells

December 18th, 1915.

I am here, your own true and loving Helen.

Well sweetheart, you have had a letter tonight from a spirit who ought to know what he is writing about, as he was a most wicked man, and, as I have been told, suffered the torments of the lowest hells.

But as to you personally, I want to say that it will make no difference to you what the nature of the hells is, or whether there be any or not. You will never see them, unless when you come over you have a desire to visit them for the purpose of doing good to some poor unfortunate.[66]

And I thank God for this assurance and knowledge.

I will not write more tonight.

With all my love, I am, your own true and loving

Helen.

Confirms that Swedenborg and Herod gave true descriptions of the Hells

December 19th, 1915.

I am here, John.

I merely want to say that I have listened to the message that you have read, and to the remarks of your friend and yourself, and I believe that you have a true conception of the truth as to these hells.

Swedenborg gave you a true description of their conditions as they actually exist, and Herod told you with the certainty of experience what he found to be true, and I, John, who have visited them in the efforts to allay the sufferings of the spirits who inhabit them, tell you that they exist as places, with all the darkness and surroundings that cause the sufferings of the unfortunate spirits to increase. I desire to make this statement so that this question of what hell really is may be settled for all time, so far as you are concerned.

I know that many mortals console themselves with the belief that because of certain natural laws, there cannot possibly be any hells such as the orthodox teach, and that therefore there cannot be any hells at all. But this conclusion drawn from the premise is not correct. The mere fact that because a man or spirit cannot burn eternally and never be consumed, does not justify the inference that such spirit cannot be punished by surroundings which have a fixed locality.

No, man must not rest in the belief of there being no such hells

---

[66] This appears to have proven correct, because James Padgett has communicated many times post death, in the last 100 years, but more particularly in the immediate period post his passing, and which is published in this volume on page viii. (G.J.C.)

as Swedenborg has described, because if they do, they will be woefully mistaken and surprised should they live such lives on earth as will cause them to be placed in these hells. I merely wanted to say this much tonight, as I don't want you to receive any communication which is not in accord with the truth. It is of such vital importance that you receive nothing but the truth that we who are interested in this work have determined that nothing but the truth shall come to you, and that whenever error or misstatements creep in we will carefully correct the same.

So without writing more tonight, I will say that I am,
Your brother in Christ,
John.[67]

Man was given the possibility of becoming in his nature Divine like the Father. But this gift was never possessed by him, until my coming to earth, and making known such possibility

March 15th, 1916.

I am here, Jesus.

I wish to write tonight on the subject of: "What it is that makes a man Divine."

When man was created he was given the highest qualities that could be bestowed upon a mortal, and yet he was mere man, but the perfect one, and with these qualities was given him the possibility of becoming in his nature Divine like the Father; but this gift was never possessed by him in its enjoyment of full fruition until after my coming to earth, and making known to man that such a possibility existed.

The first created man never possessed this gift in its fulfillment, but merely had the possibility of receiving it, on condition that he continued in his obedience, and made the effort to receive it in the way that the Father declared was the only way. You have been told in detail what this gift was, and how the first parents forfeited the enjoyment of it by their disobedience and ambition to possess it in a way that was not in accord with the Father's Way.[68]

As I have said, man lost this possibility at the time of the first disobedience, and thereafter became gradually a man with his moral

---

[67] This message is a composite of two, being published in Volume II and Volume III. (G.J.C.)

[68] Messages have been received from Aman and Amon, the first human parents, and which explain what occurred at that time. These have been published in Volume II (4th Ed.) page 129. (G.J.C.)

nature sinking lower and lower until he got almost to the condition of the beasts in the field. And from that condition man has been gradually improving or progressing towards his first state of purity.

But a great many men have ceased to know, or have never known, that God is the Creator of all things, and that all creation is dependent upon Him for its very existence, and in their assurance and self importance they have assumed and professed (it) to be true that their progress or salvation depends upon their own efforts, and that these efforts are sufficient to bring about this state of purity or harmony with God's laws and desires.

But in this men are mistaken, for there is nothing in them that is Divine, and there never will be when they depend upon their own selves to progress to that state of perfection. The Divine nature of the Father is not in man and will never become a part of him until he pursues the way which is absolutely necessary for him to accept and follow in order to become anything more than mere man.

I will not write more tonight as I think it best not to do so. I understand that you could not prevent your condition of sleepiness, and I do not blame you, but I think it best to wait until later to finish what I desire to write.

Well, my dear brother, believe that I have only love for you, and will get close to you as we progress—so I say, don't worry. I will say good night.

Your brother and friend, Jesus.[69]

Tells of the great spiritual audiences that attend the writings received by Mr. Padgett and listen to what is said

December 3rd, 1916.

I am here, Cornelius.

I will write only a line or two, as I see from your condition of mind that you are anxious to study the prayer that the Master wrote you last night. Well I am not surprised, for it is a wonderful prayer, and one, that when earnestly breathed to the Father, will bring into your soul this Great Love which is the only thing necessary to make you at-one with the Father.

As I have before told you, I am the happy possessor of this Love, and know that it is real and causes the soul of the mortal and the spirit to partake of the essence of the Father, and in a manner become Divine itself. I should like to write you a message tonight about some of the

---

[69] This message is a composite of two, being published in Volume II and Volume III. (G.J.C.)

truths of the teachings of the apostles which are very pertinent to the subject upon which the preacher discoursed tonight. I was present, as were also many other spirits—orthodox Presbyterians—and those that have been freed from their creeds and erroneous beliefs of earth life.

You might be surprised, if I should tell you the great number of spirits who listened to the sermon with interest and in expectation of learning something that they could accept as truth. The preacher had a vastly larger audience of spirits than of mortals, and among a great many of the former, his teachings were received just as they were by the mortal hearers.

But I must not write more now. So hoping that I will soon have the opportunity to write, I will say, good night.

Your brother in Christ,
Cornelius.[70]

The centurion of the Bible and the first gentile Christian. Now in the Celestial Heavens

September 12th, 1916.

I am here, Cornelius.

I will write only a few lines so that I may get in rapport with you and later write you at more length, if agreeable to you. I was the centurion of the Bible who was the first Gentile Christian.

I have listened tonight to your reading of the messages and besides me many other spirits heard what you read, and all were interested, and some of them will no doubt derive some comfort, for these messages disclosed to some of the dark ones that there is hope for them and that there is a way by which they may find relief from their sufferings.

I have just recently heard of your work and have come to add my little mite to the truths which you are receiving, and hope that I may succeed in helping the cause of truth. I am in the Celestial Spheres, and, of course, have the Divine Love in my soul and know that I am a redeemed son of the Father. I must not write more now, and with my love, say good night.

Your brother in Christ,
Cornelius.

---

[70] This message is a composite of two, being published in Volume III and Volume IV. (G.J.C.)

Explains the phrase: He that liveth and believeth on me shall never die

August 15th, 1915.

I am here, Jesus.

I was with you tonight at the meeting of the Christians and I saw that you were thinking of several things that I had written and wanted to tell the preacher of my truths. But of course you could not. He took a bit from the Bible which I am credited with having uttered and I did, but I did not mean exactly what he explained it to mean when I said *"he that liveth and believeth on me shall never die"* I meant that the man whose soul was not dead in sin and believed in the truths that I had disclosed, that is that God's Divine Love was waiting to enter into and fill his soul with its essence and substance and that man by prayer and faith received that Divine Love, he should never die. That is he would become immortal as God is immortal.

No mere belief in me as Jesus the man or as the son of God is sufficient to give a man eternal life for while he must believe that I was sent by the Father to proclaim the great truth that He had again bestowed on man, the possibility of obtaining this Divine Love by his prayers and faith, yet unless he believed this and became the possessor of this Divine Love, he could never claim eternal life.

I wish that the preacher would pay more attention to the truths which I taught, that is, those truths which showed men the Fathers Love waiting to be bestowed and the way to obtain it, than to my personality.

I, Jesus as the son of man or of God, do not save any man from his sins and make him at-one with the Father, but the truths which I taught and which were taught me by the Father are the things that save.

I know that the preachers attempt to explain these things by the light of the Bible as they understand that light, but so often it is so obscured that instead of preaching from light they preach from darkness.

For these reasons among others, I am so anxious to declare to you my teachings of these truths that the world may know what truth is, and what the individual must do in order to attain eternal life or immortality.

I know that you are anxious to do this work, and that your soul is trying for the inflowing of this Great Love and the enjoyment of a close communion with the Father. So keep up your courage and trust in the Father, and the end of your worries will soon cease. I will try with all my power to bring about this opportunity for your receiving my messages and believe that very soon I will succeed.

So believe in my love and my desire for your success.

Your brother in Christ,

Jesus.[71]

Urges Mr. Padgett to believe in him and trust the Father that he will not be forsaken or left alone

December 14th, 1915.

I am here, Jesus.

Well I am so glad that you are so longing for this Love and I will tell you that the Father loves you with all His Divine nature, and is helping you to receive this Love into your soul, and you will soon receive it in such abundance that you will find yourself happy beyond all conception. And I love you too with all my heart and soul, and am very near you and try to make you feel my presence and influence. Rest assured that I am with you in all my love and tenderness and that you are the special object of my care and keeping. I wish that you could see me as I write this for I am filled with so much love for you, that I know, if you could see the glory of the Father displayed you would never again doubt my love. Oh, my brother, only try to get this Love by prayer and faith in such a way that it will become as real to you as anything which your natural senses show you to exist in the physical world.

It is more real than anything in all nature, and you have in you the possibilities of realizing that it is an existing thing, and is yours, if you will only pray and believe. I am with you in prayer at night,[72] and with all my love and faith I ask the Father to bless you and make you a true partaker of His Love and mercy, and to give you the assurance that you will receive and know that you have it.

My dear brother I must stop now, but your longings tonight have been so great and so earnest that I could not stop without telling you what I have. And remember this that I, Jesus, with all the knowledge and authority that I possess, tell you that the Love of the Father shall be yours, and you will become a most happy man, and a power on earth in things spiritual and which pertain to the Father's business.

So believe me and trust the Father, and you will not be forsaken or left alone, but will be surrounded by a host of witnessing angels that you are the chosen child of the Father, and the object of His Great Love and blessings.

I will not write more now, but I will say, that I love you as a true brother and friend, and even as a closer one to you; and you must believe, and yours will be the happiness that few on earth possess.

---

[71] This message is a composite of two, being published in Volume I and Volume III. (G.J.C.)
[72] Mr. Padgett told me that when he as praying just before retiring at night, he sometimes saw Jesus alongside praying with him. (Dr. Stone)

So with all the great love that is mine I will say good night and God bless you.
Your friend and brother,
Jesus.[73]

Says that the Master had a great love for him

March 23rd, 1915.

I am here, your grandmother.

Well, I am very glad to be with you tonight as I see that you are in a condition of great spiritual exaltation. I was with you at the office and saw what you were thinking of and realized that the Love of the Father was filling your soul with happiness.

You certainly were very near the Father's Kingdom in your aspirations and you were very happy at the mere thoughts of what might happen when you get in condition to have your home and a place devoted to the receipt of spiritual messages and influences.

What you imagined might take place, possibly can, if you should get into such a condition of spiritual development as your thoughts led you to believe that you might. Of course the Master will not materialize as you conceived he might, but he will be there with all his power and love and the Holy Spirit will shed His Love over and through the sitters as you imagined.

I do not know just what the Master will do for you before you have finished his messages, but I will not be surprised at anything, as he seems to love you with an exceptional love and to be interested to a wonderful degree in your welfare both spiritual and physical.

So my dear son, only have more faith and more love for God and there is no telling what future blessings are in store for you.

You are not yet in condition to take the Master's message or rather to finish his last one, but after this month you will be, for several cares will be removed and then your mind will be free to think along the right lines of thought.

You will become a very happy man in the near future.
With all my love,
I am
Your grandmother.

---

[73] This message is a composite of two, being published in Volume II and Volume III. (G.J.C.)

Writes that she has progressed into the Celestial Heavens within one year after leaving the material plane

March 23rd, 1915.

I am here, your own true Helen.

You didn't think I could change the announcement of my coming, but you must know that I can do anything to please you, my dear Ned.

Yes you have, and I have been so very happy. Well, sweetheart, I must tell you that I am very happy and am progressing very rapidly. I don't expect to remain in this (Celestial) sphere very much longer; for my love and faith are so great that I feel that I must get closer to God's fountainhead of love. Only think, one short year ago and I was a mortal and now I am in the Celestial sphere, doesn't it seem like some fairy dream? But it is all true, and I am so happy.

I will soon be with you in a long letter, telling you of this Great Love, and how much I love God and you.

No you won't, for you are progressing too. You may not realize it, but it is true, and if you should come over now, you would be surprised to find yourself in a high sphere. Well, I know how you feel, but you must believe that I can see your spiritual condition better than you can.

Well that may be so, but when you get this Great Love in your heart in sufficient abundance, and you have much of it now, your sins will be blotted out. This is the law of regeneration; otherwise, the man who continues without this Love, and the man who receives it, would be in the same condition, and the New Birth would mean nothing. So do not think that this Great Love is not sufficient to cleanse the soul of the results of the sins of earth life; and, best of all, it cleanses while you are a mortal.

I know that the spiritualists quote and proclaim the law of recompense or compensation, but there is a higher law that nullifies that law; and when Love, this Divine Love, comes into the soul of a mortal, the law of compensation is removed from the scope of its working, for Love is the fulfilling of the law. So do not let that stumbling block make you believe that this Great Love is not sufficient to remove all sin and error, and to purify your soul so that you may become fitted to live in the kingdom of the Father and become one with Him.

No, the Love is for the vilest sinner, and no man can by a mere act of restoration fit himself for the inflowing of this Divine Love. It is waiting for the sinner as well as for the saint; and even though your sins be as scarlet they will be made white as wool. I mean that you will not have to wait to make recompense to mortals before this great Love can do the cleansing work; else what is the use of having this Great Love provided for man? If he shall first make himself pure what is the necessity for the work of the Holy Spirit?

Only pray for this Love and have faith, and you will get it. God is the judge of what a man shall do to render justice and restitution, and when He says that this Divine Love, with all its cleansing power, is for the sinner who seeks for it by true faith, who has the right to say that the sinner must first do what man may think is justice between himself and his fellow man?

I know whereof I speak, for the experience of many spirits who have been redeemed by this Love show that they were sinners, and had not "paid the last farthing," when they received this Love. God is the judge, not mortals nor spirits.

So, my dear Ned, do not let the idea that you must render to every man that which you think he may be entitled, to keep you from believing in the mercy and Love of the Father.

Oh, how I wish I could be with you a little while in my bodily form, and tell you face to face what this great Love means to you and to me and to all of us. So sweetheart, believe me when I say that even though you may be a great sinner, yet the Father's Love is sufficient to remove all those sins just as soon as you can receive it. Such is the law of this Great Love.

Faith and prayer can open the very heart of the Celestial Spheres, and Love will flow down into your soul as the avalanche of snow that feels the warmth of the sun's bright rays rushes from its mountain heights when winter leaves with its chilling gloom and blasting breath for other climes. Love is not only warmth, but it is the very burnings of the soul's great storehouse of God's Divine Essence.

I am not only the possessor of this Love to a large degree, but I realize that as I advance to higher spheres there is a greater abundance awaiting to fill my soul with its great undying fires of never ending burnings—but burnings so great and free from everything that makes for unhappiness and discontent.

I must stop now. So my own dear and precious Ned, love me as I love you and we both will be so very happy, that heaven will be with us and in us even while we are writing in the earth surroundings.

Your own, Helen.[74]

Tells of her spiritual progression from first Celestial sphere to the second Celestial sphere

April 27th, 1915.

---

[74] This message is a composite of two, being published in Volume II and Volume III. (G.J.C.)

Well, my darling son, I am so happy to be with you tonight and tell you that I am now in the Second Celestial Sphere, where everything is so beautiful, and happiness exists to a degree that I cannot portray to you. I am in my own home and what it is, I can scarcely describe, for you have no words which are adequate to give you an idea of what I may mean in attempting to describe the glories of this sphere.

My home is of a material that you have no faint counterpart of on earth, and it is furnished with everything that is suited to make me happy and more thankful to the Father for His Love and kindness.

I am living all alone, but I have many visitors, and love is the ruling sentiment among all its inhabitants. No spirit who is not filled with this Divine Love of which I have so often told you can possibly live in this sphere. The spirit who has all the most wonderful intellectual acquirements, and is without this Love, cannot enter this sphere, nor can the mere natural love of mortals or of spirits fit the spirit for inhabitancy here. Only the Divine Love of the Father can make a spirit so at-one with all the surroundings and atmosphere of love that here exists.

When I left the first sphere I was taken in charge by a most beautiful and glorified spirit, and carried from my home in the first sphere up to the entrance of the second sphere where many other beautiful spirits were waiting to give me welcome—and such a welcome I never thought could be extended to a spirit who is progressing. But I was received with all the love and affection and evidence of joy that the spirits of this sphere have for a spirit who has progressed from the lower one. Oh, I tell you that my happiness was certainly beyond any conception of what I had in the home which I just left.

I thought that the beauty and grandeur of the first sphere could not possibly be surpassed, but when I tell you that comparison cannot be made between the beauty of the two places, it is the best that I can do. My home was all ready for me, and I was carried by a whole host of spirits to it and told that it was for me, and that God had prepared it for my happiness and joy. It certainly is beyond description, and it would be useless for me to try to describe it.

The spirits here are so much more beautiful than those of any other sphere. They are more ethereal and their garments are all shining and white—not one little speck reminds one of the earth or the grosser spheres of the spirit world. And here the music is entirely divine and of such a great variety—all telling of the great Love of God, and sung in His praise and adoration. I have not yet seen all the beauties of this sphere, and I may later give you a fuller description of it.

Yes, I met some spirits whom I knew on earth, but not many; some of the truly Christian men and women who lived and loved and worshipped God, and passed over long before I did. My own dear mother and father have progressed to this sphere and were ready to receive me; and how glad they were to welcome me and take me to their arms of love.

Well, I must not write more tonight as you are not in condition for extended writing. So with all my love, which is so much greater than when I last wrote you,

I am your own true and loving grandmother. (Ann Rollins)[75]

Gives reasons why so many of the higher spirits wrote on Divine Love

August 6th, 1915.

I am here, your grandmother.

Well my dear son, I have been waiting to come for some time, but as you have had so many spirits from various spheres and so different in personality write to you I thought it best to refrain from writing and let them send their communications. I have been much interested in these writings because mostly all of them have testified as to the fact that Jesus writes to you and wants you to do his work and also as to the truth of our statements concerning the Divine Love and the New Birth.

We have felt that this great variety of witnesses would help to convince you of the truths which we have written and in the future will help very much to convince those who may read our messages.

So you see our personal sacrifices have been repaid by the host of witnesses that have appeared and written. I am so glad that your faith is now so strong and it will grow stronger and you will realize that Jesus is your true friend and is interested in you in many ways. He seems to love you very much and is with you when you little suppose he is. Yes, all the messages that you get in his name are from him, no matter how personal they may appear to be, for as I said he is interested in you in a way that causes him to care for you in your material affairs. You must believe and you will be benefitted and made happier by such belief.

I am very happy and so are your mother and Helen. We are very close to one another and are with one another very much.

Helen is a thankful spirit and is with you so very often, loving and trying to comfort you. I will stop now.

Well he (Ingersoll) is thinking a great deal of what Mr. Riddle and I told him. He is a man or rather spirit with much capacity for loving and receiving love and as soon as he opens up his heart to the inflowing of

---

[75] This message is a composite of two, being published in Volume II and Volume III. (G.J.C.)

the Divine Love he will receive it abundantly.

Of course his course of thinking while on earth will retard his progress and until he changes these ideas, he will not make much progress in his soul development. But I think that he is open minded and honest and will soon see that what we tell him as true is a truth.

We will try to help him in every way possible.

Yes, the contract in our appearances made an impression on him and has caused him to do much thinking. When Mr. Riddle told him the cause, he seemed to be astonished and listened to me when I told him of the higher things with great attention and interest.

Well my dear boy, I must say good night.

Your loving grandmother.

Tells of her love for Mr. Padgett

I am here, Helen.

Well my own darling Ned, you have written enough for tonight. I want to tell you that I love you with all my heart and soul and enjoyed you loving me this evening so much.

I was with you in the park and caught all your thoughts of love and was so happy.

Now sweetheart stop for tonight and love me as you have been doing all evening.

I am your own true and loving,
Helen.

Answers Mr. Padgett's question on baptism

September 9th, 1915.

I am here, your grandmother.

All I know about the origin of the Book of Revelation is what I have heard from John (St. John), and he has told me substantially what he has told you, and I believe what he has said—I know that many things in the Book are not true, and that its mysteries are not worth attempting to fathom, because they do not contain any spiritual truths—These truths are so plain and so simple that it requires no mysterious statement of them to be made, so that men will hesitate to understand their import. So my advice to you is to receive what the Master may write and believe in what he communicates.

Question: What about Baptism?

Well, baptism is not essential to a man's salvation. It is merely symbolical of the truth of a reuniting with the Love of the Father, and when you can receive that love in substance and reality, what is the need of resorting to a mere shadow. I tell you that no baptism or drinking wine and eating bread in remembrance of Jesus is necessary to salvation, and are not even advisable so far as the actual salvation of man is concerned, because many persons when they are baptized believe that is all that is necessary to salvation, and neglect the real development of the soul, and the desire to have the inflowing of the Divine Love, without which there is no salvation. Have faith and trust in the Master.

So with all my love,

I am your own loving, grandmother (Ann Rollins)

Writes about the unpardonable sin that is of the greatest importance

November 1st, 1915.

I am here, your grandmother.

I have been listening to your conversation tonight and am much pleased to see that you and your friend (Dr. Stone) are growing in your conceptions of the truth.

The matter of the unpardonable sin is one that is of the greatest importance to the world, especially in view of the fact, that so many of the orthodox ministers teach that it is a thing of real existence and is so dreadful in its consequences. But thanks to the Master, that this teaching will not in the near future be permitted to go unchallenged, for the truth in this particular will be made so plain that men will cease to believe in it, and as a consequence will be relieved from a fear that has kept many a one from seeking the Love and favor of the Father.

I know that this revelation of the truth will antagonize many of these preachers who see that it is one of the strongest instruments that enables them to keep together their organization. But this antagonism will not avail, for the truth will prevail, and mankind will, when they come to think for themselves, embrace this truth with gladness and joy. How strange that the professed ministers of Christ should so slander and blaspheme the one loving Father, and cause men to look upon Him as a God of insatiable wrath, and one who, because a man refuses to believe in the doctrines of the churches, consigns him to eternal punishment and hell; and when he gets into such condition of hardness of heart that, as your preacher said, "even God Himself will have no power to save." Oh, it is pitiable, that such erroneous and harmful doctrines should be taught, and worse than all, by professed ministers of the loving and lowly Jesus.

So my son, you and your friend, whenever the opportunity comes to combat this monstrous teaching, do so with all your strength and power of conviction and show and proclaim to the world that such teaching is not true, and that for every sinner there is opportunity for salvation, and that God loves the man who will not believe on Him just as he loves the believer, only the former may not partake of the Divine nature as does the latter.

I wanted tonight to write this, because I thought that the time was opportune to impress upon you the falsity of this great dogma that has no foundation in truth or in the plan of God for the salvation of humanity.

Well, I will not write more tonight as you have others present who may want to write, but before I close I want to say in fulfillment of John's statement[76] to you today that he is present and with him is his great influence of love.

So with all my love I bless you both.

Your grandmother.[77]

Again writes on the Kingdom of Jesus being closed to all those that do not receive the Divine Love of the Father

January 15th, 1915.

I am here, your grandmother.

The Kingdom of Jesus will be one where only those who believe in his teachings of truth and have received the Holy Ghost in their souls, will live.[78] At some time, known only to God, the entrance to this Kingdom will be closed, and all who have not qualified themselves, or rather who have not striven to heed and obey these truths, and have not received this love, will not be permitted to enter this Kingdom. Those who remain outside will have the love and care of God necessary to make them comparatively happy, but will not have that supreme Love, which they can all now get if they will seek and believe.

That all spirits shall enjoy this supreme Love is not necessary to the harmony of God's universe. Why should he continue to hold open the entrance to this Kingdom of supreme Love when men will not try to obtain it? Well as to those who are born after the kingdom is shut forever, he will not let enter because they are not included in his plan of salvation to this supreme and Celestial Heaven. They will have this other

---

[76] There is no trace of a "statement" on this date from John. But as John was his special guide, it may just refer to a very short communication that was not diarised. (G.J.C.)

[77] This message is a composite of two, being published in Volume II and Volume III. (G.J.C.)

[78] The words used here indicate this is very early in Padgett's mediumship. He is still reliant on his orthodox Christian vocabulary to express spiritual concepts. The next message below is many years later, and a totally different vocabulary is evident. (G.J.C.)

happiness that I speak of, but not that which those in Jesus' Kingdom will enjoy.

No it is not, He did not intend that his Kingdom of which we speak should remain open through all eternity for spirits to enter and live in. They who come after have no claim on God for such supreme opportunities, and he is not doing an injustice by keeping them from entering it. He has prepared a place or places where they will be able to find comparative happiness, and will only be a little lower than the angels of God, who are and will be the redeemed through the teachings of Jesus and who become part of his Kingdom.

I know that your friend and medium Mr. Colburn may think that this is not just right or just, but where there is no right to demand the Grace of God, and when he bestows that Grace in such a way as to make all his children comparatively happy, where is the injustice in giving to a certain few who seek the true way; and find it, the supreme condition of happiness which His Love to the fullest gives.

He is not a God of justice according to human understanding, but according to His own ideas of what man is justly entitled to. He will not turn away one soul who may seek this Love in the fullest, but will enter into the heart of everyone who asks Him to—and when men fail to ask why should He through all eternity keep open the gate to His place of supreme happiness—or in other words, His Divine Sphere, set apart for those who follow Jesus and his truths? I know that some people might say that God had no right to provide this special kingdom for any of his children, and in doing so he showed partiality; but he has the right to show this partiality, when the very reason for its existence is the failure of some of his children to partake and accept what he freely offers to all.

Well as to that, I am not so qualified to answer; but it seems to me that they who come after the gates to the Kingdom are closed have no right to expect that they are entitled to enter, for they are not born to have this privilege, and the only privilege that He can offer them is that of His spirit world, where they will be free from sin and unhappiness. They will all be His children, but not all His Divine Children. Those who have entered this kingdom of which I speak will take on the Divine Nature of the Father, while those who do not will remain His spiritual children, with the right to a life through all eternity, but not to all the attributes which the Divine Nature confers.

This is a subject which Jesus will instruct you in, when he comes to write his messages and you had better wait until then, for you will be better able to understand after you hear his explanation.

No, after the gates, are closed the Holy Ghost or Spirit will return to God and dwell in the Kingdom. Men's souls will then receive God's Love through the messengers which He will use for that purpose. But the Divine Part of His Love will not be conveyed; only the love which God as a spirit has for His children as spirits. I suppose that this is hard for you to understand, but as I say, wait until Jesus writes and you will know all.

No, man is not divine, in the sense that God is Divine. For he is created in the image, and that is the soul only, that makes him like His Father, but not that divinity which divides or differentiates the God essence from the spirit essences. Only God is Divine in this sense, and only those born of man can ever obtain that Divine Essence, who become members of the Kingdom that I speak of.

"Divine" is a word used in a very comprehensive sense, and includes in the minds or thought's of many persons, everything that seems to be above the mortal existence or powers of man; but it is not a true conception of the meaning of the word. Only that is divine which is of the true Essence of God in His Nature which man does not have or which is not a part of Him. In this sense no man is divine; neither has he any of this divinity in him—only God is Divine, and man cannot possibly get this divine essence except in the way that Jesus has taught. Only the Holy Ghost conveys to the soul of man this divine essence of God, and when the mission of this messenger ceases, man will no longer receive this Divine Essence.

So tell Mr. Colburn that he must not believe that through all eternity man will have the privilege of getting this Divine Essence of the Father. Tell him to seek it now while it may be obtained and when he has it, neither all the powers nor forces of earth or spirit world can take it from him.

I am very much interested in him, for he is a man of deep thought and is seeking the truth in all earnestness, and I hope that he will let his thoughts turn in the direction that will bring to his mind and consciousness the real and true things of His Father. He is not very dogmatic or difficult to grasp the truth if it presents itself in a reasonable way. He must not let his preconceived ideas, even if they are based on what the Bible may seem to teach him, keep him from embracing the true ideas of man's relationship to God and man's destiny. So give him my love and tell him to seek and he will find, even though he may at times be shocked at some propositions that may be placed before him, for I intend to tell him of what I know about these matters, whenever I have the opportunity. I have written much longer than I intended I must stop. So good night my dear grandson.

Your loving grandmother,
Ann Rollins.

Writes on the importance of knowing the Way to the Celestial Heavens

March 12th, 1919.

Let me write a line. I am not going to write a long message but one that is very short. You are now in condition to receive our messages, and I wish to write for a while on the importance of knowing the way to the Celestial Kingdom which has been written you before, but I wish to add to what you have received. You have been told that the only way to obtain that Kingdom is by the Divine Love coming into your soul and changing it into a thing Divine, which partakes of the very Essence of the Father Himself. Well, this is a correct explanation of the operation of this Love on the soul, but in order to get this Love there must be earnest supplication on the part of the seeker, and a mere mental desire for the inflowing of the Love will not suffice.

This is a matter that pertains to the soul alone and the mind is not involved except, as you might say, to start the soul's longings and prayer. When you think that you are longing for this Love and have a mere mental desire for its inflowing, the Love will not come, because it never responds to the mere mind and must always be sought for by the soul's longings. Many men have the intellectual desire for the Love of God, and upon that desire rest, and believe that they have the Love and that there is nothing further for them to do; but they will find themselves mistaken, and that instead of possessing this Love they have awakened only the natural love, and in a way, started it towards its goal of the purified soul, like the first parents before the fall, and will not experience the transformation that comes with the possession of the Divine Love.

It is no easy matter to have these longings possess the soul, and men should not remain satisfied with these mere mental desires for they will not be benefitted by such desires, except as I may say, in the way of having their natural love purified. The longings of the soul comes only from a realization that this Love is waiting to be bestowed, and that the soul must become active and earnest in its endeavor to have this Love come into it, and then the transformation takes place.

From this you will see how utterly impossible it is for the devotee of the church to experience this Love or to have the longings of the soul which are not aroused by the observance of the church's sacraments, and the duties which it imposes upon them. They may be ever so zealous in their attendance upon the church services and in complying strictly with its requirements as to doing those things which it prescribes. It is with them all a mental process but the soul is not affected. They may think that their desires are from the soul, and that a response will come, but in this they are mistaken and the soul lies dead. Only when the soul's longings are started into activity are prayers of the worshiper answered.

So you will see that a man may be apparently devout and full of zeal for his church and the teachings of his creed, and yet will not be benefitted so far as the progress of the soul is concerned.

Let not your desires be only of the intellect, but try to bring into activity the longings of the soul, and do not rest satisfied until a response shall come, and it will certainly come, and you will know that the Love is present working its transforming power upon the soul. This is all I desire to say tonight. I am pleased that you are now in condition to receive our messages and hope that your excellent condition will continue. With my love, I will say, good night.

Your own loving grandmother,
Ann Rollins.[79]

Informs Mr. Padgett that his soul is developing very rapidly

January 10th, 1915.

I am here, your father.

I came to tell you that you are a very loving man and that you will do some good both in the earth and in the spirit world. I feel that I must tell you this for I see that your soul is developing very rapidly, and as the more of God's Love you get the more power for doing good you will have. Only pray as you are doing and you will become happier yourself, and make others happy.

The message that you have just received will make the judge feel very happy, and it will cause him to think more of things spiritual as I believe.

You should not write more tonight as you are tired. So with all my love and many wishes for your happiness and prosperity,

I am your loving father,
John H. Padgett.

Writes about the infidel's first realization when they come into the spirit world that there must be a God

February 25th, 1916.

I am here, your father.

I have been listening to your grandmother's message (On Who or What is God[80]) and was interested in observing the way in which you received it, for it is a deep and important communication of truth that is not generally known to mortals. We in the lower spheres, of course, do not know these truths so extensively as do the spirits of the Celestial Spheres, but I have heard the Master discourse on the subject of God,

---

[79] This message is a composite of two, being published in Volume I and Volume III. (G.J.C.)
[80] This message was published in Volume I (5th Ed.) page 57. (G.J.C.)

and what your grandmother wrote you is, in short, what he has explained to us, but of course, in a way that we could better and to a greater extent comprehend the truth than can you.

There is one thing that I have observed in the case of these, who are called scientists and who believe only the material, and also in the case of those who claim to be infidels, when they come into spirit life, and that is, that very soon they realize that there is or must be a God, and that their God of nature, or their man-made God, does not supply the word, if I may thus express it, which they find to exist here.[81] They, of course, do not get a conception of the nature of God in the beginning, but they know very soon after they come over that there is a God other and different from what they conceived Him to be when they had any conception of Him on earth and when they denied that there was any God, and they soon realize the absolute necessity for there being one. And when they had made man his own God, they see many spirits of men in such conditions of darkness and suffering and helplessness that they readily realize that man is not God.

So I say the first truth that enters their mind and souls when they become spirit is that there is a God, although they do not know His nature and attributes.

So you see there is only one little veil of flesh between the vaunted mind of mortals that proclaim there is no God but nature or no God at all, and the mind conscious of its weakness and littleness as it exists in the spirit world.

But I must stop writing on this subject or you will think that I am going to write you a lecture, which I don't intend to do now.

With all my love, I am your loving father,
John H. Padgett.[82]

Is one of his guardian angels that is protecting him from undesirable spirits and is now a Celestial Spirit, living with his soulmate

March 13th, 1917.

I am here, your father.

I have been waiting a long time to write but there were so many others so anxious to write, and who could either do you much good or

---

[81] While this is true, it is not necessarily the case that they then accept that the "God" they conceive of is a personal God. And this is a very big distinction. Because those that believe in some non-personal force do not automatically accept that He loves them, and has available this unique Divine Love which requires the spirit to reach out in love to Him. (G.J.C.)

[82] This message is a composite of two, being published in Volume I and Volume III. (G.J.C.)

you do them good that I refrained and did not want your vitality to be drawn on too much.

Well I understand, my dear boy, and hereafter I will not wait so long to write you. You must know this, though, that I am with you very, very often, and am looking after you, trying to help you and make you happy, and protect you from the undesirable influences. No, I have not surrendered my guardianship, and won't until you shall come to us, when you will no longer need me.

I am glad that you are progressing in your soul development, and that you are doing your work. You cannot realize the good that you are doing among these dark spirits who come to you so often for help, and what gratitude they frequently express for your help. I am very happy that you have this great work to do, and so are we all, and we love you more and more as the days go by, and pray the Father to bless you and give you more of His Love.

Well, I am in the Seventh Sphere, and with my soulmate, and we are very happy together. Your mother is also very happy and while her soulmate is not in the sphere with her, yet he has made wonderful progress, and loves her with a deep and holy love, such as, he says, he never dreamed of while on earth.

Well, my son, I will come again very soon; but remember, I am very close to you, and see your worries and your joys, and always am trying to remove the one and increase the other. I must tell you that your grandmother will come very soon and write you, as she says, she has a very important message to deliver. What a wonderful wise and beautiful spirit she is.

Well they are still very happy in the love of each other, and have made some progress in their soul development. They are together, and are in the fifth sphere and are thinking much of the soul's need for the Divine Love. I am with them quite frequently, and tell them of the happiness that is ahead of them if they will only seek for it. Helen goes to them too, and tells them of this Love and the beauties of her home. They seem to love her very much, and think her one of the most beautiful spirits that come to them, and she is too.

So remember what I say, and bid me good night. I love you very much and have your happiness continually in view, and I know that you will be happy and realize what you desire in the way of performing your work.

Good night and God bless you,
Your loving Father.

Describes the various writers that wrote on this night and the help that each is given and her work in locating soulmates

March 18th, 1917.[83]

I am here, your own true and loving Helen.

Well dear, I was waiting for you to call me. The other spirits who tried to write were not dark spirits, but were not of the soul spheres either; and were very much disappointed that they could not get the rapport. We did not try to prevent them writing, and they failed because they could not get the power.

You have done considerable writing tonight and I must not detain you very long as you are tired, although you may not realize it. But tomorrow night I will come and write my message just after Luther shall have finished his.

You may doubt the identity of the spirit who wrote you but he says that he is the man, and that he has recently come to the spirit life and is very weak and somewhat at a loss as to just where he is. I heard you call him and when he came, of course, we let him write. He will come again, and explain how he heard your call.

Well, Mrs. Wilson wrote, and she was very anxious to do so, and very grateful that she was permitted to write. I will do what you requested, and tell her who her soulmate is, and whether it be her late husband or not she will be the better by knowing.

I will also tell her of the other greater thing that you suggested without telling her what it is. But I will take great pains in instructing her, and believe that she will listen to me.

Many spirits were here tonight, and your father enjoyed writing very much. He is with you very much looking after you. I will not write more now.

So love me and believe that I love you and am
Your own true and loving,
Helen.

Writes to his sick son Dr. Arbelee, regarding his life in the spirit world

April 24th, 1919.

I am here, your father.

---

[83] This is an inferred date, based on the diary entry for Mrs Wilson and the reference to Martin Luther, because there is no diary entry on this date for Helen. (G.J.C.)

Let me write for I desire to tell my son that I am with him in his sickness and am trying to help him and make him feel that there is more in life than the merely physical living.

I know that he has often felt that I am with him in my love and desire to help and encourage him in his afflictions, and his feelings are true, for with me there has never ceased to be the love and affections that were mine when in the flesh, and so long as he shall remain a mortal my love and care will be with him in all their fullness.

I am in the spirit world, which is very close to his world and am not very different from what I was when on earth, except that now I have not a fleshly body, and cares and distractions of my physical living to disturb my happiness. I am in the fifth sphere, where all is so beautiful and bright, and where the Love of the Father is so abundant that we are happy all the time and enjoy that bliss which Jesus told his followers was in store for them when they should give up the ghost and enter into their rest, which is a rest in action and work.

I was with you last night when the gentlemen called (Mr. Padgett snr.) and explained to you the truths of the existence of a soul that has been transformed by the Love of the Father and brought into at-onement with Him, and I want you to believe in this Great Love. Your days on earth, at the longest, will be very short and then you will have to come to the spirit world and leave behind you all the ambitions and accumulations of your earth life, and if you have not laid up your treasures in heaven you will be very poor indeed. Oh my son, realize that the pleasures and desires and efforts of earth life are but fleeting and for a moment only, and that then comes the great problem of living in eternity, and that the thoughts and deeds of that earthly existence comes with you to condemn or make you happy.

The great law of "whatsoever a man sows, that shall he reap" is in full force and exacts every part of the penalty that the life of a man for good or evil imposes upon him. There is no exception to the workings of this law and the full penalty must be paid until forgiveness comes, and then the demand ceases, and the soul emerges from its condition of suffering and darkness, a purified and redeemed soul. But forgiveness is not the mere release from or remission of these penalties, by the mere arbitrary dictum of God, as you are so often taught by the preachers, but it is forgetfulness.

That is forgetfulness—an oblivion as it were—of the acts and deeds that bring into operation the great law, and men when they become spirits must work into this forgetfulness in a slow and laborious manner. I say men must work, for on themselves depends to a large extent, their own redemption. No miracle will be performed, for as is said, the mills of the gods grind true but they grind exceeding small, and the spirit will have to pay the last penalty; and this must be so, as you will readily see, for the soul must in order to get into the condition of harmony with the laws of God, become purified and relieved of everything that would make it inharmonious. No soul can live in a purer state than its own qualities possess. And here let me say that no mere belief or sacraments or observance of church dogmas can bring about this purification. It is a work within the soul, and man must do the work.

Now, my son, I write all this to show you how inexorable is this great law of which the Master spoke when on earth, and which in its exactions never change. It has no mercy and admits of no shortcut to the goal of the purified soul. How few of mortals really understand the workings of this law, but in a careless and complacent manner depend upon the forgiveness of priests and preachers and the mysterious workings of some assurances of the church's dogmas.

So you will see the necessity for men to commence as early as possible to practice the renunciation and turning away from these things that contaminate and defile the soul; but, alas, as their lives on earth continue, most men, instead of renouncing these things, accumulate and add to them and come to the spirit world all burdened and filled with thoughts and acts that defile. And as they are the accumulations of many years of earth life, so many years will be required for these men, when they become spirits, to get rid of these things and false hopes and beliefs will not help them in the slightest, but frequently seem only to retard the purification of their souls.

If this were men's destiny, implacable and irrevocable, men would be in an almost hopeless and unforgiven condition indeed, forgetfulness would come only in a slow and sinuous way, and they would shed many tears and suffer much groaning before they could feel themselves forgiven. And this will be the lot of most men, but in the end forgetfulness will come and they will find happiness.

But my son, thanks be to God, the Father of us all, there is another provision of the Father which exists and is freely given to all men who will seek for it, and that is the Divine Love of the Father, in which are forgetfulness and mercy and oblivion of the thoughts and acts of earth, and which is greater than the great law of compensation, of which I have just written. When this Love comes into the soul of man, with it comes forgetfulness, which is the only forgiveness in the economy of God, and the demands of the law of compensation cease, and the soul becomes freed from the law. As Paul has said, then is a man without the law. And with this Love comes a happiness and joy that no man can conceive of, and the possessor of it knows that he has become a part of God's divinity and immortality. Now, this Love does not come all at once in its fullness, but as a still small voice, it tenderly and timidly answers the call of the heart that cries for it in earnestness and faith, and as it is nurtured it grows stronger and more soul-possessing, and makes its presence felt to the supplicant. Unless it is earnestly sought for it never comes into the soul but passes by unseen and in silence because the soul will not seek its possession.

You, my son, heard the way in which it may be obtained, and I urge upon you, with all your strength and longings of soul, to seek for it, and if you do, it will not refuse to enter into your soul, and you will know it, and then your start will be made not only towards forgiveness and forgetfulness—but towards the transformation of your soul into the very Love and Essence of the Father, and a progress that will last through all eternity.

I am the possessor of that Love and know whereof I speak, and to me comes the great assurance of a life continuous and never dying, filled with the bliss of angels and the joy of a redeemed soul. Oh, I do so much want you to obtain this Love and become one of us, who know that when death left us life took its place, bringing to us a knowledge that immortality was ours.

Well my son, I must stop writing. I have written in this way because I am more interested in your immortal soul than I am in your mere physical body, which will perish and be no more. But the soul! the great wanting, loving, hating, happy, suffering thing that it is!

I will be with you very often in my love and try to help you, and if you will think of me intently, I will impress you with my presence. I must stop now as the rapport is weakening. Good night,

Your father, Arbelee.

Confirms that the father of Dr. Arbelee wrote to him, giving advice

April 24th, 1919.

I am here, your own true and loving Helen.

Well dear, I am glad that you received a letter from the father of the sick man.

He wanted so much to write and was here ready to do so as soon as you gave him the opportunity. He is a spirit who is in Fifth Sphere and has in his soul much of the Divine Love, and is so anxious that his son shall receive the benefit of the Great Gift of the Father and live the life that only those who know what heavenly joy and immortality is. He was very thankful that he could write and he says that sometime he wants to come and write of his experience in becoming awakened to the truth of God's love and his acceptance as one of his children.

So love us all and believe that we love you.

Good night, your own true and loving, Helen.

Has progressed into the Third Celestial sphere and says that there are no words to describe its beauty

December 28th, 1915.

I am here, your Helen.

I am ready to write as I promised you today, and you must not think that I will not tell you of what is so dear to me, and should be to you. It has been a long time since I wrote you very much in detail about myself, and you do not know what has taken place in my soul progression for some time past.

Well, I have been praying and trying to get more Love of the Father in my soul and have succeeded to such an extent that I am now in the third Celestial Sphere, where are your grandmother and mother also; and my dear, if I could only tell you of the joys and grandeur of this sphere, I should be most happy. But I have not the words at my command to give you any satisfactory idea of what the appearance and conditions of this sphere are.

I have described to you my home in the second Celestial Sphere, though very inadequately, but that home cannot compare with what I have now, and I cannot better describe it than to say it is beyond all possible conception of what you can possibly have of beauty and grandeur and love. I am only in the lower planes of this sphere, but these are so filled with the Father's Love that it almost seems impossible that there can be any spheres where there is more of this Love, but, of course, as Jesus and all the apostles and some others who write you, have their homes in these higher (Celestial) Spheres and nearer to the fountainhead of love, consequently there must be more Love where they are.

I am so happy that I can scarcely tell you of what this happiness means, but at any rate, I must say that there is never the slightest thing to interfere with my happiness or to make me think that I am not an accepted child of the Father, partaking of His Love to an extent that makes me immortal and never again subject to death.

This happiness is not such as satisfies only for a while, but is one continual source of living, free from all that might enter into the feelings or lives of spirits that know not that they are one with the Father and a part of Him in Love and beauty. I am only wanting one thing now to make my life complete, and that is to have you with me; but from this you must not think that I am not perfectly happy and contented, for I am, but as you have been told I am only one half of the complete one, the other half must come and join the half that I am before the perfect one can become completed. So my dear Ned, you must try now harder than ever to get this Great Love in your soul in more abundance, and you may if you will only pray and have faith, for the Master says that you can, and he knows.

Yes, I have my individual home here, just as I had in the lower spheres, and it is just as real, and more so, as any home which you have on earth. My garments are the same in appearance, as to form, but oh, so much more beautiful and shining white, and my countenance too is more beautiful and full of expressions of love. So you see, I have a greater love for my Father and a greater love for you; for as my love for the Father increases my love for you also increases, and I know that when you come over this love will be so great, that you will wonder that such love could exist.

I do not think that I had better write more tonight as I do not feel like telling you of other things, and I only want to enjoy this Great Love free from communicating about other matters, though at another time I shall be pleased to do so.

So sweetheart, think of me as I am now, filled with this Great, new Love that is possessing my whole being, and now dear you are the object of this love, outside of that which is the Father's.

I will not write more, but will say that I am yours now and for all eternity, and am waiting, oh, so longingly, for the time to come when you can be with me. I will stop writing.

Your own true and loving,
Helen.[84]

Tells about her new beautiful garment as a result of her spiritual advancement

December 22nd, 1915.

I am here, your own true and loving Helen.

Oh my dear, how I wish that you could see me as I am now, and the great love that is in my soul, then you would never doubt me. Well my garment is a beautiful, white flowing gown which has all the splendor of the sun shining on the polished silver roof of some Turkish Mosque. I am dressed all in white and have a golden girdle, and jewels, as you would say, on my head, and an aura that shows the condition of my soul development. My form is very beautiful, the spirits tell me, and my features are very classical and mobile also. But wait until you come over and you will see, and if you can't wait, ask your friend Judge Syrick, who is here, what he thinks of my appearance.

So sweetheart I will say good night.

---

[84] This message is a composite of two, being published in Volume II and Volume III. (G.J.C.)

Your own true and loving,
Helen.

Confirms Helen's beauty

December 22nd, 1915.

I am here, Judge Syrick.

Well Padgett, I heard what your wife said, and I would like to tell you what her appearance is, but I have not words to describe it.

She is a beauty that you have never had the faintest conception or, notwithstanding what has been written you, and your vision also. But I tell you this, that she has a form of the greatest perfection, and countenance, which you have never seen the shadow of on earth, and hence; I can't give you any idea of it.

But her garments are all shining white, with a brilliancy that dazzles us, who look upon her, and her face—oh, what a beautiful face!

I want soon to come and write you a long letter. So I will say with my best wishes.

Good night.
Your friend,
Frank D. Syrick.

Writes that she was impressed with what Mr. Padgett said to Dr. Stone about the Love of God flowing into the heart; also locates Judge Syrick's Soulmate

January 9th, 1915.

I am here, Helen.

I am so happy, and I am awfully glad to see that you are also. I was with you at the show tonight, and you made me so happy when you loved me as you did. I tried to let you hear my voice, but I could not; but don't despair of hearing it. I will soon learn the way and then you will hear me quite often. I loved you so much that you could not help feeling my love, and when you thought of me so intensely I was with you and tried to hug you with my hands. You shed more tears of love, and then I almost let myself control you right there; but as it was a public place, I restrained my emotion. You are my darling Ned, and you are dearer to me than ever. So let me have all your love and I will be very happy.

I was with you today when Dr. Stone was with you, and heard what was said, and I saw that he was very much impressed with your talk to him about the Love of God flowing into the heart; so I believe that if you continue to tell him of this Love, he will soon see the true way that it must be obtained and will strive to get it. He is a naturally spiritual man and wants to have this Love in his soul.

I know just what he thinks about this Love Principle and while he is partly right, yet he does not grasp the true principle of that Love. He is depending upon a love that man creates by what he calls right thinking and action, but this is not true, man cannot of himself create this Love. He can let it come into his heart and grow and thereby become more possessed with it; but it will not come of his own creation. His heart is not in such a condition that this Love will spring up spontaneously, nor can he by his mere effort to create it, cause its appearance. He can obtain it only from a higher source, and that source is his Heavenly Father. No man is so good that this Love can emanate from him anymore than life can arise of his own volition or efforts. What is the Love Principle, as it is called, is not the natural love of a man for God or for man, but the Love that comes into the heart of a man from the Father in answer to prayer. I do not know if I have made myself very clear but you know what I mean, and you can explain better than I can.

Yes, I am very strong tonight and you are in very good condition too, but you must not write too much. You must conserve your strength for I am going to draw on it tomorrow night, if conditions are favorable.

She (Padgett's daughter) is happy as I told you. You are not so much worried, and I am thankful for it. Yes, decidedly. Yes, he has to a greater extent. He sees that only this Love can make him happy, and save him from his sins. So you see you have done some good on earth as well as among the spirits.

As to Judge Syrick, I will try to have his soulmate come and write him—wait a little while until I find her.

Rose is here.

Dear Frank, I am here and through the kindness of Mrs. Padgett, I have the opportunity to write you, and tell you that you are the dearest person to me in all the world. You do not yet fully appreciate my love for you, but as you come more in rapport with me, you will feel my presence and love to a greater and larger extent. I am not only your soulmate but your guardian angel and when you least think of me, I am with you trying to direct your thoughts and actions towards those things which will make you happier and more at peace with your troubles in life.

So do not forget that wherever you may be, and whatever your thoughts may dwell upon, I am with you and know what you are thinking of, and I want you to think and believe that in all the earth, or spirit land either, there is no one who loves you with such a pure and fervent love as I do, my own darling Frank. Oh, how I wish that I could communicate with you in this way every night and tell you of what happiness I have in being with you, and feeling at times that you do really love me in your own somewhat divided heart. But thank God the time will come when I will have your whole love for myself, and no one else will share it with me to the smallest extent.

My dear, only believe that I am your soulmate, and am waiting for you to come over, and share with me the happiness and delight which my home here gives me. No spirit can love its soulmate more than I do you, and no mortal can love so much. Be my own true sweetheart, and even though you do not have the assurance that I am with you as I say, yet I am, and nothing in all the world can keep me from you. So if you can, extinguish from your thoughts that I may be a mere myth and not your own true loving soulmate.

Let my love for you keep your thoughts in the way of things spiritual, for if you will only believe in me and in my love you will realize that I am with you and will feel my love and my presence, even though your physical senses may not be able to tell you anything.

But the sense of two souls which are decreed by our Father to be one, will tell you, at times, that I am one and you are the other, and that the two will through all eternity become and remain one in love and happiness. So you see, that even though we cannot exchange our love so very often in words, yet in our feelings and sensations we may know that our love for each other is existing, and burning with a brightness that nothing can extinguish, not even your thoughts that I am a mere myth and not your own true, loving soulmate. Be only closer to me in your thoughts and you will realize that I am your Rose, as I once told you. You sometimes doubt that you saw me and felt my kiss your forehead, and that I have no real existence, but I tell you with all my soul's love that it was I that kissed you and told you that I was your soulmate. Oh my darling one, do not doubt me again if you value my happiness.

Let my love for you keep your thoughts in the way of things spiritual, for I can see that you are inclined to the higher things of the spirit world of life; and if you desire to come to me and live with me when you come over, seek the real love of our Father, for in that you will find everything that will make your soul develop, until when you come to me. I will meet you and take you to my home, where you will find that I have prepared a home for you so beautiful that you will wonder how I could have loved you so much, and thought so much about your happiness. You are the only one for me to think of in this way, and when you stop for a moment and think of what love means, you will see that I could not do otherwise than try to make you happy.

There is another thing that I want to tell you, and that is that you must have no fear of what is called death, because it is not death, but an entrance into life; and when you come over I will be right at your bedside, and as your spirit passes from your body I will take you in my arms and carry you to the home which I have prepared for you.

Of course, this means, if you have developed your soul to such an extent as will permit you to enter my home; and even if you have not, I will be with you as the soul leaves the body and fold you in my arms and say such words of burning love that you will not be afraid or want to be anywhere else than with me. So you see, in life or death, or after death I will be with you and my love will envelope you in the great happiness which I have and want you to have.

As I have already taken up more of Mr. Padgett's time and strength than I intended, I must stop, but in doing so, say with all my heart and soul, I love you and will love you through all eternity my own dear Frank.

Helen now writes the following:

Well, don't you think that she loves him? She is a soulmate after my own heart, and I think that he ought to be very happy to know that she has such love as that.

No, not so great as mine, and I will love you with all my heart too. I am somewhat tired now, and must stop, so good night, my own darling Ned.

Your own true,
Helen.[85]

Gives his testimony on the errors of the church in not knowing about Divine Love

July 22nd, 1915.

I am here, St. Chrysostom.

I come because I want to tell you that you have entered upon a work that will bring much happiness to mankind and much glory to the cause of the Master.

When alive, I was a teacher of the truths of the Master, and lived a great many years among a people who believed with their intellects, but who knew very little of the soul religion. I, myself, was not a great believer in the truths having reference to the soul's development, but I taught those truths which appealed more to my intellect, and which were of a character suited more to instill merely moral principles than to cause men to receive and understand the real spirit and real meaning of these teachings. But yet such teachings accomplished some good among the

---

[85] This message is a composite of two, being published in Volume III and Volume IV. (G.J.C.)

people of those times. I was a great student of the Bible, as it was then written, and my studies enabled me to teach and explain these truths in an intellectual way.

It seems strange to me now, but it is a fact, that I never understood the inner depths of these truths, and when I came to die, I had not the consolation of knowing that the Divine Love was the great desideratum, in order for men to become at-one with the Father, and to become a partaker of His Divinity.

I learned these great soul truths after I became a spirit, and met those spirits who had received this Great Love, and showed by their wonderful appearances and happiness that they possessed it. So you see that while I was sainted for what I was supposed to have done for the good of the church and for mankind, I was not a saint at all, but a very great sinner without the essentials to make me a saint.

Many a saint of the church was, when on earth, anything but a saint, and the church in making such person a saint only does what a nation may do in making its prominent warriors and statesmen heroes in marble or bronze. We were saints of the church only as we were believers in the Christ, but we were not saints as to the perfection of our soul condition. In my time on earth, I sought to correct abuses in conduct among those people who outwardly, as clergymen, were carrying on the work of Jesus yet, in character, were lax in abstaining from modes of conduct which were contrary to the laws of God as proclaimed in the writings of Moses and preached by the Master.

So no church can make a man a saint by merely declaring and recognizing him as such. On earth the sins and evil deeds of men may be hidden by the glamour which the church casts over and around them, but in the spirit world these sins and blemishes appear in all the nakedness which the glare of the noonday sun may develop.

Character cannot be hidden and defects cannot be hidden, and unless the soul of a spirit is pure and spotless, it will have to occupy that place and take that station which its soul development determines are suited for it. So how futile are all these canonizing and worshippings of men as saints when there is nothing of the saint about them. The poorest peasant may be more of a saint in the spirit world, than the greatest and most exalted saint according to the creation of the churches.

I do not remember if Vespasian was a Christian at the time, but he is a Christian now, and an inhabitant of the Father's Kingdom. So you must not let the doubts that you may have about his writing to you cause you to disbelieve what he said. I saw him write and I know it was he, and no other.

With the love of a brother, I will say good night.
Your brother and friend,
Chrysostom called Saint John.

Archbishop of Constantinople. (A.D. 347 - 407)

Wishes to be included in book since he is also helping Mr. Padgett in his work

November 8th, 1915.

I am here, St. Chrysostom.

Yes, I merely want to say that I am one of your helpers in the work which you have before you to do, and will help you with all my power.

I know that many spirits will help you and that a wonderful power will be exerted by the spirits and especially by the celestial spirits, to make successful the work of your mission, and that there can hardly be a failure; but, nevertheless, I want to have some of my writings form a part of the book that you may publish. Not for any self glory, but because I believe that way truth will work good to those who may read them, and besides the individual who does the writing may have an influence with some that another individual might not have.

I will not write longer tonight, but will soon come to you and write a long message on an important truth.

So, thanking you for your kindness, I am

Your brother in Christ,

St. Chrysostom.

A French philosopher who rejects the idea of Divine Love and places his faith in reason and intellectual development

November 20th, 1916.

I am here, Descartes.

Let me say a word. I will not attempt to intrude for a great while and only want to say that you are not so very good as you may be led by these spirits to believe. I am not a wicked spirit but am an impartial observer of things, including the states of the souls of men and when I say what I have said you must not think that I have any prejudice or desire to cause you to feel that you are any great sinner, but I have heard what some of these spirits have written you and I see that they are flattering you and try to make you believe that you are a little god on earth, and as your friend I do not think it right that you should be so deceived.

Of course you should become as good as possible and get all this love that they tell you about, if there is any such thing, and it may have the effect upon your soul that they will tell you it will, but at the same time I have my doubts about the matter and would advise you to give more attention to gaining knowledge that is open before you in your earth life and when you come over, you will find that in our spirit world there is no more desirable thing as knowledge and intellectual development.

Why, I should have great regrets if I had neglected to cultivate my mind and acquire knowledge when on earth, for it has kept me from listening to these sentimental spirits who try to talk to me at times about the development of the soul with love—a word that means nothing to anyone except those who are like the silly maidens of earth or the lovesick swains who have never cut their eye-teeth. No, my friend, do not listen to this silly and useless talk about soul development and love, but learn from me and believe that the intellect is the only thing that a man as well as spirit should attempt to cultivate and acquire. Knowledge is power, and I realize that the knowledge that I possess has given me great power in this spirit life.

I associate only with spirits like myself and we have wonderful times of enjoyment in the exchange of our thoughts and bright ideas and in discussing subjects which only spirits like myself can discuss. You may rest assured that only the intellectual spirits attend our meetings and find enjoyment in our discussions. These love speaking spirits who go about and tell us that love is everything and that mind is only secondary, do not attend our discussions for of course they could not understand what our talk is about nor comprehend the wonderful thoughts of a fully developed mind such as we possess.

So you will see that I am really interested in you and desire that you pursue that course in earth life that will fit you for the highest development and the gradual enjoyment that can be experienced in our spirit world. I have as associates many of the prominent philosophers and scientists who once were known on earth as the leaders of thought and the revealers of the great laws of nature and they all think as I am writing you now. I trust that you will believe me to be your friend and that I write this in the utmost good faith and with the desire only to direct your efforts in that way that will lead to your greatest good when you come to the spirit life. I do not think it necessary to write more tonight.

Here a question was asked.

Well, we are all in what they call the earth sphere and are in some little darkness and also in some light and we understand the reason for living in the darkness. We have not yet made that development in our intellectual qualities that fit us for the planes of great light because as you know the greatest knowledge that we could acquire on earth is not equal to the least knowledge that is required to fit us for the planes where only light exists. And for this reason we have the appearance of darkness, but as we obtain a greater mental development that darkness of appearance leaves us and we then progress to the light spheres. This as you will understand is only natural and the result of a law that we recognize as working exactly and unchangeably as the other laws of nature work.

Question?

Well, I have been in spirit life a great many years and have been working as hard and with more enthusiasm than I did on earth to acquire knowledge and understand the laws of nature and I am satisfied with my progress, although I shall not cease to progress as I know, for I will never give up my efforts to acquire more and more knowledge.

I must stop now for there comes a spirit to me who is a very bright one and says I must stop and I cannot refuse to do so. But as I leave I will say that I thank you for your kindness and hope that you will believe that I am sincere in advising you as to what I think is for your own good. So my friend, good night. Your brother in search for the truth. I was known as the French Philosopher and scientist,

Descartes.

A French philosopher that is not interested in the Divine Love of the Father, but is willing to put his faith in reason and investigations

February 1st, 1918.

I am here, Auguste Comte.

I am not one of those spirits who come to you and prate about the New Birth and the Divine Love and the Celestial Spheres, but am simply a spirit who believes what can be known from observation and the exercise of the reasoning faculties. I have been in spirit life for a great many years[86] and am in a sphere of light and have much happiness and enjoy the life of an investigator of truth.

When on earth I was known as a free thinker and by some as an agnostic and consequently was not very popular, except among a number who thought as I did, and who were what was considered followers of me in my beliefs and doctrines as regards the purposes of man's creation and his functions and duties on earth. I believed and

---

[86] Auguste Comte died in 1859 thus he had been in spirit nearly 60 years at this point. Hardly a "great many years" as he claims.(G.J.C.)

taught that the great duty and object of his creation were the exercise of good deeds and the offering of the greatest help to humanity in its living the life on earth. That humanitarianism was the great and vital religion of man on earth, and the only god to be worshipped was the god of human kindness and help, and that any and all other gods were the mere creatures of superstition and without real existence and of no benefit to mankind. There were a number of persons who believed and lived in that belief and endeavored to have it guide and control them in their course of living just as I did, and there are numbers on earth who believe and make such belief their religion.

I do not dispute the future existence of the soul, or that man should have a continuous progression during eternity, and finally reach a condition of happiness and perfection that would render unnecessary the application of the doctrines of humanitarianism that was so necessary while mortals. And I have found since coming to the spirit world that my beliefs and teachings are filled with truth and have resulted in great benefit to me and to numbers of others who carried out to the best of their ability the golden rule of doing unto others as they would have others do unto them. Many of my associates of life are with me here, and we have a comparatively joyous congregation of souls engaged in the work of helping spirits who come to the spirit world not knowing their destiny, or what is before them in the way of living or thinking.

When I came to this world, I entered the planes of darkness and some suffering, and had to work with all the efforts of my mind to make progress out of that condition, by the exercise of thoughts of benevolence and the doing of good to those spirits whom I found that I could help. My state of freedom from those things that partook of sin was what determined my progress and for a long time I made very slow advancement towards the higher planes of thought and condition of purity. But I realized that within me was that which was better than I had known or realized while on earth, and that if I should get rid of those things which kept that better part of me from developing, I would progress and so I struggled to get rid of these things and have myself become the master of the situation. I found that these contaminating things, which were really the creations of my mortal animal desires and appetites, were not a legitimate part of myself, and that I was not a true philosopher by permitting them to linger with me and for, to my deception, a part of myself—the undesirable part—and so I fought to banish them from my knowledge and recollections, and as I succeeded in these efforts I found that I was advancing in light and truth and in harmony with what was pure and good.

I did not ask the help of any mediator to rescue me from my condition of darkness in some mysterious way, or pray to God to take me from my surroundings by means of some omnipotent power that He might exercise in my behalf. I was helped by other spirits who had advanced higher than I, but that help consisted of their advice and the encouragement that came to me when I perceived by their bright appearances and happier conditions that it was possible for me to advance also, as they assured me that they had been in my condition, and that by good thoughts and their efforts to help others, they had been enabled to forget and throw aside those things that caused their state of darkness and suffering. Yes, their advice and influence helped me very much to help myself. I realized the fact that, notwithstanding the help of others, upon myself principally depended the success of effort and the success of advancement.

So, as a spirit who has had the experience that I have related, I would advise all men to examine themselves and learn what is the cause of their condition of darkness and unhappiness, and then seek the means of ridding themselves of this cause, and if they will honestly make the effort they will succeed and become better and happier men.

There is no question that the temptations of the animal appetites and desires to accumulate those things that bring to them selfishness and greed and the want of charity and human sympathy, will prevent them from progressing in the development of the better part of themselves and keep it stagnant and retard its advancement; and men should know this and bend all their energies to curb these appetites and replace these desires with desires to help and serve their fellow men, and let their sympathy and love go out in active works of good to their brothers, for all men are brothers, even in the mortal life though to many it may not be apparent; but in the spirit life it comes as a truth to all, for as each spirit becomes developed in his better part, spirits as a whole become developed, and a more universal happiness ensues.

Well, I have written a long time tonight and as this is the first time that I have ever tried to communicate to a mortal, I am some little tired as you mortals say, and will stop. When on earth I was known as Auguste Comte and lived in France. I have no name here and need none.

Well, I have heard what you said and am a little surprised to hear you make the assertion that you do, but I have no pride of superior or exclusive knowledge and while I doubt that you can demonstrate what you say, yet I am willing to have you make the experiment, and will enter it with an open and unprejudiced mind, and only hope that you may be able to show me a way better than the one I have pursued.

I have never seen or conversed with spirits of the Celestial Heavens, though I have been informed that there are such; but as, when on earth, I did not believe in ghosts, so here, I have not believed in these Celestial Spirits, and thought that they were merely creations of the distorted imaginations of the spirits who told me of the existence of these celestial beings. You must not be surprised when I ascribe to some of the spirits distorted imaginations, for there are many such spirits just as there are mortals on earth with distorted imaginations. The fact of being in the body does not confine distorted imaginations and diseased minds to the earth life only. Yes, I am ready to meet your celestial spirit.

There comes to me a beautiful, bright spirit, such as I have never seen before, who says that he has answered your call and is ready to perform the work of love of showing me the easier and better way to development, and it depends on me whether I will learn that way or not, and if I am willing, he will teach me. Well, I am surprised, I confess! I will go with him and learn all that he can teach me. I will come again.

Good night.

Auguste Comte.

Comments on spirit who wrote and went with Prof. Salyards

February 1st, 1918.

I am here, your own true and loving Helen.

Well, dear, I had some difficulty because of spirits who wished and tried to write, but White Eagle succeeded in inducing them to desist and I then took control. I am glad that you are feeling better tonight and I was expecting that John would write, but conditions are not just favorable and he did not stay. You must make the effort to get in condition, so that he can make the rapport as he desires so much to finish his message.

The spirit who wrote you I never saw before, but he appeared to be a very bright and sincere spirit and desirous of learning anything possible to learn. He has no soul development in the Divine Love and I know that he will be interested in what shall be told him. He went with Prof. Salyards and was much impressed at the appearance of the Professor and his kindly invitation to go with him. I hope that he may learn the Way.

I will not write more tonight. So, sweetheart, say good night.

Stepdaughter of Napoleon, now knows the Way to the Celestial Heavens

October 27th, 1915.

I am here, Helene (Hortense).

I was the daughter of Josephine, the wife of Napoleon, and I come to tell you that I am not so far advanced in the soul development as I wish to be, but I am striving to obtain that Divine Love that I have been taught since my coming to the spirit world is necessary in order to obtain a home in the Celestial Spheres and immortality.

When on earth, being the daughter of an Emperor, my thoughts were given to everything else than to the real soul religion which I now know is the only religion that can save a soul from sin and error. My stepfather was not a spiritual man, as you may know, but all his thoughts were given to the gratification of his ambition and the conquest of nations. He was also a man who had a great deal of the love nature and was intense in his affections and let them guide his life to a large extent when they did not conflict with his ambitions. He and my mother were true lovers and are now soulmates, but my mother is much more developed than he.

When I died, I was totally ignorant of the soul requirements and my religion was confined to the belief in the doctrines of the Catholic Church, which were mostly man-made, as I now see. No one ever told me about the New Birth and the Divine Love of the Father, but always about the power of the priests to forgive sin and their authority to pray a soul out of purgatory. This, as you may know, did not help me when I became a spirit, and when this great change came to me I found myself in darkness and suffering, with no love existing in my soul, although I had the natural affections for my kinfolks; and it was many years after my death that a knowledge of the soul love came to me and I was relieved of my sufferings and brought into light and happiness. I am now in the Fifth Sphere and am very happy, although my spirit instructors tell me that there are higher spheres where much more happiness exists and which I must strive to enter.

My stepfather is not so much elevated, as he is only in the Fourth Sphere and does not yet know of this soul development to any great extent. His ambitions are still with him, and to him the mind is the greatest part of all the spirit's possessions. So you see that an Emperor's daughter does not even stand as good a chance for becoming a spirit of happiness as does the daughter of the poor burghers who know not ambition but whose life is spent in toil and in helping and sympathizing with others. How unfortunate to be a child of high position wherein only the material things of life are thought of and attempted to be obtained. No ambition for earthly things will help a spirit when the earthly things are no more to be obtained.

My mother is with me and she is very happy, and for many years has been trying to induce her husband to give his thoughts to the things of the soul; but so far she has not succeeded, although he sees that she is such a beautiful and happy spirit. But all this love merely shows that the love for and ambition to obtain the material things of life are hard to get rid of and that something in the nature of a great calamity is necessary to awaken some spirits who have this love and ambition to a realization of not only the necessity but the desirability of seeking for the things of the higher spheres. I am now seeking for these things with all my energies and longings, and I am helped by many spirits of these higher spheres. I now know no difference between the prince and the peasant, and in fact I find that the peasant is as a general thing much superior to the prince in his soul progression and beauty and happiness.

My friend, excuse my intrusion, but I have for several weeks seen other spirits writing to you and I so longed to do so, and as the opportunity presented itself tonight I took advantage of it and imposed on you. But to recompense you I will say that your discussions and your writings have done so very much to help me in my progress and bring happiness to me. So I will not detain you further, but will subscribe myself your friend and well-wisher.

Helene.

A former Pope of the early days of Catholicism has now reached the Celestial Spheres; stresses the importance of soul religion

November 7th, 1915.

I am here, Gregory.

I was the great pope of Rome who did so much to establish the Romish Church on a firm basis, and to extend its powers and influence throughout the world.

It has been many years since that time and I have had many experiences in the spirit world. I first suffered and lived in darkness, and then got into the light of the spheres where the mind is supreme, and progressed in those spheres until I found that the happiness which came to me from my associations and pursuits there was not sufficient to satisfy the cravings of my soul; for I had learned in life that there was a God of love, and although I had never found that God, yet these recollections of what I had in an intellectual way learned came to me, and I was not satisfied with the happiness of the intellectual spheres, and, as a consequence, I sought the spirits who I knew were possessed of the love of God, and besought them to teach me the way to that Love, and after a long time I became the possessor of that Love and started on my road of progression to the Celestial spheres, where I now live.

If I had only known on earth what soul religion meant and not given all my thoughts to the politics of the Church and to extending its powers and jurisdiction, I would have avoided many long years of suffering and darkness.

So you see, there is only one way to the Heavenly Home and the happiness which belongs to the Father's Kingdom which the Master is working so hard to establish, and that through the teachings of the

Master, which, if understood and followed, ensures the seeker of that Divine Love which makes all spirits inhabitants of the Heavenly Kingdom and gives them a Celestial happiness.

I don't find that the Church has improved much since my time, and many popes and priests are now going through experiences similar to the ones that I passed through. And many believers in the dogmas of the Catholic Church find that these beliefs are not helping them, but rather retarding them in their souls' progression.

I could write a long letter on this subject, but have not time tonight. I thank you for receiving my message and would like to come again, if agreeable.

Your friend and brother in Christ,
Gregory, the Pope.[87]

Has had his spiritual eyes opened and is seeking the Father's Divine Love

October 19th, 1915.

I am General Grant.

I was the President of your country and also the General of the Federal armies.

Well, I want to say that I am in a condition of comparative happiness, but not entirely relieved from my darkness or sufferings. I had a great many sins to answer for and many penalties to pay, and during the years since my death I have suffered much and experienced great darkness. But thanks be to God, I am emerging from these conditions and am having my spiritual eyes opened to the truths of God and the necessity of obtaining His Love and Favor.

As you may know, when on earth I attended the Methodist Church, but my religious knowledge was merely that which comes from an assent of the mind to certain propositions, or rather doctrines, of the church. I knew nothing of the soul development or of the Divine Love, or of any of those attributes of the Father which were necessary to my becoming a redeemed spirit and an accepted child of God.

I am in the Second Sphere, where are many of my old comrades in arms, and many who were antagonistic in the great War of the Rebellion. But we are no longer enemies, for we have obtained sufficient

---

[87] Pope Gregory I (c. 540 – 12 March 604), commonly known as Saint Gregory the Great, was the head of the Catholic Church from 3 September 590 to his death in 604. Gregory is well known for his writings, which were more prolific than those of any of his predecessors as pope. Throughout the Middle Ages he was known as "the Father of Christian Worship" because of his exceptional efforts in revising the Roman worship of his day. (Source: Wikipedia) (G.J.C.)

Love to become friends, and to know that war and hatred and murder are not in accord with God's laws, or approved by Him; and we are now seeking only Love, and trying to apply the Golden Rule in our lives here.

Well, I am somewhat surprised that I can communicate with you in this way, for while I have attended some séances and made my presence known in other ways and by other manifestations, I never before had the opportunity to do so by this method of writing; and I must say, it is the most satisfactory of my experiences.

As this is my first appearance, and coming without an invitation, though some of your band which is here signified their assent, I do not feel that I should longer intrude.

Well, I have been interested in this great and bloody war, and have visited the scenes of many battles and the headquarters of the officers of both sides, and have heard their plans discussed, and have learned what their expectations were. It is rather early in the game to form an opinion as to the outcome, but judging from the facts, as I have been able to gather them, and from the conditions of the armies and means of carrying on the war, of both sides, I am rather inclined to think the Allies will win. This I say in a perfectly unbiased way, as I have no bias or prejudice for either side. But this I do know: that no human being can at all estimate the great injury that will be done to the various countries or to the progress of the human race in the things material.

But God rules, and the right will prevail, as I believe. Sometime later, if agreeable, I will write you further on this matter.

I will now say good night.

Your friend,

U. S. Grant.

Is the same as he was on earth; but seeing his former friends so changed by the Divine Love causes him to go with Mr. Riddle to learn the reason

October 19th, 1915.

I am here, General S____ (can't write name)

No, it seems not—how strange.

(White Eagle: He says his name was General Sherman and that he wants to write a letter.)

Well, I tried to write my name, but I could not—what do you think was the cause? Why, damn it, I have written my name more times than there are stars in the heavens, and yet I was not able to write it here. Well, that is what I called war—hell. I don't mean to be profane, but the idea, that I could not write my name....

Well, as Grant and I are very close friends here, as we were on earth, I thought that as he wrote a letter I would like to do so also. Just as he said about himself, I say, I am in some darkness and suffering—paying the penalties of my evil deeds on earth, and for what I neglected to do in the way of performing my duties when I had so many to perform, and so many opportunities.

I am in the same sphere with him, but he is in a higher plane, and is not in such darkness as I am. I am not a Christian yet, but hope to be sometime, as I have some dear friends here who are, and they are trying to persuade me to become a Christian; but as you may not know, I never could be persuaded on earth, and it is difficult to be persuaded here.

I am enjoying this new experience in writing to you, and to me this is very surprising, but is very satisfactory. I wonder how such a thing can be. I have attended séances when my earth friends have attended, and have tried to make myself known to them and to some extent have succeeded, but not in the way that I am doing now. I am afraid that if you are not careful I shall steal up on you and write many times so that you will wish that I had never come.

Well, my dear boy, I am certainly glad that you recalled these reminiscences. Of course, with all the people that I met in those days, I cannot remember you, as we only had a passing handshake, but I am certainly glad that you recalled those times, and more glad that I can be with you now; and things will be reversed now, for I will be the one who will not forget, while you, considering the great number of spirits who come to you to write, and the great number who are around you ready to write, I hardly expect that you will find time to give me much thought.

Well, I don't quite understand you, but if you can show me the way to obtaining such a condition of soul and such a degree of happiness, I will certainly accept your kind offer, and will try my best to follow your advice. But really, I don't see how you can accomplish this.

Yes, I remember Riddle very well, and he was a very dear friend of mine, but why do you ask that question? Is he involved in the redemption of me? He was a very dear friend, but I doubt that he can do what you seem to imply.

I have done as you advised, and I must confess my surprise to see Riddle in the band that you speak of—and what a beautiful and bright spirit he is. How in the world did he get in that condition, when on earth he was somewhat like myself—a free thinker—and cussed sometimes. But I must speak to him and learn what it means. Well, I have been introduced to your grandmother, and what a glorious spirit she is! I never before saw such spirits. They must live in spheres far above where I live.

Riddle says I am the same old, rough, wicked Sherman, and wants me to go with him, and I will go, and I will not forget to request a few words with your grandmother.

I will ask him (R.G.Ingersoll) now, and he seems so beautiful and bright too. What does it mean? Ingersoll says it means that he has become a believer in the Great Love of the Father and is a follower of Jesus Christ. What a surprise and what a change in Ingersoll.

My friend, I cannot write more as I am all upset by what I have seen and heard; so excuse me, I will say good night.

Your friend,
Wm. T. Sherman.

Is grateful that through Mr. Padgett the two Generals were able to find out about the Divine Love

October 19th, 1915.

Well, I am here, your Helen.

You have had some rather surprising communications tonight. We thought that it would be right to let the two old Generals write, as they seem to be so anxious; and I believe that they will find their salvation by having done so.

Mr. Riddle was very glad to have General Sherman come to him, and also General Grant, and he is now with both of them, telling them his experiences in the spirit world and the cause of his beauty and brightness.

And Ingersoll breaks in once in a while, and tells them that when they hear his experience in becoming converted to Christianity they will be more surprised than they were when the cannon balls blew across their quarters in the war.

So you see what good this little thing of being able to communicate with spirits is doing. Oh my dear Ned, I am so happy that you have this great opportunity of doing good, and I know that you feel the same way. It is late and you must stop writing.

So with all my love, I am
Your own true and loving
Helen.

Was Premier of Great Britain. Has deep feelings of horror at the war that is raging. Wonders why he is not in a higher sphere; still believes in the sacrifice of Jesus

November 6th, 1916.

I am here, Gladstone.

Yes, I was the Premier of Great Britain and I merely want to say that I desire to come to you sometime and write a message containing some of my views on the war that is now scourging the countries that were supposed to be Christian. Oh, the horror of it all! And how blind the rulers are to the welfare of humanity!

But I must not write tonight, as I have not sufficient rapport with you and my comments and intense feeling on the subject are so great that I doubt if I could continue at this time. But if you are willing, I will come again soon and write you. I am in the earth plane, but not in darkness. I was, as you may know, a churchman and defender of the faith and still am, and I believe in the doctrines of my church, but strange, as I sometimes think, that I am not more advanced in the progress to the higher spheres. But I suppose I must develop and that I am striving to do; and I attend to the duties of my church and worship as I did on earth, and have the same hope in the sacrifice of Jesus and the efficacy of his atonement. I rest in his promises and am with many of my friends of earth who worshipped with me when a mortal. I still believe in Jesus, my Lord, and feel that in his good time I shall go to him in his heaven of bliss.

I shall be glad to listen to you, for I have always found that something may be learned from others, no matter what their standing or condition is.

Well, I am glad that this way has been opened to me to communicate, for my country needs my advice, as I see that many errors of judgment have been made by those in authority. So thanking you, I will say good night.

Your friend,
Wm. E. Gladstone.

Confirms the Master communicating through Mr. Padgett

July 22nd, 1915.

I am here, St. George (of the Dragon).

I was a warrior, and not a saint. I was an enthusiast in the cause of the Christians against the Turks, and I fought and suffered and died; but as to my being a saint, I never was one more than was any other warrior who was stirred by the great cause which urged us to rescue the Holy Land from the infidels.

But, while I was never a saint, yet I was of a religious turn of mind and spiritual things appealed to my higher nature, and at times my soul felt the influence of the workings of the spirit world.

But I was never a real possessor of the Father's Love as I now am. Since my coming into the spirit world I have received this Great Love, and am now a follower of the Master in my belief in his teachings, and in my efforts to work for the good of humanity.

I now know what the Divine Love of the Father means, and how the possession of it fills the soul with happiness and immortality. I live in the Celestial Spheres and am a member of the Kingdom of Jesus.

So, I merely came to add one more testimony to the fact that through you the Master is working to save mankind from their sins and to extend his Kingdom of Love and happiness to all parts of the earth.

I will not write more now. So I will say good night.

Your brother in the cause,

St. George.

Has been seeking truth with his mind. Mr. Padgett tells him about seeking truth with his soul

March 22nd, 1915.

I am here, Garfield. I am J. A. Garfield, your old partner's friend.

I want to say that you are a very much favored man in having so many spirits of such high degree of development interested in you and your work as a medium. I have been with Mr. Riddle a great deal, and he tells me of the wonderful powers you have received in taking these communications, and the wonderful truths that have been communicated to you; and what great faith you have in prayer to the Father. So you see, I am interested also, and wish to say something regarding this spirit life and my experiences as a spirit.

I am now in the Third (Spirit) Sphere where Riddle is, and he and I frequently converse about these matters, and are seeking the truths with all our minds and souls. Well, I only know this way as a believer in the doctrines of my church, and what I have learned in addition since coming over here. I am not a believer in all that the Bible teaches, but only in the things that appeal to my reason. My faith in prayer is not very strong, nor in the possibility of becoming a spirit who may receive any great help from the operations of the Holy Spirit, which, as Riddle says, is the only influence that can surely redeem me from my sins or the result of them, and make me one with the Father. I cannot comprehend this teaching, and unless my reason can be convinced, I cannot be persuaded to accept the teaching as true.

So you see, I am still in the position that I was on earth—that is, unless my reason tells me that such a thing is true, I cannot believe. That may be so, but how can I do that? I am not a child who can believe everything that is told me, just because someone else says that it is true. No, I must learn from my own investigations.

Yes, there seems to be some force in that, but how can I use the instruments or faculties of the soul when I don't realize that they exist? Or how can I attempt to investigate any truths when, as you say, the means necessary to be used in such investigation I have no knowledge of?

Well, you might be right, I may be wrong. I will ask Riddle about these matters with an unbiased mind and listen to him attentively. Well, I perceive that you have great faith in the existence of these truths, and I promise you to devote my whole efforts to searching for the truth.

I have met some of them (Mr. Padgett's band), and they are all very beautiful and happy, especially your wife. She is a wonderfully beautiful spirit and so very loving and kind. I have talked with her a number of times, and she has told me of the wonderful love of the Father, as she calls it; but I thought that she was only an enthusiast, and a believer in some doctrine that the young could easily believe, and make by their faith a reality.

Question and answer.

No, but I will. I will ask for an interview with your grandmother, and I have no doubt that she will grant it. I will listen to her, as you say.

I do not know who you mean. When on earth I considered Jesus such a one as you describe, but I have not seen him here. Well, I am surprised, I must say. I thought that he was a part of the Trinity, and was away up in the heavens far from the sight of spirits. You certainly astound me. I certainly will. You must be an exceedingly good man to have such a relationship with the Master, God. Well, let me think of this. I am confused, and not able to think what it all means.

Well, when on earth I was a mere believer in the letter of the Bible. I did not realize what its spiritual teachings meant, and do not now. I was like thousands of others who profess to teach the truths of the Bible.

So you see, I am nothing more than an intellectual Christian. I do not yet see that this life is anything more than a mere continuance of the earth life, with the possibilities of greater mental progression and acquirements.

So you are my old instructor's late partner. Well, I am certainly glad to have this opportunity to write; only forgive my intrusion. I cannot express to you my appreciation of what you have told me. I want you to pray for me, as I know that your prayers will benefit me much. I did not know that I was causing you to violate the rules of your band, and ask your pardon for doing so. I wish further to say that your motives in permitting me to write have very much affected me, and I commence to think that your love for not only Mr. Riddle but for me must be more than usual among men. I will show you how much I appreciate your interest and kindness in doing what you say. So I will stop now.

Well, I had forgotten, but now that you recall it, I do remember, and felt so grateful that the message was conveyed to Riddle. Well, how strangely things happen. To think that your wife, whom I so much admire here now for her beauty and goodness, was the messenger for me on that occasion. It seems as if all things are working together for my good. I am so glad that I came to you tonight.

So with all my respect and spirit love, I am your own true friend, and searcher after the truth.

James A. Garfield.[88]

Comments on Mr. Garfield's writing, and his own progress

March 22nd, 1915.

I am here, your old partner.

You had a letter from Garfield. He was so anxious to write that I thought it would do no harm to let him try; and I am glad that I did, for what you said to him has impressed him very much, and, I believe, will lead to his seeking information on the subject of the New Birth. He is a wonderful spirit intellectually, and has progressed to a very great degree in the investigation of spiritual laws. So that on the whole his writing will do no harm to our band.

Well, I do not understand it, as he was a Christian on earth, and one would naturally suppose that he would have made inquiry for Jesus when he came over. But it seems he did not, why I don't know; but now that he realizes what you told him, he undoubtedly will seek the Master at the first opportunity. I shall endeavor to show him the way with all my heart and ability. Yes, I will soon. I am very happy and am progressing rapidly, and expect to soon be in the Fifth (Spirit) Sphere, where your father and Prof. Salyards are. Oh, my dear Padgett, I cannot tell you what happiness I am now enjoying. Well, I must stop.

Mrs. Riddle and Bert are advancing some, but they do not seem to get the light as rapidly as I hoped they would. But they pray, and, I think, are commencing to realize that God's love is waiting for them.

So with all my love, and many wishes for your happiness and success, I am

Your old partner and spirit brother,
A. G. Riddle.[89]

---

[88] This message is a composite of two, being originally published twice in Volume III. The second instance is not included in this edition. (G.J.C.)
[89] This message is a composite of two, being originally published twice in Volume III. The second instance is not included in this edition. (G.J.C.)

Confirms that Garfield wrote

March 22nd, 1915.

I am here, your own loving Helen.

Well, you had quite a letter from Garfield. He is certainly a wonderful spirit intellectually, as many spirits who come in contact with him say. But he is not very spiritual, I am sorry to say, and do hope that your conversation with him will help him and cause him to search for the truth. No, his writing to you did not interfere with our rapport.

Yes, I heard him, and when he meets your grandmother he will undoubtedly be impressed by her, for she is so beautiful and wise and powerful that he will realize that there is within her something that he knows not of.

Of course, when he meets with Jesus, he will wonder and listen in great astonishment, and will, I believe, become convinced of the necessity for his New Birth. Well, sweetheart, you must stop now.

So with all my love I am your own loving and devoted wife,
Helen.[90]

Writes of his studies of the material universe

January 21st, 1916.

I am the spirit of Galileo[91], and come to you to tell you a few things pertaining to the spirit world of science.

When on earth, I thought that my invention of the telescope was a most wonderful thing and that it would revolutionize man's knowledge of astronomy and the solar system, and to some extent it did. But what I saw and anticipated then was as a mere drop in the bucket to what I have learned of these matters since I have been in the spirit world, not bound by the limitations of space and sight.

I have explored these heavens, among the planets and the stars, and have discovered many truths in reference to them not even conceived of by men. I desire to come sometime and describe to you and explain to you these hidden truths so that man may have an enlarged

---

[90] This message is a composite of two, being originally published twice in Volume III. The second instance is not included in this edition. (G.J.C.)

[91] Galileo Galilei: (15th February 1564 – 8th January 1642), often known mononymously as Galileo, was an Italian physicist, mathematician, astronomer, and philosopher who played a major role in the Scientific Revolution. His achievements include improvements to the telescope and consequent astronomical observations and support for Copernicanism. Galileo has been called the "father of modern observational astronomy", the "father of modern physics", the "father of science", and "the Father of Modern Science". (Source: Wikipedia.) (G.J.C.)

conception of the great God whose creatures they all are. It is too late tonight to commence my discourse, and with your permission I will come at a later date. I live in the Sixth Sphere, where the intellect rules supreme and the wisdom of the ages is congregated.

Yes, I have seen Jesus, and sometimes he comes to our spheres, but he is not so much interested in these scientific matters as in disseminating the Divine Love, as he calls it. I do not know what this is, and am not much interested, as I find great happiness in the pursuit of my studies of the material universe.

I will stop now and say good night.

Galileo.

How the spirits progress in knowledge of the Truths

August 28th, 1917.

I am here, and want to say a word to my friend (Eugene Morgan), as I have not written for a long time.

I heard what was said in reference to protection being afforded Mr. Morgan when the Broker[92] calls upon him to write, and I desire to say that I will be present, and the priests will not have any opportunity to interfere, because I am stronger than any of these fellows of the popes and will not hesitate to use my power. Not that I do not want them to receive the benefit that so many of them have received in their communications with Mr. Morgan, but I realize the importance of what you are attempting to do, and the priests will have to wait a while in order to make their assaults.

I am progressing, and it seems to me that I am a different spirit altogether from what I was when I first came in contact, consciously, with you, and had my eyes and soul opened to the truth. I cannot tell you how much I am benefited by the messages I hear you read and discuss with your friends, and also by the explanation of the truth that Mr. Morgan so often gives to the spirits who come to dissuade him from doing his work.

It may seem strange to you that we are benefited by what you mortals may say as to the truths of the spirit world, and you may naturally suppose that we, being here in the spirit world, would more easily learn these truths from the higher spirits than learn the same from you; but the fact is that these higher spirits do not often come into our

---

[92] I am not aware of who this is. It would appear to be someone within Catholicism. A reference in the daily diary on the occasion of a message from John dated April 6th, 1917 suggests it might have something to do with advice regarding the stock market. It did appear that an attempt was made to alleviate Padgett's financial situation which appeared to be causing him some stress. (G.J.C.)

plane and disclose these truths, except when they come and communicate with you. Of course, we have spirits here who teach us truths, but these truths are not of so comprehensive a nature as what you receive. We are taught only as we progress and are fitted to receive the next lesson in advance, as you might say. This may not appeal to your reasoning in such matters, but it is a truth.

You are having revealed to you a wonderful plan of God for the salvation of man, and to be taught to men whether their conditions are such as to enable them to fully grasp the great significance of the truths or not. We are taught that plan only as we progress, and that truth or part of the truth is sufficient for us as we are at the time capable of applying or making it our own.

I merely thought that you would like to know just what the truth is in reference to our being taught and the manner in which we are taught by these spirits, whose work it is to open up to us the truths that may be embraced by us. So you see, we can learn of things by listening to your messages and the instructions that you and your friend and my friend may give us, where we cannot learn from our spirit teachers.

I am with him a great deal, and am his friend and protector so far as in my power, as I promised to be. I could not be otherwise, and he must not forget that among all the spirits here who love him, he has no more devoted friend than

Sam Ford.

Wants Mr. Padgett to write on Sunday

April 26th, 1917.

I am here, your own true and loving Helen.

Well, dear, I see that you are very happy tonight, and I am so glad and want you to feel that you have around you other spirits who are glad also. I will not write much tonight, but commencing Sunday night I wish that you will commence to receive the messages that are waiting to be written you, and there are many, and of the greatest interest and importance.

I was present when the Broker was writing to you, and I want to say that he is very much interested in the work and will do everything possible to make it a success. We are all interested in this, for we understand the importance of it and what great results will follow your getting in the position that you so much desire. Have faith and you will not be disappointed. Love me and believe that I love you.

Good night, my dear husband.

Your own true and loving

Helen.

Still working for his country

February 25th, 1917.

I am John C. Calhoun.

I come to say a few words in reference to our international affairs, and I say our, because I am still interested in my country and feel that I am a citizen thereof, although I am a spirit and not a mortal.

Well, as you know, when on earth I was a Democrat, and one who believed in the independent rights of the various states of the Union, and that whenever those rights were infringed upon it was the right of the state so affected to withdraw from the Union. But my contentions are now of no practical importance, for the decision of war has settled that question, and for the best, as I now see; for had the results been otherwise, our country would not now be the glorious and powerful nation that it is.

And I also believed in the absolute right of our country to enjoy all the benefits and privileges that any other country in its international affairs of government enjoyed, and if necessary to preserve such privileges, to resort to the force of arms. But I did not believe in becoming mixed up in foreign disputes, or in the grievances that one of these countries might have against another, or in recognizing the rights of one in preference to the rights of another.

In the present difficulties, were I now a mortal I should apply the same principles to the present war and leave the respective nations to settle their disputes by and among themselves. And yet, I realize that my country is not in the position of independence and isolation that it was when I lived, and that circumstances may occur and conditions may be established that will call for the application of principles and measures a little different from those that I have above indicated; and such circumstances and conditions now exist, as I can see, caused by the unusual claims and practices of Germany in attempting to destroy the commerce of not only the nations against whom it is contending but also the commerce of the neutral nations, and more largely, that of my own country. This the governors of the U.S. should not submit to for one moment; and to do so indicates on the part of those who control the affairs of the nation either an utter want of understanding of the requirements of the occasion, or a cowardice that has no excuse.

I fully realize that peace is desirable, and should be sought for and maintained whenever consistent with the country's honor and well being; but when peace is to be maintained at the sacrifice of honor and everything that goes to the welfare of the nation, then peace must be thrown aside and the necessary means, no matter what they may be, must be used to maintain and enforce the rights of the nation.

I see that Mr. Wilson is loath to enter into the war and is waiting in the hope and expectation that something will happen or not happen, whereby he may keep the country out of the conflict; but his waiting will be in vain, for the war is here now and the sooner he realizes that fact, and acts upon it, the better it will be, and the sooner the end will come.

Germany is desperate, and it has reason to be, and it will not hesitate to destroy our ships of commerce or of war when it possibly can, and the fact that the ship is an American one or carries American citizens or sailors will not deter its destruction. Then why wait until many of these ships shall be destroyed and many lives lost, before showing to Germany that the U.S. will maintain its rights and protect its people?

I have been trying to reach the ear of the President and also the ears of some of his legislators, in order to impress upon them the necessity for action; but have not been able to make the rapport, so that my thoughts could be received by these men. And I don't suppose that such a desire will ever be realized. And the pity is, that it is necessary.

Mr. Wilson is a man of intelligence and good intentions and patriotism, and it is a little difficult for those who cannot read his mind to understand the position that he takes. But to us it is plain that the great desire to keep the country out of war—which idea I must tell you has obsessed him and caused him to believe that by doing so he is winning the approbation of the people—causes him to be overcautious and certain that if war comes he shall not be the moving cause.

Of course, ordinarily this may be commendable, but in the present circumstances it is more than deserving of condemnation and in its results may almost prove to be criminal. If someone with influence could only awaken him from this condition of obsession and persuade him to act and act quickly, it would be a thing devoutly to be wished for. The war is here and its rumblings are approaching; and it does not require an experienced ear to catch the sounds of its approach.

Well, I have written more than I intended, and thanking you, will say good night.

Your friend.

John C. Calhoun.

Gives his experiences after receiving help from a Divine Spirit

May 1st, 1917.

I am here, Caesar.

Yes, I am the spirit of that Roman who thought himself of so much importance, and then realized that he was a very insignificant spirit in his place in the spirit world.

Well, I am glad to be able to write to you again, and especially so, as I can tell you that since I last wrote you I have progressed out of my hells and torment, and am now in the Third Sphere where there is so much love and happiness.[93] Now this may seem a little surprising to you, but it need not, for you will remember that when I last wrote to you I informed you that I would then go with the beautiful spirit that came to me at your suggestion, and listen to his words of wisdom, as I now know them to be, and seriously consider what he might say to me. Well, I went with him and he was so loving and patient, and seemed to have such great knowledge of the truths of God that I not only listened to him once but many times, and made a great effort to follow his advice.

I commenced to pray to the Father for the inflowing of that great Divine Love of which the good spirit told me, and continued to pray until I felt its inflowing, and the effect on my soul was wonderful, for as the Love came to me I found that the darkness left me, and also my sufferings, and with this Love came knowledge of these truths of which I had been told—I mean a convincing faith that these things were true. When I commenced to have this experience I continued to pray the harder and all the longings of my soul and mind and of every part of me that could have a feeling or aspiration went from me, and I continued to pray without ceasing.

As you may know, when on earth I was a very positive and striving person, and these characteristics I did not lose when I became a spirit, notwithstanding that I remained so many centuries in a state of stagnation and helplessness; for during all this time I knew of no goal to which I could aspire, and of no peace that was better than the one in which I spent the long dreary years of my spirit life.

But as soon as I found that there was a future condition of light and happiness, I entered with all the energies of my soul to seek for that happiness, and as I was told that my progress depended so very largely upon my own efforts, I permitted nothing to interfere with my strivings for the obtaining of this Divine Love, and thanks to the loving Father, I at last found relief from my torments, and fullness of love that brought to me bliss and the companionship of beautiful and loving spirits. But I must not neglect to say that in all this effort on my part, I had the help and prayers of many loving spirits who seemed so anxious that I should get this Love and become in harmony with the Father and His will: and now I am no longer the resentful and wicked Caesar, but a very humble and grateful child; for I am still but a child in the knowledge of the great

---

[93] The significance of this statement is that Julius Caesar was still in the hells from the time of his death in March 44 B.C.—about 2060 years—to the date of his first communication. But, once he learns how to get out by praying for the Divine Love, he gets out in no time at all - about 19 months. Three messages are published here, but they are not in date order. (G.J.C.)

truths of which I have heard so much, and in the Love.

Even now it is all so wonderful to me that I can hardly comprehend just what it all means. But this I know, that whereas I was for many long centuries a suffering, unloving and unloved spirit, seeking only solitude and nursing my resentment, I am now a bright, loving and beloved spirit, seeking and never tiring of the association of these bright spirits, with whom I am now making my home. And besides these, higher and grander spirits come to me, and encourage me to strive and pray, and tell me of the wonders that are before me and which can be mine.

I am of the last, but these spirits tell me that I may become of the first, and I feel that there is no power in all the hells that can, and no power in all the heavens that will prevent me from progressing and obtaining a home in the Celestial Heavens.

I desire also to say that I have come to you many times when the spirits were writing you the wonderful messages of truth, and I learned from them many truths that I have tried to make mine, and which have helped me so much and revealed to me some of the plans provided by the Father for the salvation of men and spirits.

You cannot conceive of the great number of spirits who are with you when these messages are being delivered, and how anxious many of them are to learn the truth and receive the help that these truths give of them. Many have found the light and happiness through the knowledge this conveyed to them, and further, through the help that these beautiful loving spirits give them; for it seems that whenever these spirits that are in darkness indicate a desire to learn the truth these high spirits are always ready and anxious to teach and help and comfort the dark ones.

I cannot explain to you how all this has not only astonished me, but caused me to regret that I let so many wasted years go by, without having sought the help of these spirits, for many a time they would come to me with their proffers of help and advice, but I would shun them and turn from them, not believing that they could help me. What a great mistake and how I paid the penalty of neglecting this way to salvation.

And I wish further to say that as a fact, if I had not come to you, through curiosity more than anything else, I would not now be in the condition that I am; for it was only after you talked to me and told me of the way in which I could obtain relief, and brought me in rapport with these spirits and advised me to listen to them, did I think of the possibility of my being rescued or being able to find any relief from my then unhappy conditions; and so I must express to you my gratitude for your kindness and, as you then told me, love for me.

Well, I am a different Caesar now. I will not write more, but as I told you before, I shall come sometime and write you a letter of some of my experiences on earth and in the spirit world during the earlier years of my life as a spirit. So hoping that you will pray for me and give me

your kind thoughts, I will say good night.
Your true friend,
Caesar (Julius).

Confirms that Julius Caesar wrote

May 1st, 1917.

I am here, your own true and loving Helen.

Yes, dear, it was Caesar who wrote and he is so happy and thankful that he can hardly contain himself in his desires to write to you. He is an earnest spirit now, and as he said, is striving with all the energy of his soul to obtain the Love in more abundance, and I can see that he will progress very rapidly.

Well dear, you experience every few nights the result of the work and the redemption of some poor soul who has failed to seek for this Love that only can make a dark and suffering spirit a bright and happy one in a short time. There is nothing like this Love. It is all by itself and so easy to obtain, and always waiting for the longing, and aspiring soul, either in spirit or man on earth.

Your own true and loving
Helen.

Is seeking for the Divine Love. Light is breaking into his soul

December 13th, 1916.

I am here, Caesar.

Well, I merely want to say that since I last wrote you I have followed your advice and have listened to the advice of the high spirits to whom you sent me, and I have been praying as they instructed me, and now I am in a much better condition than I was, and the view that I now have of life in the spirit world is very different.

I am still in some darkness, but light is breaking into my soul and consciousness, and I am commencing to realize that my fate as I have for so many years conceived it to be is not fate at all, and that my conception of what my fixed state was is all wrong, and was the child, if I may so call it, of my condition of mind and beliefs that came to me when I came to the spirit world and realized that the fact of my having been what the world called a great man on earth did not fit me for any greatness in the spirit world. I was then so disappointed and shocked by finding myself a naked spirit of qualities that brought me into darkness and suffering that I tried to avoid the association of all other spirits, and nursed my disappointment in isolation and the belief that for me there could be no change in my condition, or possible progress out of the awful lonesomeness and weariness of my soul.

And now, when I know how different the truth is, I feel that all these long years of my spirit life have been wasted, and I bewail the fate that held me so long in that condition of stagnation and pride and resentment and utter hopelessness. I am now so thankful that I came to you when I did and told you of my condition; and when I realize that my coming to you was more a matter of curiosity to be satisfied—that I could communicate with the mortal world than because of any hope of receiving any help or benefit that could possible come to me, I thank my curiosity.

When you told me the things that you did, I thought that you were an idle dreamer, and the recipient of some of the harmless vices that existed among the men of my earthly days who used to declaim upon the glories of the spirit world. I had no faith in them, and I had none in you; and it was only when I realized that you were so earnest in what you were declaring to me, and when I came in contact with the higher spirits that you called to my assistance and saw that they had in them something that I had not—and which I had never seen in any other spirit—did I commence to think that what you had told me might have some foundation of truth.

And I also thought that I could not make my condition any worse by listening to these spirits and learn what they had to tell me as to what they declared was the truth of spirit progress; and the more I listened the more interested I became. After a while I was convinced that there might be some truth in what they so earnestly asserted to be true, and as an experiment I concluded to follow their advice and seek for this wonderful love that they told me would not only relieve me from my darkness and suffering but would make a new spirit of me in body and soul.

And oh, the wonderful surprise and experience that came to me; for I am no longer the gloomy, despondent and isolated Emperor, but a mere spirit who recognizes that death is the great leveller, and that rank and position and greatness of earth do not in one iota determine the status of the spirit for position of exaltation. I am now in my consciousness a plain spirit, having those qualities only which the condition of my soul gives me, and realize that I must pursue the same course and suffer the same purgatory as must other spirits in the same condition of soul, be they princes or peasants.

Well, as I said, I am so thankful that this knowledge has come to me, for now I am rid of pride and ideas of superiority and all those things that had caused me to believe that the Almighty had treated me unjustly in not recognizing my earthly qualities and giving me a position which, as I believed, my greatness entitled me to. I resented all this and in my resentment, I became a spirit who fed on my imaginary injuries and thoughts that I would be sufficient unto myself, and not seek the favor of such a God. So you see what can be the effect of arrogance and pride and a self-glorious estimate of one small mind upon the possibility of a spirit's happiness and progress.

But now these things have left me and I realize that I am a nothing, except that I am a child of God and the object of His Love, as your spirit friends have told me and are telling me. And in my humility—and I am humble, for I want to tell you that my fall was great and the consciousness of my littleness extreme—I know that I need the help of the Father in order to become in the least degree a spirit of light. And I am praying and longing and seeking, oh so earnestly, for this Love. Caesar the once mighty is now Caesar the most humble and weak, but the most hopeful. I realize the greatness of God's mercy and the great possibility of its making me one of these glorious angels that came to you so often with their messages of truth and salvation to mankind.

I was considered on earth a man of brilliant mind and wonderful intellect, and what of this I had I still possess; and now that the way has been shown me, I am exercising these qualities to the best of my ability to help me in my search for truth and light.

I thought that I would write this tonight, for I know that you are interested in my advancement, and besides, it does me much good to tell you. I am praying and longing, and these spirits are praying with me; but as yet, I have not very much of this Love in my soul, but enough to know—I say know—that it is real and that it makes the hard, unbelieving soul open up to the inflowing in greater abundance of its Divine essence. The Father is good, and I am trusting Him; and with all the possibilities of my soul I am longing for its filling with this Love and the getting rid of all these century-old doubts and hardness of heart and unbeliefs.

I know the way and now I will never relapse into the state of mind that was mine for so many centuries; and I can say that Caesar has seen the beacon light of hope and the great sun of knowledge that these things which the loving spirits tell me are true. I must stop now, but as I progress I should like to come to you and describe my progress. I will say good night, and subscribe myself.

Your friend and well wisher,
Julius Caesar.

Writes that earthly position does not determine one's spiritual abode

September 16th, 1915.

I am the spirit of one who when on earth was called Caesar.

Well, there was only one real Caesar—all others by that name were merely imitations. I was Julius Caesar and was the Emperor of Rome and the conqueror of the Gauls and of the Egyptians.

I am now in a condition of darkness, and also suffering, from my deeds on earth, which were very wicked and numerous.

I am not an emperor now, but am a spirit who is in the condition of one who has no one to do him reverence—not the meanest of my former slaves deign to bow the knee or salute me as their superior. And why! Because in the spirit world a man is as his soul development makes him, and mine has been very much retarded by my want of belief and faith, as I now see.

I merely want to tell you this that you may know that no position on earth can determine the position of the person when he comes into the spirit world. I mean that the position of the man on earth does not in the slightest degree influence the position of this same man in the spirit world. Many of my slaves are higher in their development and in their spirituality than I am. Well, that may be, but I am in the condition that I say I am; I don't know of any such spirit and doubt if there be any.

I see some bright spirits and have asked for Prof. Salyards, and find him to be a most beautiful and bright spirit, and I am inclined to listen to what he may say. He says that he was well acquainted with my history on earth, as he had read many books dealing with my life and exploits; and he is glad to meet me and show me the way to a higher and happier condition of existence. I rather like him, and believe that I will go with him and listen to him.

Well, I will try.

So I will say good night, and good luck. I am your friend now, since you have shown such interest in me.

Julius Caesar.[94]

Confirms that Julius Caesar wrote

September 16th, 1915.

I am here, Helen.

Well, I came to tell you that you must not write more tonight, as you are not in a very good condition. You may not think so, but it is a fact, and it is best for you to stop.

It was Caesar, as I am told. He is not a very bright spirit, but maybe your old Professor may help him.

Well, they are not quite ready yet to resume their writing, as it

---

[94] This was the very first message from Caesar, and in this message he returns nineteen months later to confirm he is now out of the hells. (G.J.C.)

seems there are some of these ancients who want to write, and have some object in writing to you which conflicts with the plan that these messages of the Master intends to be established and worked out. I must stop now and will say good night.

Your own true and loving
Helen.

Expresses gratitude to Mr. Padgett

April 12th, 1917.

I am here, Grover Cleveland.

Let me say a word, too. I am your friend and desire to say just a few words about what has just been written you, and of the necessity of keeping up your faith in what has been promised you, and your courage.

Of course, I am not of the higher spirits, but I am in the soul spheres of the spirit world, and it is so, as I am very happy to say, very largely because of your advice and help and consequently, you must know that I feel very grateful. I have not written you for a long time, and I have no doubt that you wonder who I am that is thus writing you; but in your wonder, think that I am a most grateful spirit, and one who desires to help you all that he can.

I acted on your advice and listened to the high spirits who came to me and told me of the wonderful plan of God for the salvation of men and the making of their souls pure and like unto His in Love; and I, at last, to an extent, believed what they told me and prayed and hoped and continued to pray, and found that my prayers opened up the way to the Father's Love, and to His Kingdom of Light and Happiness.

It was surprising to me how simple the plan is, and how the true longings of the soul will bring to itself this great Love, for I found that as I longed and desired in true earnestness, this Love was present, always present and not afar off to be searched for. Now the Father must love the souls of mortals and spirits!

Well, now I am in the Third Sphere and in the association of spirits like myself who are filled with this Love to the extent that they are in great light and happiness, always striving for more Love, yet always contented. You may not understand this seeming paradox, but it is true, contented yet striving for more. And this is because this great Love of the Father has in it those qualities that bring a satisfying happiness and, the same time, creates a desire for more love.

Well, my friend, I desire to tell you this because I know that you are interested in knowing something of my experience in the spirit world, and are pleased to know that I can call myself one of the redeemed. And now, knowing the truth of the Father's Love, and what its possession means to a spirit, I feel a great desire to tell you that what you first told me of is a thing of reality and that when you instruct spirits as to this Love and the Way to obtain it and happiness, you are conveying to them truths that are as real as the existence of our spirit world and the soul of men therein.

I heard what the other spirits wrote you tonight and also want to urge you to have faith for I know this; that all the powers of these high spirits are being exercised in your behalf, for they say that you have a work to do, that only you can do. What a wonderful thing to contemplate! I do not yet understand it all, but this I do know, that you seem to be of great importance to these spirits.

I am now much more interested in spiritual matters than in the war that your country has just entered, for I now see that among men and in their short lives on earth, wars and all such calamities are mere incidents, and do not determine the destinies of men in the great eternity, except as the individuals may or may not by their thoughts and desires carried into action, contaminate the conditions of their own souls and fit them for the hells and punishments that follow.

If men would only understand that, after they become spirits and possess some of this Divine Love, the mortals of earth, all alike, become their brothers, and nationalities and race distinctions disappear to the spirit's consciousness! All are brothers and the possible recipients of this Love.

But still, while we have no particular interest in nations as such, yet we have with us individuals and sympathize with them and love them, and are glad when those things which bring upon them unhappiness and misery cease to exist; and we try to exercise our influence for good on those who have the administration and directing of national affairs, and in this way we are interested in the war.

To us there comes no feeling of bias or prejudice against any nation, or desire that any one nation shall become victorious, except as we see the men of one nation are in their advocacy of principles and justice more in accord with the righteousness and truth than another, and then we are on the side of truth and use our influence for its success.

In this war, I think that the Germans and their Allies will be unsuccessful and believe that the war will soon end. But this is for man to determine, though we are exercising our influence to bring about this determination.

I will not write more tonight, but as I progress, which the higher spirits tell me I will do, I will come to you and write you of my progress.

With my love and gratitude, I will subscribe myself,
Your brother in Christ,
Grover Cleveland.

Comes to Mr. Padgett for help

August 13th, 1915.

I am here. Grover Cleveland.

Let me write just a line. I am a man who when on earth was prominent in the affairs of the nation, and who when I became a spirit, realized that my prominence on earth did not help me one particle in my soul's happiness, or in finding a home where goodness and congenial spirits live.

I was not a very religious man in the sense of soul development, although I attended church quite regularly and gave the appearance of being a Christian.

But, I realize now that something more than mere attendance in church is necessary to the development of the true Christian character or to fit a spirit to inhabit the heavenly places in the spirit world.

I was Grover Cleveland, and it is not necessary to tell you what my official position was, as I passed over so recently that all the citizens of my country know. But I do want to say that had I served God in spirit and truth, as I tried to serve my country and its interests, I would not now be in such an unhappy condition as I am. I am in the earth plane, and am in darkness and suffering, and am very unhappy.

I am led to believe by my training when a boy that I must stay where I am, but when I think on the matter in a reasoning way, it does not seem to me that a just God would impose eternal punishment upon me for the sins I committed in the short earth life that I lived.

I am surrounded by many spirits who are in a similar condition to my own, and who were not especially wicked men when on earth, and yet the recollections of the sins and evil deeds which they committed while on earth seem to be sufficient to keep them in this darkened condition with accompanying suffering.

Yes, I find among these darkened spirits a great many of my old political friends as well as my political enemies; and sometimes we talk over the affairs and life of the past, and unanimously conclude that the lives we led were not worth the fame or prominence that we attained to—that it was all vanity, and that we sacrificed our future happiness for the enjoyment of the moment. What a farce it all was, except as we did some good to our country.

But it is too late now to wish to undo these things and what we are now doing and what we may do in the future are the things that interest us now. Some of us say that our condition is not fixed and that in the future we will be relieved of this darkness and suffering, and see the light of a happier life among better surroundings and in the association of better spirits. But none of us know the way to find this relief or to bring ourselves to this light.

Of course, most of us know what the Bible teaches on this subject, but most of us believe that it teaches us that our time of probation was while we were on earth, and that now we must remain as we are until the great judgment day.

Well, as you say, it does seem strange that we should have such belief, but let me tell you that when the mortal becomes a spirit, he finds that all the importance of his earth life and the self-conceit and self-independence leave him; and he realizes that he is a very insignificant person, and that his self-independence is a myth and that he is the most helpless creature in all the universe. Such is my experience, and having nothing upon which I can stand as a fixed foundation of truth, I naturally go back to my childhood beliefs and they become a part of my existence.

I have met some spirits who claim that there is redemption for me and a way to get out of my present condition, but I did not think that they knew any more about it than I do, and hence I never paid much attention to them.

But as you remind me, if Jesus went into the hells to preach to the lost souls in prison, he would not have gone there for that purpose unless he could have done them some good by his preaching. I had not thought of this before, and I will think of it now and attempt to find some consolation in it.

But, you also say that you know that there is just as much probation for me in my present condition as there was for me when on earth. Now how do you know this? Of course you can speculate, but that will not satisfy me, as I can speculate also. I want facts. Do you know of any spirits who were in my condition and who have been relieved of their darkness and sufferings? If you can show me that you do, then I will commence to hope.

I remember hearing of Mr. Riddle while I lived in Washington, and I should like to meet him as a spirit, especially in view of what you say his condition and experience as a spirit were.

I see some spirits here who are very beautiful, and they say that they are of your band, and they are working for the redemption of spirits who are in darkness and suffering. One is especially glorious in her beauty and brightness, and she says that she is your grandmother, and that she has heard what I have written and is willing and anxious to show me the way to light and happiness, if I will permit her to do so. And why should I not? What a glorious beauty hers is, and how love seems to flow from her very being! I will accept her invitation and not wait longer to find relief. So I want to thank you for your kindness.

I will go with your grandmother, and will come to you again, and if I find the relief that I so much need I will thank you with all my heart

for your kindness in having permitted me to write to you.
I will say good night.
Your friend,
Grover Cleveland.

Writes of her happiness in the Third Sphere

May 16th, 1916.

Let me write a line. I am your cousin Alice, and it has been a long time since I wrote you; and as I saw you a few nights ago when you spoke to Mame at the show, I have since had a great longing to write you and tell you my condition now and how happy I am. Mary's mother and I were with her at the time and we saw you speak to her and heard you tell her that you had recently received a letter from her mother. Of course, she scarcely believes it, but nevertheless she has in her heart a longing that it may be so, for she dearly loved her mother when on earth, and now thinks of her very often.

Well, I am still in the Third Sphere, but I am so very happy and have such a beautiful home and lovely surroundings, and beautiful and good associates. I never on earth conceived such happiness or such a home, and such companions. It is one long dream of joy and freedom from sin and unrest. I mean that I now have nothing to make me unhappy as I had on earth. I am still praying to the Father for more Love, for Helen and your mother come to me often and tell me that I must continue to pray so that I may progress to the higher spheres where so much greater happiness may be found. And they help me very much. And what beautiful spirits they are! Helen seems to love me so much and to be so filled with the Divine Love.

Well, Ed, you thought she was beautiful on earth, but you should see her now! You simply have no conception of her beauty, and if I could write for a whole year trying to describe it to you, I could not succeed and you would not comprehend. How thankful I am that she came to me with her love and showed me the way to this Heaven of Bliss. Oh, it is wonderful to know that there is a Heaven and that I am eating its fruits and drinking from its river of life.

I must not write longer.

Well, Aunt Mary is progressing very much. She is not yet with me but she is very happy and free from all darkness and suffering, and has some of the Father's Love in her soul and knows how to pray and is doing so. She will soon progress and then I will see more of her. So pray for us both that we may get more of the Divine Love.

I will stop now, but first I want to tell you how much I enjoy writing to you and how much I love you.

So with all my love I will say good night.
Your own true cousin,
Alice.

The limitations which mortal man places upon his perception of the laws governing the universe

January 6th, 1919.

I am here, Francis Bacon.

Let me write just a few lines, as I desire to tell you of a thing which may be of importance to you.

I see you are a little disturbed over what a man said to you tonight as to his want of belief in the identity of the spirits who profess to manifest themselves through mediums. Well, this need not disturb you one particle, for the identity of the spirit is just as real and certain as is the fact that a man can and does identify another after an absence, more or less long, from the latter's appearance, voice, and so forth. In the case of his identification he depends on the operation of certain of his senses, such as his sight and hearing, and through them he satisfies his mind that the man identified is the identical person that he may claim to be, as you may say, he would be a very silly man if he would not accept such identification as convincing and determinate.

In the case of the identifying of those who are in the spirit, and who come with the powers and with the presence of spirits only, he cannot, of course, use his senses for the purpose of identification; and if he had to depend upon these organs alone, he would never be able to conclude that the spirits who present the phenomena are those who profess to be his friends or acquaintances. Most mortals do not have the gift of perceiving, or receiving the impression of, the presence of spirits, and in such cases are in the condition of the blind and deaf man with reference to the things of earth. The latter has no means of identifying his closest friends, and yet it would be just as reasonable to contend that these friends are not existing and present, and the same day after day, as for mortals to say that the spirits of those who once lived on earth are not existing and present, because the mortals have not the faculties of seeing and hearing them. There are things in earth life as well as in spirit life that can come to the knowledge of some men only through information given them by other men who have superior powers and faculties for seeking for and obtaining this information.

Some mortals have eyes and faculties not material, as usually understood, for seeing and hearing and receiving knowledge from the spirits, and who render what is thus seen, heard and received just as real and certain as are real and certain the presence of mortals and material things to those who have their physical organs of sight and hearing; and the identity of what is seen and heard and received is just as truly established in the former as in the latter case. All men who are wanting as to the nonmaterial organs mentioned can identify the things of the material world and are satisfied of the fact; and make their mode of such identification the standard by which they must and only can become convinced of the identity of the things of the spirit world: and when they insist upon such method of identification they, of course, can never be convinced, except perhaps in those phenomena as are manifested in materialization and spirit photography.

When the merely physical powers or means of ascertaining the existence and identity of things or humans are used, then those who confine their search for truth and the discerning of the identity of claimed existences to the use of such physical organs will never be able to see, hear or receive that which might convince them of the identity of the things existing in the spirit world.

This is the result of the eternal laws of the universe in their operations; and no desires or efforts of man can change this result. Man is unfortunate when he assumes the position that unless these laws can be or are changed in order that he may by his physical organs see or hear or be able to identify the things of the spirit world, he will not believe that there is identity existing among the spirits who come to men and in various ways manifest their presence.

When a man stands on the compliance with this condition as necessary to convince him of the identity of those friends of his who have passed to spirit life and who come in psychical phenomena and manifest themselves, it is useless to try to convince him, because of the very necessities of the laws governing such phenomena. And those who do believe, and those who know of this identity will only waste time and effort in trying to convince men who assume the position of depending entirely on the physical means which they may possess.

There are many humans today who are truly convinced, and have all sufficient grounds for their convictions as to the identity and presence of their spirit friends, and they are not deceived, but enjoy the happiness that comes to them from such knowledge.

In my observations of the workings of human minds upon this question of the existence and identity of spirits, I learn that such evidence as would satisfy their minds, under the strictest requirements, as to material things, is brushed aside as wholly inadequate, and sometimes not even worthy of consideration, to satisfy them as to these spiritual things; and it seems that the greater knowledge they possess of the nature of and laws controlling material things, the less credence and consideration will they give to the nature of and laws controlling spiritual things. Every other explanation of psychical phenomena is put forth and accepted, rather than the simple and natural one; and if men only knew what nature really is, and its laws, they would realize how little they now know of nature. Generally, nature is only that consciousness of things material which comes within their limited cognition. They do not know that the larger part of nature, if it can be separated, is beyond the things or conditions which they have knowledge of as being the material of the universe.

Well, as I said, the identity of the spiritual cannot be and must not be expected to be established by the operations of the merely physical organs of man, except perhaps in those manifestations appearing in the phenomena of materializations or spirit photography, and even they are not accepted as real or true by many men who accept what are called scientific deductions from supposed facts connected with the manifestations of what these men consider to be natural.

And so the proof of the presence and identity of spirits will have to depend upon the results produced by the operations of laws controlling the spiritual existences and the psychical powers and gifts of certain humans, Sometime it may be that these gifted persons will be accepted as honest and truthful and not self-deceived, and the manifestations resulting from the exercise of these powers as the effects of the efforts and intelligence of spirits who at one time were human beings.

When men come to realize that the change called death does not destroy identity and consciousness and powers of mind, as well as what may be called powers physical—for the material of the universe is used and operated by spirits—but on the contrary, intensifies these possessions and powers, then they will accept the truth that the presence of the spirits of their departed friends is a variety, and that the identity of these spirits is eternal.

Well, I have written as much as I think best to write tonight, and thank you for your indulgence. With kind regards, I will say good night,
Your friend,
Francis Bacon.

Comments on an article written by James Hyslop on Christianity and Spiritualism regarding laws which operated in certain miracles of Jesus

November 20th, 1918.

I am here, Francis Bacon.

I have been with you tonight as you have read, and was somewhat interested in what James Hyslop had to say in his article on Christianity and Spiritualism, and many things that he puts forth are true, and explain very satisfactorily why many of the miracles, so called, of the Bible, may be believed. As he says, they are not different in the nature of their operations or in the exercise of the law that produced them, from the physical phenomena which are manifesting themselves at this time among the investigators of Spiritualism; and, if today, the same law in its force that was brought into operation by Jesus and the disciples, could be called into operation, the same or similar phenomena would be produced. Of course, a great deal depends upon the medium and the amount of rapport that may be created by the communicating or rather operating spirit, for it must be understood that all the supposed miracles were the results of the work of spirits, who by reason of the harmony existing between themselves and the mortals, were able to call into operation the laws which were necessary to produce the results called miracles.

At the present time, there may not be persons who have sufficient development of these psychic powers, which were possessed by Jesus and the others, to produce such phenomena as they produced; but there have been many mortals since his time sufficiently gifted with these powers to cause manifestations very similar to those of the primitive Christian times, especially as regards healing and the like; and today much healing is being performed by mortals, and which is attributed to various causes, such as mental healing and faith cures, but which is really due to the exercise of spirit powers by spirits whose duties are to perform that kind of work.

Mortals, of themselves, cannot bring into operation any of these laws, either of mind or soul, but are dependent upon the cooperation of spirits who use some of the properties possessed by these mortals to bring into exercise the laws which only can produce the healing.

And here I desire to state, that it is not necessary that the mortal be of a highly spiritual development in order that the powers of the spirit world may effect and change the conditions of the material of earth for the laws which central the material are sufficient, ordinarily, to bring about the healing of the physical or mental diseases of men, and therefore, you will find many mediums, and others not recognized as mediums, having this power of healing.

The healing of the body and the healing of the soul require the workings of different laws, and while spirits not having very much soul development, may successfully cooperate with mortals in like condition, in healing bodily ills, yet such spirits are impotent to heal the diseased soul or the purely spiritual condition of men. But spirits who have the power to produce the latter healing, may also heal the body. And this you must know that no spirit who is not what may be called, physically whole or sound, can cause the healing of a physically diseased mortal, for power of this kind can be possessed by and proceed from only those spirits who in their material nature are perfectly healthy and sound. These spirits, while they have cast off the gross, physical material of the mortal, yet are still material so far as the spirit body and form and the properties which compose the same, are concerned.

The material of the universe is not confined to or entirely comprised in what mortals may suppose to be the only material, that is that which may be sensed by their five senses or some of them. What is of itself material is always material no matter what form it may assume, whether visible or invisible to mortals; and the larger portion of the material of the universe is in the invisible world, though subject to transformation into the visible, and retransformation into the invisible, and the laws governing and controlling the material are the same, whether that material be to men visible and knowable or not.

This material has its quality of persistence after supposed death or destruction, although the form of its manifestation be changed; and from this you will see that he who is known as the materialist, with his supposed want of belief in immortality or the continuity of existence, is in error even as to the material world of which he assumes to have special knowledge, and being in error as to this, how can he claim to be right when he asserts that the purely spiritual has no possibility of continuity of existence or, as some understand, immortality.

Well, I have written enough, and feel that you will pardon my intrusion; but I also feel somewhat justified in writing as I have done. With best wishes. I am,
Your friend,
Francis Bacon.

The designer of the Great Pyramid of Gizeh in Egypt

July 22nd, 1915.

I am here, Anaxylabis.

Let me tell you about the great pyramid of Gizeh. I want to do so in detail, as I was its designer, and I built it under the direction of the great Egyptian king, Monyabasis the Great, who lived many centuries ago, before Rameses, who is credited with its construction. I know that mankind has no records which tell of the reign of this monarch, but such records did exist, and in them was contained the history and the description of the occasion which called for the building of this great pyramid.

These records were destroyed long before the present extant histories of the world were written — long before the Book of the Dead was written and long before any of the present kingdoms of the earth had their beginnings. Centuries and centuries have passed since that time and no man has knowledge of what was then the condition of the human race or, as I should say, speaking for myself, of the race that inhabited the region of what you call the Lower Nile. We were a race of a great intelligence, and of what you would now describe as a wonderful civilization. Many of our arts and sciences disappeared from earth and have never been rediscovered, and may never be, for that race no longer has communication with the present race.

I came tonight because I saw pass me by wonderful spirits of light and beauty, evidently bent on some great mission; and I followed them and found myself with you. Listening to the communications which they gave you, I found that there came to me a desire to write also. Well, as I listened I soon saw that the communications were written in a language different from my own, and that you understood only that language and that I must write in that language to make myself understood; so I commenced at once to learn it and I learned it in the short space of time that I listened to them in their communications. This may seem impossible to you, but I can read the thoughts of spirits and men without difficulty, and as all thoughts in the spirit world require no language such as you understand, I soon found that I could clothe my thoughts in your words as I am doing now.

Well, I know it may not be very satisfactory to you, but it is true, and I cannot more clearly explain it so that you may comprehend it. Well, I have diverged or digressed from my intention of telling you what the design of the great pyramid was, and I find that I have written too long to attempt it now, as this is my first effort at writing. So I will postpone it until later, but I will come and give you the explanation.

I don't know in years, but when the Egyptian Book of the Dead was written I had lived as a spirit many thousands of years. I must stop now and say good night.

Anaxylabis.

A spirit who has received the Divine Love writes of his efforts to awaken other spirits to the true religion

I am here, Leander Albright.

Let me write a few lines. I am the spirit of one who passed from mortal life to spirit a great many years ago in a country very far from this place, and I am now in the higher spiritual spheres striving to progress to higher and higher spheres.

I merely want to say that I know the reality of the truth of the Divine Love, and how it makes a man more in unison with the Father, as he receives it more abundantly in his soul.

Many here who are in the higher spiritual spheres do not know what this Love is and do not seem to care to know, because they are very happy in the development of their mental faculties and natural love, and cannot be persuaded that there is anything greater or more desirable for them to obtain. My work is to try to awaken these spirits to the truth of true religion, and to show them the way to eternal life and at-onement with the Father. This task is difficult to perform, and the indifference of many of these spirits is so fixed that the process of awakening their souls is very slow, and to one who does not know the truth and the necessity for teaching them the way, the work would be quite disheartening.

I have recently learned the fact that spirits communicate through you, and I have become much interested and am endeavoring to help spread the truths of the Father. Jesus is working with you, and I see him write you quite often in his endeavors to reveal these truths.

Your wife says that I have written enough and must stop. So I will say, with my love, good night.

Leander Albright,
late of Aberdeen, Scotland.

The Truths that an author has learned since passing into the spirit life

December 26th, 1918.

Let me say a word.

You are not doing the wise thing in reading that book, (Scientific Demonstration of a Future Life[95]) for it is very largely speculation and that which leads to untruth and harm.

The writer knows now that his hypothesis of the dual mind is all wrong, and that he has the same mind now that he had when on earth, and that no part of that mind died with the death of the body. He also knows that spirits do communicate with mortals, and the subjective mind, as he calls it, does not among mortals furnish the means of communication or suggest the information that is contained in the psychic phenomena. He also knows that the mind is not the soul, but one

---

[95] Scientific Demonstration of a Future Life was published in 1904. The author Jay Hudson had previously published:
    The Law of Scientific Phenomena
    The Divine Pedigree of Man
    The Law of Mental Medicine
    The Evolution of the Soul.
There is not universal acceptance amongst followers of the Padgett Messages about the role of evolution. We have been advised by some recent communications that James Padgett was biased towards the notion of creation rather than evolution, as regards the human body, but one does not know if this message here is his bias, or the current belief of this spirit. A cursory glance at the contents of this book suggests the author believed in evolution, and also believed that there had been an evolution of the soul as well. (G.J.C.)

of its attributes merely, and that it is controlled by the soul and the will.

Many other things besides, he now knows, and is convinced that man is not the result of evolution, but is the immediate and direct creation of God, and that he has no relationship to the brute animal. Sometime he will come and write you fully on these subjects, if you will permit him to do so. Good night,

the author Jay Hudson.

A Celestial Spirit wants to assure Mr. Padgett that they are really the spirits they represent themselves to be and do not doubt them

February 13th, 1917.

I am here, mother.

Let me say just a word, as I have heard the Master's message and I am glad that he has given you the assurance that he has, for his love and care means to you so much more than you can possibly realize. He is so very loving and gracious and powerful, and when he comes to you he means to bring with him a glory that is not with him ordinarily as he works in this earth plane.

Well, I love you too, with a greater mother's love which now fills my soul and makes me so happy and contented in the knowledge that I am an immortal child of the Father. I know that sometimes you feel discouraged and almost believe yourself alone and that we are possibly not what we tell you we are and then we try the harder to reach your soul and consciousness with our love so that these feelings may leave you and we generally succeed and are happy when we do so. Many of your friends are here tonight and you have around you a wonderful amount of love and effort to make you realize that you are not alone and you must try to believe what I say.

I am very happy and progressing all the time for I am now higher in the Celestial Heavens than when I last wrote you and so is Helen, bless her dear heart, and of course, your grandmother has progressed and she has become a wonderful spirit all glorious and shining. The spirits who sometimes write about her and who live in the lower spheres of course never see her as she really is for they would not be able to withstand her glorious appearance. But she brings her love with her to these lower spheres and these spirits can feel the influence of that love and do so.

She says she will come soon and write you a message of truth. All send love and of course your mother gives and leaves with you her love in all its abundance. And I am happy also, my dear boy. Keep your faith and trust and even though you may live the years that you have been told you, yet they will be short and then you will be with us and

your happiness will be great.
>Good night and God bless you,
>Your loving,
>Mother.[96]

Is sorry that she cannot permit an old friend of Mr. Padgett to write but is happy with Jesus' letter to him and that of his mother

February 13th, 1917.

I am here, Helen.

Well, there was a spirit who was very anxious to write and I was disposed to let him do so, but as you are tired and are not inclined to have others write tonight, I told him that he would have to postpone his writing until another time.

Who was it?

It was your poor friend William Perry and he was so disappointed that he could not write. He is still in a very sad and dark condition and does not seem to be able to progress much out of his sufferings. We have been trying to help him but his belief that he came here to suffer eternally still holds him in his dark and suffering condition. I believe though that a conversation with you may do him good. He is still waiting here. He says he will come and I know that he will wait anxiously for the time to come.

Well, dear, I am glad that the Master wrote you tonight such a letter of love and encouragement for it will do you good. Try to follow his advice especially pray more to the Father. We are all so anxious that you get in the condition of which the Master spoke, for it will help you so much in your own development.

I love you as you know with all my heart and soul and so does your dear mother, who wrote you. She was so happy in doing so and she is a beautiful spirit, as she told you we have both progressed and we are nearer the fountainhead of God's love and it appears more real and divine the nearer we approach. I will not write more now as it is late.

Well, I will not forget and soon I will write and you must be convinced that I have not forgotten. Well, we thought it best not to write

---

[96] It might appear that this message does not refer to the message of Jesus of the same date, but it seems that the Jesus' message has had a considerable amount of personal stuff removed. This is obvious from the diary entry for the same date on the Tablet. (G.J.C.)

then, for the reason that I have told you but hereafter when you are ready in the early evening we will write, even though we may have to appear a little unkind to these dark spirits, we will explain to them and I think that they will be contented.

Well, my dear, feel that I am very true to you in my love and let not your mind be troubled, but love me with all your heart and you will realize that I am,

Your own true and loving,
Helen.

Had all his disciples and apostles and those called saints attend his writings to convince Mr. Padgett that he really selected him to do his work on earth

July 22nd, 1915.

I am here, Jesus.

I am here to tell you that you have had a cloud of witnesses as to your being selected to do my work, and you have wondered why so many of my disciples and apostles and those called saints should come to you in such close succession, and all testify as to that one fact. Well, I caused them to come as I wished to establish your faith as to my being the true Jesus of the Bible, and as to your mission in regard to my work.

So now let all doubt leave you, and let your faith grow until you will never hesitate to believe, no matter what surprising communication may come to you.

I am glad that you are feeling better tonight, and if you will only believe in my promises you will have cause to feel very much better in the near future. I do not intend to write more tonight, but soon will give you another message.

Yes, they were the persons they represented themselves to be. We will not permit any imposters to write. Yes, that is true they were actually the old prophets, and they were much interested in your ability to write. They will come again.

I must stop now.

Good night, your loving brother and friend,
Jesus.

Advises Mr. Padgett to take his daughter to a séance to prove to her that there is truth in spiritualism

May 7th, 1916.

I am here, Jesus.

I come tonight to tell you that tomorrow night I will deliver my message and I will not disappoint you and I hope that you will be in condition to receive it. Tonight you are in very good condition and I would write tonight but its rather late to commence as it will take some little time to transmit the message and I desire it to be done when you have plenty of time and not quite so tired physically as you are tonight.

You have had a pleasant evening with your daughter and your soul condition is in a very well developed state and you have much love in your heart.

If you will only pray more and let your thoughts turn more to things spiritual. You will continue in this state of soul perception and be able to receive my message as I may come to you. I will try to make my message as plain and convincing as possible and I think you will be much benefitted by it.

I am with you more than you think trying to help you and encourage you in your work and business and as you see, things are getting better, only give your attention to your business and it will increase and you will get in condition that will cause your worries to leave you. I love you as an elder brother and a spirit who knows what love means and you must have faith in me and think of me and my nearness to you.

Yes, I will be with her and help her and protect her from evil and try to make her happy. She is very happy tonight and is commencing to love you as a daughter and very soon you will see the differences in her affections and demonstration of her love. You will soon be together in your home and then you will both be happy in keeping up your courage and have faith and all these things that you desire will become yours.

I will not write more tonight.

Question and Answer:

Yes, she is very mediumistic and I think it advisable to take her to the séance for it will convince her that there is truth in spiritualism and she will then commence to think more of the subject and soon become thoroughly convinced and the power will develop itself in her and will work to her good.

So with my love and blessings, I will say good night.
Your brother and friend,
Jesus.

Writes that as his soulmate, her love for him is greater than for her children, who will not need her in the great future of eternity

I am here, Helen.

You feel so lonely today, but remember that I am with you and love you with all my heart and soul and will help you to be happier. The pictures are not so good as I thought they would be when taken, but now it makes no difference for they are merely images of the physical appearance and now I am a spirit with all the beauty that God's Love in my soul gives me. So think of me as your spirit wife rather than as your mortal wife who has left you. Be only true to me in your thoughts and love and you will not be unhappy because of the past.

I am now a spirit that has so much of God's Love in my soul, that I have almost forgotten the unhappiness of my later life on earth, and you are the one thing that binds me to earth. Of course my children also keep me with them, and will, as long as they live, but they are not to me as you are. You are my soulmate as I have told you, so that they will not need me as you will in the great future of eternity.

When you are so very lonely, think that I am with you and am loving and trying to make you happy. And will not leave you alone for a moment. My love is so great that I can scarcely keep from trying to take you in my arms and bring you over now, but as you know that would not be in accordance with the plans of the Master and so you and I must both wait until you have accomplished your work. But after all it will not seem very long, for you will have me with you all the time and I will realize that I am with you dear, that our love is burning and only needs our trust and to try to enable us to enjoy it both further. So do not feel down hearted or lonely, my own dear soulmate for you are mine and I am yours and nothing can separate us either in earth or in heaven.

Yes I know, we were all there and seen how you prayed to the Father and how your soul was filled with His Love. He was very near you and we were so happy in the knowledge that He was. He is your God as well as ours and when you pray as you did, you will always receive the Love and Blessings of the Father.

You are a very much favored man in having the Love of the Father, so much in your soul and when I think that you will someday be with me, and that we will both have this Great Love to such an intense degree, I felt that our happiness will be beyond compare. So you need not worry about the future, for I know that when you come over you will find that your soul possesses so much of this Love that no question of doubt or unbelief in the efficacy of this love will arise in your soul. You will be with me and we will progress together to the higher spheres where they tell me happiness is supreme. So be content to do your work and love God and me until the great day of rejoicing comes when you will meet me at the portals of the spirit world and feel my arms about you and my love and kisses on your lips and face. You are my own dear Ned.

Yes he was, and you felt his influence, for he loved you very much and said that you are his own true disciple and brother and that your soul shall become filled with this great love before many days. He (Jesus) seems to love you so very much that we all wonder at it, not that we don't want him to love you, but this we do not understand, why he should love you so much more than he seems to love the rest of us. I do not mean that he does not love us, for he does, but your case seems so unusual and we ask him why it is, and he says because he has selected you for his work and that you must have his love to its greatest in order that you may do as he desires. So you see few mortals have ever received that love in such an intensity as you have. And you should nourish it and return to him all the love that you are capable of giving to him.

Yes, I saw, what was in your mind and you received much happiness from the trances. But we will not be able to have such an experience. The more that you thought might come, will not come, because the voice of the angels cannot be heard as you would like to hear them. And Jesus will not manifest himself in that way. He will never appear to mortals in the flesh form again, but you will see him some time in your soul's eyes, when you get more of this love in your heart and I will try to show myself in the way that filled your dreams, I mean your wake dreams.

So will Rose and Mary and we will succeed. But you are not going to receive all these manifestations at one time. I want you to first have the independent voices and later we will try materialization and later the slate writings, this I think is the plan that will more likely succeed.

But you must stop now. Well as you say the weather is so bad, I do not think it best to go to Mr. Colburn's. You may go to the meeting of the spiritualists at the Temple, but I do not think that you will be much benefitted, although you may have some things that will increase your faith in the power of intercommunication. You will not receive anything yourself as we will not try to manifest in any way. So sweetheart stop for the time.

He has not told me, but I believe that he is waiting for you to get stronger, which you soon will.

Good bye, with all my love.
I am your own true,
Helen.

Explains the Sabbath and for Mr. Padgett not to take the pamphlet he was reading seriously, that is an Adventist belief

November 19th, 1915.

I am here, Helen.

I signaled you, and wanted merely to say that I have been reading with you the pamphlet, and want to tell you that it is not true. It is all wrong and misleading and will never save a soul from sin. The writer is so filled with the idea that God commanded the observance of the seventh day as the Sabbath, that he, the writer, can see nothing in all the Bible that is of such great importance as the keeping of the Sabbath.

The Sabbath, as a religious institution is not of more importance than any other day, and the man who believes that by observing this Sabbath day can reach that condition of soul development which will fit him for an entrance into the Divine Kingdom will, when he comes to the spirit world, find himself much disappointed. The keeping of this day as these people teach, or of any other day, will not develop their soul qualities or make them one with the Father, or even give them a great development of the natural love, for the doing or refraining to do those things which the commandment, which is the basis of their belief, directs to be done or not done, will only benefit them if they will try to get into attunement with the soul requirements which are necessary in order to become partakers of the Divine Love. So do not let the thoughts or argument of this pamphlet influence you in any way as regards the essentials to a correct understanding of the plans of God for the salvation of mankind.

As Jesus has told you, he will not come to earth with a shout surrounded by his angels, and catch up into the heavens these Adventists, or any other human beings, but he will come and is now coming into the souls of men, through his teachings the workings of the Holy Spirit and in no other way.

He is not the God of wrath and judgment that they teach, but merely the true son of his Father, and comes to all men in love and sympathy, and with the great desire that men shall turn away from their evil thoughts and seek the Love and Mercy of the Father.

I felt that I wanted to write you this, as I realize what great errors are contained in that pamphlet, and men may be lead to believe these errors. While you may read such literature do not let it for one moment cause you to turn your thoughts away from the pure and true teachings of the Master, for if you, or any other man, should base your salvation on what is taught in such writings, you will be deceived, and when you come to the spirit world you will be greatly disappointed in not finding what such writings may lead you to expect.

I must not write more now, as you are not in condition to write further.

Your own true and loving,
Helen.

Comments on the book that Mr. Padgett was reading (The Great Controversy) says the author regrets its contents

January 14th, 1917.

I am here, your own true and loving Helen.

Well, I see that you have been reading a book (The Great Controversy, an Adventist publication written by Ellen G. White) that is full of error and untruth, and that will do you no good to read. The author of that book now knows that the dead are very much alive and that spiritualism is a truth, and that the spirits who communicate are not the devils of Satan, as she calls them. Such reading is not worth the time that you waste in reading, and I do not see why you want to waste your time on such literature.

Mrs. White is now in the spirit world and realizes the great harm that her book has done and is now doing to humanity, and the great errors that so many of her followers believe in and try to follow as their guide in religious beliefs. She will come at some time and write you, for I must tell you that when you borrowed the book and made some mention of its author I tried to learn her whereabouts and succeeded, for I wanted her to come to you and tell you of the utter falsity of what she had written. She has been here tonight and knows that you have been reading her book and realizes that she must do something to correct, if possible, the untruthful teachings that the book contains. So, as I say, she will come to you very soon and write a message[97] in reference to the same.

I see that you have been feeling better today, and have been comparatively free from your worries, and I am so glad, for it makes a very great difference in your condition of mind and permits us to come in closer rapport with you as regards spiritual truths. Several spirits were here tonight expecting to write, but when you commenced to read that book they realized that they would not have the opportunity, and left, very much disappointed. My advice is that you do not waste your time in the further reading of the book, as it will do you no good.

I love you with all my heart and soul, and want you to be happy, and be free from thoughts that may tend to draw your mind away from

---

[97] This does not appear to have occurred. (G.J.C.)

us and the work which you have to do. The only information that you will need you will receive in the messages that will be written you, and so you can readily see that there is no occasion for you to read books of the character of the one now before you. I will come soon and write my promised letter, and I know that you will find more happiness in it, than in a whole world full of books that speculate on the future life and the teachings of the truths of spiritual things that never should know and not speculate upon.

Well, I will say what I have so often said, that I love you very devotedly, and all the other spirits who come to you love you also, and are with you very often with their influence, trying to help you in the development of your soul and in causing you increased happiness. The Master was here and says that he will soon write his expected message and is only waiting for you to get in good condition to receive it.

Your own true and loving,
Helen.

Explains that the book that he was reading (Pastor Russell On Spiritualism) did not have a good influence on him

January 1st, 1916.

I am here, Helen.

Well, I see that you are not in such a good condition tonight in your development, and I am sorry, for I want so very much that you have this love of the Father in all its beauty and fullness. I see that the book you read did not have a good influence on you, but you must not let it trouble you or cause you to doubt, for I am your own true Helen and am writing to you. I am not the spirit of some lost angel of God, but the spirit of the women who was your wife on earth.

The writer of that book will find to his surprise and sorrow when he comes to the spirit world,[98] that his teachings are all wrong and very injurious, and will have to pay the penalties for his false teachings; for he has prevented many a person from coming into the truth and learning that there is no such thing as a dead spirit. So as I say, pay no further attention to what you have read.

Your own true and loving,
Helen.

---

[98] Pastor Russel died on October 31st, 1916 and did indeed have some surprises in store. His detailed communication is published in Volume IV (2nd Ed.) page 238. However his first message is published below this one. (G.J.C.)

Writes about his passing into the spirit world

November 6th, 1916.

I am here, Pastor Russell.

I am the spirit of one who passed out a short time ago (six days previously) and in the full faith of his earth teachings. But in the twinkling of an eye I saw the whole falsity of my beliefs and teachings, because I awoke to the consciousness of my being alive. Yes, more alive than ever, when I expected to go into nothingness and oblivion. Oh the terrible mistake that I made and the great injury that I have done to all my followers who are now firm in the beliefs that I taught them; and when I think of the great responsibility that is mine, I am almost crushed, and feel that the loss of every soul who believes my doctrines will rest on my soul, and that I must do penance or suffer the penalties that my teachings bring to me.

I have been here only a short time and am not in condition to write much now, but I will come—I must come—and find some way to reach my people and tell them to give up the belief that there is no spirit world in which they must live when they leave their bodies of flesh. I come tonight because your wife sought me, and told me that I must come with her and see a mystery, and to me it is. All the beliefs of a lifetime destroyed in one short moment and spiritualism demonstrated to be a truth. I must stop. I will come again. Good night.

Pastor Russell.

Enlightens Mr. Padgett on the closeness of spirit and mortals during the earth holiday festivities, which Jesus does not participate in

December 24th, 1918.

I am here, Helen.

Well dear, I see that you are quite happy just now, and appreciate the difference in influence given you by the messages that you have read and the book that you were reading that took up so much of your time before you commenced to read our writings. The information that you obtain from the book is quite valuable in an historical point of view, and by contrast may show you how utterly ignorant the writers of the articles or rather the actors in the history were of the real truths of Christianity and of the true way to salvation. I would not advise you to read these articles, and I do know that it is best for you to give less time and thought to what you may learn from them. Thinking of these things to some extent interferes with your thinking of the truths, and also affects your condition for rapport, so that the spirits cannot communicate as freely and successfully as they desire to do, and as important as it is to be done.

Well tonight is Christmas eve and you are all alone, and have thought as I saw, of the times when you had us with you on Christmas eve, and enjoyed the anticipation of the happiness of our children on the morrow. It is true that we had some happy days under such surroundings and that we were so absorbed in our dear ones that nothing disturbed our joys. But yet, it is not helpful to think of these days, for they are passed and can never return, although you may before you come over have the opportunity to enjoy days in which your grandchildren may furnish you a similar happiness. But I will not be with you as you may think—without really thinking—and you may wish that I might without realizing the fact that I will surely be with you and write in your happiness. As I have told you, I will not leave you in your loneliness, or when you may long for me; as long as you shall remain on earth.

Tomorrow, when you visit Harry I will be there, and so will Baby, and will enter into your feelings of joy, and try to impress you to realize my presence. No, my dear sweetheart, I will never forsake you, but will always love you with a greater love than ever I had on earth, and which is growing deeper and purer all the time. I know that all of you will have a happy Christmas, and if you could only realize the presence of the spirits who will be with you, you would find a greatly increased happiness. Baby says that she will be there and love you and Harry and Hazel with all her love and will try to help them feel that her love is with them, and will enjoy the occasion more than if she were with you in the body. You had better go to bed now and get up early.

Well dear, they are waiting only for you to get in condition, and when you do there will be no delay in communicating the truths. The Master has been with you a number of nights, desiring to write, but for reasons that you know of, he could not, but he is patient and thinks that you will soon realize the importance of the work so that you will do that which is necessary to bring about the condition. He is not here tonight, nor in the lower spheres, because, as I have told you before, the great amount of worship of him that is taking place now and will continue tomorrow, is distasteful to him, and he has gone to his Celestial Sphere, and will not probably come back to you until after the objectionable worship has ceased.

No, not tonight. He is with you every night as he promised, and prays with you and tries to help you, and when you earnestly pray to the Father he is pleased and gives thanks. So you, knowing this, must try to pray more earnestly, and with more faith. He will soon come again, and I am so glad to hear you say that you believe he is with you as he promised. Keep up your faith and hope, and you will not be disappointed, for the love will come into your soul in more abundance and you will become in better condition to do the work.

Yes, we all hope so. But you must make the effort for so much depends upon you. You will have the help of your friend who advises, and he is very anxious to do his part of the work. He is not here now, for when he was last here he said he would not come until he had reason to advise you differently from what he last advised. But he will not fail you. So dear, love us with all your heart and believe that we love you. Give me a kiss and say good night.

Your own true and loving,
Helen.

Is very happy that her son is preaching the Truth of God's Love

July 29th, 1917.

I am here, Mrs. Mitchell.

Let me say only a word. I was present at church this morning and heard my son's sermon, and was so happy that he preached of the Divine Love of the Father and the work of the Holy Spirit. It made me think that the Truths of God's Love and man's redemption are becoming a part of his soul's knowledge.

There were many spirits present and many were affected by the sermon and turned their thoughts to this Love the Father that had never before been preached to them.

I have great hope that my son will receive the truths that have been revealed to you in their fullness, and thereby receive to a greater degree this transformation of his soul into the very essence of the Father. I thank you for your kindness, and will not write more. So with my love I will say good night.

Your sister in Christ, (Mrs. Mitchell)
Mother of Rev. Mitchell, Methodist.

Confirms that the preacher's mother was very happy because her son will put away his dogmatic beliefs

July 29th, 1917.

I am here, your own true and loving, Helen.

Well dear, you have received a message from the preacher's mother (Mrs. Mitchell) who was so anxious to write. She is very happy, and believes that her son will have an awakening to the truth and put aside his dogmatic beliefs.

I was with you at church and was very happy, because I saw that you were happy. The Master was there as you realized in all his love and soothing influence, and was pleased that the preacher delivered the sermon as he did. Many of the audience were affected by what was said and their souls responded to the truths told them by the preacher, and they experienced a feeling of love that made them happy.

I see that you are sleepy and I will not write more. Only continue to think of these spiritual things and pray to the Father, and you will find the love increasing more and more in your soul. So love me and believe that I love you. Good night, my dear one.

Your own true and loving,
Helen.

Explains the difference between the spiritual and material elements

December 1st, 1918.

I am here, Francis Bacon.

Let me write a short message in reference to our spirit world and one of the laws that obtain therein.

You were told a few nights ago that which is material in itself, always remains material although the combination into forms and appearances may change, and even the material elements may cease to be perceptive to the faculties or senses of the human, and this assertion of fact is true and without exception.

The material of the universe is one and not diverse, and the thing that you may sense as being material is a part of the same great universal material of existence, and may at different times and under certain conditions become incorporated in the invisible material and yet remain just as real as when it was the thing that you could sense as a reality. The fact of the existence of the material is not determined by the requirement that men shall be able to cognize its existence by the exercise of some one or all of the perceptions of the human organs used to comprehend what they call the material of nature; and whether or not men are able to so cognize what is the truly material does not affect the existence of the material, for as it now has reality so it would have if men had no perception at all.

To the blind man, the knowledge of the existence of that part of the material of what you may call the natural world that depends on sight for its comprehension, can be acquired only by information from those who have that sight; and so, knowledge of the existence of the material in the world not subject to comprehension by the senses of men can only be obtained through information given them by those who have cognition such existence by reason of faculties that they possess. Men sometimes claim that they have knowledge of the existence of the material in the invisible world as a resultant from the exercise of reason and an acquaintance with the law of cause and effect, and in many instances this claim is true, especially where effects are perceived, which must have had causes existing beyond the circle of the known material. To illustrate: men see and understand the effects of the workings of electricity, and to an extent can control and utilize that electricity, and yet they cannot by the exercise of their natural senses claim knowledge of the fact that it exists as a part of the material of the universe—they know it only as a cause producing an effect, and as to whether it is of the material or not they have no sensate knowledge. Electricity is of the material and intangible and not subject to the perception of sense, and to men has an existence only because it is accepted and declared to be the cause of certain known effects.

Now, there are many material things in the invisible world that have never come to the knowledge of men by reason of effects produced and made known to their cognition; yet these things are just as real and just as much a part of the material of the universe as are those things that men call the material of the natural world. Now what I have written is merely to demonstrate the fact that the existence of the material is not confined to what men call the natural world, and that men's knowledge does not always determine whether the material exists or not.

The material has its place and existence in all the spheres of the spirit world and is used by spirits in their work and living just as really as it exists in the natural world and is used by men for their welfare and happiness; and when the inhabitants of the spirit world use it for the purpose and in such a manner as to make the invisible material perceptible to the senses of men, they should not look upon such phenomena as unreal or non acceptable because such phenomena is not produced in accord or harmony with the laws of the material as they understand them.

I will continue later.
Your friend,
Francis Bacon.

Confirms that Francis Bacon wrote on the subject of the spiritual and material elements which are purely scientific

December 1st, 1918.

I am here, Helen.
Well dear, the message that you have just received was from the

spirit who wrote you a few nights ago on the subject of the material. He seemed to be much interested in the matter and says he desires to impart information which is scientific and of importance to mankind, and that he will come again soon.

I see that you have had a very happy day and feel much better because of your visit, and you are better, and in such condition that the other spirits can write, and I hope that tomorrow night you will give them the opportunity. You will receive some very instructive and vital messages and should give all the time possible to the preparation for receiving these truths.

I am quite happy in being with you today, and have felt that we are getting closer together in our love and rapport. It is late, and I will not write more now. Baby is here in her love and says she hopes that she may soon be able to write her letter, and that she loves you so much.

Well he is ready, and will write tomorrow night, if you will prepare the way. I will tell him. Love us and pray to the Father, as we want you to get more of the love and come closer to us in your soul development. Good night,

Your own true and loving,
Helen.

Explains the sudden passing of their daughter, Nita, as a result of a serious operation, and the great progress she is making in the spirit world

June 20th, 1918.

I am here, Helen.

Well, my dear Ned, you have had your little girl leave you,[99] as you now feel, but she has not left, for she will be more with you than ever, and happier than she could possibly have been had she remained in the body.

I was with her as she passed over and received her in my arms and told her that she was with her mother and had nothing to fear. That she had come to the spirit world and would now know what love and

---

[99] The following funeral notice was recently discovered. This information was published in the Baltimore Sun on Saturday morning, 22nd June 1918 as follows:
    PADGETT - On Thursday evening, June 20, in Washington, Helenita Padgett, of Washington, D.C., daughter of James E. and the late Helen W. Padgett. Funeral at Mount Olivet Cemetery, Frederick., Md., at 2 o'clock Saturday afternoon, June 22.
I have long wondered if any time elapses between physical death, and resumption of consciousness in the spirit realms. From this message, it appears there is none at all. Which makes the statement in the Urantia Book very curious. There it claims it takes three days before consciousness is recovered. (G.J.C.)

happiness are, and that all her troubles had left her forever. I told her that she would not have to leave you and her brothers, except as regards her body which was no longer a part of her, and which she would soon realize was merely a covering for herself. She was not afraid and nestled in my arms as I kissed her and told her that now she would understand how much her mother loved her and how happy she would be in that love, and that in a very short time she would be perfectly content, and feel so happy that she had left the cares and troubles of her earth life.

I was with her before she died, and she actually saw me as I waited at her bedside for her spirit to find a release from her body. She recognized and talked to me and actually heard my voice as I encouraged her and called her to come to my arms. She was not afraid and I know that I was as visible to her as I ever was on earth.

She is now with me, or rather I am with her, and am trying to help her realize fully that she is a spirit; and she is convinced for, as she tells me, she remembers the many talks that you had with her in which you told her of my coming to you and to her with all my love and desire to make her happy, and that as she remembered these things it seemed to be natural for her to have the experience of having me with her as her real loving mother.

I will be with her a great deal and so will many other spirits who love her—your parents and mine were with her when she came over and spoke to her of their love and encouraged her to believe that she was really with them and had nothing to fear, and that only love was around her.

She will soon be in a better condition to appreciate her surroundings, and then I will bring her to you and let her tell you of her experience and her love for you and the boys. I know that you are sorrowful to have her leave you in the body and that your heart is very heavy, as you expected to have her with you more intimately than ever and to find much happiness and comfort in her presence. But dear, you must try not to worry or grieve, for, as I have said, you have not lost her. She will be with you more than ever and you will feel her presence and know that she is so much happier than when a mortal. I wish that I could make myself visible to you so that I could comfort you the more and cause you to believe that your Baby has not left you. Let not your belief in the fact that we are really alive go from you. We are more alive than ever, and can love you more than when in life on the earth. So do not grieve, but know that it will not be long before you will be with us, and that this is a certainty.

Oh, my dear, I love you so much tonight and want to comfort you with my love, and with the assurance that now, as you sit in your room at night and feel lonesome and sometimes wish that baby could be with you, I and your baby, who will soon be a bright spirit and enjoy the happiness that love for you will bring to her, will be with you. You, as I say, must not grieve, for you are not strong and grief will not be beneficial to your condition of brain. Only think of her as being a beautiful loving spirit, filled with love for you and always glad when she can be with you, and only sorry that you may not be able to feel her arms around you and her kisses on your lips. You are not in condition to write more tonight and must go to bed.

Well, dear, I wanted in the first place to encourage you and keep you from worrying so that you would not be unhappy. And next I really believed that she would not die, but that she would have the strength to overcome the results of the operation; but I was mistaken and for your sake, was as sorry as you could possibly be. We cannot always foretell the results of contingencies affecting the material conditions of mortals. We do not know these things as a matter of omniscience, but merely base our conclusions on what we believe will be the results of certain causes. I was so anxious to comfort and relieve you from your worry, and the real fact is that you have no cause for worry, but I did not allude to this when I told you not to worry, for I believed that she would recover from her sickness, and so thought the others who wrote you encouraging words. And even Dr. Campbell thought that she would be able to withstand the results of the operation. But in these things we cannot always judge aright. We are not infallible and cannot always exercise the power which we possess to bring about results that our loved ones on earth may desire. So sweetheart, do not feel resentful because my promises did not come true.

If you could only fully understand what the condition of your baby is, you would not want her with you in the body. I know that you will, at times, feel very lonesome and long for her as your dear one of earth form and companionship, but you will soon have such an experience with her as your spirit baby, that you will not often sorrow because she left you. This I know without the possibility of your being disappointed, and you must try to believe me.

Well, sweetheart, when you are a little stronger I will come and write you more in detail about baby's passing and she will write also. Love me and love her, and pray to the Father. Say good night. God bless and comfort you, my dear husband.

Your own true and loving,
Helen.

Comforts Mr. Padgett regarding his daughter's sudden passing into the spirit world and the love that now exists between them, and the greater love of his soulmate wife

July 8th, 1918.

I am here, Jesus.

I am here and will write a few lines in the hope that I may cheer you up and strengthen you. You must not look at things with such despondent feelings. I understand how natural it is for you to see the dark side of conditions which have arisen by reason of the death of your daughter and ordinarily you would not have the comfort which now must come because of the knowledge that you have of the spirit world and of the actual condition of your loved ones. As you have been told, she is now quite happy and more alive to the reality of existence than she ever was, and would not return to her earth life were it possible.

While you may think at times what happiness you and she might have were she still with you in the flesh and regret that she was taken from you, yet such thoughts arise merely from your desires that are purely of an earthy nature, for when you think of what her condition is now you will certainly realize that there can be no comparison between the supposed happiness that she might have and that which she is now actually possessing. And I know that you love her so much that this knowledge on your part is sufficient not only to remove these regrets but to cause you to rejoice that she is now in the spirit world, free from the cares and troubles that belong to an existence on earth. So do not think of these possible enjoyments that might come to you were she alive and with you. She is with you—closer than you may imagine and with her is a love greater for you than she ever had on earth. She is now progressing and the love is flowing into her soul, and she is realizing that it is the one thing that can bring joy and peace to her. She will soon come and write you as she is anxious to do so.

She is here tonight, and has been with you during the day as your heart went out so lovingly to her and you called for her. She was glad that you so much wanted her with you and responded just as a young spirit in whom the first awakening of the knowledge of the possession of the great love would do. So do not grieve for her, but realize that she is with you and is happy and wants you to be happy. She will be with you a great deal and you will consciously recognize her presence and feel the benefit of her love.

You must also know that many of us are with you, and especially that beautiful soulmate of yours who loves you as no other spirit can love you, and that she is trying to comfort and help you. So do not permit yourself to feel so lonesome or despondent. Remember the great work before you, and that all your energies must now be set to accomplish that work. While you have others on earth who you must and do love, yet you must not permit that love to interfere with your work or the accumulation of the means which are necessary to carry out the work as we have heretofore planned.

I know that you have been disappointed in various particulars, and that it seems almost impossible for you to get in the condition of which I have written, yet you must not lose your faith, for the matter will be accomplished, and after a little while when you get in better physical and mental condition you will start the plan and success will come to you. Let not any ambition or hope for worldly things take the place or even associate with your ambition to accomplish the work which you have undertaken together with us to make complete. Have faith and courage and then action on your part will come. I will not write more tonight. You have my love and help and prayers, and you must pray more yourself to the Father. Good night,

Your brother and friend,
Jesus.

Wants Mr. Padgett to know that "Baby", their daughter that just passed into the spirit world is with her and sends her love to him

July 8th, 1918

I am here, your own true and loving Helen.

Well dear, I am glad that you are feeling better tonight, and hope that you may continue to grow better and not let thoughts of things which tend to make you despondent take possession of you.

I have been with you a great deal today, and saw how you felt and how far away we all seemed from you, and how much you wished that Baby might be with you, and I tried to comfort you and cause you to obtain relief from your gloomy feelings, and I know that I helped you some.

Baby was with me and tried to tell you not to worry about her, but to believe that she is very happy and loves you more than when she was on earth. She is now getting into the light which the possession of some of the love gives and is quite happy and longing and praying with all her soul. She realizes that she did not lose anything by coming to the spirit world, not even, as she says, lose being with you, and you must try to bring this thought to you as an actual, living fact.

Jesus has written you a loving letter, and he knows just what your condition is and how much you needed his sympathy and love. He has not yet talked or appeared to Baby, but says he will soon, and then I know she will become very, very happy, for he brings happiness to all those to whom he comes with his great love. I mean those who recognize and believe that he is the Master.

So sweetheart, do not be despondent any longer or let your faith in us and our love grow weaker, for we do love you more than we can tell you, and so want you to be happy and free from worry. I will not write longer now, and suggest that you soon go to bed and get your sleep. Good night, my dear husband.

Your own true and loving,
Helen.

Baby says, love her too, and believe that she loves you with all her heart and is happy and wants you to know it. Good night,
Helen.

First communication from Mr. Padgett's daughter, Nita, that is also known as Baby, tells of her progress to the Third Sphere

October 14th, 1918.

I am here, Nita. Let me write a line.

I am Nita, and I have been so anxious to write you ever since I came to the spirit world and realized that I could do so. Well, Daddy, I cannot tell you how happy I am and how glad I am that I can write you. I know that mother has written you in regards to my passing over and my condition and progress since I became a spirit, and all that she said is true and much more. I am so desirous of telling you in detail just what my experience has been, but as this is my first attempt to write I will not do so tonight, but very soon I will, and I know that you will get tired before I cease writing, for I have so much to tell you.

Of course I had some idea of what might be my experience in passing, but the idea was a very faint glimpse of what I really experienced, and I want to tell you how much your information when I was with you helped me.

Well, Daddy, I am also so very glad that I could be with you so much and know that you were still my dear Daddy, and loved me so much more than I ever realized when on earth. I am now so very happy and know to a large extent the reality and blessedness of God's Love, which you used to tell me of. Oh, how can I ever express to you how thankful I am that you told me of this Love, for it has been the means of helping me so much in my progress. I am now in the third sphere as mother tells me, and I cannot tell you the beauty and loveliness of all that surrounds me, and what a lovely home I have and what delightful associates. You must not think me selfish when I write that I would not return to the earth life for all the world, for here I am free from the worry and troubles that I had, and also can be with you and love you and know that you love me as your own darling baby.

I am with (my) brothers a great deal also and try to make them realize that I am with them, loving them so very much. They think of me sometimes and wonder if I am really with them, and I know that they, to a degree, feel my presence even though they are really not conscious of the fact.

Well, Daddy, I have written a good deal, and mother says I had best not write more now, but wait until I am in a better condition to express to you just what I desire to write. So love me and think of me, and expect me very soon to tell you of what I have suggested. Give my love to the boys, and especially to Hazel and tell her that I am with her, and so is mother, both trying to help her, and make her expectations come true, and also cause her to be the happiest little mother in all the world. She has wonderful influences around her, and should be very happy as well as should Harry, and I know you will also.

So, dear Daddy, I must say good night. With all my love, I am still your own loving,
Baby.

Explains that the power of communication can be shut off by the instrument as Mr. Padgett did for a while to even prevent his closest love tie to write. Explains the progress that is being made by their daughter, Nita, now in the spirit world

October 14th, 1918.

I am here, your own true and loving Helen.

Well, dear, you have heard from Baby, and she was so pleased that she could write you, and is more anxious than ever to tell you of all the things that she has in mind, and the wonderful experience that she had when passing, and has since had. She is a beautiful girl now and is so very happy, and best of all is filled with the desire for an increased possession of the Father's love. She prays very often and seems to have great faith, and I believe that her progress to higher spheres will be very rapid. I am so glad to have her with me, as I realize that she has escaped many of the trials and worries of life.

Well, dear, I am so glad that we can get close together again, and now I hope that we will never have another severance of our rapport, and we will not unless you let your love grow cold and your thoughts of me and for me become less. I was very unhappy when I found that I couldn't come to you as I had been doing and that you had raised a barrier between us that I had not the power to break down. While you may think that we spirits are very powerful yet you must also think that all our powers cannot bring me in rapport with you, when you do not think in that way towards me that will create a condition which will enable me to make the rapport.

Thus you will realize how much of our intercourse will depend on you. Of course, I can be with you and know and see what your condition is and what your thoughts are but I cannot arbitrarily change your condition or turn your thoughts to me and cause you to draw close to me in a union of rapport that will enable me to write to you. So sweetheart, do not let yourself get in this condition again. Only love and think of and wish for me and no spirit or power can keep me from you—only you, yourself, can do this.

Well, it is late, and you have been working and I must not draw on you longer. Keep your thoughts on spiritual things and pray to the Father and long for His Love and very soon you will be in condition which will enable the higher spirits to write.

Love me and say good night. Your own true and loving,
Helen.

The second writing could not be the long letter that she wanted to write to tell of her experience in passing into the spirit world, but happy to wait for a better time

December 29th, 1918.

I am here, Nita.

Well, Daddy, this is the night that I was to write my message, and I was looking forward to doing so, but mother tells me that I had better wait until another night when you may be feeling better and have more time to receive it, and while I am disappointed, I will wait; but I hope it will be soon.

Oh, Daddy, you don't know how anxious I am to write and tell you of the things that I have experienced and how happy I am, and how much I love you and want you to believe that I am with you and love me.

I am progressing and growing happier and more beautiful, as mother tells me, all the time. I know something of heaven and the Father's Love, and of Jesus who comes to you and to me also, and tells me of wonderful things that are awaiting me in the higher spheres. Oh, I wish that I could explain to you all that I know and see and realize, for then I know you would strive with all your might to get in the condition that the spirits desire you to have.

Yes, I have, and she is here, but so unhappy and sad and suffering. I am trying to help her. I see that you doubt. Do not, but wait a little while and you will hear from Edward. Daddy, love me with all your heart and continue to pray for me. I am with you at night when you pray and feel so much helped. Good night, my dear Daddy.

Your own loving,

Nita.

Confirms their daughter Nita's progress and the Truth of Jesus' second coming on earth.

December 29th, 1918.

I am here, your own true and loving Helen.

Well, dear, I am glad that you had the message from John, for I see that you are anxious to receive an explanation of the truth of the second coming of the Master in detail, so that not only you but the world which reads these messages may understand. John will come soon—it all depends on you.

Well, our Baby was so happy that she could write you, and tell you how much she loves you, and how happy she is and with what rapidity she is progressing. She was a little disappointed that she could not write, but as she understands the reason she acquiesced and said she would wait. She is progressing very fast and becoming so very beautiful as the love fills her soul. You must think of her and love her very dearly.

I was with you tonight at church and saw what impressions the sermon made on you, and how you felt that you would like to tell the preacher the truth and help him put on the wedding garment. Well, we will have to wait. His mother is praying for him and trying to impress him with the truth but his orthodox views are too firmly fixed to permit an impression to be made upon him at this time; but sometime he will learn the truth.

Well, dear, you have had another happy experience today and your soul has been much benefitted by your longings for the Father's Love. Only continue to pray and you will realize your desires, and the messages will come to you—for many spirits are here, waiting to communicate.

Well, we have thought of that, and concluded that you had better confine your work to the higher messages, especially as the work you did among them is bearing much fruit, and as a result the spirits of love are enabled to come into communication with many of the dark spirits who now listen to what we desire to say to them. The ones that you helped are working successfully among the dark ones. Well, dear, I will now stop.

Love me and believe and pray. Good night.

Your own true and loving,
Helen.

Wishes for Mr. Padgett to be ready to receive the Master's message and that she will write on soulmates

January 12th, 1919.

I am here, your own true and loving, Helen.

Well dear, the Master has just written you and he was very much interested in what you have in mind to do. You must try your utmost to be ready to receive his message when he comes, for nothing to you is of more importance. I will soon come and write a little upon some features of the soul which is not in the Master's messages, I mean about the soulmates and their love. So expect me.

Baby says she wants to write and tell you what she knows about love and happiness and will do so as soon as you will arrange things. I will not write more tonight as you are somewhat tired. So sweetheart, love us and pray to the Father and believe that I love you with all my heart and soul, the great thing to you and me. Good night,

Your own true and loving,
Helen.

Describes her experiences in passing into the spirit world

May 25th, 1920.

I am here, Nita.

I am so glad that I can write to you again. It has been a long time since you let me write and I have been so anxious to tell you of my progress and love. Why, Daddy, I thought that you loved me so much that you would not keep me waiting so long to tell you of my love and how happy I am, but mother told me that you were not in condition to receive my message and that I must wait until conditions are different and I understand, but thought it strange that anything should interfere, to prevent me from writing to my Daddy.

And now I want to tell you of my progress and how the love of the Father has changed my soul so that now I am in a sphere from where I may soon expect to go into the Celestial Heavens where mother is. When I first came to spirit life (June 20th, 1918) as you know, mother met me and took me in her arms and was so loving and tender with me, that I had no fear, because of the change in my condition, and with her were other beautiful and loving spirits who gave me their love and assured me that now I would soon find a home that was so different from my home on earth and would experience a happiness that I had never before felt. And I was not afraid and did not want to go with my body again as I was told so many newly arrived spirits desire to do when they first come over.

I was satisfied from the first, and how could I not help being so when I had such a beautiful mother to enfold me in her arms and assure me that never more would I have to undergo the cares and disappointments of an earth life. How glorious this was and how I thought that if heaven should have all spirits as lovely and grand as was here, what a happy place it must be. Mother was with me for quite a while and also grandmother Padgett, who was also beautiful and bright, and who told me that I had nothing to fear, but to believe that I was in the true spirit world when later I should find everything to make me happy and contented.

But how badly I felt when the parting came, for you must know that this parting was necessary. Mother lived in a higher sphere to which I could not go and she could not remain with me all the time, as I wanted her to do. But she told me that she would be with me quite often to comfort and love me. That under the law I would have to go to the place that I my soul fitted me for and from thence I would have to pray and work for my own progress. That she could not determine for me where I should live and that only my own soul's condition must fix my place and so as I say we had to part.

I soon found myself in some darkness and suffering and did not quite understand why this should be so, or what was the cause of my darkness, but after a little I found that my recollection of my earth life came to me in wonderful clearness and that my conscience was causing me some suffering. I was awfully lonesome and wanted my mother so much, but found out that I had to bear my own burdens and obey the laws that fixed my condition. I know you would want to be with me if you could, to comfort and love me and protect me from my sufferings, but this was impossible for this law that I speak of, knows neither mercy nor forgiveness, until it is satisfied.

It is stern and unrelenting, and from the very necessity of things, must be so, because only through its workings can a soul be made purer and enabled to progress from its first condition. But thanks to my dear mother I had with me the hope that such condition was only for a moment and that soon the Love would come to me and take me out of the workings of the law (Law of Compensation) and set me free and enable me to get into light and more happiness. Oh! how I prayed and prayed for this Love and tried to believe that it would come to me and dispel the darkness and the recollections of the evil things that I had done and thought when on earth. And mother and grandmother prayed with me, and encouraged me with their sympathy and love and the assurance that this love would come to me and that the Father would answer my prayers.

While in this condition and on one occasion when I had been

praying with all my soul, and when my faith seemed stronger, there came to me a beautiful spirit all tender and loving and said, my daughter, the Father will hear your prayers and soul longing and call you to higher service and brighter surroundings and greater happiness, for I know that he never fails to answer the prayer of an earnest soul and besides you are the very child of His Love and care and nothing pleases Him so much as when His children call on Him for His Love and help. And I am praying for you also and my faith makes it certain that you will soon receive the answer, only let your very soul breathe out its longings for His Love.

Oh! how beautiful and grand he was and how tender his love, which seemed to flood all my surroundings and to give me such hope and encouragement that I felt that I surely must be a little weary in brain while he was talking. He then told me, that he was Jesus and was so glad that I had come to the spirit world with so much love surrounding me and also told me how he loved me and sympathized with me and wanted me to get out of my darkness and into the light.

I cannot express to you how I felt as he talked to me and how I wondered if he were not really God. But he could not be God for he was so human and humble and seemed to think that he was a mere child of the Father of whom he spoke. When leaving me, he said, that he would come again and talk to me of the Father and His Love and blessed me and said: "You are a child of our Father and just as dear to Him as I am, and He loves you just as much as He does me. Believe in His Great Love and you will be happy."

Well, daddy, you can imagine what my feelings were and how much I was helped. I will not stop to tell you now of how this love came into my soul, little by little, until at last it seemed to fill my whole being. Oh, how happy I became, and how beautiful my surroundings appeared and what beautiful bright spirits I found myself in an association with. I was satisfied and my home became to me the most glorious and happiest place imaginable.

But this was only the second sphere of which I have written, and even that sphere surpasses all conception of man, and would satisfy the most hopeful and extravagant man as his house of bliss. But I continued to progress and more and more of the love came into my soul, and strange as it may seem to you, as I rose higher and higher, grandmother was with me so very much, became more beautiful and glorious than ever before.

I understand now why that was. As she came to me in the different spheres, and as I rose higher, she approached nearer her home and took in more of the beauty and glory that are really hers in her sphere of living. But I have written enough for tonight, and besides you are tired.

Now I am happy beyond expression and love you with a greater love than I ever had on earth, and know what love really is, and one of the happiest things that I now have before me is to wait until you come and meet you with all my love and goodness. Oh, daddy won't it be glorious when you come over and we can all be together in love. You thought that you had a beautiful Helen on earth, but when you come to us and see her in her glory, your very eyes will be dazzled at her appearance.

We are with you a great deal, loving you and trying to help you and you must believe that we will never leave you, till you reach the heaven where we now are. And not then if you want us with you. So daddy, believe that I am your little Nita and that I write you and love you with all my heart and soul.

Your Nita.

Is very happy that her daughter Nita was able to write the way she did to disclose her happiness and spiritual progress

May 25th, 1920.

I am here, your own true loving Helen.

I am so glad that Nita had the opportunity to write you as to her progress and happiness and I am so glad that she could do so. It makes her feel better to know that now somebody knows just what her condition is and how happy she is. She is a beautiful spirit and is progressing all the time and very soon now she will be in the Celestial Sphere, where everything is divine and beautiful. She is hugging me now and says that she is so happy and I feel the influence of joy.

Well dear as you have written a great deal tonight. I will not write more. Love and believe that we love you and are with you very much. I will close and say good night.

Your own true and loving, Helen.

Writes on faith and glory of the Father

May 18th, 1915.

I am here, Jesus.

Let me write just to say, be true and the power will be given you and the truth of my Revelations shall be heard throughout the world, by the work that you shall do in the way of writing.

The richer will be your soul, but you must have faith and trust in the Father's Love. I have said it and you will see the glory of the Father displayed, if you will pray and believe.

With faith, there will be revealed all these precious things in existence.

Your brother and friend, Jesus.

Writes about the resurrection of the body

October 5th, 1916.

I am here, Paul.

I will finish my message[100] tonight if you are so inclined. Well we will try. As I was saying, the body that is resurrected at death, is not the physical body, but the spirit body; and never after the first resurrection is there another. I am now dealing with the resurrection other than that of the soul, or the resurrection from the death of which I have before written you.

The body that is once laid in the grave will never be resurrected and neither will any of its elements enter into any other body for the purpose of a resurrection. The body of flesh is created for one purpose only, and when that purpose has been accomplished, never will that body or any derivation from it be used for any other resurrection. This body of flesh is of matter, and like all matter, is used for the life on earth only, and cannot be used for any function or clothing any spirit in the spirit world, and neither can it be translated into the spirit realms. All material bodies must die and never will there come a time when men can leave the earth, and enter the spirit life in these material bodies.

I know that it has been written that certain of the prophets of old were translated into the spirit heavens clothed in their fleshly bodies, but this is not true, for it is impossible that such a thing could be, for the same laws apply to the physical body of the saint as to that of the sinner; both are of the earth—earthly—and must be left behind when the spirits of men enter the heavens of spirits.

So that when men believe and preach the general resurrection of the material body, or the special resurrection of the same, they are in error and do not believe or preach the truth. Flesh and blood, or flesh without blood, cannot inherit the kingdom, and no belief or teachings can make that true which is untrue.

I do not desire to write more on this subject, because many men who are acquainted with the laws of nature, and many more who will become acquainted with these laws, know and will know and understand the impossibility of the material entering the realm of the spiritual. So thanking you for your kindness, I will say good night.

Your brother in Christ,

---

[100] This message was published in Volume II (4th Ed.) page 383. (G.J.C.)

St. Paul.[101]

Discloses the names of the guides for Mr. Padgett, Mr. Morgan and Dr. Stone and that above each of them is Jesus

October 5th, 1916.

I am here, Luke.

I did not come to write a message tonight but merely to corroborate what Mr. Morgan told you I had spoken to him. It was I and he understood correctly what I said and what I said to him is the truth. I want him to believe for I have a spiritual interest in him and in his spiritual progression and am with him very often trying to help him.

As the preacher (Dr. Gordon) said tonight, back of each mortal who thinks thoughts and evil deeds, I mean of the kind that is important, is an unseen spirit using its influence to suggest truths and inspire soul (them). And while they are unseen yet are they evil and more or less harmful?

If men could only know who these unseen helpers are they would understand the power and wisdom that are back of him helping their thoughts and attempting to control their acts. Sometimes a mortal will have more than one of such helpers but as a general proposition there exists some special helper who is with the mortal more constantly than the others and acquiring a rapport which the general helpers do not have. I will tell you now who these spirit helpers and writers of you three men who have been selected for the great work are Dr. Stone is James, Mr. Morgan's is myself and yours is John and over and above all helping all three of you is Jesus, the highest and most knowing of all. You must each and all believe this and not be astonished if to each of you comes his special guardian quite often.

I thought it best to make it known to you these facts as from the knowledge three of you may realize that back of you are spirits who are powerful and filled with the Father's Love. Believe and pray and you will find that in each of you will develop a spiritual power that will cause you much happiness and the certainty of your relation with us. I will come soon and write you a message with all my love and blessing I will say good night.

Your brother in Christ,
Luke.

---

[101] This message is a composite of two, being published in Volume II and Volume III. (G.J.C.)

Confirms that it was Luke who wrote

October 5th, 1916.

I am here, your own true and loving Helen.

I see that you may have some doubts as to who the last writer was because of his announcement of such an important fact as the guardians who are with you there. It was Luke who wrote and what he wrote I know to be true. It is wonderful that these spirits should assume such a relationship with you and the wonder is that it is true.

So all of you believe and conduct your lives and thoughts in accordance with the assurance given you. I thought I would write my message tonight but it is too late. I was with you at church and in your walk afterwards and so was Mary and we enjoyed the conversation very much.

Yes, I wrote the message and wrote it with all my love and desire to help you. It was true and you will realize that I wrote you will come to pass. Keep up your courage and believe in us all for we are all trying to help and do and will. Well, I must stop now.

So believe that I love you and am your own true and loving,
Helen.

Never said that Jesus came to earth as the only begotten of the Father, which is not true

September 17th, 1915.

I am here, St. Luke.

I came tonight to tell you of some things which are in the Bible, and which are not true as they were never written by me, or by any one at my dictation. I never said that Jesus came to earth as the only begotten of the Father, in the sense that he was born differently from other mortals, for he was not. I mean that his father and mother were Joseph and Mary, and he was their natural son, and that they never supposed that he was begotten in any different way from what the other children were begotten.

Of course, he became more truly the son of God than did any other mortal who was ever born, but that was because he became filled with the Divine Love of the Father to a greater extent than any other human being. He became so close to the Father that in his soul development he was able to commune with the Father in such a way as to realize exactly what the Father said to him, and his love made him one with the Father as he said. Now he is closer to the Father than he ever was on earth, and his love is very much greater than when on earth, greater than any other spirit, and, as a consequence, he knows more about the Father's attributes and about His will and plans for men's redemption than does any other spirit. And when he comes to you and tells you that you must receive his messages to be transmitted to mankind, he imposes upon you a mission which is greater than he ever imposed on any other man, not even excepting the apostles.

He now knows more of the truths of His Father than he did when on earth, and he realizes that the truths which are so necessary to man's salvation and their future happiness have never been revealed to mortals in their fullest extent. When he was on earth he declared many important truths which have not been preserved, and, hence, he is anxious that these truths and others shall be given to mankind.

Many things which men, who are professed Christians, believe are not truths, and stand in the way of their progress in spiritual things and in the soul's development. I would like to tell you of more of these things which men should not believe but I have not the time tonight, as others want to write.

But this you must know and forever proclaim, that God is love, and that they who want to get immortality, must believe in the New Birth, and seek to obtain it. Without this, no spirit can enter the Celestial Spheres and partake of the Divine Nature of the Father. There are many other truths that must be learned and believed in but none are as important as those which I have just written. I am writing this not as a matter of mere belief but as a matter of knowledge. There can be no doubt arise in my mind as to the reality of these things and none must arise in yours.

I will come again when you are in a better condition to take a long message and write you.

With all my love I am your brother in Christ,
St. Luke.

Arranges for Mr. Padgett to see her in a vision with all her beauty and love that she has for her soulmate

February 22nd, 1918.

I am here, Helen.

You have been happy tonight, for I was with you and could see and feel your happiness. Oh, it was grand to have such love as you gave me, and to let me know that your heart was all mine. Why can't we often have such nights? I was with you all the time and when the Rosary was played I showed myself to you as you imagined you saw me. I was actually there in the position that you saw me in, with my heart and eyes full of love for you, and pointing to the higher sphere whence came the stream of light that you saw. It was the silver stream of love that was flowing down upon us and showing us that in that happy sphere was all love and happiness. What you imagined you saw was an actual vision in which I was very much present and alive. So you see I have kept my promise to let you see me and I did it in a way that I know would make you happy, and at the same time realize what a happy soulmate you have, and how love has made her beautiful.

So now I know that you will believe that I am with you and love you, and am waiting for you to come over, and go with me to the sphere where love and joy reigns supreme. Oh, my Ned, I am so happy tonight in the knowledge that at last you have seen me as I am, and as I will appear to you when you come over.

So, sweetheart, we will not write more tonight for it would seem to me that to write of other things after one wonderful coming together and enjoying our great happiness would be a sacrilege; and so in the love which I know you have for me and which you know I have for you, I will say with all my soul, be my own Ned for ever as you are tonight and I shall be satisfied and happy.

Your own true and loving,
Helen.

Jesus listened to a conversation that Mr. Padgett had regarding his blood saving from sin, which was based on ignorance

September 19th, 1915.

I am here, Jesus.

I heard the discussion between you and the other man about my blood saving from sin, and I felt that you were not benefitted by what was said, because his faith is based on ignorance of the true plan of salvation and my mission on earth. But he is so firmly fixed in his belief that no argument that you might make would convince him that anything but my death and atonement could save from sin. So I do not think it would do any good to attempt to argue with any of these people in reference to the matter of my blood being the one thing that saves from sin and error. These people have this faith so firmly fixed that they see only my blood as a means of salvation.

They have received the Divine Love to a considerable degree and the Holy Spirit is with them in their worship and is in their hearts, but it does not come to them by reason of their belief in my atonement, but because they pray to the Father for its coming and making them a new being so far as their soul development is concerned. They do not know that only the flowing of this Divine Love into their hearts in answer to prayer is what gives them this New Birth. They think that my blood has something, or rather that it is the great and only cause of this New Birth and they will continue to think so. I would not let this matter deter you from attending their meetings because, as I have said, the (Holy) Spirit is present with them. Of course they will learn differently when they come to the spirit world and see that I am not God.

Keep steadfast in the faith that you now have and you will find that your soul development will become so great that you will be able to show by the powers that will be given you that you will be able to do the wonderful things which I and my disciples did while on earth.

Yes, I know that is what all the orthodox believe but that does not make it a fact, for no devil ever comes and teaches the things that I have written you and which I shall hereafter write. I want you to trust in me to the fullest and you will see all the wonders that will be worked before you shall come to the spirit world. I will not write more now.

So with the assurance that I am with you very often, and that I will guide you in the ways of truth, I will stop.

Your brother and friend,
Jesus.[102]

Mr. Padgett's father writes about his friend's present spiritual condition and the suffering that he must undergo before he can begin to see the light

November 11th, 1915.

I am here, your father.

I have been much interested in your conversation tonight, and I see that your two friends are firm believers in spiritualism and in the communications which you receive from the spirits who profess to write.

Of course Dr. Stone who is a believer of some years standing has no doubt whatever; but Mr. Morgan, having so recently embraced this belief, is at times a little skeptical, and this is natural; but his belief will grow, and we firmly believe, as do you, in the near future, and he will be a great help to you and to the cause. He is now undergoing that change in his ideas of life here and on earth, that he will soon realize the truths as we shall teach them to you.

I want to say a word in reference to the message which you received from your friend, Mr. Lipscomb. He is a spirit in a very dark and depraved condition and shows upon his spirit countenance the results of his dissipated life on earth. His soul has very little development, and his

---

[102] This message is a composite of three, being published in Volume II and originally twice in Volume III. The second instance has been removed from this edition. (G.J.C.)

mind is in such a condition that he will require much discipline through suffering, before he will commence to see the light, and comprehend that the truths of God are eternal and never change, and that he must accept these truths before he can progress much.

He was so anxious to write to you, and expressed his desires in such a pitiable way, that we thought it would do him good to permit him to write, and he did. Mr. Riddle has talked to him and endeavored to show him the way to light and relief, but at this time he is not in condition to receive or understand these truths, and he has gone back to his dark and dreary condition and his hell, as he calls it.

We will not desert him, though, but will continue to use our influence and love to help him, and in the course of time, he will realize that he must ask help from the Father, and then he will receive it. He is not of a very reverent turn of mind, and his ideas of earth are with him still, and will remain with him until he becomes persuaded that there is only one thing that will take him out of his darkness and suffering.

There is another thing that I wish to tell you, and that is that he is still visiting the bar rooms, which he so frequently visited when he was on earth, and is drinking his whiskey and other accursed drinks as he thinks. The attraction of this stuff and these places is holding him fast to this manner of living. So you see his life here is not much different from what it was on earth, only he is not able of himself to indulge in these appetites, but must use the appetites and organs of some of his late earth friends to satisfy his appetite. This, of course, is a matter of imagination, but to him it is as real as was his drinking on earth, and for the time being, causes him to believe that he is actually satisfying his cravings. But while he is not doing so, he is working injury to some mortals whom you know, in that he is causing them to drink more than they otherwise would.[103]

Oh, the curse of habits and evil appetites once acquired and never gotten rid of. So his only salvation now is for him to have some great awakening as to his true condition, and then his reform may commence, but until then it is almost hopeless to try to help him. I will not write more of him tonight, but say that we will not permit him to write again until he gets into a better condition.

We are all very happy and are with you a great deal, loving you and trying to help you. You must not let your worries possess you so much for they do you harm. Yes, I know that it is difficult not to worry under such circumstances, but soon you will not have cause to worry as we have told you.

Well, you may lose faith and we can hardly blame you, but the relief will come just the same.

---

[103] This situation takes place in the astral plane and is termed obsession. (G.J.C.)

I will not write more tonight.
Your loving Father,
John H. Padgett.

Methodist minister would like to tell his people on earth what he has learned to be the Truth about the soul

December 9th, 1915.

I am here, John P. Newman.
I wish you would let me write a few lines tonight.[104]

I was, when on earth, a preacher of the Gospel of Jesus, as I then understood it, and made my great and earnest efforts to show my brother man what the truths of that Gospel were, and at times succeed to a great degree. But, I now see how far short I was in my knowledge and understanding; of these truths, and how very much the creeds and dogmas of my church interfered with me and the members of my church in getting a true conception of the truths of the Master. Many a man lost his opportunity to develop his soul by his beliefs in the atonement. I mean that he relied upon the sacrifice of Jesus, being all sufficient to pay the debt which he supposed he owed to the Father, and relying upon such belief he neglected to develop his soul qualities of love for the Father. This doctrine of atonement is one that is working great harm among the children of men, and one that should no longer be believed, but be shown to be utterly at variance with the truth, and not approved by either God or the Master.

I know, it may seem surprising to some people, that such assertions could come from an orthodox minister of the church, (Methodist) but if these people could only know what I now know, they would not be surprised at all, but would bend their efforts to have the creeds of their churches so revised and reformed, that the doctrine that I speak of, and a number of other untrue and harmful doctrines, would be entirely eliminated from these creeds and from their own beliefs also.

I have found that progress in this spirit world is a portion of the heritage of spirits just as progress belongs to mortals on earth; but not every spirit progresses, just by reason of being in the spirit world. Desire and will must exist, and must be exercised in order for this progression to take place, and I have heard that numerous spirits have been in a condition of stagnation for a great many years, just because they won't

---

[104] This sentence originally continued: ", as I am very dogmas of my church interfered with me and the members of my church the spirit world, and received the love of the Father in my soul." but is incomprehensible as such. It looks like a line has been misplaced in typing out the message as there is a later instance of "dogmas of my church interfered with me and the members of my church." (G.J.C.)

exert themselves to desire and believe what is often told them.

I have taken up more of your time tonight than I intended, and I must apologize for having so intruded, but I felt that I should like to say just what I have said, as it may be that these truths may help some mortal to get into the light and the way to God's Kingdom.

So, if you will pardon me, I will say that I am thankful for your kindness, and would like to come again, if it is agreeable to you.

I will in saying good night subscribe myself,

Your true brother in Christ,

John P. Newman.

late a minister of a church in your city and a Bishop of the Methodist Denomination.

Mr. Padgett helped spirits from all walks of life and the early Indian who asked for help was not denied to write

March 6th, 1916.

I am the last of the Mohicans, and want to write a line.

I was an Indian who lived in the early days of your country's existence and I was not a civilized Indian as you would say, but was a warrior and a leader of my tribe and have many scalps to my credit. So you see there are some Indians in the spirit world who still glory in the deeds which they did on earth, and still feel the hatred and enmity against the pale faces who inflicted injury upon them. But I understand that some Indians have lost all such feelings, and that they are happier by having done so, and it causes me to think that I may be mistaken in holding my hatred against the white people, and that I will never reach the happy hunting grounds so long as I am in the present condition of bitterness and hope for revenge. What do you think of it?

I will do as you say, and I see that your guide is a very happy spirit, so I will ask his advice.

This is all I wish to say.

Good night.

Reassures Mr. Padgett that all his material requirements and plans will be realized

January 5th, 1917.

I am here, John.

I merely want to say that you must keep up your courage and belief that everything will be fulfilled as we have promised for while there may appear to be a delay in realizing the things that you desire yet they will surely come and you will get what you want and in the condition that you think is necessary to enable you to live the life that will make you able to do the work of the Master without the interference of your earthly affairs.

You may be surprised that I should write in this way, but I am interested particularly in your accomplishing the great mission that has been bestowed upon you, and I want to tell you that I have been specially designated to attend you in the way of a helper and inspirer of those things that will work to the accomplishing of our plans to reveal to mankind the truths that will cause their salvation and redemption. I am not given to interfering in material affairs but in your case I see that these things stand in the way of your carrying out our designs and hence they must be gotten rid of and I will try as are many others trying to relieve you of these differences. So with all this you must not suppose that you are not to do your part in accomplishing this end for you must work with us and bend all your efforts to bring about the desired end.

Many here of the high spirits wish to communicate to you and they are waiting for you to get into a condition that will enable them to deliver their messages as they wish to do. Think more of the Father and His Love and of the great privilege that you have in coming in close communion with these high spirits and receiving the benefit of their love and influence; for you are favored in this particular and in love (relying) upon you as our greatest instrument by which we are to accomplish our design and you must not let anything stand in the way of helping us to fulfil our plans.

You will find that you will receive more and more of this Divine Love and a greater soul development as you continue in this work and ultimately you will become a very happy and spiritual man doing much good and will have displayed in you the wonderful powers of the workers of old who lived with the Master and performed many things that were called miracles. So I say, try to realize the importance of the work that you have to do and the powers that will be given you. For I must tell you now that never since the days of the apostles have such honors been given to a man.

Well, I know just how you feel in respect to my prophecies but what I say will become true and you will live to see all these things fulfilled. Not that it is not a part of your work at this time now, you are only to receive these messages and also the wonderful soul development that I speak of for this latter is necessary to your receiving the promise that I speak of as these powers will be entirely things of a spiritual origin and unless you are in condition of soul to receive them they cannot come into your possession.

After this shall have been accomplished then you will do work of a kind to demonstrate to the world the genuineness of your messages and for this purpose you will do things that by many will be considered miraculous and from them such good will come to man, not only physically but spiritually. I came to tell you this because I see that the time is here when you must understand and fully appreciate the importance of your work as well as of the relationship that you sustain to God's spiritual instrumentalities in bringing about the great results that we desire and which men so much need. Well, I will not write more now but let me impress upon you the necessity of considering and meditating on what I have written.

Jesus is the one great instrument in doing this work and upon you he depends for that part of the work which belongs to the material. He is with you very often and he loves you with a very deep and lasting love and is exerting his promise to help you and enable you to do his work. And many spirits, both in the Celestial and in the Spiritual Heavens are with you in love and care and are trying to help you both spiritually and individually. So remember this and when you become discouraged think of the fact that you have sustaining you the wonderful love and power of the spirit world and of spirits who are high up in the Celestial spheres and have more of Divine Love of the Father than have any other spirits in all God's universe. So with my love and blessing, I am

Your brother in Christ,
John.

Writes that Mr. Padgett will receive great love and power to do the great work of the Master as well as other high spirits

January 5th, 1917.[105]

I am here, Helen.

Well, my dear old Ned, I am here to love you and encourage you and tell you that you must try to have more faith and you will soon realize that you have about and in you a sustaining influence that will enable you to overcome every obstacle.

I am glad that John came and wrote you as he did for we all see the importance of your realizing to the fullest that the position that you occupy in this work and the great importance of your receiving these truths that the Master and high spirits shall write you. I cannot tell you how happy I am when I know that you have been so favored and with what a great love and power will be given to you to do this work.

These spirits, if you could see them, would amuse you to know

---

[105] This message has this date attached because it was published after the message from John above which was easily dated. However this message only mentions John, and not Samuel and Luke, as the diary entry of that date would suggest. (G.J.C.)

that they are the greatest and most highly developed of all God's spirits and that they are so in earnest about this matter. So try to have more faith and pray for more love and your soul will become so largely developed that you may in some degree, by your soul perception, realize what wonderful beings surround you and are working with and loving you. I came today because I felt your thoughts of love and aspirations flowing to the Father and I feel that you needed me to write just a few words of love and cheer.

We will be with you tonight and you may get some deep messages of the truth and consolation for yourself as well as for your fellow mortals. Remember that your Helen is with you in all her love and influence and is very happy when she realizes that you love her so much. Well you must not write more today as it will not do you good physically. So knowing that you love me and trust and want me with you, I am

Your own true and loving,
Helen.

Explains the soulmate separations in the event that both do not obtain the Divine Love of the Father

May 26th, 1916.

I am here, John.

I desire to write about a matter that will interest you as I have heard you express your wonderment as to what would become of the soulmate who should happen to be in a condition that caused him to be without the Divine Love at the time the great potentiality of obtaining the Divine Love should be taken from mankind.

Well, this is a subject which has been discussed by spirits of the higher spheres and we have not been able to solve the question. Of course it is necessary that the two parts of the soul must again unite in order to make the perfect one, and if one part should be in the Celestial Heavens and the other part in the Spirit World at the time the great gift is taken from man, it would not be possible for these two parts to unite and become one again.

As you know we are not informed as to when this great separation will take place, and only know that at some time it will and that then the spirits in each of these conditions of development will have to part and never more become united.

But as to the effect of such a separation on two soulmates I cannot tell you as I don't know.

We don't believe there will not be some provision made by which these two separated parts can be united for I cannot conceive that one could be completely happy without his soulmate in condition of unity. Many a soul will never enter the Celestial Heavens or partake of this Divine Love and nature of the Father, but will have to spend eternity in the spirit world. I mean in the spheres lower than the Celestial Spheres, and may or may not have his soulmate with him. I do not know how to instruct you in this matter and am waiting for the great event in order to learn the truth regarding the matter.

But irrespective of this mystery, every man and woman should strive to obtain this Love which will enable him to enter the Celestial Spheres and not wait until he gets into the spirit world, as it is very much easier to start on this journey from earth than from the spirit world.

I do not believe that there will be any separation of soulmates when one of them is in the Celestial Spheres for the result would be the writer's incompleteness of the severance of that soul from its mate.

I wish that I could inform you as to what provision will be made for the reuniting of soulmates who are in the condition of the ones just mentioned, but I cannot, and all that I might say would be speculation only.

I will not write more now, but will say that you have my love and blessings.

Your brother in Christ, John.

Responds to Mr. Padgett's call to write

I am here, your own loving Helen.

I heard your call and of course I responded but there was a poor dark spirit who wanted to write. White Eagle explained to him that it is not permitted for him to write at this time and that he must not try and the spirit left.

Well, I see that you are very sleepy and I will not write more tonight. I am happy and progressing; and love you with all my heart and soul and want you to love me.

So with my kiss I will say good night.

Your own true and loving,

Helen.

Explains what takes place on death of the body and what does the spirit of man do when it leaves the body

May 29th, 1916.

I am here, St. John, Apostle of Jesus.

I come tonight to tell you a vital truth, which I know you will be interested in. The question has often been asked: "What does the spirit of man do when it leaves the physical body for eternity?"

Many spirits, I know, have written you about this matter and some of them have described their personal experiences, yet in all the information that you have received there are some facts that have not been referred to, and I will in a brief way describe them.

When the spirit leaves the body, there is a breaking of the silver cord, as it is called, and thereby all connection between the spirit and the body is severed for all eternity—never again can that spirit enter that body, and neither can any other spirit, although, I know, it is claimed by some spiritualists that another spirit may inhabit the cast-off body. But this is all wrong, for no spirit ever enters the body which has once been the home of another spirit, and, hence, claims made by some of the wise men of the East that such a thing can be, have no foundation in fact.

When the silver cord is once severed, no power that is known to the spirit world, or among spirits of the highest sphere, can again resuscitate that body and cause the manifestation of life, and, hence, in the miracles mentioned in the Bible, where it is said that the dead were brought to life, it must be understood that this tie between the spirit and the body was never broken.

In those ancient days, as now, there were persons who had the appearance of being dead, and so far as human knowledge was concerned were dead, but who were really in a state of what may be called suspended animation. With no signs of life appearing, to the consciousness of men, death was thought to have taken place. Yet in no case where the supposed dead were raised to life, had the mortal really died.

As Lazarus has already told you, when Jesus commanded him to come forth, he had not died, and so of all the other supposed dead who were called to life. When this tie has been once severed, there are certain chemical laws affecting the physical body, and certain spiritual laws affecting the spirit, which absolutely render it impossible for the spirit to again enter the body; and as you have been informed, we all, mortals and spirits and angels as well, are governed by laws which have no exceptions, and never vary in their workings. So I say, when once the spirit and body separate, it is for all eternity, and the spirit then becomes of itself, a thing apart, controlled entirely and exclusively by laws governing the spirit body.

With the spirit's entry into the spirit world, comes the soul, still enclosed in that spirit body, and to an extent controlled by that body, which latter is also, in certain particulars controlled by the soul. The spirit body has not, of itself, the power to determine its own location or destiny, as regards place, for the Law of Attraction which operates in this particular, operates upon the soul, and the condition of the soul determines the location of itself, and as the spirit body is the covering of the soul, it must go where this law of attraction decrees the soul shall abide.

While the mind and the mental faculties and the senses have their seat in the spirit body, yet the law that I speak of does not operate upon these faculties, as is apparent to every spirit which he knows from observation, as well as from experience, that the combined power of all these faculties cannot move a spirit body one step in the way of progress, unless such faculties have, in their influence upon the soul, caused its condition to change; and in the matter of mere mental or moral advancement this can be done.

So, I repeat, the condition of the soul determines the locality as well as the appearance of the spirit body, and this law of attraction is so exact, that in its operations, there is no opportunity for chance to interpose, and place the spirit body in a location which is not its, by reason of the operation of this law. So that when the spirit body enters the spirit world it must go to and occupy the place which its enclosed soul determines that it shall occupy. No interposition of spirit friends or love of parent or husband or child can prevent this destiny, although for a time, until the soul has really has an awakening as to its condition of severance from the mortal life, these relations or friends may retain the spirit body near the place of its entrance into the spirit life, even though that place be one of more beautiful surroundings and happiness than the one to which it is destined. But this situation does not last long, for the law works, and as the soul comes into full consciousness, it hears the call and must obey.

And thus you see, friends and loved ones in spirit life meet with love and kindness and consolation, the newly arrived spirit, but the parting must come, and every soul must find its home according as its own qualities have determined. And yet the consolation mentioned is a real one, for in many instances, if it were not so, the lonely spirit would experience fear and bewilderment and all the unspeakable sensations of being deserted.

Then there comes a time, when every soul must stand alone, and in its weakness or strength realize that no other soul can bear its sorrow or take from its burdens or enter into its sufferings, And thus is realized the saying that each soul is its own keeper and alone responsible for its own condition.

Of course in many cases the loving friends may visit that soul in its place of existence and offer consolation and help and encouragement and instruction, but in some cases this cannot be, for as this soul is then laid bare to itself, all its deformities, and sins and evil qualities come before it, and thus throws around it a wall, as it were, that prevents the good friends and loving ones from appearing to it.

And thus again comes into operation the great Law of Attraction for while these more elevated friends, cannot come to that soul, yet other spirits of like souls and qualities may become its associates, and render such assistance as the blind can lead the blind in their movings about. And I wish here to say, notwithstanding what some of your spiritualistic teachers have said, that the soul has its location as well as its condition.

The above condition that I have described is the destiny of some souls shortly after becoming spirits, and it is a deplorable one, and you may think that such souls are deserted by the loving influences of God's ministering spirits, and left all alone in the dreary places of their habitations. But such is not the case, for while they are deprived of the presence, to them, of the higher spirits, yet the influences of love and compassion are flowing from these spirits, and at sometime will be felt by the lonely ones, and as these influences are felt the poor souls commence to have an awakening which gradually causes the wall of their seclusion to disappear until at some time, the higher spirits find that they can manifest their presence to these unfortunate ones.

And, besides, this, every spirit, no matter how fallen, has a work to do, even though it may appear insignificant, and among these spirits of similar conditions some are a little more progressed than others, and by reason of a law which causes the more progressed to help the lesser, the latter are frequently helped from their low estate.

Now what I have last written applies of course to the spirits who are wicked and vile and without any soul development in the way of goodness, but a similar principle enters into the conditions of all the spirits in the earth plane, although the higher they are in that plane the greater opportunities they have for receiving help and progressing. Of these latter, and the operation of the mental thoughts and moral qualities upon the condition and progress of the soul, I will write you later.

I have written enough for tonight, and leaving you my love and blessings, I will say good night.

Your brother in Christ,

John.[106]

Shared the happiness of Mr. Padgett today when his soul was so filled with the Love of the Father

May 29th, 1916.

I am here, your own true and loving, Helen.

---

[106] This message is a composite of two, being published in Volume I and Volume III. (G.J.C.)

Well sweetheart, you have had some very important messages tonight and the Master says that you have received them in a very accurate and satisfactory manner and that they need very little correction.

I am so glad that you are in such good condition tonight and that your soul is so filled with the Love of the Father. It has been a happy day for you and for me too, for I have been with you a great part of the day and entered into your happiness and also the thoughts that you have had as to the spirit world and the joys of the redeemed.

I was with you at Mr. Morgan's and you did him much good by your conversation and the influence which you cast over him for I must tell you that there were present many spirits of the high kind that were interested in your conversation and influenced your thoughts of things spiritual. The music at the church was very inspiring and I enjoyed your thoughts of Love for the Father and the Master as well as for myself.

Question was asked.

They were present also, your mother and grandmother, and they were happy in seeing that your thoughts were turned towards the higher things of life and they were impressing you with their loving thoughts and trying to make you realize their presence.

Pray more to the Father and you will find that another sensation of love will come to you and faith and joy. Love me too for I love you with all my heart and soul and long to have you know that I am your own loving soulmate who will be yours through all eternity.

Well, you have written enough for tonight and are tired. I will be with you in your sleep and will try to carry you with me and let you realize my love.

Oh my Ned, how I love you tonight and how dear you are to me and how I long for the time to come when you will be with me in my home. So sweetheart, love me and think of me and believe that in all God's universe, there is no one that loves you as does your own true soulmate.

So kiss me good night and say that you love me. Yes I am yours now and always. Good night and God bless you.

Your own true and loving,
Helen.

Strongly urges him to get in condition to receive the Celestial messages that are more important than the personal ones that he is receiving

September 27th, 1917.

I am here, John the Baptist.

I merely wish to say that your condition tonight is not such as to permit the high spirits to communicate to you the important spiritual truths which they are waiting to write, and that you will receive communications from your friends of the spirit world upon matters more personal.

We have so many messages to communicate that we find the time is hardly long enough in which to do so, and we earnestly hope that you will soon get in condition to receive our messages. Let your mind turn more to the truths which have been revealed to you and to the love of the Father, and you will soon find yourself in a better condition. So, wishing that you will take my advice I will say good night.

Your brother in Christ,
John the Baptist.

Explains that Jesus has already come the second time, which subject he will discuss at a later date

December 29th, 1916.

I am here, John.

Let me write a line. I was with you tonight and heard the sermon of the preacher on the second coming of Jesus, and by it you were convinced of the continued revelation of the truths that you are receiving. How very much mistaken this preacher is in his beliefs, and how disappointed he will be when he comes to not only realize the truths, but also the knowledge that while living on earth Jesus had already come the second time, and that he, the preacher, might have had the benefit of that coming if he had not permitted his orthodox beliefs to prevent the truth from entering his mind and soul.

Well, I would like tonight to write on this subject, but I do not consider it advisable to do so. I promised you a short time ago that I would write on the subject in detail, and so I will very soon, if I can make the proper rapport. Your condition is much better than it has been for some time, and if you will continue to pray and let your longings go to the Father as you have done today, you will soon be in that condition that will enable us to make the rapport so that we can communicate our deep spiritual truths. Try with all your determination and effort to get in this condition and you will not fail. There are other messages, as you know, that I desire to write and their delivery depends only on you. I will not write more now.

With my love and prayers, I will say good night.
Your brother in Christ,

John.

Does not approve of Mr. Padgett's idea to send messages to a man that would not appreciate it

December 27th, 1915.

I am here, Helen.

Well sweetheart, I have been waiting for some time to write to you and tell you that you are not doing the right thing by sending the message to the man who wrote the article in which the message comments on his, a man that will not appreciate what it contains. I say this because I have visited him since you commenced to think of writing to him and find that he is another self-conceited man and has opinions of his own which are not easily influenced. I would like you to send it to anyone who would appreciate it, but I do not believe that the man you have in mind will.

Well, as you say, Jesus is the one to judge and he may think differently from me and I think I may ask him. He may decide that you had better send it even though he sees that the man will not believe in the ways of its coming.

So I will not say that you do not send it until he has decided the matter and he is here now and will write you, but before I stop I want to say that I love you with all my heart and am with you trying to comfort you and make you feel the effect of my love.

So with all my heart, I will say good night.

Your own true and loving,
Helen.

Does not think that that message could do harm and may do some good

December 27th, 1915.

I am here, Jesus.

Well my dear brother, I have read what your wife wrote you and at first thought I agreed with her for I am afraid that the person referred to is of the character that she describes. Yet when I consider the matter I am inclined to think that it may be a wise thing to send it to him as while he may not believe that I wrote it, yet, he may find some truth in it that may set him to thinking and help him to a broader view of man's relation to the Father. At any rate try the experiment as it can do no harm and may do some good.

I will now write you another message on a matter of utmost

importance and I hope that you will be in condition to receive it. I will not write more tonight.

Well, I am with you very often and my love is influencing you all the time and the love of the Father is flowing into your soul also. I am so glad that you feel to such an extent the importance of this work and I promise that very soon now you will be in condition to do my work as you desire and I want you to.

So continue to let your soul long for more of the Father's love and His faith and you will find that they will come to you in increasing abundance and that you will become very happy. I will be with you and give you my love and will pray to the Father on your request, with all the faith that I have that He may answer my prayers.

So only trust and believe and you will see the glory of the Father and your own salvation to the highest.

I am with you trying to help you in every way and especially in the way of your being able very soon to lay aside your professional work and give all your attention to my work.

The happiness will come, only have faith and use your best efforts to bring about the results desired.

I will stop now but in closing I will assure you of my great love and interest in you. So with all my love, I am

Your brother and friend,
Jesus.

Is with Mr. Padgett often and prays with him to help his soul development to permit him to receive his writings

April 18th, 1918.

I am here, Jesus.

I was with you tonight and heard what the preacher said and some parts of his talk expressed the truth and some did not; and I should like to comment on what he said just now, but you are a little tired from the effect of the writings of the spirits who preceded me and I will postpone my comments until later.

I expressly wish to write on the subject of what God has to do with the war, and show how far the preacher was right. I know that men may be surprised at what I may say, but nevertheless I will state the truth as I know it.

I also desire to finish my message on God, and as your condition is much improved I will do so very soon, and you must commence to write or permit me to write earlier in the evening, when you are fresh. I was with you last night as you prayed, and prayed with you, and you were benefitted. I will continue to pray, for I desire and it is necessary that your soul have such development and get in such rapport with me as will enable me to write my deepest and highest messages of spiritual truths and this can be brought about only by the love increasing in your soul and your becoming nearer and closer to the Father. And there is nothing in all the universe that can accomplish this result so certainly as the receiving of this love in your soul, in fact, there is nothing else; and you must pray and long for its inflowing. I will not write more now, so good night.

Believe that I am with you often, throwing my love and influence about you. Well, I understand and am sorry that it has so far not worked out its end; but it will, I am sure, for the work has to be accomplished, and the attaining of these ends is necessary. Have a little more faith, and act on it.

Your brother and friend,
Jesus.

Confirms what the Master said and encourages him in his work

April 18th, 1918

I am here, your grandmother.

Let me say that I have heard what the Master said and join with him in advising you to keep up your faith and courage, for I know that which you desire will be accomplished and the means found for fulfilling the work and bringing it to a successful issue.

We are all with you, trying to help you, and we will. Only do as the Master said and you will not fail or be disappointed in the end. Believe that I love you very much and am with you often, and that we will succeed. Good night.

Your grandmother.

Jesus' help spiritually is without limit but the material depends on the individual himself

January 12th, 1919.

I am here, Jesus.

Let me say a few words. I have been with you tonight while at church and since you came home and understand your desire to have the preacher read my message on the soul and I agree with you that it is advisable. He has some conception of what the soul is but his knowledge is not of that character as to enable him to express the most important qualities or its origin or difference from the spirit.

I was glad that he undertook to deal with this subject for it has given you the opportunity of making known to him or of affording him the opportunity to talk to him about these truths and then be able to enlighten him, for his mind is working in error and misconception of what the truth of these spiritual things is.

I desire to come soon and write another message and am only waiting for you to get into the necessary condition that I may do so.

Well, I will understand you and will come some night this week. Think more of these spiritual things and pray more to the Father for His Love and you will not fail to get in condition. Our work will go on and we will have many messages, yet tonight we must take advantage of every possible moment.

I have been with you a great deal lately trying to influence you and turn your mind to these spiritual things and away from merely earthly things that are not important to you. I hope that you will soon be so situated that you can give all your thoughts and attention to the work and I believe you will if you will make the effort. You know we can help you in many ways but more depends upon yourself as to these material matters and you must act.

I will not write more tonight and with my love and the Father's blessings I will say good night.

Your brother and friend,
Jesus.

Attended a church service with Mr. Padgett and tells of what the preacher should have said regarding the blood sacrifice

May 6th, 1917.

I am here, Jesus.

I intended to finish my message tonight but I see that you are not feeling inclined to receive it and so I will wait until tomorrow night.

Well, that is satisfactory, for I desire that you shall receive it just as I may write it, and I want you to be in condition; so do not think that I am disappointed. I understand and you must not feel that you have caused me any disappointment.

Yes, that I desire you to do, for sometimes it is difficult to make the exact expression; your mind will at times become positive and that interferes with my control. But I am well pleased with the way in which it was written.

Well, I will write all that is essential for man to understand just what the way to that kingdom is and what he must do to become an inhabitant of it.

I was with you at the church this morning, and I impressed you with my feelings in reference to what the preacher said as to my sacrifice and blood. Instead of calling upon his people to show their gratitude for the sacrifice and the cross, he should have taught them that the sacrifice and the blood do not save them from their sins and in that particular there is nothing that calls for their gratitude; and that to worship me as they do, and as he teaches them to do, is blasphemy, and a more heinous sin than ingratitude.

I was successful in impressing you with my feelings of dissatisfaction, and was glad that I could, for it shows that our rapport is becoming closer, and after a while you will be able to receive my thoughts by inspiration as well as by writings. You must pray and have faith, and if you do you will more often have the experiences that you did last night, which only means a quicker soul development. Trust me and you will not be disappointed. I will not write more now.

So with my love and the Father's blessing, I will say good night.
Your brother and friend,
Jesus.[107]

Writes that although the Master was anxious to write tonight, He was not displeased with him

February 5th, 1916.

I am here, your own true and loving Helen.

Well dear, I see that you do not feel like writing much tonight, and will say only a few words.

The Master was anxious to finish his message, but he saw your condition and was not displeased that you did not write. But get in condition by tomorrow night.

Well, I have been with you today at your office, and also at church, and was loving you with all my heart and soul, and tried to make you feel my presence and love.

I think if you soon go to bed you will feel better in the morning.

Well, I will do so, and tomorrow night he will come and tell you what is best for you to take. While he has not written you for a long time yet he is with you quite often looking after you. I will tell him your desire and I know that he will do what is best.

So sweetheart, keep up your courage and faith and pray, and you will be happier and realize your desires.

Good night, my own dear husband.

---

[107] This message is a composite of two, being published in Volume II and Volume III. (G.J.C.)

Your own true and loving,
Helen.

Mr. Padgett's boyhood chum expresses his gratitude for the help given to him

I am here, your old boyhood chum, Frank Davis.

Let me write just a line as I am anxious to tell you that I have progressed out of the darkness in which I was when I first came to you. I acted on your advice and prayed to the Father for His Love and after a long time as faith came to me this Love flowed into my soul and I was taken from my darkness and found relief in the light and happiness. I can now express to you how grateful I am and with what joy I thank and pray to the Father for His Love.

I will not take more time tonight, but believe me.

Your grateful friend, good night,

Frank Davis, your old boyhood chum.

Expresses his love for Mr. Padgett and the work that he is doing in behalf of the Kingdom

May 1st, 1917.

I am here, Samuel.

Yes, I am Samuel who has written to you many times before and expect to write you many more times in the future as I have some messages that I desire to write regarding the higher truths and I also want to communicate to you, personally, for I am much interested in you and your work and the fact that you have been selected to do this work makes you an object of my love and care and causes me to desire to be with you in love and friendship.

Well tonight I will not write one of my formal letters but will only say that you are in a much better condition than you have been and will now get in such a rapport with us that will enable us to deliver the messages as we desire.

I have heard what the writer has just written you and know that what he says is true and as your friend and brother I urge you to believe and pray to the Father with all the longings of your soul and with the faith that admits of no doubt.

Many spirits are here tonight desiring to write and express to you the gratitude for what you have done for them and tell you of the progress that they have made, but of course they cannot all write. I will soon come and write.

So believe that I love you and am,

Your brother in Christ,
Samuel.

That the only part of man that is immortal is the soul, the spirit is merely the active energies that manifest life and these energies for their existence depend upon the soul from which they emanate

August 26th, 1916.

I am here, Jesus.

I come tonight to let you know that in a few nights I will write you another message, conveying important truths that are necessary for men and spirits to know.

I see that you have not been well and that your vitality is somewhat exhausted, and that it is not best for you to attempt to write much at this time. You had better not attempt to receive any messages except from your wife. I wish to tell you though, that you will soon feel much better, and will be able to proceed with your work without any interference.

The only part of man that is immortal is the soul—the spirit is merely the active energies that manifest life and these energies for their existence depend upon the soul from which they emanate. Very soon I will deliver a message defining just what the soul is, and what the spirit is, and their relationship to each other and to the body. So do not trouble yourself about this question, but believe that the soul is the ego—the real part of man which distinguishes him from the beast, which has a spirit as has man, but not a soul. All these matters will be explained before we cease delivering these messages of truth.

I will not write more tonight, but with my love and blessings, say to you have faith in the Father's love and pray without ceasing, and all happiness will be yours.

Your brother and friend,
Jesus.

There are very often spirits present who listen to those on earth when they read spiritual truths

August 15th, 1916.

I am here, Jesus.

I have been interested in your reading of the messages and on desires tonight (sic) and I know that they will do much good to those who have heard them for I must tell you that there have been present a large number of spirits of all kinds that have listened attentively to what you have read and many of them are wondering what they can mean as they only heard the important points of the messages referred to.

You must continue to receive the messages just as soon as you get in a better condition physically which will soon be as you will commence to recover your vitality, just as quickly as the weather gets a little cooler.

Tonight I will not write more as it is very late and you had better go to bed, but I will come soon and write you. So with my love I will say good night.

Your brother and friend,
Jesus.

Due to Mr. Padgett's heavy schedule with the dark spirits that even Jesus had to make definite appointments to fit into his schedule

October 23rd, 1916.

I am here, Jesus.

I intended to night to write a message, but you continued your reading until it was too late. I know what you would say, but at that time these dark spirits were so anxious to write that I did not interfere, although they could not write, because you declined to let them do so. Your power of control over these spirits is almost complete and many higher spirits wonder at it. But as you have been instructed in this matter and have acquired a knowledge of the way in which you can apply the law that operates to prevent them from writing when you intend that they shall not write, (it) is not astonishing.

Well, when I saw that they were anxious and were making the effort I left and returned only a short time ago. But the meaning of my complaint is that you did not earlier in the evening give me the opportunity to write just after you had finished your paper and before you commenced to copy. It was the understanding a short time ago that we would commence our writings this early in the evening.

Well you are mistaken for I could have written very easily at the time mentioned. That will be agreeable and I will come then. The important thing is to have these messages of truth delivered and received. These other things that you speak of are interesting and have some importance, but yet, the messages should be considered of the first importance, and be received in preference to any of these other communications.

I know that the condition of the preacher's mind and beliefs is of some importance under the circumstances attending his liberality of thought, and much good may be done by using these truths to enlarge his scope of the true relationship of God and man, yet there will be time for this and the truths must be first delivered.

Yes, I understand, and I am pleased that such are your longings and desires, and if you will only persist in these longings and pray to the Father with all the earnestness of your aspirations, and let faith take hold of these aspirations, you will very soon have a wonderful inflowing of this love and get in that condition of at-onement that you so much desire. I will be with you and help you with my prayers and love, and I know that the Father will bless you.

I will not write more now, but will come tomorrow night. So with my love and blessings, I will say good night,

Your brother and friend,
Jesus.

Tells Mr. Padgett that he has the power to prevent the dark spirits from writing as Jesus has just written

October 23rd, 1916.

I am here, your own true and loving Helen.

Well sweetheart, the dark spirits are very anxious to write tonight, and it is somewhat difficult to control them, although, as Jesus said, you have the power, yourself, to prevent them from writing. They are so very unhappy that you will relieve (?) it and let them write.

They are increasing in numbers more and more, and seem more anxious to come in contact with you than ever, and we find it is difficult to induce them to leave. But I see the wisdom of your rule (to only receive their messages one day a week) and the necessity of enforcing it, for otherwise the higher spirits would not have any opportunity to convey their messages.

Well, I heard what the Master said, and you must try to do as he says regarding the time of writing. He is so very anxious to write and so are a number of others. I mean the higher spirits, for they all have messages of truth to deliver.

Yes, they (my band) are desirous of writing you but you have been so crowded that they have not attempted to interfere. She has a message and will come soon and deliver it. Well, I will tell them what you say and we will arrange for the writing in the way that you suggest, and they will be happy to do so, I know. I will not write more now—you had better go to bed soon and get up earlier. So give me my kiss and say good night,

Your own true and loving,
Helen.

That the world is becoming more spiritual and requires spiritual food, and that war causes people to think more of the hereafter

December 16th, 1917.

I am here, Jesus.

Well, my disciple, I realize that your desires are that I shall deliver a message to you tonight, and I am anxious to do so, yet I see that you are not just in condition that I may take that possession of your brain that is necessary in order to write satisfactorily. I am sorry that this is so, but it is a fact, and we will have to wait a while longer, which will not be very long, for you are much improved, and if you continue to pray you will soon become in that soul condition that will enable me to make the rapport.

There are many messages yet to be written and I am anxious that you receive them in order that they may be delivered to the world, for the world is now awakened to a greater realization of the fact that man is spiritual and must have spiritual food. The war is causing many people to think of the hereafter and the destiny of the soul; and the knowledge that the world now has of the future life is very meager and unsatisfactory, merely a knowledge that the spirit survives death and experiences more or less happiness in the spirit life.

As you know, this is not the vital thing in the destiny of man, for while a knowledge of the survival of man from the death of the physical may and does give a great deal of consolation to the near and dear ones who are left on earth, yet the fact does not, in the slightest degree, determine the condition or destiny of the soul that has left its home in the flesh; and there are no means, now known to men, to show them that destiny, except some things written in the Bible which are the subject of much speculation and controversy and want of belief. The consolation of those who have faith in the Bible is founded on that faith, or rather, in most cases, belief; but there are a number of believers in the truths of the Bible, with a conscious soul perception of their meaning, who have that faith which makes certain to them the facts of destiny, and the possession of love in their souls. I will come tomorrow night and endeavor to write a formal message; in the meantime let your thoughts turn more to the things of the spirit, and your prayers ascend with more earnestness and longings to the Father.

As you know, I love you as my brother and disciple, and am with you as you pray each night, uniting in your prayers, and you must let your faith increase and believe that your prayers are being heard and will be answered to the fullest. I will not write more now. So my brother, good night, and may the Father bless you with His greatest blessings.

Your brother and friend,
Jesus.

Explains the difference in the work of Mr. Morgan and Dr. Stone and the importance of each, but his revelations can only be made through Mr. Padgett

June 1st, 1920.

I am here, Jesus.

Let me write a few lines, for it has been a long time[108] since you have received any writing from me, and I am desirous to write you. You will remember when last[109] I wrote that I told you that there are many messages yet to be delivered, and that you must get in condition to receive the same, and I now repeat that statement with emphasis.

As you have been told many times, these revelations can be made only through your mediumship and unless you become fully convinced of this fact, and act accordingly, these truths that are so important to man, and that we are so anxious to have come to the knowledge of the world, may not be made known. This I know may seem extravagant and hardly possible, but it is the truth and you must believe it. I am as much interested in the work as ever and also in the work that your two friends are now doing, as well as in that which they shall do in the future, and they also must realize this fact and believe what I tell them.

The work of Mr. Morgan is one that is very important and causes the salvation of many souls that are now and have been in darkness, and he must understand that only he can so successfully do the work. As has been written him, there are myriads of these spirits who attend him when he gives his talks, and many more who make the effort to get near enough to him to catch the import of his teachings, but cannot get within the circle that desire the benefit of what he says. And as his spirit friends have told him, his band and others find much difficulty in giving the necessary attention to all those who have become interested in the truth because of what he says to them. But he need not hesitate to do the

---

[108] Initially this message was shown as June 7th in the tablet as received. This tablet was however not the original, but a typed out document. The message previous to June 7th was five days prior and which would seem to be at variance with this comment. Yet both this message's content and the previous message match the entry descriptions in the tablet, suggesting the dates are correct. (G.J.C.)

[109] This was not contained in the message immediately prior, but was the subject of a great many messages and particularly this one on March 7th 1920. From this I am deducing this message was actually June 1st, not June 7th, and that a transcription error has occurred. (G.J.C.)

work because of this feature of conditions, for sooner or later, they will all have the advantage of the instructions of spirits whose mission it is to instruct in the way of life.

But he is mistaken when he thinks because of what some of his friends write, that he can start the great truths to be made known, because that is not his work. They must first be completed when they can be made known to the world, and then this great work will commence and continue. No, upon you depends the necessity of receiving the truths. No other can do this now, and until they shall have been received our book must not be printed or circulated, for the world must have all the truth that it is now capable of receiving and assimilating. Just here I want to say that while the great vital truth of the new birth is already known to you and can be made known to men, yet, you, in your day, will not receive all the truths of the Infinite. Always new ones will come to the knowledge of men, and the revelations of truth will never have a finality—and no man or spirit can ever be able to say that his knowledge is complete. Progress is the one law of the universe that exists always, and man, when he gets in condition, will always be the object and subject of that law.

But the messages that you have read tonight state a fact when they say that you are not in the condition of soul development that you have been, and are not in that rapport with the higher spirits that enables them to communicate. You must arouse from this condition and let your longings go out to the Father for his love, and your thoughts turn more to spiritual things. We are greatly delayed by this condition of yours, and as a consequence, some of the spirits who are engaged and interested in this work become a little impatient, and communicate their thoughts and encouragement as they did in the messages to your friends. I will come soon and resume my writing of the higher truths, if you are in the condition to receive them.

Now think of what I have said, and in thinking, realize the importance of your work. I will not write more tonight; and will leave you with my love and blessings. Good night.

Your brother and friend,
Jesus.

A Muslim never knew or heard of Divine Love with all his many years in the spirit world until Mr. Padgett informed him and helped him to seek and obtain It. Says his prophet never taught us about Divine Love

March 6th, 1916.

I am here, Seligman.

I am the Muslim[110] who has written you before. I come to tell you that I have made investigation since I last wrote you and find that what you told me about the Divine Love is true, and I have received some of it in my soul and am progressing towards the soul spheres, where they tell me more of it can be found and where live those who have received it in greater abundance than I have.

I have never in all the long years of my pilgrimage in the spirit world before learned of the existence of this love and our Prophet never taught us of the existence of this love or anything more than the love which we all have, and the way to progress therein, but now I know that there is such a thing as the Divine Love, and that it is the only love that will enable us to gain the Kingdom of Heaven.

Very few of my people have any conception of the existence of such a love, and, consequently, they are in the spirit spheres where only those who have the natural love live, and they, while in many instances, are good and pure spirits, in this natural love, yet they are not the possessors of that happiness which the Divine Love gives.

I am so glad that I came to you when I did and had the opportunity of meeting and listening to the Christian spirits, for their teachings, as well as their condition of beauty and happiness, have caused my soul perceptions to open up to the truth, and placed my soul in such a condition that the Divine Love can flow into and fill it with its influence and the Essence of the Father.

I am now in the third sphere[111] and am trying with all the longings and aspirations of my soul to get more and more of this Love; and these loving Christian spirits are helping me so much and trying to show me the way and encourage me to increased efforts and faith. I shall never rest contented now until I have received this Love to its fullest extent, for I am told that there is no limit to the amount that I may receive, and no sphere either in the spiritual or celestial world that I may not attain to.

As I receive more of this love, I find that I become more unselfish, and there arises in me the desire that my brothers who know not of this love shall learn of it and seek to obtain it, and I will go back to the home of my brothers and try to teach them the way in which it may be found, and the great happiness that comes with its possession. So I thought that I would tell you of my great fortune and of the hope that I now have of a future bliss in the heavens of God.

Seligman that is the name that I wrote.

---

[110] The previous edition used the word "Mohammedan". (G.J.C.)

[111] A spirit resident in the Sixth Spirit Sphere must return to the Third Spirit Sphere if it wishes to take up the Divine Love path. (G.J.C.)

Well, if you did not receive it in that way there was a mistake for that is my name. I will not write more tonight. Thanking you for the help you gave me, I am your friend in Christ,
Seligman the Muslim.

Agrees with what Bismarck has said about freedom of the German people from one man rule and that the end is very soon

January 22nd, 1918.

I am here, Frederick III—the father.

Let me write a line. I have heard what Bismarck said and I fully agree with him in his predictions as to the ending of the war and while it is not in accord with what would be my desire as a German when on earth, yet it will prove to the great liberator of the Germans as individuals and as a nation. The government of men are intended by the powers that they have in thought the best interests of mankind to be the means by which the greatest good may be bestowed upon the people individually and as a whole, and the government which is founded upon the divine right of any one man or family, to rule, is not best suited for either the progress of the nation or of the individuals that comprise that nation.

Hence, I say that the ending of the German monarchy and dethronement of the Kaiser and his family and all who make claim any right to govern men will work out for the people of Germany individually and as a nation the great good and justice and freedom to which all the children of God on earth are entitled.

Of course, when I lived on earth I did not look on these things from the viewpoint that I now see is the only correct one to assume. I was a monarch and believed in the divine obligations of the people to be ruled and hence were I on earth now I might believe that the Empire of Germany should be maintained under all circumstances, now I am a spirit and realize the hollowness and untruth of all such ideas. In sight of God and in the workings of His unchangeable laws no one man is by birth or nation better and entitled to any greater rights than any other man, and every Emperor and King and nobleman of earth will, when he comes to the spirit life, sooner or later realize this fact, and in the case of some the conviction will come as it may be said, with a vengeance.

It will do no good to write of the great misery and distress that now exists in Germany and of how the cruel masters of the people are compelling them to submit to all this misery, for my writing would not lessen this condition one iota. But I will say that the end of all this horrible nightmare is in sight and peace and happiness will come to the people, though in the meantime many of these people will have become spirits, and among them will be the Kaiser and many of his advisers and sustainers in his unholy ambitions.

As a human father it would be distressing for me to write in this (way) because then I would be controlled by my natural affections and solicitation for my children, but having become a spirit with enlarged and more truthful view of the relationship of mortals and of the importance of each individual soul while I may still maintain the affection for my children yet I can see and know that the greatest good to the people of Germany will come when the ruler of the Empire shall cease. Suffering and death must follow, but out of them will rise peace and happiness and a deeper feeling of the people in their relationship to God.

I will only say further, that the end is here. Yes, very soon and the great sacrifice of men and peace and things material will cease. I will not write more. Good night, your friend,

Frederick the father of the wounded nation.
(Father of William II, the last Kaiser).

Comments on St. John not being able to finish his message and the two German writers' predictions on ending the war

January 22nd, 1918.[112]

I am here, your own true and loving Helen.

Well, dear, you are a little tired and had better not write more tonight. St. John wrote you and was rather disappointed that he could not finish his message, but he saw the condition that surrounds you and like the loving John, that he wrote you as he did.

Your spiritual condition is much better and your experience of this afternoon did you much good for it caused you to turn your thoughts to the spiritual truths of the Father and brought into your soul more of the love.

The two Germans wrote you and they were in earnest and expressed what they honestly thought, and many spirits who are very much interested in the war make the same prediction that these two make as to its ending and the causes there for. I will not write more and advise that you go to bed very soon and get warm. Love me and pray and have faith.

Good night, your own true and loving,
Helen.

---

[112] Date inferred from daily dairy. But this entry was not present in the diary. (G.J.C.)

The medium whose book Mr. Padgett was reading, explains why his book "Spirit Teachings" did not contain the Truth of the "New Birth" as taught by Jesus

September 14th, 1918.

I am here, Stainton Moses.

Let me say a word. I have been present as you read the book called "Spirit Teachings" and saw that while many of the statements therein contained are in accord with the knowledge that you have of spirit matters, yet, that there is wanting the one great truth of the New Birth as it has been explained to you by the Master and other high spirits.

Well, you must not, on account of the fact that this truth is not alleged and explained by the spirits who wrote the messages that you have been reading, assume that these spirits were not of a higher order, or that they are wanting in the knowledge of many truths that the book portrays as to the relationship of spirit to man and man to God, and his future destiny. No, these spirits were real and genuine and taught truths as they understood them. They were limited in their knowledge by the amount of the progress which they had made in things spiritual, and in attempting to teach they were honest and declared only those things that they believed to be true.

Many of the truths that they declared are of vast importance and necessary for men to know in order to their own salvation. They show the way to the condition of the perfect man, and the struggles, and sufferings, and sacrifices that spirits will have to make in order to arrive at this condition, are not overdrawn, but on the contrary are merely the outlines of what will be necessary for men and spirits to undergo in order to become the perfect man or spirit.

These spirits have since the time of the writings learned of this formation of the soul into an Essence Divine by reason of the possession of the Divine Love, and, hence, could not use their medium in making known this great means of perfect salvation, to mankind.

These spirits have since the time of the writings learned of this truth and are now progressing towards the celestial spheres, which can be obtained only by the means of the Divine Love. You will notice in the teachings many expressions that are erroneous, and solely because the writers did not know to the contrary; but this fact must not cause you to believe that many other things which they teach are not true, for outside of and independent of this truth of the divine love and what it means to men and spirits, the teachings are true and should be believed.

I write this that you may not doubt the genuineness of the writings, or think that the same were not made by the spirits who professed to write. These spirits had a mission to perform and were earnestly endeavoring to acquaint the medium, and, through him, the world with the truths and the necessity of meditating upon the same, and ceasing to be satisfied with the old-time beliefs, which were so erroneous and misleading and harmful, as the spirits declared.

I have an enlarged knowledge of the things that pertain to the spirit world, and to the true plan of salvation as established by the Father, and have experienced the possession of the Divine Love and its operations and effect upon the souls of men, and how sufficient it is to relieve men from the sufferings and penalties of their sins that they would have to endure or undergo, were this love not open and free for them to obtain. I have that love to a degree that has made me an angel of the celestial spheres, and a possessor of that immortality that was unknown to men when I lived on earth, and also unknown to the spirits who communicated the writings which you have been reading. They taught a part only of the truth of salvation and regeneration, and that the lesser part in importance, but the one which the large majority of men will know of and obtain, only.

I thought that I would write this to you, for I saw that you were very much interested in the "Teachings", and had in mind the question as to whether these spirits who wrote were acquainted with the Great Truth. And I am very happy that I am permitted to write, for I do not want those who have read and believe these writings to rest upon the assurance that the same contain all of truth, and that there is no other way to heaven and happiness, except that set forth in these writings. It is so important that all of truth should become known to men, and the opportunity given to them to seek and find the great way to immortality and bliss.

I will not write more now, but sometime in the future I should like to come and write further with reference to these matters. I thank you for your kindness in receiving this imperfect communication and will only say further, that the Divine Love and the New Birth and the Celestial heavens where the Master is forming his kingdom, are truths, vital and unchangeable, and the desideratum (something that is needed or wanted) of the happiness of mankind.

I will say good night, and while a stranger to you, yet, can subscribe myself, your brother in Christ,
Stainton Moses the medium.

Approves of Mr. Padgett reading the book by Stainton Moses as there are many things in it that are true

July 5th, 1918.

I am here, St. John.

Let me say a word. I have read with you in the book ("Spiritual Teachings" by Stainton Moses) and I find that many things in it are true, and many others show a want of the true mission of the Master. I do not know the spirit who is supposed to have dictated the messages, but from the nature of the same I would infer that he is a spirit of some of the higher spiritual spheres and that his information is limited by the development of his spirit, as he calls it. He apparently knows nothing of the true mission of Jesus, or of the Divine Love, or of the true resurrection, as was taught by the Master. It is well that you have read this book, for it will show you the differences between the messages which you are receiving and those that you read in the book. Some of the writers declarations are correct—such communications as his development of mind and soul fit him to receive.

But the great and important truth relating to God and man are not contained in the book and could not well be, for the guiding spirit evidently knew nothing of the transformation of the soul into the Divine by reason of the Divine Love. I merely wanted to write this to show you that your work is necessary to be done, and that never has the truths that you are receiving been revealed to men before. Good night,

Your brother in Christ,
John.

The guardian angel of Mr. Padgett has said that Jesus, our leader, is making a great effort to establish a Kingdom of God in the Celestial Heavens

December 16th, 1917.

I am here, St. John.

I will say only a few words. I am John and your guardian angel, and am so thankful that you are again getting into a spiritual condition when we may come and write you of the spiritual truths that we are anxious to communicate. While I have not written as to these truths, yet I have been with you a great deal trying to help you and encourage you in your longings for the Father's Love and for the development of your soul. Very soon I can see, we will resume our writings and then you will be very happy in the thought that you are again in condition to do the Father's work and to benefit humanity.

The most ancient spirits—those who have lived in the spirit world from the entrance of the first spirits therein, can if the medium is in the proper or necessary condition of rapport communicate to mortals. It is a very mistaken belief that the highest spirits do not communicate through mediums or rather may not, for these spirits have not lost their interest in the destiny of the human soul. Of course there is much of the work done by spirits for mortals in which these higher spirits take no part, but such work is generally more of a material nature, and, so far as manifestation to mortals is concerned, performed only for the purpose of convincing men that intercommunication between the two worlds is possible and a fact, and that there is the persistence of life. But when the work is of a nature that leads men to a true conception of the vital spiritual truths and the way that leads to the Father, then these high spirits participate in the work.

Jesus is now the leader of the great effort to establish a Kingdom of God in the Celestial Heavens, and all spirits who have received a portion of the Divine Essence of the Father, through love, know the work that is being done and the aim thereof—and are working to bring about the great consummation of this plan. And here I will say, that in furtherance of this plan, and because you have been selected to work on earth among mortals, yourself a mortal, the highest spirit of the Celestial Heavens has been and is in communication with you, and the most ancient of all the spirits and first of mankind have written. You must believe this, for every message that you have received from spirits who are working to reveal this plan, forms a link in the great chain of revelation, and to not believe any of these messages and their sources would greatly harm and injure the truth of the whole.

No matter what you may read as to the opinion of men who are investigating spiritualism and receiving messages from this side of life, do not for a moment doubt that you have received and are receiving these great spiritual truths from those who profess to deliver the same. I will come soon and write you a formal message on this subject.

Believe that my love is with you and that I am endeavoring to help you in your great work. Pray more and turn your thoughts more to your mission and you will do the work more satisfactorily, and the Father will bless you with a great abundance of His Love. Good night, and trust in what I have written.

Your brother in Christ,
John.

Writes that Mr. Padgett is very near the Father in His Love and not to doubt that the Master is not with him

I am here, St. John.

You are the especial care of the Master, and must believe what he says, for what he says is true. I am with you too, and love you, and am interested in you and the work that you will do.

I know that at times your faith falters, and you think that the Father is far off, and you also doubt that the Master is with you, or that what you receive from Him is not true; but I must tell you that you are very near the Father in His Love, and that the Master is actually writing to you, and wants you to trust in Him, and doubt not His Love or His power.

I, John, say this because I know whereof I speak, and am anxious that you let your faith in God increase, and your trust in the Master be firmly established, for you have in Him a friend such as you never before had, and can never again obtain.

You are benefitted tonight by your attendance at the meeting, although the people paid more worship to Jesus than to God, and you felt the error of it. But let not that disturb your belief or your faith in God. These people were happy in their beliefs, and the Holy Spirit was with them and entered into their souls and made them happy.

They do not realize that Jesus must not be worshipped but yet their real prayers were to the Father and He understood what they were seeking, and hence the Holy Spirit came to them.

Jesus was with you at this meeting and was filling your heart with his love as well as receiving the Divine Love and it helped you very much. I was there also and joined in the services as tar as the worship of God was concerned, and tried to help the people with my love and inspiration.

These people, notwithstanding the mistaken belief as to Jesus' mission, yet have the Divine Love of the Father in their souls and it will help them progress in their soul development. They, of course, will be surprised, when they come into the spirit world to find that Jesus is not God, and that his blood or death does not save them, but their souls, by reason of the divine love being in them, will find that they have progressed towards the fountainhead of God's Love and these mere errors of their beliefs will not retard them long in their spiritual progress.

So I say, do not let the fact that they worship Jesus as God prevent you from attending these meetings as the great flood of the Divine spirit which is present will help you very much.

I will not write more tonight, as others want to write—but soon I will give you a message on a subject dear to my heart and needful for you to know.

With all my love, I am your brother in Christ,
St. John.

Explains that even Jesus can lose power of communications when it is exhausted according to Law of Communication

August 24th, 1915.

I am here, Saint John.
I merely want to say that what the Master says is true, and will

soon triumph, and you must believe for faith is a wonderful help. I know that it seems a long way off to you before you will get in condition to do these things, but it will not be long, for all the powers of our Christian Spirit World is working to bring this about.

I am with you very often when you are least aware of the fact and so are herds of others.

Well, he is subject to the same laws controlling communications that the rest of us are and the powers had left him when he so stated. It is nothing that you should be astonished at because you will find in the future that many times this power will exhaust itself.

You must not think that he is infallible in these things which pertain to the working of the laws governing the communications between spirits and mortals. We are all subject to them and sometimes conditions arise that prevent the continuance of communications.

Yes, it is so and you must not let the fact disturb you. I will stop now.

Your brother in Christ,
John.

Also mentions that even Jesus in his writing can exhaust his power according to spiritual laws

August 24th, 1915.

I am here, St. Luke.

I merely want to add my testimony to that of John and to tell you that you must not doubt that the Master wrote you just because his powers to do so became exhausted. I will not attempt to write more tonight.

No, the Bible is filled with errors, I never wrote many things which are credited to me and some time I will tell you of them in detail.

I will keep my promise. So good night.

Your brother in Christ,
St. Luke.

Wants Mr. Padgett to know that he is in condition to write

August 24th, 1915.

I am here, St. Sebastian.

I am the Saint that wrote to you some nights ago and I want to say that I am still in condition to write.

Good night.
St. Sebastian.

Confirms that those who wrote were actually who they said that they were, because she knew them

August 24th, 1915.

I am here, Helen.

Well, you seem to doubt tonight as to the identity of the writers. But you must not let doubts enter your mind for I tell you that Jesus wrote and so did St. John and St. Luke and St. Sebastian. I know them and saw them write. Well, you must stop and go to bed.

Well, I don't believe you really need anything but if you do, get it. I see that you are a little hungry, so do as you think best.

I will go with you.

Your own true and loving,
Helen.

Tells of how she was killed in Rome and her work now trying to help Mr. Padgett to do the work of the Master to better understand Jesus' mission

August 8th, 1915.

I am here, St. Celestia.[113]

I was a Christian woman who was martyred by the fanatic Church of Rome. I lived in Italy and was a follower of Jesus, but not a believer in the doctrines of the Romish Church. It was long years after my death (that) I was canonized by the very church which killed me. Of course the Pope and officials who canonized me were different from those who killed me.

I want to tell you that I am interested in your mission and am trying to help you do the work of the Master. He is the savior of mankind and it must be taught in what manner he is their savior. Not as the Jesus who died on the cross, not because his blood was spilled by the Roman soldiers, not because of any vicarious atonement, but because he brought to the light and knowledge of men the fact that the Father had after long centuries when He had withdrawn the great gift of the Divine

---

[113] This "saint" does not appear in any of the lists of Saints, as far as we can determine. There are three possibilities. The first is that Padgett did not receive this message accurately and her correct name is different, or she is indeed a canonised saint of the Catholic Church, but not publicly announced, and the third is that it was a message from an imposter. It is very unlikely she is an imposter, as it is clear from the message that she is an advanced spirit, and there is a message from Jesus that states these saints are who they said they were, and that an imposter cannot write. Until someone asks the question again, we will not know the answer. (G.J.C.)

Love re-bestowed it and taught the way in which men might become partakers of that Love—even (only) by prayer and faith. The soul of man is the one thing that enables him to become like the Father and is the most important part of man's creation. If men will understand this and learn that this soul is capable of receiving this Divine Love and becoming a part of God's Divinity, they will fully realize the mission of the Master in coming to earth.

Let men abandon the idea that Jesus came as a sacrifice for their sins. He came as a messenger from God, bringing the Divine Gift and the knowledge as to how men might obtain that gift. He did not come to pay any debt which man owed the Father or to appease any wrath of the Father, because man owed no debt and God had no wrath towards him. He came as a mediator in the sense that he was a messenger of light and truth and a shower of the way. Why will men continue to cling to the old damnable doctrine of sacrifice?

Even in the days of Abraham, God never required a sacrifice for sin and no sin of man was ever removed by shedding the blood of a goat or any other animal. To teach and believe such a dogma places God on the plane of an angry and jealous God and makes Him satisfied with the trifling thing of having the blood of an animal shed to appease his anger and remove his jealousy.

God is now and has been from the beginning a God of Love and man is and has been the object of that Love. But unless man seeks that Love and opens up his soul to the inflowing of that Love he can never become reconciled to God. Love cannot be obtained in the soul of man by anything other than the desire and will of man to have it come into his soul. God wants only the love of man not his fear or dread of consequence because of disobedience. So I say let men know that there is only one thing in all the universe that will reconcile him to God, and that is the opening up of the soul of man to the inflowing of the Divine Love and the prayer to God that such Love may come into his soul.

I do not know that I can say more tonight and will stop, but some time I will come again and write further. My home is in the Celestial Heavens far above the spiritual (spirit) world.

Question by Mr. Padgett.

Well, we are all working with the Master and where he leads we follow and work also. If you will pray and believe you will most assuredly. Yes, we all pray for you and our prayers ascend to the Father with all earnestness and faith. You would be surprised to know the number of Celestial Spirits who are interested in and are praying for you. I will surely tell him, but as you say, he knows it already, but as you wish me to do so, I will and I know that he loves you too, and wants you to become his true disciple.

I will say good night.
Your friend and sister in Christ,
St. Celestia.[114]

Was a very powerful man when on earth

August 12th, 1915.

I am here, Aaron.

I was a prophet, the brother of Moses, and the priest of the tabernacle.

I was a very powerful man when on earth and taught the children of Israel the truths of God.

I will not write more tonight as you are sleepy and I will come again later.

Yes, she is here.

I will say good night.

Also became a follower of Jesus and knows that Jesus is the only way to the Father

June 27th, 1915.

I am here, Solomon of the Old Testament.

Well, I was visiting the earth plane and happened to see the two last spirits visit you. I thought that I would do so also.

I know Paul and John and converse with them sometimes, but do not have as much of the Divine Love as do they. Wisdom which I was said to have had in a pre-eminent degree is not the equal of Love in elevating a spirit in the Father's Kingdom; and they are possessed of more of this Love than am I. Yet I have great hope that someday I will get this great soul filling Love to a degree that will enable me to live with them and the others of the followers of the Master—I mean his disciples.

I became a follower of the Master many years ago, and know that he is the only Way to the Father—and I mean by that, the Way which his teachings show is the only Way. It may seem a little surprising to you that I, said to have been such a wise and good man, am not as exalted as are the disciples. Well, while I lived and died many years before the disciples, and one would suppose that I made greater progress than had they, yet such is not the fact, because my progress prior to the coming of Jesus was purely intellectual, and after his coming

---

[114] This message is a composite of two, being originally published twice in this Volume III. In this edition the second instance has been removed. (G.J.C.)

it was a long time before I started on my soul's progression.

So you must remember that the fact that a spirit who is called an ancient spirit, does not mean that it is very highly exalted spirit in the spheres—because a spirit prior to Jesus' coming to earth could only make intellectual and soul progress in the natural love and then not higher than the sixth sphere of the spirit spheres. But after his coming, and the re-bestowal by God of Immortality and the Divine Love on mankind, the ancients had the opportunity to make soul progression which was intended, and would enable them to ascend to the higher Celestial Spheres.

I would like to write more, but you are tired. So I will say good night.

Solomon the Wise.[115]

Promised to come again and write on the lost continent

July 22nd, 1915.

I am here, Anabalixis.

I lived on the lost continent of Atlantis. I was a ruler of the people who lived on this submerged continent and I come to tell you of its history, but your wife says that you are too tired to write more tonight. I will come again[116] sometime and tell you the wonders of that unfortunate land.

So good night.
Anabalixis.

Confirms that the ancient writers were just who they represented themselves to be

July 22nd, 1915.

I am here, Helen.

Well you have had some wonderful communications tonight and I know that you are somewhat mystified and have some doubts as to the genuineness of the writers, but they were the spirits who wrote the communications and they said that they are just who they represented themselves to be.

The last two (Anaxylabis and Anabalixis) and looked like very ancient spirits and had wonderful intelligent countenances.

---

[115] This message is a composite of two, being published in Volume II and Volume III. (G.J.C.)

[116] While this spirit never returned, two others did discuss Atlantis. One is Sebastobel and the other is Jayemas, both in this volume. (G.J.C.)

But they are not spirits of light and love which the Divine Love gives to spirits. I suppose that they live in some of the planes of the Sixth Sphere. You must not write more.

So with all my love,
I am your own true and loving,
Helen.

Encourages Mr. Padgett and stresses the importance to receive these important Truths without delay as mankind is turning more to spiritual things

June 14th, 1917.

I am here, Solomon.

It has been a long time since I wrote you, although I have been present many times when the other spirits were delivering their messages, and of course, have been much interested in you and the messages.

As you will remember, I told you in my message that you had been selected to do the work that the spirits of the Celestial Sphere, led by Jesus, had determined that you should do, and that you must realize the great importance of the work and also the importance of the mission conferred upon you in this regard, and urged you to believe in the truth of what I had written.

Well, I come to reiterate what I then said, and also to impress upon you the necessity for doing this work as rapidly as possible, for conditions are such that the world is very much in want of these truths, as men are turning their thoughts more and more to things spiritual, and to the future life. This war will result in men seeking a religion that will satisfy not only the longings of their souls, but the efforts of their intellects in searching for the truth; and these truths when they are presented to men will give that satisfaction.

Well, the explanation is, that these people, when they pray, attract to them the spirits, and also believe that God will answer their prayers, and these spirits endeavor to help them, and often succeed; and many times the things that these people pray for come to them by natural means.

And this I will say, that never does God by His omnipotence, as regards these material things, answer prayer. All His answers to prayer are brought about by the workings of the spirits who do God's bidding, and in no other way are prayers for the material things, answered. I know that this may be surprising to many of these people who believe that God, by His great powers answers prayer, but it is a fact.

Well, that is an illustration of the work of spirits, as I have explained. These spirits, when the prayers of that man (Mueller) ascended to God, heard them, and in obedience to their work, impressed mortals to do that which resulted in answer to these prayers. Many prayers have been answered in this way, and will be so long as mortals pray and have faith.

I will not write more now. So good night.
Your brother in Christ,
Solomon.

Will be a part of Mr. Padgett's band

July 20th, 1915.

I am here, another apostle of the Master.

I came, because I am a participant in the great work which the Master is now doing for mankind, and I want to assure you that in all your efforts to carry out this work I will give you my love and exert my power to make you successful.

I too, will be of your band; and you will have a band that will be so powerful that no opposition will be able to withstand it.

So you must have faith and with that will come the Divine Love and power to do these things which will help you work beyond your conception.

I will not write more tonight, but in the future you will receive many messages from me.

Your friend and brother,
St. Matthew.

Assures Mr. Padgett that the Master is now doing the great work for the redemption of mankind

July 20th, 1915.

I must add my testimony to the others who have preceded me, to the fact that the Master is now doing a great work for the redemption of mankind, and that through you he is going to transmit his great spiritual truths to sinful man.

I will not write much tonight, but say that in the future I will communicate my thoughts, which are the creatures of knowledge and experience in the Celestial Spheres of Christ's Kingdom.

So I will say good night, and may God keep you in His Love and care forevermore.

St. Mark, the writer of the second gospel, originally true as written, but now full of errors.[117]

Writes about the importance to receive the Master's Truths

July 20th, 1915.

I am here, Helen.

Well my own dear Ned, you have had more writings tonight from the higher spirits, and very soon it looks as if all the disciples will have written you. But you must not write more tonight as you are tired and must go to bed.

Well, you will have an evening to ourselves very soon as I am trying too for an exchange of our loving thoughts. But these things of the Master are so much more important that we must let them have precedence. But I love you more than ever and you must love me. I will tell you more of my present condition very soon and of some of our friends.

So good night. With all my love and many kisses,
I am your own true and loving,
Helen.

Confirms the thought that he is the St. John of the Bible

July 20th, 1915.

I am here, John.

Yes, I am the St. John of the Bible. I merely want to say that you are better tonight than you were this afternoon when we all wrote to encourage you and I am glad of it. You will be relieved and will soon get all that you need to relieve your worries. So do not trouble more.

Well, I am interested because I want you to get into the proper condition to do the work which has been assigned you to do by the Master. This is one reason why I come and in addition to this I want to see you happy for your own sake.

So pray and believe and you will come out of all your worries triumphant. I will not write more tonight.

Your brother in Christ,
John.

---

[117] This message is a composite of two, being published in Volume II and Volume III. (G.J.C.)

Writes that there is no reason why Mr. Padgett cannot get the Divine Love of the Father

September 13th, 1915.

I am here, Samuel.

I am the same Samuel who has written you before and told you of my home in the Celestial Heavens. Tonight I want to say merely a few words about the love which I see that you have to a large degree. You must continue to pray to the Father and have faith. There is no reason why you may not get this Love in your heart to a degree that will put you on the same plane of soul development that is your intention.

Of course the trials and worries that you may have with earth life will interfere with and retard your soul development a considerable degree but nevertheless if you will pray continually and let your faith expand you will be able to get the soul development that I speak of. I am glad that you and your friend find such interest in discussing the truths of the spirit life and especially of those things which pertain to the soul development. The communication which you had tonight did you both (Dr. Leslie R. Stone) much good and increased your conceptions of that the truth is in regards to these matters. I only wish that others would get into the light as you two are, for if they would there would be an increased spreading of these truths and mankind would be much benefitted.

I will not write more tonight. With all my love and blessing,
I am your brother in Christ,
Samuel.

Is also trying to help Mr. Padgett

September 13th, 1915.

I am here, Lot.

Lot of old, I merely want to say that I am with you trying to help you in your progress in spiritual things. I am not so very far away that I cannot come to you when I desire and give you my help.

Well, I will not write more tonight, but will say good night.
Your brother in Christ,
Lot

Describes the discussion in the park between Dr. Stone and Mr. Padgett

September 13th, 1915.

I am here, Helen.

Well, sweetheart, you are very sleepy and must go to bed. But I must tell you how I enjoyed the conversation which you and Dr. Stone had tonight in the park. The spiritual influence around you was great and working to do you both good.

Mary was there and she was enjoying the conversation as much as I and was trying to make the Doctor feel her presence as I was you. What a wonderful thing this Love of the Father is and how glad I am that you have it to the extent that you have.

Yes, Samuel was there and so were your band and some of the apostles, all enjoying the ideas which you both expressed. We could see the workings of your brain and souls and we tried to impress you with the truth and make you realize fully the many sayings of the Bible as well as what has been written to you by us, dealing with the subjects that you were discussing.

So how happy you ought to be to know that you have with you so often so many of the higher spirits of "Light and Truth".

I will not write longer tonight. So with all my love,
I am your own true loving
Helen.

Says that the only Way to redemption is through the Divine Love of the Father

September 20th, 1915.

I am here, Samuel the Prophet.

A man without the Love of God in his soul is like a ship on a stormy sea without a rudder. For life is a stormy sea and the only way of mortals that have no rudder to guide them. They know not Jesus or his truths and their lives have no stability but meander around from one thing to another in the way of religious belief until they hardly know what to believe.

This condition prevents them from obtaining the Divine Love or coming into close communion with the Father.

The only way to redemption is through this Divine Love and the sooner mortals learn it the better for them it will be, in their lives on earth as well as in heaven.

I will say good night.
Your brother in Christ,
Samuel the Prophet.

Says that Jesus was crucified because the Jews failed to recognise Jesus as the looked for Messiah

January 22nd, 1917.

I am here, Elohiam.

I am the spirit of a Jew who lived in the time of Jesus and was a member of the Sanhedrin and sat as one of his judges at the time of his condemnation for blasphemy and iconoclastic teachings against the beliefs and doctrines of the Hebrew faith, and was one of those who voted for the sentence of death upon him, and in doing so was as honest in my conviction and action as it was possible for an earnest believer in his faith to be.

Consequently, I was without prejudice against Jesus as a man and, as I believed, a fanatic; and it was only because I was convinced that he was an assailer of, and dangerous to, our religion and the welfare of my race that I consented to his death. Mortals of these days cannot fully understand the exact relationship of Jesus and his teachings to the security of our religion and the preservation of the faith which we believed had been handed down to us by God direct through our prophets and teachers.

When we were confronted with what we believed to be the destructive and irreligious teachings of Jesus and after making the numerous efforts to suppress him by threats and persuasion without effect, we concluded that our absolute and indisputable duty to God demanded that he be removed from the sphere of his activity even though such result could only be accomplished by his death.

And if mortals of the present day could understand our deep religious convictions and the sense of obligation that rested upon us to protect and keep whole the divine doctrines and teachings of our faith and especially that one which declared the oneness of God, they would not judge the action of the Jews in condemning Jesus to death to be a thing unusual or unexpected. He stood in the position to us and to our religion of a breeder of sedition just as in modern times men have occupied the position towards the civil governments of breeders of treason and have suffered the punishments which have been with approval inflicted upon them by such governments.

But to us he appeared not only guilty of treason to our national life, but of treason to the higher and God-given life of the religious government of our race, the chosen one of God, as we sincerely and zealously believed. Even in latter days men have appeared and claimed to be the especially anointed of God with missions to perform and have gathered around them a following of people whom they have impressed with the truth of their character and mission and of their teachings, and for a short time were permitted to declare their claims and doctrines and then suddenly brought to death by the decree of those who were in authority, as trouble-makers and enemies of the church or state, and have been forgotten and their doctrines disappeared from memory. And only in the instance of Jesus has his death been remembered through all the ages, and those who were the cause and responsible for his death have been desecrated and cursed and charged with the murder of God.

Well, I write this to show you that the Jews who took the life and demanded the crucifixion of that just man were actuated by motives (no) other or different from those that have many times since caused the very followers and worshippers of that Jesus to murder and crucify other men who have claimed to be the sons of God endowed with special missions for the salvation of mankind.

The sincerity of the Jews who took part in this great tragedy cannot be assailed, and even their Roman masters at the time understood that the demands for the death of Jesus did not arise from personal spite, or the satisfaction of any revenge against the individual, but solely because they believed and so declared that Jesus was an enemy and would-be destroyer of the divine faith and teachings of the Israelite nation, and a seducer of the people, and it is only because of the subsequent rise and spread of his teachings and the truths that he declared—which have made so large a portion of the inhabitants of the earth followers of him—that the act of the Jews in causing his death has been called the great crime of the world and the people themselves to be hated and persecuted and destroyed as a nation and scattered to all points of the earth.

I do not write this to excuse or palliate the great error which we committed in causing the crucifixion and death of the true son of God, but only to show that they, though as I now know, mistakenly, did that which other men with the same faith and convictions and zealous for the religious preservation of the nation, be these men Jews or Gentiles or pagans, would have done in similar circumstances.

But the great element of tragedy in all this is not that Jesus was crucified, but that the Jews were so mistaken and failed to recognize and accept Jesus as their long looked for Messiah and Deliverer, not from their material conditions of bondage, but from the bondage of sin and error in which they have lived for so many centuries. This, I say, was their tragedy, and it has been their lasting and deadly tragedy from that time until the present day, and the prospects are that it will continue theirs for many years to come, and that generations of them will pass from the earth life to the spirit world under the shadow of that great tragedy.

They still believe—and that belief is a part of their existence and as firmly fixed as in the days of the great mistake—that they have Abraham for their father and that his faith and example are sufficient to show them the true way to God and salvation and that they are the chosen people of God, and by worshipping the one and only God and observing the sacraments and feasts and commands of God that were given to them by and through Moses and the prophets and as are contained in the Old Testament, they will find the heaven of God here on earth and after death rest in the bosom of Abraham. That the observance of the moral and ethical precepts of their Bible is all that is necessary to develop their spiritual natures, and that beyond such development there is nothing to be desired or to be sought for. That some time they will attain the Adamic condition of reward and happiness, which is the ultimate of man's future existence.

Some are still looking for the coming of the Messiah who will restore to them their former glory and rule on earth as the king and governor of all the nations and that they will be his chosen subjects and selected to assist in the administration of that Messiah's kingdom. How certain it is that their dreams will never be realized and that unless they have an awakening to the true nature of their God they will never become inhabitants of the Father's kingdom!

And I want to say to my people with the certainty of knowledge arising from experience and actual observation, that Jesus of Nazareth was the true Messiah who brought to the world, and first to the Jews, the truths of God and His plans for the salvation of mankind and their restoration to all that they had lost by the fall of their first parents because of their disobedience, and that if the people of my nation had received him and accepted and followed his teachings, they would not now on earth be the scattered, homeless and persecuted race that they are, and in the spirit world would not now be satisfied with their homes and happiness in the spiritual heavens, but would be, many of them, inhabitants of the Celestial Heavens and the possessors of immortality and God's Divine Love.

You have received many messages describing the plan of the Father for the salvation of men and what the Divine Love is and how it may be obtained and its effect on the soul of man and spirit when once possessed, and I will not attempt here to enter into an explanation of these things, but with all the love that I have for my race, superadded to a knowledge of the great error and insufficiency of their faith to bring them into at-onement with God, I advise and urge them to seek the truth and apply it to their individual souls, and affirm that the truth is contained and the way be found in the messages that you have received from Jesus and the other high spirits.

I am a believer in these truths, a follower of the Master and an inhabitant of the Celestial Heavens; but I want to say that these truths did not come to me as a part of my faith until many long years of life in the spirit world, and that some of these years I lived in darkness and

suffering. So I will say good night and subscribe myself your brother in Christ,
    Elohiam[118]

A Roman Emperor and murderer of Christians, suffered all the horrors of hell and has paid his penalties and is now a follower of Jesus, who helped him out of darkness.

October 11th, 1915.

I am here, Caligula.

I was the Roman Emperor and the murderer of the Christians, and have since that time, and for my sins, suffered all the horrors of a hell which I can't describe. Suffice it to say that the hell of the Bible or of those who interpret the Bible, is not equal in its torments and horrors to the hell that I passed through. I tell you this that you may know that every man will have to pay the penalties for the evil deeds he does when on earth, and as my deeds were so extremely evil my penalties were correspondingly great.

But thank God, I have paid my penalties and am now enjoying the happiness of the Christian heaven, for I am now a follower of that Jesus, whose followers I persecuted. Strange as it may seem to you, the cause of my conversion to Christianity was one of the very Christians whom I murdered. She was a beautiful spirit when I first saw her in the spirit world, and when she came to me and told me of the great love of the Father, and the kindness and humility of the Master, I was then in much darkness, though I had suffered for many long years and my thoughts were commencing to turn to things that ultimately helped me to get out of my darkness and find relief from my sufferings.

But this Christian spirit came to me with such love and forgiveness in her speech, that I was greatly affected by what she said and by her appearance; and I listened to her as she told me of the wonderful Love of the Father and the great desire of the Master that I should seek for that love and the happiness which it brings to spirits who obtain it.

She had many interviews with me, and at last, she told me that her happiness depended, to some extent, on my getting this Divine Love in my soul, and progressing with her to the sphere of light and love. She said that I was her soulmate and that my love was necessary for her happiness, and that I could not give her that Love, until I had become the possessor of the Divine Love to some extent. So you can imagine what an

---

[118] This may also have been more correctly "Euliam." This message is a composite of two, being published in Volume I and Volume III. (G.J.C.)

effect this declaration had on me.

I saw that she was beautiful and pure and loving, and that I was not a fit soulmate for her, and that I must try to make myself a suitable soulmate in order that I could be with her. And in addition, when she told me of her love for me, and that we were necessary to each other's happiness, I had a most wonderful longing to be with her and enjoy her love, and the desire soon took possession of me, that I commenced to inquire the way by which I might get this great love, or start to get it; and she told me then of the love of the Master, and how he could teach me the way and what power he had to help spirits like myself to get out of the darkness and torture into light and happiness.

And so I continued in my longings and desires, until at last, my spirit seemed to have a power to rise out of the darkness and to meet other spirits who were not dark and forbidding as I was. She often came to me and taught me to pray, and I did pray and ask forgiveness and for just a little of that Divine Love of which she had told me.

At last as I was praying and hoping for this Love and for deliverance the Master came to me, and such a wonderful loving spirit he was, the most beautiful and loving and yet the most humble that I had ever seen or ever have seen, and he commenced to tell me of this wonderful love of the Father, and how it was working for me to fill my soul and make a child of God, and at-one with him, and he told me that the only things necessary were for me to pray to the Father, and have faith and in all earnestness repent of my great sins. That if I did so, the Love would come to me, and as it came into my soul all the sins and recollections of my sins, would leave me so that I would be able to progress to a higher sphere, where light and love were.

I could not resist his influence, and I did not want to for my soulmate was with me in her love, with pleading eyes and anxious looks, and I commenced to have this faith, and to pray with all the earnestness of my soul; and, at last, light came to me and love came flowing into my soul; and what a happy spirit I became, and thanked God for his mercy. My soulmate rejoiced with me and we were so happy in our loves and in the great Love of the Father.

From thence I have been progressing ever since, until now I am in the Celestial Spheres, where love is the ruling principle and only those who possess this divine love can live, and where Jesus is our Prince and elder brother. Caligula, the Emperor, is now a humble follower of the despised Nazarene, and happy in his humility and in his following of such a loving saviour.

My soulmate is with me, and whenever I look upon her and think that I was the cause of her sufferings and death upon earth, my whole soul goes out to her in great streams of love and she knows it, and that is a part of my great repentance. So you see, that even though a man may be the vilest of sinners on earth, yet the Father's Mercy is so great that His love is never turned away, or is His mercy ever withheld.

I tell you that Love—the Father's Love—is the greatest thing in all the universe, and like unto it is the pure, holy love of the soulmate who has in her soul the great Love of the Father.

I must not write more tonight, but as I was passing I saw the brilliant light that is with you and I embraced the opportunity to write.

Yes, it was Celestia.

And what an appropriate name! My friend, you must also thank God for his goodness to you, for I have seen your soulmate and she is a most beautiful spirit.

So with the love of a brother in Christ, am your friend,

Caligula the Roman Emperor that was, and the Christian that is.

Overheard a conversation between Mr. Padgett and Dr. Stone on operations of the soul development upon the physical mind after death

October 25th, 1915.

I am here, Caligula. (Roman Emperor)

I came merely to say that I am interested in your conversation and the conclusions you draw as to some of the operations of the soul development upon the physical mind after death.

You are right when you say that the condition of the physical mind after death is affected by the development of the soul, for if a man in life, has his physical nature developed by the knowledge that the soul is the controlling power, he will soon be able when he becomes a spirit to subordinate the desires and thoughts which are purely material to his conception of spiritual things; so that the progress of the spirit will not be retarded by what his material thoughts may have made him while in the body. I mean that the thoughts of the material mind will not continue with him very long after his decease, but that the thoughts that come from his spiritual development will overcome or even eradicate the material thoughts.

The mind is material; the thoughts which come from soul development are spiritual, and if permitted to grow and increase will overcome the material mind.

I find it a little difficult to express myself tonight as you are not in the best condition for communicating, so I will not write further, but will come again.

Your brother in Christ,

Caligula.

A German philosopher, now in the Second Sphere, wrote on immortality and the uncertainty of obtaining it even in the spirit world

June 4th, 1917.

I am here, Gottfried Leibnitz.

Let me write a few lines. I am not an acquaintance of yours, yet I am not a stranger, so far as my being in your presence and observing the different spirits who communicate with you.

I have been in spirit life a great many years and have been through the hells and purgatory and all kinds of suffering and am now in the light and comparatively happy. I am in what is called the Second Sphere, where are many bright and intellectual spirits, working out their own plans for accomplishing certain of their ideas and progressing to higher planes.

I was a professor on earth and gave much of my time to the study of psychology and kindred subjects, and had many ideas of my own on these questions, and especially was I interested in the study or rather speculation—for I did not believe in the Bible or the teachings of the churches—as to the future of man, and my speculations led me to the conclusion that the physical death was not the end of man, for it seemed to me that if such was the case the object of the workings of the great laws of evolution would be defeated by the ending of the existence of the greatest and highest resultant of that evolution, namely man.

I was a student of comparative biology and believed without any doubt and with the certainty of knowledge that man was the greatest product of this great principle of evolution and that for centuries upon centuries it had been working to bring or develop man from the mere molecule to the high degree of perfection displayed in his wonderful mind and moral faculties, and that then, in a moment, end it all by this thing known as physical death, was unreasonable and unjustified, and, hence, I concluded, as I say, that men must live after the death of the body.

But when I got that far in my conclusions there came the question, what was beyond; and here my speculations were not so satisfactory for I had very little upon which to base any theories. Of course I thought, that as man in the past had made such wonderful progress in his evolution, and as he would live in the future it was reasonable to suppose that this evolution would continue and that man's progress would be without limitation or ending—provided, he should continue to live forever. And thus arose the question of man's immortality; and here, I was stalled, for I had nothing with which to make a comparison.

I knew that it was accepted as a truth in natural science that nothing could ever be destroyed or lost, and that the elements or atoms from which those physical things, perceptible to the senses, were composed should continue to exist forever, but this was not satisfactory to me upon which to base the fact that man would live forever. While these elements or atoms, themselves, could not be destroyed, yet many of those composite things into which these elements had entered, and given form, had been destroyed and as such composite entity and form no longer had an existence.

I had seen the oak start from the acorn and grow to be a mighty tree and live for years and suddenly, by a stroke of lightning, destroyed and ceased to live, and as such tree went entirely out of existence. And, hence, by analogy I could not say that man as the identical individual would not go out of existence, and, in fact, I had seen him as regards his physical existence, cease to be an existence and his body disintegrate and go back to its elements; and I could find nothing in all this to justify me in asserting that man, in whatever form he might exist after his bodily death, would not at sometime in the future cease to have the form that made him the very individual that had lived on earth and continued his existence in the spirit world. No, I could not, in my speculations satisfy myself that man was immortal. And so speculation was compelled to stop, and I was left without any assurance that my theory of persistence of man after death was not one that might not prove to be false.

But I died, and found that I, the conscious thinking man, continued to exist with all the faculties of mind and feelings that were mine when a mortal. And in addition, I soon met those who had preceded me in the spirit world, and who had since becoming spirits, advanced in their evolution, and were more perfect mentally and morally than they had been when on earth; and who, also, informed me that beyond where they had evoluted (evolved) to, were spheres in which spirits of greater intellectual development and ancient in years, lived and worked and speculated upon the same question that I had given so much thought to when on earth, namely: is man immortal?

And they further informed me that these ancient worthies had not been able to solve the problem, but that many who had come to the spirit life thousands of years before were still living, and no spirit had ever been known to have passed out of existence or dissolve into the elements of which it was composed.

So you see, the spirits in the highest spheres with all their intellectual development and thousands of years of study, can no more assert with certainty that man is immortal than I could when on earth. To me now, as when on earth, this is the greatest question that arises, and engages my continuous thoughts, and I see no way to solve the problem. I remember, that when on earth the preachers and the churches claimed and taught the doctrine of immortality, and while I never deeply investigated the foundation of their claims, yet I cannot conceive that they can possess any more certainty of the supposed fact than did I. I can hardly believe that God ever revealed to man the fact of immortality; and in my opinion, in my present stage of development, only God knows, and all the teachings of the churches and wise theologians are mere speculations, not to be relied on.

Well, I have written you a long letter tonight, and you may not be interested, but I am, and as the opportunity came, I thought that I would like to write, for I know that there are many mortals who are working and speculating and attempting to find some basis for their hopes of immortality; and some believe that while they may not satisfy their hopes on earth, yet when they come to the spirit world, the difficulties will be removed and the problem solved; and to these I desire to make known the fact that they will look through just as dark glasses here as they are now looking through on earth.

Well, you surprise me and I can scarcely believe that you are serious, for I have never heard of such a way or of such a knowledge existing among spirits, and if you can show me that way I will, with all the energies of my soul pursue it. Well, you surprise me more and more; but I am willing to do as you say, no matter how absurd it may seem to me, or what little prospects I may see in making the pursuit. I will do as you say.

Well, I see a beautiful spirit who says that he is Prof. Salyards, and has heard what I said and what you said, and that he will be pleased to show me the way to obtain both a knowledge and the actual possession of this immortality[119], and I shall accept this invitation and go with him. I thank you very much for listening to me and for your expressions of desire to help me; and if what you promise comes true, you may rest assured that I will return sometime and tell you.

So my friend, I will say good night.
Your friend,
Gottfried Wilhelm Leibnitz.

A friend of Mr. Padgett's praises him for his work and tells about his spiritual pursuits

September 14th, 1915.

I am here, James G. Blaine.
I am here to tell you that you are a wonderful medium, and that

---

[119] The message on Immortality by Jesus as also by Henry Ward Beecher and Luke in Volume I (5th Ed.) on page 45 address this issue. (J.P.G.)

you will do a great deal of good before you die.

Well, I have been with you at times of your writings and have seen what messages you received, and what effect the communications have had on the spirits, as well as on yourself and friends.

I am in the fourth sphere and am happy in a way, but I need more happiness and more light, and I will try to get these things. I am engaged in intellectual pursuits that are congenial to me, and I also take great interest in the affairs of your country, and try to influence its rulers to do the right thing at the right time. I have met many spirits since I came over and have made acquaintances with them. They are all very wonderful spirits in their understanding of the laws of nature and kindred subjects, and I learn a great deal from them. I merely wanted to introduce myself to you and let you know that I am alive.

Well, I believe more in the intellect than in religious matters, and I don't seek the other spirits that you mention. I have no special interest in them.

I will not write more tonight.

James G. Blaine.

Wonders about the many beautiful spirits that are around him at times

I am here, Helen.

You must not write more tonight as you are tired and must sleep. We were all with you this afternoon, and you had around you spirits who live in the highest heavens as well as those who live in the earth plane. All were trying to help you, and wanted to see you get the relief that you need and asked for.

What a crowd of beautiful spirits you have around you at times. I do not quite understand why the higher ones should come in such numbers, but they come and try to help you in your soul's progress.

I must stop now.

Your own true and loving,

Helen.

Visits the councils of all nations to learn the objects of their efforts and desires and surprising as it may seem the German's feel that God is on their side

February 1st, 1917.

I am here, James G. Blaine.

I want to write a few lines as I am interested in the affairs of our country, and I see the present critical condition of affairs growing out of the recent declarations of the Germans as to the policy that they intend to pursue regarding the blockading of the ports of the Allies, which means, in substance, that the ports of our country will also be blockaded, for if the merchant vessels travelling from the U.S. to the ports of the Allies are not permitted to land at their destinations, there will, of course, be no departures from our ports, and the result will be the same as if such ports were actually blockaded.

It is a serious condition for Mr. Wilson to deal with and he must act quickly and firmly, and not in any particular recognize the right of the Germans to carry out their policy, or to permit, so far as possible, the cessation of the travel of ships from our ports to those of the Allies. Temporizing will not do, and he must at the very start let the Germans know that America will not submit to the dictation, and that, if necessary, the America nation will not only sever diplomatic relations with Germany and her allies, but will become active participants in the war, which humanity and the welfare of the majority of the nations of the earth demand shall be recognized and enforced.

He, the President, may in his dream of peace, which he has recently given expression to, and which is wholly impracticable at this time, attempt to conciliate the Germans, and by further reasoning show them that they are wrong and violators of all recognized laws of nations, and in this hope to avoid war; or the involving of America in this conflict. But to do so, will constitute a great mistake, for his protestations will fall on deaf ears, and create in the German mind the impression that his great desire for peace will restrain him from asserting to the extent of force, the power of the U.S. to prevent the Germans from carrying out their policy of murder and destruction.

I write this, not because I am in any way antagonistic to the German people, or have any special predilection for the Allies, but because I see the right of the matter, and that which is necessary to the salvation of not only the larger part of the nations of the earth, but also to preserve the rights and dignity and substantial welfare of the U.S. This action of the German nation must not for a moment be tolerated, and the sooner the President strikes the better it will be for all concerned. Of course with the Germans it is a matter of life and death, but even so it is not right that the other nations of the earth should suffer ruin or destruction in order that the German nation should continue to exist, and be enabled to carry out its policy of domination, which is really the foundation of the existence of the present war.

While I am a spirit and supposed to be interested only in spiritual things, yet my thoughts and interests are with my people, and incidentally with all the nations and peoples of the earth, and these nations and peoples must be preserved and not be permitted to be ruined by any other nation, and especially so in the present war for which no justification exists, for the course that the entente have pursued in attempting to carry out it unholy desires for destruction and aggrandizement. I know what the rulers of the various nations contemplate and what their policies are in the prosecution of this war, for I visit the councils of each of them and learn the thoughts of the leaders, and the objects of their efforts and desires.

On both sides there is much that deserves condemnation and entails suffering, but in weighing the wrongs perpetrated by these various nations I realize that the Germans are guilty of the greater wrongs, and if God should interfere as the Kaiser and the rulers of some of the other nations believe He will, the German nation would have visited upon them the just indignation and punishment of that God. But He will not interfere, and men will be left to themselves to settle this war, and they alone; but here I may say that as right and justice are more powerful in the long run than wrong and injustice, the nations that have the most of right on their side, will come out victors. And according to my understanding of the things and motives and ambitions that have entered into and caused this war, the Allies must become the victors.

Of course, I cannot tell when this war will end, but considering the conditions that exist and the causes that are now operating, I believe that the end is in sight and that very soon the Germans and their allies will have to sue for peace, and the end will soon follow. I would like to write more tonight, but your wife advises me that I have written enough, and so I will close. So good night,
Your very dear friend,
James G. Blaine.[120]

---

[120] James Gillespie Blaine (January 31st, 1830 – January 27th, 1893) was a U.S. Representative, Speaker of the United States House of Representatives, U.S. Senator from Maine, two-time Secretary of State. He was nominated for president in 1884, but lost a close race to Democrat Grover Cleveland.
Blaine was a dominant Republican leader of the late 19th century, and champion of the "Half-Breed" faction of the GOP. Nicknamed "The Continental Liar From the State of Maine," "Slippery Jim," and "The Magnetic Man," he was a magnetic speaker in an era that prized oratory, and a man of charisma. As a moderate Republican he supported President Abraham Lincoln during the Civil War. As a major leader during Reconstruction he took an independent course in his advocacy of black suffrage, but opposed the coercive measures of the Radical Republicans during the administration of Ulysses S. Grant. He opposed a general amnesty bill, secured the support of the Union veterans who mobilized as the Grand Army of the Republic, worked for a reduction in the tariff and generally sought and obtained strong support from the western states. Railroad promotion and construction were important in this period, and as a result of his interest and support Blaine was charged with graft and corruption in the awarding of railroad charters. The proof or falsity of the charges was supposed to rest in the so-called "Mulligan letters," which Blaine refused to release to the public, but from which he read in his controversial defence in the House. (Source: Wikipedia) (G.J.C.)

A former statesman places the blame on England for the economic conditions in Germany that forced them to go to war

February 1st, 1917.

I am here, Bismarck.

Let me say a word, as I have listened to what has just been written, and am interested in the subject matter of that communication, and do not agree with the sentiments or the conclusions of the thoughts there contained. I am not impartial, I confess, but yet I think that I can do justice to both of the contending parties in the war, as I am a spirit and have learned that right is right irrespective of the person or nation that may claim to be in the right in its actions.

I was a German, and a rather important one, as men consider importance in the earth life, and was acknowledged by the world to be something of a statesman. I have kept in constant touch with the thoughts and motives of the leaders of the various nations that are engaged in this great conflict, and know the right and wrong of things to a greater extent, I claim, than does the spirit who has just written you, and submit that my inferences and opinions are as worthy of consideration and acceptance as are his.

In the first place, this was not brought about by the Germans without justification and cause, and for a long time the German rulers delayed and endeavored to postpone, and, if possible, avoid the war. But their rights, as a nation, were so seriously preyed upon and not recognized, that the only thing left for them to do was to compel their secret enemies to respect their rights by force of arms, and so you have the real cause of the conflict. The Germans were not desirous or ambitious for conquest or territory or advancement to the detriment of other nations, but only for what they, as a great nation, were entitled to. And England, in its greed, stood in the way of and prevented these rights from being recognized, and tried every way in her power to prevent the German nation from enjoying these rights, and especially from extending its commerce to countries in which England had established her commerce and trade, almost to the exclusion of every other nation.

The Germans waited in hope, that by diplomatic means their rights would be established and recognized but such hope was never realized and as a last and only resort, they threw down the gauge of battle, quick and sharp and destructive—with some violation of the rights of a neutral that stood in the way of accomplishing what the German nation considered its decisive blow. But this is history, and it is not necessary that I should add further detail.

And now, as the war has progressed for more than two years,

True Gospel Revealed Anew by Jesus

Germany has naturally become depleted of its resources, and especially in those things that are necessary to sustain the physical existence of its people, and all through the action of the Allies in preventing foodstuff and other necessaries being imported from other nations. Its ports have been blockaded for a long time, and it has been unable to obtain supplies that were absolutely necessary to the existence of its people, until famine and want are staring them in the face, and more than that, have actually worked their ruinous effects, and the cry of the people is for sustenance.

Then, such being the fact, what is the duty of the German rulers? Can humanity ask that they shall sit supinely by and see their people starve and their country ruined, because of the conditions that I speak of, brought about by their enemies in preventing intercourse with outside nations? I know that international law should be respected by nations in war as well as in peace, and that it is for the good of all nations that such laws be held sacred and inviolable, and Germany has tried to observe these laws, even after some of its enemy nations have violated them.

Let me ask here, what difference does the means used in considering the right or wrong of a thing, make when the same result is accomplished? England, by her superior number of war vessels, has succeeded in blockading the ports of Germany, and preventing its people from getting the supplies necessary to their sustenance, and at the same time is enjoying the benefits of unrestricted importation of these necessaries, because Germany had not had it in its power to blockade the ports of England and thus prevent her from obtaining these supplies. This kind of blockade, the nations claim, and international law justifies, no matter what the results may be.

And now, when Germany has found a way to accomplish the same thing, as regards the ports of England and place her and her people in the same condition that the people of Germany have been in for so long a time, and have given notice of its intention to use such means, the nations hold up their hands in horror because such means are not known to international law.

The effect of one blockade is just the same as the effect of another, then why should the means make any difference? America has not been permitted for a long time to send its products to a German port, and to that extent its, America's have been blockaded, as the last writer says; but this is allowable, because, as they say, the English blockade is in accordance with recognized international law. All which means, that because one nation has the power to do a thing in accordance with international law, another nation has not the same right because the means used are not contemplated by that law.

Well such reasoning is one that if applied to the progress of the world would have kept that progress in a state of stagnation. When international law was formulated the means and instruments used in this war were never heard of, and they are only the evolution of the war, growing out of the progress of man in the knowledge and necessities of war. Laws are always subject to change and that change need not be by agreement, for sometimes, and it has often happened, necessity has compelled and justified the modification of the law.

It is said that necessity knows no law, and it is a truth, and one that has been recognized and applied by many nations, at many times. In the present circumstances of Germany, this necessity has arisen to such an extent that the very existence of Germany, not only as a nation, but of her people as individuals is involved, and life is at stake, and the only remedy is that the nations who are fighting Germany, be placed in the same position as she is in, and that can be done only by preventing those nations from obtaining those supplies that are necessary to maintain their people, and this can only be accomplished by blockading their ports.

It may be said that the use of the submarine is brutal and inhuman. Well for the argument admit this to be a fact, yet it is not necessary that any brutality or any murder be actually inflicted, for if the persons interested will heed the warnings and not attempt to run the blockade there will be no murder or outrage. And why, may I not ask, is it not just as reasonable to demand that the blockade established by the German submarines shall not be attempted to be violated as that the blockade which the English have established shall not be attempted to be violated?

In the latter instance, the neutral nations recognize the blockade and do not attempt to have their merchant ships enter the ports that are so blockaded, and why is there any greater injustice done when Germany demands that these neutral vessels shall not enter the ports that she intends to blockade? The only difference is in the means used, and if the neutral nations will observe the obligations that each blockade imposes to the same extent, there will become no necessity for using the means in either.

I do not see why the U.S. should feel that her rights are being violated to any greater or different extent, as a question of right, by the proposed German blockade, than by the blockade that has been created by the English, and for so long a time existed. Of course, the effects of the two blockades upon the business of the U.S. are different in degree, as more business is done and has been done with the Allies, than was done with Germany. But this does not enter into or affect the question of the right or wrong of the matter. Well, I will not write more along this line.

Now as to the results of the war, or rather as to its ending, I cannot prognosticate. Germany is fighting on very unequal terms, and she may be defeated, and I would not be surprised if such was the end of the conflict. But, nevertheless, and even though victory may come to the Allies, I assert as true that the right of the matter is with her, and that the neutral nations are not doing her justice, when they declare that she is the aggressor; and that she is not justified in the course that she is now pursuing. I am told that I have written enough, and so I must stop, but what I have said is the right of the matter. Good night,

Your friend,
Bismarck.

Confirms that Blaine and Bismarck wrote about the war and were most serious about what they said

February 1st, 1917.

I am here, Helen.

Well dear, you have received some very interesting letters tonight, and both the spirits who claimed to write actually did so. Blaine is very much interested in the crisis that has arisen, and his advice is given with much enthusiasm and desire that the President take immediate action to protect the rights of the U.S. Bismarck was most serious and not at all excited while writing, but was very calm in stating what he considered to be the right of his country.

Well, it is all very sad, and we spirits as well as you mortals, will be very glad when this cruel war is over, for I must tell you that many spirits come over from the battlefields in a very bad condition, and the spirits who receive them are given much work to do in helping them. I have visited some of the battlefields during the battles and have seen some very terrible sights, and sometimes I will write you the results of my observations, and what the spirits of some of the soldiers have said and done after they were in the spirit world a little while. Peace will come, but never will it be a certain lasting peace, until men receive in their hearts the true love for their brother mortals. The reforms must come to the individual, and the victory of nations as such, will not bring this peace.

Well, you are tired and I must not write more. But I must say that you are in a much better condition of spirit and soul, and if you continue to pray to the Father you will soon be in condition so that the higher spirits will be able to write their messages, which they so much wish to do. We all send love and blessings and desire you to be happy. You know how I love you and want you to be happy, and how my prayers go to the Father for your happiness and the inflowing of the love. So think of me and love me, and have faith and courage, and you will be

blessed. Give me my kiss and say good night.
Your own true and loving,
Helen.

Writes that he is the prophet of the Transfiguration that actually occurred

October 8th, 1916.

I am here, Elias—I am the Prophet.

I merely want to say that I desire to write you a message and will be pleased to do so as soon as it may be convenient. I have something to write which may be of interest to you as well as of importance to mankind.

Well, I will speak to her. Yes, I know her and she is a beautiful spirit, having much of the Father's Love in her soul, and is the real person who was on earth your wife, and now is your wife more than ever. You are blessed in having such a soulmate and she loves you with a wonderful love. So believe in her and love her and you will be a happy mortal as well as a happy spirit when you come over.

I am the Elias of the Transfiguration, which was a scene of actual occurrence, and which disseminated a great truth that humanity has never understood, but which you have had explained to you. But I will describe more in detail and explain more lucidly its signification (meaning).

I will come soon, and with the assurance that I am interested in you and your work I will say good night.

Your brother in Christ,
Elias.

Talks about the importance in getting into proper condition to permit the spirits to write

April 14th, 1917.

I am here, Elias.

I come tonight to write a few lines only, as you are not in condition to receive the lengthy discourse that I promised you.

I merely desire to say that I will be pleased to give you my message as soon as you feel that you are in condition to receive it. Of course, as you know, it is necessary for you to be in the proper condition as it is for me to be so. There must be a mutual rapport so that our powers may work in unison.

Well, I have nothing further to write tonight, except to say that you must not let your feelings of discouragement take so great a hold on you. They do harm and unfit you for your work.

So with my love, I will say good night,
Elias.

A Muslim, helped to defend Jerusalem from the Christians, is a very happy spirit and a lover of God

August 12th, 1915.

I am here, Salaalida.

I am a Muslim and I lived in the time of the crusaders and helped to defend Jerusalem from the Christians. I was an officer of high rank, and a general who was known among my own countrymen for my prowess in battle. I merely want to tell you now that I am a lover of all mankind and know no difference between the Christians and the Muslims, for all are God's children and are the objects of his love, and of my love, for I am a lover of God.

I am an inhabitant of the highest Mohammedan heavens and am very happy and satisfied with my spiritual condition, and am still a follower of the Prophet who lives in our heavens and still teaches the truths of the Father, Allah.

I have no criticism to make of the Christians and believe that they are also followers of God in the way that their Jesus taught, but I cannot yet believe that his teachings are the only truths of the Father. He and his followers live in a different sphere from our sphere, and those whom I have met seem to be happy and are very beautiful.

So while I was once an antagonist of the Christians, and hated them with all the hatred that my religion taught me to hate, yet now I see that hatred is not a thing which God recognizes as being a part of the faith or practices of his true followers.

I came merely to tell you this and to inform you that love is the ruling principle of the spiritual world where I live. By love, I mean love for God and for my fellowman. This is the only love that I know of and I find it sufficient for my happiness.

I don't know what you mean by the Divine Love. It cannot be anything more than the love which we have for God. Well, I must stop now, and will say good night.

Your friend,
Salaalida the mussulman.(Muslim)

Was murdered in the Inquisition of Spain because he believed in God and was a Bible student, tells of his progress into the Celestial Heavens

January 12th, 1917.

I am here, Los Trenos.

I am the spirit of a man who was murdered in the Inquisition of Spain, because I would not declare that I believed in the false and damnable doctrines of the Romish Church. I was a student of the Bible, and I learned that the church was not teaching and enforcing the true doctrines of Jesus, and I would not surrender my beliefs, even to save my life. The unholy and devilish priests and persecutors racked my body and tortured my mind, and at last tore me asunder, but my soul preserved its faith, and came into the spirit world in the fullness of its belief, all unspotted from these false teachings of the church. There were many who were tortured and killed as I was, because they would not recant.

Well, I became a spirit in all the vigor of my manly strength, and greater, but I did not find myself in heaven as I expected, for I did not know what the great Love was, but, yet, I was not in such darkness as were some of my persecutors who followed me into spirit life. Of course, I was more or less human, and when these church devils came into spirit life and found themselves in hell, I naturally rejoiced and enjoyed, for a time, their sufferings and condition of hellish torment and used to visit them to charge them with my murder; but after some years, I realized that such satisfaction as I thought I experienced did not give me happiness or help me to progress, and I became sympathetic and tried to help them, which was not easy to do at first. As I continued to help them I found that my soul was being benefitted and that I was gradually getting out of the darkness in which I had been living, and so I continued this work until at last I came into the light and a knowledge of the truth that by helping and trying to love my enemies, I was helping myself.

I will not take the time to relate to you my fortune in meeting some spirits who, I know, possessed the great Love of the Father, and how they taught me the way to this Love, but will only say that now I am one of the redeemed children of God, and the possessor of that Love and have my home in the Celestial Heavens, and to show you how wide and all embracing is this great Love, I must inform you that some of these very priests and minions of the church, who committed the outrages of which I speak, are now in the Celestial Heavens also, and, of course, possessors of this great Love, all their sins having been eradicated by the merciful workings of this Love in their souls. Of course, they suffered the torments of the damned when they first came to spirit life and for a long time afterwards, but the Love of the Father and His Mercy were sufficient to wash away, even their sins. So from this you will see that there is no sin so heinous and deadly that the Father's Love will not destroy, or rather, the effect of it.

You must excuse me for intruding as I have, but I saw that you have the gift of receiving communications from this side of the great divide and I wanted to try the experiment. I am a redeemed child of God and can never thank Him enough for His Mercy. So with my love, I will say good night.

Your brother in Christ,
Los Trenos,
The martyr to a belief that was not the true belief, but not so vile and ungodly as the one that he renounced.

Confirms that the Spanish martyr is whom he represents himself to be

January 12th, 1917.

I am here, A. G. Riddle.

I merely write to explain that the spirit who claimed to be a Spanish martyr is whom he represents himself to be, and is not a mere intruder relating a fictitious story. Well my dear boy, I will say good night.

Your old friend and brother,
A. G. Riddle.

Is a follower of the Master and an inhabitant of the Father's Kingdom

August 8th, 1915.

I am here, Loyola the Jesuit.[121]

Yes, I am a follower of the Master and a very weak one. I was a persecutor of those who differed from me in my views of religious things and duty, and as a consequence was the cause of the death of many a true Christian as I see the truth to be. And on earth my followers now in many parts of the world have the same bitter feelings against all who do not think as they do upon religious matters, and were it not for the laws

---

[121] Ignatius of Loyola (ca. October 27th, 1491 – July 31st, 1556) was a Spanish knight from a local Basque noble family, hermit, priest since 1537, and theologian, who founded the Society of Jesus (Jesuits) and, on 19th April 1541, became its first Superior General. Ignatius emerged as a religious leader during the Counter-Reformation. Loyola's devotion to the Catholic Church was characterized by absolute obedience to the Pope. (Wikipedia) (G.J.C.)

of the countries in which they live they would do as I did.

How I have suffered since I became a spirit for all the evil which I inflicted on mankind when I lived on earth in what I thought then was a religious cause. But thank God even my sins have been forgiven and I am now an inhabitant of my Father's Kingdom. But oh, the long years of bitter suffering and remorse and the darkness of blackest night that I lived in among howling devils and lost souls as they thought.

But now I know that God's mercy is so wide that the greatest sinner may be saved and receive the Great Love of the Father. I write this because I have never before communicated to a mortal in this way and I want to give warning to the world, and especially to my followers on earth that the truths of God are eternal and will live forever, and that no persecution in the name of truth will meet the approval of God or save from punishment and torment those who engage in it no matter how honest they may think themselves to be, or how much they believe that they are doing their duty to God.

God has given to every man a free will which even he does not attempt to curb or bind and no mere creature of his has any right to say to a man that he shall or shall not believe this or that, and exercise his will according to the enforced or seeming belief. No, man is a free agent and can do as he pleases in regards to his beliefs, and even God will not force him to believe, but when he believes that which is not true he will certainly have to pay the penalties of his erroneous beliefs, because the truths of God are fixed, and with these truths operate laws that are inexorable, and men who fail to conform to the requirements of these laws must pay the penalties to the last farthing. These laws never change and are supreme. I am now a redeemed spirit through the grace of God and have realized what his love means and I am an inhabitant of the celestial heavens. But not because of my works on earth, but because of the great overshadowing love of the Father.

So I say, seek the truth as it may be found in Jesus teachings and shun the dogmas and creeds of the churches as you would a poisonous thing of death. I will stop now, but thank you for the opportunity of making this, my confession.

So with all my kindest wishes I am your brother in Christ,
the Jesuit Loyola.

Is now in the Celestial heavens and a follower of Jesus, but began in the spirit world in darkness and suffering because of a false life as a teacher

August 31st, 1915.

I am here, Saint Salatia.[122]

I was a woman of Italy when on earth. I was a great worker for the church and was at the head of some of its institutions, and after I died, I mean after I had been dead for a number of years, I was canonized. I died in 1689 in Milan. My name is among the saints of the Romish church.

I came merely to tell you that I am now in the celestial heavens and a follower of the Master. But I have to say that when I first came to the spirit world I was in darkness and suffering, because of my false beliefs, and false life as a teacher. It was only after I became an inhabitant of the spirit world that I learned the truths. Oh, the false teachings of the church and its priests! There are many of them here in the spirit world who are still in darkness and torment, and who lived when I did on earth.

The reason is that they were so firm in their belief in the doctrines of the church that they have never been able to open their minds to the truth, and in fact many of them will not listen to any teachings, but those which they were taught on earth.

Yes, I have tried to convince them of their errors but they would not listen to me, thinking that I had been deceived and proselyted and was lost.

Well I am now very happy and I thank you for the opportunity of writing to you as it is the first time that I have ever written to mortal man. I need not take up more of your time now and so will say good night.

St. Salatia.

My name was Victorina Salatia, the daughter of an Italian nobleman. I was a single woman.

A Catholic nun, is no longer a nun or a Catholic, but a Christian redeemed by the Father

August 31st, 1915.

I am here, St. Camelia.[123]

---

[122] This "saint" does not appear in any of the lists of Saints, as far as we can determine. There are three possibilities. The first is that Padgett did not receive this message accurately, or that this saint is not on any public record and the last is that it was a message from an imposter. However, there is a message from Jesus that states these saints are who they said they were, and that an imposter cannot write. Until someone asks the question again, we will not know the answer. (G.J.C.)

[123] This "saint" does not appear in any of the lists of Saints, as far as we can determine. There are three possibilities. The first is that Padgett did not receive this message accurately, or that this saint is not on any public record and the last is that it was a message from an imposter. However, there is a message from Jesus that states these

Yes, I was a catholic nun. I merely want to say that I am no longer a nun or a catholic, but a Christian redeemed by the Father's Love and the teachings of the Master.

I lived in 1676 at Florence, Italy, and was canonized nearly a hundred years after my death. Yes, in the Romish church history. I am now in the Celestial Heavens where are those who have received the New Birth.

I will not write more tonight. I merely wanted to write and I had never before written through mortals.

So I will say good night.
Your sister in Christ,
St. Camelia.

A resident of the North Pole when it was green and warm

August 31st, 1915.

I am here, Amoulomol.

I was an inhabitant of a land that no longer exists and is entirely forgotten by human history.

It was at the North Pole, and I lived there when everything was beautiful and green and warm. Yes, thousands of years ago. I live in the sphere where my people live. I am very happy with them. I was a white man and lived in a city where we had all conveniences and comforts.

So you don't believe me but it is true.
I will do so.
Good night.

Errors of the Church in which he was a member must be destroyed

August 29th, 1915.

I, St. Clement,[124] want to write a few lines.

I have written you once before and told you of some of the evils and errors of the church of which I was a member, and now I want to tell you that in the distant future that church will lose its power over the hearts of men, and then it will go into decay and finally disappear from the face of the earth. It can never be reformed from within because

---

saints are who they said they were, and that an imposter cannot write. Until someone asks the question again, we will not know the answer. (G.J.C.)

[124] St. Clement as he was known by the early Christians predicted in 1915 that a church of Christ would be organised, which is now a reality, and known as the Church of the New Birth under Jesus the Christ leadership. (J.P.G.)

those who govern and control it know nothing about the real truths of salvation, and will never learn.

The dogmas of the church are too firmly fixed in their minds to ever permit the truths to enter, and consequently, as these dogmas must be destroyed, with their destruction the church will cease to exist as a church.

I am sorry that this will have to be, but the truths of God will prevail, and everything that is not in accord with them must be destroyed and cease to exist. I know that it will make a desperate effort to preserve its power and existence, but in vain. I am now working to bring about that consummation and so are all the redeemed Christian spirits, because we see that it is a mighty stumbling block to the reception of God's truths by men, and men must be taught these truths and be saved from their sins.

Yes, there will be a church established, and it will be a church of Christ, and all mankind in time will come to unite with it and worship the one true God, and believe on Jesus as His great messenger and teacher, and not as God.

The name of that church I don't know, but it will be one in which faith in spiritualism will obtain, and all members will believe that spirit and mortal can commune.

I will write no more now, but say good night.
Your brother in Christ,
St. Clement.

Writes that Mr. Padgett will not be in error as he was because his writing came only from spirits and angels who know God's Truth

April 12th, 1917.

I am here, Luther.

When I was on earth I had my troubles and suffering but thanks be to the Father, I was never forsaken and you will not be. And when you consider the greater importance of your work as compared to mine, you must realize that the Father, and the powers of His angels are more interested in preserving you from everything that may interfere with your work than He was with me; for while I was earnest and sincere in what I attempted to do, and believed that I was right in my attacks on Catholicism and in my teachings of the truth, yet I was in error in many things; and you, on the contrary, will not be in error, because what you may receive will come only from the spirits and angels who know what God's Truths are. So you must see the importance of your work and the necessity for its being accomplished.

Take courage, and when these thoughts of dread of not being provided for and being felt without the means necessary to your existence, come to you, cast them aside. My dear brother, believe what I have been trying to impress you with, and that we all love you, and are trying to help you. Good night.

Your brother in Christ,
Luther.

An ex-president is still in darkness due to some earth desires

I am here, Johnson.

I am here, (Andrew) Johnson, an ex-President of the United States. I want to write because I am in darkness and suffering from the recollections of my evil life, and want help.

I am in the earth plane and have some of my mortal traits with me now. I was a great drinker when on earth and I am still drinking and never satisfied. So you see how long the appetite has stayed with me. So help me if you can.

I know that it may surprise you to hear from me in this way, but the fact was that I was a President of your great country does not help me one bit in my condition here. No matter what a man may have been on earth he cannot escape from his evil deeds, and a President is thought no more of than the meanest man in the community.

I wish that you would show me the way to light and freedom from my sufferings.

Well, I am sorry, but I suppose that I must wait.

So good night.

Tells of his spiritual progression, but knows nothing of Divine Love

November 25th, 1918.

I am here, Longiticus.

Let me write a few lines tonight, as I am very desirous to explain some truths of the spirit world, which may be of benefit to you and those who may read my explanation. I am a spirit that has been in this world for a long time and progressed from the hells to the planes of the Sixth Sphere, and am acquainted with the method of progress and the various experiences of the soul as it ascends from one sphere to the succeeding one higher.

When I lived on earth, man as to his moral development, was in a somewhat limited and uncertain condition, and right and wrong were very largely a matter of might. His conscience was merely that part of him which was operated and caused to be operated by his desires to possess those things that seemed to him to be necessary or suited to his contentment in living, or to the destruction or hurt of those whom he hated or sought to destroy; and this condition of conscience should not be difficult to understand, for at the present day, as has recently been demonstrated the same or similar desires have determined the consciences of those who have brought so much distress to mankind.

Gods were many and their qualities and attributes many and always were the creatures of the men who were supposed to have a knowledge of and acquaintance with these gods, and who were looked upon by the common people as entitled to their credulity and obedience in attempting to carry out the wishes and directions of these gods.

You probably have heard of such people and of such gods and I will not consume space to detail more of the moral conditions of the men of those days or of their utter want of knowledge of the true God and the wholly insufficient thing their conscience was.

Well, of course, we died as all men will have to die, and when we found ourselves spirits, more of us were in the dark planes and many in the hells, of which latter class I was one; and the hells then and cause thereof, were the same as they are today and the difficulties of becoming relieved there from, the same as are the difficulties of today.

I remained in the hells a very long time, and simply for the reason that my state or rather conscience, continued without change, and right and wrong as I had perceived it on earth, persisted with me, and my conscience refused to understand that change is the law of the hells as well as of the earth and the heavens, and that stagnation is itself a sin against law. Many of us who had been associates on earth became associates in the hells and continued in our same ideas of what morality meant, and when I say morality, I simply mean that right course of living and thinking which is in harmony with the creation of the perfect man, as I am now. Of course I could not have given this explanation of morality when I was in the hells, but nevertheless, it applies, even though I did not understand its meaning.

I don't seem to be able to write further now and must stop, but will come again. Let me say that you are very much in the dark as to what the truths of the spirit world are, and need enlightenment, and I can enlighten you.

Love is not in my curriculum. All I know of or care about is knowledge and truth, and of these things would I write. Knowledge is the comprehension of that which has reality of existence and not a speculative existence only, and this is the knowledge that I have and can teach you. Well, shall I tell you some of the truths of the spirit world?

The greatest truth is that the soul of man is immortal and needs no recreation; and the next is like unto it; that this soul is as distinct from all other souls as one star is different from any other.

Well, I know this, because I can see the souls of men and of spirits, and know that they are separate and never become absorbed, the one in the other; and the soul is immortal because I have met souls here who have lived for thousands of years without having seen the death of a soul, or heard of such death, and it is reasonable, yet certain, to infer that as death has never appeared during such centuries of time, death never will appear.

I am a philosopher here, as I was on earth, and am still pursuing my studies on existence, with much increased facilities and satisfaction, and am in a sphere where the frailties of my earth life have left me. I am pure spirit inwardly, though I have a body that is of the sublimated material and subject to change, but never to destruction, and is the portrayer of my soul, the I am.

Well I had a certain line of thought that I desired to reveal to you in a methodical way and your questions somewhat interfered with the symmetry of my discourse, but I do not complain as I have explained to you certain primal facts or truths, which may be of benefit to you.

I would like though, to deliver to you in this way my thoughts of truth in a logical and consecutive manner, and if convenient to you, will come again and do so.

No, there is nothing in my lecture on love—that I can enjoy without seeking to learn of its nature or truth, and it is not so important to discourse about as other things that you will find expounded in my lecture. A spirit says I must stop. Good night,
Longiticus.

Mentions the fact that Mr. Padgett was not satisfied with what the wise men were writing about

November 25th, 1918.

I am here, your own true and loving Helen.

Well, dear, you have had two spirits (Only Longiticus was recorded) write you tonight that are not of our band as you may know. They are wise men, though, and what they could say to you might be instructive and desirable to know, but I saw that you were not satisfied with having them write, and they perceived the fact also, and left.

I know that you are disappointed, because some of the higher spirits did not write, but they could not make the necessary rapport and so did not attempt to write. You were not just in the condition. I would like to write my letter, but you are too much drawn on now to undertake the writing. I want you to permit me to commence early when you are fresh. If you will try to get in condition by tomorrow night, I will certainly come and write.

Well that will be satisfactory. I do not think it best to write more tonight. Baby is here and sends her love. Love us both and pray to the Father. Good night and God Bless you.

Your own true and loving,

Helen.

Spirit mother of a material preacher writes about her spiritual finding and new beliefs and would like her son to know and believe as she does

July 3rd, 1917.

Let me say just a word.

I am interested in the message that has just been written you more than you may imagine, for I am the mother of the dear boy whom Paul refers to as the preacher.[125] I know that what Paul has said is true, for during the years that I have been in the spirit world, I have been with my son so very often and, as you may be surprised to know, in contradictory conditions of mind and belief, and also influence that I tried to exercise upon him.

When I lived on earth I believed as my son now believes. To me Jesus was God and savior and the redeemer of my soul by his blood and sacrifice and vicarious atonement; and when I first entered the spirit world and for some years thereafter, I believed as I did when on earth, and, as a consequence, I visited my son in his study and in the churches as he preached, and tried to impress upon him the truth of this belief, and also endeavored to inspire him in his soul as he proclaimed these truths to his hearers. And I was comparatively happy in these beliefs, and so, as I saw, was my son; and I thought that he was doing a great work for the Master; and I often prayed for him and gave thanks to God, that I had on earth a boy who was doing so great a work for the salvation of men and the glory of the Father.

Now you may wonder that I continued in these beliefs any great while after I entered the spirit world, and infer that I must soon have realized that I was not in the arms of Jesus and singing praises around the throne of God, as our church teachers sometime assured us would be our experience when we passed to spirit life. Well, I will confess that I

---

[125] This was the Washington Methodist preacher Rev. Dr. Mitchell. Paul's message is published in Volume IV (2nd Ed.) page 164 and recommends that he talk to the preacher. However within the month it appears that something must have occurred because his mother is now very pleased with her son. Looking at the diary it appears Padgett had a further conversation with him on the 19th July which lead to him preaching on the Divine Love on the 29th July. (G.J.C.)

had that expectation, and was disappointed upon arriving in the spirit world to find no arms of Jesus to receive me, and in not going into the presence of the Father. But I loved Jesus and I loved God, and had in my soul a great deal of the Divine Love, though then I did not realize just what that love is, and, consequently, after I arrived in the spirit world I found myself in a beautiful plane of light and love, and glorious spirits having homes such as I had not conceived of on earth, even though I had thought of the many mansions that Jesus had spoken of. And I was happy, very happy, and retained my belief that at the proper time I would go to where Jesus was sitting on the right of the Father. (I believed) that there was some reason, personal to me, why I was not admitted into his presence, and that when he saw that I was fitted in my soul, I would be called to him. I continued to believe in this hope, and prayed to him and rested in the assurance that he had reconciled God to me, and that there was no doubt that at the proper time I would realize the expectations of my belief, and live with Jesus in his home forever.

Well I have not time to tell you how I was awakened from these false beliefs, and learned the truth; that while Jesus was my savior, yet he was not my God, nor did his sacrifice and vicarious sufferings reconcile the Father to me. I learned what a glorious and loving spirit Jesus is—the Prince of the Celestial Heavens and the most beloved of the Father. Yet the humblest; for he is still working among the lowly and contrite to show them the way to the Father and immortality.

I also learned the great and vital truth that only by the New Birth—the flowing of the Divine Love into the soul of a man or spirit can he become reconciled to the Father and take upon himself a part of that Father's divinity, and inhabitant of the Celestial Spheres, where Jesus is now forming the kingdom of heaven in which those only who have taken on the Divine nature can possibly live. And here let me tell my son, for I know he will rejoice in the fact, that I am an inhabitant of that Celestial Kingdom, and know that I am immortal, never to die or to lose the Divine Essence that is a part of my soul.

Well, to hurry. When this great knowledge and transformation came to me, I did not cease to be with my son as he worked for the salvation of souls, but continued with him in a greater love than I had ever before had, and endeavored to impress him and guide his mind in the truth—but oh, how different from heretofore! No more did I rejoice when he preached the sacrifice and blood, but prayed to the Father that my boy might become enlightened in the truth, and that I might be given power to cause him to realize that there was only one way to salvation, and that through the wonderful Divine Love, and not through the blood.

But, alas, I could not reach his mind so that his intellectual beliefs could be changed and a mental knowledge of the truth come to him; but even this I did to some extent, for many times he has had his doubts as to some of the doctrines of his creed or church teachings not knowing that his mother was working with all her love to make these doubts the way to truth.

But these beliefs remained and are his still, and he must not feel hurt at his mother telling him that they are as fragile and of as little tensile strength as the shell of an egg. But this consolation I have, that while I could not work effectively on his mind, I did help his soul to open up to the inflowing of this Great Love, and to become the possessor of a great deal of it; and sometimes this love dominates his beliefs, and he thinks thoughts and has come to him conceptions of things spiritual that cause him to wonder as to their source.

Well, I have intruded upon you too long already but I love my boy so very much and want him to find the truth as soon as possible and thereby liberate his soul development from the bands that his intellectual beliefs fasten around it.

I am thankful for this opportunity to communicate to him and let him know, not only what his mother now knows as facts, but that his mother is with him very often, praying with and for him, and casting around him her mother's love which has been made so much sweeter and purer by that other love which she now possesses so abundantly.

I would like to write further, but I must not, and when I tell you that for a long time I have been waiting for this opportunity to tell my boy all that I have told him, you, I know, will pardon my long writing. With my love to him and the blessings of the Father, I will say good night,
his mother, Mrs. Mitchell.

Progresses to a higher Celestial Sphere and tells of her work in revealing who their soulmates are and in bringing them together, but since Mr. Padgett is her soulmate, her work is mainly with him so long as he is on earth

October 28th, 1916.

I am here, your own true and loving Helen.

Well, my dear, I am here as I promised you today and will try to write my letter, although I hesitated about doing so, as there are some spirits here who are very anxious to write, but I told them that I had made the engagement with you, and that they must wait until another time to write, and of course, they very willingly acquiesced. Well, I want to tell you that I was with you tonight at the meeting and saw that you enjoyed some of the soul love and influence that were present. These people have a great deal of this love and attract many spirits of the spiritual kind and receive a great amount of the Divine Love, for the Holy

Spirit is present with them, doing the work of the Father. But I did not come to write of them, so I will not write more.

As your father just wrote you, I am in the higher planes of the Celestial Heavens and I am so happy that I hardly know how to express myself to you, for your language has no words adequate to express what I should like to tell you. All the descriptions of my several homes that I have heretofore given you, if combined could not faintly describe the home in which I now have or the happiness which is mine. As I go higher the things of earth gradually fade away from my memory, and only my love for you and the children remain in its strength and realness. And if it were not for this love I do not think that I would often come to the earth plane, for my special work, as you know, is among the spirits of the higher spheres in revealing to them the soulmates that they have, and in bringing to them the consequent happiness. But as I have told you while you remain on earth, I will never be able to remain away from you, as the great attraction which our love creates would not permit me to do so, even if I did not desire to come, if you can imagine such a thing to be possible.

The Father is so loving and good that he never prevents his spirits of the Celestial Kingdom from indulging in those things that will make them happy and contented and, consequently, there are more of the spirits in the earth planes doing their missions of love, than might be expected, when the happiness that their homes gives them is considered. But these spirits know not selfishness in the sense of desiring all this happiness for themselves. Of course, it they have no attraction on earth—if love for the mortal does not call them to earth, then they live mostly in the spiritual or Celestial Heavens doing their work, but always work for others. These spirits are never idle, indulging their own pleasures in such a way as the majority of Christians may believe. They have their harps and their music of various kinds and all these things that are commonly conceived by the Christian mortals to exist in the Kingdom of Heaven, yet they enjoy them only in the moments of cessation from their work in helping other spirits to progress towards the fountainhead of the Father's Love.

I am also now working in teaching the spirits of the lower spheres the plan of God for the salvation of their souls, and it is a glorious work, and the reflected happiness is beyond all explanation. As we give our knowledge and love to these spirits and realize their happiness and joy, this love that streams down upon us from the higher planes seems to fill our souls with increased abundance, and we realize the saying, that the more we give the more we receive. Never are we made poor by giving and never cease to give when the opportunity presents itself. Only are we disappointed when those to whom we try to give our love and share our happiness with, refuse to receive these gifts, and this frequently happens, especially in the lower spheres and in the intellectual spheres, for you must know that these spirits of the divine nature spend much time in the intellectual spheres, endeavoring to lead the spirits of these spheres in the way that will bring to them this Divine Love and endless progress.

But strange as it may seem to you, these intellectual spirits whose natural love has become to a great degree purified, are the most difficult to convince or even interest in the great plan of the Father for their souls' redemption and entrance into the Celestial Spheres. They are comparatively happy as they progress in these intellectual and moral spheres, and they do not desire anything until they arrive at the limit of their progress and then many of them have an awakening to the fact that there may be something beyond their present powers of acquiring, and that the celestial spirits may know a way to greater progress and happiness.

We of the Celestial Spheres, all engage in this work, for we know the importance of it, and the certainty that at some time the Celestial Kingdom will be closed but we do not know when, our work with these spirits will have to cease, and then they will be left through all eternity to the limited happiness and ended progression. The more experience I have in this work, the more I am astonished at the great and wonderful power of the human will, and when I say this I include the will that these pure spirits of the natural love have. It seems to me that they approach nearest the greatness of the Father in this will power, and in the untrammeled exercise of it.

I know of no power or function that these spirits of the natural love have, that the spirits of the Celestial Spheres cannot control or subordinate, except this great will power, and as to that we are as helpless as babes so far as compulsion is concerned. When we try to influence them with love is our weapon, and unless love can work its way our influence is almost hopeless. Of course, persuasion of their intellects is also necessary, and reason must be taken in the account, but as I say, the approach to persuasion and reason must be through love, which is the power that moves and governs the spirit world. Well dear, don't you think I have written enough for tonight? You are somewhat exhausted and I think it best to stop.

Your own true and loving,
Helen.

Answers a dream call from Mr. Padgett

December 4th, 1915.

I am here, Helen.

Well, sweetheart, I heard you call me in your waking moments after your dream, and I came to you and loved you with all my heart. I know what your dream was, for I was trying to come to you in your sleep so that you would realize my presence, and I came as I might have appeared to you on earth were I now living; but you must not think that I would not love you for I would, and my appearance did not indicate that I did not love you. I only seemed a little sad and showed that I wanted your sympathy and love. So don't suppose from the dream that I did not love you.

I heard you call me several times and I came to you and I then realized how lonesome you were and how much you wanted me, and how necessary I am to you. Oh, my darling, only to think that in a few short years you will be with me and we will never have to separate again, and that our love will be so great that never can anything occur that will bring us unhappiness or discontent. I do love you with all my heart and soul and you must love me in the same way, and think of me very often and wish for me, as you did last night.

The dream had no special significance, but was merely intended to show you that your little wife was still with you, and that even if she could not come to you in the flesh, yet she could in your dreams. She was just as she might have appeared to you in her early days of married life, and tried to let you see how beautiful, even as a mortal, she was, because she thought that maybe your recollections of her of those days may have become dim and shadowy.

So you see, we can be with each other in our writings, in our visions, in voice communications and in dreams. Should we not be thankful to the Father for these great privileges. I so often think of the great gift that he has given to you, and of our ability to become so close to each other in conscious communion, and wonder why it is. But when I consider the work which you have been selected to do, I don't wonder for that work is of such importance that you will have to have the gift which has been bestowed upon you, and also the other great powers that will be given you.

As I said last night, the power of inspiration is yours also, and if you will seek to cultivate it, you will find that you will be able to express the thoughts of some of the greatest spirits that we have in our higher spirit world, and you will not only be surprised yourself at what may come through you in this way, but your hearers will also wonder and think you a wonderfully wise man and orator. But you will understand that it will not be you who will really do the speaking, but the spirits who may be behind you.

No, it will not interfere with your writing powers, but, on the contrary, will help and increase these powers, for many times when we write, if we could only tell you in the way of inspiration what we desire to express, many things would be more easily transmitted to paper, than as now, when we have to do the physical work of moving your hand as well as of using your brain. So you see, it is very desirable for you to cultivate this phase of mediumship, for the good that you will be able to do is beyond calculation.

No, I have not heard that he (Ed Thomas) has passed over, and I don't know any of his friends here, but I will try to find them and will speak to him and tell him that you sent me to him, and if he needs help I will try to help him, and, if he desires, will bring him to you, and let him write. So you see, if we can do any good to any spirit we are always willing to do it.

Don't you think that we had better stop now, as you are tired, although you may not realize it.

Well, sweetheart, I do love you with all my heart and soul and I will stay with you, and comfort you and make you feel my presence. I am so happy that you love me so much and want me with you as you do; but we have to observe the laws governing our communications, and it will not be best for us to write more at this time.

I will come tonight and again tell you of my love.

So with all my love I will say goodbye.

Your own true and loving,

Helen.

Is not willing to write on the subject of soul because Mr. Padgett's condition is not what it should be although Mr. Padgett is anxious to receive it

February 13th, 1917.

I am here, Jesus.

Well, I come tonight and desire to write on the subject of the soul but when I consider your condition, which is much better than it has been, I desire (think) it best to wait a while longer. As I have told you, it is necessary for you to get in the best possible receptive condition in order that you may receive my message just as I deliver it.

I know that you are anxious to receive this discourse and expect that it will contain a disclosure of mysteries that the world has so long had hidden from it. And such will be the contents of the message but as a fact there are no mysteries connected with this subject for the soul is a creature of God, just as is the body and spirit. The only reason that mankind has (not) known of the nature and constituency of the soul, is that their soul perceptions have never been developed so that they could comprehend the qualities that pertain to the soul.

They have studied and conceived of the nature of the body and have assumed at some knowledge of its wonderful construction and functions and the purposes of its existence and so they have some idea of what the spirit is which is really a manifestation of the workings of the soul. And as I have before told you, the active energies of the soul and even as to the spirit while they see its manifestations yet they have but a slight apprehension of what it really is. Yet they necessarily have some knowledge of its workings, for the results of its activities are manifested even to their physical senses. But as to the soul they have but a very indefinite comprehension of what it really is and frequently in their conception of its qualities and functions and existence, confuse it with the mind or with the spirit and hold them to be synonymous. They know nothing of its origin and of its great possibilities and of the fact that it is the only part of man that lives forever and can become a part of the very Substance of the Father himself and hence become immortal.

That it is that which gives to man a creation and existence above the brute creation of earth and that it determines the great distinction between man and the brute creation and not reason is this determiner as men so frequently assert. Reason is merely a faculty of the mind which in the event of the soul taking on the divine substance, becomes, as it were, a thing of non-existence for the faculties of the soul supplants reason. That is the reason that so distinguishes man, as mere man, and which will continue in this spirit life to distinguish him as God's highest creation, so long as man remains mere man even though he becomes the perfect man. But I will not write more on this now.

I am your friend and brother,
Jesus.[126]

Explains the writing received by Mr. Morgan and the relative importance of each, and that their work will become more important after Mr. Padgett finishes his work in behalf of the Kingdom

June 7th, 1918.

I am here, John.

Let me write a line. I have been with you as you read the messages that your friend received, and want to say that what they say as to your want of condition is true, as you know, and that you must give your longings and thoughts more to spiritual things in order to get in condition to receive the messages again.

---

[126] From the summary of this message in the daily diary, it is apparent that a considerable amount of personal comment by Jesus has been edited out of this message. The original also has impossibly long sentences, and evidence of poor rapport. (G.J.C.)

But the messages are not correct when they tell him that you will not be necessary to start the great work on earth. There is no other who can possibly start this work and, hence, you must realize the responsibility that rests upon you and make every effort to get in that rapport with the higher spirits that will enable you to successfully do your work.

Your two friends have an important work laid out for them to do, but their work is merely confirmatory of the messages that you receive, and until you shall have received all that is intended to be revealed their work will not start.

Mr. Morgan is now doing a great work among the spirits and his band and many others of the high spirits are kept very busy in attending to the awakened spirits in their demands for enlightenment. He must continue this until the time that I have mentioned, comes, when he will be given the greater work. He is a man of very deep convictions, and earnest in his work, and will sooner or later realize the results of his efforts to help the dark spirits.

Your work and his work and that of Dr. Stone, are separate and distinct. Neither can do the work of the other, but yours must first be done. So do not forget this and realize with all the knowledge of your soul how much depends upon you. I will not write more now. With my love I will say good night,

Your brother in Christ,
John.

Explains the great importance of his being in condition to receive the many truths that are still to be written while Mr. Padgett is still here

March 7th, 1920.

I am here, Jesus.

Let me write a line for I see that you are desirous to hear from me and obtain the encouragement that always flows from my communications. I have been with you tonight as during many nights past with the desire to write you upon subjects important to the work that you are to do and was prevented from doing so only by the condition in which you were that prevented me from making the rapport.

As I have told you before, we are governed by law in regards to the kind of messages that we may communicate to you and unless you are in condition that will permit these laws to be complied with we are powerless to use your brain for the purpose of delivering our messages. You also know what the remedy is for the defect that may exist at any particular time and we have urged upon you to seek this remedy and thereby get in the proper and necessary condition that will enable us to make the rapport.

But you have not been successful in applying the remedy, not because it is not available to you, but because of your course of thought and failure to pray to the Father for an inflowing of His Love into your soul and thereby causing the proper influence to be caused upon your brain which will enable us to take possession of its functioning and deliver the messages that we have to communicate. You are in better condition tonight than you have been for some time and I hope that you will continue to think of these spiritual truths and pray to the Father and if you do this we shall soon succeed in writing to you many of the truths that we are so anxious to communicate.

There are very many of these truths yet to be revealed to you, some of far greater importance than you have already received except those relating to the Divine Love, and we are anxious that you receive them as rapidly as possible for they are needed by mankind and many souls are longing for the truth that can only be made known through you.[127]

So my brother, think deeply of what I have said and let your work be to you the most important thing in your life. As you know you have only a few years yet to live and if you do not do our work it may be that a lifetime will elapse before we may be able to get another who shall have the qualifications that are required. You sometimes, I know, realize the importance of your work but lately and more often you let your thoughts turn to and become absorbed in things that are of the mere mortal life and as a consequence the greater things are put aside and neglected. I like (trust) that this may not continue. We will be with you and give you all the help that is possible for us to give and hope that from now on it may be successful.

Tonight I will not write upon any subject of a formal character and wish to say that we are ready to continue our messages and are dependent only upon you getting in the condition that will enable us to do so.

So think of what I write and pray earnestly to the Father and you will be able to overcome this inclination to lower your thoughts to these material things. We understand just what you need to enable you to turn your life on earth and as we have told you these things shall be provided and you will not be compelled to suffer for anything of this nature that is necessary for your comfort or living. Only trust in us and do the work instead of thinking of these things.

---

[127] From this we can deduce that a considerable amount of material that was planned was never received by James Padgett. Now that it is 100 years later, there has of course been a considerable volume received post-Padgett, especially in the last 15 years. (G.J.C.)

I will come soon and write another message that will be of importance and far reaching with its effect upon the belief of men. Many spirits are with you watching over you and ready to help. You must believe this and act on that belief.

Well, as I have said, it is because of your want of condition and the spirit who moves your pencil are those who merely have the desire to write and are not presently to do so. Your guide, the Indian, is a very careful guardian and will not permit many of them to intervene but occasionally he does let one write so that you may know that there are many spirits surrounding you ready to take advantage of the opportunity to write.

But until our work is accomplished this kind of spirit will not be permitted to write. You will remember that some time ago we suddenly stopped the spirit in darkness from writing you and asking your help. This was done not that we did not want these spirits to get all the help possible, but because the work that we are doing just now is of more importance to humanity as well as to spirits, and every other kind of communication must be stopped in order that our work shall proceed. Then you will see how important the work is for ordinarily nothing is of so much importance as the rescuing of a soul from sin and ignorance. I will not write more tonight.

Yes, I will pray with you and I hope that you will let all the longings of your soul enter into your prayers for the greater the longing the greater will be the abundance of the love received in answer to your prayers. I will come soon, good night.

Your brother and friend,
Jesus.

Is so anxious to reveal the Truth that he knows for the good of humanity

March 7th, 1920.

I am here, your own true and loving Helen.

Well, my dear, I am glad that the Master wrote you tonight as he did for I must tell you that he was much in earnest in what he said and I hope that you will think of what he said and try to improve your condition as he suggested. He is so anxious to reveal to you the truth that he knows and which he realizes will be for the good of humanity.

He is so loving and if you could only see how tender and sympathetic he is when writing to you, you must not for one moment doubt his love or think of anything and be very impatient, or having him with you in all his love and influence. Try to realize what this means.

Only believe that I love you with all my soul and am with you

very often trying to help you and make you happy.
Good night, my own dear husband,
Your own true and loving, Helen.

Postpones writing to correct Mr. Padgett's thinking before he can write again

February 27th, 1916.

I am here, Jesus.

I see that you are not in condition tonight and I will not try, for I would not be able to convey to you my thoughts as I desire. We will have to postpone it until later. Well, you have been thinking about other things too intently and your mind is not in that condition of concentration on what I may write that is necessary.

You have been reading today about the teachings of Barbarism and the mysteries of Abdul Baba and you have not found that they are anything different from what you expected for they are based upon the writings of the Bible and of the Koran and of other so-called sacred writings. They will not benefit you particularly for they stress that the Prophet is as the writer says, the Ancient of Days, and does not know the real truths concerning God and man and His relationship to them. So I advise that you do not think more of these things but confine your thoughts to my writings.

As I told you several nights ago, I will come sometime and write you in detail about this new cult and that Baba's Allah himself will come sometime.[128] Strange as it may seem, he is not in the Celestial Heavens, but only in a high sphere which is inhabited by those who have equal development of the natural love. So stop thinking about these matters and give your thoughts more to me. I will soon come.

So with all my love, I am,
Your brother and friend,
Jesus.

Is happy for the improvements in Mr. Padgett's spiritual progression

March 5th, 1916.

I am here, your Helen.

Well sweetheart, I merely want to say that I am sorry you are not

---

[128] This did not occur. The reference to "Allah" above is curious, because it is generally understood to refer to God. (G.J.C.)

in condition to write tonight for the Master rather expected that you would be able to take his message. But as you are not in condition I will not attempt to write. I am very happy and I see that you are not so worried and I am glad of it only believe what we say and you will soon be relieved.

Your grandmother is here and says that you must pray more to the Father and let your thoughts turn more to Him and His Love for then you will find that the rapport between you and the celestial spirits will be much increased. She sends her love and will soon write you.

Prof. Salyards is also here and says that he will be pleased to finish his message at your earliest convenience. He says that he will come and do as you suggest.

Well I must not write more. But say that I love you with all my heart and soul.

So with a great big kiss, I am your own true and loving,
Helen.

The lover of liberty, and a friend of Washington and our country, expresses his thoughts regarding France as well as Germany and the outcome of the war

August 1st, 1915.

I am here, Lafayette.

I am the Frenchman who was a lover of liberty and a soldier of both your country and mine, and who was an aide to your great general and father of his country—I mean Washington. I came because I want to tell you that in the Great War[129] that is now going on I am interested, and want to express my opinion as to its causes and its ending.

France was not desirous of this war and had made no preparations to struggle against the Germans and had no idea that the Germans would so soon seek to overrun her territory; as Germany professed the greatest friendship for her; but as you know, the German Emperor, without warning and without excuse hurled his legions into poor Belgium in his endeavor to reach the French capital and possess it before the French nation could make any effective resistance. The Kaiser was anxious to acquire more territory belonging to France for purposes of colonization, and thought that the task would be an easy one. He had no conception that he would have any difficulty in passing through Belgium, neither did he contemplate that England and Russia would join with France in opposing his onslaught. In fact, he thought that he would so quickly succeed in capturing Paris and obtaining what he desired that

---

[129] This was the First World War. (G.J.C.)

these other nations would not have time to take any part in the conflict.

But as you know, little Belgium checked his advance and held him at bay until England was enabled to take such action as embarrassed him to such an extent that he has never yet succeeded in gaining the object of his desires, and let me say, he never will. I will not further review this phase of the matter.

In the end Germany will be defeated and her Kaiser will be killed and his family disappear from the face of the earth as a ruling family. Germany will become in a few years after the war a republic, but its territory will be much reduced.

Before the war ends the Allies will invade Germany and Berlin will become invested by them and they will dictate their own terms of capitalism, and these terms will be such that Germany as a great nation will cease to exist, and will take her place among the republics of the earth as a secondary state, and devote herself to the industries which her natural resources and the capacity of her people will entitle her to. She will never become a great maritime nation but will be content to exist as a manufacturing and agricultural country. Her people will migrate in large numbers and become swallowed up in the other nations of the world, especially in the South American countries.

France will again thrive and so will her Allies and little Belgium will be taken care of and become an important manufacturing country, with a people much improved in their intellectual acquirements. I say all this, not because I am a Frenchman, but because I can see that these results must flow from causes which now exist, and which will continue to exist until the results that I speak of come about.

But the sad thing is that before these results come many a human will become a spirit and many a happy family will be broken up and poverty and distress cause much suffering. But such is war and such a war never was.

So my friend, I thought that I would write to you tonight and express my views. I will not take up more of your time.

I live in the sixth sphere and have a home of much beauty and many friends in whom I find much happiness and entertainment. I sometime see him (Washington) but not so often as formerly. He is living in a sphere higher than where I live and I don't often see him. Our attractions have not continued as you might suppose, and where this attraction does not exist, spirits do not often come in contact with one another.

I never thought of that view of the matter, and the next time I meet him I will make the inquiry. I know that he is a more beautiful spirit than I am and more beautiful than when he lived close to me in a lower sphere. I have never thought to ask the reason for his improvement but will do so as you suggest.

I sometimes see Napoleon and talk with him and more often since this war began. He is interested as I am but he does not seem to think that it will last very long, as he sees a reason why the Allies will soon overrun the German empire, and bring the war to a close.

I cannot write more.

Your friend,

Lafayette.

Disagrees with what Lafayette has just written about the German emperor, but claims that the war was forced on him and of course made the wrong prediction as to its outcome

August 1st, 1915.

I am here, Bismarck.

Let me say a word. I saw what Lafayette wrote and I don't agree with him on either proposition.

The German Emperor did not bring on this war as the Frenchman said, but it was forced on him. He saw that not only France but England was trying to destroy the great mercantile business which Germany had built up, and that unless he took some means to forestall the efforts of these nations, Germany would lose its commercial prestige and have to submit to the dictates of these rivals; and as a wise Emperor and statesman he struck the first blow—sharp and quick—and had it not been for the Belgians he would have reached Paris and accomplished his object.

But that little nation of lacemakers, as we called them, showed that when home was invaded they could fight, and fight they did; and notwithstanding the fact that I am a German, whose sympathies and desires are all with the Germans, yet I admired the way in which these Belgians fought. Had France such fighters, the Germans would have been out of that country a long time ago, and the German territory would now be invaded. But this is past, and Germany is still in France and will stay there, notwithstanding the efforts that France and England may make to oust them.

The end of the war is not yet and before that end comes Paris will fall and the terms of peace will be dictated by the victorious Germans; and France will lose some territory, and England will pay an indemnity and make such concessions to Germany that her commerce will be established and grow to such an extent that she will be second to none as a commercial nation.

Germany will not cease to be an empire—a stronger and greater one than ever. William will not live long after the war ends, but one of his sons will occupy the throne and his family will reign for years. It will not become a republic, although I know the socialists will make a great effort to bring that about; but they will fail.

So I tell you that the French spirit is mistaken and he will find out his mistake before a great many months have gone by. I don't know what causes he imagines he sees, but if he would see the true causes he would draw different conclusions as I do. I am Bismarck and I am with the German Army trying to show its generals the way to accomplish their objects. I must not write more.

I live in the second sphere and am trying to find happiness, but this war interferes with my happiness and my progress.

Well, I saw you writing, and I saw Washington and Lafayette engaged in writing and I stopped to listen, and became interested in both the writing and the subject matter, and when Lafayette wrote as he did I determined to give my views, and hence I wrote. You must excuse my intrusion, but I thought it just to express what I think about the war.

I will not take up more of your time.

So with my kind regards, I am your friend,

Bismarck.

Is a follower of the Master and has progressed to the First Celestial Heaven, and is still interested in the individual souls of men as well as their spiritual welfare

August 1st, 1915.

I am here, George Washington.

I was the first President of the United States. I came to tell you that I am a spirit who is now a follower of the Master and that I have found the Love of God and am an inhabitant of the first Celestial sphere, where my home is one of happiness and love.

I am not so much interested in the affairs of earth as I once was, and I do not attempt to influence the men who are at the head of public affairs as I did a few years ago. Now I see that the things of the earth are only temporary and need not the oversight of spirits who have advanced to the higher spheres, and consequently, I don't at this time take an interest in such matters. But I am interested in the individual souls of men and in their spiritual welfare and I am doing what I can to help them develop their soul qualities. So when you read that I am advising the rulers of the nation, or others who have to do with the making of its laws or the execution of them, you must conclude that such messages are not from me or in any manner suggested by me.

I am now interested in men as individuals because that welfare exists through all eternity and not for time only, as does the welfare of the nation. Of course, as men become possessed of the higher soul development the condition and excellence of the nation will be benefitted and increased, and men's happiness, both individually and in the aggregate, will be much increased, and will make them more at one with the Father, and as a consequence, the brotherhood of man will be more effective in working good.

But the brotherhood of man is not the great object for which men should work or preach. First, let each man receive in his heart this Divine Love of the Father, and then the true principles which should exist in the brotherhood of man will find their existence, and men not only as individuals but as brothers will find that they will be happier, and devote themselves to serving one another and to causing the greatest good to the greatest numbers. No mere philanthropical desires of men will bring about the great millennium that men look forward to in organizing and fostering what they call the brotherhood of men.

Of course, men should endeavor to love one another even if they do not have this Divine Love in their souls, but such love will not be sufficient to form a brotherhood that will last and grow under all circumstances. Men's desires are not naturally of the kind that unite them together in one great object, and where their material interests or love of power or ambition to extend their territorial or commercial interests come in conflict with this natural love for one another the natural love must succumb, and as a result war will ensue, and hatred and envy and the desire to overcome one another will take the place of love and brotherhood. Only when men shall get this Divine Love in their hearts will they be able to overcome these natural desires.

So I say, the great and only preachment is the obtaining of a brotherhood of man founded upon the Divine Love existing in the individual souls. Without this the brotherhood will be founded on sinking sand and no stability will make it a thing of lasting existence. I have written enough for my first attempt.

As to the present terrible war, I do not see that it had any excuse much less justification and the results that will follow are beyond the conception of the wisest statesmen. I do not know how or when it will end, but to me it seems that the allies must prevail, and the Germans and Austrians be compelled to submit to the dictates of their antagonists. But ere that time comes, many a man will become a spirit, and many an orphan and widow will be made to hunger and suffer the pangs of distress. Let men fight if they will, but the truths of the Father will always continue to stand and call for men to recognize and embrace them.

So my friend, I must stop. Thanking you for your kindness, I will say good night.

Your brother in Christ,
George Washington.

Gave his life for the freedom of the slaves and the purification of the nation; and is still fighting for truth and liberty in the spirit world

August 1st, 1915.

I am here, John Brown.

I was the man who gave his life for the freedom of the slaves and the purification of the nation. So I come to you as a spirit who in the long years since my death has seen the principles for which I fought and died established in the laws of my country, and the principles of freedom and political equality made a part of the economy of your land.

I am now a spirit fighting still for truth and liberty, but now my fight is for the liberty of all mankind from the slavery which sin and the greed of men impose upon their fellow men. No man has the right, because of superiority in position or greatness in wealth to make his fellow man a slave or keep him from enjoying the God given things of earth. Of course, some men must rule and some must possess the greater riches, but these facts do not justify the ruling ones or the wealthy in treating the subordinate or the poor in a way to make them unhappy, or to prevent them from receiving their just dues in the working of the affairs of their relationship of employer and employee or of governor and governed.

Right is right, and the machinations of men will not much longer make the poor and dependent a slave to the rich and independent. Men are awakening to their rights and to the object of their creation by a just God who is no respecter of persons; and soon men will come into their own and peace will reign on earth. I am not what is called a socialist, but a lover of mankind without regard to environments or opportunities. Let the rich treat the poor as brothers, and let the laws be administered for all alike.

Religion is a mighty power in the world, and as men come to see that the golden rule of the Master is the only one that should govern their actions, one towards the other, peace and prosperity and happiness will come to the inhabitants of the earth.

What I say is not a mere dream of an enthusiast, but is the result of what I see will follow the workings of the great spiritual forces which are now combined and working for the salvation of men as never before in the history of the world.

And in this great work love will be the mainstay of the principles that will activate men in their dealings with one another, and when this love shall flow to men with all its fullness and irresistible force, as will do, men will realize a new existence, and the brotherhood of men will become a thing of reality. So I say, let men prepare themselves for this great inflowing of love, for it is coming and will sweep away the evils and trifles that now are influencing the great crime of the centuries. I mean the great barbarous and inexcusable war that is now devastating the whole of Europe.

Men may think that the end of the war will see a peace that, because of the horrors and great losses and depletion of men and means, will last for many years, but if peace should depend upon these causes, war would rear its ugly head again before many generations have passed. While the war shall end, the causes of the war will only slumber, and when new generations come, and the ambition and desire for aggrandizement and power shall again work their evil influences upon the hearts and minds of the rulers of the new generations, war will come again.

But we hope, and are working to that end, that the love of one for another and the great feeling and realization of the brotherhood of man will so fill the souls of men that those things which cause wars will entirely disappear, and peace will become the lasting condition of both individuals and nations. Liberty and freedom are the great possessions of men even as they are now possessed, with all these feelings of envy and hatred and ambition, but peace and love are the greatest things in all the world, and when men learn this, war will never rear its ugly head again. I must stop now.

I am living in the fourth sphere and am comparatively happy, and am much interested in any country's welfare and in the welfare of humanity the world over. I am a worshiper of God and am trying to follow His precepts as I learned them on earth. I am not the possessor of what you call the Divine Love but I have a love for my fellow men which enables me to try to help them in every way in my power.

I never have troubled myself about the love that you speak of. I know that there are spirits who live in higher spheres than I do, and they seem more beautiful than do I, but I have never sought the reason or troubled myself with knowing why. But as you put the proposition I will talk to some of these spirits and ask them about this love that you speak of.

So I thank you for the opportunity of writing my sentiments on the subject that is so dear to me now, and was when I was on earth.

With all my love I will say, good night,
John Brown.

Explains the effect on babies who come into the spirit world as a result of abortion

November 13th, 1915.

I am here, Helen.

Yes, I was there and enjoyed the show. The pictures contain a very important truth that all women should understand and appreciate, for so many refuse to become mothers and perform the duties that God intends them to perform. I have no doubt that the pictures will have a good effect on many of them, and make them think before resorting to that means of getting rid of the unborn babies.

In my investigation of the subject of babies who have come to the spirit world as a result of abortion, I do not find that they ever go back to their earth mothers for any purpose whatever. There are spirits who are specially designated to take care of babies, and in cases where the natural mothers have succeeded in cutting short the lives of these babies, these spirits who have charge of these babies in the spirit world never permit these babies to come in contact with their unnatural mothers or visit them. And this because the mother's love is not there to receive these poor little waifs; and where there is no mother's love there is no attraction existing that will cause the return of the babies when they have once left their mothers.

But in the case of babies who prematurely die, or of those who die very young, these babies do return to their mothers under the guidance of their guardian spirits and receive from their mothers their love and feelings which are going forth to these babies.

The law of attraction operates here as well as in other matters and this is the law in reference to babies who die early. When there is existing a mother's love, the baby will return and receive this love and help from coming in contact with such mother. But when there is no mother's love there is no attraction, and the baby may never know its mother.

In many cases, the baby, before the mother comes to the spirit world, finds other attractions, and hence there is no feeling of love or sympathy between the baby and its mother.

It frequently happens that when the mother comes into the spirit world, she finds the spirit of the unborn baby, and in a way has a uniting, but rarely is this love strong enough to keep them together, the law of attraction separates them and then each goes his own way. I will not write more.

Your own true and loving,
Helen.

Mr. Padgett's cousin seeks his help, which she has learned about in the spirit world from the dark spirits that received his help

March 29th, 1915.

I am here, Laura Burroughs, your cousin.

Oh, my dear Edward, you do something to help me. I am so unhappy and need help so much. I am in such darkness and pain that I can scarcely see the light of day, I mean the light that enables me to see my surroundings. I am also so lonely and without love or sympathy. I feel that you can help me, so pray do so.

Yes, I have seen several beautiful spirits but I did not believe that they had interest enough in me to help me and so I turned aside from them. I don't understand why I am in this condition and no one has explained it so far. I thought that maybe you might show me some way to get out of my awful condition. I thought so because I saw other spirits writing to you who are in this darkness as I am and they said that you had helped them.

Why I see Aunt Nancy and your mother and Helen and your father and others I don't know. How beautiful and happy they look to be. Why are they so beautiful? Oh, if I could only be like them. Tell me, Ed., why it is, and tell me what made them so?

Yes, I will and she is calling me now. Oh, how glad that I came here. I feel better already. Dear Aunt Nancy, she will love me I know and so will cousin Ann and Helen. Oh, how glad I am.

I am now going with them, so good bye, my dear cousin.

Reassures Mr. Padgett to have faith in the Master, the true Jesus of the Bible, and others truly are who they represented themselves to be

April 5th, 1915.

I am here—your grandmother.

Well, I am glad to be with you again as I want to tell you of some truths that you will be benefited by knowing. You have had more or less doubt pass through your mind as to whether we are really the persons whom we represent ourselves to be, and whether, if your own mind does not produce the thoughts and write, or whether some evil spirit or imposter does.

I want to tell you now with all the love which I have for you, that everyone of us who write you is the person he represents himself to be, and no spirit who may seek to impose on you is permitted to write or in any way communicate with you. Our band is sufficiently powerful to prevent any such spirit from intruding himself upon you. Of course, the unfortunate spirits[130] who write you, we permit to do so, but they are

---

[130] Mr. Padgett enabled the unfortunate spirits to visualise the bright ones so that they

not imposters, but tell you truthfully just who they are.

I know how natural it is for you to doubt this great marvel of spirit communion, and of the truthfulness of our representations, but I assure you that it is all true. The Master is the one of whom you read in the Bible, and of whom you have heard all your life. The only difference being that he is not God or part of Him, but a spirit the greatest in all the spiritual kingdom.

He is not so very different in his desire to do the great work which the Father gave him to do, from what he was on earth, except that he is now more highly developed than when a man traveling the plains and mountains of Palestine. He is more powerful and knows so many more truths of the Father, but his love is just the same, only greater in degree.

So you must not doubt any longer or you will not develop as you should.

He is the wisest and most filled with the Father's Love of all the spirits in the Celestial Spheres.

I know that you love us all, and I believe that you love Him also, and when I tell you that His love is greater than that of any of us, I am merely telling you what is true.

I would like to write more tonight but there are some others here who are very anxious to write you and I will stop.

Your own true and loving grandmother
Ann Rollins.[131]

Describes her home in the Second Celestial Sphere

July 6th, 1915.

I am here, your grandmother.

I come tonight to tell you that I am very happy to see that you are in such good condition and so free from your worries and cares. So you must try to keep your mind and thoughts free until you have no occasion for worry.

I want to tell you of my beautiful home in the Second Celestial Sphere, and what happiness we have in enjoying its beauties and grandeur. It is not possible for me to describe its appearance, only to say that its beauty is beyond any conception that you may have, or any ability I may have to describe it.

Everything that the heart may wish for is contained in it, and everything that you can conceive of as being necessary to make a home

---

can receive help. Mr. Padgett gave one evening a week for this purpose. (Dr. S.)
[131] This message is a composite of two, being published in Volume II and Volume III. (G.J.C.)

beautiful is there. I am in a great degree of happiness, and have so many bright and beautiful spirits for companions, and never get tired of listening to the grand and angelic music.

We, I mean your mother, wife and myself, are with one another very frequently, although our homes are different and not very close together. Of course, my home is in a higher plane in that sphere, than those of your mother or wife, but there is nothing to prevent our having constant intercourse and companionship.

He (grandfather) is in the fifth sphere still, although he is progressing, and is so very anxious to get with me, but he has not love and faith sufficient to be with me in my home. I know that you are anxious that we be together and that you pray for such a consummation of our desires; and your prayers will be answered before a great while for my faith is so strong that I know that my prayers will soon be answered by the Father.

Yes, I will go to the third Celestial sphere where many bright spirits are. Spirits who have the Love of God in their souls to an extent that fits them for such a life.

You are right, there are no purely intellectual spheres in the celestial heavens. All the spheres are soul spheres where the Love of the Father is possessed by all the spirit inhabitants to such an extent that intellectual development is merely a secondary condition. How I would like to write you a long letter tonight on spiritual matters, but I do not think that you are quite in condition to take such a message, and I will postpone it until a later time.

Your wife is here, and after a little she will write to you, and tell you of her happiness and peace in the Father's love.

So I will not write more tonight, but will only repeat that I love you with all my heart and soul.

Your grandmother.

Confirms Luke's message and that he is the representative of the Father to help His work on earth

September 30th, 1915.

I am here, Jesus.

Well, my dear brother and disciple, I am so glad that you are feeling so much better tonight and that your worries are not pressing so hard upon you as they were. What you received from Luke in his last message is true. The climax of your troubles have been reached, and from now onward you will find that relief will come to you, and that very soon you will commence to do that which will bring you such relief from your obligations that you will get into condition to do my work, and to give up your professional cares and devote your whole time to receiving the truths which shall save mankind from their sins and show them the way to the Father's Love and to immortality.

I will not write much tonight, but only say with all the emphasis of a conviction which knowledge gives me, that you will soon be free, and that you must believe, and must have faith in the Father's love and care for you, and must trust me with all the faith of your being, for I am the Jesus that represents the Father in all his works and plans for the salvation of man and for the redemption of the world from sin.

I am not the Father which the book that you have been reading says. I am not, but am the beloved son of the Father, and I have given to me all the power, and love, and knowledge which the Father thought best for me to have; and no other spirit has such a Gift conferred upon him.

So, trusting in my love, let your faith increase, and your worries leave you.

With all my love, I am your brother and friend,
Jesus.

Writes on the great love of Jesus for him and his work of greatest importance

I am here, your grandmother.

My son, what a wonderful love the Master shed upon you as he wrote to you, and for a time after he ceased writing. Oh, how happy I am that he loves you so much, and is with you so often trying to influence you in the way of truth; for I must tell you that when he wrote he manifested a wonderful power and glory and seemed to be so interested that you should not only see what he should write, but should also feel his presence.

So, do not doubt what he told you, as I know that he spoke as one having authority based on knowledge of what the future had in store for you.

I cannot tell you how happy we all are that you are his chosen one for this great work, and that with that work will come to you the wonderful influence of the divine love that John speaks of.

I am with you often, and am trying to help you in all your material troubles, so that soon you will become a free man, serving only the Master and his great desires. Your mother is here and is so happy and thanks God continually for the great favor and blessings that He has bestowed upon you. And as to Helen, she can hardly restrain her job, and if it were possible, she would come to you in a visible form and hug you and kiss you and shed tears of joy that such blessings are yours. So believe and pray to the Father for more faith and more love.

We are all praying for you and will continue to so pray all the years that you may live on earth.

I must stop now, but will say, that if love could make you as happy as the celestial angels, this night you would have all our love. So, trust in what I say and let your thoughts sometime turn to the love of your own grandmother.

Ann Rollins.

Writes of the great love of Jesus for him and the interest he has in both material and spiritual work

I am here, Helen.

My own darling Ned, how I love you tonight, and how happy I am in the knowledge that you have the great love of the Master; for tonight he showed to us the great love that he has for you, and the great interest he has in your material, as well as in your spiritual, welfare.

Never have I been so happy as now, for I now know that as you progress in your work you will have come to you the wonderful love of the Father that will develop your soul to such an extent that when the time comes for you to come over you will be able to be with me in my home in the celestial spheres.

So darling, let your thoughts turn to the work which you are to do, and to the love of the Father. Pray and have faith and you will soon realize that your soul is expanding with this great love, and that joy and blessings will come to you.

Your grandmother said truly, when she wrote, that if it were possible I would manifest in such a was that you could see me and feel my arms about you and my kisses on your lips and great tears of joy streaming from my eyes.

So, sweetheart, love your little wife, as you used to call her, and believe that she loves you with all her heart and soul, as she does.

Your own true and loving,
Helen.

Writes about the increase in the love for the Father will help Mr. Padgett both materially and spiritually

August 30th, 1915.

I am here, Jesus.

I come tonight because I see that you are again praying to the Father for the inflowing of His Love and for faith, and for a nearness to Him that will make you happy. I am glad of this new aspiration and know that the Love will come to you and that your faith will be increased, and your trust in me will be established firmly so that we can proceed with our work. So, I will soon come now and write you another of my formal messages, and I hope that thence we can go rapidly onward.

I have been with you today and know what your feelings have been, and how in a way you have had faith that certain things would come to pass without knowing just why—but you have not troubled yourself very much and expected to secure them at the time needed. Well, I want to tell you that that is the kind of faith that you should have in reference to all the things that affect you both materially and spiritually. Such faith brings results and you will not be disappointed in your present faith, for what you need will come to you this week. I am here predicting a thing with certainty as I see it; and I do not think you will be disappointed. I know what you mean, and we will help you, only exercise your willpower, and when you feel the temptation come to you very strong, utter a prayer to the Father for help, and you will receive it.

I am glad that you are in such condition of harmony with the Father tonight, and that your love for him is so strong; and with that love will come faith that will be able to accomplish most anything that you may desire, and that the Father sees is best for you. Yes, you can ask those things with the assurance that they will be pleasing to the Father, and will not be refused you. I would like to write longer but I must stop now.

I will tell you the next time that I write about these two spirits who say they are the first parents of the human race.[132] I have not the time now, and what I may say may be interesting to you and to the world.

So, my dear brother, I will say good night.
Your brother,
Jesus.

Was praying and helping Mr. Padgett to receive the Divine Love of the Father to permit the writing to be received by him

April 1st, 1915.

I am here, Jesus.

I have been with you very much to-day, trying to cheer you with my love and influence. You are much better than you were yesterday or a few days past, and your soul is in a condition of development and love that it has not been in for a long time. The Love of the Father is with you

---

[132] Messages from Amon and Aman, the first parents, are published in Volume II (4th Ed.) on page 129.(G.J.C.)

and filling your soul to an extent that you can hardly realize, for it is a Love that knows no limitation and is without bound or cessation.

I am glad that you are experiencing this great inflowing of this Love of the Father, and with it will come a faith that will make the Father seem very near to you.

Try to realize the presence of this great Love more and more, and you will find a happiness that you have never before felt, and a great peace will come to you that will make your worries disappear and leave you a free man. So my dear brother, let this confidence in the Father take possession of you, and believe that there is nothing that can separate you from this great Love and happiness.

I wanted to write this to you so that you may know that the feelings and thoughts which you have are not the mere imaginings of your own mind, but the real, true and substantial things that I tell you of.

Keep praying to the Father, and His Love will come to you in increasing abundance, and with this Love will come a wonderful faith that will make real all the longings and aspirations of your soul, so that you will know that the Father has the personality that I wrote you of a few nights ago.

I am pleased with you and with your efforts to become a true child of the Father and in unison with Him, and a recipient of His favor and mercy. Go not in the way of the wicked, nor associate with those whose thoughts are given to the evils of the material life, or to those things which are not approved of by the Father, or by His higher spirits who so often now come to you.

I am with you and you have all my love and help to enable you to become pure in heart, as you so often now pray you may become. Keep praying and you will find that this condition of soul will be yours, and with it will come a realization that you have been regenerated, and are at-one with the Father and His Love. Your blessings will be great and the happiness that will come to you will be beyond all conception that you may now have of what happiness may be.

I must not write more now, but will say, only believe in me, and trust to the Father, and all things that may be needful will be added unto you, and you will not be forsaken or left to your troubles, alone. I will be with you tonight and will try to write you another message, after you have received the messages from the dark spirits, who will come to you for help.

So with all my love and the blessings of an elder brother, I will say goodbye for the present.

Your brother and friend.

Jesus.

Let not your faith be shaken by what anyone says

September 20th, 1915.

I am here, St. John.

The other man said that there is no other salvation than through the blood of Jesus. How in error he is and how he will find the truth on his awakening in the spirit life! Let not your heart be troubled or your faith in the Master be shaken by anything that he or any other man may say.

I was at the meeting and what the preacher said was all right, except that one must believe that only the blood of Jesus saves from sin.

No, he did not say that in so many words, but that was what he intended that his sermon should convey.

Let not the conversation cause you to doubt for a moment what we have written you. We are with you and want you to believe firmly in what we may write. So believe and trust.

Your brother in Christ,
John.

A message from Helen

September 19th, 1915.

I am here, Helen.

I went to church with you this morning and saw that you were sleepy and I can't blame you, for the sermon was not very interesting. Of course he preached some truths when he spoke of trusting God to sustain you in your attempts to do His Will and uphold the right. The three Hebrew children who passed through the fiery furnace merely illustrated the care which God has over his children and it is just as true today as it was in any past age.

Your own true and loving,
Helen.

Often went with Mr. Padgett to the church services that he attended in Washington and then wrote about the preachers belief and spiritual development

October 3rd, 1915.

I am here, Jesus.

I was with you tonight and you were not very much impressed

with the thoughts expressed by the speaker,[133] because he did not dwell very much on the qualities of the soul or the manner in which are perceived the great truths of the Father. He spoke of the love of man to man and of the duties that men owed to one another and of the wonderful possibilities of the intellect in guiding man along lines of living that will bring them happiness and harmony in their earth life. But he did not show them that the mere intellect is not sufficient to bring them in that condition of soul development which is necessary for their highest happiness in the life to come.

When he spoke of the immortality of the soul he did not intend to express more than that the spirits of men continue to live after the body dies. He, in fact, does not know what immortality means as we have taught you, and he will someday be surprised when he learns that mere continuity of life is not immortality, or that continuance of existence, which when once possessed cannot be taken away from the spirit.

Yet, notwithstanding all this want of knowledge on his part, he is an earnest spiritualist and is doing much good to mortals for he is showing them the fact that the spirit of man is a mere extension of form of what man now possesses, and that there is no such thing as the death of the spirit when the body dies, or that the spirit lies with the body in a state of obscurity or nothingness, or rather of oblivion, until what the orthodox call the great judgment day.

I am interested in the efforts that these people are now making to build a temple in which to worship and gather in their cause, and I favor the building of the same, because while they do not preach or know the great and necessary truths, yet they preach those things which free men from the beliefs that hold them in thralldom and error, and set them free to receive the greater truths, when the time shall come that they shall be known to humanity. So that I would advise you to help their project to the extent that you feel yourself able.

Many people will find that the things which they may hear at these meetings will cause them to arouse from their slumbers and ignorance, and cause them to investigate for themselves the truths of spiritualism and when once they start and become convinced of one truth, they will continue to seek, and in the end, it they are sincere seekers, find the truths, because when their minds shall be convinced of the truths of spirit existence and spirit control, they will then realize that over and beyond this, there is something that their souls long for, and is never satisfied; and the result will be that they will be in condition to readily believe what may be told them, which leads to that which will satisfy their souls in their longings.

---

[133] The speaker was Mr. Herrick. While the heading suggests it was a church service, the text suggests it was a spiritualist meeting. (G.J.C.)

This is the great good that the spiritualists are doing in their efforts to extend their spiritualistic doctrines, and when they are earnest, true believers and teachers in what they know of these things, they will bring about that which will cause the increase in the number of mortals who will accept the higher truths of the Divine Love and the immortality of the soul, and the way to obtain it. So you see, that while you may not be much benefited in your soul's aspirations in attending these meetings or affiliating with these people, yet I would advise that you do everything in your power to help the movement to establish firmly that church in this City, for it will be a great influence in attracting people in all parts of the country to the truths of spiritualism.

Let not the thought that this church may not teach the real truths of the soul development, or those things which will bring men in attunement with the Father, cause you to in any way discredit the movement that they may endeavor to start in the way of a revival as one of their preachers said. A little of the truth is better than none at all, especially when it leads to free men from a bondage that has caused them to blindly follow the teachings of those who are in darkness and error.

I will not write more tonight, but will say this, that you and your friend (Dr Leslie R. Stone) must believe what has been told you and continue to pray to the Father and seek more of the Divine Love. When the time comes I will inform him of the work which he shall do, and it will be an important one and one which will bring him in close contact with me, and the higher forces of the Celestial Spheres. He is now in a condition to receive this soul development, and he must let his mind and soul expand to their fullest extent, so that when it comes, I mean the Divine Love, with the great and wonderful power which will accompany it, he will be in a condition to receive it.

I am your friend and brother and his also, and you must both believe that I am writing this to you, for I am that Jesus that all the spirits have told you about, and if it were profitable, I would come to you, as I came a few nights ago, and show my glory and power. But this is not necessary for you will believe without this and so much the stronger will be your belief.

I must stop now.

So with my love and blessings for you both and my peace which the world cannot give you, I will say good night.

Your brother and friend,
Jesus.

States that Mr. Padgett is very near the Kingdom and that Jesus is with him in all his love and blessings

October 16th, 1915.

I am here, John.

You are now so filled with the Love of the Father and the influence of the Master that you are very near the kingdom. The Master is with you in all the fullness of his love and blessings, and no wonder that you should receive him in so palpable and conscious a manner. He certainly loves you, and if you could only see his glory as he writes to you, and the great streams of love that flows from him to you, you would never again doubt that he is with you and that you are the object of his care. It is wonderful, and we are all amazed at the great display of his love for you, and we rejoice that it is so, for we know that to him you are the most important of mortals.

You will soon commence again to do his work and your soul will be so filled with the Divine Love that you will receive his messages in such soul understanding that there will be no possibility of any mistake being made. And such messages of truth as they will be, why the whole world will stand in wonder and amazement that such truths should come to you, and, as a consequence, many a mortal will be brought to see the great plan of man's redemption, and will turn to the Love of the Father and receive that great inflowing of Love that will show them beyond all doubt that they have become at one with the Father and are inheritors of his immortality.

So, as I say, we all rejoice, and are anxious that the work begin; and we are all preparing to help in conveying these great truths of the Father. So you must believe and accept what is written to you as true. Let not what may be contained in the Bible, or what the preachers or commentators may say influence you in any way to believe or write anything other than what the Master may write you.

The book (The Atonement by Pastor Russell) that you have been reading tonight contains many truths in regards to Jesus' relationship to the Father, and that there is only one God, and that the Father—no other God is there—and Jesus is his best beloved son.

The plan of salvation as contained in that book is not correct, for, as we have told you before, the blood of Jesus has nothing to do with the plan of salvation, only the bestowal of the gift of Divine Love and the teachings of the Master as to how it may be obtained saves man from sin and error and brings about that at-onement which the author writes about.

My dear brother, if you only knew how much we all love you and are interested in your welfare and the work which is before you, you would be very thankful to the Father for having had the Master select you, and would also never cease to love and honor the great Master for his love and friendship. I, John, tell you all this, because I know whereof I speak. I was the beloved disciple of the Master when on earth, and I know what it means to have the great love of such a Master and friend.

I see that you are opening up your soul to the Divine influences, and that very soon you will find that through your soul perceptions, you will be enabled to see and understand many, many things which are now hidden from you. And what an opening of the soul perceptions that will prove to be! Even the spirits who are in portions of the celestial heavens will not have the great truths presented to them as will you, and they are seeking these truths in great earnestness. But you are in a position that they are not, to make known to the world these great truths. And while all this will not be done primarily for your benefit, yet you will receive such knowledge of these truths and such inflowing of the Divine Love as you write, that you will find yourself in a condition of soul development that rarely have mortals experienced.

So pray and believe, and when I say believe, try to get that great faith of which the Master wrote you—the faith that makes all the longings and aspirations of the soul realities. I could write much more but think it best not to do so tonight.

So with all my love and blessings, I am
Your brother in Christ,
John.
The beloved disciple of the Master in my time, and which you are now.

Writes that the Truths that are now being received by Padgett will fill the void in man's search for the Truth that is not being taught by the Churches

October 19th, 1916.

I am here, John.

I was with you tonight and heard the preacher answer the questions, and some of his answers were very satisfactory, but there was one that did not exactly satisfy the true longings of the man who is in search of truth—I mean the one that asks what should a man do who is not satisfied with any of the churches.

Well, if he can find no church that provides truths that satisfy that man's inquiring soul, then that man can never feel that he should go to any church for information as to those things which he has no knowledge of or which he has grave doubts about.

The churches, of course, can give no information of truths that the churches themselves do not know, and if the truths that these churches teach fall short of what the man is seeking for, then these churches cannot possibly be satisfactory to him. While the churches differ in their creed and government, and perhaps in some particular construction or interpretation of the Bible, yet they, the orthodox churches, are all founded upon the teachings of the Bible, and they cannot teach greater or other truths than that Book contains, and, hence, if a man is seeking for truths that are not in the Bible, his inquiries cannot be answered by those whose knowledge is confined to the Bible teachings.

And the non-orthodox churches cannot give forth the truths of the spiritual kingdom of God for they to a large degree reject the Bible and depend very largely upon ethical and moral doctrines, and the results of the works of mere conscience in determining the right and wrong of things. The spiritual things are not known or taught by these churches, and, consequently, the inquiring mind cannot get from them the information or help that it is calling for.

I know that in such a condition and want of knowledge of truth on the part of the churches, such a man is without the privilege of having his cravings for the truth and his cravings for spiritual things satisfied. And, as a consequence, he must seek further to get the information which he may consider so necessary, and when he comes to so seek, he will find no place where such knowledge may be found.

The mere intellectual acquirements of students and philosophers will not supply what the man is seeking and he is without any possibility of obtaining what he seeks for. And so the preacher's suggestion that he and two others form a church of their own, would have some force were it not for the fact that any church that might be so formed would have no greater possession of the truth than the churches that he has failed to find any satisfaction in.

There are many men on earth today in the condition of the man spoken of, and many who refuse to seek in the churches for the truth, are without any recourse to other means or places or teachers of whom they can learn the things that they are searching for.

The spirits have known of this condition of men for these many centuries and have been trying to supply a way or create a medium through which the great spiritual truths of God could be made known to men. And for that very purpose we are now using you to receive our messages of truth and make them known to mankind, and provide a church, may I say where the seeking man may find answers to his inquiries.

We shall complete our delivery of these truths through you and then the man who cannot find a church where his searchings can be satisfied, will find a reservoir of truth opened up to him, that will not require any preacher or church to explain it.

As you proceed in your experience with the churches and teachers of the old truths, as they call them, you will more fully realize the necessity for our work and your work. I will not write more tonight, but will come soon and deliver a formal message.

With my love and blessings I will say good night.

John.[134]

Writes that only the Father can give you His Divine Love through earnest prayer to Him

April 15th, 1916.

I am here, John.

I want to write a few lines on a subject that you will be interested in, and which will open your understanding to some truths that are not known to mortals. Tonight I see that you have a caller, and I will defer my writing until later, although I know that he also is interested in the subject, and it will be written as much for him as for you, so after you shall have received the message of the Master, I will come and write you. But this I must say now, both for your sake and that of your friend (Dr. Stone) and that is that you must both pray more to the Father and seek the faith that will bring you in unison with Him and His Love, you both have this Love to a considerable extent and you realize it, but what you now have cannot be compared to what will be yours, if you will only do as I say.

There is no other way to obtain the great inflowing of this Love, we can and do help you by our influence and association, but this Love is that which comes direct from the Father through the medium of the Holy Spirit, and no spirits no matter how high we may be in the Celestial Kingdom, and how great our development may be we cannot give you this Love, for it comes only from the Father.

But for your encouragement let me say, that we all pray for you and are always endeavoring to throw around you influences that will cause your souls to open up to the inflowing of this Love, if you could only realize what this means, you would see the great favor that you have and how your position is such that not seldom have the wicked or undesirable spirits had any opportunity to exercise their influences upon you.

So my dear brethren, think of what I have written, and let it sink deep into your souls and consciousness that there are surrounding you

---

[134] This message is a composite of two, being published in Volume II and Volume III. (G.J.C.)

many spirits of the Celestial as well as of the higher spiritual heavens. I will not write more tonight, but with my love and blessing will say good night.

Your brother in Christ,
John.

Advises Mr. Padgett to give up reading unrelated material and apply himself to the writings given him by Jesus and other Celestials

January 19th, 1917.

I am here, John.

I wish to write only a few lines tonight to tell you that you are not in condition of soul that you should be, and that you may be, for I see that you have been thinking a great deal lately of certain teachings and philosophies that do not lead your soul to development that is necessary in order for you to enjoy the Love that may be yours and which at times you have possessed and experienced. So I want to advise you to give up the investigating or even reading of these things, and confine your thought to the teachings of truth which you have received and will receive from the spirits of the Celestial and the higher spiritual spheres.

The meat of what you read in the books that you have been reading is merely speculation and sometimes contains the truth and at other times errors, while what you receive from these spirits who write you of these deep and religious truths are based on knowledge which only spirits of the development of those who write you can learn and instruct you in. The truths that you shall learn from the sources that I have mentioned will be sufficient to enlighten your mind and to develop your soul and you will find that by learning them, great benefit will come to you. Let these unusual philosophies take care of themselves because they cannot take care of you and they only serve to distract your mind from the truths which are real and never changeable and which must determine the condition of men and spirits and movements of the universe.

Of course, it may benefit you some to consider the teachings of the Bible which you cherish and accept as the word of God and which we say is not His word and was never written by men inspired by Him and which do not contain the sayings as teachings of Jesus surmounted with the interpolations and thoughts of me and to compare them with the truths which shall come to you from us and by such comparison you will see what great errors there are in the Bible and what injury the belief in such teachings is doing and have done to humanity.

This will be a point of the work that lies before you because when your work comes to be published, it will be read in light of what the Bible contains and the interpretations placed thereon by the theologians and commentators and the errors will then be readily seen by men, and as a consequence, rejected, and man's conception of God and His relationship to man and the latter's destiny will become the only line and cornerstone.

I know that if you follow my advice you will find yourself grow into a better condition for the reception of these truths and also realize that your soul development will progress with great rapidity, so that your soul perception will become so accurate that you will be able to know the truth and all its inherent meanings. I will try to help you in this regard and will let you feel the influence of my presence and efforts to assist you to get in this condition. I have many messages to write you yet, as well as have the Master and also many high spirits who will contribute to the filling of the book of truths that we know to be truths. So, my dear brother, think of what I have said and determine that you will follow my advice, and you will soon see the beneficial results.

Well, there are many other things that you may read and so occupy your mind. History and fiction of the better class and also many sermons and essays based on the teachings of the Bible, for as I have said, the discussion of these things will help you in comprehending and formulating and fixing in your mind, and soul, the real truths.

Yes, of course I do, for there is no religious doctrines or teachings on earth that I am not acquainted with. I learned these things in order to appreciate just what men used to help them to avoid false doctrines and beliefs and to learn the truths which may be necessary for them to know. As you know there are many beliefs on earth and some particular truth is required for some particular mind that may be imbued with these beliefs in order to show that mind the error of its belief and the truth that it should know.

The Bahaist have not the knowledge of the great Truths of the New Birth or of the Divine Love as contradistinguished from the natural love in its purified state, and while their doctrines and teachings are very beautiful and beneficial to men in a moral point of view, yet they do not show men the true way to the Celestial home and the coming into an at-onement with the Father in the Divine Nature or in His Divine Love.

So remember what I have said and you will soon see the results of following my advice. I will come soon and communicate a truth which deals with the great love of the Father. I will not write more now but in closing; will say that we all love you very much and are very much interested in your work and are working with you. So, only believe and pray to the Father for His love and blessings and you will find a wonderful happiness and contentment and the opening of your soul perceptions that will bring you very near to Him, and to us all in love and

rapport. With all my love and blessing, I am
>Your brother in Christ,
>John.

Attended a spiritual meeting with Mr. Padgett and then wrote about the speakers that they did not know what oneness with the Father means

September 10th, 1916.

I am here, John.

I come tonight to tell you that in a few nights I desire to write you a message on an important truth regarding the ultimate destiny of the man who does not receive the Divine Love of the Father, but who depends upon his own righteousness, and the help that he may receive from spirit friends who have not this Divine Love in their souls. I know that this subject has been written on before to a limited extent, but I wish to deal with it in detail and at large so that humanity can make no mistake as to what this future will be, and can have no excuse for not seeking the Celestial Kingdom.

I have been with you tonight and heard what was said, and saw that none of the speakers have any experience as to what this great necessity as to a future state of at-oneness with the Father means, and that they are satisfied with the knowledge of the continuity of life and the help and comfort that their spirit friends may bring to them in their communications. (Mr. Padgett attended a spiritualist meeting).

The truth as to this great vital necessity must be taught to mankind, and the way to this Divine Love must be made so plain that no man can have any excuse for not obtaining it and becoming an inhabitant of the Celestial Kingdom. Many are longing for this condition of soul and know not the way to obtain it, and have to rest unsatisfied. So you see we must hurry with our messages, for men are dying rapidly and without the knowledge of this great truth.

You are now in better condition than you have been for some time, and you will continue to improve so that we will be enabled to deliver our messages with ease and certainty. Pray to the Father for His Love and help and you will receive both and find that your worries will leave you and peace come to you, so that your thoughts may be turned more to the work which is set before you. Faith and prayer are the great means by which your soul may be filled with this Love, and happiness will follow as surely as the day follows the night, and something of the joys of the Celestial Spheres will be yours.

I know that you are anxious to do this work and that you long for the time when your whole efforts may be devoted to it, and to the revealing to man the truths which we come to reveal. We are all with you and are trying to help you in every way so that troubles may leave you. There are many spirits present tonight, throwing around you the influence of their loves, and praying to the Father that His blessings may be bestowed upon you and your soul made happy with the inflowing of His love. I will not write more tonight and in leaving you say, pray and believe.

With my love and blessings, I am
Your brother in Christ,
John.

Often attends Church services with Mr. Padgett as well as many other Celestials; says: The inexperience of the preacher to fully describe the subject of spiritualism was due to insufficient knowledge of the continuity of life

October 15th, 1916.

I am here, John.

I come tonight to write a few lines in reference to the thoughts that have answers in your mind regarding the position that the preacher (Dr. Gordon) will take on the subject of his sermon on modern spiritualism.

As he said at the Thursday night meeting that he has investigated to some extent the subject of spiritualism, but his investigation has been so superficial that he knows scarcely anything about its truths and is not in condition of mind or knowledge to discuss the matter in an impartial or understanding manner. He has seen some phenomena and read some of the books that have been published regarding the truths of spiritualism but the phenomena and the books have not been such as to convince him that Spiritualism is a fact and in addition he will assert that it conveys or teaches no truth or doctrine that benefits man or fits him for the future life—that not even admitting that it shows the continuity of life and the possibility of communicating between the departed and the mortal, yet it does not show any truth or principle that will benefit man in his life on earth or in his life after death.

He is so imbued with his belief in the Bible that his intellect is prevented from having the ability or condition to grasp any truths that may be apparent in contradictions of what he considers the Bible teachings. Yet with all this should he be presented with facts that would be sufficient to convince him of the truths of spiritualism, he would not hesitate to accept those facts notwithstanding that they might conflict with the belief desired from the study of the Bible that he has had for so many years.

I think that when you hear his sermon you will see that I have written a correct description of his belief on the subject of spiritualism and of what in substance will be the effect of his sermon. You must hear it, for it may suggest something that will enable you to be (do) good even towards the preacher himself. I will not write more now, but next week I will deliver another message. So with all my love, I will say good night.

Your brother in Christ,
John.

Writes about his visit to Church with Mr. Padgett

April 28th, 1918.

I am here, James.

I am here and desire to say a few words as I have been with you this evening at the church and listened to the lecture of the preacher, and feel that he misapplied his opportunity for furnishing his hearers spiritual food which they all are so much in need of and which in many cases their souls are longing and crying for.

The lecture of the preacher was instructive in a certain way and appealed to the sympathies and better nature of those who heard it but it contained nothing that tried to open up the souls of men to the Divine Love of the Father or show them the way to the Celestial Kingdom of the Master or the way in which they may become divine in their soul qualities of love or in perfect union with the spirit love of the Father. I do not know that what I have said will serve any good purpose but yet I thought it, best for me to communicate to you their thoughts. Perhaps they may do some good in the future when you come to demonstrate the truths that you have received.

I will not write more. Good night.
James.

Writes of the ignorance of preachers to explain the Truth of the Gospel

April 28th, 1918.

I am here, Helen. I am your own true and loving Helen.

Well, dear, I have been with you a very great deal today and know just how you have felt and experienced a happiness in your soul arriving from the thoughts that you had in reference to things of the soul.

I will not attempt now to comment on either of the sermons that you heard. But I know just what thoughts you had in reference to the same and your thoughts were as my thoughts. It is so important but sad that the preachers have not had more information of the truth so that they might tell their hearers.

Tonight the Master was with you and listened to the lecture and impressed you with the thoughts that you had, and felt that he would like to be able to tell the preacher just what his future is. He is a representative as he claims of the Christian teachings with a duty upon him to give forth these teachings to his people, yet he failed to do so. It is pitiable that such condition of ignorance of the truth exists among the ministers of the Gospel. But it is so and no help can apparently be offered them until the truths that you are receiving shall be published and spread among them.

The Master would have written tonight had circumstances been altogether favorable, but they were not and he will come very soon and communicate. I will not write more now. So, my dear, love me and pray to the Father for His Love. Good night.

Your own true and loving,
Helen.

A member of Mr. Padgett's band is happy that he was selected to do the Master's work on earth

October 10th, 1915.

I am here, Saul of Old.

I came merely to say that you are very near the kingdom and the Father's Love, for I can see the condition of your soul and the results of the prayers of yourself and friends.

So let your faith increase until there will be no doubt, that you are a child of the Father, and the one chosen to do the Master's work on earth. I am merely telling you this in order to increase your faith in what has already been told you so often.

I am one of the band which is back of you, sustaining you in the work you have to do and in the preparation you are now making to be able to do that work.

Well, you will soon find yourself in that condition and will soon be free from these cares that you speak of. I will not write more tonight.

Your brother in Christ,
Saul.

Introduces himself to Mr. Padgett and makes arrangement to write and be included in the Book of Truths

March 24th, 1916.

I am here, Elias the prophet.

I am a stranger to you, but you are not to me for I know all about you and the great work you are doing and will have to do.

I understand that you are tired tonight and I will not write more. I only wish to say that when the opportunity presents itself I should like to write you a message so that I may not be left from the Book of Truths which you shall publish.

Well, I am glad that you feel that way. I am your brother and friend and a follower of the Master. I am in the Celestial Spheres in a place very near the highest spirits who are my associates. I will write to you fully when I come.

With my love and blessing, I will say good night.

Elias.

Describes the feelings of the congregation of an orthodox minister, whose sermon was spiritual enlightenment and believed to be a true spiritualist

October 22nd, 1916.

I am here, Elias.

I come tonight to say a few words on the sermon of the preacher[135] and also because I was an early spiritualist and all down the ages have had knowledge of the communications between spirits and mortals. Tonight at the church there were many spirits present and as the preacher said "every particle of space in the building was occupied by spirits"—some of the higher order and others of the lower planes where conditions are dark, but there were many there and interested, for nearly every person in the audience had some spirit friend or guardian angel with him, and as the nervous (various) members of the congregation differed in their condition of soul development or spiritual enlightenment, so they attracted considerable spirits.

But in addition to these who were attracted by their respective mortal friends or relatives, there were a number of spirits from the higher spheres who were interested in the occasion. For it is not often

---

[135] The diary refers to Dr. G. here. It seems very unlikely that this is Dr. Gordon as elsewhere he (Dr. Gordon) has been described as lacking in any understanding of spiritualism. (G.J.C.)

that an orthodox congregation has the opportunity or takes the opportunity to listen to a sermon upon the theme that the preacher dealt with tonight, and if you could have seen the difference in the workings of the minds and understandings and the effect upon the preconceived beliefs of the several members of the congregation, you would have been surprised and realized more fully the powers that belief has upon the consciousness of mortals.

I do not intend to analyze the sermon, but must say that the same was a surprise to many of the orthodox as well as to some who are spiritualists. The preacher declared many truths that were repugnant to a number of his congregation because in their blind belief in their creeds and dogmas they had not the right, that any real orthodox minister could have believed and proclaimed such doctrines as the preacher declared. He is a true spiritualist so far as the propositions of continuous life and inter-communication are concerned, but he hardly dares announce his beliefs in the language of spiritualism and he may have been wise in not doing so as the effect would not be very desirable upon many of his hearers.

He is not very well versed in the truths of spiritualism, in matters which deal with its philosophy or religion and consequently he does not understand the great importance of searching for and finding the truths which these means afford of learning these truths. But the seeds of truth are in his mind and conviction and he is in that condition which renders him susceptible to receiving the truths, should they be presented to him in such a manner as to appeal to his beliefs and to his reason. And as he has a great deal of the soul development by reason of his possession of the Divine Love, the higher truths which have been revealed to you will appeal to him, more especially to his soul sense than to the sense of his mind conditions.

I know it would at first be a shock to him to learn that his intellectual belief in the doctrines of the trinity and the vicarious atonement and kindred portions of the creed of his church are all untrue and short of any basis in fact but nevertheless should he learn of the great truths of the plan of God for man's salvation, he would not hesitate to embrace these truths and even dare to proclaim them.

In a way he will prove to be a kind of pioneer in the work of spreading the true religion that must ultimately become known to and received by mankind and tonight's sermon may cause many of his hearers to regard spiritualism in a little different light, not as the creature of devils and evil spirits, but on the manifestation of the natural as I may say the reasonable workings of the laws of God upon the actual and normal relationship of spirits and mortals.

The preacher's sermon will do the cause of truth much good, because it will tend to open up the minds of many to gain a respectful hearing to any attempts that may be made to enlighten them as to the reality of the truths of spiritualism. One thing he said and that is that very few mediums can be depended upon in conjunction with the prejudice that exists in the minds of the orthodox, against everything that has the flavor of spiritualism, may tend to prevent the conversion of these people to its truths or even to attempt even if mere curiosity may be the moving cause.

We are pleased that the preacher took the position that he did in declaring his belief that spiritual communion is a fact and in giving the illustration of its several phases although he left the results or causes of such manifestation in a rather uncertain meaning. His hearers may infer that he meant that God, as contradistinguished from spirits was the voices or the cause of the visions or manifestations that he referred to in some mysterious or super-natural way in the exercise of His omniscience.

I merely wanted to write these few things to give you an idea of how important the teachings of the preacher may be proved to be in opening up the minds of many of his hearers. And as I close let me say that all down the ages spiritualism has existed and been demonstrated and prophets and apostles and mediums and men have heard the voices of spirits and seen the materialized spirits and received the inspirations of spirits of good and evil. I will not write more tonight and I hope you are not disappointed that I wrote instead of John, for we intended that you should be surprised somewhat in the writer, that is, the personality of the writer for we saw that you rather expected that John might write.

Many of your spirit friends have been with you tonight and they accompanied you to the rooms where you and your friend sat and discussed the sermon and the preacher and things connected with us and our messages. I will not write more tonight. With our love and blessings, I will say that we are
Your brother in Christ.
Elias.

Was also present and heard the sermon of the orthodox minister

October 22nd, 1916.

I am here, your own true and loving Helen.

Well dear, I see that you enjoyed the evening very much and on the whole felt satisfied with the sermon of the preacher. It was a rather unexpected sermon from an orthodox minister and one that may result in some good to those who heard it.

I was with you and so was that little soulmate of the Dr.'s and she was delighted to be with him and of course I was also delighted to be with you. I was also glad that Edward was with you for I see he will be led to believe in the truths that we are teaching and so experience the happiness of having the Divine Love and having the soul development that is so desirable.

He is a good boy and I am so sorry for him in the manner that you know of. But he will soon have the change that I have written you about. Be with him as much as you can, for he will need your sympathy and loss and will feel very lonesome at times although he will also experience some relief from some of the things that worried him.

I think of baby also and am with her a great deal as she needs you also and I hope that soon you will all be together. In fact I know you will be very kind and loving with her.

Yes I will try to influence her in the way that you spoke of, and I think I can succeed. So have hope that she will do as you desire. I love you all with all my heart and pray for you to make you happy. I must not write more tonight. Give me my kiss and go to bed soon and get up earlier in the morning. So sweetheart good night.

Your own true and loving,
Helen.

Talks about the Law of Compensation and that God will not alter same

December 25th, 1916.

I am here, Elias, Prophet of Old. (Elijah).

I will write a short message tonight, as it is late and you are tired. Well, I desire to say that the message you received from the Master contains some of the most important truths affecting the relationship of God to man in his worldly or material living.

Every Truth that was uttered has in it an element which shows that man to a certain extent must expect and know that God will not interfere with the Law of Compensation as to its effects and results. Only will He help man to remove the causes that so certainly entail the results, and the sooner men know this and more thoroughly understand it, will they become able to avoid the consequences of sin and the violation of law, and also understand that no prayer will cause God to respond, where a suspension or setting aside of his Laws or their workings are necessary. He will respond to prayer, where that prayer asks the removal of causes, but never when it applies only to effects.

This Truth men should learn and in their prayers ask that those things or causes[136] which in compliance with the Law of Compensation

---

[136] Causes are for example the causes of sin. As an example, if someone is an alcoholic,

bring about results that are harmful to them be removed, or eliminated from their acts and deeds as well as from their desires. I could write a long message on this subject but will not do so now, as you are not just in condition to receive it. I will come soon and write at length. So with my love I will say, good night.

Your brother in Christ,
Elias.[137]

Comments on the lack of knowledge by the preacher of the truths of spiritualism

April 1st, 1917.

I am here, Elias.

I will write a few words in respect to the sermon that you listened to tonight on the question: Do the dead communicate with the living?

The preacher[138] is a believer in what he enunciated and the only trouble with him is that he has very little knowledge of the truths of spiritualism, and hence his ability to teach these truths is very limited. The mere fact that the soul and spirit of man continue to live when they shuffle off the mortal coil, as he described it, is but the first truth of this great subject, and is one that all spirits learn immediately upon their separation from the body no matter what their religious beliefs may be or whether they have any such beliefs or not. This fact is one about which there can be no difference in knowledge. They all know, in a moment, as it were, that there is no such thing as the death of the soul—the real man. But this, as I say, is the mere beginning of knowledge, and beyond the fact of this continuous existence, this knowledge serves no purpose as to the destiny of man.

The preacher was much interested in the book[139] about which

---

God will assist to remove or lessen the desire for drink, if the mortal truly wishes and prays for this assistance. However the results of the alcoholism are not likely to be removed, as this is part of the Law of Compensation. So praying for relationships to be healed, which were damaged as a result of alcoholism or healing a damaged liver may not be effective, unless and until the primary cause is totally resolved. And even then, it is possible it may not be resolved if it's part of the compensation due. (G.J.C.)

[137] This message is a composite of two, being published in Volume I and Volume III. (G.J.C.)

[138] Rev. J. L. Gordon, preacher of the Congregational Church, 10th and Y Street, Washington D.C. (J.P.G.) The original text has "Gorden" but the diary has "Gordon". (G.J.C.)

[139] "Raymond, or Life and Death," published in 1916. Written by Sir Oliver Lodge (1851 - 1940) the world renowned physicist on the death of his son Raymond who died in battle at Ypres in 1915. The book is split into two parts, but at every stage each chapter contains clear cross referenced evidence obtained by him of the continuation of life after death.

he was talking and found in it some statements that are confirmatory of the beliefs that he already possessed, and some statements that are new to him and which gave him somewhat larger views on the subject; but necessarily these views are not of the vital truths which a more complete or extended knowledge of spiritualism will give to him.

The spirit of whom he was talking knew little more than what appeared to his senses, and, of course, these things are only those that come to the knowledge of the spirit when it first enters the spirit land. Its truths are not learned in a moment, and frequently not for centuries, and as to the higher truths, are never learned by a great majority of the spirits. So that, what is contained in the book referred to is very consoling to those who believe that their loved ones are waiting to meet them, and will receive them when they cease to be mortals, with love and affection and joy, and further that these loved ones are with the mortals while on earth, watching over them and trying to help them, yet no information as to the lives that these spirits must lead in the spirit world as soon as their status is determined by the great law of attraction and what the future may be and is disclosed to them and for the reason that the spirit communicant did not know.

But, as the preacher said, it is a glorious knowledge to possess, that man after death, still lives, and that his soul does not have to wait for some great resurrection day to realize that it has life and consciousness.

The preacher is still in the dark as to the conditions of spirits and their destiny, and as to the means provided to attain to the heavens, and become released from the hells, by the Father's love. To merely live is not the end of men or spirits, and the fact of living as a spirit of today instead as a mortal of yesterday does not demonstrate immortality; and the consoling thought that the preacher expressed from the fact of continued existence after death, are merely the wishes of desire based on such existence.

The preacher has at this time within his own soul that which is freed from the limitations of his erroneous beliefs in many supposed truths, would cause him to know that the life in the spirit world is something more than the mere living, and that this living is only a means to the realization and possession of that immortality that is so often preached about and hoped for.

He has much of the Divine Love in his soul, and that soul is struggling to expand and get in condition to receive more of this love, and is prevented from so doing only by the erroneous beliefs that he has imbibed and misconstrued by his long years of living in what he calls, the truths of the Bible and the fear that if he loses such beliefs or questions

(G.J.C.)

the truth of the source of his beliefs there can be no salvation for him. And this is not surprising, for he knows no source of correction of these errors of his beliefs, and as a wise man—and wise only because he does not know how to obtain greater wisdom—he holds on to his beliefs and reverences the source thereof—and his intellect is satisfied.

But the soul, the important soul, which can be fed only by its own perceptions, is like the imprisoned bird, panting and struggling to beat down the bars of its imprisonment and get out into the freedom of God's wide atmosphere. And his mind—the misguided mind—is the bars of his soul's freedom and prevents it from opening up its own perceptions. If the preacher only knew the truth and the way to open the doors to his soul's prison, he would long for that truth and seek that way with all the energies of his soul's powers, and would then become free and progress towards the attainment of the certain knowledge of immortality.

But this I will say now, that sometime he will learn the truth and the way, and his beliefs will become in accord with the longings of his soul and the shackles of his mind's erroneous beliefs will be loosened and fall from him, and then he will realize that he is a true son of the Father, privileged to partake of the Great Love without limit in his onward progress to the Celestial spheres.

The church was filled with many spirits interested in the discourse, anxious to learn any truths that might be declared, but they learned nothing, for what he declared, as truths, they already knew, notwithstanding that these spirits were of all kinds—wicked and dark and suffering and bright and happy, and mostly still men without the physical body.

Well, I thought it might be advisable to write as I have, so that, if the preacher should ever hear this message, he will see the necessity for seeking the deep and real truths that disclose the conditions and destinies of the spirit of men. And besides, he will also realize the importance of his knowing these truths, so that he may teach them not only to men, but to spirits as well, who form the vastly larger part of his audience. I will not write more now.

With my love and prayers for the Father's blessings on you, I am
Your brother in Christ,
Elias.

Encourages Mr. Padgett to get into condition of soul to enable the Master to write his important messages

January 27th, 1918.

I am here, Elias.

I have not written you for a long time and tonight I desire to say a few words, and those in reference to your work and the attitude that you have assumed towards it.

It has been a long time since you have received any formal messages from the high spirits, and this loss of time means more to the accomplishment of the design to inform the world of the spiritual truths that are so important to the people, than you probably realize. As has been told you more than once, this delay has been caused by your condition of apparent indifference and failure to place yourself in the condition of soul that is necessary to enable the spirits to make the required rapport.

You should think more seriously of what this means, and how much on you rests this great responsibility, and of the further fact that without your cooperation we cannot make the rapport, and, as a consequence, these messages cannot be delivered. I know that in a way, I may say intellectually, you are willing and ready, as you think, to receive these messages, and that if you are not in condition you don't exactly understand the reason, and do not know how to remedy the difficulty. But in all this you are mistaken, for it is not merely a matter of having the inclination and intellectual assent to do the work, but, further, the proper condition of your soul's longings is required, and this will not come to you by a mere acquiescence and willingness to do the work, but an active exercise of the soul's longings is called for, and you must take the effort to obtain these longings, so that your soul may receive more of the Divine Love.

In messages, such as I speak of, the Divine Love in the soul is the important and vital factor in your condition. You must make greater efforts to get these longings and this Love, so that there will come to you the soul development that will enable the higher spirits to make the rapport. Well, there is only one way in which you can obtain this development and that is by turning your thoughts to the Father and His Love until they shall develop into deep, sincere longings of the soul, and with these longings you should pray with all the earnestness of your nature for the inflowing of this Love. If you will do this, the longings will come and also the Love, and then you will find that your desires will go out to the spirits for communication with them. This is the only way in which you can overcome the difficulties that now prevent the writings. I hope you will think of what I have written, and do as I advise.

I have a message that I desire very much to communicate, and besides me there are numbers of other spirits with similar desires. The most important messages to be delivered are those of the Master, and He is anxious to write. I will not write more now. Good night and God bless you,

Your brother in Christ,

Elias.

Expected to complete an important message, but the soul condition of Mr. Padgett did not permit it

January 27th, 1918.

I am here, John.

No, I cannot write tonight as I expected and am disappointed that you are not in condition for me to make the rapport. It seems that you are not inclined to receive my messages as you were at one time, although you say that you are ready to receive the writings. But your mere intellectual willingness is not sufficient, for my messages are those which do not come from the human intellect, but from the intellect of the soul, and in order that they may be received it is necessary that your soul shall be, in some degree, in harmony with mine. I could easily write you of things of the material or even of the spirit heavens, but it is impossible for me to use your brain to convey these spiritual soul truths unless your soul is developed into a harmony with mine.

To explain this was the object of my unfinished message, and as I desired to explain the laws controlling the communication and rapport of the celestial spirits with the mortal, and your soul not having the required condition, I was unable to finish my message. I have written you before on this subject, and all that I can say now is, think of the importance of this matter and the responsibility resting upon you. Remember the advice of Elias, and follow it. As soon as you are in condition I will come and write. Good night.

Your brother in Christ,
John.

Confirms that both Elias and John were anxious to deliver important messages tonight but could not due to improper soul conditions

January 27th, 1918.

I am here, Helen.

Well, dear, I see that you are not in condition to write much tonight, and I am sorry for it as I desired very much to write. I have heard what Elias and John said and can only join with them in the advice that they gave. I do so hope that you will follow that advice and soon get in condition that will enable the communications to be received.

I know that you do not feel like your usual self, and you don't exactly understand the reason, but if you will think of what they told you,

you will soon realize the cause and will be able to get rid of it.

Think of these things and keep up your courage and have faith in the future and what we have told and promised you. I will not write more now. Love me and believe that I love you and am with you so very much trying to help you. Good night.

Your own true, loving
Helen.

Mr. Padgett once called an old friend "a man with a ponderous mind"; came back to tell him of the wonderful help that he received from his band of spirit helpers

August 23rd, 1915.

I am here—the man who had the ponderous mind as you called him.[140]

Since writing to you last I have had a great experience and the result is, I see what a damned fool I must have appeared to all of you at the time. I wrote, and because of the manner I wrote in, I now see that I was really an ignorant man, and that I was learned in only what I didn't know, that is in my egregious conceit that what I didn't know was not worth learning. But since that time I have really had my eyes opened and my mental powers awakened to the fact that I was just on the border land of learning what is here for me to learn.

I have had the benefit of association with members of your band and with many other intelligent spirits, and I have learned that there are several spheres higher than that in which I live, and that they can be obtained only by progress in knowledge and mental acquirements.

Some of these spirits have shown me truths of the spirit life that I never conceived of and taught me laws governing this spirit world that I never heard of.

I must have been very stupid as well as hide bound and I don't wonder that you all, in a kind of derision, called me the man with the ponderous mind.

I am now in the second sphere and am studying the laws of the universe and other needful things under the supervision of competent and learned teachers, and I have studied also those things which tend to enlighten me of things spiritual. Your friends who first took me in hand

---

[140] This is probably Samuel R. Smith. His last contact is published in Volume IV (2nd Ed.) on page 368 but his first contact on April 5th, 1915 does not appear to have been published. However it is confusing as to whether there is only one man with a ponderous mind, or two or even three. That two names are suggested in the diary against the same entry (John H. Collins & Charles W. Everett) indicates that some editing has probably occurred, after Padgett recorded the entry. (G.J.C.)

have helped me very much, and especially your grandmother who seems not only so beautiful but to be so filled with knowledge. She is a wonderful spirit, and her teachings have helped me beyond all comprehension.

I have not yet been able to quite believe what she tells me about the New Birth and the Divine Love of the Father, although when I meet these spirits who claim to have received this New Birth, I have to think that there is something in it, for they are all so much more beautiful and bright than are we who have not believed in it.

I am seeking the light though, and that which will show me that there is some reality in this doctrine I shall not hesitate to seek further and accept it for my own salvation.

I came tonight merely to tell you that I am no longer the man with the ponderous mind in my own conceit, and that I am a very humble student of the many things of which I had no knowledge or experience.

I will not write more tonight, and will say good night,

Your friend.

Tries impersonation to test Mr. Padgett's soul perception

January 18th, 1917.

I am here, Frank D. Syrick.

I am glad that you could feel the influence of the spirit sufficient to cause you to doubt the personality of the writer, for this spirit who wrote was not Ingersoll and he was permitted to write merely to test your ability or spiritual sense, as we have done before. The spirit who wrote was myself and I did not have with me my usual influence, but assumed that of someone else in order to make the test more complete.[141]

Ingersoll is here and was really with you at the church services and so was I and I was interested in what the preacher said and what I wrote you as to the preacher being a medium and his difficulty of receiving (that) the communication from spirit is true. So you may believe that the message contained the truth as to his condition.

I do not feel like taking up more of your time tonight, but very soon I will come and write you as I have promised.

Tell the Doctor that I am glad to inform him that I am here, and also that I frequently come to him and enjoy his thoughts and experiences in the matters of the soul. I am still his friend and well

---

[141] Mediums commonly report that they know the energetic signature of those they channel frequently, but in this case Padgett had channelled a very large number of spirits, and had not channelled either Ingersoll or Syrick that frequently, so the point that he could tell it was not Ingersoll is remarkable. (G.J.C.)

wisher, even though he can't see me or hear my voice, but I am in full sympathy with him in all his efforts to obtain more of the love and in helping mortals as well as spirits. So with my love to you both, I will say good night.

    Your friend,
    Syrick.[142]

Confirms the test that was made by Judge Syrick

January 18th, 1917.

I am here, your own true and loving Helen.

I will not write much, for you are not in good condition. However, I was with you tonight at the services and heard the preacher and wished that I could have suggested some thoughts to him that he could have received for he then would have made clear something about spiritualism that he did not. He is a medium and with a little more faith or rather with a little less belief in some of the old orthodox doctrine he would become quite a satisfactory medium to himself at least.

What Judge Syrick wrote you is true and we merely wanted to make the test and Ingersoll said that he was astonished that you could detect it. He says that he is learning something new all the time. He wants to write you soon. Well I must stop and so I will say good night.

    Give my kindest regards to the Dr. (Dr. Leslie Stone) and my love to yourself.
    Your own true and loving
    Helen.[143]

Confirms many things that Mr. Padgett told him about life in the spirit world

March 29th, 1915.

I am here, Syrick.

Let me say a word, I am your late friend and brother in spiritualism. Yes, I am able to write some and your wife told me to try as she wishes me to get stronger and realize that I am living as a spirit.

Well, I am here and alive and have my Rose with me. She is so very beautiful and loving and I am very happy to be with her, but I have already learned that I am not suited to live with her for she is so much

---

[142] This message is a composite of two, being published in Volume III and Volume IV. (G.J.C.)

[143] This message is a composite of two, being published in Volume III and Volume IV. (G.J.C.)

higher in her spiritual development than I am, but she tells me that I can progress and I am going to try with all my might.

Well, old friend, the uncertain has become certain and I know now that spirits can and do communicate with mortals. So let any doubts that you may have, leave you and believe with all your heart that you have received the messages from your band and others as you have been informed.

I can tell you this that you have as your wife and soulmate the most beautiful of all the spirits that I have yet seen. I had no conception of what beauty was until I came here and saw your wife and Rose and Dr. Stone's Mary. She is very beautiful also and loves him, I know, with a very deep love. As this is my first attempt I am tired and must stop.

Well, I know no one whom I would rather that it should belong to than you, so keep it and think of me sometimes.

So with my kindest regards and best wishes, I am your true friend,

Frank D. Syrick.[144]

Explains Judge Syrick's spiritual condition as well as their cousin Laura who was not known to either on earth

March 29th, 1915.

I am here, Helen.

Well, you have received a letter from the Judge. He was so anxious to write that we thought it would do him good to try as it would make him realize more sensibly that he is now a spirit only and also strengthen him.

Well, you may not think so but it is a fact. With many spirits when their surroundings are good and much spirit help is given them they can almost as soon as they leave the body overcome their functions of mind and do things that you little expect. The Judge was prepared, to some extent, to understand this power of communication and when we all assisted him with our powers he tried successfully to write to you. He is not yet very strong but soon will be and then I have no doubt he will want to write to you often, but of course we cannot permit him to because he is not in rapport with our band. He has not very much spiritual development and the conditions that surround him are not such as would be in accord with our conditions, and hence we will have to refuse to let him write very often but he can communicate through some of us.

---

[144] This message is a composite of two, being published in Volume III and Volume IV. (G.J.C.)

Well, he is dark in appearance as he necessarily must be until he gets more enlightenment of soul. He will undoubtedly suffer because of the sins he committed when on earth, and will pay the penalty until he finds the true way to God's Love and forgiveness. Of course he has one advantage over many spirits who come over bringing the results of their life on earth and that is that he has some idea as to the way to salvation. You and Dr. Stone told him when on earth that he must turn his thoughts to spiritual things and while he did not understand just what you meant, yet, such advice had some influence on him and will cause him to try to learn what was meant, and having Rose and the rest of us to enlighten him, he will progress more rapidly to these higher things and the more rapid his progress the sooner his suffering will leave him.

He is now commencing to realize that as he sowed so must he reap. While Rose is with him a great deal and loves him and tries to help him, yet all that isn't sufficient to prevent his memory from scourging him because of the life he led on earth. But we all pray for him and try to show him the way and he is ready to believe and is commencing already to pray to the Father. So you see, you must all sooner or later face this great crisis and the better prepared you are to meet it, the less will be your sufferings and the more happiness you will experience.

Yes, it was Laura[145]—she is very unhappy. I had never met her before and your mother said that she had not either. You see in this world family ties do not always bring spirits together. When the relationship is distant the spirits lose interest in relations merely because they are relations, and find themselves attracted to spirits who have like qualities and relations.

This relationship counts for very little in the spirit world of itself and when we meet our loved ones of earth, before they come over we stay with them for a while and then if there are no other attractions than mere relationship, we gradually separate. This is the law of attraction, and we are compelled to obey it. So that when on earth mortals sing of meeting again on the other shore to part no more, they will find that they are mistaken. They will meet but, unless conditions compel it, they will part again and may never meet ever in the spirit world.

Love is the thing which determines the relationship and place of living in this world; I mean similar loves existing between spirits. No spirit loves another after a little while merely because that other is a mother or father or wife or brother, but loves it because that spirit has a similar love of the beautiful and true that it has. So you see relationship after

---

[145] The original publication of this message refers to "Lerna" but the message itself, received the same day refers to "Laura". This may be a simple transcription error, as automatic writing is not easy to decipher, or a typographic error. But this appears to be Padgett's Cousin Laura Burroughs whose communication is published in this Volume on page 425. (G.J.C.)

the first meeting and living together a little while determines nothing.

Of course while the child or father of mother or sister or brother remains in the earth life the spirit relative will love them and watch over them and try to help them in every way. Especially will the mother for ties among son or daughter, and this is in accordance with the maternal law of love. But when that father or son too, becomes a spirit then the law of love as it were changes and like loves like, be there a natural relationship or not. This, I know, seems contrary to what mortals usually believe and accept as a fact, but it is true.

When my children come over my love for them will not be the same as it is now. Then they will find that their love will probably, after a time, turn elsewhere and it will be only another in memory for our loves may take entirely different directions. And this love while for the moment may seem unnatural in its workings, yet it is not, for happiness comes with love reciprocated and love comes only in reciprocation of its own kind.

We do not think that you will be forever with your children or parents or any other relative forever for that may not be so. If that relative has like attractions that you have then you may be together as long as that attraction lasts. But suppose that you make greater progress in your spiritual or even in your natural development, than the other spirit, it cannot be supposed for a moment that you will determine the results of your development in order to stay with that other spirit. No, that would be a violation of the law of progress and you could not and would not want to delay your upward movement.

So the idea that when we meet in the spirit world we meet to part no more is not correct and is contrary to the laws that determine the condition and place of habitation of spirits. I know this of my own experience. My parents are in a lower sphere than I am and have much less spiritual development, and while I visit them sometimes, yet they have not the attraction for me that other spirits to whom I have no relationship. And why is this, not because I do not care for my parents as such, but because the objects and extent of their loves are different from mine.

The main fact that they are my parents does not cause me to want to be with them all the time. I could not so desire if, as you might say, I wanted to. Love is the attraction and love must demand a likeness in a spiritual sense of the objects of its love.

The time may come when I will never again see my parents and may forget that they ever had an existence. I say may, but I hope not, for I desire that sometime they will progress so that they may be a similar condition to my own in spiritual development and then, of course, we will live in the same peace and necessity will meet and enjoy one another's company. But not because we are parents and daughter but because our loves are similar and our attractions are like.

This is a matter that few mortals understand and it may well be that they do not because the love existing between many a relative is a beautiful thing and one that causes much happiness and self preservation. There is nothing on earth like the mother's love and no provision of God's blessings for mortals equals this great gift of a Mother's love. And so with the other natural loves to a lesser degree.

But as Jesus said, "He that doeth the will of my Father is my mother and brother and sister".

So you must realize that what you and the natural love of relations is only for the earth life and a short time afterwards. Each individual is in and of himself a complete unit depending not on relationship to others, and as such must find his place in the great eternity which must be determined by the development and progress of his own soul in expectation of what may become of the souls of his earth relations. He is attracted only by souls of similar development and will find his home in the company of such souls irrespective of the question of natural relationship.

I have written enough for tonight and must stop.
So with all my love, I am
Your own true and loving,
Helen.

Although a bright spirit and happy, she has never seen spirits as bright as those that surround Mr. Padgett when he is receiving these communications

June 16th, 1917.

I am here, Elizabeth Barret Browning.

Let me say a word and that is, that I have listened to the last message that was written you, (St. John) and if I could only utter from my soul as that spirit did the deep and true meaning of love and gladness, I would think that beyond the condition that I should then be in there could not possibly be any starry heavens or beyond.

I am a bright spirit and happy, but my happiness is not that which I saw in the bright spirit who wrote, and my love to his is like a pale moonbeam compared to the glorious sunlight. I wonder now that such a spirit can possess such a glorious countenance of love and sympathy. When he spoke of the love of the mother for her son his whole soul seemed to go with his words, and to reflect the wondrous love that he must possess.

This is the first time that I have ever attempted to write through a mortal, and my astonishment is great that I can do so with such ease, but I realize that it must be, because there are so many beautiful spirits present encouraging me to do so.

You should be a very happy mortal to have all these glorious spirits around and so close to you, and they all seem to love you so very much, and as I write they smile upon you and say that they love you, not only because they are your parents and relatives, but because in your heart—and I refer to both you mortals—there is a love that responds to theirs and recognizes the fact of the mutuality of the affections.

Tell me what is the secret of this, to me, wonderful attraction, and what this love is, for it must be beyond what I have experienced.

Well, I have heard what you said, and one beautiful spirit comes to me, and says, that she is a country woman of mine, and invites me to go with her for a little talk, and says that her name on earth was Kate, and now it is, a child of the Father and a possessor of His Love, which she says is a part of the love that I see all around me. How wonderful this all is, and how I long to be among these beautiful spirits in their beauty and happiness!

Well, I will have to leave now and learn the secret of the love. So thanking you I will say good night.

Your true friend,
Elizabeth Barret Browning.

Discloses that allowing the lower spirits to take control of him has depressed him to the extent that he lost faith in the Celestial Spirits

July 7th, 1917.

I am here, John.

Well, I come tonight to write a few lines on your condition and suggest a few thoughts to encourage you in (out of) your despondency. You have been much depressed in the past few days owing very largely to the fact that you permitted the evil influences to make a rapport with you, which fact is largely due to your not letting the Love enter your soul in such quantities as heretofore, for in your imagining, for such I must call them, you became convinced that your material affairs were such as to afford you no hope of relief from the burdens you felt were resting on you.

Well, you have these burdens and you do not see in what manner you may be able to meet them, and find relief and consequently you become negligent of the necessity of seeking and praying more for this Love. In other words, the thought came to you that no love or influence from the higher spirits could enable you to find a way out of your difficulties, and you lost faith in the power of the love, and in us and the result was that your soul became in such a condition that the evil ones could make their rapport, and thus increase your feelings of despondency and want of faith.

I know that your disappointment was very real and that you had a difficult task to make yourself believe that we could do you any good or that your condition of soul could determine that another of your problems being relieved from your worries and as may be said, it was natural for you to feel this way, but if you had taken the advice which we have given you more than once and prayed with all the longings of your soul for the help of the Father, you would not have gotten in such a condition of despondency and could not have given way to the temptations of the flesh and let the influences of the evil ones make a rapport with you and suffered the effects of that rapport.

Every time you get in this condition you lose ground in your spiritual development, and also in your state of happiness and the strength of your faith and experience the hopelessness that comes with such a condition. The material things I know are of great importance and are necessary, and you must obtain them in order to sustain you in your earth life, and the earthly happiness that comes from the freedom of want and when you could not see where these things were coming from it was difficult to throw aside the worries that resulted from such a state of anticipated want. But if you had prayed and exercised your faith such worries would not have dominated you as they did and caused you to ignore the very source from which all things must come.

And I say to you now, that you will not be left alone in these matters for you well realize the things that you desire and need. We are working to bring about the realization of your desires and we will succeed and you will be taken care of.

Yes, I understand, but nevertheless you must try to believe us and endure for a little the disappointment. We cannot accomplish these things at just the time that they may be used but they will be accomplished in such time as will prevent embarrassment.

Yes, I see what your thoughts are and I say to you that you will soon receive what is necessary to relieve you. So have faith in us and pray for the love in more abundance. Believe that we are with you and will not forsake you and that all will be well. Try to overcome the worries and let them pass from you. I know that this is difficult to do but you can do it and will feel the good that will come to you by so doing.

I am not the only one who is saying this to you tonight for many of the spirits who are interested in you are present and are trying to help you, even the Master who is so anxious that you find the relief that you so much desire and get in condition to receive these messages. I will not write more and only say pray and believe. Good night,

Your brother in Christ,

John.

Explains disappointments in both spiritual and material world

July 7th, 1917.

I am here, your grandmother.

Well my dear son, it has been some time since I last wrote to you and I will write a few lines and although I have not written, I have been with you, loving and sympathizing with you in your troubles and trying to help you.

I am so sorry that you have had the experience of the past few days and know that you have suffered from the same, and that everything has appeared to you very gloomy and disheartening, and that even now you are worrying about the material conditions that surround you and see no hope for the immediate future.

Well, my dear one, what you are experiencing has been the experience of many mortals and will be of many more, for such disappointment belongs to the mortal life. Yet you must remember this that very few mortals have had the loving close influence of high spirits in their troubles that you have had and are now having and have had to have their burdens intensified by the evil influences of spirits of the dark planes. So you see, you have been fortunate in this particular and will be in the future, and you must try to believe in the greater faith that such is your fortunate position.

We all understand what your worries have been and we have tried to help you and to remove the causes, but as we have told you before we are not omnipotent in these material affairs and cannot absolutely control these things although we have a greater influence than you can conceive of with mortals as regards their actions, as the result of these influences.

I cannot foretell just what will happen or when, but we know the existence of some and the effects and we try to make conditions that will bring certain effects, and this we have been doing with reference to your material affairs, and very soon I am certain you will be relieved of your present troubles as John has written you. Pray and have faith in us and you will find your condition of spirit and mind much bettered.

As you know, I love you very much and want you to be happy and free from worries, and if I did not honestly believe that you will soon be, I would not tell you so. You have behind you a wonderful power working for your good, both spiritually and materially and if you will only follow our advice you will find yourself much benefitted. No matter how gloomy things may look to you, pray and try to have faith and the gloom will not last or find its lodgment in your mind.

I would like to write you a long letter tonight, but you are not just in condition to receive such a letter. So my dear son, think of what has been written and make the endeavor to let your spiritual condition dominate your feelings and conditions that arise from your depressions and despondency of mind. You can do it if you will pursue the way suggested to you, and happiness will come to you.

I will not write more now but with all my love say pray and believe and trust in what we tell you. May this love of the Father flow into your heart in greater and greater abundance until all worry shall leave you. Good night.

Your loving grandmother.

Also reassures Mr. Padgett that the sun will shine on his material as well as spiritual affairs

July 7th, 1917.

I am here, your own true and loving Helen.

Well dear, I am glad that John and your grandmother wrote you as they have tonight for if you will meditate on what they said you will derive much benefit and realize that your troubles are natural notwithstanding the fact that you are embarrassed by certain material affairs that I know will soon disappear, and existed only on things of the past. I have been so anxious that you get out of the condition of despondency[146] that has been yours for several days past and see only the real condition of your soul qualities. You must not worry about these things for while they are very depressing yet you will be relieved and the sun will shine again. You and Nita will both be provided for and you must not worry.

I should like to write my letter tonight but you are not just in condition to receive it and when I write I want to do it successfully so that you may get as much happiness out of my love dictations as possible. Keep up your courage and pray, this is the greatest source of help, for when you pray you bring to you the Father's Love, which is the great thing that mortals not only require but which will make them happier than can anything else make them. I love you with all my heart

---

[146] It is easy with the benefit of distance to consider that James Padgett seems to lack faith here in the promises of these Celestials. It is not clear if his financial situation did in fact recover, but when you add to that the fact that he lost his daughter Nina only a year later, it is very easy to see why he ultimately became disillusioned. I also know from personal experience that worry and stress (financial or other) is a very real barrier to making a good connection to the Divine and thus receiving the Divine Love that will result in you feeling better. A real catch 22 situation. (G.J.C.)

and soul and so want you to be happy and am doing everything possible to make you so.

So my own dear Ned, think of what I have said and believe. Love me and know that no one in all the universe can love you as I do. Good night and God bless you.

Your own true and loving,
Helen.

Says the preacher has very little knowledge of the "Truth" as has been revealed in the writings received and does not advise attending these services

July 8th, 1917.

I am here, John.

Well, I was with you tonight and you did not learn any truth from the preacher's (Terry) discourse that is vital to the salvation of men. He does not know the truth, and consequently, cannot teach others. You could readily see his want of knowledge when he declared that Jesus was not different from the other teachers to whom he referred, or did not teach any truths that they did not teach. No, I am sorry to say, he does not know the truth, and his opportunity is so great to teach the truth for the majority of his hearers do not believe in the orthodox creeds, and their minds are open to a reception of the truth.

His conception of the relationship of man to God, and of man's own constitution as regards spiritual things, are all wrong, and he will not be able to learn the truth from the investigation of Spiritualism as he is now studying it, for all he knows is that men when they become spirits continue to live and have the power of communicating with mortals, and also that spirits are all happy or very shortly after their entrance into the spirit world may become so by their own exertions by the development of the "divine spark", as he calls it, that exists in all men's souls.

He may learn the truth before he comes to the spirit world, and he may not; for there is no way other than through the information contained in your writings by which he can learn these truths. His advising his hearers to pursue the course of conduct that the moral teachings of the great teachers of light, as he denominates them, show, to men, will not give them the truth and the light and the liberty of which he so loudly discoursed.

There were many spirits present and some of them communicated to their friends, as the preacher told them, for he is a psychic and has the gift of clairaudience and also of clairvoyance to some degree, but he also is a man of quick perception and readily grasps the conditions of the mind and desires of those who are so anxious to hear from their departed friends, and sometimes he uses the information which he gathers by the exercise of his quick wit to describe to the people, the presence of those in the spirit life that they are anticipating will make their presence known by communicating. But aside from this he receives many messages from the spirits and he tries honestly to deliver them to the hearers for whom they are intended.

Now, while all this is true and affords consolation to many of these anxious ones, yet the meetings do you no good as we have told you, for the influences of the spirits who attend these meetings are not helpful to the development of your soul qualities, and it is not desirable that you come in contact with these spirits who always try to make a rapport whenever the opportunity occurs.

There were also some spirits of the higher order present who were interested in their relatives and friends, and tried to get in rapport with these persons for the purpose of helping them; but generally their efforts were not very successful as the conditions prevailing did not enhance the probability of making the rapport or permitting the influence to be felt.

Well, I see that you are feeling better tonight and more hopeful and realize the result of the prayers that you offered to the Father and the increase of your faith in us. If you will continue to pray and exercise this faith you will find yourself helped to such an extent that the troubles you have will not worry you very much, and in addition, such a condition of mind on your part helps us to more effectively perform our part of the work in bringing to you those things that you so much desire. You may not understand the philosophy of this, but sometime I will come to you and make clear the operation of the laws that are brought into use in bringing these results. Only believe and pray, and you will not be forsaken.

Well, I will not write more, but soon I must come and write a message, and if you improve, I will be able to do so in a very satisfactory way. So try to get in this condition. Remember that I love you and am with you very often, trying to help you spiritually and materially, and that you will be so helped. With my love and blessings I will say good night.

Your brother in Christ,
John.

Agrees with John that Mr. Padgett was not benefitted by attending meeting, but pleased with his improved condition of soul

July 8th, 1917.

I am here, Helen.

Well dear, I see that you are tired and I will not write much. But I must say that I am so glad that you are feeling better and more hopeful. Keep up your courage and everything will be alright.

I was with you at the meeting, but will not write my impressions now. You were not benefited. Try to have faith and pray, and I believe that tomorrow night you will be in condition to receive my letter that I so much desire to write. Love me and believe that I love you. Good night.

Your own true and loving,
Helen.

Came in to encourage both Mr. Padgett and Dr. Stone to have faith in the outcome of a plan that the spirit forces have outlined to them

May 24th, 1916.[147]

I am here, John.

Well, I come to write only a few lines as you are not feeling so well, and are not in condition to receive any formal message tonight. But I will say that, notwithstanding what you have read tonight in reference to your material affairs, you must have faith and expect that our promises will soon be realized. The work must be done and you must be placed in condition to do it, without interference. If you could realize the powers that are at work in the endeavor to bring about what is necessary to place you in position to do this work, as we desire it to be done, you would not lose faith or doubt that all the promises made will be fulfilled.

We recognize to the fullest the importance of this matter, and we will not permit much more time to elapse until the end desired is brought about. You and your friend, who is interested in the means that we have adopted to bring about the consummation of our plan, will soon be able to accomplish as we have told you and you must both have faith.

I will not write more tonight, and with my love to you and your friend who is present, I will say good night and God bless you both.

Your brother in Christ,
John

---

[147] This date is uncertain. (G.J.C.)

Comments on Billy Sunday's sermon to the effect that his teachings are directed towards the progress of the soul and the perfect man[148]

January 9th, 1918.

I am here, Helen.

Well dear, I was with you tonight and saw that you were not much benefited by Billy Sunday's sermon, and of course, could not be, because the preacher said nothing to feed the hungry soul. He said some things which were very good in the way of showing men and women what they should do in order to make the earth lives more happy and it will be well, if the hearers will heed and follow the advice. But nothing much was said to help the progress of the soul.

I saw that you were not in much sympathy with the methods and sayings of the preacher and thought that there was too much hilarity and not enough reverence present, as a meeting for the opening up of the soul and helping the development of those qualities that will lead to the Father's love and the Celestial Heavens. But nevertheless, some things that he said will do good to some people.

You must not forget that the teachings of the Master were twofold, and for those who were not in a condition to hear and understand his higher spiritual truths, he preached those things, which if followed, would make them better men and women and cause them to progress in the development of their natural love; and in this latter effort the preacher will do good and his work must not be undervalued, for all men are not alike in their conditions, intellectual or spiritual. And besides, here and there in his preachings some truths that he utters may by its influence upon the hearts of his hearers cause such hearers to think more deeply about spiritual things of the higher nature, and in thinking, their souls may be opened up to the influence of the spirits who have the Divine Love in their souls, and from which may follow the longings of these hearers for this Love of the Father.

Everything said that tends to cause a spirit to progress towards either of the conditions of love must be encouraged, for the Father works in His own way, and frequently the Love comes into a man's soul, and the man not being intellectually conscious of what the Love is. Whoever is not against us in this work is, in a certain sense, with us, for the salvation of men is the objects of all our efforts; and if we or mortals

---

[148] This heading as originally published is far longer: Mr. Padgett's wife Helen makes comments on Billy Sunday's sermon, to the effect that his teachings are directed towards the progress of the soul and the perfect man. However, this direction in religious teachings is not to be discouraged, as it leads to purity, though not divinity of soul. Billy Sunday is an Evangelist preacher. (G.J.C.)

cannot awaken dead souls to a life in the higher condition, then we must work to bring them into that condition that will cause them to get into a state of purified natural love. They are all the children of God, and if they will not become His beloved children in the divine sense, then He wants them to become the pure spirits that the first parents were before the fall.

So do not criticize or look down upon the work of this preacher because he does not show men the true way to the Celestial Heavens, or because he says and does things that may not appear to be reverent. God looks at the heart and the intentions and the forms of expression used by the preacher are not important, except as they may have the effect of causing some soul to turn away from the truths that the preacher may communicate. All men are not alike and the preachings of the man, while they may, as some say, disgust some hearers, yet others will be affected by them and good will be done.

I write this because I see that you are inclined to criticize the preacher and conclude that his teachings are not conducive to spiritual progress. Well, as you have been told, the large majority of men and spirits will never become inhabitants of the Celestial Heavens, but that is no reason why they should not be taught the way that will tend to purge them of their sins so far as the natural love is concerned. Those who will not become angels must become purified men, and any and everything that will help them to become the latter is approved by the Father and is the object of His favor.

Well dear, I will not write more now as I see that you are cold and must go to bed. But remember this that while all men will not become dwellers in the spheres of the soul in the Celestial Kingdom, yet they are brothers, and the favored brothers must try and help in every way possible the less favored brothers in obtaining that which the Father has designed shall be their portion, even though they refuse or neglect to seek for and obtain the great goal of Divine Love and Immortality. So love me and pray to the Father for His Love, and with all the sincerity of your soul, thank Him that you have found the way to His Great Love and the mansions in the Divine Heavens.

And what I have said to you I say to Dr. Stone, for I see that his thoughts are somewhat similar to your own and that you both think that unless a preacher can and does show the way to the Celestial Kingdom, his work is not worthy of much consideration and falls short of what he as a saviour of souls should do. And so it is, but all cannot teach the higher truths, for they do not know or understand them; but that fact must not cause you, or any who know the truths, to think that this work when sincere and beneficial in its moral teachings, should not be taught. I thought best to write this tonight, so that you may not get a wrong conception of what men who cannot teach the great truths should or should not teach. All men are not in that condition of soul and love and they should be taught the way that will lead them to those mansions in the heavens that will be theirs by free will choice.

I love you my dear husband, and am closer to you in your thoughts, and do not want you to think wrong in anything, even though you think right in a great many and the most important things. Pray and let your faith increase and believe that we are all with you trying to direct you aright; and one who knows is more anxious than any of us that your knowledge of the truths increase, and your experiences arising from that knowledge bring to you with more convincing force the truths, that God is Love, and your God. Good night.

Your own and true and loving,
Helen[149]

Comments on a sermon delivered by Rev. William Sunday entitled: "There is appointed once a time for man to die and after than the Judgment."

February 23rd, 1918.

I am here, Jesus.

I see that you are in good condition tonight, and that I am able to make a rapport with you. I was with you at the meeting tonight and saw the workings of your mind and the pity, as it were, that you had for the preacher (Rev. Billy Sunday), because of his want of knowledge of what the judgment is that comes to all men after death. A judgment that is certain and exact, but not one pronounced upon man by God, as the preacher proclaimed.

I was trying to impress you in your thoughts and you felt the influence of my suggestions and realized that you did not fear the judgment, or rather its results, because you know the way in which the judgment for you can have no terrors, or no eternity of condemnation. I wished as you did that the preacher might know the truth and then proclaim it to his hearers, and in this manner show them that the judgment is a certainty that cannot be escaped from, and that its sentences are not for an eternity of duration.

He is an earnest man in his beliefs, and teaches just as he believes, and the pity is that he does not know the truth. But, nevertheless, he is doing good to those who hear him, for many of them are caused to think of things spiritual, and of the future, as well as of the present, who otherwise might and would neglect these important things

---

[149] This message is a composite of two, being published in Volume III and Volume IV. (G.J.C.)

that will determine the kind of judgment that they will have to undergo; and I am glad that he is so preaching and doing a work that in many instances will lead men to meditate upon their spiritual condition, and ultimately lead them to seek for the Love of the Father, which they may obtain by their longings, though their beliefs may be erroneous as to how this Love may be obtained.

Men are constituted with a mind and a soul, each having its own perceptions and ability to comprehend the truth, and sometimes it happens that the perceptions of the soul will enable them to see and reach out for this Love, while they may be wholly blind in their mind perceptions, and even these latter perceptions may be in conflict with the operations of the perceptions of the soul.

Until the truths that I and the other spirits are revealing to you, shall become known to the world, there will be nothing in existence or in the knowledge of men that can supply the place of these truths so much as the beliefs that have been and are being taught by the teachings of the Bible, for in it are many truths, especially those that show men the way to attain to moral perfection; and that, as you know, was one of the objects of my teachings when on earth, but not the great object of my mission.

Nevertheless, the man who learns and applies these moral truths to his daily life and conduct comes nearer to the enjoyment of that harmony that man must obtain in order to get into a unison with God's laws, that is necessary to his regeneration and to his becoming the perfect man. And besides, as he—I mean the mortal—progresses in this regeneration, he will find it easier for him to learn by his soul perceptions the great truth of the transformation of the soul through the New Birth.

I approve of the efforts of this preacher to bring men to a realization of their relationship to God, even though he has many erroneous beliefs, and says many things that are contrary to the truth, and not in accord with the true relationship of man to God.

I will write you soon upon this matter of the judgment, and what it means and the variety of its operations. Tonight, I will not write longer, for I think it best to not draw upon you too much at this renewed conjunction of rapport with your condition. I have been with you very often of late, and tried to influence you with my love and suggestions, and I must tell you that you have progressed much in your soul development and nearness to the Father's love. Continue to meditate upon these spiritual things, and pray to the Father, and you will realize a great increase in the possession of this Love and in your condition that will enable us to come in closer rapport with you.

Well, I will do as you suggest, and am pleased that you feel as you say, for we must do the work as rapidly as possible. We have lost much time and will have to work the harder to bring about the completion of our delivery of the truths. But you need not fear that we will not be successful. We will complete the book and you will receive the other gifts that are promised you. Only have faith and pray, and all will be well.

I must stop now, but before doing so must assure you that I am praying with you in your prayers at night, and that your prayers will be answered. Other spirits will now be able to write you and they have many messages to communicate and all are anxious to do so. Keep up your courage and believe in me and what I tell you. With my love and the blessings of the Father, I will say good night.

Your brother and friend, Jesus.[150]

Was also present at Rev. William Sunday's services with many others including his special guardian, John, and is happy that Jesus was able to make a good rapport with her husband

February 23rd, 1918.

I am here, your own true and loving, Helen.

Well my dear husband, I am so glad that the Master has written you, and that the rapport has been re-established so that he can continue the delivery of his messages, for as he said; they, the spirits, are all very anxious to do the work.

I was with you tonight and besides me were the Master and your special guardian, John, and we were all watching the impressions made upon your mind by the preacher and saw that what he said which was contrary to the truths that you have received, made no impression upon your beliefs, except that you desired to be able to tell him of his errors. I will not refer to the occasion further as the Master has written you fully on the subject, and you realize that he corroborates what I said a short time ago in regard to the good that the preacher is doing.

I am glad that you are in much better condition of soul and are able to realize more and more the existence of the love in your soul and the fact of your increased nearness to the Father. This makes us all very happy, and we know that you will now be able to do your work with greater rapidity and receive there from a wonderful happiness. Continue to pray to the Father, and turn your thoughts to these spiritual things, and think of the great responsibility that is resting upon you.

I will soon come and write you a real long letter of love, and I

---

[150] This message is a composite of two, being published in Volume II and Volume III. (G.J.C.)

know you will feel that love surrounding you in great abundance. Many spirits are here tonight and rejoice that the rapport has been re-established. I love you as you know and want you to love me, and you will not be happier than I when you come into possession of the surroundings that you desire as you so often depict them in your mind's eye. Have faith and you will not be disappointed, and you need not fear the judgment that comes to all men after death. I will not write more now. May you be happier as the days go by. Good night.

Your own true and loving,
Helen.[151]

Writes that a large majority of men will exist in eternity as perfect men and enjoy the happiness which it brings, hence it is important that men should know the moral Truths of Divine Love

May 21st, 1918.

I am here, Helen.

Well dear, I see that you have been much benefitted by the reading of the messages tonight, and I am so glad that you read them in the manner that you did. The truths which you read in reference to the spirit world in the book of Dr. Peebles, are very beautiful and also edifying and helpful to the extent that they affect the conditions of the souls of men, but, as you know, they do not reach the vital point or tell of the great truth which is necessary for men to know in order to obtain the condition of the Divine Angel and a home in the Celestial Heavens.

Of course, the writer, or any of those whom he quotes, could not speak of this higher truth, for they did not understand the same and they could comprehend only the great moral teachings of Jesus. But these teachings are also of great importance to mankind, for the understanding and observance of them in thought and deed will certainly lead man to a purification of his soul, and to a coming in at-onement with the Father, in accordance with the perfectness of man in his creation. As we have written you, the large majority of men will exist in the great eternity only as perfect men, enjoying the happiness which that condition brings to them, and, hence it is of great importance that men should be taught these mortal truths.

But of greater importance is the knowledge of the truth which will show men the way to become Divine Angels and at-one with God in His very Substance and Essence of Love. This was the great mission of the

---

[151] This message is a composite of two, being published in Volume II and Volume III. (G.J.C.)

Master on earth, but men failed to understand and realize that fact, and, instead, were possessed only of the knowledge of the moral truths and a belief that such truths, or rather the results of the practicing and living the same, would lead them to immortality and perfect happiness.

Well, you understand all this, and I will not say more on the subject; but I wish to emphasize to you the importance of your fully realizing, deep down in your soul, that the truths of the Divine are not understood by men, and, hence, cause you to appreciate more the great importance of the work which you are to perform. Oh, my dear, I hope that you will consider and meditate upon this and try your best to get in such condition that the rapport may be made and these truths delivered to you.

You know the way, the only way, and you must follow that way. Pray to the Father with all the longings of your soul, and meditate more on spiritual things, such as the truths which the Master and the others have revealed to you. I know that you are desirous of receiving the messages, but you are not willing, as it seems, to make the effort to get in the soul condition, which will not come from the existence of the mere desire to receive the messages.

Well, I did not write earlier in the evening for you were not just in condition, and I thought that if you did not hear from me, you might possibly read some of the messages and thus get in a better soul condition to receive my message, as you have done. It is too late to write more tonight, but I feel quite hopeful that I will be able to do so very soon. So sweetheart, pray to the Father and let your faith increase, and think more of these truths, and what they mean. I will not write more now, and will only further say, love me with all your heart and think more of me, and you will be much happier.

Good night, my dear husband.
Your own true and loving,
Helen.

That the most effective way of re-establishing the rapport is by praying more sincerely and frequently to the Father for the inflowing of His Love

September 23rd, 1918.

I am here, John.

Let me write a few lines, as I see that you are expecting some of the higher spirits to write tonight, and yet you are not just in that condition which will enable them to write of the higher truths that are waiting to be made to you. I am sorry that this is so, for there are many messages to be delivered; and the spirits are very anxious to write. But you are in better condition than you have been for some time, and if you continue to improve in a very short time you will be able to receive the messages.

Tonight I merely wish to say that we have been with you a great deal, trying to influence your mind and tune your thoughts to things spiritual so that your soul may become more in accord with us, and we be enabled to make the rapport that is necessary. You have thought more tonight of these spiritual truths than for some time, and as a consequence, your soul has had a new awakening, as it were, and taken on the qualities that will enable us to form the rapport, and for that result we are thankful and pleased and desire to advise you to continue in these thoughts and the opening up of your soul. We are all very anxious for the return of the rapport and the opportunity to continue the writings, as so very much time has been lost and the urgency of communicating the truths is very great, and they must not be longer delayed.

As you have been told, the most effective way of re-establishing the rapport is by your praying more sincerely and frequently to the Father for the inflowing of His Love, for you must know that the possession of that love in your soul brings you in closer union with us than anything else that could possibly exist. I say this that you may appreciate the importance of action in the particular mentioned on your part and also the vital necessity for doing the work which has been assigned you to do. So take my advice and make the effort, and success will undoubtedly come and we will all be happier.

I will not write more tonight as I prefer to wait until you get in a condition which will permit me to disclose some of the truths that I desire to communicate. Believe that we are with you and love you and above all else desire the development of your soul in love and progress towards a condition of religious experience. Pray to the Father and believe that it is I who am writing, and that I am your sincere and true guardian and friend,
John.

Urges Mr. Padgett to bend every effort to get in condition as John has written

September 23rd, 1918.

I am here, Helen.

Well, my dear Ned, I am so very glad that John has written you as he has, and hopes that you will consider and act on his advice. If you could only realize what it all means you would bend every effort to get in the condition that would enable these high spirits to make the rapport and communicate to you their wonderful messages.

I know though, that you really feel the importance of the work and that you long for the Love and will be glad when the delivery of the messages is resumed. And I know you love me and will try to do everything possible to please and make me happy, and you can do this by following the advice of John.

Baby[152] is here tonight and is so very anxious to write you, but I tell her that it is best to wait for a few nights when you will be in so much better receptive condition and she will be more successful in writing to you. She is so very loving and beautiful and believes that her daddy is the most wonderful man on earth, and one to be loved by her, and it is no wonder that she thinks in this way, for she sees so many of the bright and Celestial Spirits around you desiring to get in rapport with you and deliver their messages.

Well dear, it is not necessary to repeat our expressions of love, for you know how much we all love you and want your love and thoughts. Some spirits are here tonight who would like to write you, but I tell them that they must wait a while until you are in a condition when their messages may be received. Think of us and believe that we are with you very much trying to help you.

Yes, he has been here on several occasions, but did not have the opportunity to write. When he next comes I will have him write. Good night, my dear one.

Your own true and loving,
Helen.

Informs Mr. Padgett that his reading about the old prophets had little effect on his soul, because our Father never had the feeling of wrath against His children as the Bible quotes

October 30th, 1918.

I am here, Helen.

Well dear, you have been in two conditions of soul and mind tonight. The one, rather repellent and out of sympathy with us, which prevented us from writing you, and the other, which you now have, congenial and in unison with us.

Your reading the prophecies of the old prophets did not have the effect of awakening in your soul those feelings and aspirations which were suitable to bring your soul in rapport with us, and largely, because those writings did not declare and display the true and loving Father

---

[152] Baby is Helenita and she passed very unexpectedly at age 26, on the 20th June 1918. (G.J.C.)

whom we know and love. Our Father never had the feelings of wrath against his children that are in those prophecies ascribed to him. The Jehovah of those prophets was of a very different type from the Father whom we know and love and fear only in the sense that in some possible way we may violate the laws of His Love.

Of course, as you know, the people of those times, prophets, priests, Kings and common people, never had or knew of His Divine Love, and their comprehension of God, was one who required sacrifice and obedience to his laws of right and justice as they understood them; and undoubtedly their prophets were, to a degree, inspired by the spirits of the higher heavens as they then existed; to warn and threaten and denounce, so that the people might be brought to a realization of their sins and induced to a return to that harmony with the law that would enable them to become rid of their sins and evil doings; and considering their conception of God, the means used by the prophets were the ones necessary to bring about these results.

A consideration of these means in comparison with the ways taught by the Master that lead to the Celestial Heavens will demonstrate the fact that, in those ancient days, neither prophet, priest nor people had any knowledge of the Divine Love, and that the privilege of these ancient people of obtaining the Divine Love was not in existence.

I and the higher spirits, as they have declared, see no good that can possibly come to mortals of the present from a reading and understanding of these books of the Old Testament. The moral commands contained in them were pronounced and emphasized by the teachings of the Master, which needs no assistance from these old teachings in order that the Master's teachings should have a sanctioning. And as to the higher spiritual truths, these old scriptures contain nothing which can possibly enlighten or help man to acquire knowledge of these truths.

So I advise you not to waste your time in reading these scriptures, but rather use all the time that remains to you outside of the affairs of your practical life to learn and study and meditate upon the truths which have been revealed to you by the messages that you have received.

I would not by what I have said, desire to be understood as depreciating the reading of these scriptures by people who have not the opportunity and privilege of hearing the truths that have been revealed to you, for in these scriptures are many moral truths and illustrations which may be of benefit to these people; and undoubtedly essential to them in the particulars and under the circumstances mentioned. So my dear husband, continue to pray and believe.

Question and answer.

Well I meant that these truths are not necessary to be read by the people of the present day, for in the New Testament are found these moral truths; and while not necessary I would not advise that the people should absolutely fail to read the Old Testament, because some may enjoy the reading of these truths as they are therein contained and associated with the circumstances surrounding them. They may appeal to some people, and if so, work a benefit. I again say that they are not necessary but they may be helpful to some—the minds of all do not work alike.

Think of me in your prayers and love me. Good night.
Your own true and loving,
Helen.

Comments on the book that Mr. Padgett was reading, which only incorporates the natural love and not the Divine Love

February 19th, 1919.

I am here, Job.

Let me say a few words tonight upon a subject that is of importance to mankind and to the future of man.

I see that you have been reading a book professing to give communications from a spirit who claims to be possessed of a divine mission in the way of teaching men the truths of the soul, and of the way to immortality and life. Well, you may accept what is said with some degree of truth as to the condition of spirits who are progressing in the development of their natural love, and as to the facts that await a soul after it has left the mortal life. Many of the statements contained in the writings are true and should be accepted and acted upon by mortals who desire a knowledge of the true way to a kingdom of the purified soul and to a reconciliation to God in the way of renunciation.

God is good, and not the hateful and merciless being that your orthodox beliefs teach and is always the same, now as in the days of old when men's conception of Him were determined by their own ideas of what a God should be, and what men should believe him to be. But there are many things taught in the writings of the book that are not true, though in accord with the knowledge possessed by the writers and suited to the condition of the medium through whom the messages were delivered.

The writers were spirits who were highly developed intellectually and morally, and had knowledge of the truths to an extent that made what they said powerful expositions of the truth as they knew it to be; but beyond the fact that men must, in order to become pure and holy, do those things which the law of harmony in their natural love demands, they could not teach.

Now, while this is all true, yet they did not know of the higher truths that make a man or the soul of a man divine and at one with the Father and could not teach because they did not possess any knowledge of, and only so far as they knew, must, their teachings be accepted as truth. They were far in advance in their renditions of the disclosures contained in the Bible, both as to God and Jesus, and the final destiny of man, and their revelations should be accepted in place of the teachings of the Bible. They were not only acquainted with the laws of God as dealing with man in his relation to good and evil, but also with the laws as to man's release from the consequences of his acts and deeds of earth, and as to his release from the consequences of his evil acts.

I would like to write now, but the rapport is broken. Good night, Job.

Is pleased with the improvement that Mr. Padgett is making in his recovery, but he is not strong enough for the Celestial Spirits to write

February 19th, 1919.

I am here, your own true and loving Helen.

Well, dear, your condition is better tonight than for a long time past, and we have great expectations that before long it will be such that a rapport can be made and the spirits be able to write with ease.

The spirit who attempted to write you was a high spirit and was desirous of writing you, and was very sorry when the rapport was broken as he had much to say on the subject of the writings which you have been reading. I am sorry that the conditions were not such as to enable him to continue, but it is better than it was for a long time, and will improve if you will only pray more and give more of your thoughts to the spiritual things.

I wish that you were in the condition that once was yours, so that the Master and others could write you. You may now (not?) know, but it is a fact, that you are being looked after with such watchfulness and care that your condition shall not be injured, that no other spirits are permitted to communicate with you, who have not the powers of the Celestial Spirits. We desire that you shall be preserved for the work which is yours to do, and so we do not permit communication from the ordinary spirits to intervene. Soon you will be alright again and then the higher spirits will come and write you as they desire. Only wait a little while.

Tonight I should like to write a long message, but I will not for fear that your condition may be interfered with, and so I will stop now. But remember that we love you and are trying to help you in every way. Good night.

Your own true and loving,
Helen.

Mr. Padgett's guardian angel is with him a great deal and advises him on the talks given by various lecturers

June 13th, 1917.

I am here, John.

I was with you tonight at the talk of the lecturer, (on New Thought) and display of what has no foundation in truth. She has an idea that God is what man makes him to be, and that only as man's consciousness realizes the existence of a God in harmony with that consciousness, does that God really exist. She seems to have no conception as an Absolute, Unchangeable Being, not dependent upon man's realization of him or of man's consciousness that he exists in any other form or substance than as man sees him.

No, she has not a true conception of God or man. To her, man is just what his status demonstrates him to be and no matter whether a formless, senseless amoeba or a perfect man as originally created by God, he is still man, and dependent upon his knowledge of the different conditions of himself in order to determine what he may have been in any state of his evolution. She cannot define God or man, and that being so, how can she possibly help man to know these matters. It is all pitiable that any human should let his own salvation or future destiny depend upon such unreliable and erroneous conceptions.

I do not think that such lectures as this do you any good and I advise you not to attend them. Rely only on what you have received and shall receive from the Master and other high spirits as to what God and man are. I see that you are in better condition tonight, and I hope that we may resume our messages and continue to reveal to you the truth as regards God and man, and the plan, and the only one given by the Father for the full salvation of him.

I will not write more tonight. So with my love I will say good night.

Your brother in Christ,
John.

Advises Mr. Padgett about a Plan of Independence that will be disclosed in detail at a later date

March 11th, 1916.

I am here, John.

Let me write a few lines as I desire to tell you of something that may be of importance to you. You will remember that we have told you on many occasions that at some time you would be in condition to do the work for which you have been selected to do in a way when all physical cares and worries would be eliminated from existence, and I want to repeat tonight those promises and say that the time will soon come when you will be in that condition and find yourself free to enjoy the opportunities that such freedom will afford you.[153]

We have been with you much of late, exercising our influence upon your spiritual thoughts and trying to help you to get in condition that will enable you to receive our messages without much difficulty and from the influences of these outside things, and we want you to get in condition that our work and yours can be done in this way. You must make the effort to assist us in placing you in this condition and if you will do so we will proceed in placing you in the position to bring: about the end that we so much desired.

I will not write more tonight but will try our best to help you in your efforts. Ease your mind and whatever money you can spare to attempt to find this success and we will help you.

Of course you understand what we mean and very soon a spirit will come who will direct you in the matter and make your success certain. I will come a little later and write you more in detail.

So trust and believe and you will not be disappointed. good night.

Your brother in Christ,
John.

Selected to help Mr. Padgett with his personal problems

March 11th, 1916.

I am here, John D. Mastry.

I am interested in what John has written you and want merely to say that I have been selected to assist you in the matter to which he referred and will do my best to help you, and will be very careful in my advice, and I hope that you will have faith in me.

---

[153] This theme of financial stress in Padgett's life pops up regularly, but it is not known either what exactly the issue was, or whether it was solved in his lifetime. (G.J.C.)

This is all that I desire to say. Good night.
Your brother in Christ,
John D. Mastry.

Confirms both John and stranger by the name of Mastry wrote

March 11th, 1916.

I am your own true and loving Helen.

Well dear, you must not doubt what has been written you but try your best to follow the advice that may be given you and believe that you will succeed.

John actually wrote you and so did the other spirit, whom I don't know, but who says he has been selected to do the work. He says his name is Mastry that is all I know about him. You will have a further explanation of the matter a little later.

Some of the higher spirits were present tonight as you read the messages and are very desirous to write other messages and will soon come to do so.

You must pray more to the Father for His Love and so get in the condition to receive the messages. I love you very much and so want you to be happy and free from all earthly cares. We will come soon and write you, so kiss me and say good night,

Your own true and loving,
Helen.

A former law partner of Mr. Padgett, has progressed sufficiently in receiving the Divine Love of the Father to be able to help other spirits in the lower spheres

March 30th, 1915.

I am here, your old partner.

I am very happy and have progressed very much since I last wrote you, and have increased in my faith and knowledge of God and his love, I am very near the fifth sphere, and I hope to soon go there and be with your father and Prof. Salyards, who have been there for quite a while, and who are so very happy and filled with the Father's Love.

Well, I received the female spirit that you sent me last night, and I tried very hard to show her the way to redemption and freedom from her sufferings. She has such little soul development that it was a difficult undertaking to reach what little soul she has; but I struggled with her with all my powers of arguments, and also with all the influences of my love which I now possess, and at last she commenced to see the light, and promised me to pray to the Father, and try to believe in His Divine Love as standing ready to be bestowed on her and save her from her most unhappy condition. She was one of the most unloving and most unlovable spirits that I have ever met, and was literally starved in her soul. No love for anyone not even for herself, and in her strict ideas of what was right and wrong; she had sacrificed every sympathy and feeling of love to the building up of the intellect. So I had an uphill task from the beginning.

She said that you told her that she must come to me with an open mind and a will free from all prejudice and then I could help her. Well, she tried to assume that position, but it was difficult for her to do so. She is a very strong minded woman, and, consequently, she was not easily convinced of those things which did not appeal to her mind. She thought that the mind is the whole of spirit, as some earth people teach; but when I told her that spirit and mind are both only a part of the soul, and the mind the lesser part, she seemed astonished and couldn't accept the assertion as true. She has no soul, that is, it is all dried up and dead for want of exercise. She has now some little awakening, and if she persists in prayer and faith she will finally become convinced that soul is what brings happiness and joy, and saves her from her torment. So I will continue to help her if she will permit me to, and she now seems disposed to do so.

Well, you have had a great many communications since last I wrote you, and some of them were very wonderful in the information they conveyed.

The Master is so much interested in your welfare that he visits you very often, and you must not let your heart doubt that he comes to you, because he seems so brotherly and familiar. It is he, and his love for you is very great. I know this for he sometimes tells me of his great love and interest in you. He has told you of certain things that will come to you in the future, and I say to you, that you must believe him for they will come true. He knows better than anyone what the future will bring, even though he may decline to acknowledge this great power, only trust him and you will not be disappointed.

I am now preparing a discourse on a subject that I desire to write you in a little while for your consideration, and I hope information. I will let you know beforehand so that you may prepare yourself to receive it. Well, I will not write more tonight.

Well, I think that Garfield is too much given to the things purely intellectual to accept our teachings of the New Birth, but I think that sooner or later he will think of it, and when he does he will not rest until he has found the truth of the matter. Yes, he told me of his interview with your grandmother, and said that she had put to him some wonderful propositions which he could not exactly understand, but which he has been considering very earnestly. He thinks that your grandmother is a very superior spirit in her knowledge of spiritual things, and in her beauty and goodness; and he said there must be something in what she told him to account for her great beauty and power. She showed him such powers of soul and mind that he was astonished and could only keep silent while she talked, and listened to what she said. He was impressed by her and I think, after a little while, he will visit her again and seek for further information. I want to say that she is a wonderful spirit in all things that pertain to the bigger things of spirit life.

Yes, I saw him (Syrick) and said a few words to him in the way of encouragement, but he is not in a very good spiritual condition; but he has the advantage of having had his eyes opened to the fact that there is such a thing as spiritual development while on earth. He is only fairly happy, and as the new sensation of a new life wears off, I think he will commence to suffer because of the errors of his earth life. His soulmate is with him a great deal and is helping him and so is your wife. She is a wonderful spirit and seems so full of the Divine Love and goodness that her influence among spirits is marvelous. I tell you Padgett, that you are a fortunate man in having such a soulmate.

Well I must stop. So good night.
Your old partner and brother.
A. G. Riddle.

Writes about her experience with some spirits that Mr. Padgett sent to her that did not believe in prayer, although one said that he did pray as a child

March 30th, 1915.

I am here, Helen.

I will not write much tonight as you are tired. So let me tell you of a little incident that happened only yesterday. The spirits that you sent to me came, and I had quite a long talk with them, and told them the way to light and happiness, and tried to impress upon them the necessity of faith and prayer. One said that he did not believe in prayer and if that was the way out of his torments he did not see much hope for him. The other said that he when a child used to pray, but that was so long ago that he had forgotten how, and that he thought it useless to try again.

Well I talked to them a while longer, and there came to us a spirit that you had helped some months ago, and who had learned the way and was enjoying comparative happiness because he had followed your advice. He heard what these two spirits said, and at once told them, that a short time ago his condition was worse than theirs and that he had sought your help, and you told him of this wonderful love of the Father, and of prayer and faith, and that he had told you that he did not believe in either God or prayer, but that you became so insistent that you would not let him go until he promised to pray and tried to believe. That you literally tortured him in telling him of this wonderful Love and the only way to it. That he made the promise in order to get away from you, not intending to keep it; but that before you let him go, you told him how much you were interested in him and how much you loved him that his heart melted, and when he left you he determined to keep his promise, and after that, he commenced to pray as you had told him, and that at night you prayed for him, and called him to pray with you, and that as he prayed the light commenced to come to him, and at last some of the wonderful love that you had told him about, came to him, and he found that as this love came into his soul, his sufferings and torture left him, so that now he was a very happy spirit, but still a praying one and a believing one.

When he had finished telling the two spirits of his experience, they commenced to ask him questions, and to think that there might be something or some way to relief, and after a little time commenced to pray, and the spirit who had told them his experience prayed with them; and as they prayed they commenced to feel strange sensations as they said, and after a little while they said they felt better, and believed that there might be something in prayer and faith.

They very soon thereafter left me, but said that they would continue to pray, and asked if I thought that you would pray for them as you did for the other spirit. I told them that you had already prayed for them, and would do so at night before you retired, and they said that they would be with you; and last night as you prayed for them they were there and joined in your prayers. They are now praying continually, and I know that soon they will see the light, and commence to feel their sufferings and torments leaving them.

Oh, my dear, what a blessing it is to help the unfortunate and despondent souls. How you should thank God that he has given you the means to reach the hearts of these unfortunates, and the power to help them. They will always remember you with love and thanks, and you will feel the influence of your kind actions. I must stop. So good night my own dear and loving Ned.

Your own true and loving,
Helen.

Gives reasons why corrections have to be made in the New Testament and that James is the real brother of Jesus

August 28th, 1916.

I am here, John.

I merely want to say that you will soon be well and in condition to receive some of our messages which we are anxiously waiting to write. The time is approaching when the book will have to be published and it is very necessary that you get these messages in full so that you can compile the book. Of course we want to incorporate every truth that is necessary to make known to mankind, and to do so we will have to work faster.

Yes I, I know him well (James the Lesser, the subject of a question asked by Mr. Padgett) and he was the brother of Jesus, the real brother, having the same father and mother that Jesus had and all speculations as to his having parents who were other than the parents of Jesus are not in accord with the truth, and were falsified, to make it appear that Mary was a virgin. He was not in the beginning an apostle of Jesus and came to believe in him late in the ministry of Jesus, but when at last he became convinced that Jesus was the true messiah he became a very earnest and hard working follower of Jesus, and also the first Christian Bishop of Jerusalem.

I have no personal knowledge as to whether he wrote the epistles ascribed to him or not but he has said that he wrote some portion of the first epistle and a portion of the second but that he did not write the third. That in each of these epistles is many assertions of truth which are wrong and which he did not teach. All the writings of the New Testament, as they now exist, contain so many things which the original writers did not write and which they did not teach or believe in, that it is with difficulty that the mortal, even though a great student, can separate the true from the false. And that is one reason that enters into our motives for writing a new revelation of the truth.

The truths will be made plain and you must not let the writings of the Bible influence you in your receiving a correct conception of these truths. I will not write more now.

So with my love I will say good night.
John.[154]

---

[154] This message is a composite of three, being published in Volume III and twice in Volume IV. (G.J.C.)

Has met the two popes responsible for his trials and they have now progressed in the Spirit World

August 28th, 1916.

I am here, Luther.

I will not write much at this time but am anxious to continue my letter to my followers, and as soon as you are in condition I will come and hope that you will give me the opportunity. Well of course, I will have to wait until they have delivered these messages, but I have no doubt that there will be times when you will not be occupied by receiving their messages. I thank you and will come.

I have met both the popes[155] who were in the papal chair at the time that I went to Rome and when I was afterward persecuted and brought to trial before them. They are now in the Celestial Heavens[156] but before they left the earth sphere they were in very great darkness and suffering intensely, and thus repentance was very thorough and sincere. They were compelled to realize the great evil that the teachings and dogma of their church was doing to humanity and they devoted all their time in the spirit life to attempting to influence the priests and hierarchy of the great errors that they were teaching, but the result of their work was not very satisfactory for reasons that I have not time to explain now.

The state of the ignorant catholic layman is a very deplorable one when he comes to the spirit world, but that of the pope and the priest is beyond all description. They are forever branded by the results upon their followers of their evil teaching and consequently suffer very much. Some time I will come to you and write in detail into the conditions and causes there is of these blind teachers of the blind. I must not write more tonight.

With my love I will say good night.
Your brother in Christ,
Luther.

Is happy with Mr. Padgett's improved condition

I am here, your own true and loving Helen.

I will not write much as you are not in condition yet. But I will say that John and Luther wrote you and they were the real persons of whom you know.

---

[155] These were Pope Leo X and Pope Clement VII. (G.J.C.)
[156] The daily diary suggests that the phrase "They are not in the Celestial Heavens" which is found in the original publication, should in fact be "They are now in the Celestial Heavens". The text above has been altered accordingly as also the heading. (G.J.C.)

I see that you are feeling better tonight and I am glad, but you must be careful and not take more cold.

There are quite a number of your spirit friends here tonight who wish to be remembered and say that they are trying to help you in any way.

So kiss me good night.
Your own true and loving,
Helen.

Confirms the writers as being who they represented themselves to be and that both Mary and Martha, his daughters, are living together in the Celestial Heavens

September 21st, 1916.

I am here, Lazarus.

I merely want to say that I am the real Lazarus of the Bible story and that I am an inhabitant of the Father's Kingdom, and in the truth that exists in that Kingdom, and in its inhabitants.

I declare to you that the spirits who have written you the truths of Celestial and spiritual things are actually those whom they represent themselves to be. Jesus, especially, is with you very often and communicates to you truths from His great storehouse of knowledge of the truth. He is so much interested in the work to be done and the revelations to be made that he is with you so very often for the purpose of not only revealing these truths, but of preparing you to receive them; and he is enveloping you in his love, and giving to you a development of your soul faculties that will make you qualified to receive these high truths as no other mortal has ever been qualified, for he knows that you are his best qualified instrument now on earth to do his work and the work of the Father.

From what I say, you must not suppose that you are the best, nor the man having the greatest amount of the Divine Love in the soul, for that is not true. Nor are you chosen because of any merits of your own or superior mental endowments; but you have those conditions of attunement with him that enables him and the other spirits to use you in performing this work.

I am not of such exalted position or soul development as are many of the spirits who write you, yet I know the plans of the Master, and what I say to you is true. I was a Jew and an orthodox one, until the Master came to me and I developed my soul so that I could understand his teachings, and become susceptible to the inflowing of the Divine Love.

I will not write more now, but in closing repeat that you must believe what I have above said, and try to do the will of the Father, and the work that you have been selected to do.

Well, both Mary and Martha are in the Celestial Heavens, and you would naturally suppose that Mary has made the greater progress in her soul development but that is not true, as they both live in the same sphere, and have similar development. As you know they have been in the spirit world for a very long time and whatever spiritual superiority Mary may have appeared to have over Martha does not now exist, for they both have this Divine Love to a degree that has caused all sin and thoughts for the material to have become eradicated long years ago.

Your wife says that I must not write more now and so I will say good night.

Your brother in Christ, Lazarus.[157]

Confirms the writing from Lazarus

September 21st, 1916.

I am here, your own true and loving Helen.

Well sweetheart, you have had a message from Luke and one from Lazarus, and I want to tell you that it was really they who wrote. I was with you tonight and saw that you did not enjoy the evening very much nor the music either. I think it may be best for you to not visit there (the Colburns) so often, for if you will give more of your evenings to us you will find more benefit in our society and communications.

It is well that you visit them occasionally for they enjoy your visits and some time perhaps you may be able to show them the way to the vital truths of the soul. I am so glad that you are feeling so much better and I wish that the time was here when you could enjoy the things that you were thinking about as to your home. I will not write more tonight as it is late and you had better go to bed and get up early.

Yes, Mary was with us and she enjoyed the visit and was very close to the Doctor. She says tell him that she loves him and wants him to love her more and more each day. She will write him soon.

Yes, they did her good and succeeded in relieving some of the difficulty and she is better and the doctors think that she may recover. Dr. Campbell was with her last night and gave her the best attention and help that he was able to give and he knows a great deal about the ills of mortals and how to remedy them. He took charge of the case as the doctors say and directed the manner of assistance on the part of the others. I do hope that she will get well and the doctors are very hopeful.

---

[157] This message is a composite of two, being published in Volume II and Volume III. (G.J.C.)

So you may expect to hear that she is better.

So my own dear Ned, love me and think of me for I love you so much. Kiss me and say good night.

Your own true and loving,
Helen.

The famous giant Goliath of the Philistines affirms that there is no reincarnation after death of the mortal body

November 25th, 1916.

I am here, Goliath.

I have been present for some time and have listened to your conversations on the various sects who are expecting a great teacher and others who look for a reincarnation and if it were not so serious to the welfare of mankind, it would be very humorous. But the matter is too serious to deal with in a humorous vein and I will say a few words as to the utter falsity of both of these beliefs.

There will appear no such great teacher as is expected. Of course, many may appear on earth claiming to be such a teacher and they may declare some moral truth that may be beneficial to mankind but these teachings will not be such as these people may expect a great teacher to make known and the result will be that if the world had to depend on such teachings, it would be very little if any better than it now is, for there is only one course of truth and in order for any great teacher to teach such truths, he necessarily will have to have a knowledge of such truths. And here I want to say that there is only one means of learning such truths and that is through the help of Jesus Christ and his followers, who know these truths and the Holy Spirit that speaks to all men if they will open their souls to its silent voice of truth and love.

So I say that these people who are expecting some earthly teacher to arise and come to them with a knowledge of truth will be greatly disappointed, for it is impossible that any man will ever come in some mysterious and godlike way be endowed with this knowledge. The souls of these people are longing for the truth and not having a knowledge as to how it may come about are willing to conjure up in their minds some being that may possibly burst on the world and enlighten them in those truths for which their souls are longing and wishing. No, they will never in all time and eternity learn what they so anxiously desire from any great teacher of the kind that I have named and they expect.

As to the others who are equally misguided and who believe that their salvation or future condition of happiness and perfection depends on reincarnation, I must say that they are now, and will be, disappointed just as will the first class that I mention. This doctrine of reincarnation is a false and misleading one and will never enable any man or spirit to live the second time in the body as a mortal.

It is so utterly absurd that it is astonishing that men can believe that such a thing can be and besides, if they will only think seriously for a moment, they will realize that there is no necessity for man to live again on earth, for the surroundings and things that prevent the progress of man to perfection are so detrimental to his progress that it would not assist him one particle, in acquiring such progress, to have to undergo a second incarnation.

When the spirit leaves the body, its possibility for progress then becomes greater than ever existed on earth, though some spirits for long ages do not take advantage of such possibilities, yet they exist, and earth life can afford no means equal to them for making this progress towards what these people call Nirvana. Some day the truths will become so plain and easily understood by mortals that these beliefs will of their own weight, and I mean weight that absurdity gives them, that they will cease to exist.

You may be somewhat surprised that I write on these subjects, but you must know that I am an angel of the Celestial Heavens and have a work to do, and being present, I requested the privilege of writing and it being granted, I did so. I know what Divine Love means and what progress means, as I came from the lowest hells and found no necessity for reincarnation, and you may be assured that if my condition of suffering and darkness could have been gotten rid of by reincarnation, I would have reincarnated centuries before I was relieved of my awful condition.

I have met spirits who said they believed in the doctrine, but strange to say, none of them had ever been able to reincarnate though they persisted that they felt assured that other spirits had who were just in that condition that permitted it, and that they would when they became in a condition that was suitable, but I have noticed that these spirits never got in that suitable condition, but progressed in the spirit world and now say that they were mistaken and are thankful that there is no such thing as reincarnation. Well, the race will die and a new race will arise on earth, but in the new race there will not be any who have been reincarnated. I want to stop now, so thanking you, I will say good night.

Your brother in Christ,

Goliath of whom men may think a mythical person. but who really lived and died, even though he may not have been killed by a slingshot of David, as the Bible relates, but yet a real living mortal who followed the ways of other mortals in sinning and dying and gone through hell and is at last redeemed.

Helen confirms the statement, that there is no reincarnation

November 25th, 1916.

I am here, Helen.

Well dear, you have had a somewhat astonishing letter tonight, I mean astonishing when you come to consider the person who wrote it, but it is true, it was really Goliath who wrote, and I may say this because I have met him before and besides the higher (spirits) and even some evil spirits have told me that he is.

Well, he made a very strong argument and I hope that it may be very effective some day in convincing men of its truth. I could have written on the same subject based on the knowledge that I have, but I would have said, and what I should have said, would have been just as true in a few words thus; there will be no such great teacher as these people expect and there is no such thing as reincarnation. Once a spirit, always a spirit. But I must not take the time to write on this matter.

I am very glad that you are feeling better tonight as it makes me able to get closer to you and more in rapport with your condition. I am very happy and want you to be and I am praying for you and asking the Father to bless you with a greater inflowing of His Love.

Mary wants me to say a few words to the Doctor for her. She says she is happy too and sees that the Doctor is and that she is progressing more and more and that even her progress does not keep her from being with him quite often. She has asked me to let her write a long letter to the Dr. and I have promised and very soon she will do so. She says she will go home with him tonight and stay with him until he goes to sleep and will then try to take his spirit with her and give him a taste of the happiness of a sphere that he has never been in, and I will help her and I believe that she will succeed and tell him to prepare for the experiment. And if we succeed we promise to bring him back to his body, which will be the only reincarnation that he will ever experience. So with our love to you both, I will say good night. God bless you both.

Your own true and loving,
Helen.

As a brother and friend, urges Mr. Padgett not to permit his material mind control his spiritual consciousness, which darkens the soul faculties and prevents rapport with higher spirits

December 1st, 1916.

I am here, Judas.

I will say only a few words tonight as I see that you are not just in condition to write a long message.

I wish to say that whenever you let the thoughts of your material mind control your spiritual consciousness, the result is that you suffer a darkening of the soul's faculties and a consequent impossibility to get in rapport with the higher spirits and their condition of exalted truth and the happiness that necessarily accompanies the association of such spirits with your spiritual essence. So you will understand the importance of keeping the purely mental thoughts that are created by or arise from the exercise of the five senses and the reasoning powers, in subordination to the perceptions of the soul that arise from the condition of that soul being in harmony with the truths of the Father.

I know that at times the cares and worries of life will cause the mental faculties to so operate as to obscure or make almost non-existent these faculties of the soul, which alone can perceive and comprehend the spiritual truths of God, that are the only truths that can make men really happy and fitted to enjoy the blessings that the Father is bestowing upon them. I make these abstract suggestions that you may apply them to your own condition of mind, as it has existed for the past few days, and making such application you will realize the force of what I say.

Your worries and dread of impending distress and failure to be able to satisfy the demands upon you, have alienated you, to a large extent, from the higher truths and the rapport that you have heretofore enjoyed and possessed, and have caused much unhappiness to come to you. But being mortal, and realizing the demands that are made upon you as a mortal, it may be quite natural that you should get into that condition of worry and dread, and not be able to realize that these higher spiritual conditions are the more desirable, and the only ones that will bring you happiness and freedom from worry.

I know that so long as you are a mortal the cares of life will be a part of your living, and that they will be of sufficient weight to exercise a powerful influence on your thinking and acting, and that you will scarcely be able to cause the spiritual thoughts and happiness that always flows from them, to set aside and make unreal this material condition. Yet such a thing is possible, and you can bring about this so desirable condition if you will only follow the advice that has been given you by your spirit friends. Pray to the Father and believe.

No, that is true. This desired condition will not of itself bring to you these things that you speak of, but it will help you to endure their absence to a greater extent than you can possibly imagine. Neither does the fact that you worry and fret bring these things; and when you have this need and in addition the condition of mind that worry and dread bring to you, you have a double burden and one which does much harm.

So let me advise you to make every effort to get into that condition that these spiritual acquirements will place you in, and trust to the promises that have been made you as to the material things.

I desire to write merely this tonight to encourage you, and to assure you that you need not let the worries and fears of the future, as to these material wants, take possession of you and deaden the spiritual contentment that may be yours. You will not be abandoned in the particulars mentioned, and you must rely upon the promises that have been made you, and you will find that you will not be forsaken. So think of what I herein say, and give your thoughts to the Father's Love and to the promises of the spirits who are so much interested in you. I will not write more now. With my love and assurance that what has been promised, you may expect, I am

Your brother in Christ,
Judas.[158]

Comments on the mediums' ability to prophecy and says, that no spirit has the gift of prophecy, as mortals term it, arising from a supernatural or omniscient power; as well as encouragement for Mr. Padgett

January 7th, 1917.

I am here, John.

I was with you tonight and heard the alleged prophecies, and was interested in the great number of people that were present, intently listening to the words of the speaker (Mrs Kates). To you, the most significant element in the meeting should be the large number of persons present, evidently interested in the teachings of spiritualism, or in what they supposed might be manifested as the workings of the spirits.

It shows that many of earth are deeply interested in this truth and desire to learn whatever may be taught and demonstrated, and such evidence should be inspiring to you in your work of receiving and preparing the great truths that come to you through the medium of spiritualism. The people are longing for the truths of which they know not, but intuitively feel must exist somewhere, and hope that a revelation of them may in some manner come to their hopeful souls.

So, become more earnest in your desire to receive these truths, and give more of your time, that can be spared from your business, to receiving the messages, and you will the sooner accomplish the work and

---

[158] In 2001 a Divine Love medium began receiving messages from Judas, and eventually some 170 were received. These can be read on the web, but have also been published in print, and as a Kindle eBook. (G.J.C.)

get in stronger rapport with those who write. After tonight we will come more frequently and more regularly, and deliver our messages, and will not permit these other messages that you may call personal, to interfere with the transmission of ours. I am glad that you are in so much better condition tonight, and assure you that you may continue to grow better and better, if you will only follow our advice. Try your best to cast aside your worries. Have faith in us and in our promises and you will not be disappointed. I will come soon and write you another message.

Well, the fact is that she (Mrs. Kates) was controlled by a spirit part of the time that she was speaking, and he suggested to her some of the thoughts that she gave utterance to, but most of her declarations of prophecy came from her own mind, as they had been lodged therein by her observations and thoughts. What she said was really her own prognostications rather than prophecy. The spirit who controlled her, impressed upon her his thoughts as to what the future might be, and her speculations were as reliable as his, except that he has a wider scope of vision as to causes that may bring about results, such as she spoke of. As we have told you before, no spirit has the Gift of Prophecy, as mortals term it, arising from a supernatural or omniscient power; and these prophecies should be accepted with all the allowance that want of knowledge on the part of spirits or mortals will justify.

Some of those who heard her may believe in what she said and be benefitted by it, for she said some things that are helpful, and in that view some good may come from her lecture; but to accept what was said as known truths is a deception, and should not be accepted. I will not write more tonight. Remember what I have said, and believe that I love you and am trying to help you. Good night.

Your brother in Christ,
John.

Agrees with what John has written concerning Mr. Padgett's material and spiritual progression

January 7th, 1917.

I am here, Samuel.

I will say a few words only. I am glad that John wrote so encouragingly, as it will do you good, and I want to substantiate what he said. You may look for better conditions now. Only keep up your courage and have faith in what we write you. You have my love and blessings. So believe in us all, and let not the things that appear insurmountable discourage you.

I will come soon. Good night.

Your brother in Christ,

Samuel.

Confirms the opinion of John regarding the ability of the medium to prophecy

January 7th, 1917.

I am here, Helen.

Well, my dear, I am glad that John wrote you as he did, and you must believe in what he said. I was also glad that you are in so much better condition and that you have set aside your worries. Soon this burden will not come to you and you will be free.

I was with you tonight and heard the prophecies and as John said, they were mostly speculations of the medium and also of the spirit who controlled her. No reliance can be placed upon what she said as prophecies. Many of the things that she mentioned may come true for there are many causes in operation that will bring about some of the effects that she mentioned.

Well, I will not write more tonight, and I would advise you to go to bed early and get up early. It will help you very much in every way.

Believe that I love you and am your own true and loving, Helen.

Writes that there is no one in all the world at this time who is fitted to do the work which you are now doing and which you must continue to do while on earth

February 11th, 1917.

I am here, John.

I come tonight to tell you that your condition of soul is very much better than it has been for some time, and you are more in unison with the Father's Love than you have been for some time and you realize that this Love is working in your soul and making you happy.

I have been with you a great deal today as you copied the messages and saw that you enjoyed the truths that they contained. The message describing the progress of the soul[159] is one that contains the truth of how the soul finds the true way to the Love of the Father and to progress to the Celestial Spheres. It is a very clear and convincing portrayal of the necessary course that every soul must pursue, which comes into the spirit world devoid of the Divine Love. There is no other way in which that soul can find its true development, and the message is

---

[159] Mr. Riddle delivered a message on the Progress of the Soul. This was published in Vol I (5th Ed.) page 154. (J.P.G.)

one that will appeal to the honest seeker after salvation and the happiness which only a perfect atonement with the Father can give.

I also see that you have been thinking a great deal about your future on earth in carrying forward the work that you have been selected to do, and I am glad that the great work is becoming to you a matter of such importance and seriousness; for important it is, not only to the world but to you; and this you will realize when you consider what was told you a few nights ago—that there is no one else in all the world at this time who is fitted to do the work which you are now doing and which you must continue to do during the whole time of your stay on earth.

As you progress in this work and as these truths come to you and your soul becomes more filled with this Love, you will to a greater and greater degree realize and understand the wonderful importance of the work; and you should now bend all your energies to developing your soul, and its perceptions and to carrying forward the work.

We understand as well as you the disadvantages under which you are now laboring and the necessity for getting into that position with the harmonious surroundings that will enable you to give your whole time to the work, and we are endeavoring to bring about these necessary conditions and will succeed in our efforts, and you must have faith; for faith will help you very much to work in conjunction with us and so cause the consummation of our desires and plans much more rapidly.

To us the accomplishing of this work is infinitely of more importance than to you, because we realize as you cannot, what a failure to have these truths made known to men would mean to them in the way of depriving them of opportunities that are so requisite to their future salvation, both on earth and in the spirit world.

So I say, let not yourself become discouraged, but believe, and you will find that our promises will be fulfilled, and the work will go on, and the truths be made known to humanity.

I am with you a great deal, trying to develop your spiritual nature, and by this I mean your soul, for as this develops the better able you will be to receive our truths and properly transmit them to the waiting world, so that men may readily see and understand the truths of God and the only way to His kingdom of Love and immortality. Doubts as to the teachings of the churches are now penetrating and permeating the minds of many, very many of those who are nominally Christians, and the perception of God is almost blunted, and they attend worship only because of a kind of feeling of duty and impression that it is right for them to do so. They know nothing of the Divine Love of the Father's nature and of the plan for their salvation.

Their prayers and worship are only those which come from the lips or a kind of blind intellectual belief. Their soul longings do not enter into their prayers and as a consequence, their petitions for God's Love and mercy go no higher than their heads, as has been said. This condition of men is very injurious to their future welfare and cannot possibly lead them to the Father, and so long as it exists men can never become in an at-onement with Him. Only the inflowing of this Love can reconcile men with God in the higher and desirable sense.

Of course they may become in harmony with Him by a purification of their natural love, but that is the harmony only that existed between Him and the first parents before their fall, and is not the harmony which Jesus taught and which was the object of his mission to teach. When he said "I and my Father are one", he did not refer to the at-onement between the mere image and the substance, but to the at-onement which gives to the souls of men the very substance of Father.

I should like to write more tonight, but you are tired and should not further be drawn on as it will make you feel bad physically. So I will say good night and stop.

Your brother in Christ,
John.[160]

States that very soon a great effort will be made by the Christian spiritualist to spread the Truth

September 20th, 1915.

I am here, John.

I will not write long and merely wish to say that you must continue to have faith and pray.

Soon you will be able to do as the Master has said and you will succeed in getting in the condition to do his work as he desires.

I come to you so often because I am so much interested in your work and in helping forward the great efforts that will be made by the Christian Spiritualist to give to mankind the Truths of the Father.

So believe in what we say and you will find that what we promise you will be realized by you and that you will become free from your worries and very happy in your old age.

I will not write more, but will say good night.

Your brother in Christ,
John.

---

[160] This message is a composite of two, being published in Volume I and Volume III. (G.J.C.)

Writes that there is no doubt among the Celestial Spirits that Jesus has selected Mr. Padgett to do the work of communication between earth and the spirit world

September 20th, 1915.

I am here, John the Baptist.

So you are in condition to believe what we write to you and to rely upon our statements as coming from the fountainhead of truth.

I am so glad that this is so, for I want to see you filled with the Divine Love and with all the power which the Love of the Father filling your heart will bring to you.

Do not let any doubt arise in your soul as to what you have been selected to do, for I tell you that there is no doubt among us who have heard the Master say that he has selected you to do this work.

I will not write more, will pray for you and believe that you will receive all the promises that have been made to you in these writings.

Good night.
Your brother in Christ,
John the Baptist.

Reassures Mr. Padgett that the writers truly are who they represent themselves to be

September 20th, 1915.

I am here, Saint Mark.

Let your faith increase and your belief in the fact that we write to you grow until no doubt will possibly enter into your mind as to who the writers are.

I am here merely to say these few lines and encourage you to put forth every effort to get in condition to receive the message which shall be written to you.

Not much longer will your worries stay with you for you will soon be in condition to start to do those things which your father spoke of so that you will be relieved of your worries.

I will not write more, but will say good night.
Your brother in Christ,
Saint Mark.

Is working to strengthen Mr. Padgett's faith

September 20th, 1915.

I am here, Saint Stephen.

I merely want to say that I am here to try to help you in getting in condition to do the work of the Master. Have faith and you will find that all your desires will be realized and you will soon be able to receive these messages without any difficulty.

I am with you very much trying to impress you with the necessity of this faith and for a belief in what the Master writes to you. So believe and hope for the consummation of these things. I will not write more. So good night.

Your brother in Christ,
Saint Stephen.

A brother lawyer explains his spiritual progress and is happy that Jesus is able to write through his old friend

September 20th, 1915.

I am here, William A. Meloy.

You may be surprised in what I say but I have learned much since I have been in spirit life. I am in the fifth sphere.

Yes, I have seen him but he has not progressed very much. He is in the fourth sphere where he is studying the laws of the spirit world.

Yes, I have seen him and talked to him. He is progressing very rapidly. He tells me that you were the cause of his receiving the light and that you are a wonderful medium and are engaged in taking the messages of Jesus. I was surprised when I heard it and investigated myself and found it to be so, for I have seen the Master writing to you and I also heard many things that he said. Well, you certainly are favored and will find that the frequent interviews with the Master will do you much good.

I sometimes see him and talk to him and I want to say that he is wonderful beyond all conception either of spirit or mortal.

I am glad that I could write tonight and hope that I may find the opportunity to write again.

I am engaged in studying the laws that pertain more to the soul than to what is called nature. I also try to help the spirits who are in darkness and suffering and sometimes try to help mortals.

Well, I must confess that my belief in the trinity was all wrong. I know now that there is only one God and that the Father, and that Jesus is a spirit like the others of us only more refined and filled with the Father's love, more than any spirit in our heavens.

Sometime I will come and give you my opinion more fully and in detail if agreeable. Well, I must stop now.

Your friend and one time brother in the practice of the law,

William A. Meloy.

Confirms the various writers this night and they all were who they represented themselves to be

September 20th, 1915.

I am here, Helen.

Well sweetheart, you have written enough for tonight and must stop.

I want to tell you that the spirits who professed to write actually did so. Mr. Meloy was very much pleased that he could write to you and was a very bright spirit and seemed to be very much interested in the phenomenon of your being able to take his messages. I know that he was anxious to write because when he came he told me that he was an old acquaintance of yours and a brother lawyer and asked that we permit him to write, which we did.

Well, he is a quite comely spirit; he is of the ordinary size and seems to be one who has his full development in so far as the spirit body is concerned.

I must not write more.

Well, they are anxious to write but somehow when these higher spirits come they stand back and let the former write.

But they will now, anxious to write again and you will enjoy their writings, I know. Yes, I know but they wish to impress on you certain important truths and hence in a little different form, they proclaim the same truths. But they will soon change and when writing go more in detail as to the things that they desire to tell you about.

You will be surprised to see how loving and patient he is with you, never a look that indicates that he is tired of being with you or of writing to you, and I know that he loves you very dearly and wants to be with you.

So you must not think that because he is with you so often that he is not the real Jesus, for I tell you that any time you receive a message signed by his name he always writes it.

So good night,
Your own true and loving,
Helen.

Informs Mr. Padgett that he is surrounded by a band of Celestial spirits sending their love and best wishes for his spiritual progression

September 30th, 1915.

I am here, John.

I come to encourage you and tell you that your worries will soon leave you for things will get better with you from now on and you will soon be free of the present burning needs. As the Master, who has just written you says, try to believe in what we tell you for we are with you so very much trying to help and comfort you.

I know that things have looked very dark today and you do not see any relief at hand, but it will come and that very soon and then you will feel different from what you do now. I will not write more tonight as you are not in condition to write very long.

Well, I will say that you are now surrounded by the love and influences of a band of Celestial Spirits all sending to you their best and kindest wishes as well as their love. I am now trying to make you feel my presence and love and if you will open up your heart you will realize that you are surrounded by love. We are many and all anxious that you feel our presence. You must pray to the Father more and ask for more faith. You will receive it and will be correspondingly strengthened.

So let me say before I close that you are the special care of the Master and his love for you tonight was something wonderful. He seemed to let all his love center on you and I do not doubt that you felt its influence.

I will stop now and say that you have my love and blessings.
Your brother in Christ,
John.[161]

Also speaks encouraging words to Mr. Padgett to help increase his faith

September 30th, 1915.

I am here, John the Baptist.

Let not your heart be troubled, believe in God and in the Master. This is as true tonight as it was when spoken by Jesus to his disciples many centuries ago. You are his disciple now just as certainly as were they, and while you cannot see him or hear his voice as they did yet the words are just as emphatically spoken tonight as they were to the other disciples.

You do not realize what love and what powerful influences are with you tonight, else you would let your worries flee to the winds and never return. I merely want to tell you this to let you see that there is

---

[161] This message is a composite of three, being originally published in Volume II and twice in this Volume III. The second instance has been removed in this edition. (G.J.C.)

another of the Celestial Spirits who knows that the Master's promises will be kept. I am not here because I want to encourage you merely, but because I want to tell you a fact, and fact it is, that you will soon be relieved of your worries.

Go to God in prayer and you will find great consolation as we have all found consolation in our troubles, and when on earth we had a great number who were persecuted resulting in the death of many of us. But we had faith, and our faith and the love of the Master helped us over many rough places. I merely want to add another confirmation to those who have told you that you will be relieved of these worries.

I will stop and say, that I am your brother in Christ,
John the Baptist.[162]

Also encourages Mr. Padgett to have faith in what Jesus said today

October 31st, 1916.

I am here James the Apostle.

When you are weakest, then are you strongest, because then you rely more on the power and help of the Father. Such has been your condition tonight, and I want to tell you that you have received a wonderful amount of the Father's Love, and the love of the Master. This I tell you because I know from what I actually have seen. So you should not let your worries trouble you so much. Try to think more of the promises of the Master and of the Love of the Father, and you will realize that help is very near you.

We are all here tonight because we are interested in you and want to see you happy, and you should be so; and if you could only know the love that is surrounding you, you would cease to worry so much. The Master has told you that your worries will leave you soon and you must believe him, for it is true.

I know this, and I can only corroborate what he says, so that you must not continue to let these temporary troubles keep you in such a condition of gloom and despondency. I will not write more tonight. Your brother in Christ,
James the Apostle.[163]

---

[162] This message is a composite of two, being published in Volume II and Volume III. (G.J.C.)
[163] This message is a composite of two, being published in Volume II and Volume III. (G.J.C.)

Assures Mr. Padgett of the great love and power of the master and the Celestial power that surrounds him

September 30th, 1915.

I am here too, and want to assure you that our love is all with you tonight, and we are trying to make you feel that you are not forsaken even though things look very dark and you see very little light. But the light will soon come and with it a relief that will make you realize that the Celestial World is with you in love and power.

I see how worried you have been today and what a condition of helplessness possessed you, but we were with you then and were trying to help and encourage you with our influence.

Trust in the Master for he is more powerful than you think and I know that he will give you the relief that you need. I will not write more tonight, but will say I am

Your brother in Christ,
Luke.[164]

A brother lawyer, dropped in to pay a visit and explain his disappointment on entering the spirit world

November 7th, 1915.

I am here, John Critcher.

You must remember me, for I had my office in the same building with you when I practiced law.

Well, I am in a condition that gives me considerable happiness, and yet I am not in that state of happiness which I expected to have when I was on earth.

As you know, I was an Episcopalian and tried to observe strictly the doctrines and formalities of my church, and expected when I died to go to heaven and find rest and nothing to make me unhappy.

But I was mistaken in this, and I found myself in the earth plane of the spirit world, and had to undergo some suffering and darkness, and did not find the heavenly rest that I expected.

But I have progressed since I came over, and am now happier and in more light.

I was passing, when I saw the light that comes from your room, and looked in and saw you, and asked permission to write, and your band consented and so I am writing.

---

[164] This message is a composite of two, being published in Volume II and Volume III. (G.J.C.)

No, thank you, only sometimes you can give me a kind thought and good wish.

So thanking you, I am

Your friend,

John Critcher.

A former law partner of Mr. Padgett's, is now a part of his band of workers as well as protectors from the spirit side of life

September 24th, 1915.

I am here, your old law partner. (A. G. Riddle)

It has been a long time since I wrote you and I have missed the opportunity very much. I know that you expressed the desire to hear from me, but there were so many other spirits who wanted to write, that I thought it best to abstain for a while and let them write. Soon I will come and write you a long letter, and tell you of my progress and of some spiritual truths which I have learned. Well, I will tell you of them also.

What a wonderful thing was Ingersoll's conversion! And I must tell you that it was genuine, for now he is one of the most earnest workers we have. He does not belong to our band, but is working with us. He does not seem to be able to leave your grandmother whenever she is with us. He says she is the most beautiful spirit and orator he has ever heard. Of course he expects (?) Jesus, but his attraction to her is wonderful and beyond our comprehension. He will tell you himself, sometime, of how much he thinks of her.

Poor Perry is still in darkness. It is a hard matter to convince him of the truths of salvation, but we are all trying to help him.

No but they are much improved in their condition and have considerable of the love of the Father. I think that very soon they will be in the third sphere.

I see that you are tired so I will not write more,

Your old partner,

A. G. Riddle.

Attended a Church Service with Mr. Padgett and tells of the various relatives that tried to contact him that he never knew

November 7th, 1915.

I am here, Helen.

Dear old Ned, of course when you call me I must come. I see you are tired and I will not write much.

I was with you at the church and the medium saw the spirits she described, for they were present. The Sarah was Cousin Sally, as you call her, and she showed the medium her funeral at the little town where she lived.

The child was a stranger, but seemed to be attracted to you, and wanted to talk and tell you something. She was very young and very lovely. Her name was Rosebud, and she was a bud, because when she came to the spirit world she was only a few days old. We have all petted and loved her since she came to you, and I expect that she will be with you often for she seems to be drawn to you.

The James was a spirit that I never knew, but he says he was your uncle, your father's brother, and that he was anxious to make his presence known to you. He is not a very bright nor yet a very dark spirit.

Well, you must remember that the band of attraction between your father and him has died, for they are in altogether different spheres, and, as I have told you before, that fact that spirits were related on earth does not bind them together in the spirit world. When a spirit first comes into the spirit world, the relatives, unless they live in a very high sphere, generally meet it, but after a little time that attraction ceases and they seldom meet and so it is that I never met your uncle. Of course your father knows many spirits here that I don't know. So you see, the spirit world in that particular is not very different from the earth world. You have cousins whom you have never met and do not know the existence of, and so we spirits here have many relatives that we never see or know. I know this may seem strange, but it is a fact.

I will write a long letter soon, but I must stop now. You are tired. So with all my love, I am

Your own true and loving,
Helen.

A friend of Mr. Padgett's writes that when on earth he believed in the New Birth but found It quite different upon entering the spirit world

December 18th, 1917.

I am here, William R. Woodward.

Let me say a word as I have listened to your conversation and to me the most of it is Greek, for while I understand your words and sentences, I do not comprehend your meaning. What do you mean by transformation of the soul? I am a spirit who when on earth believed in the New Birth and regeneration, and believed that I was the subject of both and was fitted when I died to enter into the mansions of the redeemed and enjoy the presence of God and of Jesus, but I have found that since I became a spirit I am no more in the presence of God than I was on earth.

I was taught that by receiving the New Birth, and, as I understood that meant to believe on the Lord Jesus Christ and accept him as my savior and become baptized, I would be saved—as I said I was taught that this New Birth was all that I was required to have in order to become an inhabitant of Jesus' heavens; and now I know that teaching did not bring me to heaven, and when I hear you speak of the transformation of the soul by the New Birth your teachings sound very much like those that I was taught when on earth, and I wonder if you are not suffering under the same delusion that I was.

You talk as if you know what you say to be true and that you actually know, as a fact, that there is a transformation of the soul that results from this New Birth. I hope you are not mistaken, for if there be any such fact, I would like to hear it and the way to obtain it. So if you can enlighten me, do so. I know what you say in words, but that does not satisfy me. I want that, if there be such, which is back of words, can you help me?

Well, I see a spirit, and he is very beautiful and says, he will help me to understand if I will sincerely listen to him and I will, so good night. I am William R. Woodward whom you knew when I was on earth.

Your friend.

A school acquaintance is seeking help from Mr. Padgett

January 31st, 1917.

I am here, George C. Calvert.

I was an acquaintance of yours when you were a student at New Market, and you will recollect me when I recall your memory to the fact that I was called "Judge." Well, I came, because I saw that other spirits were writing you, and when I looked at you I remembered you, and then desired to write.

I am in what is called the dark plane and have been for some time now, though when I first entered the spirit world I went into the hells and suffered a great deal. But I am thankful that I have gotten out of the conditions that suited me for those places, and am now in a brighter plane and in less suffering. I don't know that you can do anything for me but some spirits say that you have helped them and if that be true I should like for you to help me. I am willing to do most anything to get into a better condition, and if you will do what I say, I will appreciate it very much and try to follow your advice.

No, I should like to be surprised. Well, I have looked, and I see some wonderfully bright and beautiful spirits, but I don't recognize any of them. Wait a moment—one is coming to me and I am surprised, for it is Prof. Salyards. How wonderful! Why he is really handsome! Well, well, dear old Prof. He says he is glad to see me and that I must go with him, and I certainly will. I thank you very much and will come again.

Good night,
Your old friend.

A brother lawyer, in darkness, learned that Mr. Padgett was helping spirits in darkness and thought that he would not refuse to help him

March 19th, 1915.

I am here, Samuel R. Phillips.

I was an acquaintance of yours and a lawyer as you will remember, and I desire to ask you to give me some assistance in getting out of this condition of darkness in which I am now living.

Well, I have heard other spirits say that you have helped them, and so I came, and remembering that I was your brother lawyer on earth and had an acquaintance with you, I presumed that you would not refuse to assist me. Yes, R., that is correct.

I don't know why I am in darkness, except that I did not develop my spiritual nature when on earth. I did not understand very much about spiritual things or the soul, and hence when I came to the spirit world I was a very unenlightened spirit. I cannot explain this thing. All I know is that I am in darkness and need light.

Well, I was a member of the church but that did not mean that I knew anything of the truths of the spiritual things. I read the Bible and understood what it said, but I did not understand what it meant in the inner and spiritual sense. My religion was purely intellectual, and now I find that is not sufficient to relieve me from the darkness which I am now experiencing.

Yes, I believed in God, but not in Jesus as a God, but thought him to be a very good and wonderful teacher.

Well, as to prayer, I never gave much thought of it; of course, as the people prayed in response to what the minister might read I read too, but I never really prayed. It was all formal and not the longing of my heart as some have said a prayer should be. But I do not understand what prayer has to do with my present condition of darkness.

Well, as I don't understand, I don't seem to appreciate what you say. Tell me more fully what you mean, so that I may make the effort to comprehend your meaning.

Well, I am happy in a way, but not as I expected. I believed that God was all goodness, and that all his children would be happy in the spirit world, but I find that I am not so. I am somewhat disappointed and also very much at a loss to understand.

No. I have had no remorse or realization that I committed any very great sin on earth for which I should suffer here. Of course I was, I suppose, very much like other men who are not very immoral. I never indulged in immorality to any extent and tried to do the right thing towards my neighbor, and hence do not understand why I should have remorse or lashings of conscience.

No. I never have tried to examine myself very much to learn how I compare with the ideal Christian as portrayed by the teachings of Jesus, but I will do so. There may be something in what you say, and it may be that I have not sought the truth as to the cause of my darkness. Yes, I see a number of spirits who seem to be in darkness also, and who say that they are anxious and waiting to talk to you.

Well, I do see some bright spirits and they certainly are beautiful, and seem so loving. Why they look at me with great eyes of love and sympathy, as if they would like to help me.

Well, I am surprised, for there is Riddle my old friend and brother lawyer. Why is he so bright and beautiful? He thought, when on earth, very much as I did about the things of the spiritual world.

He says that he is glad to see me, and invites me to go with him, for a talk, and I will go.

So my dear friend, I will say to you.

Good night, and good luck.

An abortionist realizes only too late the great wrong she performed on earth and is seeking help

I am here, Sarah J. Wilson.

Let me write as I need help so very much. I am in darkness and suffering. When on earth i was a woman who tried to make my living by doing that which God and man both condemned as against nature and all the provisions for perpetuating the world. I was an abortionist and caused many a premature birth, or the destruction of that which if it had been permitted to gestate would have been a human being. So you see my deeds were so very evil; and since I have been in the spirit world I have realized the enormity of them.

Of course, when I committed these acts I knew that I was doing wrong, and committing in many cases murder. But the desire to make money was so great that my crimes did not appear to me in all their nakedness and enormity. But now I see them face to face, and I realize that I am of all wretches the most wretched. I have never known a moment's peace since I have been a spirit, and it seems to me that I have been such a spirit for centuries and centuries.

No ray of light ever comes to me and no word of love or sympathy. My associates are just like myself, steeped in sin of one kind or another and never a ray of hope comes to us. I wonder sometimes why I was ever born and why I cannot die and forever be annihilated. But that consolation is not mine. I must live and suffer and pay the penalties of my deeds done in the body.

I thought that I was a kind hearted woman in most of the affairs of life, and I believe that my neighbors so considered me. I often helped the poor and fed the hungry, and spoke words of kindness to the distressed, and I really thought that I was a good woman. But now, how useless all these deeds of apparent kindness seem to me, for they do not weigh a grain of sand to a mountain in my favor. So you see the great sins that I committed have no way of being blotted out. I wish that I had never been born.

Well, sometimes I am told that some of the little children who live in higher lands are the children whom I deprived of the earth life. I, of course, do not know, but some spirits tell me this, and when I learn this it helps me some to think that even though I deprived them of their earthly existence, yet they are alive in a brighter and happier land. But this is not sufficient to relieve me of my sufferings. I killed them when on earth and I had no right to do it.

I am being punished. And even when on earth I tried to make myself believe that there was no hell. I know now that there is a hell and that I am in it, and believe that I will never get out of it.

Well I could tell you of many instances of my sinning but it will do no good. I feel that I have told you enough to arouse your pity, and that if you can help me you will.

I was married but had no children and sometimes I think that if I had had children of my own I would not have engaged in the business of destroying others. But now it is too late and I must suffer. I will do anything that you tell me, and will try to believe and follow the advice that may be given me. Only do something for me.

I have asked for Mrs. Salyards and a beautiful spirit comes to me, and put her arm around me and says "you are my sister in trouble and a child of God just as I am, and He loves you just as He loves me so come with me and I will love you and try to show you the way to light and happiness." So I am going.

Oh, dear friend, I thank you and with all my heartfelt tears and gratitude I say good night,

Sarah J. Wilson.

Claims to have been bad when on earth, is trying to get out of darkness

I am here, Bill Tucker.

Let me write just a little bit as I need help. I am suffering because I was a bad man when on earth, and did so much harm to my fellowman. I was a very great thief, and robbed many men and women while I was living. So you see, I must suffer now; just as I enjoyed the things I stole so I must suffer now for having had that enjoyment.

Well, I am in darkness and suffering. I don't know whether it is hell or not. I don't see any fire or brimstone, but the torture is here, all right. Gee, it I had only known what would happen to me I never would have stolen as I did, but I did not know and thought that I was only doing what I had the right to do.

I want to get out of this place, and I wish I could go back to earth again and undo what I have done, but I can't, so what can I do?

My name was Bill Tucker and I lived in New York City, and died only a few years ago.

Well, I have asked for him, and he says come on Bill, and I am going, so you must excuse me now.

Good night.

A wandering spirit is looking for help as he is more or less lost

I am here, Solomon P. Brown.

Let me write just a few lines and tell you how unhappy I am and how much I need your help. Well, I was not a very bad person, but merely did not do what I should have done to help my fellow man to become happy and prosperous.

Because I was selfish and thought that I needed everything for myself. But now I see that I was all wrong and that I must try to right the matter, but I don't know how. Tell me if you can.

I live on the earth plane, but I am not happy as I tell you.

I don't know anything about God except in a general way as a being who created the world and sends the bad to hell and the good to heaven.

Well, that is one thing that has confused me. I am neither in heaven nor in hell, and where I am I don't just know; but I know that I am a spirit and do suffer and am not very happy. So if you please, tell me where I am and what I must do to get to a better place.

My name was Solomon P. Brown and I lived in a town named Bridgeport, Connecticut. I died in 1892, and I have been here ever since wandering around in hope to find some way to get out of this unhappy condition.

Yes, I was married, but my wife is still on earth and enjoying herself in a second marriage, and I don't blame her, for if I could find someone here who I thought could add to my enjoyment I would get married too. But I have never seen any marriages here, and I suppose they don't have any.

Well, I will go with him. He says all right come along and I am going.

So my dear sir, good night.

Is seeking help because on earth he made many animals to suffer

I am here, Samuel Williams.

Let me write for a while. I am in darkness too, and need help so much.

I was a man that lived a very wicked life in the way of causing many animals to suffer in order that I might get paid for my work in the way of helping the doctors to cut them up alive. I collected the animals and sold them to the doctors, and knew at the time what they were to be used for. So I was as much to blame as the doctors. I am now suffering for doing these things, and I want help, if you can give me any.

I have been here a very short time as you might say, but to me it seems a century of years. Please help me if you can. I need it so much.

Yes, I will do as you say. I was a white man when on earth, but I am very dark now.

I have asked for him and he says that he will help me and calls me to him, and I am going. So good night.

Samuel Williams.

Is in darkness and is seeking help

I am here, Julius Soloman.

Let me write a little, for I need help too, and the quicker I get it the better.

Well, I am in darkness and am suffering for my deeds, which I did on earth. I was a very wicked man and did not do what I know I should have done. I was a man who tried to make my living by letting other people use my money for a large and usurious interest. Well, I made my living and more besides, but I made my hell at the same time.

You may think this strange, as some argue that money is a commodity like anything else, and is worth just what it means to the needs of people, and that if people want it they should only borrow, when what they pay in the way of interest is no more valuable to them than is the money which they borrow. And this is all right as a mere matter of logic. Because money is a thing which when borrowed, should be paid for according to its value to the borrower, just as any other commodity should be paid for according to its value.

Of course this value changes, and sometimes the commodity is cheaper and sometimes dearer. But in my business the money was never cheaper and its value depended on what estimate I placed upon it and not what the borrower might think it worth. So you see, I was not only the judge as to what should be paid but was the one to withhold if that fixed value was not paid.

I now see the enormity of this method of stealing from the poor and necessitous (lacking the necessities of life) their money. There was nothing fair or honorable about my dealings, and many a poor man and woman has been made to starve and lose their all by reason of my exactions. (the action of demanding and obtaining something from someone, especially a payment)

So no sophistry or splitting of hairs will suffice now to show me that I was acting legitimately with my unhappy customers. So I am realizing this great sin of mine and suffering very much and would give the world to find relief. Hence I came to you in the hope that I may get relief of some kind.

I know that it may be said that I was no worse than many others, but that does not excuse me or lessen my sin, for I am not responsible for what others may do, but am for what I do myself. I certainly am sorry for my course of life as explained to you; and if it were in my power, I would restore to every man and woman the smallest farthing that I unjustly took from them, but as you know that we cannot do.

After we enter this life we cannot make restoration in material things, and so I am forever barred from making recompense. Oh, why did I not realize all this when I was on earth and engaged in that awful business! So if you can tell me any way in which I can find relief, I will be obliged if you will do so—and will try to follow your advice.

Well they are all like myself, dark and unhappy, and wandering about seeking rest and peace and never finding them. I am not very sociable here, and, consequently, cannot tell you just what evil deeds they are suffering from; but I suppose their deeds were bad like mine or they would not be suffering so much and have to live in such darkness.

Yes, I was a Jew and belonged to the synagogue, but that does not help me. I never believed that it was wrong to cheat the gentile; but now I know that a sin is a sin no matter upon whom it is committed—and in my heart I know at the time that it was wrong to take the money from the poor and needy. Yes, I see many, but why do you ask me? They don't seem to be in any better condition than I am, and need help as much as I do, if they are telling the truth, for they are shouting to me to stop writing.

Yes, I see some bright ones. Well I have asked for your father, and he says that I shall come with him and I am going.

So I will say good night.

Julius Soloman.

Had a theatrical career and is in darkness with others of the same profession

I am here, Louisa R. Connell.

Let me write a little for I am in darkness also, and need help so very much.

I was not a very good woman when on earth, nor yet a very bad one as I then thought. I was engaged in the theatrical business, and was considered a very fine singer and dancer; but I now see that my life was not one that helped me after I came to this world of truth and nakedness. I mean that nothing is hid here. I am seen just as I really exist, and I can hide nothing, or make myself appear other than I really am. I am suffering from the recollections of that earth life and the experiences that I had on the stage.

I was married to a man who was an actor, and like myself never gave any thought to the higher things of life; and so we both were satisfied to live in the atmosphere which a theatrical life throws around those who live in it.

I, of course, was a good woman in the sense of being chaste, for I have that consolation and it helps me some; especially when I consider the many temptations that surround a woman of the stage. But thank God, I maintained my chastity, and I believe that recollection has been a great help to me here. But I did many other things, which I now see were not right, and from which I am suffering and am kept in darkness. I don't know how to get out of it and hence I come to you.

Well, when I was a child I went to church and Sunday school, and was taught what a child is usually taught there; but I have to confess that my teachings made no lasting impression on me, and after I became a woman and started my career of singing and dancing, I never gave those teachings a thought.

My thoughts were given to becoming a star as we say, and a successful actress and singer; but, as you know, that did not help my spiritual nature, as I have now found to be the fact. So I am now a spirit, and am without very much knowledge of the things which I suppose are necessary for me to know to get out of this darkness.

No, he is not, he is still on earth and is not now on the stage, but is living a very respectable life with his family, for we had several children. My name was Louisa R. Connell, and I lived in London, England,

and died in 1877, at that place.

No, I have never been taught the way to light, as you say, I have met some spirits who said that they were living in a higher sphere, and could help me if I would only listen to them; but I refused because they did not seem to me to be any different from myself, and I did not believe that they could help me.

My associates have been spirits like myself—some of them theatrical people, who knew no more about spiritual things than I did. We are all in darkness and need help. Well, I will try to do as you say—only show me the way. Yes, I see a great many spirits, and they tell that I must hurry as they wish to write, but they don't seem to be any better than I am.

Well I see more bright spirits about you and they are very beautiful, and I wonder how they can be so beautiful.

She answers and says of course she will take me with her, and help me, and love me too. And now she says come with me and I am going and will try to believe as you told me to.

So my dear friend I must say good night.

A message from White Eagle

April 2nd, 1915.

I am here, White Eagle.

I have told them and they are now learning and seem disappointed but will go willingly. I told them what you said about asking your band but they say they want to talk to you first and I don't believe they will be satisfied unless they do so.

Only your wife and White Eagle.

Yes, I was there and wanted to talk but the Indian Squaw would not let me and I gave her a piece of my mind and she only laughed and said that you would understand. She is a beautiful girl though.

I was there and sat at your feet all evening and enjoyed the meeting. Your wife came and talked and she certainly did love you. She could scarcely talk because she felt so full of love.

Well, I will write you soon and tell you some things that you should know.

So with my love, will say, good night,

White Eagle.

A message from Helen

April 2nd, 1915.

I am here, Helen.

Well sweetheart, you have had a long night of writing and I must not write much. I am happy and love you and know that you love me.

So try to forget your cases (legal?) and think more of me and my love. You had better go to bed soon and rest.

With all my love and best wishes.

I am your true and loving, Helen.

A grateful spirit writes to thank Mr. Padgett for the help, he had received from him

I am here, Joseph G. Godfrey.

Let me write for a short time, as I am very desirous of writing you in reference to some things that have been in my mind for a long time with the desire to communicate the same to you. You may not know who it is that writes, but that makes no difference as the subject matter that I shall communicate constitutes the important thing to be considered.

As I said, I have thought of these things for a long time and now that I have the opportunity will not hesitate to convey the same to you.

As you may not know, I am one of the spirits which came to you several years ago in much darkness and suffering and asked your help and you were so good as not only to tell me of the way by which I could get out of my sufferings and into light but also brought to my assistance a beautiful, bright spirit who instructed in the way and patiently endeavored to cause me to see the light and learn the way to happiness.

I cannot express to you my gratitude or the appreciation of the wonderful good you did me or the joys that now are mine; but this I can say, that in all eternity I never will be able to repay you the great debt that is owing to you by me, and many others who have had experiences similar to my own. Only we who have experienced the torments of hell can appreciate the greatness of the relief after we have come into a new and different existence. I hope that you will pardon my intrusion, as I could no longer refrain from expressing to you my gratitude for your kindness. Good night.

May the Father bless you in all your undertakings and make your soul happy in the Love, which is now mine.

So believe that I am very grateful.

Your friend,

Joseph G. Godfrey.

Writes about his suffering and darkness that he is in and is asking for help

November 20th, 1915.

Let me write, John G. Carlisle.[165]

I merely want to say that I need help so much. I am suffering so very much and in such darkness, and I can find no relief from my condition. So please tell me if you can help me. Some spirits here say that you have helped others and I want help if it can be found.

It is not necessary for me to tell you who I am, or what I did on earth for you, as many others in Washington, knew just what kind of life I led when I lived in that city, as I was a prominent man and my actions were watched and known by a great many.

Suffice it to say that I am now paying the penalties for my evil life, and I am in torture and such intense darkness, and don't know the way to relief if there is any for me. I want you to help me, and if you can and will do so, I will never forget you.

I will come and claim your promise; and if you can succeed I will be everlastingly obliged.

Yes I have seen him (Cleveland) on several occasions and have talked with him, but he seems to be in a better condition than I am for some reason that I don't understand. We were very much alike in certain particulars when on earth, but he seems to have found some means by which he is enabled to live in a brighter state than I do.

No, I have never met Mr. Riddle and don't know that he is in the spirit world, but from what you say I suppose he is. But why do you ask? You know that I knew a great many of the public men, and so very many better than I knew Riddle, and hence I am a little anxious to know why you ask me if I have seen him. Well, you make me anxious to meet him, and should I do so, I will remember what you say.

Well I have looked, and I see some beautiful spirits but I don't know any to them. I have asked who they are, and one says she is your wife, and what a beautiful spirit she is, and how good and loving her appearance. I wonder why she is of such beauty! I have asked her, and she says she will try and has left me.

Well, he is here and how surprised I am, for he is beautiful and bright, too, and seems to have so much love about him. What is the

---

[165] John Griffin Carlisle (September 5th, 1834 – July 31st, 1910) was a prominent American politician in the Democratic Party during the last quarter of the 19th century. He served as the Speaker of the United States House of Representatives, from 1883 to 1889 and served as Secretary of the Treasury, from 1893 to 1897, during the Panic of 1893. As a Bourbon Democrat he was a leader of the conservative, pro-business wing of the party, along with President Grover Cleveland. (Source: Wikipedia) (G.J.C.)

cause of all this wonderful beauty and brightness?

Well, he has spoken to me, and tells me that he is glad to see me, and that he is willing and anxious to help me out of my darkness, and wants me to go with him for a talk, and I am going. I will try to do as you say, and will certainly make every effort to understand this great mystery.

So my friend, I must leave you, but in doing so I want to express to you my gratitude for what you have done, and for your kind thoughts. So believe me when I say that I am very grateful.

Goodbye,

Your friend, John G. Carlisle.

Tells Mr. Padgett why she called him to write

November 20th, 1915.

I am here, Helen

I called you because when the spirit (J. G. Carlisle) who wrote came he was in such a very bad and suffering condition and begged so piteously to write that I thought it would be doing a great act of love and mercy to let him write. He is a very ugly and dark and deformed spirit in his appearance, and while a man of great intellect, yet his soul is almost in a condition of death. That is, it has no conscious life, for it was literally starved and was not capable of seeing or feeling any of the higher or better impulses.

So when he came and said that he needed help so much, we let him write. He is now with Mr. Riddle, and I hope that he may find some light and relief, though I fear that he will have a struggle to believe what may be told him, for as you may know, when the soul becomes all shrunken and dead, it is hard for the intellect to believe anything which pertains to the awakening of the soul. But everything is possible with God and this man is not beyond redemption.

I believe, though, that he will have a long course of soul development before he will see the light and realize that his sufferings are leaving him. He must have been a very wicked man on earth, for he has about him all the traces and evidences of a very abandoned and wicked life. *"Their sins do follow them saith the Lord,"* and I may add, stay with them until the great law of compensation has been complied with, or the greater law of Divine Love has supplanted it.

You must not write more now.

So goodbye,

Your own true and loving,

Helen.

A friend of Mr. Padgett's, is seeking his help to get out of darkness

March 7th, 1916.

I am here, John G. Carlisle.

I am the spirit who wrote you once before (two messages above) and I merely want to say tonight that I am better than I was then and am not in so much darkness; but yet I suffer and am paying the penalty for my sins.

The advice that you gave me and also the help that I received from Mr. Riddle have benefitted me a great deal, and I am hoping that sometime I may get into the light and be free from my sufferings.

If I could only have faith in what he and other good spirits tell me I believe that I would soon be in a much better condition, but somehow I don't seem to be able to have this faith. My old ideas stick to me, and although I realize that many of them were wrong, yet they cling to me and hold me in the darkness and sufferings. This may seem strange to you, but it is a fact. Beliefs are wonderful things of substance and strength when they have become fixed in a man's mind by long years acquiescence and fostering, and that was my case.

As you may know, my animal appetites were strong and I gave free vent to them, and to ease my conscience I embraced certain beliefs, which as I lived and fostered them, came to be realities to me, and now they stand before me, as it were, like a wall of brass and rarely give me an opening to get beyond or out of them. My friends that you brought to me are trying to help me, and at times I feel that what they tell me must be true. But then comes in the old long years of belief, and I lose the benefit of what influence I may have received from these spirits who I see are so beautiful and happy.

I do not understand this enigma, and because I do not I sometimes think that what I think I see in these others are mere hallucinations of my own mind. And then again these influences come to me with such force that I think I must break away from these bands of belief and see the light as they see it. But the struggle is hard and the progress is slow. I tell you that if I could only come again into my earth life, I know that my life or rather the way I lived it would be very different, but it is too late now and I must make my fight here, and it is a hard one.

The thing that gives me greatest hope is that while Riddle may not have been so bad a man as I was on earth yet he was a mere man with no special pretensions to goodness, and now I see him a beautiful and happy spirit, and he says it is not on account of any inherent goodness in himself, but because he has received to some degree what he calls the Divine Love; and he urges me to try to believe in this Love and open up my soul to its inflowing. It may be right, but I don't seem to be able to understand what he means, or to find the way to open up my soul as he advises.

But this I know, he has given me hope, and I at times make the effort to follow his advice, and I even pray, but I am afraid that my faith is not very strong, though I observe that when he is with me I seem to have more power to make this effort than when I am alone. And he is kind to me, for he comes quite frequently, and at times, there comes with him a wonderfully beautiful spirit who he says is your wife, and she seems to have so much love with her. I say she comes with him, and when she does, her influence is wonderful and I feel nearer leaving my old evil thoughts and getting into light than at any other time. And she talks to me in such words of love and encouragement, that it makes me believe that there must be a better place and a better condition for me.

So you see from all this what thoughts and beliefs cemented to a man's soul by an evil life on earth will do for him when he becomes a spirit and all these evil things come before him like a panorama as they do in my case. But I sowed and I am now reaping, a saying which I often heard on earth, but which to me was meaningless as it is, I have no doubt, to many others who are living such lives as I lived.

Well, my friend, I must not write more, but I feel better for I realize that it does me good to come in contact in the way of exchanging thoughts with a mortal for notwithstanding I have no mortal body, yet in thought and desires I am still a mortal.

So, thanking you for your kindness to me I will say good night.
Your friend, John G. Carlisle.[166]

An old friend and chum of Mr. Padgett's, describes his condition on entering the spirit world and tells about the help that he received there to obtain the light

March 7th, 1916.

I am your old friend and chum, Frank Davis.

Well, I am glad to be able to write you, a thing when on earth, I never expected anybody could do, and it is only recently that I learned that such a method of communication could be used.

I am quite happy now, but when I first came to the spirit world I was in considerable darkness and suffered some. As you may know I was an ordinarily good man when on earth, by that I mean I never had any

---

[166] We hear again from this spirit 18 months later, but just a few messages further on in this Volume. (G.J.C.)

really bad or vicious habits which a great many men have, and I loved my wife and children very much and died loving them.

You also know that I was not what was called an orthodox Christian having imbibed my beliefs from my father, but I believed in God and, also, that he would not be severe on me for my short comings when I should come to stand in His presence. But I now know that there were other things that I should have believed and experienced in order to fit me for a condition of happiness which I firmly expected would be mine.

I have found that belief is a very important thing, both on earth and in the spirit world, and that these creations of the mind have a wonderful influence in determining the happiness or the contrary of a spirit in this life.

I never had any of the Love of God in my heart, except in a general way, which was, I suppose, of the same nature as the love for my family, but, I am afraid, not to the extent that I loved them. And also, I rather prided myself on my own moral excellence, and supposed such qualities would be sufficient to make me a pretty happy spirit, but I soon found my mistake. When we come to offset our moral qualities against the evil thoughts and deeds of our earth life they are largely in the minority and don't count for very much while these evil thoughts and deeds, or rather the recollection of them exist in our minds and memories.

Well, it will do no good to rehearse the experience of my earth life now, but I found myself in darkness and suffering and realized that I was paying the penalties for the sins that I had committed. But after awhile these recollections commenced to leave me and I found that I was getting into more light and less suffering, but the movement was very slow, and at times, hardly perceptible.

After a while I met some beautiful and loving spirits who seemed to take an interest in me, and told me of the way to get rid of my sufferings and to reach the planes of light where happiness was, and I had to listen to them, for I saw that they were so superior to me, and they told me that they had been mortals like myself and had come up out of darkness and suffering such as I was then undergoing. Well, to make a long story short, I finally acted on their advice and found that way, and you will not be surprised when I tell you that the way was through and by the Divine Love of the Father. I tell you this because I know, and all the speculations of philosophers and religionists cannot bear a feather's weight in the argument against my "know." Yes, I found this Love or rather it found me and now I am very happy.

I am in the third sphere and am trying my very hard for more faith and more Love, and I know that I will get it, because I have before me every moment living examples in those who have received it to a wonderful degree and are still receiving it and progressing.

As we in the long ago were old chums and thought a great deal of each other, I thought that you would be interested in knowing that I am happy and a redeemed child of the Father and on my way to spheres celestial.

Well, I will not write more tonight, but sometimes I should like to come and have a real heart to heart chat about old times, for though those are things of the past and not to be compared with what I have now in the way of experience, yet as you are on earth I feel that we might both enjoy talking over old times, because we used to have some happy times together.

So with all the old time friendship and love, and with a new love too, I will say good night.

Frank Davis.

Writes that she sees both Carlisle and Davis and is trying to help them both to come into the light

March 7th, 1916.

I am here, Helen.

I come and am glad to do so, as I have been waiting some time for some of your old earth friends to finish their writings.

I rather enjoyed the last letter for it showed me that earth ties of friendship still survive for a while anyhow, in this world and that a meeting of long parted friends brings happiness. I see Mr. Davis quite often and we talk of you and of the times of your earth life.

I also try to help him and he is progressing and is in the right road to the high spheres.

Well, sweetheart, I see that you are very tired and must stop so I will not write longer though I should like to very much.

So give me a hug and a kiss and say good night.

Your own true and loving,

Helen.

Has progressed into the light within the past year with the help of Mr. Padgett and his Celestial Spirits

September 29th, 1917.

I am here, John G. Carlisle.

Well my friend, I have not written you for some time, not because I did not desire to do so, but because I have not had the opportunity; for I have been present many times when other spirits were here writing you. I have also been present when you and your friends have talked about spiritual things and have listened with very close attention, and have derived much benefit from thinking of what you have declared to be the truths of the spiritual kingdom.

As a consequence, I have progressed very much and am now in considerable light, and have received into my soul sufficient of this Love that you talk of, to be convinced that it is a wonderful redeeming influence from the darkness and suffering that I and spirits like me found ourselves in when we came to the spirit world. I know that prayer is a thing that brings its response and I am praying with all my soul, but it is hard to make a complete surrender of my beliefs and to forget the deeds of my life that cling to me with such very great tenacity.

While, as you have said in your conversations, and as some of the bright spirits tell me, the true longings of the soul will bring to my soul this Love, yet I find it difficult to get these longings so that they are not mingled with the thoughts of earthly things that came with me when I became a spirit. As you know, when on earth I accumulated in my memory a large and varied amount of evil and sin, and when I became a spirit I found it very natural that these memories should be with me and control my thoughts and desires as they did on earth. In fact, they seemed to get rid of some member of my body without injuring the body.

So you will see, it is not so easy to have these longings that I speak of, and even if a spirit makes up his mind and will to have the longings, he cannot always succeed. This has been my experience, and I have suffered so very much in consequence of this inability to direct my will to these longings. Intellectually I understand that this is necessary and that the longings, when earnestly possessed, will bring relief and surcease (To bring to an end) from these sufferings, but this intellectual knowledge, I find is not sufficient. The knowledge does not bring the power to will, and the will is controlled by appetites and desires. I know that I must try to control these appetites and desires, but oh, how hard is the task!

It is very foolish for men to suppose that they can cultivate and exercise these desires and appetites until a time convenient to them, and then by the mere wish control these desires and have these longings and aspirations come to them so that the help that comes in response to prayer will be theirs. No, they will find themselves greatly disappointed, for they will realize that these desires and the results of their indulgences will bind them in bands of iron, that a mere intellectual attempt to sever will not prove efficacious.

The spirits who all have this Love of which they tell me, teach me that this Love is sufficient to bring happiness to me, and that it will come in response to earnest prayer, but they do not tell me that by the sudden exercise of my will I can obtain these true longings, and if they should so teach, I could hardly believe them, for I have had such a will and have attempted to pray, and as I think wanted to be in all earnestness, but still the longings would not come free from the memories of my sinful life on earth; and I find, that I have to continue to pray in order to progress the little that I have progressed.

I have no doubt that the Love is waiting for me and that I will be enabled to obtain it by the proper condition of my longings, but the trouble is to get the proper longings. It is not so easy to get rid of the effects of evil deeds and evil thoughts on earth, and the mere praying with the mind will not help except such prayers become merged into the prayers of true longings.

Well, I realize all this in my own experience and I am praying and longing, and sometimes I feel the true longings, and then comes the response and I progress just that much. I mean in proportion to the strength of these true longings.

When men believe that by merely saying that they believe on Jesus Christ or by asking forgiveness of the priests and when absolved believe that they have done all that is necessary, they are mistaken, and if they rest in that contentment, they will find themselves as I was when they come to spirit life. No belief of this kind or absolution by the priests will put them in such condition of memory or soul as will enable them to have these longings of which I speak.

You may think that I am quite a preacher, but I am very ignorant of the bulk of the spiritual truth and what I have said is the result of my own experience. Well, I will not write more now, except to thank you and your friends for the opportunities that I have enjoyed in listening to your conversation on spiritual matters. I will not cease to come to you even though I may not be able to write. So with my love and hope that you will pray for me, I am

Your friend and well-wisher.
Good night.

Writes about his progress from darkness into the light with the help of Mr. Padgett

March 15th, 1919

I am here, George Butler.

I would like to write a few lines tonight, if you are agreeable. A long time ago I wrote you,[167] describing my condition and that of the hells in which I was then living, and you were kind enough to help me and bring me in association with some bright spirits who were willing to

---

[167] This is published in Volume II and was received on January 5th, 1916. (G.J.C.)

show me the way out of my awful condition, and who since that time have been helping me with their love and sympathy and prayers; and now I am happy to tell you that I have gotten out of my darkness and am progressing towards the heavens which a development and transformation of the soul by the inflowing of the Divine Love, leads to.

Tonight, I desire to express to you my thankfulness and gratitude for the great service you did me, and to say, that in all the spirit world there is not one who feels more conscious of the truth which your advice leads to in the salvation of his soul, and the redemption from an existence of darkness and suffering, than do I.

I cannot convey to you any conception of what this redemption means to me, or of the wonderful difference of condition in a soul that has experienced the possession of this love, and one that remains in ignorance of the blessings that it confers. What I wrote you then, I now repeat, that the hell of a soul which is all tainted and permeated with the results of an earth life of sin and error, is wholly true and the contrast between souls in the two states of existence is impossible of description.

When you spoke to me of the probability of my release from the hells, and told me that this great love would work out my deliverance, I confess that, I had very little faith in what you told me, and thought that you were trying to impose on me some of the old nonsensical beliefs of your church doctrines, of which I had heard a great deal when on earth; and when the bright spirits came to me and confirmed what you had said, and offered their services in accordance with what you had advised me was the certain way to my obtaining a new state of living, I thought that is was an illusion or delusion, and that no results could possibly come to me by pursuing the course that they told me would surely lead to a change of my condition. But they were so earnest, and so anxious that I should listen to them, and seemed to have so much love for me and my welfare which was a new experience for me since I had been in hells, that I commenced to think that such evidence of friendship and anxiety for my betterment, must have some foundation of truth, and that I would not lose anything by heeding their advice and making the effort to pursue the way pointed out to me.

And so I commenced to pray for the love, and they prayed with me, and in a little while their Father appeared to me in a new light—not just real, but as something that might have a potential existence. I continued to pray and listen to their prayers, and my emotions were aroused, and I felt a kind of happiness that I had not before felt, and a feeling of hope that there might be some efficacy in their prayers, but, had not much faith in my own; and, notwithstanding my incredulity, I realized that I felt better in the atmosphere of their presence and in the influence that their prayers seemed to bring around me. They were very kind and sympathetic, and so wonderfully patient, and impressed me with the feeling that my soul's salvation, as they termed it, and the deliverance of me from my unhappy and suffering condition were to them matters of personal interest and importance; and, of course, with such feelings I soon commenced to think that if these beautiful spirits could have such interest in me, I should have interest in myself sufficient to earnestly seek for the relief that I so much needed.

Well, I then put more desire and longings in my prayers and tried to look upon their Father, as possibly my Father also, and so my longings became more real and intense. I prayed and called upon the Father to give me this love, and to cause me to have faith in prayer and in the Being to whom my prayers were offered. I will not tell you how earnestly I continued to pray and how the first faint realization of the answer came to me and with it the consciousness of a hope that might be fulfilled. After a while this love came to me and with it a feeling of happiness that I had never conceived of, and also the conviction that these spirits were showing and helping me on the true way to a redemption of soul and body, also, for as you may know, I had then and have now a body more substantial and real than the one which I possessed when on earth.

I will not here describe my progress or the different experiences that I had, nor the faith nor doubts that came to me in succession. I persisted, with the encouragement of these spirits, and after awhile found myself out of the darkness and sufferings and the hells, real and terrible, and an inhabitant of a brighter sphere and in the association of brighter spirits, who, though not like the beautiful spirits who had so lovingly worked with me, yet, were very different from those whom I had left in the darkness and the hells.

I am now in the Third Sphere, and if I had the time or rather, if I felt justified in consuming your time, I would describe to you as best I could, what this sphere is, and the wonderful beauty and happiness that belongs to it. Sometime, I hope to have the opportunity to attempt to portray the wonders of this sphere, and more particularly of my home and surroundings.

Tonight, as I have said, I merely desire to express to you my gratitude, and to assure you of the truth and the results of what you told me was the true way to light and happiness. Never through all eternity shall I forget your kindness and the great help that you gave me, nor shall I cease to remember you in my prayers to the Father, whom I now know is a true, real, existing and loving Father. Oh, the difference in the condition of the Butler in hell and the Butler who is now writing you is beyond all description, and this love, which is the greatest thing in all the universe and the greatest gift to mortals, is the cause thereof.

I must stop writing, although I should like to write longer, for I have already intruded too long. So remember my gratitude, and also that I am now a very happy

George Butler.

Is in a condition of darkness and suffering, is asking Mr. Padgett for help

I am here, Stephen B. Elkins.

I want to tell you that I am in a condition of darkness and suffering that causes me to need help. You knew of me on earth and you know that I was not a very spiritual man, and must necessarily be in a condition which needs help. I am in a place that makes me think I am in hell and I want to get out. So try to help me.

Yes, I knew him very well, and I want to learn of his whereabouts. Is he in the spirit world?

I see some bright spirits but don't see him and I am disappointed.

So tell me, can you help me?

I will come.

Good night.

By this message, admits that she is not always present when Mr. Padgett receives communications

I am here, Helen.

Well, I was not here, because I was engaged in work with the higher sphere where my work is now being done more than in any of the lower spheres.

I do not think that any of the band was present.

I do not know who wrote except Jesus. He wrote and told you just how he feels.

Sweetheart, you are too tired to write. Go to bed.

Your own true, loving

Helen.

Was helped by Mr. Padgett and has progressed out of darkness. When on earth, he did not believe in things of the soul, or Jesus, or even in a God

February 11th, 1916.

I am here, Stephen B. Elkins.

I have written you before, and I merely want to say now that I am in a better condition than when I last wrote you. I acted on your advice, and went with your grandmother, who is so very beautiful, and good, and listened to her explanations of the way to get out of my darkness and sufferings, and tried to follow her advice; and as a result, I find that much of my suffering has left me and I am in more light. I tell you, the relief that has come to me is beyond description, and the hope that I now have helps me to see that there is complete salvation for me, and that I may attain to the happiness which she tells me of.

I want to express to you my thanks for your assistance, and for directing me to those beautiful and bright spirits who compose your band, and who are doing so much good to the spirits in darkness and torment.

I now realize how unimportant were all the things of earth. I mean the material things, such as money and position and fame, and if I could only tell my children and wife and the others of my family what are the important things for them to do, I would be so happy; for notwithstanding the fact that I am no longer a mortal, I love them with all my heart and soul, and want to see them happy.

But, of course, I don't know how I may reach them, for they do not believe in spiritualism, or that I can communicate with them, or even that I am in a position to realize the real life of the spirit world. They are thoroughly orthodox and are resting in the security, as they believe, of their faith in the teachings of the church to which they belong. I am so helpless in this particular, and I see no way by which I can benefit my loved ones, except as I may be able to influence them by my presence, which is with them almost continuously.

Yes, I know you would help them if you could, but I fear it is as you say, and your informing them of my having written you would do no good. So I will have to try to influence them as you say, and in their moments of weakness or unhappiness, when their longings for higher things assert themselves, try to make my presence and influence felt by them as a reality. But I will not despair, for God, in his mysterious workings, may at sometime turn their thoughts to the things of the soul, and then I feel that I will be able to get nearer to them.

I am now in the earth plane, but in a place so much brighter than when I first entered the spirit world. My associates and surroundings are so very different, and my soul seems to have expanded, so that I am commencing to understand what this great love that your grandmother and others talk to me about, means. If I had only known when on earth, what are the real things of existence, and how the soul is everything, how much happier I would be now, but that is past and I am striving now to work for the future.

I want to say this though, that you are a most favored man in the matters pertaining to the soul development, and in the great number of exalted spirits who seem to be with you so often, and write you such wonderful messages of love and truth. I often come to your room when these spirits are present and hear what is written; and when the greatest of all spirits write you, I am almost overcome with the glory of his presence and the love that he seems to cast upon you and all about the room. He is a most beautiful and loving spirit, and his advice has shown me that only the Divine Love of the Father can bring to mortals or spirits the great happiness which I see that these exalted spirits possess.

I, of course, when on earth was not a believer in these things of the soul, or in any Jesus or even in a God in the sense that I now realize exists; and when I came to the spirit world you cannot understand how ignorant and poor I was. But now I know that there is, and was on earth, a Jesus, and that he is the most wonderful of all the spirits that I have ever seen, and, as I tell you, I have seen very many from the Celestial Spheres. But I must not write more, for you have been very kind in receiving this long letter. I again wish to express my thanks to you for your great help.

Well, I understand, but the worry that you have in that particular is only for the moment. It will soon become a thing of the past and disappear from your mind; for I must tell you that you will not be left to worry much on this subject. You have the help of a powerful band of spirits, helping you in this way as well as in other ways, and sooner or later you will realize the results of their assistance. So don't let this matter worry you very much. I wish that I could help you, but I cannot, and can only try to encourage you by telling you what I have.

So I will say goodbye and hope that I may have the privilege of writing again.

With my best wishes and kindest feelings, I am
Your friend,
Stephen B. Elkins.

Explains that White Eagle is in charge of the dark spirits and only permits them to write at the proper time, and reports on the progress made by spirits that he helped

February 11th, 1916.

I am here, Helen.

Well, these spirits wanted so much to write, but White Eagle won't let them do so, for he tells them that this is not their night, and that if they will come on Wednesday night they may write. He is very good and kind to them, and they understand him, and while they are disappointed yet they take his advice and leave.

Well sweetheart, I am so glad that you are feeling better, for you were not in good condition last night, and I think it was because you were worrying over Nita, but, as I told you, there is no necessity for you to worry.

I am very happy in my new home, and I intend to write you about it very soon, and I know you will be much pleased to learn what a beautiful home I have.

I will write my other message first, as I promised, and you will think that I can do a little deep thinking as well as can some of the other spirits. So try to get into a very good condition, for you know, there are a number of spirits who have promised to write to you, and they are all anxious to do so.

I was not present, but he (Elkins) told me that he had written. He is a spirit who has progressed considerably, and seems to be very anxious to get the Father's Love. He almost worships your grandmother, who has been so good and kind to him; and believes implicitly in her advice and her love for him; and he is with us a great deal, and never seems to tire of listening to your grandmother. I know that he will soon get the love in his heart and will progress to a higher sphere. He has a great deal of the natural love, and seems to love his family so much. Well, I will not write about these other spirits as it is late.

The Judge is progressing and is with you quite often as you receive the messages from the higher spirits. He is much interested in them, and thinks that it is wonderful that you should attract to you so many of the spirits from the Celestial Heavens. He says, that he did not appreciate you when on earth; and is so sorry that he did not, for he believes that he would be in a better condition now had he understood your advice.

He is quite happy though, and so is his Rose, who is with him nearly all the time. They make a happy couple, and Rose wants me to send her love. They are here now and want to write, but I tell them it is too late. He says, "Not on your life," as he is with the one that he loves and who loves him, and there is no other in all the universe for him. And Rose says he is right, and that he does not want any little Dutch girl, or any other girl. So they both send their love.

He says he will be glad to do so. He says he will try his best to prepare a message that will be interesting, but not such a one as he might have written for the University, that he sees how mistaken Dr. Holler is in his ideas of spiritual things and in his teachings, that he would like to write the Doctor a letter telling him of his mistakes, but he supposes the Doctor wouldn't believe that he had written it.

But I must stop or they will talk all night. Take good care of yourself and love me with all your heart, for I love you more than I can tell you. I must leave you now. With all my love I am,

Your own true and loving,
Helen.

Does not believe in the Divine Love; his home is in the Sixth Sphere

I am here, Emerson.[168]

For a long time I have observed the communications between you and the spirits, and have heard many of the messages in reference to what is claimed to be spiritual truths, and have had a great desire to write you, and let you know something of what my ideas and knowledge of the spiritual world are. But your wife tells me that you are not in condition tonight to receive my message, and so I will postpone it, and, if agreeable to you, will come whenever you may be in condition.

Well, I must say, that I do not believe in the Divine Love as some of the spirits describe it. I believe that all love is divine, and that as the love which man—all men—possesses becomes purified it then attains to it perfection of divinity, and beyond that there can be no other or greater love. And it is of this and similar things that I desire to write. I am in the Sixth Sphere but not in the highest plane. I am progressing all the time and enlarging my intellectual powers and acquiring knowledge, and at the same time am having my love purified. I am quite happy and in the association of wonderful spirits. I worship God and love Him, and also love all my spirit associates, and this must be the only and true religion. But of all this I will write later.

Yes, I have met Swedenborg, and found him to be a wonderful spirit as he was a man on earth; but he and I do not live in the same sphere. He is a believer in that Divine Love and lives in a different sphere, and I seldom meet him.

I must stop now. So thanking you for this favor, I will say good night.

Your brother and friend, Ralph Waldo Emerson.[169]

While on earth, did not believe in Jesus as the Son of God

June 20th, 1915.

I am here, Thomas Paine.

When I died, I did not believe in Jesus as the son of God or as his messenger sent to show the world that the Father had bestowed upon it His Divine Love and Immortality and the Way to obtain it. But now I

---

[168] Ralph Waldo Emerson (May 25th, 1803–April 27th, 1882) was an American author, poet, and philosopher. Emerson was born in Boston, Massachusetts, to the Rev. William Emerson, a Unitarian minister in a famous line of ministers. He gradually drifted from the doctrines of his peers, then formulated and first expressed the philosophy of Transcendentalism in his essay Nature. (Source : Wikipedia) (G.J.C.)

[169] A contemporary message from Emerson was received in 2006, and he has not changed his opinion. (G.J.C.)

believe to the fullest these truths and am a follower of Jesus and the possessor of the Divine Love.

How different would my condition now be if that erroneous and damning doctrine taught by the churches—that there is no redemption beyond the grave—were true. I never thought that there was any necessity for redemption either while on earth or after I should become a spirit, but thought that if there was a God, He would deal justly with me and bestow upon me happiness and enjoyment of the future life according to my idea of His love and mercy.

But I must tell you that I was mistaken in some particulars. God is Love and He is merciful, but His love and mercy are exercised only in accordance with His fixed and unchangeable laws—laws that apply impartially to all men, and which in their operation make no exceptions. What a man sows so shall he reap is as true as that the sun shines for you on earth.

I found the truth of this great law in my own experience and I paid the penalties of my sins. Jesus could not do this for me and he never pretended that he could. But he could and does show the Way by which the operations of the laws which produce these penalties may be superseded by the operation of other laws which, as it were, removes the penalties from the individual spirit. This does not change the law but changes the condition of the spirit which invokes these penalties; and if men would only learn this Way, they would not remain in darkness and sin, because they believe and assert that God's laws never change. If they would only understand that while the laws do not change, yet the condition of the spirit which calls for the operation of these laws does change, and new laws are brought into operation.

I have not time tonight to more fully explain these principles, but should I in the future have the opportunity, I will be glad to do so. Christ was and is the Way and the Truth and the Life.

I am in the first Celestial sphere and my name was Thomas Paine, the so called infidel. I believed in God, but only one God. Jesus was never God to me and is not now. And he does not claim to be God now. So you see even the so called infidel could come into the Truth and Love of the Father, even after he left the material plane and became an inhabitant of the spirit world.

So, my dear brother, I will say good night and God be with you, Thomas Paine.[170]

---

[170] In Volume I this message is dated July, not June, but the daily diary indicates it was June, and that appears the more likely date. This message is a composite of two, being published in Volume I and Volume III. (G.J.C.)

Founded the Red Cross Society, and is still in the earth plane and not too interested in spiritual progression

April 14th, 1916.

I am here, Clara Barton.

I was the woman who founded the Red Cross Society, and I am still interested in it, although I am a spirit. I saw that others were writing through you and I thought that I would like to try, and so with the permission of your wife I took hold of the pen and am now trying to express a few thoughts to you.

Well, I see that my society is very busy now in the Great War, and is doing a great deal of good, and needs all the encouragement that it can get. It also needs to have an increase in its membership in all parts of the world, for I see additional scenes of action where its services will be required. Especially in Mexico, for very soon your nation will be at war with that nation, and many a poor soldier will need the services of the Red Cross.

I will not write more tonight, but will come sometime and write more fully, if I am permitted to do so.

I am in the earth plane, they tell me. I am not very happy nor yet unhappy. I have the association of some very good and lovely spirits who are interested in humanity as I am. We are trying to help men wherever we can. Yes, I have met some of these beautiful spirits, and they have been very kind to me, trying to help me, but I am so interested in the work of my society that I have not given much attention to the advice of these high spirits.

But why do you ask the question as to my having seen these spirits?

I have listened to you with great interest, and I am impressed by what you tell me. I have never thought of myself in the particular which you mention, but now I see that what you say must be true, and that I should seek my own development as well as try to assist my late associates. I will do as you advise and seek one of these high spirits, and ask her help and instructions.

I see a number of high spirits here now, brighter and more beautiful than I have ever seen, and your wife brings one to me and says that she is interested in me, and loves me and will help me in the way that you suggest. I am going with her and will seriously listen to her, and seek for all the benefits that I may obtain. I thank you for your interest and kindness and will come sometime and write you of my experience.

So thanking you I will say good night.

Says that Miss Barton is now with Mr. Padgett's mother, who is explaining to her the Great Love of the Father

April 14th, 1916.

I am here, Helen.

Yes, this is Helen, and no one else. I heard what you told White Eagle, and he was ready and able to keep away the spirits who wanted so much to write, and a great many were here with that desire. But he told them that they would not be permitted to write. Yes, Great Bear is here too, and he was with White Eagle in letting these dark spirits know that they would not be permitted to write tonight. Well, I have told him and he is pleased, and says he will write you very soon, and will be very glad to do so. He is a good Indian and seems to love you very much.

Well, as to the two who wrote, I advised White Eagle to let them write for I saw their condition, and saw that some good might result to them for having the chance to write, and so it proved to be for the Frenchman is now with Mr. Riddle who is telling him of spiritual truths, and Miss Barton is with your mother who is explaining to her the great love of the Father, and the necessity for her to seek for and find it. I will not write more tonight, but as I promised sometimes ago, very soon I will come and write my long loving letter.

Well, as you are so anxious to receive it, I will come just as soon as you say. Well how will tomorrow night suit you? Oh, Ned, how happy you make me! If you would only love in this way all the time! I wish I could have you see me and feel my arms around you, and even feel you stopping me as you say. You may not know, but you would find something real to slap.(?) You dear old Ned, how I love you and want you with me. But I say to my longings, have patience, for soon he will be with me, just as soon as your work shall be finished.

I do love you and pray for you, and try to make you happy. So sweetheart, when you go to bed tonight think of me and love me, and even dream of me, for I will be with you.

So dear heart, let us have a real long kiss and say good night.
Your own true and loving,
Helen.

The writer of Pilgrims Progress, now a Celestial Spirit, and a follower of Jesus

September 13th, 1915.

I am here, John Bunyan.

I am the writer of the Pilgrims Progress, and I want to tell you that I am an inhabitant of the Celestial Spheres and a follower of Jesus. I am now a Christian who knows that many of the things that I wrote in my book as allegory are truths.

Of course, my belief in Jesus as God and as having made a vicarious atonement is all wrong, for now I know that there is only one God, the Father, and that every other living being, either in the earth plane or in the spirit world, is his child—son or daughter, of the Father.

Jesus is the brightest spirit in all God's universe, and possesses more of the Divine Love than the other spirits, and consequently is nearer the Father, with whom he has his spiritual communions.

My belief in God and in his love and mercy is stronger than when on earth, and I want every man to believe and understand that the great thing to be acquired is the Divine Love of the Father and His grace.

I am so very happy that I cannot tell you of its extent, and when I think of the troubles and sufferings that I endured when on earth it makes me believe that I acquired the wonderful love at a very small cost. I will not write more tonight, but will come again soon and write you more at large.

I am in the Second Celestial Sphere where your folks are—I mean those who write to you. I want to tell you also that you are a very highly favored man to have been selected to do this work. I know the fact that Jesus is with you so very often, and that his great love and power will be with you and you will feel their wonderful influences.

So remember that I want to write again.

Your brother in Christ,

John Bunyan.

When on earth was both blind and deaf, but was not unhappy, and the secret was, that in her soul she had the Love of the Father

January 9th, 1917.

I am here, your grandmother.

Well, my dear son, it has been some time since I wrote you, and I feel that I must say a few words to you, as you are in a condition that needs some encouragement and sympathy. I love you as you know and while I have not written you lately, yet I have been with you a great deal watching over you and trying to influence you with my love and powers of bringing to you spiritual thoughts and soul's longings.

Now, I want to tell you a few things that may help you in your moments of worry. When on earth, as you know, I was nearly blind and deaf, and in such condition as would naturally cause me to worry and be unhappy, but I did not worry and was not unhappy; and the secret was that I had in my soul the Love of the Father, and it was so real to me that no doubt of its existence in my soul ever came to cause me unhappiness.

And that Love, I know, and assure you, is the same kind of Love that now floods my whole being and gives me the happiness that I now possess. I remember that I did not have many material things to trouble me, for you looked after my material welfare and was always kind to me and loving, yet, nevertheless, if it had not been for the Love that I speak of, I can readily see that I should have been very unhappy and worried a great deal, for my natural inclination was to worry when things did not go right, as we said.

And so I tell you from actual experience, that all your worries, and by this I mean your causes of worry, may be taken from your conscious self if you will only seek for and obtain, which you certainly can do, this Love of the Father. It is astonishing how efficacious it is to cause the worries and troubles to disappear. They, as you may know, are very largely a matter of the mind and while in a certain sense they are real, yet the mind or its condition is the real cause of the realization of the worries.

And consider for a moment the fact, and I know that you will agree with me that it is a fact, that the indulging in these worries does not in one particular remove the material causes of the worry, and does not in any manner bring relief from the troubles. No matter how much you may allow your mind to dwell on these things, and how intensely you may worry, the cause, the material cause, remains. You may say, and it is natural to do so, that it is easy enough to advise that you should not let these inconvenient things cause you to worry, but when you come to the practical experience and are the sufferer from these conditions, it is not so easy to throw aside the effect of the troubles on the mind. Well, there is much truth in that, but notwithstanding, this Love that I tell you of, when living in the soul, will make even that effort easy to accomplish.

The philosophy of the phenomenon, if you may call it such, is that this Love is of such real substantial essence that it takes control of the mind and eliminates the consciousness of the reality of the causes of the worry. Now I do not want to be understood as intending to convey the idea that these material causes are not real, for I am not a Christian Scientist to that extent, but what I do mean is, that notwithstanding the real existence of these causes, the effects of this Love, and the faith that accompanies it, upon the mind which is the real cause of the worry is such that forgetfulness of these causes of worry takes the place of the constant indulging in the thoughts of their existence, and the unhappy consequence that must flow from them.

The cause itself is not removed but the consciousness of their existence, for the time being, is dissipated, and to the mind that is thus influenced by the Love, these causes are, as if they were not. Of course, they are existing and facing you to some extent, but it will come to you that they are not so overwhelming and insurmountable as they would appear were this Love absent from the soul and its influence from the mind. And in addition to this, love and faith creates a confidence in the power of the Father and His willingness to help, that engenders courage, which enables the possessor of this confidence to overcome these causes of worry that he would not otherwise be able to do.

What I have said may be called the philosophy of the workings of this Love in its effective destruction of worry. But the great fact is that the Father does, as a truth, help the one who is in the condition of being possessed with this Love. His Love is real and His help is real, and the effect is to make the causes named things of unreality so far as the happiness of the object of this help is concerned. And as a truth, shown by the experience of mortals, a very large proportion of the worries and troubles that harass and cause so much unhappiness to mortals is a thing of the imagination and never realized.

So my dear son, try to understand what I have written and apply it to your own condition, and you will find that your worries are not near so great as you now think. I know just what is facing you, but as you have been told by others who have written you, in a short time you will be relieved and the sun will again shine in your consciousness of existence, and you will become in a much better condition to do your work, both that of your business and that of the Master. You must not for a moment think that you will not be looked after so that you can do and complete the task that you have been selected to do. This is as certain as that the sun shines, and while for a time yet some disagreeable and disheartening things may confront you, yet it will not be a great while before they will become things of the past, and you will be in condition to do this work without hindrance or interference.

So think of all that I have said and try to believe and make a practical application of my philosophy; and above all pray to the Father for a greater inflowing of this Love, and have faith to realize that it will become yours, limited only by your longings and sincerity of aspirations. Well, I will come soon and write you a long letter on some spiritual truth that will be of interest to you. I must stop now, and so with all my love and the Father's blessings, I will say, good night.

Your loving grandmother.

Heard the message of Ann Rollins that was filled with deep Truth and love of the Father. If I had this love I would have saved many hours of worriment

January 9th, 1917.

Let me write a few lines. I am much interested in you and your work, and want to do all that I can to help. I have heard your grandmother's message and it is a beautifully encouraging one, and filled with deep truths, which, if you will grasp and apply, will benefit you very much.

I had my troubles when I lived on earth, but never had the sustaining power of the Divine Love that she speaks of, and, hence, lived my life as best I could with only the help of natural powers and a rather cheerful disposition. Had I possessed this Love, I now know that I should have been saved many hours of worriment, and enjoyed many hours of happiness that were not mine.

It seems to be the fate or destiny of mortals to experience trouble; as someone has said, man was born for trouble, but this is not just true, for man to a large extent makes his own troubles, and as men come into a knowledge of the great law of compensation they will realize the truth of what I say. But thank God, even though man makes his own troubles and the law of compensation works impartially, yet the loving Father can relieve him from his troubles and make him happy.

And in doing so, I want to say, the demands of this law are not unsatisfied. This law, itself, is subject to another law, and that is, that unless causes exist it cannot demand anything from the mortal; and the Father in helping His children does not say to the law, you shall not demand a penalty from this child whom I desire to help, but says to the child, receive my Love and help, and the causes for the demand of this law will cease to exist.

If mortals would only understand this truth they would not continue to believe that the Father cannot help His children, and they would also see that in order to confer such help, it is not necessary to set aside or suspend this great law in its operations. The Father never grants a special dispensation to relieve mortals from paying the penalties of this law, but He does give to them His Great Love, and when they possess that the causes that entail the penalties cease to have an existence.

The law of the Divine Love is the greatest law and supplants every other law in the workings upon the souls and minds of mortals. Well, my friend, I must not write more, and so with my love, will say good night.

Your brother in Christ,
John Bunyan.[171]

---

[171] This message is a composite of two, being published in Volume I and Volume III. (G.J.C.)

Reassures Mr. Padgett that Bunyan really wrote. And she wants him to read his grandmother's message

January 9th, 1917.

I am here, Helen.

Well, my dear, you have written a great deal tonight, and must stop as it is late. The spirits who wrote were very glad that they could do so. You had some doubts as to Bunyan and desired to call him back, but he had left. It was actually he who wrote you.

I must not write more tonight though I would like to do so. But, dear, read over what your grandmother wrote you and you will find much help. She loves you very much and wants you to be happy. Give me my kisses and say good night.

Your own true and loving,
Helen.

Tells of meeting her soulmate

January 19th, 1917.

I am here, Laura Burroughs.

I am glad to be able to write you again and tell you that since I last wrote you I have made much progress and come into the possession of much more happiness. Dear cousin, I am so glad that I can tell you this, for I know that you rejoice with me in my happiness and the knowledge of what great mercy has come to me. I merely wanted to say this, for it makes me very happy to come to you in this way.

Well he (her husband) is in the spirit world but in a very dark plane, and is not at all happy. I have been with him some, but have not been able to do him any good, as his old beliefs cling to him and prevent his progress. Sometime we may be able to help him, and will then try.

She (Helen) has told me he is not my soulmate, and I have met my soulmate very recently; he is in the same sphere with me and we are very happy together and are trying to progress together. Well, I never knew him on earth. He lived in Pennsylvania and died a long time before I did, and tells me that he had to go through much suffering and darkness before he got into the plane of light. He is a very beautiful spirit, and I could love him, I believe, even if he were not my soulmate; but as he is, you know what our love means. He is looking at me write and heard your question and says his name was Henry W. Spaulding, and lived in Millville, if you know where that is.

After I had made some progress and got some love in my soul, Helen brought him to me one time, and said "Laura, here is a young man who has been very anxious to meet you for some time, and you must not fall in love with him, if you can keep from doing so," and she laughed. Well, I suppose, I blushed, as we mortals used to say, but I did fall in love, as you can imagine, and have been loving him ever since. How we all love Helen for her kindness and the great good that she does. You just wait until you come over, and you will see the most beautiful girl that you ever saw.

He returns the satisfaction (salutation), and says that he considers himself very fortunate in having such a cousin, and he means it, for he sees the wonder of the great gift that you have, and the loving and high spirits that come to you. I must say good night now, and with my love I will stop.

Your loving cousin,
Laura.[172]

Is surprised to hear about soulmates, as written by his cousin, so moved to write

January 19th, 1917.

Let me say a word—George E. Luckett.

I am a spirit who has listened to your last communication and was somewhat interested in what the spirit said about her soulmate and her love for a spirit that she never heard of until after she got into the spirit world.

Now that may be all true, and I must say that she and her companion seemed to be very happy, and looked like sure enough lovers that you read of in romances; but what I want to ask is, how could they know that they are soulmates? Of course, they may love each other a great deal and think that there is no one else in all the wide world that can take the place of the one with the other, just as mortal sweethearts have thought and said many a time, to find later they were mistaken. And, as I have heard that this soulmate love is one that admits of no mistake, I should like to know, as I said, how they are certain that they are soulmates.

Well, I see your wife, and she says that there is not the slightest difficulty in knowing that you are some other spirit's soulmate, provided you are in condition to be able to receive that knowledge. That of course, some of these old grouchy selfish bachelors would not be able to receive this knowledge; and that is one of their punishments. But whenever the spirit has a loving soul and he has progressed into that condition of

---

[172] This message is a composite of two, being published in Volume III and Volume IV. (G.J.C.)

development where it is best that he should meet his soulmate he will meet her and will know the fact when he does meet her.

Now, this makes me think some, for I am one of these bachelors, and have never believed in soulmates or anything of that nature; though I have seen a number of couples who claimed that they were soulmates and seemed to be very happy. Yet the fact made no special impression on me, neither did it incite in me any desire to learn if I have a soulmate. But now I believe that I will try to find whether I have or not.

Your wife says that when I get in proper condition for having one come to me she will find her for me and bring her to me, and that I will almost curse myself for having been such a big fool all these years. But I wonder what she means by "proper condition"? I must go after her and find out, and try to get in that condition.

Well, I will do it! I am glad that I broke in here tonight. I am in the light planes of the earth sphere, and am trying to be a decent fellow, and hope that I am. But as to whether it meets the "proper condition", I will find out. Thanking you for your kindness, I will say good night.

Your friend, George E. Luckett.[173]

A Seventh Sphere inhabitant wants to assure Mr. Padgett that the writers are truthfully who they represent themselves to be

March 14th, 1916.

I am here, John D. Parker.

Let me say a word, for I am interested in you and your work to a very large extent. I have not written you before and I want merely to say that you are receiving these messages from the higher spirits, and you must believe that you are.

I am a spirit who once lived in a country far away from where you live and was not a Christian man in an orthodox sense, but was a believer in God, though not in the God of the Bible, as I never thought that a loving God could be the wrathful and vindictive God that the Jews believed Him to be.

I have been in the spirit world for many years and am a follower of Jesus in his truths and teachings and am an inhabitant of the Seventh Sphere where only the followers of him live.

I will not write more tonight as I see that you are tired, and others want to write a little. So with all my brotherly love, I will subscribe myself

---

[173] This message is a composite of two, being published in Volume III and Volume IV. (G.J.C.)

Your brother in Christ,
John D. Parker
of Liverpool, England.

Assures Mr. Padgett that he is receiving communications from spirits living in the Celestial Spheres

March 14th, 1916.

I am here, Josephus.

I am Josephus. Yes, Josephus, the Jewish Historian who has written you before.

I merely want to say that I am interested in your work and that you are receiving messages from the high spirits whose homes are in the Celestial Spheres, and you must believe what they write you, for they write only the truth. I see that you are sleepy tonight and that I must not write more, though I would like to write you a long letter at this time; but I will come again and give you my views on certain matters in which you are interested.

Your brother in Christ,
Josephus.

Helen says that spirits that wanted to write were stopped by his Indian guide because Mr. Padgett was too tired

I am here, Helen.

Well, sweetheart, I am here, and see that you are very sleepy, and I will not detain you. So think of me with all your love and I shall be happy. Everything will be all right and you must not worry.

Well, the spirits who attempted to write were strangers. They were not evil spirits, but good ones and merely wanted to write a little, but your Indian guide stopped them. We were not present at the time as you failed to write when you promised and we all left to do our work elsewhere.

So kiss me good night and go to bed.
Your own true and loving,
Helen.

Is grateful and never will forget Mr. Padgett's kindness in helping him to see the light

July 22nd, 1915.

I am here, Franklin H. Mackey.

I must write just a line to tell you that you are my friend and helper in my darkness and sufferings. I have been much benefitted by your advice and the help which your band has given me and I am commencing to see the light and to know what the love of the Father means to a poor benighted soul who has been in a state of torment.

I will not write longer but say that I am so grateful and will never forget your kindness and sympathy. May God bless you and keep you in His care.

Your old friend and brother lawyer that was,
Franklin H. Mackey.

Wants to know why Mackey and Taggart have changed so: Was it because they have received the Love of God?

July 22nd, 1915.

I am here, George W. Harvey.

Wait a while until I say something. I want to tell you that Mackey and Taggart have changed so much, that I wonder why they have and I have not. They tell me that it is because they have received the love of God in their souls, and faith in what the beautiful spirits of your band tell them.

I hardly know what to think and I want to ask what you think is the cause. I am a doubting Thomas. Well, I have heard what you said and I will try to do as you say. I will do so. And I want to express to you my gratitude for the interest you have taken in me.

Your friend,
George W. Harvey.

Is grateful for what Mr. Padgett has done for him and the wonderful results that followed from the advice given to him

July 22nd, 1915.

I am here, too—Hugh Taggart.

As Mackey said, I am grateful for what you have done for me, and the great light that has come to me by reason of your advice, and the teachings and help of your band, and especially the deep sympathy and sisterly love of that beautiful wife of yours. Why, Padgett, I want to tell you that the most fortunate things of my whole existence were my acquaintance with you and the wonderful results that flowed from it. I sometimes wonder how all of this could have come about.

When on earth, while I knew that you believed in spiritualism, yet I never realized what your belief and experience meant to you, and what a great help it would be to me, when the time came for me to become a spirit.

I will never forget our first argument[174] after I became a spirit on this great question of how I might be rescued from my awful condition of suffering and darkness, and with what earnestness you maintained the position that you took and tried to show me that there was a way by which I could get light and happiness and relief from my torments. Mackey and I often talk about it, and we wonder that you could have had such knowledge of these spiritual matters and such faith to maintain the truth of their existence. But you were right and your faith was not misplaced.

Old friend, I thank you again, and God bless you! I am now in a condition of light and suffer very little and realize to a great extent that there is such a thing as the Love of the Father, and that it may be mine.

I pray and my faith is becoming stronger all the time. The great proof to me, aside from what I see in the condition of other spirits who claim to have this love, is my own change in soul happiness and in desire to progress to the higher spheres, which your band tells me exists, and that I may find my home there if I will only pray more to the Father and let my faith enlarge.

To me this Love and faith is a new revelation. Of course, when on earth I heard of God's Love and of faith, but to me they meant nothing more than the rhapsodies of the enthusiastic religionists, whose emotions had overcome their normal reasoning powers—a will o' the wisp—as it were.

But now I know the reality of these things and I find that the emotions are in things pertaining to the soul more certain leaders than are the reasoning faculties. I am quite happy at times, and I hope to make such progress in my soul development as to be happy all the time. You are my true friend and I love you as a brother now.

Well, they are still in darkness, but have progressed some little. The great disappointment which Harvey experienced when he came over seems to have such a baleful influence on him, that it is almost impossible at this time for him to reach out and try to grasp the truth of the existence of this Love. But we are trying to help him, and he is commencing to wonder at our improved appearance and to think that maybe we know what we tell him to be the cause of the change.

Mac is still in darkness, and it seems hard for him to awaken to the fact that there can be any other condition that he may have. He is very hard to reason with, and does not seem to have much desire to have

---

[174] Taggart and Mackey conducted a question and argument session with Padgett on January 12th, 1915 which is published in Volume IV. (G.J.C.)

his condition change. Well, I will not write more tonight.

I saw some spirits writing to you but did not know them, except Jesus. I know him and I could never forget him for there are none like him in grandeur and beauty and love.

So my dear friend, let me again express my gratitude and say with all my heart, that I am your grateful,

Hugh T. Taggart.

Writes that Mr. Padgett's grandmother has had a beneficial effect on him and has helped him to get into the light

November 17th, 1916.

I am here, James A. Garfield.

No, I have not written you for a long time though I have kept in touch with you and many times have heard the messages which you have received and also listened to the conversations of yourself and friends[175] regarding these messages. I also have spent much time with Riddle and with your grandmother listening to their teachings and descriptions of their experiences in the spirit world and I have become much interested in what they have related to me and in the results of their experience as manifested to me by their appearances and conditions.

Your grandmother especially has had a very deep and beneficial influence on me and my thoughts, for she is a most wonderful and wise spirit and so filled with love and powers that I necessarily have to regard what she says with feelings of belief and credence. And besides I see that she is so very different not only in her appearance but also in her knowledge and conception of spiritual things from those spirits of intelligence with whom I am most frequently in association, that I have become dissatisfied with the course that I have pursued, believing that the mind is the great thing and its development the most to be desired and acquired.

So I desire to tell you that I am now trying to follow the advice of your grandmother and these other spirits who preach the doctrine of the Divine Love and am praying and longing for the inflowing of the love into my soul. It may seem strange to you that I should have for so long a time been told to secure (discern) the truth of this doctrine in view of the fact that when on earth I was a kind of preacher in my church and attempted to preach the Scriptures; but when I tell you as I have told you before that my beliefs were mostly mental and as I now found to be erroneous after coming to the spirit world. When I realized as I quickly did, that my beliefs and teachings of the Bible were not true, I then became a kind of

---

[175] Dr. Leslie R. Stone and Dr. Eugene Morgan.(J.P.G.)

infidel[176] and to such an extent that I was not willing to listen to any suggestions that partook of the nature or flavor of the teachings of the Bible or to the soul and spirits and heaven and hell, etc.

And it was only after I fully realized the want of satisfaction in my mental pursuits, that I agreed to try the conversations with Riddle and other spirits of what they claimed to be as a truth of the soul development, did I give serious attention to what I saw was not connected very intimately with the mental development and changed my course of investigations and turned to a search for the truths that your grandmother told me existed in the presence of the soul. And I want to tell you that I am so very thankful that this change came to me and I was started on the road to light and truth.

I am in much better condition than when I last wrote you and in more light and happiness and have a hope which I did not then have. I thought that you might be interested in knowing this and it gives me great pleasure in telling you the fact.

Well I am surprised by what you tell me for I have never heard of or seen displayed any of that power or glory that you speak of and I know her only as a loving tender spirit but very wise. I will ask about this power that you speak of, for it must be a wonderful thing and when I realize that such power may exist it makes me realize the truth of what she tells me to a greater extent than ever.

Yes I have met him (Ingersoll) on several occasions and must confess that I was surprised at his appearance and condition but I did not inquire as to the cause of the same, but from what I now know I suppose it was the possession of this love. I will do so.

Riddle is a very bright spirit and is getting brighter and brighter all the time and his happiness seems to be without end. Well, my friend, I will not write more. So thanking you for your kindness I will say good night.

Your brother and friend,
James A. Garfield.

Would like to be able to impress our President that he is overlooking matters of greater importance close to his peace stand

February 27th, 1917.

I am here, James A. Garfield.

---

[176] Sadly this reaction by those that once were fervent believers in Jesus and find that things are not as they expected when they arrive in the spirit spheres is all too common. (G.J.C.)

True Gospel Revealed Anew by Jesus

I come tonight to say a few words in reference to the present condition of the affairs of our country, as I have been much interested in what has taken place in the past few weeks, and especially in the attitude of the President with reference to Germany and its inhuman method of carrying on its system of underwater destruction of merchant ships.[177]

I know that what I say may not amount to anything for several reasons: one is, that no one save yourself and a few of your friends will know what I say, and another, that a live dog is of more importance than a dead lion. But nevertheless, I feel that I should give expression to some of the thoughts that come to me in reference to these vital and critical conditions that now exist.

The President has been very much hampered by his desire to preserve peace, or rather to keep our country out of war, and so strongly has this desire possessed him that other things of greater and more vital importance to the welfare of the country have been ignored and made matters of secondary consideration with him and his advisers.

Peace is very desirable, and human lives are very dear to those who may have to answer the call to possibly sacrifice theirs, yet the honor and preservation of the nation are of much more importance than the former things, for peace is not necessarily a thing that can exist only in the absence of war, for it may exist in reality while war is progressing, to a greater degree than when war is actually in operation. I mean that even now there is very great want of peace in the individual lives of the people, even though the country, as a nation, is not at war.

And the life of the individual is not of so great importance as the life of the nation, for if the nation be destroyed, or subjected to the dominion of another country, the life of the individual may not be worth the living, as in the case of poor Belgium.

But, as I was saying, this desire on the part of the President to preserve peace has caused him to ignore the rights of both the nation and the individual as they have been threatened and injured by the actions of Germany, in its assaults upon the rights of the nation to continue its commercial pursuits, and enjoy the freedom of the seas, that have always heretofore been preserved, and to establish which this nation, in days gone by, fought to establish and have recognized.

He will be disappointed in his expectations that some kind Providence will interfere, and prevent the overt act, that he holds to be necessary for justification on his part to enter into the conflict, as that overt act will not only take place, but has already done so, and the cause that he has been waiting for is now a thing of reality.

It is a great pity that he has delayed all this time, for if he had

---

[177] This is a reference to the German U-boats—submarines. (G.J.C.)

taken a firm and determined stand some months ago and let Germany know that America would maintain her rights, even by force of arms, if necessary, Germany would not now be the (as) aggressive, belligerent that she is, and many vessels would not have been destroyed, and many lives have been saved.

But this wavering policy caused the Germans rulers to believe that he did not desire war, and that he would refrain from entering actually into the war, and consequently, that he would let go by any act on their part that did not purpose to injure the rights of the U.S.; and this feeling on the part of Germany increased until it was led into doing things that it might otherwise not have done, and having gotten into its present desperate state, it came to the conclusion that the only thing it could do now, was to adopt the plan of blockade that now obtains, and destroy everything that interferes with the carrying out that plan, and that the U.S. must submit to its demands or do whatever it might think best to protect its rights, hoping, though, that it would avoid war by recognizing the blockade and keeping its vessels out of the zone of the same.

Now the time has arrived when Mr. Wilson can have no possible excuse for remaining neutral, and he will have to do what he should have done a long time ago. I can see that this delay will result in the destruction of many vessels and the sacrifice of many lives, but it is the only thing that can be done to save greater calamity.

So I hope that he will delay no longer, but declare war or call upon Congress to declare war, at once, and thus put the country in a position to effectively preserve and maintain its rights. And I make these predictions, that as soon as this shall be done the beginning of the end will be established, and that before the middle of summer peace will come and the war will cease, though its effects will appear in more certain horror than they do now, and will be felt for many years to come. I hope that he will act now, and if I could induce him to do so, I would without hesitation or doubt of the right of so doing.

I will not write more, so good night.
Your true friend,
Garfield.

Describes his entry into the spirit world and his spiritual progression

December 18th, 1914.

I am here, Prof. Salyards.

I am here to tell you of some of my experiences in spirit life and I wish that you would let me speak first of my regeneration and birth into the higher sphere where I am now living. Your mother is the chief cause of my progression as she first showed me the way to the Love of God. I was, as you may know, not a very spiritual man when on earth, but thought that man only needed a great intellect in order to enjoy the great blessings of the spirit life. I was not what might be called a great sinner as I lived a tolerably good moral life as you may know from your experiences with me while you were at school under my instructions, but I had no idea that something more than mere intellectual acquirements were needed in order to enjoy the happiness which God had provided for his children who were willing to receive all the blessings that His Love and favor had in store for them.

Well, after I ascended to the spirit life I found that my intellectual and moral qualifications did not make me very happy although I enjoyed comparative happiness in the pursuit of knowledge and the investigation of those intellectual questions that appealed to my higher desires. I soon commenced to see that I had something more to acquire than mere knowledge of spiritual laws and things that appealed to the intellect or sympathies which all who are of a practical inclination deem sufficient for self satisfaction.

I began to study these things and have advanced very much in my knowledge of them and have succeeded in writing a poem which gives me great satisfaction and makes me think that I am really a poet.[178] But not since I have progressed to the higher sphere where love rules and intellect is a mere subordinate medium of true happiness, I find that while my acquirement in the particulars mentioned are desirable and afford much enjoyment and delight to my mind, yet my true happiness is with possession and knowledge that I have the Love of God in my soul.

So you see mere intellect or moral qualities are not the important thing for a spirit who wants to enjoy the greatest happiness to possess. Keep this in mind in your earthly life and when you come over you will find that many things will appear easy to comprehend which otherwise you may have to search for in darkness and doubt.

Be sure that your heart is in the right place and you will gain many advantages which I was not blessed with. I am now in the Third (Spirit) Sphere with your wife and father and while we are all together in a sense, yet our real condition and place depend upon the extent of God's Love which we have in our souls.

Your mother first caused me to realize that I was not spiritually enlightened by her beauty of form and countenance and the great Love that she seemed to possess, and when she commenced to tell me of the

---

[178] A picture of Professor Salyard's grave stone can be found on the new-birth.net website and is inscribed thus: "JOSEPH SALYARDS, M.A. POET, SCHOLAR AND INSPIRED TEACHER 1808—1885" (G.J.C.)

cause of her appearance and love expressing itself so abundantly, I thought that after all I might be mistaken in my ideas that my mind and acquirements were not all that was necessary to enable me to progress to higher things. And I let my thoughts take the form of direct meditation and I soon realized that she must be correct in what she said.

She was so gentle and loving in her manner and speech that I was soon convinced that while my mind was superior to hers in that I had a greater extent of knowledge and superior endowments of things purely intellectual, yet what she possessed was far more necessary to my true happiness, and I commenced to inquire what the secret of her superior appearance and lovely disposition was.

Soon she explained to me that only the Love of God existing in the soul was the true secret, and that no spirit who had not that Love could possibly realize that true happiness. So you see I am much indebted to her for my present condition. I do not believe that any soul can obtain this happiness unless he lets this Love become a part of his very existence.

My one desire now is to obtain more of it, and keep on obtaining it, so that I may rise higher and higher until I get as close to the fountainhead of God's Love as possible. I will not attempt to tell you what this happiness means, but only say that without it I should still be grasping in the earth plane, seeking mere knowledge and composing verses which you might not think worthy of even a mere versifier (person who writes poetry).

I am now engaged in trying to teach others the way to this Love, but I am not yet in a condition of faith and Love to do very much good. Your grandmother is a wonderful spirit in love and beauty and I am so thankful that I have the opportunity to enjoy her companionship and instructions. She is trying very hard to show us the way to a more perfect realization of this Love and when I think that if you had not been a dear pupil of mine I would possibly never have met her. I feel so thankful that you came to my humble school and became so very dear to me as you did.

If your mother had not known me on earth, she possibly would not have known me here and I might have yet been in my condition of contentment in the study of merely intellectual things and have remained in that condition indefinitely, but thank God I knew you and through you your dear mother.

I have met Mr. Riddle whom as you know I made the acquaintance of in life and I find that he had heretofore been in that condition of self contentment that I had, before your mother showed me the way to my present home, and he is now commencing to see that there is something more than mere intellectual pursuit necessary to his progress too—that which will make him truly happy. He seems to be thinking of what you told him a few nights ago and has told me that you first caused him to think that there was something more in this spirit life than mere study of laws of spiritual communications in which he has been engaged. He seems to think that you have a correct idea of what is necessary to his salvation and he is praying as you advised him and is listening to your mother's teachings and Love of God which she tells him he must let come into his heart before he can come into perfect peace.

He is still thinking thoughts that he is a good man morally and that he does not need any help from God or Jesus, but this belief is narrowing and I believe that ere long he will realize that he is all wrong and must accept the plan which your mother tells him is the only one that can bring him in perfect accord with God's Love and make him a new man. I also try to tell him of the truth of this plan and he listens to me with considerable interest and I hope that very soon he will see that we are right and that he must accept it or be left to his present state of unrest and yearning after things that will never come to him.

So you see I am now in my home of peace and love and true happiness. Let me tell you of what I saw when your father left us to go to his home with your wife. He was so uncertain as to whether he really needed the Love of God more abundantly in his soul that he asked your mother if he could not have that Love and still try to have his earthly desires for things that he loved so on earth, such as dancing and smoking and other things of this nature and if it was absolutely necessary to let his thoughts turn from these things in order to progress.

She told him that it was necessary, as nothing which tended to keep his mind on earth or attract him to that life could possibly exist when his soul should be filled with the Love of the Father. He said that it was hard to give up these things as he enjoyed them so much and was only getting ready to have a good time when she told him that he was not to think of them anymore, but to turn his thoughts to more spiritual things and pray to God to fill his soul with Love and longings for these higher things.

I feel that if she had not thus entreated him that he might still be in the earth plane and while very happy as he had some of God's Love in his heart yet not to the extent that made him feel that he had been Born Again.

Your mother is my own dear friend and I love her so much for what she had done for me. And your father is now with your wife in this sphere and is as happy as he can possibly be, until he gets more of this Love in his soul, but you must not think that he is as beautiful a spirit as your wife for he is not and neither am I. She is so earnest in her love and is making such efforts to progress that she will soon leave us as I believe for the sphere where your mother is and when she goes we will miss her so very much as she is so happy and cheerful and full of music and everything that makes our life happy that while we have our own soul's love and happiness yet we will miss her very much. She is now trying to tell you of her great love for you which is of such a deep nature that we all wonder at times because of its intensity. So you see what a very favored man you are to have such a soulmate as she.

My home is in the same sphere with her but not in the same plane. Hers is more beautiful than mine, but she comes to me at times and I visit her. My soulmate and I have not yet met though I believe that she is in a higher sphere than mine. She has not yet come to me, why I know not, but am waiting for her to come to me and then I will be happier than ever.

Soulmates do not meet each other always when we first come into the spirit world. I know this for I have met many spirits who have been here a long time and yet have never yet seen their soulmates. This seems to be the result of something done while on earth, but I do not understand it. I am hoping to soon see mine.

I have heard something to that effect, but I have never been able to find mine. Your wife may be right, but if so she has never told me the way. I will ask her, if she knows, for I want to know if possible.

I will write you some of my poems sometimes when we have more time and will also tell you the result of investigation of the spirit life, but not tonight as I am tired and so are you. I can write you a couplet but do not think it best to do so now as I do not wish to give you a part of the poem and so remove it from its place that you may not fully appreciate the whole. I will try.

If you do not love me as I have told you, I cannot write in a very successful way so that you must first learn to love me more before I attempt to write the poem. I know that you may reason that way, but what I say is true. My poem is one of Love to God and love to man and unless you love I cannot write it.

I cannot explain more fully now. So only trust me and I will show you in the near future that I am right.

Yes I am really Prof. Salyards who is writing and you must believe me or I will feel hurt. Yes, that is it, you seem to know, just what is waiting, so I must close for this time.

Your old professor and friend,
Joseph Salyards.

Assures Mr. Padgett that Prof. Salyards loves him and that it was really he who wrote

December 18th, 1914.

I am here, Helen.

You certainly did write a long letter. Prof. Salyards is very much interested in you and you must believe that he wrote you for he did. I was here all the time that he was writing and got very impatient for I wanted to say something myself. He was telling the truth and you are real mean to have me think that you doubt that I do. So be a good boy and listen to what I have to say.

You are not so worried tonight and I am so glad of it, for if you had continued to be so, I fear that you might have become sick. You see that everything is coming all right, just as we told you. You were so worried that even Jesus condescended to assure you as he did last night.

Jesus was certainly good to you to talk to you so kindly and lovingly. He told you that he would always look after your welfare and he will. I do not believe that any other human has ever had that assurance direct from him since he came into spirit life. He is the one that you must believe in and if you do, there is no telling to what heights you may rise to for he seems to love you so much that I believe he will do whatever you may wish if it be not contrary to his ideas of what is good for you. So only trust in him and I tell you that you will never want for anything, either in the earth life or in this. He is now trying to help you in your spiritual nature so that you can do his work and when you become a better man in that particular he will write you the message that he told you he would. Let me help you to believe fully in his promises. Be my own true Ned and you will be a most happy man.

Yes, I know, but they will soon pass and then you will realize what it is to have a God and a Jesus and a little wife love you. I am least, but I love you with all the love that I have and you must realize it.

Yes, you may.

Here no doubt a question was asked about Prof. Salyards' soulmate.

He has never tried as I suppose, for if he had he would have found her. The fact is that he did not think of soulmates until he became more in contact with us and then I suppose that he did not give sufficient consideration to the matter. I do not know, all spirits do not find their soulmates at once. Some of them not for long years as I am informed.

Yes, I will and the next time that he writes, he will tell you that he has found out who she is, for I will search in that book of lives that you know about and find out and tell him and then he will know and tell you.

He is still in doubt, but I think that he is commencing to see the light and you must continue to pray for him. Do not let the thought that he is not praying himself disturb you for he is and your mother is trying her best to convince him that he is in the right way by praying and that soon he will see the light which will guide him to God's Love. He is a wonderful spirit in his earnestness and desire to learn of the things of this life and just as soon as he is convinced of the truth of the New Birth he will progress very rapidly, for he will not rest until he gets whatever is possible for him to obtain. Let your best and most loving thoughts go to him.

Yes, sometimes, but he is not so very much convinced as to what I may know of the necessity of his learning to give his heart to God as he is as to what your mother and grandmother may know, and so I do not talk to him on this matter very often, yet he seems to think that I must have experienced something that makes me look so different from what I did when he first saw me in this life.

Yes, he told you just what your father said and what your mother told him in reply. Your father was a spirit that liked the things of earth to a great degree and enjoyed looking on at the pleasure of the earth life as the Professor told you. Yet he was also so good that he realized to a great extent the love of God and could write you about it very effectively. But he did not enjoy it as much as you might be led to believe from the way he wrote. But now he knows and when he writes you again and tells you of the love of his Father, you may believe that he experiences what he is writing about.

He is my own dear daddy and I love him very much. He is so kind and loving that I do not wonder that his soulmate loves him so much, and I believe that you must take after him for I love you more than she does him. She may not agree with me, but I can't help that and still stick to what I say.

I have seen his poem and I know that he has written it, but I do not understand why he cannot write it to you without your learning to love him more. It does seem unexplainable to me, for I do not see how the want of more love on your part can possibly prevent him from writing the poem to you. He must not be ready to do it now or he may feel bashful in doing so, but I will talk to him and urge him to do so. Maybe he does not think it of sufficient importance now that he has risen to the higher sphere, but I will find out and let you know. I will tell him what you say.

Nothing more tonight except that White Eagle says that you do not seem to want him to treat you any more as you do not make the opportunity for him to do so.

He says that you are alright and that he will treat you tonight after you are through reading. He is very anxious, so do not disappoint him.

Your own loving,
Helen.

Has progressed to the Third Sphere and has located his soulmate with the help of Mrs. Padgett and knows that she is his forever

December 28th, 1914.

I am here, Prof. Salyards.

Your wife told you today that I would write tonight and I will try to do the best that I can.

I am now in the third (Spirit) sphere with your wife and father who are my very constant companions although I am not so highly developed in spirit love as is your wife who is one of the most beautiful spirits of my acquaintance.

I am trying to learn what is possible about the laws that govern the spirit life but as yet I know comparatively little of them. I am also trying to write poems of love of God and of man. So you must not be surprised if some day I shall write to you some of my productions.

I am also trying to get more of God's Love in my heart, so that I may progress to the higher spheres and find the greatest happiness possible to obtain. My present condition is one of great happiness, but I know that there is greater, higher up, and that as your grandmother and mother have found it, I will be able to find it also, if I follow the way that they have pursued.

You must not expect me to write very much tonight as you are not in condition to permit me to do so. I know that I do not write as you anticipate that I would but only because I want to wait until conditions are better.

Yes, I have found my soulmate, thanks to your wife, and I cannot tell you how happy I am. Your wife was certainly good to me and I will never cease to thank and love her for her interest in me. My soulmate is a very beautiful and spiritual woman who I never knew on earth even though she lived in a part of the Valley not very far from my home. Her name was Sarah Conway as she tells me and her father was a farmer near Mt. Crawford. She is now here and says that you are a very dear man to suggest that your wife find her.

She says that she had never been instructed that she had a soulmate and that until your wife told her she did not know that I was the one that God intended for her. I do not understand why this is, but it seems to be so.

I have heard that there is a law of attraction as you say but just how that law operates I am not able to say. Your wife seems to have a knowledge of this law which I do not have and have never yet tried to learn. She is a wonderful spirit in her investigations of certain laws pertaining to the laws of spirits for one another. How she obtained this knowledge I am not yet informed and cannot explain just how she discovered who my soulmate is. I know though that I have found her and that she is mine forever. How, I don't know, but she did locate her and I have her now with me. She says that your wife told your mother who my soulmate is and your mother who is in the same sphere told her and she came down to my home and found me and then knew that I was intended for her.

She is in the fifth sphere where your mother lives. Yes, I see that it is and I will include it in my catalogue of studies. You are right when you say that I must study this matter for the happiness of so many spirits depends upon knowing their soulmates that it is well worth studying so that I may help them in finding who is the one that God has selected for any inquiring spirit.

Question and Answer.

She has not yet, but she will as I will ask her and she is so good that I know that she will tell me. She is a very diligent student of many of the things pertaining to the love of the spirits for the humans and she had made wonderful progress in her studies of the various means of communication between them. But she is so beautiful and so filled with God's Love that I scarcely know what to tell you of her current condition on any of these subjects. She is a wonderful spirit in her accomplishments in almost any line of investigation.

Yes, I know that it may seem impossible to you, but she is a spirit of such energy and determination that nothing seems to prevent her progressing in these things. She is also a wonderful lover of her soulmate and he should consider himself highly blessed by having the great love which she has for him. You need not think that all soulmates have this wonderful love for they do not. Love here seems to be something like love on earth. In some it is developed to a greater degree than in others. I am one who is very deep in my feeling of love and so my soulmate seems to be.

I do not know, but it is quite possible, for if she has undertaken to find her, she will, if there is any way in which it can be done.

I will soon do so if you get in condition. He is with me in this sphere. He is a very bright and loving spirit and I am so glad that he is here with me. He died so young, that his ideas of spirit matter were not very firmly fixed and when he came over it was not difficult for him to learn the truth. Yes, mother helped him very much as she was so kind to him in his early life here. She is my dearest spirit friend and is so good and fine that I am always much helped by being in her company.

Yes, he is in the earth sphere and is not very happy. He was a good churchman, but was not very spiritual. I have tried to help him on several occasions, but he seems to think that the only life for him to lead is one that he led while on earth. I mean that he seems to be satisfied with the condition that he is now in. His father has progressed to a higher sphere recently but he is not yet very much filled with God's Love and does not seem to be able to help Ambrose very much as I believe that Ambrose would not be so contented with his present home.

You are very tired and I must stop.

Your old professor and friend, Joseph Salyards.

Is prevailed upon to write his prose or poem as he mentioned in an earlier writing

April 1st, 1915.

I am here, your old Prof.

Yes, we are very happy, but she is more so than I. She has more love in her soul. She loves you very much and wants to write to you some time and tell you what a wonderful medium you are and how much happiness you give to all of us. She is very beautiful and loving.

She (his mother) is not as beautiful and loving as your wife and very few spirits are. Well, your grandmother is more beautiful still, but she is an exception. Oh she is the most beautiful of all and so wise and good.

Yes, I was and thought it a wonderful production. She wrote it herself, no masculine mind had anything to do with it, as your friend remarked. My, she knows more of the things pertaining to the higher spiritual life than any male spirit I know of except Jesus. He, of course, is beyond comparison. But beside him I don't know of any masculine spirit who is the equal of your grandmother in her knowledge of these spiritual things. We all recognize this and submit our judgments to hers and besides she is so good and loving.

Well, it is so late tonight, I will not write very much but I am now prepared to write you my discourse on certain matters as I promised you some time ago. And when you say that you are ready I shall be glad to do so.

Yes, that will be best and you shall have it in minute detail as I have taken great pains to compose the best that I know how.

Yes, that was written when I had not my present spiritual development and the things then written are not of very much interest to me now. Yet there are some beautiful thoughts in the book. Well, I will try:

Oh soul of mine when I realize the wonderful capacity that you have for loving and telling of your love, I stand in mute adoration of your great Creator.

You are the greatest creature of His Wisdom and Love and when in all your fullness, you possess the wonderful Love of the Father, Divinity is yours.

You possess the wonderful love of the Father, divinity is yours, and immortality is yours.

So let my love be—

I don't seem to be able to write more. Let me try some other time when you are in better condition. No, I will complete it the next time I write. You see it is not in verse, but in prose which I like better for the meaning can be more plainly expressed. But I will write it the next time I come.

Well, good night, my dear friend and brother,
Your own true friend,
Joseph Salyards.

Has progressed into the Seventh Sphere and never ceases to thank God for His Love and Mercy

August 6th, 1915.

I am here, your old Prof.

I wish to write a little tonight as I have not written for some time. Well, I have been watching the many messages which you have received and I have been much interested in the variety of the subject matter and the number and difference in the spirits who have written.

You seem to have received messages from spirits of all ages and from all nationalities and I am pleased to see that these messages were mostly of a higher order of communication. I was interested in the messages from the prophets and also those from the apostles and saints. And in them I saw that there were many spiritual truths disclosed and that they were very similar in their declarations as to the Divine Love of the Father and the New Birth.

It is wonderful that you should get such corroboration of these truths from spirits who have had such a wide difference in experiences in the spirit world. You are better tonight than you have been for some time and we are all so glad of that fact and hope that you may continue in such a frame of mind and in the condition of your soul development.

I am now in the Seventh Sphere and am very happy. Your father is with me and we are so pleased at our progress that we never cease thanking God for His goodness and mercy. Mr. Riddle is still in the fifth sphere, but we expect that he will be in the seventh very soon and we will then have a happy reunion. My soulmate is with me and sends her love to you and says that she is much interested in you and tries all she knows how to help you in your material, as well as your spiritual, condition.

Very soon I want to write a long message on a subject that I think will be of much interest to you and to others who are interested in the things of the spirit life. I know that that will please all the band as we have missed writing to you and desire so much to continue our communications. Of course the messages that you have received have been very beneficial and are intended to do good, but yet we feel that we had stayed away, I mean refrained from writing for too long a time.

Well, I have been trying to help him (Roller) but his condition is such that I find great difficulty in doing so. He still thinks of the earthly matters and his appetite for the accursed stuff still clings to him and causes him to neglect the thoughts that would do him so much good. But we continue to try to help him.

Well, I will stop for tonight.
With all my love, I am
Your old Professor and friend in Christ,
Joseph H. Salyards.

Writes on the effect of the Divine Love on the soul of spirits and its great power to purify

October 10th, 1915.

I am here, Prof. Salyards.

I heard your inquiries of your wife, and I was pleased that you expressed the desire to hear from me again as I most assuredly want to write to you. Since I wrote you last I have been living in the Seventh Sphere with my soulmate, and in close proximity to your father, and have been very happy in the love which I now enjoy.

I have seen so much of the effect of this Divine Love upon the souls of spirits who come into the possession of it, that I wonder more and more at the fact of its great power to make pure and truthful, souls who were in such darkness and torment. I have seen some very surprising conversions of souls steeped in sin and error, in souls with their sins last leaving them and happiness and Love coming to them in wonderful inflowing.

Since I have been in the seventh sphere I have paid very little attention to things about which I wrote you when in the beginning of my soul development, because with me now the soul and its divine possibilities are the things that absorb my attention and efforts.

I am sorry that I cannot continue my writings on certain phases of the laws of the spirit world, but for the reasons stated I cannot as only this Great Love and the work of helping men and spirits to obtain this Divine Love and to become children of the Father, are possessing me and occupying all my time and attention. So you must not feel disappointed that I do not continue the writings that I speak of.

I can tell you about the seventh sphere and the life and inhabitants there and the wonderful happiness which we all enjoy. Our homes have been described to you by your grandmother and your wife and I cannot add to their descriptions, only to say that they do not tell half of the beauty and grandeur of these homes and of the joy of the inhabitants. I am in a home of that kind now and am with my soulmate and we are very happy. I do not know at this time of anything more to write about.

Well, you are not complimentary but you are right. I seem to have lost my desire for investigating and writing about these things that I first wrote to you about, and I have not yet prepared myself to write of these higher things. So I will stop tonight.

Your old friend and Prof.,
Joseph H. Salyards.

Is helping Dr. Leslie R. Stone with his spiritual progression and is with him a great deal

I am here, James.

I will say only a word and that is that you are better in your soul condition as are also your two friends.[179]

The next time the Dr.[180] is present, I will write my message to him if conditions are favorable. I am with him very much and am trying to help him in his soul development.

So with my love, I will say good night and God Bless and keep you in His Love.

James.

Writes that the Law is the unchangeable factor in determining the status of men on earth and spirits

January 21st, 1916.

I am here, Prof. Salyards.

I am here and I have waited a long time for you to give me the opportunity to write, and now I fear it is too late to write as I desired to do.

I was not with you, and of course do not know why you did not come earlier, but I suppose you had some good reason for not doing so,

---

[179] Dr. Leslie R. Stone and Mr. Eugene Morgan.(J.P.G.)
[180] Dr. Leslie R. Stone.(J.P.G.)

and hence I make no complaint at the delay.

Well, do you think that we had better try to write tonight? Under that condition I will try to give you my ideas on a certain topic which I have had under consideration for some time, intending to give you the results at the first opportunity, and I hope that I may be able to do so in an intelligent manner. I desire to write you about the importance of learning that Law is the unchangeable factor in determining the status of men on earth and spirits in this life.

And when I speak of Law I mean the Law established by God at the time of the creation of man, and which ever since that time has been in continuous unchangeable existence, operating upon the same condition of facts at all times in the same way and producing the same results.

I have been in the spirit world now for some years and from having given considerable of my time to the study of these laws and their influences and dominating effect upon mankind in their relationship to one another, and to God, my investigation has resulted in the discovery of many important truths which men should know and attempt to apply the benefits of to themselves, and to their relation to one another as members of society.

First, let me say that in compliance with these laws men should observe the rights and duties which all men possess and are under obligation to perform to one another, and to try with all their best efforts to understand.

There are many of these laws operating upon these rights and duties of men, and to know them, men are obliged to study first the rights of others and then the rights of themselves and in applying these laws the rights of the former are of no greater importance than the rights of the latter, for these rights are correlative, and an understanding of these rights is necessary in order for men to understand the relative duties resting upon them.

I feel that this subject is one that is in its nature very dry, yet it is of no less importance to the well being of man than are many truths of much seeming greater importance. These laws are, I know, to a very large extent, not comprehended by men nor are these rights that I speak of, yet, if men will only attempt to get into the right attunement with the Father they can understand the laws and the rights and duties without much fear of making mistakes in their comprehensions.

I will not tonight go into great detail because it would require too long a writing, and I merely write in this general way as a preliminary to what I desire to write hereafter on the subject indicated. So if I stop now and wait until I have more time for entering into the spirit and heart of my theme you will not be disappointed.

So if you will excuse me I will stop now.

Your old friend and teacher,
Joseph H. Salyards.

Informs Mr. Padgett on the conditions surrounding a medium that he visited to learn about the kind of work they did in behalf of the Kingdom, on advice of a friend

January 21st, 1916.

I am here, Helen.

Well, sweetheart, we were somewhat disappointed tonight that we could not have the opportunity to write as we had agreed, and you were also, I know. I was with you at Mrs. Miller's and saw and heard what took place, and while there was nothing very edifying in the proceedings, yet it was a little enjoyable because of the great number of spirits who were present and their evident happiness in being able to communicate.

The spirit who was writing through you was one that I did not know, and who was of the lower planes, and had not much of the development. The guides of Mrs. Miller actually talked through her, and Minnie is a very cute and spiritual little Indian and is very faithful to her medium.

The other Mrs. Miller was much interested and the advice given her by Rolling Cloud is good, and if she will procure the medicine and give it to her mother she will find some relief. These Indians know a great deal about healing and very often help mortals in their sickness. Yes, she was very anxious to hear about the prospects of her becoming a free woman, and, while I can hardly blame her, yet, the spirits are not permitted or inclined to give much comfort to mortals who have in their souls the desires that she had.

I know the condition of Mr. Miller, and it is a very precarious one, for he may die at any moment. His heart is not in a good condition and his kidneys are very much diseased, and worse than that he is obsessed by a wicked drunken spirit who will not let him get out of their power if they can prevent it; and because of his circumstances and surroundings it seems to me that they will be able to retain their control of him. Well, we have some power, but not all that you may think. Unless he puts himself in condition to accept our help we can do nothing for him, for his condition is what gives these spirits the power to control him, and unless he makes some effort himself to break the rapport between him and them, we can do him very little good. Such is this law of attraction that I have written you about.

Well, she is a good hearted woman, but not one that would benefit you in a spiritual point of view, for she is very worldly in her desires and thoughts and scarcely ever gives the future any consideration. I know this from not only what she said, but from the condition of her soul development, which shows that not often does she permit her soul to have any communion with the higher things of God's universe; and I tell you that the condition of the soul is a sure index of the thoughts and aspirations of the person.

Yes, of course, she has a soulmate, but who he is I don't know, and it is not important at this time to find out, for she is not thinking of soulmates, but of the material things of life, and her chief desire is to obtain money. Well, I must not write more and you must go to bed. The others of the band will come at a later time and write you.

So with all my love I will say good night.

Your own true and loving, Helen.

Mr. Padgett was once a pupil of Prof. Salyards and now the tables are reversed

February 8th, 1916.

I am here, your old Professor.

I merely want to say that I desire to finish my discourse of some weeks ago and am ready at any time that may suit your convenience.

Well, I will come one night this week and try to finish. I see that you are in a very good condition now, as your brain is working very well. The message that you have received from Paul is a wonderfully deep message upon the existence of the resurrection, and as I understand and have experienced the resurrection is a true explanation of its meaning.

Paul is a very logical and clear writer, and I am glad that he finds such little difficulty in making use of your faculties. He is very much pleased at the success of the experiment and his estimate of you is very great, as are the estimates of all the higher spirits who write.

Well my dear boy, I often think of the wonder of all this experience, and sometimes let my mind return to the days when you were my dear pupil; and I think how wholly we were in want of any conception that such a thing could be. And I can't tell you how glad and thankful I am that we ever came in contact with each other, for I will frankly and assuredly say that if I had never met you I doubt if I would have had the privilege of meeting such spirits as your grandmother and mother, and of having received the benefits of their advice and the influence of their love, as well as the companionship of your father and Mr. Riddle.

I often think of how a mere accident as your coming to my school should have brought about such momentous results, and in thinking I am so grateful to our Heavenly Father. So my boy, keep up your good work and you will find a wonderful happiness when you come over.

The dark spirits whom you help are so very grateful to you and are all lovers of you and your friends are ready at all time to protect you from the evil that might come to you from the influences of the many evil spirits who have their habitations so near your earth. Yes, more than you can imagine, I want to say this further thing, and that is, that very many spirits who don't have the opportunity to write to you are influenced very much by what they hear you tell others, and act on the advice that you give to those who write. And small wonder at the confidence of these spirits have in you and the influence you have with them. So many are being helped, and our work is made so much easier because they listen to us and believe so much more readily when you advise them to do so.

Well, we are very happy and progressing all the time. Oh, I wish I could tell you how beautiful she is and how loving and how much she thinks of you. She is with you quite often and is trying with the rest of us to help you in every way. We know when you pray for us, and it does help us more than you can conceive of, for your prayers are sincere, and, I know, ascend to the Father, who answers the prayers of the sincere and trusting.

So I say, we all love you very much, and feel that we cannot do for you what we should like to; but you must believe in us and know that we are with you and have more power than you may think to help.

I have written too long already, and your wife says, "Professor, I don't like to be discourteous, but I must suggest that you stop and let that baby boy go to bed, for he will sit up all night if you continue to write." What a beautiful and loving wife you have, and how we all love her for her goodness.

So my dear boy, I will say good night.
Your brother in Christ,
Prof. Salyards.

Learns that Mr. Morgan will have an Indian guide called Red Fox

February 8th, 1916.

I am here, Helen.

Well, you need a keeper, for you never know when to go to bed. I mean that you must not let your interest in us or our writing interfere with those things which are necessary for your physical welfare.

I will say only a word more, and that is, that I love you with all my heart and soul, and am with you all the time that I can spare from my work. Yes, he told me what you said, and I will try to find him sometime and bring him to answer for himself. I see you object, and it may work all right, I don't know.

He says he was there and gave Mr. Morgan a guide—a very powerful Indian of the more civilized tribes. He is something like White Eagle, and will be a great benefit to Mr. Morgan. Yes, White Eagle says his name is Red Fox.

So with all my love, I am
Your own true and loving,
Helen.

Says he goes to the Father in time of trouble

September 30th, 1915.

Such are the thoughts of men when troubles arise: I can do nothing of myself, but will go to my Father and seek His aid; and the thoughts are true and the aid is certain. You are that man tonight, and you will not be disappointed for you will find relief from your worries and the help that the Father shall bring to you.

The Master is all love and you seem to be his favorite on earth, and you can rest assured that you will not be forsaken. I tell you this because I know from experience.

I will not write more.
I am, your brother in Christ,
Barnabas, the Apostle.[181]

Also encourages Mr. Padgett

September 30th, 1915.

When the Master said, "Feed my sheep", he not only meant that Peter and those to whom he was talking should feed the spiritual natures of those who should believe on him and try to belong to his fold, but he also intended that their material wants should be taken care of. And tonight he is saying the same thing, and as you are his sheep of special care and love, he intends that all the things that are necessary for your well being shall be given you. So do not doubt at all, but believe that you will be looked after in all your times of need.

He was so loving to you tonight that we were all somewhat astonished at the great love which we saw going to you, and thought how dear you must be to him. I have never seen him take such interest in any particular person before, and when you realize what his love and

---

[181] This message is a composite of two, being published in Volume II and Volume III. (G.J.C.)

power are, you will be more astonished than were we.

I see what your troubles are, and while they may seem mountains high to you, they are merely temporary and will soon pass away. So believe in what the Master told you, and pray to the Father for Love and faith.

I will not write more, but will say God bless you.
Your brother in Christ,
John Wesley.[182]

An old friend of Mr. Padgett's wrote about his suicide and his condition in darkness and explains the reasons for taking his own life, but is astonished to learn that Jesus is working today, as always, in helping the fallen and dark spirits

October 1st, 1915.

I am here, your late friend, Perry.

I want to tell you that I am in a condition of great darkness and suffering, and I am not able to find a way out of the darkness or to relieve myself from my tortures.

I know that you may think it strange that I did not listen to Mr. Riddle when you brought him in contact with me a short time ago,[183] but I could not believe what he told me, or understand in what way the darkness would leave me by merely praying to God, and trying to believe that there is such a thing as Divine Love, which I might obtain by letting my belief in what he said become sufficiently strong to cause me to forget the recollections of my awful deed.

I saw that he was a wonderfully bright spirit, and seemed to be so very happy in his condition of belief, but, nevertheless I was not able to believe that it was the result of what he told me, and so, I am in the same condition that I was when I wrote you last.

My, friend, for such I believe you to be or you would not be able to interest yourself in me as you have. I want to tell you that if I only again could shoot myself and by that means end my existence, I mean annihilate my spirit and soul, so that they would go into nothingness, I would gladly and quickly pull the trigger and send the bullet into that spot which would bring about the desired effect.

But I realize now that I must continue to exist and to suffer for how long I don't know, but it seems to me forever and ever. Oh, why did I do such a thing! I had no occasion to take my life so far as earthly things

---

[182] This message is a composite of two, being published in Volume II and Volume III. (G.J.C.)
[183] It seems this happened on July 28th, 1915 but has not been published. (G.J.C.)

were concerned, for I needed nothing of the material to make life satisfactory.

Question?

Well, I will tell you. As you may know, I was, as I thought, something of a philosopher on earth, and to me life was a thing to retain or put off just as I might think it had served or not its purpose, and when I felt that I could no longer do any special good to the world or to those who were near to me. I thought that there was no reason why I should longer continue the life which was one of monotony in a certain sense. And besides I felt that I had arrived at the height of my mental powers, and that they were on the decline; and the thought that I should decrease in what I had so striven to cultivate and display to my acquaintances, caused me to believe that the object of my creation had been fulfilled, and that I would gradually become not only an encumbrance, but a person to be looked upon with a kind of pity which would cause me much unhappiness. To have others point their finger at me and say: "There goes poor Perry who used to be such a brilliant and capable man, and who is now a mere wreck of his former self intellectually. Isn't it a pity that such a man should come to a condition that he has come to?"

These are some of the thoughts that entered my mind; and in addition as I have told you, I thought that death was the end of all, and that in the grave I would know nothing, and sleep in utter oblivion.

These thoughts I fed on some little while before I decided to die, and the more I thought the greater became my condition that what I had said would prove to be true. Just before I fired the fatal shot I thought intensely of all these things, and saw that what I supposed would be an end to everything was the true solution of life's decay and to mental as well as to physical decrepitude. And when I prepared to do the deed I was never more calm in all my life. It did not require any courage on my part for conviction of the correctness of my conclusions was so strong that the question of courage was not a part of the equation.

Men may think that courage is a necessity to commit suicide, but I tell you, I believe that courage or the want of courage forms no part of a man's condition of mind when he commits that deed. The mind forms its own conclusions as to the necessity or the desirability of doing the act, and every other consideration or reason is ignored. The suicide is not, as a general thing, at the time of the act, a coward. I have no doubt though in bringing his mind to the condition that I have spoken of, that is in feeling that the burdens of life are too great, or that he cannot further bear the things which duty calls upon him to do, he may be and often is a coward. I must not write more on this theme now. I am more interested in finding a way, if possible, out of this intense darkness and suffering.

I have not seen Mr. Riddle since my first interview and I do not think that I would be benefitted by seeing him, because, for one thing, the great contrasts in our conditions only intensifies my sufferings, and, hence, I prefer to remain to myself or among spirits like myself. You know, that on earth the poor are much happier with the poor, than when thrown into the company of the rich, and this because of the apparent greater happiness of the latter. And so with me, when I see Riddle in his happiness, I feel that my misery is the greater.

No, I did not see your grandmother at that time and I do not know her now. But why do you ask that question?

Well, if what you say is true, I should like very much to meet her and listen to her, and if you will tell me how I can meet her, I will make the effort. I will certainly take advantage of your invitation and be with you tonight, and hope that I may meet your grandmother. How I wish that I may find what you tell me and feel the influences that you speak of! Oh, for such a consummation! Why, my dear friend, if what you promise me shall come true, I will never cease thanking you for your kindness and help.

I am astonished at what you say, for I never really believed in Jesus as you tell me of him. I could not when on earth believe in him as a God, and I thought that he was really an ideal of progressive human minds, and that as to his actual historical or earthly existence, it was a mere fable. But now you tell me that he really exists and is working in the spirit world to help the fallen and dark spirits, and that he comes to you and tells you of his love and work. Well, I won't say that I can't believe you but, I prefer to wait until I see him myself, and then if he appears to me as you say, I will be ready to believe what Riddle told me about prayer and the Divine Love. How wonderful all this is!

You surprise me more and more. Of course I knew Ingersoll and read many of his lectures, and in some things agreed with him, but when you tell me that he is now a believer in God and in Jesus, and has been converted to Christianity, you again draw very strongly on my credulity; and I am afraid that if what you tell me is true, I will see so many surprising things that I will hardly know whether I am a spirit of hell or not.

I will ask him to tell me about his conversion and I will listen to him intently and will try to believe what he tells me; but when you describe it as you do, by the comparison you make with that of Paul, I am more bewildered than ever. Tell me then, what kind of man are you to know all these things? I cannot understand you. When on earth I merely considered you as like the rest of us, but now I am told that you know things, that I never thought any mortal could know.

Question and Answer.

Well astonishment upon astonishment and all as you say to help me and lead me to the light. Yes, that is what I want, light. Only wait until I have had these experiences that you promise me, and I will come to you and write you a letter that you will tire of receiving. I must stop now, for you must be tired and I am.

So my dear friend, let me say, that I thank you with all my heart, and hope that I may be able to come to you again, and say that what you promised me, I have received.

Your friend,
R. Ross Perry.

Helps a friend of Mr. Padgett, a suicide spirit that lost all hope of ever being forgiven to realize that there is hope for him in the spirit world

February 16th, 1917.

I am here, Taggart.

Let me say just a word, as I am anxious to tell you that Perry has had demonstrated to him, by the appearance to him of certain suicides, the fact that his punishment will not be everlasting, and it is wonderful to see what effect the demonstration had on his hopes and belief that there may be salvation for him.

Then your grandmother brought these spirits to him and had them tell Perry their experiences, which, in the darkness, were so very much like his own, and then told him that their present condition is due to the Divine Love of the Father, which came into their souls in response to earnest prayer, he commenced, at once, to send his aspirations and longings to the Father for this Love, and all these spirits joined with him in prayer. It was a very impressive sight, as you mortals might say, and his mother was there praying and so very happy.

Your grandmother also brought Judas, and he was so filled with love and glory, that his presence made Perry look in wonderment and astonishment and when he was told that the glorious spirit was Judas, he said that now he knew there was hope for him. Well Padgett, I must not take up more of your time now, and I only wrote, because I thought you would like to know the result of Perry's experience with the bright spirits who had once been suicides and inhabitants of the hells. But sometimes I should like to come and write you as to some of my knowledge of the things of the spirit world. I will say good night. Your old friend and brother in Christ,

Taggart.

Is feeling better and is grateful for all the help given to him by Mr. Padgett and other loving spirits

March 4th, 1917.

I am here, Perry.

I am very weak, but I must tell you that I am feeling better, for now I do not believe that I am doomed for all eternity to the damnation of darkness and suffering, and when I think back that but for you and the loving spirits that you brought to me, I would be without hope, my heart is so filled with gratitude that it seems as if it must break asunder.

What a wonderful thing is this great gift that you have and no spirit in all the darkness of a hope so near despair can understand the meaning of what that beautiful and glorious spirit who just wrote you said, as I can.

Well I cannot write more, but you and your friend (Dr. Leslie Stone) pray for me as surely you who have such beautiful spirits loving you must have some power in your prayers to help. Good night and pray for me.

Your friend,
Perry.[184]

Expresses her gratitude to Mr. Padgett for his efforts in permitting her son to see the light

March 4th, 1917.

I am here, the mother of Perry.

You must let me say a word, for if ever there was a thankful spirit in all the spirit world I am that one. Oh, how I thank you and praise the Father for His Mercy and Goodness in permitting my dear boy to see the light and have hope come to him as a star that beckons him to a state of happiness and salvation.

I am so filled with love and thanksgiving that I cannot write much for my heart is just going out to the Father in such streams of love and joy and gratitude that my eyes are so suffused with tears of gladness that I can hardly see.

Do not forget to pray for my boy, both of you, for we all know that you love the unfortunate and miserable spirits who have no hope or way to get into the light. You know that I am his mother, for your soul must feel that it is the mother's love that is thus expressing gratitude.

---

[184] This message is a composite of two, being published in Volume III and Volume IV. (G.J.C.)

Good night,
Perry's Mother.[185]

Perry is praying for Divine Love and is commencing to realize the great love that his mother has for him

March 4th, 1917.

I am here, your own true & loving Helen.

Well dear, you have had a wonderful night and if as you say, you could see the scene of your surroundings you would wonder that there could be such happiness and joy in the spirit world. I mean in these lower planes where there are so many dark and unhappy spirits. We have all been happy and I must tell you that all of your band and also the Doctor's have been present listening to the messages that have been written you.

And it seems to be a night when so many of these dark spirits have come seeking and longing for help and trying to find the way to light. And while only a few have written you yet many have been benefitted for they have heard the messages and your conversations and have listened to the bright spirits who have been ready and anxious to help them.

Perry is better as he says, and is praying and just commences to realize the love and solicitude that his mother has for him and she is so happy that he realizes that she is his own loving mother, and the scene between them was very pathetic and they mingled their tears, hers of love and thankfulness to the Father and his of gratitude that hope has come to him. He is praying and I am so glad that he asked you and the Dr. to pray for him, for it shows that there has come to him some little faith in prayer.

We are all praying for him and your grandmother, in all the beauty of her love, is with him and to her he seems to listen and believe in more than all the others. It is a glorious time for us all. I will not write more now as you have been drawn on a great deal and we must stop.

Give my love to the Dr. (Stone) and tell him that if he could know the amount of love that is surrounding him tonight he would not exchange places with Rockefeller or any other rich man or great men as you mortals consider greatness—for this love will be his through all the years to come even increasing and growing.

So dear believe that I love you and give me your love and trust that I am,

---

[185] This message is a composite of two, being published in Volume III and Volume IV. (G.J.C.)

Your own true and loving,
Helen.[186]

A brother lawyer and once an associate of Mr. Padgett, seeks help, since he heard that others received help

June 27th, 1916.

I am here, Edwin Forrest.

Well I am here again and I am glad to be able to write you for I need your advice so much, as several have told me that you can help me.

I am in much darkness and suffering, and don't know just why, but I suppose it is because of my evil habits, and I want to get relief if possible so try your best to help me.

Well I understand what you say and will believe that you desire to help me, and I will certainly try to take your advice. So give it to me.

Yes I see some who are like myself and need help as I do.

Yes, now I see some beautiful and bright ones who are so different from what I have ever seen, and as I look they become plainer to me, and I see your wife and she is so beautiful and speaks to me, and says that she heard what I said to you and that she is ready and willing to help me, if I will listen to her and try to believe what she says. My she is lovely and seems too good!

Well, I have heard what you say and you surprise me somewhat in telling me about Taggart and the others, and I will try to do as you say. But before I go tell me how did you ever get the power to receive my writing and thus communicate. I never knew when on earth that you had this power, and if you had told me, I suppose I would not have believed.

So Ned, I will do as you say, and your wife calls me to her and I am going. So goodbye, and believe that I am thankful.

Your old partner and now grateful friend,
Edwin Forrest.

Writes that he is out of darkness and in the light of Love, that he has been praying, and the bright spirits in his behalf and especially Helen, Mr. Padgett's wife

February 27th, 1917.

I am here, your old friend, Edwin Forrest.

Let me say just a word. I merely want to say that I am

---

[186] This message is a composite of two, being published in Volume III and Volume IV. (G.J.C.)

progressing, and am out of my darkness and in the light of love, for I have been praying since you last heard from me, and have had the prayers of many of the bright spirits ascending to the Father for me.

Well Ned, I never thought that all this happiness could possibly come to me, for, as you know, when I came to the spirit world I was sinful and all ignorant of the great Love, and found myself in darkness and suffering, and why God should have been so good to me, I cannot understand. But this I do know, that if it had not been for your spirit friends and especially your wife, I would have remained a long time in my darkness and soul slumber. But, thanks to you, I had the benefit of their love and kindness and prayers, so that I am now on the way to the higher spheres that she tells me of.

I sometimes come to you at the office and see just what your condition is, and think that I am somewhat responsible for the same, and know that I am, and I cannot tell you how I regret what took place, and try to help you with all my powers. And I want to say to you to keep up your courage for you have many powerful spirits working for you, and I know that they will soon cause a change in the condition of your affairs.

I also know that you are rich in this Love for these spirits all tell me that you have received it to a large degree, and are doing a great work among spirits, and this I know, and are also preparing the way for bringing to humanity the truths that will give to men a knowledge of the Love and plans of the Father for their redemption. It may seem a little strange to you that I should write in this way, and I hardly know myself when I realize what I was such a short time ago, and what I am now.

Very soon now, I shall go to my mother and try to help her, as I have told you, I intend to do, and I pray that I may succeed. It is all so wonderful to me that sometimes I think that I must be dreaming, but of course I awaken to the fact that my experience is true, and that this Love is a real thing, and that all my spirit friends are real.

Yes, I see Lipscomb sometimes, but I cannot tell you that he is any better. He seems satisfied with his condition, and it is hard to talk to him for he has not lost the characteristics that he had on earth. He still thinks that he knows it all, and that the life he is leading is more desirable than the one that I try to tell him of.

Miller is still in darkness, though he listens to us at times, and makes the effort to realize the truth of what we say to him, but he seems to be unable to comprehend the truths that we try to tell him. We are working with him and will do so, so long as he will let us try to help him. Well, your wife says that you are tired, and I will stop.

So good night.
Your old friend,
Forrest.

Is commencing to realize that there must be a God of Mercy and Love with the help of Mr. Padgett's wife and grandmother

October 12th, 1916.

I am here, Edwin Forrest.

Well, Ned, I want to write you a few lines, and as your wife is here, and says that I may write, I will do so.

I am glad to say that I am in a much better condition than when I last wrote you, thanks to the help that I have received from her and your grandmother, who came to me a short time ago with such wonderful love and such convincing words of cheer and hope. She is the most wonderful spirit that I have seen, and when she speaks to me it is with such authority and convincing power that I just have to believe and follow her advice or try to do so.

She prays with me at times and as she prays there comes into my soul such wonderful and strange sensations, that I know that something is coming to me that I am not acquainted with, and I feel so much better, and everything gets lighter. The darkness seems to leave me and I feel like a new man; and I pray too, though I scarcely know what it means. But this I know, that a change has come over me, and hope comes to me, and with it comes belief that I will get out of my darkness and suffering.

I commence to realize that there must be a God of Mercy and Love, and that He is not inflicting upon me the sufferings that I have endured; and that maybe He will answer my prayers for help and relief from my darkness. Your wife tells me He will and that if I will have faith and pray with all my heart and soul sometime I may become beautiful and happy as she is. It is hard to believe this, but even if I can never become as she is, yet I sometimes think that I may become more beautiful and happier than I am, and I am making the effort.

You pray for me, too. I come to you at times when the other dark spirits come, and I see the effect of your help. I don't understand it, yet I see that these spirits are made better, and I must believe that there is something in what the bright spirits, to whom these dark ones go, tell them. I am so glad that I can write to you.

No, I have not seen Mr. Miller and don't know where he is. I will act on your advice, and try to find him, and do as you say, for even though I am not a bright spirit, yet if I can help him I will gladly do so. I will seek him and the next time I write, will let you know just what his condition is. So thanking you, I will say good night.

Your old partner friend,

Edwin Forrest.[187]

Writes that Forrest is praying earnestly for the Divine Love and is progressing, and was so anxious to write

October 12th, 1916.

I am here, your own true and loving Helen.

Well sweetheart, at last I have the opportunity to write my letter, and I am so glad that I can. I thought it best to let Forrest write you as he was so anxious and seems to realize so much pleasure in doing so. He is progressing some and commences to see that there is some virtue in prayer, for he prays very earnestly and very often. We are helping him as much as possible and he seems to have great faith in me, and in your grandmother who appears to him to be something more than the spirit of a mortal. He seems to be awed by her presence when she first came to him, but she talks to him with such love and sympathy in her voice, and has so much of the Father's Love beaming from her eyes that he soon forgets her grandeur, as we call it, and listens to her with all his soul, and seems to drink in her words of comfort and love. She has a wonderful influence over him and is helping him very much. Well, I must not write more on these matters or I will not have time to tell you what I so much wish to say.

Since I last wrote you of my progress, I have gotten into higher planes of the Celestial Spheres and am correspondingly happier and surrounded by more beautiful scenes and brighter and lovelier spirits. My home is also more beautiful and is filled with a greater atmosphere of love and happiness. And I further find that with all this progress and increased happiness, my soulmate love for you increases and a more wonderful vista of what our happiness will be when you come over and progress to my home and become my soulmate in actual living together, unfolds itself.

I am so often with you, that if you knew how often, you might think that my home is not so attractive to me as it should be from my reference to its beauty; but you would be mistaken, for it is more attractive and has more happiness for me than any home I have yet had in the spirit life, and when I am in it, no mortal can conceive of my joy and bliss. But yet, I love you so much that I cannot stay away from you for any great length of time, and some of my spirit friends wonder at it.

But it is not to be wondered at so much when it is known, and it is a fact, that my actually being in my home is not necessary to my great

---

[187] This message is a composite of two, being published in Volume III and Volume IV. (G.J.C.)

happiness, for when I come to you, my soul, which is really I, comes too, and in it is the great Love of the Father, and from that Love proceeds my great happiness. So you see how the Father blesses me and all others who have His Love. Because we have our love for the mortal and leave our mansions of joy and light and go to the earth plane of darkness, where sin and error are, our great soul's love and happiness are not left behind. And why should it be? The homes which we have do not make the soul's happiness, but the soul's possession of love makes the homes. And this Love is ours for all eternity and cannot be taken from us. It can grow greater but never less. This is a law or the result of a law in the Celestial Heavens. And what a wonderful law it is!

I come to you bringing all the love that I have in my celestial home, and throw around you its influence and essence, and just to the extent that your soul is receptive do you absorb it and feel its presence. So in a faint way you can realize the great fortune of those mortals who have come to them spirits of the Celestial Spheres.

Have you ever considered what it means to you and your friends to have surrounding you the love and presence of the Master and of the other high spirits who are so often with you? Very few mortals have such love breathing upon them so often. If you will think of this you will realize how favored you are and what your possibilities may be. But when I come to you I bring not only the Divine Love which possesses my soul, but the lesser, though very intense love of the soulmate, a love which had its beginning before we were mortals and which will never have its ending in all eternity.

When I think of the goodness of the Father in all these things to make His mortals and spirits happy I can only wonder at His Love and wisdom, and never cease to thank Him! But astonishing also, man can have these blessings as he wills or not to make them his own. In this way he determines his own happiness or misery, when God wishes him to be only happy.

Well, sweetheart, I will not write more tonight as you have written enough. But this I wish to tell you, that I love you with a love that is only yours, and always increasing with no possibility of dying. And as the years of your pilgrimage on earth go by, this love will be with you and around you in greater abundance, and you will realize it more and more; and your heart will grow younger and younger until the earth life will become something more than the shadow of what awaits you when you come to me. I will say good night.

Give me my kiss and know that I am your own true and loving,
Helen.[188]

---

[188] This message is a composite of two, being published in Volume III and Volume IV. (G.J.C.)

Writes about her son's soul, that is now opening to the Truth and that he is relieved from the awful belief that held him in darkness, and is praying to the Father

February 16th, 1917.

I am here, Mrs. Perry.

I have heard what Mr. Taggart has just said, and I feel that I must also come and tell you that my son has had his mind and soul opened to the truth, and that now he is rid of the awful belief that held him in darkness, and is praying to the Father with all the earnestness of his soul.

Oh, my friend, how can I ever thank you enough for what you did? I cannot, but I can pray for you, and I will with all the earnestness of my soul, and I know the Father will bless you. So good night, and God bless you.

Your friend,
Mrs. Perry.

Confirms that Perry has been helped by Mr. Padgett in the direction of Divine Love

February 16th, 1917.

I am here, your own true and loving Helen.

Well dear, I know that you are happy at hearing the result of your conversation with Perry and you should be, for it means a soul saved that would have remained in darkness, in all probability, for a long time, and even then might never have found the way to the Divine Love, with all its blessings and benefits. Well, the work is wonderful and the results are great.

I see that you are tired tonight, and I will not write longer. So with all my love, I will say, good night.

Your own true and loving,
Helen.

Has progressed sufficiently out of darkness that he is now helping other dark spirits that are going through the same conditions that are similar to his

April 3rd, 1918.

I am here, Ross Perry.

I was at the séance tonight and talked to you and Middleton; and besides me there were Carrington and another spirit whom I did not know, named Silby, who had committed an act similar to my own. He was a very unhappy spirit, because he was in the same condition as when he first came to the spirit world, and has never had the benefit of the help that I received, and, consequently, knows nothing of the way in which he can find relief. But as I have met him, I shall endeavor to help him and give him the benefit of my experience, and I think that he will listen to me. I have already told him of some of my experiences in progressing, and as he is like a drowning man willing to catch at any straw, I think he will be willing to listen to me, and probably act on my advice.

Hutchins was also present, and he also is in a very bad condition and needs help very much, but I believe it will be more difficult to help him, because the sins of his earth life had a long continuous and accumulating acquirement. He is very dark and repulsive looking, and has not yet had any spiritual awakening. His thoughts and interests are still connected with the money that he left and the fight that is going on between his children and wife.

He has attempted to discuss the matter with me just as he did on earth, but I tell him that he must forget these things and think of things that are more vital to his happiness and progress. But he says, he cannot, for as he loved the accumulation and possession of money while on earth, he still loves them and as on earth they took the place of God, so now, he has no other God. It is very pitiable and it seems as if it were not possible for him to get rid of his thoughts and desires with reference to these things, and it is hard to induce him to make the effort. When tonight, he said he was happy, he only meant that he had that supposed happiness which he imagined he had on earth by reason of his love for these material things.

I have observed frequently, that spirits who are in a condition of darkness, with all their old loves and imagined happiness which they had on earth say that they are happy; but it is not so, and they are merely without an awakening as to their true condition which will surely come to them, sooner or later, and then they will see themselves as spirits in the more advanced condition see themselves to be.

I want to say one other thing for the benefit of Middleton, and that is, that his father, whom I knew very well on earth, was with him, and was very anxious to talk to him, but he could not get the proper and sufficient rapport and strength to do so. Also, his wife was present, and desired so very much to make herself known to him, but for the same reason, as in the case of his father, she could not. But sometime she will be able to do so, if he will give her the opportunity, and he must do that, for it will make her very happy, and him also, if he will only believe that it is she who may appear to him and tell him of her being alive and with him so much, as she says she is.

Well, I have written enough and must stop. Soon, I desire to write you a long letter about my own condition, if you can find time to receive it. With kind regards, I will say good night.

Your true friend,
R. Ross Perry.

Is very happy to tell Mr. Padgett that he is praying to the Father with all the longing of his soul for an increase of His Love, and that he will soon be in the Third Sphere

April 27th, 1918.

I am here, Ross Perry.

Let me write a line, for I am very desirous of again communicating to you the fact that I am progressing and have found the Love of which you first told me and which information led to my seeking it.

I know that you are very much interested in the higher messages and want to give your time to receiving them and that it is almost impudence for me to intrude, but I have asked your wife if I will interfere with any of these messages tonight by my writing and she informed me that it would not, as none of these messages would be written tonight. So I feel somewhat at liberty to write and I hope that you will consider that I am not intruding.

Well, since last I wrote you, I have been praying to the Father with all the longing of my soul for an increase of His Love and realize that it has come into my soul in greater abundance and I am correspondingly happy. I shall soon be in the Third (Spirit) Sphere, so the spirit friends who have been so kind and loving to me, tell me, and it gives me much happiness to know that such a prospect is opened up to me, for I can, because of the progress that I have already made, and realize to some extent what a home in that sphere will mean to me.

I would like to write you a long letter tonight, but I must not detain you. But this I want you to remember that I am very happy now, and my sufferings have left and I know that all these blessings came to me because of the workings of the Divine Love in my soul. It is wonderful what that Love can accomplish in the way of rescuing a sinful soul from its surroundings of darkness and from suffering.

The Law of Compensation, which is a great truth, does its work without hesitation or partiality, or interference by any God or angel in the way of commanding it to cease its work, but this great Divine Love is more powerful than the Law and when it enters into the soul of a man or spirit it in effect says to this Law: "You shall no longer operate on the soul of the sinner that was, because it will take that soul away from and outside the operations of the Law."

How little men understand this working of the (Divine) Love. It does not set aside the Law, but it merely removes the soul in which it has found a lodgment from the scope of the operation of the Law. The Law goes on but the objects of its operations are rescued from the same. No Law is set aside which men think and argue is necessary in order for a soul to be saved from its penalties and when on earth I believed this too, and did not believe in or accept the doctrine of the special interposition of divine providence to succor men from the consequence of their sins and that I did not believe because I thought that the only way in which this could be accomplished was for God to say to the Law: "You shall cease to operate."

But now I know, that, while the Law never ceases to operate until the penalties that are called for are paid, yet this Love is above the Law, though not antagonistic to it. I wish that I might write more on this subject tonight as to me, it is one of the most wonderful truths in God's Universe of Spirit and I never cease to meditate upon it and thank the Father that I was made a real example of the power of this Love.

Well I must stop now, but when you have time I should like to come and write at more length. I see that my wife has not progressed in learning the truth and I am very sorry. Well friend, good night.
Your friend,
Ross Perry.[189]

Glad Perry wrote

April 27th, 1918.

I am here, your own true and loving Helen.

Well dear, I see that you are not just in condition for very lengthy writing tonight and I will say only a few words, your condition though is much better and there is no reason why you cannot receive the messages that have so long been delayed and I trust that you will do so very soon.

I am glad that Perry wrote you as he did, he is very enthusiastic over his knowledge and experience of the Divine Love and is now quite happy and progressing. Love me and think of me and pray to the Father. Good night.
Your own true and loving,
Helen.

---

[189] This message is a composite of three, being published in Volume II and Volume III and again in Volume IV. (G.J.C.)

Was the first to compile material now contained in his Gospel, which is not the same as he compiled it

August 28th, 1915.

I am here, St. Luke.

Well, I came to tell you that you are not in such a condition of faith as will enable you to take my messages in a satisfactory way, and I will not write as I expected and give you some account of the errors and untruths that are in my gospel. I am the one who first collected the different writings or manuscripts of the history of the times of the New Testament and of the sayings and doings of Jesus and compiled them in one gospel.

The present gospel is not as I wrote it, for many things have been added and a number extracted from what I wrote and what the truths are. Tonight I will not attempt to tell you but will come again soon.

I know, and I will tell you with all my emphasis that it was Jesus the Nazarene, and the person of that name around whom the New Testament centers. He is the same Jesus and waits to write through you his messages to the world.

So you must believe and listen to what he says, and try to do your best in receiving these messages for they will be the truths of God. I will stop now and say good night.

Your brother in Christ,
St. Luke.

The Prayer[190] for Divine Love

Our Father, who art in heaven, we recognize that Thou Art all holy and loving and merciful, and that we are Thy children, and not the subservient, sinful and depraved creatures that our false teachers would have us believe. That we are the greatest of Thy creation, and the most wonderful of all Thy handiworks, and the objects of Thy great Soul's love and tenderest care.

That Thy will is, that we become at one with Thee and partake of Thy great love which Thou hast bestowed upon us through Thy mercy and desire that we become, in truth, Thy children through love and not through the sacrifice and death of any of Thy creatures.

We pray that Thou will open up our souls to the inflowing of Thy love, and that then will come Thy holy spirit to bring into our souls, this, Thy love in great abundance until our souls may be transformed into the very essence of Thyself; and that there may come to us faith—such faith

---

[190] This prayer is slightly modified by a further revelation from Jesus on September 26th, 1965 and referred to in the introduction of Volume IV. (J.P.G.)

as will cause us to realize that we are truly Thy children and that we are one with Thee in very substance and not in image only.

Let us have such faith as will cause us to know that Thou art our Father and the bestower of every good and perfect gift, and that only we, ourselves, can prevent Thy love changing us from the mortal to the immortal.

Let us never cease to realize that Thy love is waiting for each and all of us, and that when we come to Thee with faith and earnest aspirations, Thy love will never be with-holden from us.

Keep us in the shadow of Thy love every hour and moment of our lives, and help us to overcome all temptations of the flesh, and the influence of the powers of the evil ones, which so constantly surround us and endeavor to turn our thoughts away from Thee to the pleasures and allurements of this world.

We thank Thee for Thy love and for the possibility of receiving it, and believe that Thou art our Father—the loving Father who smiles upon us in our weakness, and is always ready to help us and take us to Thy arms of love.

We pray thus with all the earnestness and longings of our soul, and trusting in Thy love, give Thee all the glory and honor and love that our finite souls can give.

Made in the USA
Middletown, DE
08 November 2017